# ADVANCES & INNOVATIONS

# BOND AND IN THE MORTGAGE MARKETS

## FRANK J. FABOZZI

### EDITOR

Visiting Professor
Alfred P. Sloan School of Management
Massachusetts Institute of Technology
and Editor
*The Journal of Portfolio Management*

# DEDICATION

To Peter Bernstein
Former Editor of
*The Journal of Portfolio Management*

# Contents and Contributors

## PART V
## FUTURES AND INTEREST RATE AGREEMENTS

## PREFACE

In 1985, I edited a book titled *The Handbook of Mortgage-Backed Securities,* which included a chapter written by Richard L. Sega, then an investment officer at the Traveler's Insurance Companies. In the opening paragraph of that chapter he wrote:

> The familiar expression, "shooting at a moving target," alludes to the difficulty involved in dealing with a problem where conditions are constantly changing. Consider now a strange situation where the target is fixed, but instead, the gun in your hand is moving and twisting such that you can barely keep your grip on it. If you can imagine this, you begin to appreciate the challenge a portfolio manager faces in the use of mortgage-backed securities. However, the yield and flexibility they offer can make the effort well worth it for the astute manager. Realizing these benefits requires careful attention to the particular features of mortgage products.

While Richard Sega's comments were confined to the mortgage-backed securities market, most portfolio managers will probably agree that the statement is equally applicable to all sectors of the bond market.

Not too long ago, yield to maturity was accepted as the "true" measure of potential return for corporate, Treasury and agency bonds and yield to 12-year life was viewed as the potential return for a mortgage pass-through security. Not too long ago, market participants made no attempt to quantify the value of the call option embedded in callable bonds and the impact of that option on the potential price performance of the bond.

Today, well-trained portfolio managers recognize the limitations of "yield" numbers. They employ the latest developments in option pricing theory to value bonds with embedded options and to analyze the potential performance of these bonds over different investment horizons.

*Advances and Innovations in the Bond and Mortgage Markets* was prepared to keep bond market participants abreast of the latest products, market developments and analytical techniques. The latest strategies that can be employed in managing a bond portfolio are covered in a companion book, *Fixed Income Portfolio Strategies.*

I would like to express my appreciation to the contributors to this book and to the following individuals who provided me with assistance at various stages of this project: John Carlson (Security Pacific Merchant Bank), Ravi Dattatreya (Shearson Lehman Hutton), Dessa Fabozzi (Merrill Lynch Capital Markets), Sylvan Feldstein (Merrill Lynch Capital Markets), Harry Kavros (First Boston Corporation), Lisa Pendergast (Prudential-Bache Capital Funding), Sharmin Mossavar-Rahmani (Fidelity Management Trust Company, Boston), Chuck Ramsey (Bear Stearns) and Koichi Sakamoto (Mitsubishi Bank).

*Frank J. Fabozzi*

# PART I

# Risk, Return and Volatility in the Bond Market

# Introduction

FRANK J. FABOZZI, PH.D., CFA
VISITING PROFESSOR OF FINANCE
SLOAN SCHOOL OF MANAGEMENT
MASSACHUSETTS INSTITUTE OF TECHNOLOGY
AND
EDITOR
THE JOURNAL OF PORTFOLIO MANAGEMENT

Prior to the 1970's, the securities issued in the U.S. bond market had a simple structure. They had a fixed interest rate and a fixed maturity date. The only option that was available to the issuer was the right to call all or part of the issue prior to its stated maturity date. For a small number of issues, the only option available to the bondholder was the right to convert that bond into a fixed number of shares of the issuer's common stock.

The high and volatile interest rates that prevailed in the United States in the late 1970's and early 1980's made the cost of borrowing for issuers of even the highest quality rating expensive. To reduce the cost of borrowing funds for their clients, investment bankers designed new debt instruments that were more attractive to investors. These included original-issue deep-discount bonds, zero-coupon bonds, putable bonds, commodity-backed bonds, non-dollar denominated bonds and contingent take-down bonds.

While corporate floating rate bonds were first introduced into the United States bond market in 1974, declining interest rates in the years that followed made these bonds unattractive to investors. Very few were issued between 1974 and 1979. But in the high and volatile interest rate environment that followed, new floating rate structures with frequent coupon reset and put options made them more attractive to institutional investors who had begun to realize the investment merits of these securities for asset/liability management. For floaters, the coupon rate could be benchmarked to some market interest rate, non-interest rate financial index or commodity index. Some of the issues could be exchanged either automatically at a certain date or at the option of the issuer into fixed rate securities. A few issues were convertible. Bonds in which the coupon interest rate floats in the opposite direction of the change in interest rates, known as inverse floaters, were subsequently introduced because institutions found them useful for asset/liability management.

Studies of the low quality or "junk" bond market found that the historical default rate of these securities was low. The large spread to Treasuries for bonds in this sector of the market coupled with low default rates suggested that a diversified portfolio of junk bonds could produce above average returns. Empircial studies of the long-run investment performance of diversified portfolios of junk bonds confirmed these expectations, resulting in increased institutional interest in this sector of the bond market. The development of the junk market to finance leveraged buyouts and recapitalizations in this decade saw the introduction of new junk bond structures. Examples include payment-in-kind (PIK) bonds, extendible bonds, and deferred coupon bonds.

Innovation and growth have characterized the mortgage-backed securities market in recent years. Using the basic instruments in the market (whole loans and pass-through securities), derivative instruments such as collateralized mortgage obligations and stripped mortgage-backed securities have been created to fit the specific needs of a broadening range of institutional investors. These derivatives can be employed by institutional investors to hedge mortgages and bonds, to better match assets and liabilities, to create synthetic instruments, and to create risk/return profiles that were not available or were too costly to replicate with pass-through securities and whole loans.

Increased interest rate volatility in the 1980's resulted in greater use of interest rate futures by institutional investors to control interest rate risk. Other interest rate risk control contracts were introduced. These included exchange-traded and over-the-counter interest rate options, interest rate swaps (as well as options on swaps or swaptions), interest rate agreements (caps, collars and floors) and compound or split-fee options.

In the early 1980's, an increasing number of bond market participants began to recognize the important contribution option theory could play in the valuation of bonds. There was wider recognition that a bond could be viewed as a security comprised of an option-free bond and a package of options. To value such a security, it would be necessary to value these options. Moreover, it was also necessary to value interest rate risk control tools such as interest rate options and interest rate agreements (which are, in effect, a package of options).

However, almost all of the initial work in option pricing theory (Black-Scholes and binomial) focused on the pricing of options on stocks. These equity option pricing models were then applied to the pricing of options on fixed income securities. It did not take long before bond market participants began to realize the shortcomings of applying equity pricing models to price fixed income options. Research in the mid-1980's focused on developing models that would be more appropriate for pricing fixed income options. Examples of such models included yield diffusion models and arbitrage-free models that incorporate the term structure of interest rates.

In the 31 articles that follow, new bond structures, market developments and analytical techniques are presented. While not all of the instruments covered are new, what is new are the frameworks proposed to assess their investment merits.

# Risk and Return in the U.S. Bond Market: A Multifactor Approach

RONALD N. KAHN, PH.D.
MANAGER, SPECIAL PROJECTS
BARRA

## I. INTRODUCTION

Bonds are exposed to many sources of risk. The term structure of interest rates can shift and twist in different ways. Issuers may call bonds before maturity; or default as a result of sector-wide problems or individual credit difficulties. For mortgage investors, prepayment is a significant risk source. Only a multifactor model can adequately capture bond risk exposure. Duration, the traditional bond risk assessment, is but a single number, and measures only the risk arising from parallel term structure shifts.

Risk analysis underlies all the central functions of bond portfolio management: benchmark tracking, immunization, active strategy implementation, and performance measurement and analysis. All of these involve comparing the risk exposures of two portfolios, or of a portfolio and a liability stream. Matching an investment portfolio's risk exposures to those of a benchmark should lead to investment returns which accurately track benchmark returns. Matching the portfolio's risk exposures to those of a liability stream should immunize the portfolio's liability coverage against market changes. Deliberately choosing risk exposures which differ from those of a benchmark is an active strategy aimed at exceeding benchmark returns.

Identifying these active bets and studying their past performance can measure bond manager skill.

This article will present a specific multifactor risk model of the U.S. bond market.[1] First, a valuation model will identify and measure the various sources of risk. Bond values in the heterogeneous U.S. market depend on the term structure and on a set of yield spreads corresponding to sectors, quality ratings, and other factors.[2] Analysis of the historical variance and covariance of excess returns[3] to these factors will then lead to the risk model. Individual portfolio risk will depend upon the portfolio's exposures to the risk factors. This model has proven effective in predicting risk, and has successfully contributed to all the functions of bond portfolio management.

## II. THE VALUATION MODEL

The price of a bond represents the market's assessment of the present value of its expected future cash flows. For a bond with expected coupon or principal payments at $\{t_1, t_2, \ldots, t_N\}$:

$$
\begin{array}{l}
\text{cash flow } (t_1) \times \text{discount } (t_1) \\
+ \text{ cash flow } (t_2) \times \text{discount } (t_2) \\
+ \qquad\qquad \cdots \\
+ \text{ cash flow } (t_N) \times \text{discount } (t_N) \\
\hline
= \text{PRICE}
\end{array}
$$

These discounts—the term structure—are a property of the market as a whole. The cash flows depend on the individual bond. This distinction between marketwide properties and individual bond characteristics does not hold for the traditional yield curve, since yield is a bond specific property.

Still, there exist many elements of heterogeneity which distinguish bonds with identical promised cash flows. Consider for example, a Treasury bond and an electric utility bond with identical coupon and maturity. The Treasury bond price will exceed the utility bond price because the market perceives utility bonds as riskier than Treasury bonds. Investors demand higher yield as compensation for assuming this risk. We can model this effect through an electric utility yield spread off the Treasury term structure:

---

[1]This model of the U.S. bond market was developed by BARRA.

[2]Michel Houghlet, "Estimating the Term-Structure of Interest Rates for Non-Homogeneous Bonds." Ph.D. Dissertation, School of Business Adminsitration, University of California, Berkeley, October 1980.

[3]Excess return is defined as the total return minus the risk-free rate of return.

cash flow $(t_1) \times$ discount $(t_1)/(1 + $ electric utility yield spread$)^{t_1}$
$+$ cash flow $(t_2) \times$ discount $(t_2)/(1 + $ electric utility yield spread$)^{t_2}$
$+$                       $\ldots$
$+$ cash flow $(t_N) \times$ discount $(t_N)/(1 + $ electric utility yield spread$)^{t_N}$

$$= \text{PRICE}$$

By assumption, this electric utility yield spread is a marketwide property which applies to every electric utility bond. In general there exist marketwide yield spreads for every element of heterogeneity in the U.S. bond market. Overall, the price of a bond depends upon its specific characteristics, i.e., its cash flows and distinguishing factors; and upon marketwide parameters, i.e., the term structure and the yield spreads off that term structure.

The following multifactor model clearly elucidates factors of value present in the U.S. bond market. This model estimates bond prices as:

$$P = \sum_{i=1}^{N} \frac{CF(t_i) d(t_i)}{\left[ 1 + \sum_{j} \alpha_j x_j \right]^{t_i}}$$

where          $P =$ bond price
$CF(t_i) =$ expected cash flow at time $t_i$
$d(t_i) =$ discount for horizon date $t_i$
$x_j =$ bond exposure to factor $j$
$\alpha_j =$ market's assessment of factor $j$.

The bond specific exposures include the cash flows $CF(t_i)$ and the set $\{x_j\}$. The characteristics of the market as a whole are the term structure $d(t_j)$ and the yield spreads $\{\alpha_j\}$ (the market assessments). This model clearly enumerates how a bond's total exposure to the various factors of value determines its price. Bond market assessments result from fitting this model to actual trading prices.

The model assigns one $x_j$ to every identified factor of value in the market. Most of these identify sources of default risk. They naturally fall into several groups. First are the sector factors. All industrial bonds are subject to a certain common sector risk. The same holds for all electric utility bonds. In all, the model identifies 20 distinct sectors in the U.S. bond market. On average over the past ten years, market assessments for these factors have ranged between 25 and 60 basis points; with oil bonds and industrial bonds exhibiting relatively low average spreads, and railroad bonds, foreign issued bonds, and electric utility bonds exhibiting relatively high spreads.

The quality factors form another general group. Moody's Investor Service, Standard and Poor's Corporation, Fitch Investors Service, and Duff & Phelps, Inc., provide quality ratings for corporate bonds. These are rating service estimates of default risk. The bond market constantly assesses an excess yield which issuers must pay for each additional grade of credit risk. An industrial bond rated AAA is exposed, by definition, to only the industrial sector factor. An industrial bond rated AA is exposed in addition to the AA factor. Over the past ten years, AA-rated bond issues have traded with a yield in excess of AAA-rated issues by 19 basis points. This quality spread has averaged 43 basis points for A-rated issues and 104 basis points for BBB-rated issues.

A third group of factors pertain to the equity of the underlying issuers. One measures the equity specific risk: that part of the equity risk not correlated with general market movements or whole sector movements. Another factor measures financial risk of the issuer as evidenced by leverage, coverage of fixed charges, debt to total assets, liquidity, and net monetary debt. The net yield spreads due to these factors have averaged less than 10 basis points over the past ten years.

A fourth group of factors fall into the miscellaneous category. The size of the bond issue measures its liquidity. Illiquid issues are riskier—investors demand additional yield for them. This spread has averaged less than 8 basis points over the past ten years; however, liquidity considerations can influence other spreads. Another factor is the current yield effect: domestic investors value lower coupon issues which traditionally have received beneficial tax treatment. In the past, government bond investors have demanded 4 basis points for each percent by which current yield exceeded the government market average, and corporate bond investors have demanded 13 basis points for each percent by which current yield exceeded the corporate market average. Since the capital gains tax advantage no longer exists, this effect may disappear. However, many foreign investors—increasingly important participants in the U.S. bond market—have a demonstrated desire for high coupon bonds. Hence the behavior of this effect in the post-tax reform era is still unclear. Investors also value Treasury bills because of their particular safety and convenience, and their use for reserve requirements; and so Treasury bills are exposed to their own special factor in the U.S. market. Treasury bills are such short instruments that yield spreads can be deceptive; however on the par equal to $100.00 basis, this factor has increased prices by only $0.05 on average over the past ten years.

The final step in the valuation model involves adjusting the fitted bond price to reflect the influence of call and sinking fund provisions and mortgage prepayment provisions. These issues include embedded options, whose values depend on interest rate volatility. Since the issuers retain these options, we can view the marketed securities as portfolios, long an equivalent non-optionable security, and short the option. For a callable bond for example:

$$\text{callable bond} = \text{noncallable bond} - \text{call option}.$$

A stochastic model which estimates a probability distribution for future interest rates can simulate the call and sinking fund option values. Simulating mortgage cash flows requires an additional behavioral model to accurately account for prepayment decisions of individual homeowners.

## III. THE RISK MODEL

Bond price changes over time in response to three phenomena: bond maturities shorten, the term structure shifts, and the market assessments change. Bonds are risky because the last two of these three phenomena are uncertain. The core of a bond market risk model is an estimate of the variances and covariances of excess returns to the term structure and the market assessments. The risk model focuses on returns to the factors because total returns are observable and are the ultimate goal of bond portfolio management. Building the risk model therefore requires a history of the behavior of all relevant market factors. The valuation model identifies these relevant factors and, by fitting it to past market prices, estimates their past histories.

Consider first the behavior of the term structure. We can characterize it by a discrete set of discount factors at fixed vertices:

vertices in years  $\{0, .25, .5, .75, 1, 1.5, 2, 2.5, 3, 3.5, 4, 5, 6, 7, 11, 15, 20,$  $25, 30, 35, 40\}$

discount factors  $\{d(0) = 1, d(.25), d(.5), \ldots, d(40)\}.$

The discount factor $d(v_i)$ represents the price of a \$1.00 pure discount bond maturing at time $v_i$. The return to vertex-$i$ at time $t$ is the return to the following strategy:

Invest \$1.00 at time $t - \Delta t$ in pure discount bonds maturing at time $t - \Delta t + v_i$. These bonds have a maturity of $v_i$. Hold for a period $\Delta t$. Then sell the bonds, which now have maturity $v_i - \Delta t$.

The excess return to vertex-$i$ at time $t$ follows then by subtracting off the risk-free rate of return. This risk-free rate is the return to the strategy:

Invest \$1.00 at time $t - \Delta t$ in pure discount bonds maturing at time $t$. These bonds have a maturity of $\Delta t$. Hold for a period $\Delta t$. Then redeem the bonds, which have now matured.

The fixed holding period $\Delta t$ is a defining constant of the risk model.

The historical variances and covariances of the excess returns at each vertex constitute a measurement of term structure risk. Of course these excess returns are not completely independent sources of risk. In fact, analysis of the U.S. bond market shows that three modes of collective motion—shifts, twists, and butterflies—almost entirely capture term structure variance. These are the first three principal components of term structure risk.[4]

The shift, where all returns move in the same direction, accounts for 89.6% of all term structure risk in the U.S. bond market over the period from July, 1979 through April, 1988. Exhibit 1 shows this collective motion, normalized to a 100 basis point shift in the 30-year spot rate. Except for the 91-day rate, short maturity spot rates here are more volatile than long maturity spot rates. However for a given change in spot rate, the associated pure discount bond return varies in proportion to maturity:

$$P(T) = \exp(-s_T T)$$
$$\left(\frac{1}{P}\right)\frac{\partial P(T)}{\partial s} = -T$$

and so returns to long maturity pure discount bonds are more volatile than returns to short maturity pure discount bonds.

**EXHIBIT 1**
**FIRST PRINCIPAL COMPONENT: SPOT RATE SHIFT**

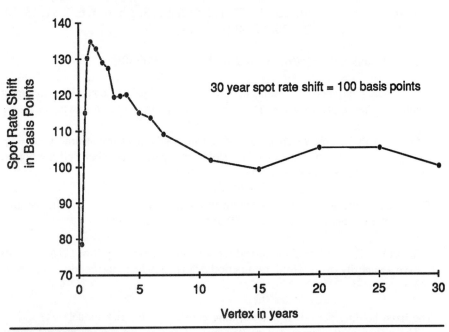

*Source:* BARRA

---

[4]While there exists considerable covariance between excess returns to adjacent vertices, the principal components are defined to have zero covariance. They result from diagonalizing the covariance matrix of excess vertex returns. The 20 vertices map into 20 principal components; however for U.S. bond market term structure risk, the first three principal components account for over 99% of this risk.

**EXHIBIT 2**
**SECOND PRINCIPAL COMPONENT: SPOT RATE SHIFT**

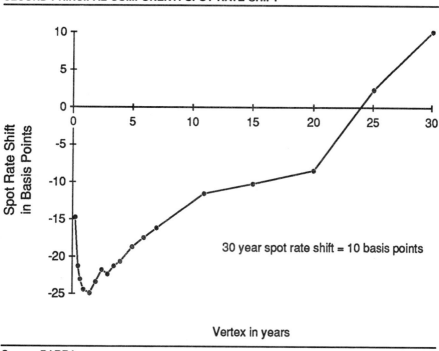

Vertex in years

*Source:* BARRA

The twist, where short returns and long returns move in opposite directions, accounts for another 8.1% of total term structure risk. Exhibit 2 shows this motion, normalized to a 10 basis point shift in the 30-year spot rate, because the amplitude of this second principal component is roughly an order of magnitude below the amplitude of the first principal component. Here again, the short maturity spot rates are more volatile than the long maturity spot rates. For this principal component the 25-year spot rate and the 30-year spot rate move in opposition to all the shorter maturity spot rates.

The butterfly, where short and long returns move together and intermediate returns move in the opposite direction, accounts for another 1.4% of total term structure risk. Exhibit 3 shows this motion, normalized to a 1 basis point shift in the 30-year spot rate, because the amplitude of this third principal component is roughly an order of magnitude below the amplitude of the second principal component. For this third component also, the short maturity spot rates are the most volatile.

In the idealized world of parallel yield shifts, duration measures the first order change in price and convexity measures the second order change in price due to a yield shift:

$$\frac{\Delta P}{P} = -DUR \; \Delta y \; + \frac{1}{2} CONV \; (\Delta y)^2$$

**EXHIBIT 3**
**THIRD PRINCIPAL COMPONENT: SPOT RATE SHIFT**

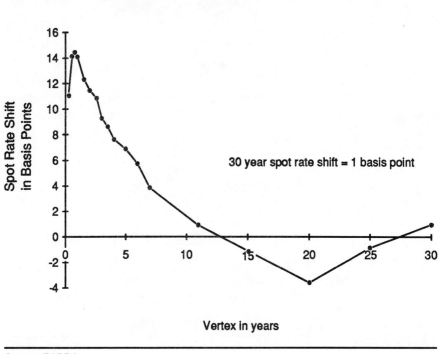

30 year spot rate shift = 1 basis point

Vertex in years

*Source:* BARRA.

In the language of risk, duration measures exposure to the risk of parallel yield shifts and convexity measures exposure to the risk of large parallel yield shifts (since for small $\Delta y$, $(\Delta y)^2 \ll \Delta y$). Now generalize to a world of parallel shifts and linear shifts:

$$\Delta y\,(T) = a\Delta y_1 + bT\,\Delta y_2$$

where $a$ and $b$ are constants and $bT\Delta y_2 \ll \Delta y_1$ (the parallel shift is the dominant effect). For pure discount bonds now:

$$\frac{\Delta P\,(T)}{P} = -\,T\,\Delta y\,+\frac{1}{2}T^2(\Delta y)^2 + \text{higher order terms}$$

$$\frac{\Delta P\,(T)}{P} \approx -\,T\,[a\,\Delta y_1 + bT\,\Delta y_2] + \frac{1}{2}T^2[a\,\Delta y_1 + bT\,\Delta y_2]^2$$

$$\frac{\Delta P\,(T)}{P} \approx -\,T\,[a\,\Delta y_1] + T^2\left[-\,b\,\Delta y_2 + \frac{1}{2}(a\,\Delta y_1)^2\right]$$

where we ignore terms smaller than $(a\Delta y_1)^2$ and $bT\Delta y_2$. Since the duration of a pure discount bond equals its maturity, and the convexity of a pure discount bond equals the square of its maturity, duration measures exposure to the risk of parallel yield shifts and convexity measures exposure to the risk of both large parallel yield shifts and also linear yield shifts.

But as this principal components analysis shows, parallel term structure shifts and linear term structure shifts do not describe term structure risk in the U.S. bond market over the period from July, 1979 through April, 1988. In fact, duration acts as no more than a rough proxy for exposure to the first principal component of term structure risk, accurate only to the extent to which the curve in Exhibit 1 resembles a horizontal line. And, since this first principal component captures only 89.6% of the term structure risk in the U.S. bond market, and none of the market assessment risk, duration clearly fails to adequately capture bond market risk. Convexity, likewise, is only an inaccurate measure of exposure to large movements of the first principal component and movements of the second principal component. The first principal component is not a parallel shift, and the second principal component is not simply the sum of a parallel shift and a linear shift. So even duration and convexity together do not adequately measure term structure risk, and of course they do not measure market assessment risk at all.

Now consider in more detail the risk associated with market assessment movements. The excess return to market assessment-*j* at time *t* is the return to the following artificial strategy:

Invest $1.00 at time $t - \Delta t$ in a portfolio exposed only to factor *j* and to term structure risk. The portfolio duration is set to the average U.S. bond market duration over the risk model history. Hold for a period $\Delta t$, *and assume that the term structure simply rolls down over this period.* Sell the portfolio at time *t*.

This strategy is artificial because it assumes a deterministic term structure roll down. The return to this strategy is the change in market assessment-*j* over the holding period, multiplied by the average bond market duration. Duration, the fractional change in price accompanying a change in yield, enters into this formula to convert a change in yield spread into a price return.

With the historically estimated excess returns to each of these factors, we can estimate their variances and covariances to assess their risk. We can once again identify principal modes of collective behavior, however, for the market assessments these are not easily visualized.

Finally, there exists covariance between term structure movements and market assessment movements. This covariance is quite small on average over the period from July, 1979 through April, 1988. In general, correlations between the term structure first principal component and the sector and quality excess returns are not statistically significant.

## IV. PORTFOLIO RISK CHARACTERIZATION

Historical analysis captures the inherent riskiness of the factors of value present in the U.S. bond market. The riskiness of a particular bond portfolio depends upon its exposure to these sources of risk.

The fraction of portfolio present value at each vertex measures the portfolio's exposure to term structure risk. Two portfolios with identical distributions of present value along the vertices face identical term structure risk. Traditionalists will note that these two portfolios have identical durations. However, two portfolios can have identical durations without having identical distributions across the entire set of vertices. Such portfolios will not face identical term structure risk.

What about market assessment risk? Consider for example the risk associated with the sector market assessment. The fraction of the portfolio in each sector, multiplied by the duration of the bonds in that sector compared to bond market average duration, measures the portfolio's sector risk exposure. Risk exposures for quality factors and other factors follow analogously.

Beyond the marketwide factors of value which the model identifies, there also exist risk factors associated solely with individual issues. By definition, the specific risk for each issue is uncorrelated with all marketwide factor risk and with the specific risk of all other issues. We can estimate this specific issue risk historically as the realized excess return risk of each specific issue not explained by the model.

Total risk finally follows from combining the risk exposures which characterize a given portfolio with the variances and covariances of the underlying risk factors which characterize the market, and adding in specific issue risk. This number is the predicted total variance of the portfolio excess return.

## V. SUMMARY

This article has identified the many factors of value operating in the U.S. bond market, and presented a multifactor risk model of this market. Over the period from July, 1979 through April, 1988, the traditional risk measurements of duration and convexity did not adequately capture bond risk. This multifactor risk model, however, has successfully predicted portfolio risk, and proven to be a valuable tool in bond portfolio management.

# The Implied Volatility of Fixed-Income Markets

WILLIAM M. BOYCE, PH.D
SALOMON BROTHERS INC

WEBSTER HUGHES
SALOMON BROTHERS INC

PETER S. A. NICULESCU
SALOMON BROTHERS INC

MICHAEL WALDMAN
SALOMON BROTHERS INC

## I. EXPECTED VOLATILITY AND THE VALUATION OF CALLABLE, FIXED-INCOME SECURITIES

Most U.S. fixed-income securities carry embedded call options that allow the borrower to redeem the liability before maturity. The loans underlying mortgage-backed securities can, in general, be prepaid at par at any time and about 75% of outstanding corporate bonds are callable at the issuer's discretion at some time before maturity. Until recently, participants in fixed-income markets lacked effective tools for evaluating these options. Some commonly used valuation measures

17

assumed that interest rates would not change, that is, that interest rate volatility would be zero. Thus, mortgage-backed securities were quoted on a cash flow yield basis, on the assumption that prepayments would proceed according to a fixed schedule, and callable corporates were bought and sold on the basis of their "yield to worst" (the minimum of the yield to maturity and the yield to call). The impact of changing rate levels was analyzed by viewing the security's performance for a small number of arbitrarily chosen scenarios.

Two related concepts—*effective duration* and *option-adjusted spread (OAS)*—provide a more precise measurement of the relative value and performance characteristics of securities carrying differing degrees of call protection.[1] The effective duration of a callable corporate or mortgage security gives the sensitivity of the issue's price to interest rate changes; the OAS is the basis-point spread offered by the security over U.S. Treasuries, after adjusting for the effect of its option features.

Unlike the yield to worst or the cash flow yield, the OAS explicitly accounts for the possibility that interest rates might change. Consequently, the value of a given callable security, as measured by its OAS, will vary depending on how much interest rates are likely to change. For example, consider a callable bond trading at a discount. If interest rates are not expected to vary beyond a very narrow range, then it is unlikely that the issuer will exercise the option to call the bond before maturity. Thus, at low volatility levels, the embedded call option will have little effect on the bond's value, and the OAS of the bond will be close to the standard spread over Treasuries given by the bond's yield to maturity. The effective duration of such a bond would be approximately equal to its nominal duration (the modified duration based on the cash flows to maturity). By contrast, if interest rates are expected to be highly volatile, then there is a much greater probability that the issuer will call the bond before maturity. In this case, the effective duration of the callable bond will be shorter than its nominal duration, and the OAS will be narrower than the yield to maturity spread.

## II. HISTORICAL VOLATILITY

Thus, the valuation of callable securities depends on expectations regarding the future volatility of interest rates (see Exhibit 1). Because the future course of interest rates is uncertain, the question arises: What volatility should be used to evaluate any given callable security? One guide is provided by historical rate movements.

---

[1]For detailed descriptions of these valuation techniques see William M. Boyce, Mark Koenigsberg and Armand Tatevossiani, *The Effective Duration of Callable Bonds: The Salomon Brothers Term Structure-Based Option Pricing Model,* Salomon Brothers Inc, April 1987 and Michael Waldman and Mark Gordon, *Evaluating the Option Features of Mortgage Securities: The Salomon Brothers Mortgage Pricing Model,* Salomon Brothers Inc, September 1986.

**EXHIBIT 1**
**OPTION-ADJUSTED SPREADS: PACIFIC TELEPHONE 9.875s OF 2016 AND GNMA 10s**
**EVALUATED AT ALTERNATIVE VOLATILITY LEVELS**

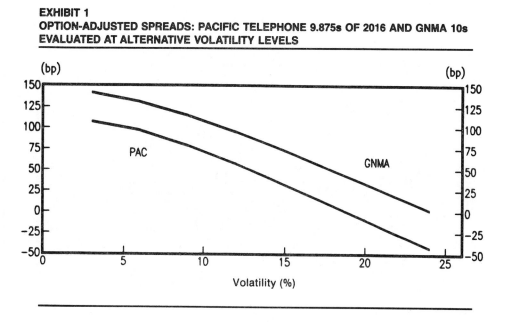

The historical, or realized, volatility of the fixed-income markets has varied widely over short periods of time (see Exhibit 2). On average during the 1980s, however, the intermediate-term U.S. Treasury and corporate markets and the current-coupon mortgage market have experienced yield volatilities of approximately 18%.[2]

Since the introduction of the Salomon Brothers corporate bond and mortgage security option pricing models in 1986-87, the base case assumptions used for our standard reports of OAS and effective duration have ranged from 12% to 20%. These reports currently assume 16% volatility.[3]

## III. IMPLIED VOLATILITY: THE CONCEPTUAL BASIS

The concept of implied volatility is familiar to participants in exchange-traded options markets. For these short-dated options, relatively simple models can be used

---

[2]For purposes of this article, interest rate volatility can be described as the annualized standard deviation of percentage changes in yield.

[3]In applying the corporate and mortgage option pricing models, we explicitly assume a volatility for short-term interest rates. This assumption then translates into (somewhat lower) volatility levels for other interest rates, such as long-term corporate bond or mortgage yields. Details on the models' treatment of volatility are given in the reports cited in footnote 1.

**EXHIBIT 2**
**12-WEEK ROLLING HISTORICAL VOLATILITIES OF YIELDS ON TEN-YEAR U.S.**
**TREASURY NOTES, NEWLY ISSUED, A-RATED, MEDIUM-TERM INDUSTRIALS, AND**
**CURRENT-COUPON GNMAs (JANUARY 1982-OCTOBER 1987)**

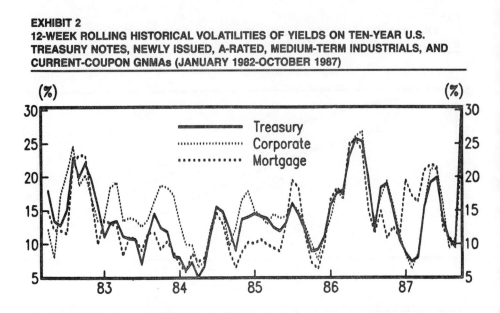

to calculate the option's price as a function of a small number of variables, including the assumed volatility. Because the other parameters are either known or have comparatively little impact, it is possible to determine the volatility level implied by the option's market price.[4]

Callable corporate bonds and mortgage securities present more complicated situations. First, for corporate bonds, neither the price of the embedded call nor the price of the underlying noncallable security is observable. Similarly, the market does not separate the prices of mortgage securities into their fixed cash flow and variable prepayment components. Second, both types of instruments involve options that can be exercised over long periods, extending as much as 40 years. Finally, the value of these options depends on the potential movements of both short-term and long-term interest rates. For these reasons, evaluating these securities requires relatively complex option pricing models.

Nevertheless, for a given corporate bond or mortgage security, we can calculate the volatility implied by the security's market price if we know the appropriate OAS. Identifying the right OAS is the problem. A logical choice for corporates would be the yield spread over Treasuries of noncallable bonds of the same issuer. However, many categories of corporate bonds do not include noncallable issues. Furthermore, clear-cut benchmarks for the OASs of mortgage pass-throughs do not exist.[5]

---

[4]For a discussion of options pricing theory and its applications, see Cal Johnson, *An Introduction to Options,* Salomon Brothers Inc, October 1987.

[5]The yield spreads over Treasuries of noncallable agency debt define logical minimum OASs for agency pass-throughs.

## IV.  ESTIMATING IMPLIED VOLATILITY

Without noncallable benchmarks, it is still possible to estimate the market's assumed interest rate volatility by examining the *relative* pricing of various callable issues. For example, consider two hypothetical 30-year bonds issued by the same corporation, a 9% issue callable at par in ten years and an 11% bond callable at par in five years. Assume that the 9% and 11% bonds are priced to yield 10% and 10.40%, respectively.

The 11% bond offers the investor a higher yield (40 basis points) than the 9% bond as compensation for its greater degree of call exposure. Exhibit 3 displays the OAS of each bond for a range of volatility values. There is one volatility value, 14%, at which the OASs are equal. Thus, the 40-basis-point nominal yield spread between these bonds implies an interest rate volatility level of 14%.

**EXHIBIT 3**
**ESTIMATING IMPLIED VOLATILITY: OAS OF TWO HYPOTHETICAL BONDS**

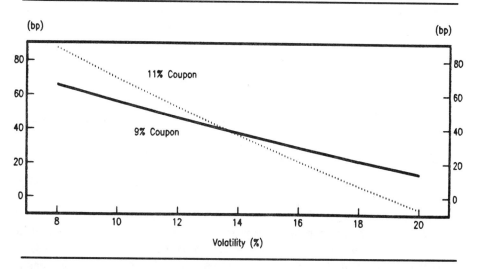

## V.  BONDS OF THE SAME ISSUER

This technique can be extended to a larger number of securities. First, consider a group of securities of the same issuer but with differing coupons, maturities and call features. The outstanding bonds of the General Motors Acceptance Corporation (GMAC) provide a good example. We define the implied volatility as the level, based on results from the Salomon Brothers option pricing model, that produces the smallest deviation from the average OAS for all GMAC securities.

The estimation technique is illustrated in Exhibits 4 and 5. When a 16% volatility assumption is used in the pricing model, deviations from the average OAS-effective

**EXHIBIT 4**
**OPTION-ADJUSTED SPREADS OF GMAC SECURITIES COMPUTED AT**
**16% VOLATILITY (OCTOBER 31, 1987)**

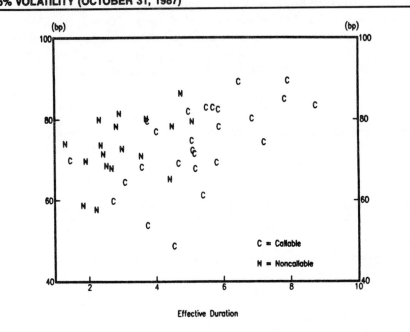

Effective Duration

duration relationship are quite wide. In addition, the OASs of callable bonds are much smaller typically than those of noncallable bonds. In other words, the market, through its pricing of these securities, appears to be assuming a smaller probability that GMAC will exercise its call options than would be generated by a random walk in interest rates with a 16% volatility.

In this case, the volatility level that produces the smallest sum of squared residuals is about 12%. Furthermore, when this estimate is used in the pricing model, the results indicate no particular pattern of cheapness or richness for callable or noncallable bonds.

## VI. BONDS OF DIFFERENT ISSUERS

To compute the implied volatility of a broader market, we will divide all securities in that market into narrowly defined cells. Specifically, securities are stratified into cells according to the following:

- Market sector, such as GNMAs, FHLMCs, finance companies, electric utilities, and energy companies;

**EXHIBIT 5**
**OPTION-ADJUSTED SPREADS OF GMAC SECURITIES COMPUTED AT**
**12% VOLATILITY (OCTOBER 31, 1987)**

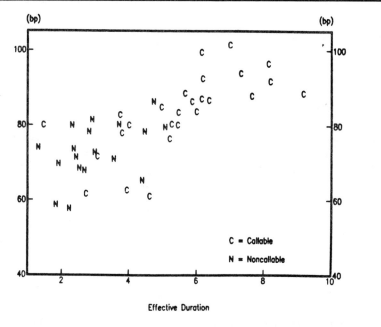

Effective Duration

- Credit rating; and
- Effective duration.

The implied volatility of the market is the single volatility estimate that minimizes the sum of squared deviations of each individual security's OAS from the average OAS of its cell.

This method can be used to estimate the implied volatility of fixed-income markets as a whole or of any given sector of the market. In particular, it allows us to analyze spreads between call-vulnerable and call-protected securities in the corporate and mortgage markets.

## VII. HISTORICAL PATTERNS IN IMPLIED VOLATILITY

The method described above allows us to calculate the implied volatility of the corporate and mortgage markets and to track trends in these statistics over time. We have computed the end-of-month implied volatilities for the past two years of the (nonsinking fund) corporate and mortgage sectors of the *Salomon Brothers Broad*

**EXHIBIT 6**
**IMPLIED[a] AND 12-WEEK ROLLING HISTORICAL VOLATILITY OF THE**
**MORTGAGE AND (NONSINKING FUND) CORPORATE MARKETS**

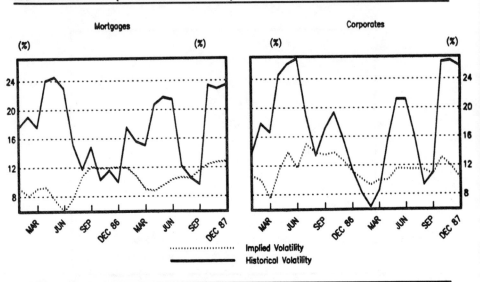

[a]Exponentially smoothed for mortgage securities.

*Investment-Grade Index.*[SM] These estimates are compared with the actual trailing 12-month yield volatility of current-coupon GNMAs and medium-term corporates in Exhibit 6. The statistical results reveal a completely new dimension of relative value in the fixed-income markets.

Although the implied volatility of both markets has varied over time, implied volatility for each has been consistently lower than the average realized yield volatility; the implied volatility for both the corporate and mortgage markets has averaged less than 12%, compared with these markets' average volatility of around 18% for the previous two years. At present, the implied volatility of the corporate market is approximately 10% versus 13% for the mortgage market.

There are several reasons that may explain why implied volatility has been consistently lower than historical realized volatility:

- Investors focus on securities' yields rather than on their total return potential; thus, buyers systematically place too low a value on call-protected bonds with their lower yields.
- Many investors evaluate securities on the basis of their yield to worst or cash flow yield; that is, on the implicit assumption that interest rate volatility is zero.
- Investors expect realized volatility to decrease in the future from the unusually elevated levels of the 1980s. Historical realized volatility was substantially lower during the 1960s and 1970s compared with levels in the 1980s.

● Investors have more information regarding the probability of corporate bonds calls than is incorporated in the OAS models. The model provides a worst case estimate of an option's value from the investor's point of view by assuming that any call will be exercised with perfect economic efficiency. Any additional information about individual issuers can only reduce the value of the option, and this will be reflected in a lower implied volatility.[6]

To the extent that the first two explanations are true, the low market implied volatility reflects a persistent market inefficiency and points to ways of systematically outperforming the corporate and mortgage markets as a whole over time.

However, if the latter two explanations hold, it may be appropriate to evaluate bonds under the assumption that expected volatility will be close to 12%. At present it is difficult to determine the relative importance of these explanations. Thus, it is not possible to determine a single "correct" volatility estimate that should be used in evaluating embedded options under all market conditions and for all applications.

When comparing option-adjusted spreads across fixed-income markets, however, we believe that investors should assume a volatility number nearer the actual volatility levels reached during the 1980s. We have reached this conclusion for two reasons:

1. We see no signs that realized market volatility will return to the lower levels of the 1960s and 1970s. Fundamental imbalances in the world economy are likely to continue to agitate financial markets for the foreseeable future.
2. We believe that most corporations exercise their call options with a considerable degree of efficiency. Furthermore, even if the exercise of options has been somewhat inefficient in the past, the growing availability of a wide variety of vehicles by which issuers can hedge refundings will tend to increase efficiency in the future.

## VIII. USES OF IMPLIED VOLATILITY: TRADING OPPORTUNITIES

The concept of implied volatility can be used by portfolio managers both to enhance portfolio performance and to identify inconsistently priced securities.

### Swap Into Call-Protected Securities

Exhibit 7 compares the aggregate characteristics of two sectors of the long-term industrial bond market, based on detailed issue data taken from the Salomon Brothers Broad Index. The first consists of *call-protected issues*—noncallable securities

---

[6]See C. Douglas Howard and Andrew J. Kalotay, *Efficiency and Optimal Bond Refunding*, Salomon Brothers Inc, March 1987.

and those with coupons below 7%. The second is a *call-vulnerable sector* comprising callable issues with coupons between 8½% and 10%. For assumed volatility of 12%, these two sectors offer about the same OAS, on average. However, at a more realistic 16% level, the call-protected issues provide a 19-basis-point wider OAS. At volatility of 20%, the advantage expands to 42 basis points. Thus, given the actual volatility levels of the 1980s, call-protected issues appear to be undervalued relative to the call-vulnerable sector.

**EXHIBIT 7**
**LONG INDUSTRIALS—BUY CALL-PROTECTED ISSUES, SELL 8½%-10% ISSUES**
**(DECEMBER 31, 1987)**

|  | Sector | Average Maturity | Effective Duration[a] | OAS by Volatility | | | |
|---|---|---|---|---|---|---|---|
|  |  |  |  | 8% | 12% | 16% | 20% |
| Buy | Call Protected | 25.6 Yrs. | 9.2 Yrs. | 90bp | 90bp | 89bp | 87bp |
| Sell | Call Vulnerable | 21.3 | 6.1 | 112 | 93 | 70 | 45 |

Call Protected: Less than 7% coupon and noncallable.
Call Vulnerable: 8.5%-10% coupons.

[a]Evaluated at 16% volatility.

**EXHIBIT 8**
**FHLMC PARTICIPATION CERTIFICATES—BUY 15-YEAR 8s,**
**SELL 30-YEAR 10s (DECEMBER 31, 1987)**

|  | Sector | Coupon | Effective Duration[a] | OAS by Volatility | | | |
|---|---|---|---|---|---|---|---|
|  |  |  |  | 8% | 12% | 16% | 20% |
| Buy | 15 Year | 8% | 4.4 Yrs. | 121bp | 114bp | 103bp | 89bp |
| Sell | 30 Year | 10% | 4.3 | 125 | 100 | 69 | 36 |

[a]Evaluated at 16% volatility.

In Exhibit 8 we compare the OASs of 15-year FHLMC 8s and 30-year FHLMC 10s. The 15-year issue is less exposed to the impact of interest rate volatility because of its lower coupon and shorter maturity, As indicated, the 15-year 8s provide a significantly wider OAS over a broad range of volatility estimates. Only at an unrealistically low 8% volatility level does the OAS of the 30-year issue narrowly exceed that of the 15-year security. On a relative basis, the market once again is underpricing the issue with a greater degree of protection from interest rate movements.

Another way to take advantage of the market's low implied volatility is to buy underpriced, high-coupon callable bonds or "cushion bonds." For these securities, the issuer is likely to exercise the first available call option because the option is well "in the money." For example, consider the Commonwealth Edison (CWE) bonds displayed in Exhibit 9. Under all volatility scenarios, the 14.375s of 1994 (callable

**EXHIBIT 9**
**COMMONWEALTH EDISON BONDS—BUY 14.375s, SELL 10.625s**
**(DECEMBER 31, 1987)**

| | Bond | Next Call Date | Call Price | Price | Effective Duration[a] | OAS by Volatility | | | |
|---|---|---|---|---|---|---|---|---|---|
| | | | | | | 8% | 12% | 16% | 20% |
| Buy | CWE 14.375 of 1994 | 15 Jul 89 | 104.11 | 111.30 | 1.7 Yrs. | 139bp | 126bp | 105bp | 81bp |
| Sell | CWE 10.625 of 1995 | 1 Sep 90 | 102.86 | 104.12 | 3.4 | 86 | 62 | 39 | 15 |

[a]Evaluated at 16% volatility.

at 104.11 on July 15, 1989) offer a significantly wider OAS than do the 10.625s of 1995 (callable at 102.86 on September 1, 1990). At the same time, as with discount securities, the OAS of the high-coupon 14.375s is less sensitive to changes in volatility than that of the 10.375s.

## Identifying Inconsistencies in Pricing

Because implied volatility is lower than historical volatility, investors who sell call-vulnerable issues and buy call-protected securities of similar quality can expect to outperform the market over time. The concept of implied volatility provides another benefit by identifying securities that are inconsistently valued, *given the market's own view of expected volatility.*

Exhibit 10 displays two examples using pairs of GMAC securities. In general, the OASs of GMAC issues are consistent when we assume 12% interest rate volatility. In both cases shown, however, one issue provides a significantly wider OAS at the market's implied volatility level of 12% as well as at levels that are closer to the historical average. This result reflects an inconsistency in market pricing over and above the market's undervaluation of call protection.

**EXHIBIT 10**
**OPTION-ADJUSTED SPREADS OF GMAC SECURITIES (JANUARY 22, 1988)**

| | Coupon | Maturity | Next Call Date | Next Call Price | Effective Duration[a] | OAS by Volatility | |
|---|---|---|---|---|---|---|---|
| | | | | | | 12% | 16% |
| Buy | 8.000% | 15 Nov 94 | NCL | | 4.7 Yrs. | 91bp | 91bp |
| Sell | 10.375 | 1 Sep 95 | 1 Sep 92 | 100.00 | 4.0 | 80 | 68 |
| Buy | 9.875 | 1 Nov 89 | 1 Nov 88 | 100.00 | 0.9 | 124 | 114 |
| Sell | 7.125 | 15 Oct 89 | NCL | | 1.5 | 114 | 114 |

[a]Evaluated at 16% volatility.
NCL Noncall life.

The undervalued security is not necessarily the discount or noncallable issue. In the first example, the noncallable 8s of 1994 provide a wider OAS than the callable 10.375s of 1995; in the second example, by contrast, the callable 9.875s of 1989 provide an OAS that is wider than or equal to that of the noncallable 7.125s of 1989, even though the high-coupon issue has a substantially shorter effective duration. The securities that are undervalued at current market implied volatility offer potential performance benefits if and when their spreads realign with those of other issues.

### Trade on Changes in Implied Volatility

During the 1980s, implied volatility has generally been lower than historical volatility. However, there have been significant changes in this statistic over time. For example, in July 1986, the implied volatility of the corporate market rose to nearly 16% only to return to 8% later in the year. These changes in implied volatility reflect substantial shifts in the relative values of call-vulnerable and call-protected issues and, thus, present opportuniites. When implied volatility is relatively low, as it is in the current market, investors should take the opportunity to increase the call protection of their portfolios. When implied volatility is relatively high, investors should swap into more call-vulnerable sectors.

At year-end 1987, the implied volatility of the nonsinking fund corporate market was approximately 10% compared with 13% for the mortgage market. Thus, the case to swap from call-vulnerable to call-protected corporates is particularly compelling because corporate bond implied volatility is even lower than usual.

## IX. SUMMARY

- The option-adjusted values of callable corporate and mortgage securities depend on expectations regarding the future volatility of interest rates. Thus, the market prices of these issues implicitly incorporate a volatility estimate. Salomon Brothers has developed a technique for assessing the implied volatility in the corporate and mortgage markets. Estimates of this statistic reveal a new dimension of relative value in the fixed-income markets.
- We define implied volatility as the single volatility estimate that minimizes the differences among the OASs of securities with similar effective duration, market sector and credit quality characteristics.
- Implied volatility for both the corporate and mortgage markets has averaged slightly less than 12% during the past two years. This is considerably lower than the 18% average historical yield volatility observed over the period and, indeed, during the 1980s as a whole. At year-end 1987, the implied volatility of the corporate bond market was approximately 10%, and that of the mortgage market was about 13%.

- We believe that the difference between implied and realized volatility presents an opportunity to outperform both the corporate and mortgage markets over time by buying undervalued call-protected securities, such as noncallable bonds or discounts. At present, this undervaluation is even more pronounced than usual in the corporate market.
- The concept of market implied volatility highlights several general and specific investment opportunities. The specific opportunities in the current market include:

  Sell "call-vulnerable" securities and buy duration-matched call-protected issues, such as noncallable bonds and low-coupon mortgages.

  Take advantage of pricing inconsistencies by selling securities with a narrow OAS and buying securities with a wide OAS, where both are evaluated at current market implied volatility.
- The more general strategic approach involves swapping into call-protected securities when implied market volatility is unusually low and into call-vulnerable securities when implied volatility is unusually high.

# Duration and Volatility in International Fixed-Income Markets

Vilas Gadkari
Director/Research
Salomon Brothers Inc

Chee Thum
Research Assistant
Salomon Brothers Inc

## I. INTRODUCTION

In today's world of "high-tech" mathematical models, concepts such as duration and convexity are used every day on bond trading and sales desks, particularly in U.S. domestic markets. Can these analytical techniques be carried over to international markets? With some modifications for differing market conditions across countries, we believe that they can be effective tools for multicurrency portfolio management.

## II. ILLUSTRATION

As an illustration, consider two ten-year bonds: a U.K. gilt and a Japanese Government bond with current coupons of 9% and 4.5%, respectively. The duration of the ten-year Japanese bond would be 1.5 years longer than that of ten-year gilts. If these bonds were to exhibit similar yield volatilities, contrary to most assumptions, such as 15%, which bond would have a higher price volatility?

Contrary to most assumptions, the Japanese Governments—with higher duration—would exhibit significantly lower price volatility during a period of equal yield volatility. This behavior can be explained by analyzing the situation in greater detail, as shown in Exhibit 1.

**EXHIBIT 1**
**COMPARISON OF VOLATILITY AND DURATION**

| Assumptions | Japan | United Kingdom |
|---|---|---|
| Current Yield (Coupon) | 4.50% | 9% |
| Yield Volatility | 15 | 15 |
| Modified Duration | 8.0 years | 6.5 years |
| One-Standard-Deviation<br>Change in Yield Level[a] | 67.5bp | 135bp |
| Percentage Change in Price<br>Corresponding to One-<br>Standard-Deviation Change<br>in Yield Level | 5.4% | 8.8% |

[a](One-Standard-Deviation Change in Yield Level) = (Yield Level) × (Volatility).

The percentage change in price corresponding to a one-standard-deviation change in yield level is an estimate of price volatility for the bond market conditions described above. This example emphasizes the fact that a bond with lower duration can have higher price volatility: In this case, the yield change corresponding to a one-standard-deviation shift is much higher in the lower duration market. This analysis also suggests that even if the yield volatility of ten-year yen bonds is twice that of ten-year gilts (about 25% in the above example), the two bonds could still have similar price volatilities.

## III. EFFECT OF YIELD LEVEL ON YIELD/PRICE VOLATILITY

In recent years, yield levels in most major bond markets around the world have fallen significantly from their peaks in the early 1980s. The effect of this drop in yield levels could be analyzed in a constant yield volatility environment in the following way:

- A drop in yield level will increase the duration of a bond, thereby making its price more sensitive to yield changes. This will tend to increase the price volatility of the bond.
- A drop in yield level, at constant yield volatility—a constant percentage change environment—will result in smaller absolute yield changes and, therefore, will

reduce the magnitude of average price changes. This will lead to a decrease in the price volatility.

● The decrease in price volatility resulting from smaller yield changes tends to dominate the increase in price volatility from an increase in duration, reducing the volatility of the bond.

In addition, in a constant price volatility environment, a drop in yield level will increase the yield volatility of a bond because the change in yield level will now appear larger in percentage terms. As the yield level continues to decline, its effect on yield volatility increases exponentially. Thus, it is necessary to be careful when comparing yield and price volatilities over long periods of time.

The Japanese bond market presents an interesting case in point. Compare the two periods: 1980, which had yield levels of about 10%, versus 1987, when yields averaged about 4.9%. In 1980, yield volatilities of around 35% produced price volatilities of about 25%; during the recent backups, yield volatilities as high as 50% led to price volatilities of only 20% (see Exhibit 2).

It is also possible to find periods of similar price volatilities for varying yield volatilities. Exhibit 3 shows periods with price volatilities of about 15% and the different yield and volatility levels for the Japanese Government bond market.

**EXHIBIT 2**
**TEN-YEAR JAPANESE GOVERNMENT BOND YIELDS VERSUS THREE-MONTH MOVING YIELD AND PRICE VOLATILITIES, JAN 80-MAR 88 (Weekly Data)**

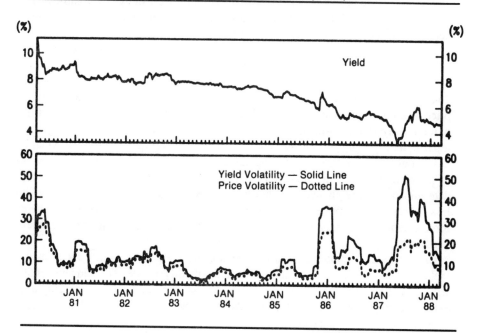

**EXHIBIT 3**
**JAPANESE GOVERNMENT BONDS—EXAMPLES OF VARYING YIELD LEVELS AND VOLATILITY LEVELS FOR 15% PRICE VOLATILITY**

| Period | Average Yield Level | Yield Volatility | Price Volatility |
|---|---|---|---|
| 4 Dec 80-5 Mar 81 | 8.7% | 18.0% | 15.1% |
| 1 Aug 85-31 Oct 85 | 6.2 | 31.4 | 15.5 |
| 19 Feb 87-21 May 87 | 4.3 | 41.3 | 15.7 |

The historical relationship between yield and price volatilities in the major fixed-income markets can be seen in the data presented in Exhibit 4. The lower yielding bond markets, such as the Japanese and West German Governments, have experienced much lower price volatilities, even though their yield volatilities have been in line with higher yielding bonds, including U.K. gilts or U.S. Treasuries. An exception to this rule has been the volatility in the Japanese Government through most of 1987.

## IV. WHAT IS THE RIGHT MEASURE OF RISK, PRICE OR YIELD VOLATILITY?

The question then becomes, what is a more useful measure of market volatility? The better measure of risk is price volatility. Yield volatility has been traditionally used because it is a much more convenient measure for market participants and because coupon and duration differences in a given bond market do not need to be taken into account. There are several ways that participants use market volatility estimates: Portfolio managers looking to maximize their risk-adjusted total returns use market volatility as a measure of risk associated with an asset class. For these investors, price volatility is of greater relevance because it is virtually identical to the volatility of total returns on fixed-income assets. Option traders, who use yield volatility as an input in their pricing models and concern themselves primarily with yield volatilities, should be aware that their pricing models perform the transformation from yield to price; thus, up in the branches of their binomial trees, the option payoff is determined by price changes and not by yield fluctuations. Option traders may be less concerned with price volatility if their option expirations are short, and therefore, a significant change in yield level may not be expected during the investment horizon.

Exhibit 5 demonstrates a method of estimating the price volatility for a known yield level and volatility. For example, a yield volatility of 25% at a yield level of 5% will imply a price volatility of 10% (point A), while a similar price volatility also exists in a market with a much higher yield level, of 15%, and at a much lower yield volatility of about 15% (point B).

# EXHIBIT 4
## AVERAGE THREE-MONTH YIELD AND PRICE VOLATILITIES AND AVERAGE YIELDS OF TEN-YEAR CURRENT-COUPON GOVERNMENT BONDS

| | U.S. | | | Japan | | | Germany | | | U.K. | | |
|---|---|---|---|---|---|---|---|---|---|---|---|---|
| | Yield Vol. | Price Vol. | Average Yield | Yield Vol. | Price Vol. | Average Yield | Yield Vol. | Price Vol. | Average Yield | Yield Vol. | Price Vol. | Average Yield |
| 1982-1986 | 14.1% | 12.9% | 10.95% | 10.6% | 7.7% | 7.04% | 11.5% | 8.5% | 7.50% | 13.4% | 12.5% | 11.40% |
| 1986 | 17.6 | 13.1 | 7.68 | 17.6 | 10.8 | 5.47 | 14.6 | 9.5 | 5.97 | 13.8 | 10.0 | 10.04 |
| 1987 | 16.7 | 13.8 | 8.39 | 29.2 | 14.6 | 4.83 | 15.1 | 9.8 | 6.21 | 16.1 | 13.7 | 9.61 |
| 1Q 87 | 5.8 | 5.4 | 7.15 | 12.3 | 6.4 | 4.96 | 11.7 | 5.4 | 5.96 | 14.6 | 14.9 | 9.80 |
| 2Q 87 | 18.5 | 15.6 | 8.32 | 50.9 | 20.0 | 3.86 | 13.6 | 9.3 | 5.72 | 14.3 | 12.1 | 9.02 |
| 3Q 87 | 9.4 | 7.3 | 8.83 | 35.5 | 20.3 | 5.18 | 13.3 | 10.2 | 6.43 | 19.0 | 17.6 | 9.90 |
| 4Q 87 | 31.8 | 29.1 | 9.12 | 27.0 | 15.9 | 5.28 | 30.4 | 20.6 | 6.67 | 22.6 | 16.9 | 9.70 |

**EXHIBIT 5**
**PRICE AND YIELD VOLATILITIES AND YIELD LEVELS FOR PAR BONDS WITH A TEN-YEAR MATURITY**

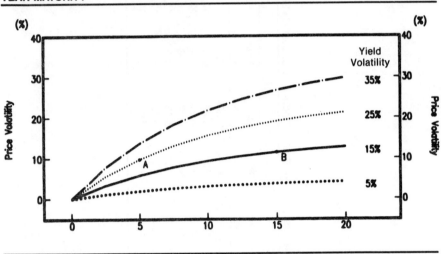

## V. APPLICATIONS

### Management of Multicurrency Bond Portfolios versus a Benchmark

In recent years, bond market performance has commanded more attention and has led to an increased interest among portfolio managers to compare the expected performance of their portfolios with benchmarks like the Salomon Brothers World Government Bond Index. This can be done by identifying the extent to which a portfolio deviates from a benchmark in terms of expected total returns and risk. (Risk in this case could be measured as the volatility of deviations in returns from the benchmark.) *Once again, duration is the key measure currently used to estimate such deviations. Unless these durations are normalized across markets, a portfolio could be more out of line with the benchmark than typically expected by a portfolio manager.*

### Example

Consider a portfolio manager who believes that sterling will strengthen versus Deutschemarks in the coming months, but does not expect the performance of the two bond markets to differ significantly and, therefore, wishes to overweight the sterling sector of his benchmark relative to the Deutschemark segment. He could express his view in one of two ways:

(1) He could buy sterling versus Deutschemarks in the short-dated forward exchange market without changing the local currency bond weightings relative to his benchmark. This alternative may not be available to some portfolio managers who have restrictions on the use of futures, forward and options contracts.

(2) He could buy more gilts relative to Bunds to overweight the sterling sector. This method of acquiring currency exposure is widely used. In this case, however, the portfolio manager is also picking up a different risk/return profile for his bond portfolio. Exhibit 6 shows total returns on five-year duration gilts and Bunds in local currency terms.[1] The monthly mean absolute deviation of 138 basis points (not annualized) between the return series illustrates the fact that the two bonds are not perfect substitutes.

**EXHIBIT 6**
**LOCAL CURRENCY TOTAL RETURNS ON FIVE-YEAR DURATION U.K. GILTS AND BUNDS AND THE SPREAD BETWEEN RETURNS**

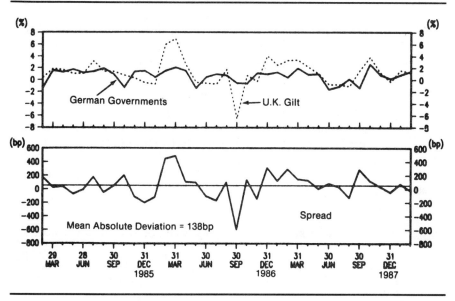

The price volatility characteristics of these two markets are also quite different. Exhibit 7 shows duration and volatility relationships in the major Government bond markets. *Local currency total returns on gilts and Bunds, with durations of five*

---

[1]Exhibits 6 and 7 were created by choosing several bonds in each of the major Government bond markets with different durations and then building portfolios that maintained constant durations throughout the three-year period for which monthly data from the Salomon Brothers World Government Bond index data base was used. This set of bonds was updated every six months, while their weights were updated monthly to maintain constant duration.

*years, have had volatilities of 8.1% and 4.0%, respectively, during the past three years. Different yield levels and volatilities in the two markets lead to varying patterns of yield changes. Therefore, duration—which measures percentage price change for a unit change in yield—becomes ineffective as a tool for comparing the relative riskiness of bonds in multicurrency portfolios.*

The U.K. gilt market provides a good case in point when analyzing differences in the risk/return characteristics of international fixed-income markets. In Exhibit 7, the shape of the duration-volatility line for the gilt market is rather different relative to other markets. Although the volatility of shorter durations in the United Kingdom is the highest in the major international fixed-income markets, the rate of increase in volatility decreases as durations increase above five years. Consequently, long duration gilts end up with lower volatilities relative to U.S. Treasuries. For the United States and Japan, the slopes of the lines in Exhibit 7—which represent the rates of increase in volatility—are roughly constant throughout the duration spectrum. The behavior of the U.K. gilt market can be attributed to the following:

- Short-term interest rates in Britain fluctuate more in response to currency changes relative to other countries used in this analysis. As the shorter maturities respond to these fluctuations in the money markets, the price volatility of lower durations increases.
- In Exhibit 7, the rate of increase of volatility (the slope of the U.K. gilt line) declines around durations of five years. The decrease in volatility may be due to the fact that most of the short-term bond portfolios in Britain (building society portfolios, for example) have a maturity limit of seven years, and their investment decisions (made in response to shifts in money market rates) affect bonds with durations of up to five years much more than those with longer durations.

**EXHIBIT 7**
**VOLATILITY OF LOCAL CURRENCY RETURNS VERSUS DURATION (Jan 85—Dec 87)**

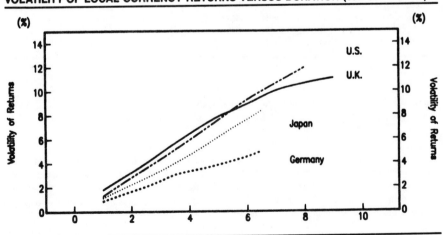

These differences in market behavior are important for analyzing the risk/return characteristics of multicurrency portfolios, particularly those that deviate from their benchmarks. To obtain a common ground to compare the relative riskiness of investments in bonds from different countries, we need to shift from a measurement using duration to price volatility. To remain consistent with the market convention of using yield volatility, investors could normalize durations by multiplying the modified duration by the yield level (see the first equation below). The resultant number can be used, along with expected yield volatilities, when developing bond market strategies. Specifically, an estimate of price volatility can be obtained by using an estimate of yield volatility (see the second equation below).

$$NMD = MD \times YL$$
$$PV = (MD \times YL) \times YV = NMD \times YV.$$

where

$NMD$ = Normalized Modified Duration
$PV$ = Price Volatility
$MD$ = Modified Duration
$YL$ = Yield Level and
$YV$ = Yield Volatility

## VI. CONCLUSIONS

The duration of a bond is a widely used indicator of bond price sensitivity to yield changes.[2] However, duration may not be an accurate measure with which to compare bonds from different countries (in local currency terms), because durations represent price sensitivities to bond yield fluctuations in various domestic markets. For example, five-year duration U.K. gilts have very different price volatilities versus five-year duration West German Government bonds (Bunds), as yield volatilities in the two markets are typically dissimilar.

Even if yield volatilities are similar across markets, this measure could provide misleading signals about relative price volatilities, because differing yield levels translate similar yield volatilities into unequal yield changes. This, in turn, results in different price changes and volatilities for bonds with similar durations.

To compare the relative riskiness of bond investments from different countries, we believe that investors should use local currency price volatilities instead of

---

[2]The formula used for estimating bond price sensitivity to yield change is as follows:

$$\triangle P/P = MD \times \triangle Y$$

where for a given bond $\triangle P$ = Change in Price; $P$ = Full Price; $MD$ = Modified Duration; and $\triangle Y$ = Change in Bond Yield.

durations. Since duration and yield volatility are key measures used by multicurrency portfolio managers in the day-to-day management of their assets, we recommend a way of normalizing durations for varying yield levels across countries and establishing a relationship between local currency price volatility and normalized durations and yield volatility.

# Reagan—Changing the Rules of the Game*

CHRIS P. DIALYNAS
MANAGING DIRECTOR
PACIFIC INVESTMENT MANAGEMENT COMPANY

## I. PREAMBLE

The economic policies of the 1970's consisted of rapid monetary growth, increased rates of taxation and increased rates of Federal expenditures. These policies resulted in rapidly increasing prices, economic stagnation, a gradual reduction in the growth of an underground economy and the proliferation of real asset based tax shelters and escalating prices of real assets.

At the time Ronald Reagan took office in 1981, the Consumer Price Index was increasing at an annual rate of 9%, real Gross National Product was 1.9%, three-month Treasury bills yielded 14.75%, 30-year Treasury bonds yielded 11%, the annual budget deficit was less than $50 billion, the trade balance was in deficit by $36 billion and the unemployment rate was 7.6%.

The Reagan Administration abruptly changed both monetary and fiscal policies simultaneously in an effort to control inflation, deregulate and restore economic incentives. Monetary policy was tightened dramatically in the early years and eased dramatically in the latter years. Taxes were cut dramatically in the early years and gradually in the latter years.

The magnitude of the changes were so great that unpredictable outcomes resulted. The budget deficit increased dramatically to over $200 billion and eventually stabilized at a $150 billion structured prosperity deficit. The value of the dollar doubled

---

*Adapted from a talk given on October 13, 1987 at the Pomona College Centennial Celebration.

during the 1980-85 period and subsequently declined by half. The balance of trade reached a record monthly deficit of $15 billion and stabilized at a $10 billion monthly deficit even though the dollar is lower against most currencies than it was in 1980. Inflation rates plummeted and bankruptcies roared even though real economic growth prevailed. Volatility in asset prices was dominant throughout the period.

The Reagan Era is ending with an economy buoyant with prosperity, masked by poverty. The many various policies implemented have resulted in extraordinary persistent budget and trade deficits. Savings levels are at 4%, less than half the 1981 rate. Moreover, private debt, both corporate and personal, have escalated well beyond those levels ever experienced during peacetime prosperity. The magnitude of the pre-Reagan and post-Reagan debt level differences are staggering. The country's future fiscal and monetary flexibility have been mortgaged. Absent new meaningful breakthroughs in productivity in the United States, the economic outlook is one of gradual relative decline at best. Living standards will deteriorate with the deterioration of the dollar value and volatility will persist as tomorrow's policy makers attempt to grasp with the future. The potential for new international conflicts is very great.

## II. INTRODUCTION

The economic policies implemented by the Reagan Administration have resulted in historically high volatility in the prices of both real and financial assets. As a result, massive transfers of wealth have occurred between the owners of real assets and the owners of financial assets. The desirability of wealth transfers is a topic best left for social philosophers. Understanding the aspects of public policy that create volatility and the financial and economic implications of changes in volatility are most interesting topics.

Reaganomics allegedly represent a transition from demand side economics to supply side economics. More generally, though, Reaganomics is merely a policy of frequent, abrupt, meaningful changes in economic policies. The policy changes induce volatility and result in wealth transfers. For example, the policy of increasing the investment tax credit is a subsidy to capital intensive industries. The general public will pay either higher direct taxes to compensate for the lost revenue, pay the indirect tax of increased inflation, a weakened dollar, or both and eventually a reduction in employment resulting from tax-induced rather than economic-induced investment. Major policy changes transfer large amounts of wealth. Large wealth transfers lead to direct economic dislocations and indirect dislocations as the expected value of financial contracts and production plans are exogenously changed.

Wealth transfers are accomplished by the change in the marginal prices of assets. The new price reflects the discounted after-tax, risk-adjusted present value of the new expected income flows and asset value. The price changes create volatility. By inference, macroeconomic policy changes create price volatility as wealth transfers.

Expectations of volatility, in turn, displace endogenous economic effects which impede the efficiency of the policy changes.

## III. VOLATILITY AND INVESTMENT

Expectations of forward volatility retard economic growth. Volatility premiums affect economic activity in many ways. All of the effects increase the risk-adjusted cost of economic activity. By definition, high expectations for volatility means high risk. Therefore, expected returns must increase or investment incentives are diminished.

We can examine the dynamics of inventory investment as an example. The decision to add to inventory is primarily predicated upon the future price of the product and the liquidity or turnover rate of the product, as well as the product's profit margin and financing rate. No distributor would want to purchase inventory if he knew the price would instantaneously go lower since instant losses occur. All distributors would want to purchase inventory if they knew prices would instantaneously increase and the turnover rate was greater than zero during the period of price increase. The greater the uncertainty about tomorrow's price and the lower the turnover rate and profit margin, the lower the incentives for inventory investment. Since greater expectations for volatility imply greater uncertainty about forward prices around a random mean price, inventory investment is dampened with increased expectations for volatility. The reduction in inventory investment exerts a direct effect on production and Gross National Product which serve to reduce the turnover rate and feed back into higher risk-adjusted inventory holding costs.

Insurance exists for the purpose of encouraging risk-taking. Insurers pool risk takers and rely upon the law of large numbers to centralize their risk about a mean volatility. The premium charged for the insurance is primarily a function of volatility. The greater the chance of the adverse event, the greater the premium.

Economic agents may alter their intrinsic risk-reward profile with the purchase of an insurance policy. With the purchase of an insurance policy, the costs associated with risky behavior are limited to the cost of the insurance policy. Increased costs of insurance decreases the return on investment and therefore the desire for investment. A decision not to insure increases the return on the investment but also increases its risk. Parties who cancel insurance because of increases in the premiums probably cancel investments since they presumably view them as containing higher risks than previously perceived, and the new insurance costs render the risk-adjusted return on investment inferior. The more conservative investment policy which results from volatility's affect on insurance premiums and the new investment policy adopted constrains investment and reduces production. Moreover, volatility increases the value of liquidity. Marketable financial assets become preferred to capital projects as the investment of choice because the costs of changing an investment decision when macro policy changes is relatively small.

## IV.  VOLATILITY AND THE SOCIAL STRUCTURE

Volatility's influence manifests in the social structure as well. All else equal, the greater the volatility, the greater are the costs associated with mistakes and the greater the benefits associated with brilliance. New meritocratic rules develop with regard to employment policies. Inefficient employees are displaced by employees with state of the art skills. Wall Street is a prime example and a leveraged example of this. New MBA's with state of the art financial, statistical and computer skills dominate the business. In fact, when Stan Diller, foremost among practical applied bond theorists was at Goldman Sachs, he joked about how the firm used to hire bond traders by the size of their liver, but how today they hire traders based upon their ability to solve differential equations. So, the old are displaced by the new in employment as well as production. Both substitutions disrupt the economic structure and impose new constraints upon public policy.

## V.  VOLATILITY AND CONTRACTUAL ARRANGEMENTS

The ability and willingness of economic parties to contract is a basic requirement of capitalism. Increased volatility increases the risks associated with engaging in long term financial contracts. A lender or borrower who knew interest rates would never change would, all else equal, prefer to minimize transaction costs and lend (borrow) long term rather than frequently rolling short term debt. The lower the certainty of stability, the greater the premium the lender will demand if, as is normally the case, the borrower reserves the option to repay the loan if rates decline. In fact, we know from option pricing theory the value of that option is most influenced by the amount of volatility experienced. Since these options are associated with virtually all long term bond contracts from home mortgages to the borrowings of industries, public utilities, and municipalities, volatility increases the cost of financing. The amount of volatility, ex post, determines the ultimate economic effects of volatility and the value of those contracts.

## VI.  VOLATILITY AND RISK TAKING

Commercial banking is an industry within which the a priori and ex post volatility assumptions are perhaps most dramatic. The importance of differentiating between economic flows and economic stocks is very apparent with asset based lending. The lending policies of the banks during the real asset inflationary boom exemplifies the risks. Loans were extended to borrowers based primarily upon the expected value of the assets rather than the ability of the borrower to repay the money. So, for a point up front and a 2% spread, money was available. Two percent margins were quickly eliminated as real asset price volatility increased and the asset's price fell by 50%. The enterprise of asset based commercial banking is rendered obsolete in volatile economic environments. Naturally, loans extended on financial assets also fit into this category and will probably prove to be the next Achilles heel of the banking industry.

Investment banks have suffered the tax of volatility as well and will, most likely, suffer more of a tax in the future. As a group, the market-making investment banks have experienced trading losses exceeding a billion dollars recently. The losses of some investment banks have been well publicized; others have not. The incentive compensation structure embedded within the industry made it ripe for the losses which have occurred. Once again, the importance of the differentiation between asset prices and economic flows was ignored. Traders, controlling hundreds of millions of dollars of leveraged capital have their compensation tied to non-risk-adjusted profits. A recent loss of $25 million on a $300 million position is easily explainable. A gain of $25 million which should have resulted if interest rates had decreased rather than increasing as they did, may have created $2.5 million of income to the trader. Instead, it cost him his job. On a 75-25 bet, assuming you were privy to valuable trading information, would you trade your job for the prospect of $2.5 million?

## VII. VOLATILITY AND GREED

Ivan Boesky was presented with similar circumstances. Trading on information which assured large price changes on the assets he controlled and, therefore, extraordinary profits for himself, encountered another asymmetric economic condition created by extreme price volatility and amoral greed. On the downside, Boesky was confronted with the prospects of jail. The upside promised money beyond the imagination. Such risk-reward tradeoffs render bank robbery obsolete without even considering the potential of death in the latter case. Our actions are indeed influenced by the higher order macroeconomic conditions and the micro behavioral changes are also observed on a macro level by changes in the velocity of money, the demand for money, in money multipliers, in savings rates and a whole host of other ex-post observatives of economic activity.

The combination of misspecified incentives and volatile policies have affected the financial behavior of Corporate America also. Just as the 1970's executive compensation schemes, whose functions related to revenue and income production, created merger mania and conglomeration, so to the *price* of the company's stock created incentives for the leveraging of American enterprise for the purpose of stock buy-back. Increases in executive wealth are easily accomplished through bondholder expropriation. ESOPs encourage and accomplish similarly motivated events and outcomes for a company's employees. Moreover, the increases in leverage increase the probability of volatility which subsequently increases the benefits of leverage. So, once again an arena dramatically changed combined with a changing of the rules of the game create natural economic outcomes, but outcomes with harmful macroeconomic effects because of their short term orientation.

## VIII.  VOLATILITY AND THE BOND MARKET

Finally, a few comments about the Great American Bond Market. Bonds are uniquely quanitfiable with respect to volatility changes. Bonds, as you will recall, are contractually defined by a fixed coupon rate, a maturity date and are offered at a price which translates into a yield to maturity (YTM). In a world without volatility, the YTM is of greatest importance. A world with extraordinary volatility holds as its most important element the price elasticity of the bond with respect to changes in market interest rates. Bonds themselves may be thought of as a crude set of options wherein investors are able to buy or sell "insurance". The market place is full of examples. Bond mutual funds which emphasize yield or dividend rate are very volatile. On the other hand, long term U.S. Government bonds have tremendous price elasticity as interest rates vary but sacrifice yield to obtain this good price character. Most of the debt of issues other than the U.S. Treasury contain explicit refunding and/or sinking fund provisions. Virtually all corporate and mortgage debt fall into this category and because of these "refunding options," the value of these bonds is directly related to the variability of interest rates. In choosing bonds as an investment, a conscious decision about the volatility expected for interest rates as well as the direction of rates must be considered.

## IX.  ECONOMIC POLICY IN A VOLATILE ENVIRONMENT

In conclusion, the extremely volatile budgetary, monetary, regulatory and tax policies implemented have induced extreme volatility in asset prices, dollar volatility and encouraged speculation. Short term price changes inherent to the volatility are an increasing factor of income as volatility increases. The motivation to game volatility (legally and otherwise) or to speculate increases with volatility increases. The importance of short term results dominate long term considerations. The present value of the long term flows represented by income from a job, profits, dividends or interest payments are dominated by bonus payments, stock price changes, changes in housing prices, currency fluctuations and bond price changes. Extraordinary risks by economic agents in all camps are undertaken because of the short term myopia. The subsequent results of increases in volatility and leverage require a greater reliance upon the public as the large losses accrued are transferred to the public while the tremendous gains reaped remain private. Public policy acceptance of the losses as assurance that the "system works" encourage further speculation, further volatility, greater short term myopia and greater system reassurance. The destructive forces of volatility eventually dominate because the public system is unable to absorb the losses without taxing the private gains.

The recent formation of a Western world economic cartel as manifested in the "G" meetings will only serve to perpetuate volatility. Cartel formation has been motivated historically by a desire to stabilize conditions but cartels have ultimately resulted in great economic displacements and instability. The Western alliance, while similarly well motivated will, most likely, result in significant economic dislocations inducing substantial volatililty and the eventual reduction of wealth.

So, volatility has reduced many mighty men from Texas to New York to mere mortals. The greatest threat today is that extreme volatility reduces this mighty nation to merely another nation.

# PART II

# Corporate Bond Market

# Takeover Event Risk and Corporate Bond Portfolio Management

N. R. VIJAYARAGHAVAN, PH.D.
VICE PRESIDENT
DREXEL BURNHAM LAMBERT

RANDY SNOOK
ASSOCIATE
GOLDMAN, SACHS & CO.

## I. INTRODUCTION

The recent surge in takeovers and restructuring has brought to fore a previously known, but latent peril in high grade corporate bond markets—"event risk." Knowledge of its existence, however, has not provided great comfort to those bond investors who faced substantial drops in the values of their portfolios after the announcement of the management-led leveraged buyout (LBO) bid for RJR Nabisco. There are structural reasons which have promoted this form of risk to prominence in the current takeover boom. The markets certainly have witnessed cyclical

This article was completed when Mr. Snook was an Associate with Drexel Burnham Lambert Inc. The authors would like to thank David J. Askin, Llewellyn Miller, Terran Miller, Scott Redstone and George Varughese for their very helpful suggestions.

upturns in takeover activities in the past. However, there are qualitative and quantitative differences in the current market for takeovers from those of the yesteryears. Noteworthy among them are the following.

1. Current acquirors not only include corporations but individuals and small partnerships (backed by takeover funds from large institutions) as well.
2. Takeovers have grown in terms of transaction size—the bid for RJR Nabisco exceeded $24 billion, an amount deemed impractical even just a few years ago.
3. They have undergone a metamorphosis in terms of the structure of the financing—from all equity transactions to bank financed leverage transactions to public (high yield bond) and bank financed leverage transactions.
4. LBOs are no longer confined to "mature, cash cow" oriented industries. This was the case earlier, ensuring that the total leverage of the restructured firm (operating plus financial) was not excessive. High operating leverage no longer is an insurmountable constraint in an LBO. The result is the use of LBOs in virtually every type of industry—from publishing to entertainment to high technology.
5. There is a richening trend in the valuation of takeover candidates based on their cashflows. For example, only a few years ago the typical valuation multiple on earnings before interest and taxes (EBIT) was in the range of 4 to 6. Now, it ranges from 8 to 10. To some extent, this trend is a result of too much money (with the increasing inflows of overseas capital) chasing too few transactions.

In combination, these trends have contributed to the current visible effects on the high grade industrial corporate bond market.

"Event risk" could relate to a variety of events in the context of different industries. For example, nuclear plant cancellations in the utility sector and special provisions for loans and losses in the banking sector were issues which contributed to risk under this category, in the past. The focus of this article, however, is on the takeover, restructuring, merger, acquisition and LBO risks. These will broadly be referred to by the generic term "event risk" in the remainder of the discussion. The topics addressed are: the rationale for and the risk structure of a takeover, its effect on the underlying securities of the corporations involved, the spillover effects into related securities and effective ways of hedging or controlling such risks.

## II. THE RATIONALE FOR TAKEOVERS

The objective of most takeovers, from the point of view of the acquiror, is to either create arbitrage profits from the inefficiencies inherent in asset markets or to enhance value through efficient management of the firm for future realization of profits. For the target shareholders, a takeover provides an opportunity to participate in part of the revaluation of the assets through enhanced share values. The underlying premise, then, is that target stocks are undervalued. A variety of reasons are offered for the undervaluation, but they usually relate to "inefficiencies," taking the following forms.

a. *Operational inefficiencies*, as in non-optimal utilization of the basic inputs to added value—labor, capacity utilization, etc. A restructuring of the firm, resulting in reduced labor and increased manufacturing efficiency could lead to higher earnings. The higher estimated earnings is used to arrive at a "fair price" by using an appropriate price/earnings (P/E) multiple. In acquisitions, operational synergies often lead to improved efficiency for the combined firm.
b. *Structural inefficiencies*, as in unrelated business activities under one firm, inefficiently valued because of the commingling of independent P/E multiples. By selling the unrelated businesses at their (higher) P/E, a gain can be achieved. Increasingly, better focused businesses utilizing the franchise values, brand names and other such intangible assets are seen as strategies for increasing shareholder wealth.
c. *Valuation inefficiencies* with hidden tangible assets such as real estate, commercial buildings, natural resource reserves, etc., which can be sold separately to increase share values.
d. *Capital structure inefficiencies*, as in underutilization of the available debt capacity. As returns to debt (interest payments) are tax deductible to the firm whereas returns to equity (dividend) are not, a higher leverage for the firm is viewed as contributing to additional shareholder value. (Note that the same reason may result in worsening credit quality of existing bonds.)

The last point is particularly important. It emphasizes the dual role of leveraging—it is used not only as a *means* for takeovers, but also, in many cases, as an *end* in itself, as it adds (shareholder) value through tax advantages.

The current increased pace of mergers could also be partly explained by the participants' risk aversion to policy uncertainty when a new administration takes over. There is also an increasingly palpable concern among members of Congress and regulators at the growing leverage at all levels in the economy—the consumer, business and government. This is likely to lead to more stringent anti-trust enforcement and closure of at least some of the current tax advantages in M&A.

## III. EFFECT OF TAKEOVERS ON OUTSTANDING SECURITIES

The target firm utilizes a given capital structure (debt to equity) to produce its current earnings. The debtholders' priorities depend on their existing covenants.

They have claims on the earnings of the firm in accordance with the assigned priorities. For example, bank debt may have a priority over senior debtholders, who, in turn will be followed by junior debtholders and other subordinated claims. When an LBO is attempted, this priority structure is disturbed. For example, the new capital structure might be an attempted substitution of current equity with higher debt, with, say, 50% of the new financing coming from bank loans, 30% from public high yield bond issue (which is usually preceded by bridge loans from investment banks) and the remaining 20% in new equity. A typical LBO might attempt to change the debt/equity ratio from, say, 60/40 to 90/10. Exhibit 1 depicts the typical change in capital structure associated with an LBO and the accompanying change in credit quality. (For equity, interpret credit quality to be its risk.)

The restructuring of current equity to debt/equity disturbs the valuation of existing high grade debt securities. This happens due to the fact that the firm is likely to retain lower earnings after the LBO (with lower build-up of equity), because of increased debt servicing. This might lead to a lower cushion for existing high grade debt with reduced interest coverage, leading to a deterioration of its credit quality.

The change in the status of the existing debtholders' priority of the claim on the cashflows of the firm also affects their valuation. If the new debt issue is always assigned a lower priority, then the existing debt securities will be less affected compared to the case where the new debt issue is at a higher priority, if other things remain the same. The change in prioritization could be due to:

a. the fact that the existing debt securities might not have (foreseen) the adequate covenants to protect their priorities even with respect to the scheduled new public debt issues and/or

b. the new debt in the form of bank loans typically are assigned a higher priority, scheduled with some asset collateralization.

Additionally, there is a volatility effect which redistributes wealth from existing bondholders to stockholders. The bond investors perceive an increased riskiness of

**EXHIBIT 1**
**IMPLICATIONS OF CHANGING CAPITAL STRUCTURE ON CREDIT QUALITY**

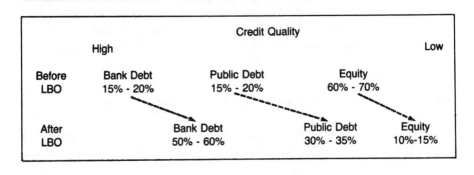

the firm, due to the higher uncertainty of new management/policies, new projects or other factors. This contributes to a decline in the credit quality on bonds. For a given value of the firm as a whole (equity plus debt), the increased volatility, therefore, has a net effect of transferring wealth from existing bondholders to stockholders.

However, as new bondholders buy under current market conditions, their securities will tend to be fairly valued.

Firms within a given industry are also correlated in terms of event risk. Acquisition debt has a spillover yield effect to securities of other firms in the same industry, usually at an attenuated level. This effect can be explained due to the following factors:

a. An event announcement in one firm lowers the credit quality of its high grade bonds which might not have adequate protection.

b. The announcement, apart from lowering the credit status of the high grade bonds of the target firm, also often signals other attractive targets within the industry. This happens due to the fact that "undervaluation" of firms within a given industry could be correlated. This portends likely event risks for other firms in the industry.

Exhibit 2 illustrates the effect of the announcement of the management-led LBO bid for RJR Nabisco on its high grade debt. Exhibit 3 shows the correlated effect of the announcement on three other investment grade industrial bonds.

**EXHIBIT 2**
**RJR NABISCO—THE IMPACT OF THE INITIAL LBO BID ANNOUNCEMENT
ON YIELD SPREADS**

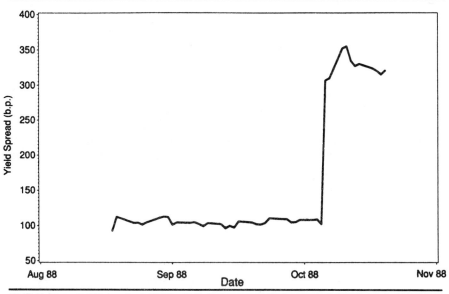

*RJR Nabisco 9 3/8 due April 2016 - U.S. Treasury 8 7/8 due August 2017.

**EXHIBIT 3**
**ANHEUSER BUSCH, SARA LEE & UNION PACIFIC—EVENT RISK FEARS CAUSED**
**THESE YIELD SPREADS TO WIDEN**

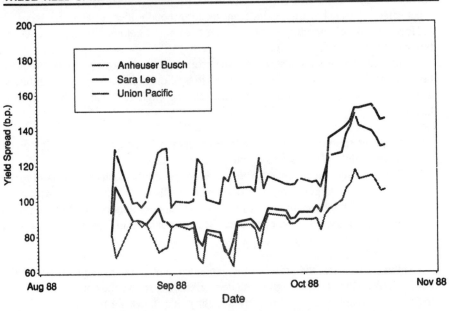

*Corporates are Spread to the U.S. Treasury 8 7/8 due August 2017.

A combination of such events in an industry affects the overall credit quality of existing securities. As equity is replaced in takeovers, there is an increased supply of bank debt and high yield debt supporting such transactions, increasing their relative yields and resulting in slippage of their credit quality. If existing high grade issues do not have pari passu protection with new bank debt, their credit quality slips as well toward that of low grade issues as was shown earlier in Exhibit 1. They are effectively downgraded because bank debt replaces their position with stronger covenants and because interest coverage is lower with the higher level of debt in the capital structure. The question then is, can existing bondholders protect themselves under such circumstances? What are the mechanisms available for debt already in place? And what precautions should new high grade holders take for future event risk protection? This is the focus of the discussion in the following section.

## III. PROTECTION AGAINST EVENT RISK

In this section, some of the common features, instruments and procedures available to provide protection against event risk in bond portfolios are discussed. Note that with many instruments, risk protection is available only for the total package of event risk, other forms of credit risk and interest rate risk combined together. More specialized forms of protection are emerging currently to provide insurance against each of these risks separately. Such forms provide for more efficient risk allocation among market participants by increasing their ability to attain selective risk exposure.

### Equity

Hold a combination of equity and high grade debt, rather than stand-alone issues of debt. In the event of a takeover, the drop in bond prices will be compensated by the rising stock price of the target firm. An apropriate hedge ratio has to be used by considering the likely movement in the bond and stock prices. Obviously, this is an extremely difficult task and calls for judgmental positions. Further, this ratio may have to be adjusted dynamically to rebalance the hedge. An equivalent effect can also be obtained by using calls on the underlying stock. However, in this case, one has to be careful about the dissipation of the time value of the option. Alternatively, because of the correlation of stock price movements within the same industry, equity of a similar firm could be used as a successful substitute.

The problem with using equity as event-risk hedges is that they may have unintended side effects, especially when the holding period is uncertain. For example, there may be a situation when both stock and bond prices fall together, as with rising inflation. Against such non-event risk factors, equity ends up increasing the relative risk exposure. Investors, therefore, should be careful in assessing the global hedging characteristic of an instrument against multiple risk factors. However, by timing the holding period of the hedge, selective hedging can be achieved effectively.

### Convertible Bonds

Convertible bonds allow investors to participate simultaneously in both the debt and equity of the issuer. In particular, investors should look for convertible bonds that are trading at substantial discounts to their conversion prices. Such bonds are likely to trade similar to the issuer's straight debt. If there is a substantial move in the stock price, the bonds will begin to trade like equity. This transition from a straight bond to equity therefore provides an "intrinsic" dynamic hedge ratio adjustment. Minor moves in the stock price will probably not impact the convertible trading at a steep discount.

This approach is somewhat restrictive since the majority of the convertible bonds outstanding tend to be highly leveraged non-investment grade debt. Also, they may not be available in the firm (or industry) of interest and may not be liquid.

### High Yield Securities

Swaps into high yield securities can be appropriate for both investment grade bonds and for "fallen angels." Investors holding high quality bonds may find that these are generally underleveraged companies with strong cash flows. Rather than hold bonds of these firms, investors might protect themselves from takeover event risk by swapping into the high yield sector. This strategy holds the view that by and large, high quality AA and AAA industrial credits are in a long-term deteriorating credit trend (because of takeover or restructuring risk or industry maturation), whereas high yield non-investment grade securities are in a long-term improving credit trend.

Investors holding what once were high quality investment grade bonds that have fallen below investment grade are faced with several choices:

a. Swap back into investment grade issues,
b. Hold the issue to maturity, or
c. Swap into high yield issues.

Performance-oriented investors need to compare this situation to an equity investment with a loss. Their current investment should be evaluated against other high yield alternatives. The credits that offer the best potential for improvement should be purchased. On the other hand, investors with accounting constraints, who do not want to mark to market, may be satisfied that their coupons are adequate. While these investors may feel that with principal repayment at maturity the accounting ramifications of the event risk are lessened, they have taken on much greater credit risk. There may be opportunities in the high yield sector to achieve the same return with lower credit risk or much greater return with the new level of credit risk.

### Put Features in Bonds

The sequence in this section describes various kinds of put protection used, proceeding from the most specialized version to the most general version.

**Poison Puts—Protect Against Hostile Takeover Risk.** Corporate issues that contain poison puts typically allow the holder to put the bond back to the issuer in the event of a restructuring, causing either a change in management or a set percentage change in equity control. Oftentimes, this must be accompanied by a ratings classification downgrade. Most of the poison puts in place give management considerable latitude in deciding when the put option is enforceable. Typically, if company management supports the restructuring, the bondholder will not have the put option. The performance record of such puts is somewhat questionable as they are yet largely *untested*. In the future, it is very likely that more favorable terms will be sought by the bondholders in the design of these instruments. Poison puts generally have an American exercise in that the put can be used over the life of the bond.

Poison put exercise prices are usually either the prevailing call price at the time of the event or 100%. Exhibit 4 gives an example of a poison put.

**Spread Puts—Protect Against Credit Risk (Including Event Risk).** Bonds with spread puts allow the holder to put the bonds back to the issuer at a spread to Treasuries. This ensures protection against erosion in credit quality but not against rising rates. Bonds with these provisions are rare, but their popularity may rise with increased event risk concerns. Note that this put is more general than a poison put in that the credit risk protection applies for more than hostile takeover event risk. This may be more attractive to the issuer than the straight put option (described in the next section) which provides credit risk protection when the bond is under par and additionally provides rate risk protection to the holders. This forces the issuer to refinance at higher rates, if the straight puts are exercised due to higher rates. Of course, other things remaining the same, efficient valuation of this additional feature will mean that straight putable bonds may be priced higher to reflect the extra protection available to holders. The spread puts, on the other hand, represent a division of risks between the issuer and bondholder, the former bearing the credit risk and the latter the rate risk. Spread puts typically have a European exercise feature at a predetermined date. Exhibit 5 gives an example of a spread put.

**Straight Puts—Protect Against Credit (Including Event) and Rate Risk When Below Par.** Bonds with embedded puts have typically been viewed by investors as defensive instruments. In a rising rate environment, investors would have the option

**EXHIBIT 4**
**EXAMPLE OF POISON PUT**

| | |
|---|---|
| Issuer: | Ralston Purina Company |
| Coupon: | 9½% |
| Maturity: | 06/01/16 |
| Call Provisions: | Deciining call schedule, non-refundable '96 |
| Sinking Fund: | Minimum of $13.5 million nor more than $40.5 million per year beginning with the year 1996. |
| Amount Issued: | $300 million |

**Put Terms**

| | |
|---|---|
| Put Trigger: | Hostile Change of Control of 40% of Stock. 'Change of Control' is defined in the indenture as the time when (a) any person or (b) affiliation shall have become the beneficial owner of at least 40% of the outstanding common stock or 'Continuing Directors' shall have ceased to constitute a majority. A 'Change in Control' must be deemed to have occurred by a majority of Continuing Directors. |
| Put Price: | Prevailing Call Price |

**EXHIBIT 5**
**EXAMPLE OF SPREAD PUT**

| | |
|---|---|
| Issuer: | Transcontinental Gas Pipeline Corporation |
| Coupon: | 8⅛% |
| Maturity: | 01/15/97 |
| Call Provisions: | Non-callable |
| Amount Issued: | $100 million |

**Put Terms**

| | |
|---|---|
| Put Date: (Strike Date) | 01/24/89 (Repayment Date) The holder has a tender period commencing December 15, 1988 and ending on the close of business on January 16, 1989 (the Strike Date). |
| Put Price: (Strike Price) | The Strike Price is the sum of the present values on the Strike Date of the principal and remaining interest payments discounted at a rate equal to the yield to maturity of the U.S. Treasury 7¼% note due 11/15/96 on the Strike Date plus 1.325%. |

**EXHIBIT 6**
**EXAMPLE OF STRAIGHT PUT**

| | |
|---|---|
| Issuer: | Tenneco Inc. |
| Coupon: | 10% |
| Maturity: | 03/15/08 |
| Call Provisions: | Non-callable |
| Amount Issued: | $250 million |

**Put Terms**

| | |
|---|---|
| Put Date: | 03/15/98 (Repayment Date) The bondholder may elect repayment within the period commencing on January 15, 1998 and ending at the close of business on February 15, 1998. |
| Put Price: | 100% of principal amount. |

to put the bonds back to the issuer at par. However, these bonds also allow the bondholder to put the bonds back to the issuer at par should the credit quality erode. These puts, therefore, provide simultaneous insurance against credit risk (including takeover event risk) as well as interest rate risk when the bond trades below par. Note, however, that the straight puts may not give credit risk protection when the bond trades above par, as the spread puts do. The puts have a European exercise and are typically exerciseable at a predetermined date, though, they may have multiple puts on various dates. An example of a straight put is given in Exhibit 6.

Exhibit 7 shows the impact of an event (which is associated with a 200 basis point instantaneous widening of yield spreads on the straight bond) on the relative performance of a straight bond compared to bonds with various types of embedded puts.

**EXHIBIT 7**
**IMPACT OF A 200 B.P. CHEAPENING "EVENT"**

No initial Change in Absolute Level of Interest Rates
Base Case: 9½% due in 11/01/98
Market Price = 100%, Yield to Maturity = 9.50%
Event causes a 200 bp cheapening to the base case

| | | MARKET PERFORMANCE | | |
|---|---|---|---|---|
| PUT BOND TYPE | INVESTOR COST (4) | WITH PUT | WITHOUT PUT | SAVING (POINTS) |
| Poison Put<br>*Put Terms*<br>1  Bondholder can put<br>bond back to issuer<br>under change in control | Relatively small | Price = 100.00<br><br>YTP = 9.50 | Price = 88.31<br><br>YTM = 11.50 | 11.69 |
| Spread Put<br>*Put Terms*<br>2  Put Date: 11/01/93<br>Put Spread: 125 bp<br>Put Price Calculated: 98.84% | 35 - 40 bp | Price = 92.98<br><br>YTP = 9.80<br>(8.55 + 200 + 65) | Price = 88.31<br><br>YTM = 11.50 | 4.67 |
| Straight Put<br>*Put Terms*<br>3  Put Date: 11/01/93<br>Put Price: 100.00% | 15 - 25 bp | Price = 93.65<br><br>YTP = 11.20<br>(8.55 + 200 + 65) | Price = 88.31<br><br>YTM = 11.50 | 5.34 |

*Assumptions:*
1. 10-Year Treasury: YTM = 8.85%.
2. 5-Year Treasury: YTM = 8.55%.
3. AA Industrial, little perceived event risk.
   Pricing Spread = +65 bp = 9.5% YTM.
4. Invesor costs reflect pricing levels prior to the wave of recent events. In the current environment, investor costs may be larger. However, in practice, these costs will usually be borne by
   the issuer since these provisions enable financing consistent with current rating levels.

This analysis assumes that the term structure of interest rates does not change and
that the cheapening from the event is uniform across the corporate yield curve. The
potential savings for poison put bonds is large and can be realized immediately on
the occurrence of the event. However, investors will seldom realize this benefit due
to the restrictive clauses associated with these provisions. On the other hand, bonds
with straight or spread puts give the bondholder added flexibility in terms of latitude
of exercise. Note, however, that in these cases the put can only be exercised at a
future date. Therefore, the investor usually continues to hold the debt of the impacted company, until the put can be exercised. However, with the realization of an
event, the put goes further into the money and causes the overall duration of the bond
to drop. Consequently, the price declines from potential future events (and rate
increases) are mitigated due to the shorter duration of the put bond. Bullish investors

concerned with event risk protection should, other things being equal, prefer the spread put as the put strike price can potentially rise with the market. The straight put will generally be preferred to the spread put in rising rate scenarios as the put strike price holds constant at 100.0%, rather than falling with the market.

It should also be added that in the event of a bankruptcy, there will be no protection for the bondholder through the option components. A put bondholder will be treated the same as a straight bondholder. A bankruptcy filing, therefore, reduces the option components to zero values.

### *Shorten Duration*

**Shorten Maturity.** The obvious way of shortening duration is to shorten maturity. As shorter maturity issues are paid off earlier, other things remaining the same, their credit quality is higher under the condition that the firm is not in imminent default. With imminent default, the duration of the bond will not make a material difference to its credit quality.

**Trade up in Coupon.** Trading up in coupon class, other things being equal, ensures that a greater portion of the total return comes from coupon cash flows and their reinvestment. As a larger portion of the value of the bond is paid off earlier, similar to short maturity bonds, these are likely to have a better credit status compared to low coupon bonds. Also, typically, investors are paid (by higher yields) to trade up in coupon for the additional call risk assumed. In event risk situations, investors should look to swap into such shorter duration securities which will have reduced price depreciation if a restructuring occurs. Also note that to maintain the same par value of bonds, higher coupons may require an additional outlay of investment.

### *Diversification*

The portfolio should be diversified with a large number of issues, particularly focusing on industry diversification. As mentioned earlier, takeover events create correlated price responses for firms within the same industry. This portion of the risk can be reduced by diversification across unrelated industries.

### *Takeover-Proof Bond Selection*

By concentrating on industries which are more likely to be takeover-proof, such as utilities and financial companies, takeover event risk can be substantially reduced. Another alternative is to concentrate on companies that are still "too large" to be taken over—for example, IBM and Exxon. However, such selection increases the specific idiosyncratic firm/industry risk exposure. Assets can also be diverted to the non-corporate sectors which provide comparable yields—for example, mortgage-backed, (taxable) municipal securities or selected Yankee bonds. However, these may have differential interest rate risk characteristics.

### Bonds of Firms Under Workout

In quite a few cases, firms which violate their indenture provisions are subjected to workouts to maintain continuity of operations. The bonds of these firms are attractive candidates to be included as part of a portfolio, as they are often substantially discounted in relation to their expected payoffs. In other words, their expected return could be in excess of what they should provide for their underlying risks. By consciously devoting a part of the overall portfolio to include a diversity of such bonds, a manager can enhance the returns on the portfolio.

### Credit Research

Ongong credit research puts the investor on the offensive. Continuing efforts to identify break-up values of firms will enable pro-active event risk management. Early warning systems of event risk should be of great value to portfolio managers in their strategic asset allocation schemes. Such a system enables identification of swap opportunities from high event risk rated securities to ones that have low ratings. This will be particularly useful for managers who face allocational constraints of maintaining a certain fraction of the portfolio within the corporate industrial sector.

## IV. CONCLUSION

Takeovers, which replace equity with debt, increase the chances that existing bondholders will face a deterioration in the credit quality of their securities. Steps to provide protection against such risks (and other similar risks) are discussed in this article. The degree of protection available in such mechanisms varies widely. Managers should focus on the risk exposure of their portfolios and ensure that they tailor the use of such mechanisms to their specific information and requirements. As the market demands varying prices for different degrees of protection, managers should optimize based on the available choices. For example, spread puts may be less expensive than straight puts, other things being the same, as the former gives protection only against credit risk and the latter against (partial) credit and rate risks. For a manager who believes strongly that rates are headed down, the latter instrument is superfluous. Such information-specific strategies will enhance the returns of portfolios while simultaneously minimizing the risk.

# The Yield Measurement for Bonds with Embedded Options: The Option-Adjusted Duration-Adjusted Yield

KI-YOUNG CHUNG, PH.D.
KOREAN MONETARY ECONOMIC INSTITUTE
SEOUL, KOREA

## I. INTRODUCTION

Yield is one of the most quoted numbers in the bond market. By traditional definition, the yield on a coupon bond is the single discount rate that would equate the price of the bond with the present value of the cash flows to be received from the bond. Thus, the bond's yield is its internal rate of return. The yield, $y$, is obtained from the familiar bond pricing equation:

$$P(t) = \sum_{i=1}^{N} C_i e^{-y(t_i - t)} \tag{1}$$

This article was written when the author was a vice-president at Gifford Fong Associates.

where     $P(t)$  = the bond's price at time t
          $t$     = the evaluating time
          $t_i$   = the coupon payment time, $t_i > t$
          $C_i$   = the cash flow at time $t_i$
          $y$     = the bond's yield[1]

$t_N$ is not necessarily the stated maturity. When $t_N$ is the stated maturity, $y$ is the so-called "yield-to-maturity."

The yield-to-maturity of an ordinary coupon bond is well-defined because $N$, $C_i$, $t_i$ in Equation (1) are values know in advance. However, many bonds have option-like features such as callable bonds, puttable bonds, extendable bonds, retractable bonds, and mortgage-backed securities. Cash flows of these bonds are conditional on the interest rate environment because of embedded option features.[2] In other words, $C_i$ or $t_N$ is uncertain in the bond pricing equation. Therefore, the yield on a bond with an embedded option is not well-defined from Equation (1) without further assumptions.

This article shows how to calculate the yield on a bond with an embedded option, and the appropriate measure of the yield for a contingent claims security. Since the best known example among bonds with embedded options is a callable bond, and other contingent claims securities are similar to the case of a callable bond, I will focus on the yield of a callable bond. There are several conventional methods to calculate the yield of a callable bond such as yield-to-stated-maturity, yield-to-call, yield-to-worst, and yield-to-effective-maturity. More recently, the option-adjusted yield is considered as the appropriate yield measure for a callable bond by applying option pricing theory.

This article reviews all these different methods to calculate the yield of a callable bond, and then proposes an alternative measure of the yield which is theoretically superior. It is the option-adjusted duration-adjusted yield of a bond with an embedded option. This option-adjusted duration-adjusted yield is based on contingent claims pricing theory which is consistent with the intertemporal general equilibrium theory of the term structure of interest rates developed by Cox, Ingersoll, and Ross.[3]

## II. YIELD-TO-STATED-MATURITY

Yield-to-stated-maturity is conventionally one of the most commonly used yield measures for a callable bond. Substituting the actual price of a callable bond for $P(t)$ in Equation (1) and setting the stated maturity to $t_N$, the yield-to-stated-maturity of a callable bond is calculated from Equation (1)

---

[1]This yield is compounded continuously.

[2]Bonds with embedded options are also called interest rate contingent claims.

[3]John Cox, Jonathan Ingersoll, and Stephen Ross, "A Theory of the Term Structure of Interest Rates," *Econometrica*, March 1985, pp. 385-407.

The value of a callable bond is lower than that of a non-callable bond, all other things being equal, because a callable bond has the call risk which would arise from the uncertainty of cash flows due to the callability of a bond. In other words, the lower price of a callable bond reflects the call risk premium. Using Equation (1), the yield-to-stated-maturity of a callable bond is obviusly higher than that of a noncallable bond. And, the higher yield-to-stated-maturity of a callable bond represents compensation for the call risk. Accordingly, the yield-to-stated maturity of a callable bond includes the call risk premium.

Suppose there are two hypothetical bonds. Bond A is a noncallable bond with 10 years to maturity and a 10% coupon. Bond B is a callable bond with 10 years to maturity and a 10% coupon, which is callable at par after one year. Bond A is currently priced at par, and Bond B is at $98. Here, the $2 difference in Bond B's price reflects the call risk premium of a callable bond. From the information given on each bond, we can compute the yield-to-stated-maturity on each bond using Equation (1).

Yield-to-stated-maturity on Bond A  =  10.00%[4]

Yield-to-stated-maturity on Bond B  =  10.33%

Since the two bonds are identical except for the call feature, then the 0.33% higher yield on Bond B represents compensation for the call risk which may have an adverse effect on the holder of a callable bond.

## III. YIELD-TO-CALL

Yield-to-call is another yield measure for a callable bond. If a callable bond is called by the issuer at a call date, this call date will be the actual maturity date of the callable bond. Then, the appropriate yield of this callable bond may be computed by substituting the call date for $t_N$ in Equation (1). Using the call date as the last payment date, and the call price as the redemption price, the yield-to-call of a callable bond is calculated from Equation (1). Because most callable bonds have more than one call date and call price, we can calculate the yield-to-call for each future call date in the schedule. Bond B is callable at par and has one year to the call date. Now we can calculate the yield-to-call on Bond B.

Yield-to-call on Bond B  =  12.18%

Bond B has a 12.18% yield-to-call, which is much higher than the 10.33% yield-to-stated-maturity as well as the 10.0% yield-to-stated-maturity on Bond A. When

---

[4]These yields are bond equivalent rates, i.e., semi-annually compounded rates.

the actual price of a callable bond, which is callable at par, is below par, the yield-to-call is higher than the yield-to-stated-maturity of the callable bond. On the other hand, when the actual price of that callable bond is above par, the yield-to-call is lower than the yield-to-stated-maturity of the callable bond.

Compared with the 10.0% yield-to-stated-maturity on a noncallable bond (Bond A), the yield-to-call on a callable bond (Bond B) also includes compensation for the call risk. In fact, the yield-to-call and the yield-to-stated-maturity of a callable bond have significantly different call risk premia because one year to the call date and ten years to the stated maturity date make a dramatic difference in cash flows of the bond.

## IV. YIELD-TO-WORST

Because the issuer controls the call option attached to the callable bond, the yield-to-worst model assumes that the issuer will redeem the bond on the date which results in the lowest yield to the investor. Therefore, as we calculate the yield-to-stated-maturity and the yield-to-call for each future call date in the schedule, the yield-to-worst of a callable bond will be the lowest yield among them:

$$\text{Yield - To - Worst} = \min_{k} \left\{ y_k : P(t) = \sum_{i=1}^{k} C_i e^{-y_k (t_i - t)} \right\}, \qquad (2)$$

where $t_k$ = each future call date and stated maturity date.

According to Equation (2), the yield-to-worst on a callable bond, Bond B, will be the lowest one between yield-to-stated-maturity and yield-to-call.

$$\text{Yield-to-worst on Bond B} = 10.33\%$$

The yield-to-worst of a callable bond also has a call risk premium, which is the smallest premium among those of yields-to-call and yield-to-stated-maturity. *However, it should be noted that the yield-to-worst neglects the probabilistic nature of future interest rates.*

## V. YIELD-TO-EFFECTIVE-MATURITY

A callable bond can be redeemed by the issuer anytime between the first call date and the stated maturity date, which causes the major difficulty in obtaining the appropriate yield measure for a callable bond. The effective maturity date is defined as the redemption date when the callable bond is called by the issuer. Using time to the effective maturity date as the last payment time, the yield-to-effective-maturity of a callable bond will be calculated from Equation (1).

There are several ways to estimate the effective maturity date. Since the yield-to-effective-maturity reflects the probabilistic nature of future interest rates, the effective maturity date might be calculated as the probability weighted average of each call date and the maturity date. In general, the weighted average of the first call date and the stated maturity date may be obtained as the effective maturity date:

$$t_{EM} = w\, t_c + (1 - w)\, t_{SM}, \quad 0 \le w \le 1 \tag{3}$$

where    $t_{EM}$   = time to the effective maturity date
             $t_c$    = time to the first call date
             $t_{SM}$   = time to the stated maturity date

The weight of Equation (3), $w$, may be a function of the term structure of interest rates, the coupon rate, and the call price. We may interpret this weight as the probability with which a callable bond would be called at the first call date. When $w=0$, a callable bond will be redeemed at the stated maturity date, the yield-to-effective-maturity on this bond will be equivalent to the yield-to-stated maturity. On the other hand, when $w=1$, a callable bond will be called at the first call date, and the yield-to-effective-maturity will be equivalent to the yield-to-first-call. Therefore, the yield-to-effective-maturity of a callable bond is bounded by the yield-to-stated-maturity and the yield-to-call.

Suppose that $w=0.75$ in the case of Bond B. From Equation (3), Bond B has 3.25 years to the effective maturity date, and thus the yield-to-effective-maturity on Bond B is calculated from Equation (1).

Yield-to-effective-maturity on Bond B = 10.73%

Apparently, a 10.73% yield-to-effective-maturity on Bond B is higher than a 10.33% yield-to-stated-maturity, but lower than a 12.18% yield-to-call. And, the yield-to-effective-maturity of a callable bond also has a call risk premium. It is noteworthy that the yield-to-effective-maturity considers the probabilistic nature of the future term structure of interest rates while any previous yield measure does not.

An alternative yield measure to take the probabilistic nature of future interest rates into consideration is the probability weighted average of each yield-to-call and yield-to-stated-maturity. However, it is not identical to the yield-to-effective maturity when the effective maturity date is defined as the probability weighted average of each call date and the stated maturity date.[5] Theoretically, this alternative yield measure is more reasonable than the yield-to-effective-maturity in considering the probabilistic nature of future interest rates.

---

[5]Mathematically, this can be demonstrated based on Jensen's inequality.

## VI. OPTION-ADJUSTED YIELD

Recently, contingent claims pricing theory has been applied to the valuation model for bonds with embedded options. Under this approach, a bond with an embedded option can be considered as a portfolio of two securities. One security is a bullet bond without any option feature and the other is an option. Therefore, option pricing theory can be used to value the attached option of an underlying bond.

The net value of a bond with an attached option is the sum of the value of the pure bullet bond and the value of the option when the option is the long position to the investor, such as a puttable bond, a retractable bond, and an extendable bond. However, when the option is the short position to the investor, such as a callable bond and a mortgage-backed security, the net value is the value of the bullet bond less the value of the option. For example, the price of a callable bond is

Price of a callable bond =

Price of a noncallable equivalent bond  −  Price of an option          (4)

The conventional yield measures for a callable bond we have discussed so far have extra spread that compensates for the call risk, since the call is to the detriment of the bondholder. Therefore, the yield of a callable bond would clearly be expected to be higher than that of a noncallable bond. The two bonds, however, cannot be compared as investment alternatives on the basis of yield alone if we don't adjust the call risk premium. In order to make an appropriate comparison of the yield of a callable and a noncallable bond, an adjustment should first be made to net out this option feature of a callable bond. In other words, if the yield is adjusted for the call option feature, the yield would be a measure of investment attractiveness regardless of whether the bond is callable or not.

Because we can value an attached option fairly by using option pricing theory, we add the price of an option to the price of a callable bond so as to net out the option feature of a callable bond. The result will be the price of the remaining bullet bond, that is, the noncallable equivalent bond after adjusting for the value of the option. Substituting the adjusted price of a noncallable equivalent bond for $P(t)$ in Equation (1), we can calculate the yield-to-stated-maturity of a noncallable equivalent bond from Equation (1). The result is called the *option-adjusted yield of a callable bond*.

The option-adjusted yield of a callable bond depends on the term structure of interest rates on the evaluation date because the value of the attached option is affected by the term structure of interest rates. Generally speaking, in a high interest rate environment, the value of the attached option is relatively smaller than that in a low interest rate environment.

Suppose we price the attached option of a callable bond, Bond B, using a contingent claims pricing model, and find it to be worth $2.33.[6] The price of a noncallable equivalent bond is the price of Bond B plus the price of the attached option, or $100.33. The call-option-adjusted yield on Bond B is then equal to the yield-to-stated maturity on a 10% coupon, 10-year maturity, noncallable bond priced at $100.33, which is 9.95%.

$$\text{Option-adjusted yield on Bond B} = 9.95\%$$

After purging the option feature of Bond B, the option-adjusted yield is now 9.95%. That is much lower than any conventional yield measure on Bond B because the option-adjusted yield does not include the call risk premium of a callable bond. Therefore, the option-adjusted yield can be directly compared with the yield of a noncallable bond. Even though all of the conventional yield measures on a callable bond are higher than the yield on a noncallable bond, the option-adjusted yield on Bond B, 9.95%, is lower than the 10.0% yield on Bond A. In other words, after netting out the call feature on Bond B, the noncallable bond, Bond A, is more attractive than Bond B in terms of yield if the two bonds are equivalent except for the call provision.

## VII. OPTION-ADJUSTED DURATION-ADJUSTED YIELD

In this section, we introduce the option-adjusted duration-adjusted yield of a callable bond, which may be theoretically superior to any other yield measure, in order to provide an appropriate yield measure that reflects more reasonable investment return from holding a callable bond. Here, duration is defined as the price elasticity with respect to interest rate shift. This option-adjusted duration-adjusted yield will be obtained using interest rate contingent claims pricing theory.

An embedded option has an effect on the duration of a callable bond as well as on the value of that bond. As in Equation (4), the value of the attached option can be added to the price of a callable bond to give us the price of a noncallable equivalent bond, so that we net out the option feature of the callable bond. Furthermore, the duration of a callable bond becomes shorter than that of a noncallable bond because of the call option feature. When the value of an option is close to zero, the duration of a callable bond is very close to that of a noncallable bond. But, when the value of an option is large, the duration of the callable bond becomes much shorter.

The option-adjusted yield only considers the price adjustment if we need to purge the option feature of a callable bond. This price adjustment, however, is not enough to exclude the call risk premium from the conventional yield measure, because the

---

[6]The embedded option of a callable bond, Bond B, is priced using the actual term structure of interest rates on March 31, 1988. The short rate, *i.e.*, the spot rate of a one-month Treasury bill was 5.97% and the long rate, *i.e.*, the spot rate of a 30-year Treasury bond was 8.77%.

option feature affects not only the price of a callable bond but also the duration of a callable bond. Therefore, we need both a price adjustment and a duration adjustment in order to net out the call option feature completely in calculating the appropriate yield of a callable bond. The result will be the option-adjusted duration-adjusted yield of a callable bond.

$$y = y_{op} - \left( y_{nc}^{D} - y_{c}^{D} \right) \tag{5}$$

where   $y$ = the option-adjusted duration-adjusted yield
$y_{op}$ = the option-adjusted yield
$y_{nc}^{D}$ = the yield-to-duration on a noncallable equivalent bond
$y_{c}^{D}$ = the yield-to-duration on a callable bond

The yield-to-duration on each bond is computed from Equation (1) using duration[7] as the last payment time, $t_N$. The option-adjusted yield was already explained in the previous section (that is, the yield-to-stated-maturity of a noncallable equivalent bond after adjusting the value of an option). The difference between the two yields-to-duration arises from the fact that the embedded call option affects the duration of a callable bond. For the complete adjustment of the call risk premium, the yield differential arising from the duration differential should also be adjusted.

The magnitude of the yield differential depends upon the shape of the yield curve, which is directly related to the term structure of interest rates on a specific date. In the case of a flat yield curve, the yield differential is zero because the yield-to-duration on a callable bond is equal to the yield-to-duration on a noncallable equivalent bond. In other words, the duration differential arising from the attached option cannot make any yield differential, and thus the duration adjustment has no effect on the option-adjusted yield. The option-adjusted duration-adjusted yield is the same as the option-adjusted yield. When the yield curve is rising, the yield differential becomes positive, and thus the option-adjusted duration-adjusted yield is lower than the option-adjusted yield. On the contrary, when the yield curve is falling, the option-adjusted duration-adjusted yield is higher than the option-adjusted yield because of the negative yield differential. Therefore, the option-adjusted duration-adjusted yield is also highly dependent on the term structure of interest rates on the evaluation date because not only the price adjustment, but also the duration adjustment, is affected by the term structure of interest rates.

In the case of a callable bond, Bond B, the contingent claims duration of a noncallable equivalent bond is 6.20 years, and the contingent claims duration of Bond B is 3.36 years. Since we had a rising yield curve on March 31, 1988, the yield-to-duration differential is calculated as 0.36% using an interest rate contingent claims pricing model. Therefore, the option-adjusted duration-adjusted yield on Bond B is computed from Equation (5).

---

[7]Duration, defined as the price elasticity with respect to interest rate shift, can be calculated consistently with the interest rate contingent claims model, which is named contingent claims duration. This contingent claims duration captures the option-like character of a callable bond.

Option-adjusted Duration-adjusted Yield on Bond B = 9.59%

Because of the rising yield curve, the option-adjusted duration-adjusted yield on Bond B, 9.59%, is slightly lower than the option-adjusted yield, 9.95%. The difference, 0.36%, is a portion of the duration adjustment in purging out the option feature. After adjusting the call risk premium on Bond B completely, the noncallable bond, Bond A, is a much more attractive investment instrument than Bond B in terms of yield.

Exhibit 1 is the price/yield table of of different yield measures for a callable bond, which is a 10-year maturity, 10% coupon bond, callable after one year at par. We used the actual term structure of interest rates on March 31, 1988 to calculate the option-adjusted yield and the option-adjusted duration-adjusted yield. The values of embedded options are also shown in the last column. Since the yield curve was rising on March 31, 1988, the option-adjusted duration-adjusted yield is lower than the option-adjusted yield because the yield differential is positive. When the value of the attached option is large, as in the case of a high bond price, the duration adjustment becomes significantly important. On the other hand, when the value of the attached option is negligible, as in the case of a low bond price, the option-adjusted duration-adjusted yield is very close to the option-adjusted yield.

Exhibit 2 shows different price/yield relationships according to different yield measures. The curve AOB represents the price/yield-to-stated-maturity relationship. If this bond is currently priced at $98, the yield-to-stated-maturity on this callable bond is 10.33%. The curve COD shows the price/yield-to-call relationship, and the yield-to-call on this bond is 12.18%. The yield-to-worst curve consists of a part of the yield-to-stated-maturity curve and a part of the yield-to-call curve. Here, the curve COB represents the price/yield-to-worst relationship, and the yield-to-worst on this bond is the same as the yield-to-stated-maturity, 10.33%. The curve EOF represents the price/yield-to-effective-maturity relationship, and the yield-to-effective-maturity on this bond is 10.73%.

Finally, the curve GH stands for the price/option-adjusted duration-adjusted yield relationship, which is derived from the contingent claims pricing model. The shape of the option-adjusted duration-adjusted yield curve is affected by the term structure of interest rates on the evaluation date. This is because the value of the embedded option and the duration adjustment depend on the term structure on that date. The curve GH is drawn using the actual term structure of interest rates on March 31, 1988, and the option-adjusted duration-adjusted yield on this callable bond is 9.59%. The option-adjusted yield curve is skipped in Exhibit 2 to avoid complicating the figure because it has a shape similar to the concave curve GH.

## VIII. SUMMARY AND CONCLUSIONS

This article has reviewed several conventional methods to calculate the yield of a callable bond such as yield-to-stated-maturity, yield-to-call, yield-to-worst, and

**EXHIBIT 1**
**PRICE/YIELD TABLE OF DIFFERENT YIELD MEASURES—**
**10-YEAR MATURITY AND 10% COUPON BOND, CALLABLE AFTER ONE YEAR AT PAR**

| Price | Option-Adjusted Duration-Adjusted Yield | Option-Adjusted Yield | Yield to Stated Maturity | Yield to Call | Yield to Worst | Yield to Effective Maturity | Value of Option |
|---|---|---|---|---|---|---|---|
| 104 | 5.72 | 6.87 | 9.38 | 5.82 | 5.82 | 8.56 | 18.38 |
| 103 | 6.54 | 7.57 | 9.53 | 6.85 | 6.85 | 8.91 | 13.81 |
| 102 | 7.27 | 8.20 | 9.68 | 7.89 | 7.89 | 9.26 | 10.10 |
| 101 | 7.97 | 8.75 | 9.84 | 8.93 | 8.93 | 9.62 | 7.23 |
| 100 | 8.58 | 9.22 | 10.00 | 10.00 | 10.00 | 10.00 | 5.04 |
| 99 | 9.12 | 9.61 | 10.16 | 11.08 | 10.16 | 10.36 | 3.46 |
| 98 | 9.59 | 9.95 | 10.33 | 12.18 | 10.33 | 10.73 | 2.33 |
| 97 | 9.98 | 10.23 | 10.49 | 13.03 | 10.49 | 11.11 | 1.59 |
| 96 | 10.31 | 10.48 | 10.66 | 14.44 | 10.66 | 11.50 | 1.09 |
| 95 | 10.59 | 10.70 | 10.83 | 15.59 | 10.83 | 11.89 | 0.78 |
| 94 | 10.83 | 10.90 | 11.00 | 16.77 | 11.00 | 12.28 | 0.59 |
| 93 | 11.05 | 11.10 | 11.18 | 17.96 | 11.18 | 12.68 | 0.46 |
| 92 | 11.26 | 11.29 | 11.36 | 19.17 | 11.36 | 13.09 | 0.37 |
| 91 | 11.46 | 11.49 | 11.54 | 20.40 | 11.54 | 13.50 | 0.29 |
| 90 | 11.66 | 11.68 | 11.72 | 21.65 | 11.72 | 13.91 | 0.23 |
| 89 | 11.86 | 11.88 | 11.91 | 22.93 | 11.91 | 14.34 | 0.19 |
| 88 | 12.06 | 12.07 | 12.10 | 24.22 | 12.10 | 14.76 | 0.15 |
| 87 | 12.26 | 12.27 | 12.29 | 25.54 | 12.29 | 15.20 | 0.11 |
| 86 | 12.46 | 12.47 | 12.49 | 26.88 | 12.49 | 15.64 | 0.09 |
| 85 | 12.67 | 12.68 | 12.69 | 28.25 | 12.69 | 16.09 | 0.06 |
| 84 | 12.87 | 12.88 | 12.89 | 29.64 | 12.89 | 16.54 | 0.05 |
| 83 | 13.08 | 13.09 | 13.10 | 31.06 | 13.10 | 17.00 | 0.03 |

**EXHIBIT 2**
**PRICE/YIELD CURVES OF DIFFERENT YIELD MEASURES FOR A 10-YEAR MATURITY AND 10% COUPON BOND, CALLABLE AFTER ONE YEAR AT PAR**

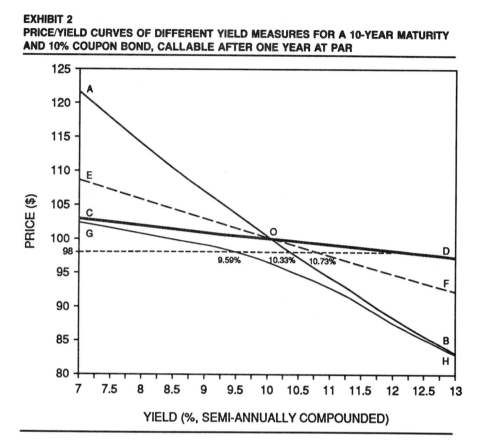

yield-to-effective-maturity. As the embedded option can be priced using the modern option pricing model, the option-adjusted yield has been suggested to be another yield measure for a callable bond.

All of these conventional yield measures include extra spread which compensates for the call risk of a callable bond since the call may have an adverse effect on the bondholder. However, in order to make an appropriate comparison of the yield of a callable bond with that of a noncallable bond, we need to adjust the call risk premium. This adjustment is made to net out this option feature of a callable bond. The option-adjusted yield is calculated after adjusting the value of an option.

Although the embedded option has an influence on the duration of a callable bond as well as on the price of that bond, the option-adjusted yield only considers the price adjustment in netting out the option feature. In fact, not only the price adjustment but also the duration adjustment should be made to purge out the option feature completely. Correspondingly, this article proposes the option-adjusted duration-adjusted yield, which may be a more appropriate yield measure for a callable bond. Obviously, this option-adjusted duration-adjusted yield can be readily applied to other bonds with embedded options, such as puttable bonds, extendable bonds, retractable bonds, or mortgage-backed securities.

Calculation of the option-adjusted duration-adjusted yield on a bond with an embedded option is based on the interest rate contingent claims pricing model which is consistent with the intertemporal general equilibrium theory of the term structure of interest rates. The value of an embedded option and the contingent claims duration are computed from this pricing model. The contingent claims duration captures the option-like character of the bond.

# Measuring the Duration of Floating-Rate Debt Instruments

JOHN D. FINNERTY, PH.D.
PROFESSOR OF FINANCE
FORDHAM UNIVERSITY
GRADUATE SCHOOL OF BUSINESS ADMINISTRATION

## I. INTRODUCTION

*Duration* is a statistic that measures the sensitivity of the price of a debt instrument to a change in market yield. The concept of duration was developed by Macaulay[1] nearly 50 years ago. A large number of studies have described how to calculate and interpret various measures of duration for fixed-rate debt instruments.[2] As shown in

---

[1] F. R. Macaulay, *Some Theoretical Problems Suggested by the Movements of Interest Rates, Bond Yields and Stock Prices in the United States Since 1856*, New York: National Bureau of Economic Research, 1938.

[2] See for example Gerald O. Bierwag, "Measures of Duration," *Economic Inquiry*, Vol. 16 (October 1978), pp. 497-507; Gerald O. Bierwag, *Duration Analysis* (Cambridge, MA: Ballinger Publishing, 1987); John Caks, William R. Lane, Robert W. Greenleaf, and Reginald G. Joules, "A Simple Formula for Duration," *Journal of Financial Research*, Vol. 8 (Fall 1985), pp. 245-249; J. H. Chua, "A Closed-Form Formula for Calculating Bond Duration," *Financial Analysts Journal*, Vol. 40 (May-June 1984), pp. 76-78; J. E. Ingersoll, Jr., J. Skelton, and R. L. Weil, "Duration Forty Years Later," *Journal of Financial and Quantitative Analysis*, Vol. 13 (November 1978), pp. 627-650; and Richard W. McEnally, "Duration as a Practical Tool for Bond Management," *Journal of Portfolio Management*, Vol. 3 (Summer 1977), pp. 53-57. Calculating the duration of securities, such as fixed-rate mortgages, that can be prepaid at little or no penalty when interest rates drop remains a difficult problem. Any closed-form solution would have to assume a particular prepayment pattern. Pinkus and Chandoha develop a useful approach based on an analysis of relative price volatilities of comparable securities. See: Scott M. Pinkus and Marie A. Chandoha, "Implied Duration," *Secondary Mortgage Markets*, Vol. 3 (Summer 1986), pp. 7-13; and Scott M. Pinkus and Marie A. Chandoha, "The Relative Price Volatility of Mortgage Securities," *Journal of Portfolio Management*, Vol. 12 (Summer 1986), pp. 9-22.

Exhibit 1, floating-rate debt issue volume in the United States has increased dramatically within the past few years.[3] Of the approximately $33 billion of domestic floating-rate corporate debt securities issued during the 1982-1985 period, roughly one-third have coupon rates indexed to interest rates other than Treasury rates. The vast majority of these are indexed to one of the London Interbank Offered Rates (LIBOR).[4] In addition to the volume of floating-rate debt securities reported in Exhibit 1, many billions of dollars of adjustable-rate and variable-rate mortgages (referred to generically as floating-rate mortgages) have been issued within the past decade. A large percentage of these have been repackaged into mortgage pass-through securities that now reside in thrift and other institutional asset portfolios.

**EXHIBIT 1**
**DOMESTIC FLOATING-RATE DEBT SECURITIES ISSUES (MILLIONS OF DOLLARS)**

| Index | 1974 | 1975–77 | 1978–81 | 1982–85 |
|---|---|---|---|---|
| Prime Rate, Commercial Paper Rate, Certificate of Deposit Rate | – | – | – | $ 2,200 |
| London Interbank Offered Rate: | | | | |
| 3-month LIBOR | – | – | – | 8,868 |
| 12-month LIBOR | – | – | – | 225 |
| Treasury Bill Rate: | | | | |
| 3-month (1) | $1,150 | – | $ 250 | 10,197 |
| 6-month (2) | – | – | 2,592 | 475 |
| Constant Maturity Treasury Rate (3) | – | – | 785 | 11,066 |
| Nonfinancial Indexes (4) | – | – | 52 | 75 |
| Total | $1,150 | – | $3,679 | $33,106 |

(1) Includes issues indexed to the 91-day Treasury bill auction rate (bond equivalent basis) and issues indexed to the 3-month Treasury bill secondary market rate (interest yield equivalent basis).
(2) Includes issues indexed to the 6-month Treasury bill auction rate (bond equivalent basis) and issues indexed to the 6-month Treasury bill secondary market yield (interest yield equivalent basis).
(3) Includes issues indexed to one (or to the maximum of a set) of the Treasury constant maturity indexes corresponding to a maturity of one year or longer.
(4) Includes issues indexed to the price of crude oil and issues indexed to average trading volume on the New York Stock Exchange.
*Source*: Richard S. Wilson, "Domestic Floating Rate and Adjustable Rate Debt Securities," in Frank J. Fabozzi (ed.), *Floating Rate Instruments* (Chicago, IL: Probus Publishing, 1986).

[3]For an overview of floating-rate instruments that explains how a variety of floating-rate debt instruments are structured, see: Frank J. Fabozzi (ed.), *Floating Rate Instruments* (Chicago, IL: Probus Publishing, 1986).

[4]In addition, most floating-rate Eurodollar debt instruments are indexed to one of the LIBOR, London Interbank Bid Rates (LIBID), or an average of the two (LIMEAN). See: Sarah Allen and Lizabeth L. Palumbo, "Eurodollar Floating Rate Notes," in Fabozzi, *Floating Rate Instruments*.

Because of the growing importance of floating-rate debt instruments in institutional portfolios, portfolio managers need a means of measuring the price sensitivity of such securities. The coupon rate index can have a significant impact on the price volatility of a floating-rate debt instrument.[5] It is therefore important that any formula for calculating the duration of a floating-rate debt instrument correctly reflect the impact on price volatility of the responsiveness of the coupon rate index to changes in market yields. This article develops procedures for calculating the duration of a floating-rate non-sinking-fund bond and for calculating the duration of a floating-rate mortgage, both of which incorporate the sensitivity of the coupon rate index to changes in market yields.[6]

## II. DURATION OF A FIXED-RATE BOND

The formula developed below for calculating the duration of a floating-rate bond is expressed in terms of the duration of a fixed-rate but otherwise identical bond:

$$D = \frac{\sum_{t=1}^{n} tr (1+y)^{-t} + n(1+y)^{-n}}{\sum_{t=1}^{n} r (1+y)^{-t} + (1+y)^{-n}} \tag{1}$$

where $D$ is the duration of a bond that pays interest at the fixed rate $r$ per period for $n$ periods and repays principal in the amount of \$1 at maturity and where $y$ is the market yield with respect to which duration is being measured. $D$ is referred to as the Macaulay duration measure when the bond's yield to maturity is used as the market yield $y$. An equivalent but more convenient formula than equation (1) for calculating duration is:[7]

---

[5]See: John D. Finnerty, "Measuring the Duration of a Floating-Rate Bond," *Journal of Portfolio Management*, Summer 1989; Robert A. Ott, Jr., "The Duration of an Adjustable-Rate Mortgage and the Impact of the Index," *Journal of Finance*, Vol. 41 (September 1986), pp. 923-933; and Neal M. Soss, "The Choice of Interest Rate Index on Performance," in Fabozzi, *Floating Rate Instruments*.

[6]The development of the procedure for calculating the duration of a floating-rate non-sinking-fund bond is based on Finnerty, "Measuring the Duration of a Floating-Rate Bond." The development of the duration formula for floating-rate mortgages is based on Ott, "The Duration of an Adjustable-Rate Mortgage and the Impact of the Index." Other contributions to the literature dealing with the duration of floating-rate debt instruments include: Don M. Chance, "Floating Rate Notes and Immunization," *Journal of Financial and Quantitative Analysis*, Vol. 18 (September 1983), pp. 365-380; Don M. Chance and George E. Morgan, "Immunization of Floating Rate Notes," in Fabozzi, *Floating Rate Instruments*; George Emir Morgan, "Floating Rate Securities and Immunization: Some Further Results," *Journal of Financial and Quantitative Analysis*, Vol. 21 (March 1986), pp. 87-94; and Jess Yawitz, Howard Kaufold, Thomas Macirowski, and Michael Smirlock, "The Pricing and Duration of Floating Rate Bonds," *Journal of Portfolio Management*, Vol. 13 (Summer 1987), pp. 49-56.

[7]See Caks et. al.

$$D = \frac{r\,(1+y)\left[(1+y)^n - 1\right] + ny\,(y-r)}{ry\left[(1+y)^n - 1\right] + y^2} \qquad (2)$$

For the special case of a bond whose coupon rate equals the market yield ($y=r$), equation (2) simplifies further:

$$D^* = \frac{(1+r)\left[(1+r)^n - 1\right]}{r\,(1+r)^n} \qquad (3)$$

$D$, and more particularly Macaulay duration, represents an accurate measure of duration when the term structure is flat.[8] However, empirical evidence indicates that, in practice, Macaulay duration is as accurate a measure of price volatility as the more sophisticated measures of duration that are intended to take into account non-level term structures and non-parallel shifts in the term structure.[9]

## III. DURATION OF A FLOATING-RATE BOND

Let $B$ denote the duration of a floating-rate non-sinking-fund bond. The duration of a bond can be interpreted as that point in time at which the future value of the debt service stream is invariant to changes in market interest rates.[10] When the term structure is flat, the future value of the debt service stream of a floating-rate bond as of the $B$-th period is:

$$FV\,(B) = (1+y)^B\left[\sum_{t=1}^{n} r\,(1+y)^{-t} + (1+y)^{-n}\right] \qquad (4)$$

At some point in time $j$, the coupon rate $r$ begins to adjust in response to changes in market interest rates. Normally, $j=1$, that is, the interest rate adjusts for the first time at the end of the initial interest period, but this need not always be the case.

An expression for $B$ is obtained by differentiating $FV(B)$ in equation (4) with respect to the market yield $y$, keeping in mind that beginning with the payment at time $j+1$, $r$ varies as a function of $y$. The resulting equation is then set equal to zero and solved for $B$. This leads to the following expression for the duration of a floating-rate bond:

---

[8] See Bierwag, *Duration Analysis.*
[9] See Bierwag, *Duration Analysis*, Chapter 12.
[10] See Bierwag, "Measures of Duration."

$$B = \frac{\sum_{t=1}^{n} tr(1+y)^{-t} + n(1+y)^{-n} - \sum_{t=j+1}^{n}(dr_t/dy)(1+y)^{-t+1}}{\sum_{t=1}^{n} r(1+y)^{-t} + (1+y)^{-n}} \tag{5}$$

Note that $dr_t/dy$ in equation (5) must be evaluated for each time $t$, $j+1 \le t \le n$. Equation (5) can be simplified by substituting in terms of equation (1) to obtain:

$$B = D - \frac{\sum_{t=j+1}^{n}(dr_t/dy)(1+y)^{-t+1}}{\sum_{t=1}^{n} r(1+y)^{-t} + (1+y)^{-n}} \tag{6}$$

The duration of a floating-rate bond equals the duration of a fixed-rate but otherwise identical bond minus a quantity that reflects the sensitivity of the floating-rate bond's coupon to changes in market interest rates.[11]

Define the *adjustability coefficient* $a_t$ of the index employed in adjusting the coupon rate as:[12]

$$a_t = \frac{\sum_{t=j+1}^{n}(dr_t/dy)(1+y)^{-t}}{\sum_{t=j+1}^{n}(1+y)^{-t}} \tag{7}$$

When the index adjusts perfectly to changes in market interest rates, $dr_t/dy = 1$ for each period $t$, $j+1 \le t \le n$, so that $a_t = 1$. But the index may adjust on a lagged basis. For example, if the London interbank offered rate for three-month Eurodollar deposits (3-month LIBOR) is the index on which coupon rate adjustments are based and if duration is measured with respect to the 10-year constant maturity U.S. Treasury yield, then the value of $a_t$ will depend on how the value of 3-month LIBOR

---

[11]Equation (6) is similar to Chance and Morgan's formula [p. 299]. In their formula, the coupon rate adjusts monthly and interest is paid quarterly. Adapting their formula so that coupon adjustments and interest payments occur at the same frequency, as in equation (6), their formula agrees with equation (6) when (i) the coupon rate $r$ is indexed to the market yield, so that $dr_t/dy = 1$ in equation (6), and (ii) the durations in equation (6) are modified by dividing each side of equation (6) by $1+y$ so as to measure percentage bond price changes.

[12]See Ott.

in the current period *and* in future periods adjusts in response to an instantaneous change in the 10-year constant maturity U.S. Treasury yield. When the index adjusts imperfectly, equation (7) expresses the adjustability coefficient as the weighted average of the period-by-period adjustments, where the weight for each period equals the present value of a dollar (of interest) received that period divided by the present value of a stream of dollar payments received over the remaining life of the bond. A procedure for calculating the adjustability coefficient is presented later in this article.

Substituting equation (7) into equation (6) and rearranging terms, the duration of a floating-rate bond can be expressed in the following form:[13]

$$B = D\left[1 - \frac{a_t y (1+y)\left[(1+y)^{n-j} - 1\right]}{r(1+y)\left[(1+y)^n - 1\right] + ny(y-r)}\right] \qquad (8)$$

The duration of a floating-rate bond is a fraction of the duration of a fixed-rate but otherwise identical bond, where the expression in brackets in equation (8) represents the *factor of proportionality*. The value of the factor of proportionality depends on the adjustability coefficient $a_t$, the current coupon rate on the bond $r$, the market yield $y$, the maturity of the bond $n$, and the length of the period until the next coupon adjustment occurs $j$. Note that if the coupon rate never adjusts, $a_t = 0$ and equation (8) simplifies to $B = D$.

To interpret equation (8), suppose the index adjusts perfectly to changes in market interest rates so that $a_t = 1$. If $r = y$, then $D = D^*$ and equation (8) simplifies to:

$$B = D^*\left[\frac{\left[1 - (1+r)^{-j}\right](1+r)^n}{(1+r)^n - 1}\right] \qquad (9)$$

Substituting equation (3) for $D^*$ simplifies equation (9) to:

$$B = \frac{(1+r)\left[1 - (1+r)^{-j}\right]}{r} \qquad (10)$$

For an instantaneous adjustment period, $j = 0$ in equation (10) and hence $B = 0$; the floating-rate bond has a duration of zero.[14] If the rate adjustment occurs at the end of every interest period, $j = 1$, and thus $B = 1$; the floating-rate bond has a duration of

---

[13]Equation (8) is analogous to Morgan's equation (5).

[14]While, in general, the duration of a floating-rate bond is between zero and the duration of a fixed-rate but otherwise identical bond, it is possible mathematically for the duration of a floating-rate instrument to be less than zero (see the Morgan and Ott articles). Two examples of securities with negative duration are presented later in the article.

one period. In this case, the duration equals the length of the adjustment period regardless of the bond's maturity. The floating-rate bond behaves like a fixed-rate bond that pays interest and matures in one lump sum on the next interest rate adjustment date. Portfolio managers often use this simple approach when calculating the duration of the floating-rate instruments in their portfolios.[15] But this approach is valid only if (i) the adjustability coefficient equals one and (ii) the floating-rate bond's coupon rate equals the required market yield ($r=y$).

## IV.  SENSITIVITY ANALYSIS

Exhibit 2 illustrates the sensitivity of the duration of a par-value floating-rate bond to the maturity and coupon rate of the bond. The exhibit assumes for the sake of illustration that the adjustability coefficient is 0.75 and that the coupon rate adjusts semi-annually. The longer the floating-rate bond's maturity and the lower its coupon rate the greater is the bond's duration. The duration of a perpetual par-value floating-rate bond is:

$$ B = \frac{(1 + r)\left[1 - a_t (1 + r)^{-j}\right]}{r} $$

Thus, for example, for a collection of floating-rate bonds each of which pays interest at the current rate of 10% and is currently worth par, a 10-year bond has a duration of 2.01 years, a 30-year bond has a duration of 2.86 years, and a perpetual bond has a duration of 6.00 years.

Exhibit 3 illustrates the sensitivity of the duration of a floating-rate bond to the value of the adjustability coefficient and the length of the period until the next coupon adjustment occurs. It assumes a 20-year floating-rate bond that currently pays interest at the rate of 10% when the required yield is also 10%. Duration decreases as the adjustability coefficient increases. The more responsive to market interest rates the index to which the coupon rate on the floating-rate bond is tied, the greater is the degree of price protection afforded, and hence the smaller is the floating-rate bond's duration. The more frequent the coupon adjustment the greater also is the degree of price protection afforded, and hence the smaller the duration. At the extremes, of course, if the coupon rate never adjusts ($a_t = 0$ or $j = n$), the duration is that of a fixed-rate bond.

For the bonds in Exhibit 3, the fixed-rate bond has a duration of 9.01 years. A 20-year floating-rate bond would have a duration of 0.25 years when the coupon rate adjusts quarterly and when the adjustability coefficient is 1. The floating-rate bond's duration is greater than 0.25 years if the adjustability coefficient is less than 1 or if the coupon rate adjusts less frequently than quarterly but is substantially less than the duration of the fixed-rate bond over a wide range of adjustability coefficient values.

---

[15]See Yawitz et al.

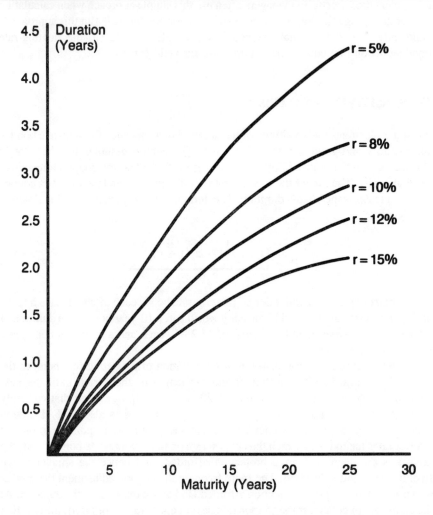

**EXHIBIT 2**
**SENSITIVITY OF DURATION TO MATURITY AND COUPON RATE FOR**
**A BOND WORTH PAR**

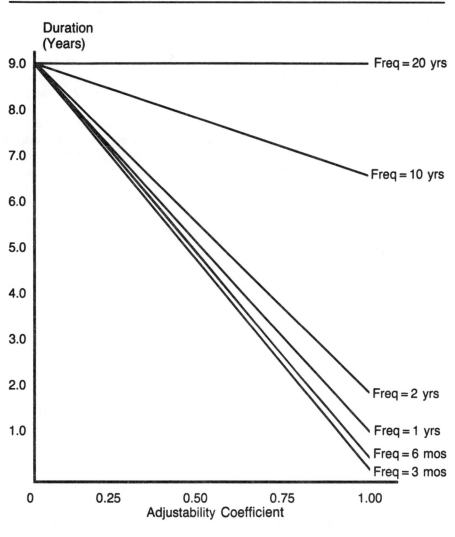

Exhibit 4 illustrates the time pattern of the duration of a 20-year floating-rate bond assuming that the coupon rate adjusts annually. The exhibit assumes the bond's coupon rate is 10%, its adjustability coefficient is 0.75, and the required market yield is 10%. Duration follows a saw-tooth pattern. The duration of a floating-rate bond decreases as each coupon adjustment date approaches. It then "jumps" immediately following the coupon adjustment because the length of the period until the next coupon adjustment is scheduled to occur "jumps" from zero to one year. Each peak is lower than the preceding peak, however, because the duration of a floating-rate bond, like the duration of a fixed-rate bond, tends to decrease as the bond approaches maturity.

Exhibit 5 illustrates the sensitivity of the duration of a 20-year floating-rate bond to the current coupon rate on the issue and to the required market yield. The exhibit assumes that the adjustability coefficient is 0.75. Given the bond's current coupon, the duration of a floating-rate bond is inversely related to the currently required market yield. This is also true for a fixed-rate bond. However, given the required market yield, the greater the current coupon the greater is a floating-rate bond's duration, which is the opposite of the relationship between the coupon and the duration of a fixed-rate bond. The sensitivity of the factor of proportionality in equation (8) to changes in the coupon rate is responsible for this behavior. The factor of proportionality varies directly with the coupon rate $r$.[16] $D$ decreases as $r$ increases but the factor of proportionality increases at a faster rate, and this causes the duration of a floating-rate bond to increase with $r$.

## V. CALCULATING THE ADJUSTABILITY COEFFICIENT

The adjustability coefficient for a floating-rate bond can be calculated in the manner described by Ott.[17] First, measure the responsiveness of the index to which the floating-rate bond's coupon is tied to changes in the level of market interest rates (as reflected in a particular benchmark yield) by fitting the following equation:

$$I_t = a + by_t + cI_{t-1} + U_t \qquad (12)$$

$I_t$ denotes the value of the index in period $t$; $y_t$ denotes the market benchmark yield in period t; and $I_{t-1}$ denotes the value of the index in the prior period. Equation (12) is fitted to data for an appropriate historical period to obtain estimates for the parameters $b$ and $c$, which together characterize the speed of adjustment of the index $I_t$ to changes in the market yield $y_t$. When $b=1$ and $c=0$, adjustment is complete in the initial period; $dr_t/dy = 1$ for each period. If $b=0$ and $c=1$, as in the case of a fixed-rate bond, adjustment never occurs. In between, the index adjusts to changes in the required market yield but on a lagged basis.

---

[16]See Finnerty.
[17]See Ott, p. 928.

**EXHIBIT 4**
**TIME PATTERN OF DURATION OF A 20-YEAR FLOATING-RATE BOND**

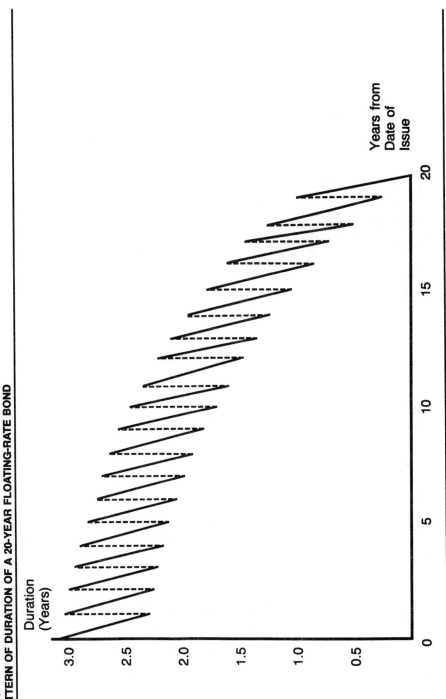

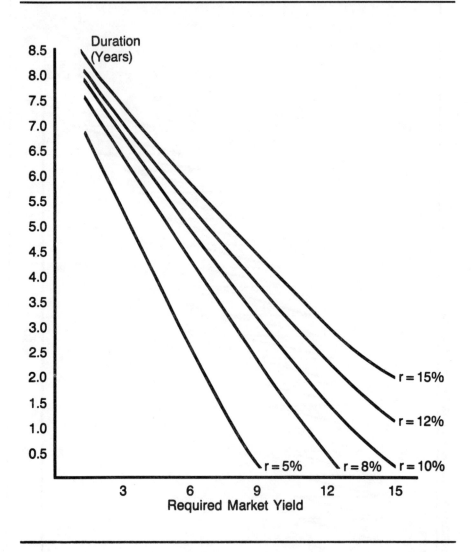

When the initial coupon adjustment occurs $j$ periods after the floating-rate bond is issued and the coupon rate readjusts each period thereafter, the value of the adjustability coefficient is calculated in the following manner. The first coupon payment to adjust occurs at the end of period $j + 1$. The change in market yield causes the index to change by $b + bc + bc^2 + \ldots + bc^j = b[1-c^{j+1}]/(1-c)$. In virtually all floating-rate bonds, the coupon rate is obtained by adding a fixed markup to the index so that the index and the coupon rate change by the same amount. Hence, $dr_{j+1}/dy = b[1-c^{j+1}]/(1-c)$. Similarly, coupon payments between periods $j + 1$ and $n$ change by $dr_t/dy = b[1-c^t]/(1-c)$, $j + 1 \leq t \leq n$. Substituting these values for $dr_t/dy$ in equation (7) leads to the following expression for the adjustability coefficient:

$$a_t = \frac{b}{1-c}\left[1 - \frac{c\left\{c^j(1+y)^{n-j} - c^n\right\} + (1+y-c)}{\left\{(1+y)^{n-j} - 1\right\} + y}\right] \tag{13}$$

where $y$ and $n$ are as previously defined.

### An Example

As illustrated in Exhibit 1, roughly one-fourth of all domestic floating-rate bonds have a coupon rate that adjusts quarterly based on 3-month LIBOR. An issue the Chase Manhattan Corporation sold in 1984 contains a typical coupon formula.[18] The notes pay interest quarterly, and the interest rate for each quarterly period equals ⅛ of 1% per annum plus the average of 3-month LIBOR as quoted by a set of reference banks two business days prior to the beginning of the interest period.[19]

The notes mature 12 years from the date of issue. The initial interest rate was 11⅛%. The 10-year constant maturity U.S. Treasury yield is used as the proxy for the market interest rate in the duration calculation. At the time the notes were issued, the 10-year constant maturity U.S. Treasury yield was 12.50%. Converting the parameters of equation (8) to a quarterly basis, $y = .031250$, $r = .0278125$, $n = 48$, and $j = 1$. It remains to estimate $a_t$. The *Federal Reserve Bulletin* regularly publishes weekly and monthly estimates of 3-month LIBOR and the 10-year constant maturity U.S. Treasury yield.[20] Fitting equation (12) to end-of-quarter data for the five-year period spanning the fourth quarter of 1981 through the third quarter of 1986 produced the following parameter estimates:

---

[18]The Chase Manhattan Corporation, Floating Rate Subordinated Notes Due 1996, prospectus, April 4, 1984.

[19]The Chase Manhattan issue also has special features that may have affected its pricing. These are ignored in the interest of keeping the illustration simple.

[20]The *Federal Reserve Bulletin* publishes weekly figures that represent the averages of business day data. Each end-of-quarter estimate for 3-month LIBOR and for the 10-year constant maturity U.S. Treasury yield is the weekly average for the week that contains the last business day of the quarter.

$$I_t = -2.313 + 0.836\ y_t + 0.281\ I_{t-1} \qquad R^2 = 0.86 \qquad (14)$$

Applying equation (13) with $j=1$, the value of $a_t$ is 1.1577. Substituting into equation (8) gives a duration of $B=-4.87$ quarters, or -14.61 months. The negative duration has an interesting interpretation. The coupon rate $r$ rises faster on a present-value basis than the market yield $y$ (note that $a_t=1.1577$, meaning that it effectively rises 15.77% faster when the present values of the lagged effects are taken into account), more than offsetting the downward effect of the higher required yield on the price of the security.

If instead it had been assumed simply that $a_t=1$ and $y=r$, formula (10) would have indicated a duration of 3 months, a difference of nearly 1.5 years from the actual duration. Taking into account the sensitivity of the coupon rate index to changes in the market rate of interest can be very important in correctly calculating the duration of a floating-rate bond.

## VI. ROLE OF THE TERM STRUCTURE OF INTEREST RATES

$B$, and more particularly, the duration $D$ of a fixed-rate bond incorporated in formula (8), only approximate true duration when the term structure is not flat. But, as already noted, the available empirical evidence suggests that, in practice, Macaulay duration is as accurate an indicator of price volatility as the more sophisticated measures of duration that are intended to account for different shapes of and shifts in the term structure. In the case of floating-rate bonds, there is one additional factor related to the term structure to consider: How will a non-flat term structure affect price volatility as the coupon rate adjusts over time?

The coupon rate of a floating-rate bond typically adjusts according to a market interest rate that corresponds to the length of the period until the next coupon rate adjustment is scheduled to occur, for example, the 91-day Treasury bill rate or 3-month LIBOR in the case of quarterly coupon rate adjustments. When the market is efficient and when interest rates evolve over time in accordance with the term structure of interest rates that prevailed at the time duration was calculated, the evolution of interest rates along a non-flat term structure will not affect the price volatility of a floating-rate bond.

Let $r_{i-1,i}$ denote the forward rate that corresponds to the period between interest adjustment dates $i-1$ and $i$; $F$ denote the principal amount of the floating-rate bond; and $P$ denote the floating-rate bond's price.

Let $\{R_t\}_1^N$ denote the term structure of interest rates.

$$\text{Then } 1 + R_t = \prod_{i=1}^{t}\left(1 + r_{i-1,\ i}\right). \qquad (14B)$$

On each interest payment date $k$, the price of the floating-rate bond would be

$$
P = F \left\{ \frac{r_{k, k+1}}{1 + r_{k, k+1}} + \frac{r_{k+1, k+2}}{\left(1 + r_{k, k+1}\right)\left(1 + r_{k+1, k+2}\right)} + \ldots \right.
$$

$$
\left. + \frac{1 + r_{N-1, N}}{\left(1 + r_{k, k+1}\right) \cdots \left(1 + r_{N-1, N}\right)} \right\} = F ,
$$

(15)

that is, par provided interest rates follow the term structure.

Evidence presented by Fama[21] and others indicates that forward rates are the best predictors of future spot interest rates, even though these predictions are not especially accurate. In an efficient market these predictions will be fully reflected in required yields and market prices. Therefore, expected changes in future spot rates as reflected in the prevailing term structure, regardless of its shape, should not affect the price volatility, hence the duration, of a floating-rate bond in an efficient market.[22]

Thus, when the term structure is not flat, formula (8) rests on the assumptions that (i) formula (1) accurately measures the duration the bond would have if its coupon rate were fixed *and* (ii) interest rates during the remaining life of the bond will move in accordance with the current term structure. Depending on the shape and assumed manner of shift in the term structure, formula (8) could be extended to incorporate these particular assumptions by proceeding along the lines of Bierwag's extension of Macaulay duration.[23]

## VII. DURATION OF A RETROSPECTIVELY INDEXED FLOATING-RATE BOND

The preceding discussion has assumed that interest is paid prospectively. The interest rate is adjusted at the beginning of each interest period, and interest is paid at this rate at the end of the interest period regardless of how market interest rates change during the period. But interest payments could instead be based on the change in

---

[21]Eugene F. Fama, "Forward Rates as Predictors of Future Spot Rates," *Journal of Financial Economics*, Vol. 3 (October 1976), pp. 361-377.

[22]A floating-rate bond will not necessarily trade at par between interest payment dates when accrued interest is calculated on a straight-line basis, as is current market practice. However, it is easily shown that if interest rate changes between interest payment dates subsequent to any particular point in time follow the term structure prevailing at that point in time and if accrued interest during any period is paid in accordance with forward interest rates at the beginning of the interest period, a floating-rate bond would always trade at par.

[23]See Bierwag, "Measures of Duration."

some index during the interest period. To reflect this, set $j$ equal to zero in equation (7) and equation (13) and apply equation (8). The duration of a bond for which the interest rate is indexed to the price of some commodity or service or to some financial index, as for example the recent issue of SPINS (Standard & Poor's 500 Index Subordinated Notes)[24] which indexes the coupon rate to the Standard & Poor's 500 Index, would be calculated in this manner.

Formula (8) can be simplified under certain circumstances where interest is paid retrospectively. Suppose that the bond is sold at par, so that $r = y$. In that case, $D = D^*$ and formula (8) simplifies to:

$$B = (1 - a_t)D^* \qquad (16)$$

which is just the product of one minus the adjustability coefficient and the duration of a par-value fixed-rate bond that is otherwise identical to the floating-rate bond.

When the coupon rate is perfectly indexed to market interest rates, $a_t = 1$, and duration is zero.[25] But if the index is the price of a commodity, a stock market index, or some other quantity that does not adjust perfectly to changes in market interest rates, duration is nonzero. That is, if the coupon rate adjusts instantaneously to the index, there is no basis risk with respect to the index. But if the index does not adjust instantaneously and perfectly to changes in market interest rates, there is basis risk with respect to market interest rates. Consequently, the duration of such a floating-rate bond is not zero with respect to market interest rates.

Consider for example the issue of SPINS mentioned earlier. According to the prospectus for the issue, the securities were sold at par on August 21, 1986. The notes mature four years from date of issue, pay interest semi-annually at the rate of 2% per annum, and at maturity the bondholder receives the greater of (i) $1,000 (the principal amount per bond) and (ii) $1,000 increased in proportion to the increase in the S&P 500 above 270.38. The 270.38 value represents a premium of 8.25% over the value of the S&P 500 at the time the SPINS were offered to investors. At the time of the SPINS issue, less risky four-year Treasury bonds were yielding approximately 6.75% and so SPINS purchasers must have expected the S&P 500 to increase significantly above 270.38 by the maturity date. The present value of the 2% per annum interest payment stream serves to offset the effect on SPINS value of the 8.25% premium.[26] Accordingly, the SPINS can be viewed as a floating-rate bond

----

[24] Salomon Inc, 2% Standard & Poor's 500 Index Subordinated Notes, prospectus, August 21, 1986.

[25] This corresponds to Cox, Ingersoll and Ross's default-free bond that accrues interest at a rate that adjusts instantaneously to the prevailing spot default-free (i.e., Treasury) rate of interest. See John C. Cox, Jonathan E. Ingersoll, Jr., and Stephen A. Ross, "An Analysis of Variable Rate Loan Contracts," *Journal of Finance,* Vol. 35 (May 1980), pp. 389-403.

[26] The closing value of the S&P 500 on August 20, the day prior to the SPINS offering, was 249.77. The 270.38 threshold thus represents an 8.25% premium. The preliminary prospectus for the SPINS issue proposed no premium but also no semi-annual interest payments. The 2% interest rate compounded semi-annually over 4 years represents a future value of $1.0829 per initial dollar invested in SPINS, an increase of 8.25% when rounded to the nearest ¼ of 1%. By transforming a portion of the prospective future value into more certain interest payments, the issuer made the SPINS more attractive to investors.

the coupon rate on which adjusts instantaneously to changes in the S&P 500 and on which interest payments are made retrospectively at maturity, subject to a floor rate of 2% per annum payable semi-annually.

The 10-year constant maturity U.S. Treasury yield is again used as the proxy for market interest rates. End-of-quarter values for the 10-year constant maturity Treasury yield were obtained from the *Federal Reserve Bulletin,* and end-of-quarter values for the S&P 500 were taken from Standard & Poor's *Daily Stock Price Record.* Fitting equation (12) to end-of-quarter data for the four-year period spanning the fourth quarter of 1982 through the third quarter of 1986, the length of which matches the maturity of the SPINS, produced the following parameter estimates:

$$I_t = 10.744 - 0.664\ R_t + 0.129\ I_{t-1} \quad R^2 = 0.06 \tag{17}$$

The estimated value for $y$ is 8% per annum. Substituting into equation (13) with $j = 0$ and $n = 8$ semi-annual interest periods gives $a_t = -0.7463$, reflecting the fact that percentage changes in the S&P 500 and percentage changes in the 10-year constant maturity Treasury yield tended to move inversely during the 1982-1986 period of estimation. The SPINS were sold at par. By equation (16), the duration of the SPINS was -5.23 semi-annual periods, or -31.38 months.[27] Due to the inverse relationship between the S&P 500 and the 10-year constant maturity Treasury yield, when interest rates drop payments on the SPINS would be expected to increase, not decrease. The price of the SPINS would get the double benefit of higher interest payments and a lower required yield. However, the opposite would occur if interest rates instead increased. In any case, the duration of the SPINS, and by implication their price volatility, is highly sensitive to how the S&P 500 to which interest payments are indexed responds to future changes in market interest rates.

## VIII. DURATION OF A FLOATING-RATE MORTGAGE

Formula (8) applies to floating-rate debt instruments that repay in a single lump sum at maturity. A mortgage amortizes over the life of the instrument. Formula (8) must be modified before it can be applied to floating-rate mortgages. As in the case of non-sinking-fund bonds, the formula for the duration of a floating-rate mortgage is expressed in terms of the formula for the duration of the comparable fixed-rate instrument.

The duration, $F$, of a fixed-rate level payment mortgage can be expressed as:[28]

---

[27]This calculation ignores any impact the 2% interest rate floor might have had on the price volatility of the SPINS. However, the floor is so low relative to the prevailing level of interest rates that it would have had little impact on bond price volatility on the issuance date. Nevertheless, if decreases in the S&P 500 make it increasingly likely that investors will only realize the floor rate of return, the existence of the floor would affect the bond's duration. In particular, if the S&P 500 were to decrease sufficiently so as to make it very unlikely that the 270.38 threshold would be exceeded on the maturity date, the SPINS price volatility would approximate that of a 2% fixed-rate bond.

[28]See Ott.

$$F = (1+y)/y - n/((1+y)^n - 1) \tag{18}$$

where $y$ again denotes the market yield with respect to which duration is being measured and $n$ again denotes the maturity of the instrument. For the special case in which the interest rate on the mortgage equals the market yield ($r = y$), equation (18) becomes

$$F* = \frac{(1+r)}{r} - \frac{n}{(1+r)^n - 1} \tag{19}$$

Let $M$ denote the duration of a floating-rate mortgage. A formula for $M$ can be obtained by proceeding in the same manner as in the development of formula (8). Ott develops the following formula for $M$:

$$M = F\left[1 - \{a_t(1+y)F*/((1+r)F)\} \right.$$
$$\left. \times \left\{1 - \sum_{t=1}^{j}(1+y)^{-t} / \sum_{t=1}^{n}(1+y)^{-t}\right\}\right], \tag{20}$$

where $a_t$ is defined by equation (7), $F$ by equation (18), and $F*$ by equation (19). Equation (20) is analogous to equation (8). The duration of a floating-rate mortgage equals a fraction of the duration of a fixed-rate but otherwise identical mortgage, where the expression in brackets in equation (20) represents the *factor of proportionality*. Note that if the mortgage rate never adjusts, $a_t = 0$ and equation (20) simplifies to $M = F$.

Equation (20) has an interesting interpretation. Suppose the index adjusts perfectly to changes in market interest rates so that $a_t = 1$. If $r = y$, then $F = F*$ and equation (20) simplifies to:

$$M = F\left[\sum_{t=1}^{j}(1+y)^{-t} / \sum_{t=1}^{n}(1+y)^{-t}\right] \tag{21}$$

Equation (21) represents the duration of a floating-rate mortgage that adjusts fully on each reset date. When equation (20) is rewritten as

$$M = \left[1 - a_t(1+y)F*/((1+r)F)\right] \cdot F$$
$$+ \left[a_t(1+y)F*/((1+r)F)\right] \cdot F \cdot \sum_{t=1}^{j}(1+y)^{-t} / \sum_{t=1}^{n}(1+y)^{-t} \tag{22}$$

it becomes clear that the duration of a floating-rate mortgage, expressed in equation (20), equals the weighted average of (i) the duration of a fixed-rate but otherwise identical mortgage and (ii) the duration of an otherwise identical floating-rate mortgage that adjusts fully on each reset date. The bracketed terms in equation (22) serve as the weights.

## IX. SENSITIVITY OF DURATION TO THE INDEX

Ott calculated the duration of a variety of floating-rate mortgages. He examined five different indexes: The Federal Home Loan Bank Board monthly median annualized cost of funds for FSLIC-insured institutions (COF), the Federal Home Loan Bank Board national average mortgage contract rate for major lenders on the purchase of previously occupied homes (MR), and the 3-month, 6-month, and 12-month Treasury bill rates (TB3, TB6, and TB12, respectively). He also investigated four different rate adjustment frequencies: 6 months, 1 year, 3 years, and 5 years. He calculated duration in each case using the Treasury yield that corresponds to the length of the interval between rate adjustments as the market yield benchmark. The results of Ott's numerical analysis are summarized in Exhibit 6.

**EXHIBIT 6**
**SENSITIVITY OF THE DURATION OF A FLOATING-RATE MORTGAGE TO THE INDEX**

| Coupon Rate Index(1) | Duration (in months) When Market Yield Benchmark Is(2) | | | |
|---|---|---|---|---|
| | TB6 | TY1 | TY3 | TY5 |
| COF | 40.56 | 48.00 | 55.00 | 59.76 |
| MR | 10.14 | 19.04 | 24.93 | 32.69 |
| TB3 | −3.58 | 3.85 | 5.05 | 19.45 |
| TB6 | NR(3) | 11.47 | 10.62 | 22.58 |
| TB12 | 19.62 | 23.52 | 21.36 | 30.47 |

(1)  COF = Federal Home Loan Bank Board monthly median annualized cost of funds for FSLIC-insured institutions.
  MR = Federal Home Loan Bank Board national average mortgage contract rate for major lenders on the purchase of previously occupied homes.
  TB3 = 3-month Treasury bill rate.
  TB6 = 6-month Treasury bill rate.
  TB12 = 12-month Treasury bill rate.

(2)  TY1 = 1-year Treasury yield.
  TY3 = 3-year Treasury yield.
  TY5 = 5-year Treasury yield.

(3)  NR = no value reported.

Source:  Robert A. Ott, Jr., "The Duration of an Adjustable-Rate Mortgage and the Impact of the Index," *Journal of Finance*, Vol. 41 (September 1986), pp. 930-931.

For each rate adjustment frequency, there is considerable variation in duration depending on the particular index used as the basis for adjusting the mortgage interest rate. For example, the duration of floating-rate mortgages that provide for annual rate adjustments vary between 3.85 months, when the 3-month Treasury bill rate serves as the index, and 48.00 months, when the cost of funds (COF) serves as the index. In particular, when COF serves as the index, the duration is four times as great as the length of the adjustment interval. The index used as the basis for adjusting the interest rate evidently has a significant impact on the price volatility of a floating-rate debt instrument.

## X. CONCLUSION

This article has presented formulas for calculating the duration of a floating-rate non-sinking-fund bond and for calculating the duration of a floating-rate mortgage. In addition to the current coupon rate, the required market yield, and the maturity of the instrument, all of which affect the duration of any debt instrument, the responsiveness to changes in market interest rates of the index to which the floating-rate debt instrument's coupon rate is tied and the frequency of coupon rate adjustment each has a significant impact on the duration of a floating-rate debt instrument.

# Valuing Convertible Securities

LUKE KNECHT
VICE PRESIDENT
FIXED INCOME MANAGEMENT DEPARTMENT
HARRIS TRUST & SAVINGS BANK

MIKE McCOWIN
VICE PRESIDENT
FIXED INCOME MANAGEMENT DEPARTMENT
HARRIS TRUST & SAVINGS BANK

## I. INTRODUCTION

With over $12 billion of new convertible securities being brought to market annually, the need for effective convertible valuation tools has never been greater. Innovative new features and increasingly complex call and put features, challenge portfolio managers to carefully weigh the value and use of convertibles.

In the past, convertible securities were characteristically issued by small, emerging companies or those in financial distress. Sometimes, warrants were added as "sweeteners" to entice investors to buy otherwise unmarketable debt. Such issues were typically purchased by insurance companies and by "special situations" portfolio managers.

Today this has all changed. Blue chip firms such as IBM, Unisys and Westinghouse are issuing convertible bonds by the hundreds of millions of dollars. Interestingly, these same blue chip companies are also allocating comparable amounts from their pension funds to be specifically invested in convertibles.

97

This article is intended to help investors who are already reasonably familiar with the analysis of stocks and bonds to better understand the unique attributes of convertible securities, and more importantly, how to evaluate them and employ them in carrying out investment strategy. The material is presented in the form of three basic topic areas. First, convertible securities are described in terms of how they are created, their behavioral characteristics, and who uses them. Next, valuation theory is presented, together with tools and techniques for estimating the value of individual convertible securities. Finally, applications to the achievement of specific investment objectives and strategies are discussed, together with the practical problems of execution, anticipating calls, and deciding when and whether to convert. The appendix provides a glossary of terms.

## II. WHAT IS A CONVERTIBLE SECURITY?

A convertible security is defined as any investment instrument which is not currently common stock, but which can be converted into common stock at the holder's option. This would include convertible bonds, convertible preferred stocks and bond/warrants deals. Due to the convertibility feature, such instruments will reflect changes in the value of the underlying common stock, as well as movements in interest rates. For this reason, convertibles are sometimes referrred to as "hybrid" securities, to reflect their dual nature. Later, the term "hybrid" will be used in a more specific way.

Typically, a new issue convertible bond will carry a fixed maturity of 25 to 30 years and a coupon (dividend in the case of a preferred stock) rate below a comparable non-convertible bond. In exchange for the lower income rate, the issuer grants the purchaser the right to acquire an equity security at a price which is usually 20% to 30% higher than today's price. The conversion privilege remains in force for the life of the convertible security.

There are many variations on the above described "typical" convertible structure. They range from zero coupon convertibles with very small conversion premia to higher coupon securities with premia in excess of 40%. However, all convertibles can be viewed in terms of two essential components: a fixed payment stream analogous to a bond and a call option on the underlying equity security. Both of these components interact to determine value and price behavior as will be explained in the valuation section.

## III. HOW ARE CONVERTIBLE SECURITIES CREATED?

Convertible securities can come into existence in a variety of ways. Corporations seeking to raise capital are the most common source of new issues. In addition, however, substantial quantities of convertible securities are the result of mergers and acquisitions. Notable examples are the $1 + billion issue of Unisys convertible preferred stock resulting from Burroughs acqustion of Sperry and the $400 million convertible debenture issued by Amoco Canada to acquire Dome Petroleum. Convertible securities can also result from corporate restructuring, often by troubled companies.

Convertibles can also be created by companies wishing to divest themselves of another firm's common stock. These are sometimes called "exchangeable" bonds, since they are "exchanged" for *another firm's common stock*, rather than converted into the issuer's common stock. This unique combination of one company's credit with another's equity, together with the often limited size of the issue (i.e. limited by the amount of common stock held by the issuer), tends to make such issues popular with investors. Examples of such issues would include: Internorth 10.5% bonds of 2008 Exchangeable for Mobil common stock, General Dynamics 5.75% bonds of 2011 exchangeable for Federal Express common stock, and IBM 6.375% Eurodollar bonds exchangeable for INTEL common stock.

The most important source of new convertible securities is the corporate issuer. As noted earlier, this was historically the smaller, more speculative company, but now includes major blue chip corporations. This change reflects a growing recognition that convertibles offer benefits to issuers, as well as to investors. What are the benefits to the issuer?

First of all, the issuer is able to obtain debt financing at a lower coupon rate than would be necessary for straight debt. If the stock price does *not* rise (so that the company is *not* able to cause the bonds to be converted into common stock), the annual savings of 1% to 2% (sometimes more) can be quite significant over the life of the bond. More typically, however, the issuing corporation expects the common stock price to rise, resulting in conversion into common stock.

In this event, the benefit to the issuer is that of having sold common stock at a premium to the price that existed at the time of the financing. Additionally, while waiting for the stock price to rise, the issuer has enjoyed a reduced rate on its debt obligation. Thus, the convertible security is often perceived by the issuer as a lower cost method of raising equity capital.

In addition to these advantages, the covenants associated with a convertible security are generally less restrictive to the corporate issuer than they would be for straight debt. Finally, the subordinated position of convertible debt in the capital structure, while a slight disadvantage to the investor, represents a modest advantage to the issuer insofar as it facilitates the ability to issue more senior debt.

## IV. CATEGORIZING CONVERTIBLES

Convertible securities can behave in a variety of ways depending on movements in the underlying common stock price and interest rates. To demonstrate this point, examine Exhibit 1.

**EXHIBIT 1**
**CONVERTIBLE BOND PRICE RESPONSE CURVE**

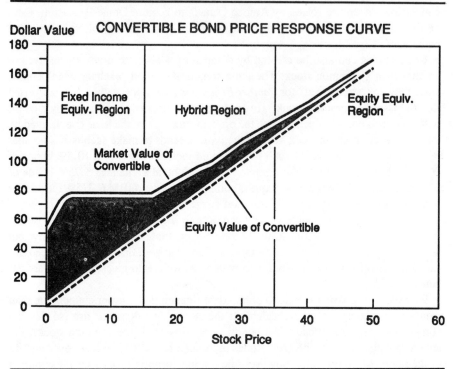

The solid line represents the price behavior which might be expected of a typical convertible bond relative to the value of its underlying common stock. The straight dashed line is simply a linear representation of possible values for the common stock. For each stock price, the underlying equity value of the convertible security may be plotted as shown. The distance between the dashed line and the solid line represents the "premium" value in the convertible bond.

As the common stock price moves higher (to the right), the equity value of the convertible will begin to dominate its behavior. Eventually, the convertible price will move in close lock-step with the common stock price. In this region the premium value of the convertible is negligible and is largely determined by the issue's call provision and coupon or dividend rate of the convertible in relation to the underlying common stock. Because this type of convertible's price response is dominated by changes in the price of the underlying equity, it is commonly referred to as an "equity equivalent."

As the common stock price declines (to the left), the fixed income value of the convertible security becomes more dominant. As the premium over the underlying equity value becomes greater, the favorable bending of the return distribution becomes more apparent. However, in the extreme (i.e., bankruptcy, etc.), the bond value will also drop sharply, as indicated by the sharp downward slope of the convertible security line as the stock price approaches zero. Of course, as interest rates change, the bond value of the convertible will also change. The bond value of the convertible will also be affected by the time remaining to maturity and default risk premiums in the marketplace. For obvious reasons, convertibles in this region are called "fixed income" or "bond equivalents." They are sometimes also referred to as "busted convertibles."

Earlier, the term hybrid was used as a generic description of the behavioral characteristic of convertibles. In this section, the term hybrid is used to denote a specific type of convertible. Specifically, convertibles whose price behavior is sensitive to both stock price and interest rate moves can be classified as hybrids. Typically, most new issue convertibles come to market as hybrids and through subsequent market action become bond or equity equivalents. In Exhibit 1, hybrid convertibles fall in the middle region where the characteristic line bends. In general, convertibles which trade at a premium of 15% to 40% of their equity value may be classified as hybrid.

Although the distinction between these three regions may occasionally seem blurred, this treatment is helpful when focusing on investment strategy and in understanding the type of investors to which a particular convertible might appeal.

## V. BEHAVIORAL CHARACTERISITCS OF CONVERTIBLE SECURITIES

Exhibit 2 illustrates the characteristic behavior of a convertible securities portfolio relative to that of an equity or bond portfolio under the assumption that stock and bond prices are generally moving in the same direction.

Overall, a stock portfolio is expected to exhibit somewhat more volatility than a bond portfolio and therefore offer a somewhat higher return.[1] This is reflected by the steeper slope of the stock portfolio line. Since convertible securities should reflect the underlying common stock values in a period of rising market prices, the convertible portfolio line is shown approaching, but not reaching, the stock portfolio line in the upper right hand quadrant.

In a period of declining market prices, the stock portfolio will drop in value more rapidly than the bond portfolio. During such a period, the convertible portfolio should respond less and less to the downward movement of the common stocks and begin to more closely approach the bond portfolio. This is shown in the lower left hand quadrant.

This hybrid behavior produces a non-linear distribution of expected returns for the convertible security portfolio. *This non-linearity of expected returns is probably the single most important attribute of a convertible security portfolio!*

---

[1]Roger Ibbotson and Sinquefield, *Stocks, Bonds, Bills and Inflation*, Financial Analysts Research Foundation.

**EXHIBIT 2**
**RETURN DISTRIBUTIONS STOCKS, BONDS, CONVERTIBLE SECURITIES**

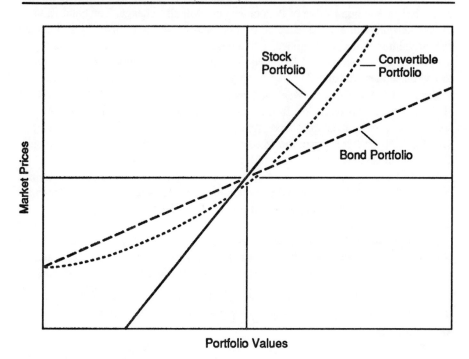

It is important to note that the favorable bending of the return distribution is essentially inherent in the convertible security itself, i.e., it does not depend on the judgment or action of a portfolio manager. In a period when the underlying common stock value is declining rapidly, the behavior of the convertible security will automatically move in the direction of a fixed income instrument. Conversely, in a period of sharply rising equity value, the convertible security will automatically begin to take on the behavior of the common stock.

The convertible security will normally not rise as rapidly as the common stock in a favorable market environment, nor will it be quite as defensive as a straight bond issue in a declining market environment. Nevertheless, a portfolio of convertibles will often exhibit superior behavior to either instrument alone over complete market cycles. What is more, it will sometimes be possible to achieve returns which are superior to an all equity portfolio with a volatility of return which is less than that of the overall equity market!

If this portfolio characteristic sounds familiar, it should, for it is in many ways equivalent to so called portfolio insurance. Generally, portfolio insurance is an asset allocation strategy whereby the stock/bond ratio is managed in direct response to the price behavior of the underlying assets. That is, as stocks appreciate, fixed income holdings are liquidated and moved into stocks. Declines in stock price trigger the opposite response and result in more money moving into the bond component. The goal of this responsive allocation strategy is to ensure the portfolio some minimum return while offering the possibilities of the higher returns associated with stocks.

As stated above, this is an inherent quality of a diversified convertible security portfolio. As stock prices rise, the portfolios price behavior will be increasingly responsive, while declines in stocks will result in an increasing bond equivalent portfolio. Unlike portfolio insurance which requires active intervention, convertibles offer this transition as a natural behavioral element.

This bending of the return distribution and the automatic nature of the transition which takes place enable a convertible securities portfolio to outperform a balanced portfolio of stocks and bonds. Although the stock and bond portfolio might appear to have similar attributes at the outset, it would suffer from two disadvantages. First, the adjustment of the relationship between equity and fixed income would not be automatic. That is, the balanced portfolio requires an active, "manual" adjustment process to rebalance the stock/bond mix. Market discontinuities and transaction costs are unavoidable elements of such a strategy. Secondly, the responsive behavior could not be tailored to the action of the individual common stock.

It should also be noted that the bending of the return distribution tends to be sharpest in the hybrid region described in Exhibit 1. In the equity equivalent range, the convertible price behavior will very closely parallel that of the common stock and in the fixed income region, it will be relatively unresponsive to common stock price change. In the middle range, then, is where the "action" occurs. Therefore, *to the extent that an investor wishes to exploit the naturally favorable attributes of convertible securities, it is desirable to operate in the hybrid region.* Unfortunately, this is where the valuation process is most challenging.

## VI. WHO USES CONVERTIBLE SECURITIES?

One of the more fascinating aspects of convertible securities investment is the wide variety of participants in the market. Each type of investor brings a unique perspective to the valuation process, thereby creating a wide diversity of attitudes in the marketplace. A "junk bond" manager may want to sell a bond equivalent when the company's prospects improve and the security begins to behave more like a hybrid. The hybrid manager who buys this security may later sell it to an equity portfolio manager, when the common stock rises to the point where the security becomes an equity equivalent. Each manager is making a decision which is rational and sensible from his own perspective, yet each may feel that he has had the better side of the trade.

Types of convertible investors include:

*Risk Average Equity Managers*—Common stock portfolio managers who wish to hold a somewhat more defensive instrument.

*Income Oriented Equity Managers*—Common stock investors requiring more income than is provided by the common stock.

*Convertible Specialists*—Investors dealing exclusively in the management of convertible security portfolios.

*Bond Managers Seeking Equity "Kickers"*—Junk bond managers and other fixed income managers willing to sacrifice a certain amount of income to obtain some equity exposure.

*Arbitrageurs and Hedgers*—Investors oriented to exploiting perceived disparities in the spread relationship between the common stock and the convertible security.

Each type of investor may place a different degree of emphasis on particular variables in determining which convertible securities are attractive or unattractive. The more equity oriented investor will tend to restrict activity to the equity equivalent end of the spectrum, whereas junk bond managers will tend to be more active in the bond equivalent range. Convertible specialists will employ the full range of securities, but may have a preference for the true hybrid convertible security, for reasons which will be discussed later. Arbitrage tends to be most easily accomplished with equity equivalent issues, but can take place over a broad range of security types. In each case, the valuation tools given greatest emphasis will vary with the investor's perspective.

As a convertible bond passes from one category to another, market segmentation must be overcome. An issue which was widely held by convertible specialists as a hybrid may become unusually cheap before it attracts the attention of debt portfolio managers. This is especially true when the price action is as abrupt as it was in October of 1987. Many investment grade convertible bonds could be purchased at yields in excess of their straight debt counterparts due to massive selling by equity oriented holders. Bond portfolio managers in general were slow to recognize the tremendous value some of these securities offered. This brings us to the topic of valuation.

## VII.  CONVERTIBLE VALUATION

Like most things in life, there are many ways to approach the valuation of convertible securities. Before examining these different views, it is worthwhile to briefly restate the obvious. The most obvious method for selecting a good performing convertible bond, convertible preferred stock or warrant is to choose a good common stock. Getting the common stock right will make up for numerous errors in convertible security valuation. Conversely, the most careful convertible analysis will only partially mitigate a really bad stock choice. Assuming that you have solved the problem of equity issue selection, a sound convertible valuation technique will further enhance investment performance.

Until very recently, the most common convertible valuation technique revolved around the concept of *payback* or *breakeven time* (these terms are used interchangeably). The object of this analysis is to determine how long the higher income on the convertible must persist to make the investor "whole" relative to the dividend income from an equivalent dollar amount of the underlying common stock.

For example, assume XYZ Company stock is currently selling at $25 per share and pays a $1 dividend annually (i.e., 4%). Further assume XYZ Company has a convertible security outstanding with an 8% coupon due in 30 years. Each $1,000 face value of XYZ convertible may be exchanged for 32 shares of XYZ common stock. This equates to a conversion price of $31.25 per share ($1,000/32) or a "conversion premium" 25% above today's actual $25 stock price.

Some investors attempt to calculate a simplified breakeven by dividing the conversion premium by the difference in the current yields. In the case of XYZ, this method would produce a breakeven of 6.25 years (.25/ (0.08 - .04) = 6.25). As will be explained below, this answer is incorrect. Although still inaccurate, a better approximation of the true breakeven is produced by substituting (1 - equity value/market price) in the numerator of the equation. For XYZ, this approach yields (1 - 800/1000)/(.08 - 0.04) or a breakeven of 5 years which is much closer to the truth.[2]

The following example demonstrates the correct calculation of breakeven. Consider an equity investor who owns 40 shares of XYZ stock trading at $25 (i.e., a $1,000 investment). This investor chooses to sell the common and use the $1,000 proceeds to purchase the convertible at par. However, by doing so the investor has decreased his common stock exposure from 40 shares to 32 shares. To maintain a 40 share exposure, $1,250 par value of the convertible must be purchased (i.e. ($1,000/$31.25) x 1.25 = 40). Assuming the investor borrows the additional $250 at 8% and applies the entire incremental cash flow of $60 (i.e. $1,250 x .08 - 40 x

---

[2]This relatively simple method yields the same result as the somewhat more cumbersome "dollar" method, as follows:

$$\frac{(\text{bond price} - \text{equity value})}{(\text{bond income} - \text{income from equal amount invested in stock})}$$

or in the case of XYZ:

$$\frac{(\$1000 - (32 \times \$25))}{(\$80 - \$1000/\$25 \times \$1))} = \frac{(\$1000 - \$800)}{(\$80 - \$40)} = 5.0 \text{ Years}$$

However obtained, this result is superior to the previous answer, 6.25 years, or to the answer obtained using another popular but much inferior method, which assumes conversion of the bond into common stock, as follows:

$$\frac{\text{Bond Price} - \text{Equity Value}}{\text{Bond Income} - \text{Income obtained if bond is converted into stock}}$$

or, in the case of XYZ:

$$\frac{(\$1000 - \$800}{(\$80 - \$1000 / \$31.25 \times \$1)} = \frac{\$200}{(\$80 - \$32)} = 4.2 \text{ years}$$

$1) to the repayment of the debt, the loan would be repaid in 5.26 years.[3] The following table demonstrates how this repayment would take place:

| End of Year (a) | Beginning Loan Balance (b) | Incremental Cash Flow[4] (c) | Interest @ 8% (d) | Debt Reduction (e)=(c)−(d) | Ending Loan Balance (f) |
|---|---|---|---|---|---|
| 1 | $250.00 | $60.00 | $20.00 | $40.00 | $210.00 |
| 2 | 210.00 | 60.00 | 16.80 | 43.20 | 166.80 |
| 3 | 166.00 | 60.00 | 13.34 | 46.66 | 120.14 |
| 4 | 120.14 | 60.00 | 9.61 | 50.39 | 69.75 |
| 5 | 69.75 | 60.00 | 5.58 | 54.42 | 15.33 |
| 6* | 15.33 | 15.65 | .32 | 15.33 | 0 |

* Interest and incremental cash flow figures shown in year 6 are 26/100 of a whole year.

After 5.26 years, the "free and clear" ownership of $1,250 par value XYZ convertible is, at a minimum, equal in value to the prior position of 40 shares of the common stock and thereby insures our investor a "breakeven" position. Indeed, if the stock has fallen in value over the period, the convertible may be trading at a price substantially in excess of its equity value. Of course, if the borrowing rate is above or below the coupon rate the breakeven would change, as it would if we introduced a non-static dividend assumption.

Breakeven calculations are frequently used by equity portfolio managers to compare a convertible against the underlying common stock. In this context, short paybacks (i.e. less than 3 years) are considered good, while long paybacks are undesirable. Paybacks are frequently compared against the call protection a convertible offers. A convertible with a properly calculated 3 year payback and 4 years of absolute call protection offers equity investors a nearly riskless trading opportunity versus the underlying common stock. In contrast, paybacks far in excess of the convertible's call protection period are more difficult to defend under this methodology.

Breakeven is only one method to evaluate convertibles. What merit this approach does have is limited mainly to the comparison of a convertible to its underlying common stock. The use of breakeven to compare different convertibles is suspect at best. For that task, more complicated techniques are needed that incorporate additional factors.

---

[3]The formula which solves this equation for the number of years, N, is as follows: $N = (\ln(R) - \ln(R-i))/\ln(1+i)$, where i is the annual interest rate expressed as decimal, R is the ratio of the annual repayment to the original loan balance, and ln is the natural logarithm.

[4]In this simplified example all cash flows from coupon payments and dividends are assumed to occur at annual intervals.

## VIII. MORE COMPLICATED VALUATION TECHNIQUES

Convertible bonds and convertible preferred stocks present similar valuation problems. While different in nature and frequency, both promise the investor a future
stream of cash payments. Both also carry a provision allowing the investor to
exchange a fixed claim against earnings for a variable (equity) claim on earnings and
the residual value of the firm. Although the convertible bond holder usually enjoys a
priority claim against the firm in the event of default, a similar valuation technique is
applicable to both.

To facilitate the valuation process, it is convenient to view a convertible security
as consisting of a fixed payment stream attached to a long-term warrant on the equity
of the firm. The convertible preferred's cash flow is in the form of a known dividend
rate, while the convertible bond offers the investor periodic coupon payments. The
income aspect of the valuation process is fairly straight forward. In the case of the
bond, a standard valuation given by the following formula can be used:[5]

$$IV = (.5C/Y) + ((1/(1+Y)t) \times (100-(.5C/Y)))$$

where     IV    = Investment value or market value (price) of the bond
           C     = Coupon rate in dollars per 100 face amount
           Y     = Yield to maturity as a % per semi-annual[6] period
           T     = Number of semi-annual periods to maturity

For the XYZ bond, if we assume that a 10% annual (5% or .05 semi-annual) yield
would be required for straight debt, the formula would give:

$$(8x.5)/.05) + (1/(1 + .05)60 \times (100-(8x.5)/.05)))$$
$$= (4/.05) + (.053533 \times 20)$$
$$= 80 + 1.07 = \$81.07$$

In the case of a convertible preferred, the formula can be modified to derive a
similar valuation, using the dividend stream and specific or assumed redemption
provisions.

The next phase of valuation deals with the convertible's equity conversion feature. This feature is very similar in nature to a long-term warrant with special
redemption features. Accordingly, a logical place to begin the valuation process is
with the application of a typical warrant model. Assuming that the warrant is non-
callable prior to expiration and may be exercised at any time, a Black-Scholes option

---

[5]This formula does not account for sinking funds and will, therefore, somewhat understate values for
sinking fund bonds.

[6]Quarterly in the case of convertible preferred stock.

valuation framework would suffice.[7] Although this approach would entail a number of unrealistically simple assumptions regarding dividend policy and the stock's volatility, it is adequate for quick approximations of the convertible's non-callable warrant value.

Unfortunately, few if any convertibles exist with absolute call protection for the life of the issue.[8] The inherent callability of most convertibles precludes the use of a Black-Scholes valuation framework. Fortunately there are alternative "option" valuation approaches which can cope with the callability issue.

The most straight forward of the available techniques is a Cox-Ross-Rubinstein option valuation model[9] (also known as a binominal model). This approach generates a tree of future stock prices to determine the warrant value and allows us to deal explicitly with early redemption provisions.

It is beyond the scope of this article to examine in detail the application of a binominal option valuation framework to convertible securities. It can be emphasized, however, that investors must recognize the general tenets of option/warrant valuation when comparing different convertible issues. The factors to be considered in determining value are well known and include:

- The strike price of the option (i.e. conversion price)
- The current stock price
- Variance in the stock's return (volatility)
- The risk free interest rate
- The time to expiration
- The dividend rate of the stock

How these factors come together to produce an option or warrant value is often counter-intuitive. However, some generalities of option valuation are equally applicable to convertibles. All other things equal:

1. volatility in the underlying stock increases an option value
2. call options are worth more when interest rates move higher
3. longer maturity options are worth more than shorter options
4. options on "no dividend" stocks are worth more than options on high dividend stocks

These generalizations can be transferred to the convertible market in the following fashion:

---

[7]Unlike call options models, such as Black-Scholes, warrant valuation models usually adjust for their potential dilutive effects.

[8]In fact if such a warrant existed its value would quickly approach that of the underlying equity itself!

[9]J. Cox, S. Ross, and M. Rubinstein, "Option Pricing: A Simplified Approach," *Journal of Financial Economics*, September 1979, pp. 229-63.

1. The more volatile the underlying stock, the greater the warrant or option value will be. Reconsider the payback form of analysis. Assuming you are indifferent between two stocks with similar convertibles outstanding, ask yourself "would I rather own a 2 year payback on a .85 beta stock or a 3 year payback on a 1.5 beta stock?" Volatility has a direct and large impact on warrant value and cannot be overlooked.

2. The value of holding your equity exposure in warrant form and keeping the bulk of your funds invested (e.g. Treasury bills) increases as rates rise and decrease as rates fall. This has a direct influence on option and warrant valuation.

3. Convertibles with greater call protection (i.e. longer options) are worth more than equivalent securities with less call protection. Time value is a powerful component of an option's value.

4. The greater the disparity between the dividend rate on the underlying common stock and the convertible, the greater the warrant value will be.

Serious investors must appreciate how these and other basic components of option valuation influence a convertible security's price behavior. One need not have a complex model to recognize relative value if these general principles are understood.

## IX. CONVERTIBLE STRATEGIES

Earlier, we described some of the different types of investors using convertible securities. The significance of individual valuation parameters will be heavily influenced by the perspective of the investor. If one is driven by a minimum income requirement, for example, the coupon or dividend may be quite important. If one is attempting to acquire defensive characteristics in an equity portfolio, the conversion premium may be of primary importance. A junk bond manager may be concerned primarily with credit analysis and how much he is paying for the equity "kicker." Convertible specialists, hedge funds, and arbitrageurs would each similarly bring their own unique perspective to the valuation process.

What are some of the strategies these different investors might consider?

One strategy is simply to view the convertible strictly as an extension of the equity selection process. In other words, first determine which common stocks are attractive and then, and only then, look at the availability of convertibles. The convertible security's primary appeal could result from a favorable disposition to the common stock, coupled with concern about the general market outlook. This strategy is essentially one of hedging against an adverse market environment. In such a case, the investor might be willing to pay slightly more than the theoretically correct value for the convertible.

In another case, the holder of a common stock may find that a convertible security is available on sufficiently attractive terms that he would prefer it to the common stock regardless of his market outlook. If the analysis and valuation indicates that the convertible would share in most of the stock's appreciation, while still offering significant downside protection, it might make sense to swap from the common stock into the convertible. Similarly, if the income gained by using the convertible would fully absorb the premium before the bond becomes callable, a swap would make sense.

These are equity oriented strategies. Such investors will pay particular attention to valuation parameters such as payback period, conversion premium, and call protection. They may place relatively less value on coupon and investment value.

Fixed income oriented investors, on the other hand, might place heavy emphasis on investment value and much less on the conversion premium. Here, the strategy would be to achieve the objectives of the fixed income portfolio (e.g. immunization), while still obtaining *some* exposure to the common stock, albeit distant, through the convertible. A 5-year or longer payback period may be much less important than a comparison of the amount being paid in excess of investment value to the theoretical warrant value.

Convertible specialists and arbitrageurs will be looking for disparities in value between the convertible and the underlying common stock, wherever they may occur. Although it is generally unwise to purchase a convertible security if the common stock is expected to decline in price, it nevertheless might be desirable to purchase a convertible security when the stock price outlook is indifferent. This is provided that the valuation analysis indicates that the convertible is underpriced relative to the common. A hedge fund or broker/dealer can, of course, maintain a long position in an undervalued convertible and a weighted short position in an offsetting amount of common stock, so as to exploit such undervaluations with relative indifference to the direction of stock price changes. Conversely, a short position can be maintained in an overvalued convertible against a properly weighted long position in the common stock.

After establishing objectives and guidelines for the use of convertible securities, perhaps the most important factor for any individual investor to bear in mind is that *other* convertible investors may have very different strategies and objectives. This may facilitate execution of his own strategies. What is perceived by one participant as a gross overvaluation of a security may be perceived by another participant with different objectives as a great opportunity. To a significant extent, then, a convertible security's attractiveness is in the eye of the beholder.

This is not to say that a theoretical valuation scheme aimed at estimating the "intrinsic value" of a convertible security is not worthwhile. Rather, the point is that when substantial deviations relative to such a theoretical value seem to appear, it may simply mean that another point of view is prevalent among investors.

## X. PRACTICAL PROBLEMS AND SPECIAL FEATURES

### Trading

Most convertible bonds are traded away from the popular exchanges in what is essentially a negotiated or over-the-counter market. Although many of the larger convertible preferred stocks and convertible bonds are listed on one of the major exchanges, the latest reported trade data will not always accurately reflect the true market conditions. This lack of visibility of the "real" market puts a premium on the ability of a good trader to get programs effectively executed.

Many of the smaller issues trade infrequently and have very few active market makers. For larger and more active issues, however, an informal network of "street brokers" maintains a reasonable level of market efficiency. To assure effective executions, a trader must maintain active surveillance on a daily basis of all issues in which trading activity is likely. *It is only through active participation in the marketplace that true market levels can be ascertained.*

### Anticipating Calls and Redemptions

In the 1970's and early 1980's, a period of high and rising long-term interest rates, very few convertible issues were called as a result of refinancing. It was generally a safe bet that a call was intended to force the holder to convert into common stock. In more recent years, refinancing calls have become more common and it is, therefore, necessary to anticipate both types of calls.

When the call is intended to "force" conversion into common stock, the issuer will normally not risk having the common stock decline sufficiently during the 20-30 day call period to make conversion unattractive. In other words, the price level of the common stock will have to be sufficiently above the conversion price of the convertible to provide a "cushion" against a market decline. The size of this cushion will depend on the volatility of the stock, market conditions, the length of time which must be allowed between the announcement and the redemption, and any possible adverse reaction to the dilution which the conversion might cause. There is no simple "rule of thumb" for estimating the appropriate amount of cushion, but experience has shown that companies rarely force conversion unless the convertible price is at least 15% above the call price. In the case of more volatile issues, a 20-25% cushion may be necessary.

After a convertible security becomes callable, the most conservative assumption is that a forced conversion will take place whenever the bond price rises more than 15% above the call price. This enables the convertible holder to estimate the probable price action of the convertible relative to the common stock. (Since the conversion premium will normally disappear when the issue is called, the holder should assume that a convertible lacking call protection will trade at conversion parity when it is 15% to 20% above the call price. The corresponding stock price level is thus also determined.)

A call which is not intended to force conversion, i.e., call intended to redeem the issue, will depend, in large part, on the issuer's ability to obtain capital on more favorable terms. The coupon and premium level of the existing convertible should be compared to the probable terms at which the issuer could bring a new convertible offering to market or some other measure of the issuer's marginal cost of capital. The issuer's internal cash flow projections and likely need to obtain more capital in the future might also be important. The holder of the convertible security, to take the most conservative approach, should estimate the yield-to-call for all issues trading significantly above the call price.

### Deciding Whether to Redeem or Convert

When a convertible security is called for redemption, the price of the issue will normally move very quickly to either the call price or the equity conversion value, whichever is larger. Generally speaking, the correct action will be quite obvious. Naturally, a convertible whose equity conversion value is significantly above the redemption price should not be redeemed. It should be converted into common stock prior to the redemption date. On the other hand, when the equity conversion value is well below the redemption price, it is clearly best to redeem. However, if the equity conversion value is not too far below the redemption price, it is often wise to wait as long as possible before acting on the call notice.

As an example of the value of waiting to redeem, Allied-Signal called their $6.74 convertible preferred for redemption in August of 1986 at a redemption price of $57.00. When the call was officially announced in early July, the equity conversion value was below the $57.00 redemption price. By month end a company announcement concerning a possible stock buy-back program briefly caused the common stock to rally above the conversion price. This gave the convertible preferred holder an opportunity to sell shares at more than a dollar above the redemption price. The stock subsequently declined again and the preferred issue was redeemed at $57.00.

### Indenture Terms

Convertible securities can be offered with quite a wide variety of terms and special features. This makes a careful reading of the offering prospectus quite important. There are no hard and fast rules for what to look for, but careful attention should be paid to the protection provided to the convertible holder against dilution of the common stock (splits, stock dividends, acquisitions, etc.) or in the event that the company is taken over or undergoes a massive change in its capital structure. The call provisions should also be carefully reviewed, since there is sometimes language permitting the issuer to escape payment of the final coupon when calling an issue to force conversion.

### Put and Call Provisions - Two Examples

Most convertible securities become callable (by the issuer) 2 or 3 years after the date of issue. In addition, most have a provision permitting earlier call, if the price of the common stock rises above a specified level (usually 40% or 50% over the conversion price). In some cases, most notable Eurodollar issues and zero coupon convertibles, an issue will contain put provisions, which enables the holder to "put" the security back to the issuer for redemption at a specified price (often above the original issue or "par" price). As noted earlier, these features can complicate the valuation process. As an aid to understanding such effects, the following two examples are provided.

In February 1986, with common stock at $30½, Cal Fed issued a 6.5% Eurodollar convertible bond due February 20, 2001 with a conversion price of 35¼. The bond can not be called before February 20, 1993, unless the common trades above $45.83. There is a put provision allowing the bond to be put back to the company in February of 1993 at a price of $123.

By the fall of 1986, the bond had "seasoned" and was being traded in the U.S. at a price of $112, with common stock trading at $31½. This represented a conversion premium of about 25% and a breakeven time of 5.2 years. A straight forward estimate of bond investment value and warrant value suggested that the warrant feature in this issue might be worth as much as $45-$46 (per $100 par value) and that the straight bond or investment value, ignoring the put feature, would be about $67-$68. Thus, the issue might have appeared to be "fairly priced" by a model not able to cope with put features.

However, when the put feature is taken into account, the $67-$68 investment value (based on a 6½% coupon and 15 years to maturity) is increased, to about $90, reflecting the shorter maturity and the premium ($123) put price. On this basis, the bond would have appeared to be substantially undervalued.

As evidence of the importance of strong call protection, the Student Loan Marketing (Sallie Mae) 7 3/4% convertible bond due November 15, 2009 is instructive. This bond was issued in November of 1984 and provided for five years of absolute non-callability. Nearly two years later, despite a doubling in the common stock price, this bond continued to sell at a significant conversion premium and had provided the holder with over 80% of the return he would have received from holding the common stock. Had this bond been issued with only two years of call protection and a provisional call feature 40% above the conversion price, a doubling of the stock price almost surely would have caused the bond to trade at (or even below) conversion parity. This would have produced only about 66% participation in the common stock return for holders of the convertible issue.

## *Eurodollar Convertible Bonds*

A growing number of U.S. corporations have chosen to issue dollar-denominated convertible bonds in Europe which are backed by the full faith and credit of a U.S. parent. A Eurodollar convertible financing may reflect the issuer's perception of more favorable market conditions, a desire to diversify sources of capital, or merely the need to raise the funds quickly, since Eurodollar offerings do not require SEC registration.

Eurodollar issues cannot be sold to U.S. investors until they have "seasoned," a process which normally takes four to five months. Eurodollar convertibles typically pay coupons only annually and frequently have put provisions (sometimes at prices above par). On the other hand, they usually provide somewhat less attractive call provisions, such as only two years of call protection with a 130% provisional feature (as opposed to three years and 140% or 150% which is more typical in the U.S.). After the seasoning period, Eurodollar convertibles often trade actively in the U.S. market.

## XI. SUMMARY

Convertible securities represent a unique combination of equity and fixed income attributes which offer the investor a favorable, non-linear distribution of expected returns. In a period of sharply rising equity values, the convertible will automatically assume the behavior of the underlying common stock. When the stock price declines, the convertible will increasingly behave like a straight debt instrument. The benefit of this favorable bending in the return distribution is most readily captured when the convertible is in the middle or "hybrid" range between these two extremes.

The primary advantages of convertible securities arise from this ability to provide participation in the upward movement of the underlying common stock, while providing a limit to the downside as a result of the "floor" provided by the straight bond value. In addition, convertibles generally provide more income than the common stock and may permit investors who are precluded from owning non-dividend paying common stock to participate in the equity of smaller, growth oriented companies.

Needless to say, convertible securities also have certain disadvantages. In addition to providing less coupon income than a comparable straight debt issue, the convertible is also (normally) subordinated to other debt of the issuer. The convertible security will rise less rapidly than the underlying common stock and will, therefore, provide a lesser total return in a rising market.

Convertible securities typically provide less restrictive covenants (limitations on dividend payments, etc.), than straight debt issues. While this is favorable from the point of view of the issuer, it is a modest disadvantage to the purchaser. Finally, convertible securities tend to be less efficiently traded than either common stocks or straight bonds, placing a premium on the ability of a convertible manager to effectively execute trades.

Valuation methods tend to revolve around the concept of payback or breakeven time. The most accurate way to quickly estimate breakeven was presented in the article. However, the breakeven concept, while useful for certain equity-oriented investors, is less useful (and less rigorous) than a warrant valuation model (such as the Cox-Ross-Rubinstein model adjusted to allow for call features) together with a standard bond valuation formula.

Strategies for the use of convertible securities will tend to reflect the perspective of the investor using them. Such investors will range from risk averse equity managers to bond managers seeking an equity kicker. To some extent, the attraction of a convertible security is in the eye of the beholder.

The combination of a well focused strategic direction and a good set of valuation tools can enable the convertible investor to significantly enhance investment performance. Although effective convertible evaluation cannot make up for poor common stock selection, the naturally defensive nature of the true hybrid convertible security can provide a very favorable risk/reward trade-off to the investor.

## APPENDIX: CONVERTIBLE GLOSSARY

*Bond Equivalent*—(See "Fixed Income Equivalent").

*Bond Value*—(See "Investment Value").

*Breakeven Time*—The time required for the added income from the convertible to offset the conversion premium. This is also referred to as the *payback period.*

*Call Provisions*—Indenture provisions describing the date, price and other circumstances under which the issuer may redeem a convertible.

*Conditional Call*—(See provisional call).

*Conversion Premium*—The poriton of the market value of the convertible in excess of its value if immediately converted into common stock. Typically expressed as a percentage relative to the common stock value.

*Conversion Price (or Exercise Price)*—The price at which common stock can be purchased through exercise of the convertible instrument.

*Conversion Ratio*—The number of shares of common stock into which a convertible security can be exchanged.

*Equity Conversion Value*—The value of the convertible security if converted into common stock at the current common stock price level.

*Equity Equivalent*—A convertible whose price behavior is dominated by changes in the common stock price, with relatively little sensitivity to changes in interest rate levels.

*Fixed Income Equivalent*—A convertible whose price behavior is dominated by changes in interest rates, with relatively little sensitivity to changes in the common stock price.

*Floor Value*—(See "Investment Value").

*Forced Conversion*—When an issuer attempts to redeem a convertible for cash, while conversion parity exceeds the redemption price the investor is "forced" to convert into common stock to realize the higher conversion parity value.

*Hard Call*—A convertible which does not have any provisional call feature is said to have "hard call" protection.

*Initial Premium*—The conversion premium at the time of offering of a new convertible issue.

*Investment Value*—The price at which a debenture would have to sell as a straight debt instrument. This is also referred to as the bond value or "floor" value.

*Investment Value Premium*—The difference between a convertible's market price and its investment value, expressed as a percentage of investment value.

*Parity or Conversion Parity*—The value of the convertible security if converted into common stock at current prices. Also referred to as "conversion value" or "equity conversion value".

*Payback*—(See "Breakeven Time").

*Point Premium*—The conversion premium expressed as the dollar price of the convertible less the dollar value of the equity conversion.

*Provisional Call*—Indenture provision which permits the company to call a convertible security prior to the stated call date if the common stock price rises above a preset level. Typically expressed as a percentage (such as 140% or 150%) of the specified conversion price of the convertible.

*Unit Offering*—A combination of notes and warrants which subsequently may be traded separately but initially are issued and traded as a unit. Sometimes also referred to as a "synthetic" convertible.

*Yield Advantage*—The difference between the current yield of the convertible and the current yield of the common stock.

*Yield to Call*—Rate of return provided from the current price level, assuming the issue is called at the first available put date.

*Yield to Put*—Same as above to the first available put date.

# Extendable Reset Bonds: A New Addition to the High Yield Landscape

LAURIE S. GOODMAN, PH.D.
VICE PRESIDENT
FINANCIAL STRATEGIES GROUP
GOLDMAN, SACHS & CO.

ALAN H. COHEN
ASSOCIATE
HIGH YIELD GROUP
GOLDMAN, SACHS & CO.

## I. INTRODUCTION

In 12 months, since October 1987, 21 high yield bond issues have come to market with provisions for resetting the coupon rate and extending the term. Under such provisions, the issuer must reset the coupon on specified dates so that the bond will trade at a predetermined price. The coupon rate will generally be the average of rates suggested by two investment banks.

While the reset provisions of recent bond issues all share certain similarities, they may differ from issue to issue in several dimensions: the number of resets, the reset formula, the call structure of the bonds, the presence of caps and floors on the resets, and the availability of investor puts. We will discuss the basic structure and its variations in Section II.

Issuers of extendable reset bonds appear to be motivated by the desire to pay short-term rates while still being assured of the long-term availability of funds. Thus, they apparently believe that the upward sloping yield curve reflects a liquidity premium rather than bearish market expectations about future interest rates.

On the other hand, bearish bond market sentiment has spurred a great deal of investor interest in these securities. The extendable reset bond is the first high yield instrument that provides flexibility for investors who are expecting Treasury rates or high yield credit spreads to rise. In a rising rate environment, high yield investors have historically faced a dilemma: either hold a relatively short-term, low yielding instrument until rates rise, or buy a longer-term bond and hope that as high yield rates rise generally, the credit spread will improve on the particular bond purchased.[1] Extendable reset instruments eliminate this dilemma by allowing the coupon to move up as market conditions warrant. In Sections III and IV, we discuss the advantages and disadvantages of these securities for issuers and investors.

Extendable reset issues are too new to allow for empirical studies. Thus, important questions remain as to whether the reset will work as they theoretically should. The first of the reset structures was issued by GACC on September 29, 1987, with a two-year reset. The only bond to reset thus far is the Western Union bond issued on December 16, 1988, with resets on June 15, 1988 and June 15, 1989. This bond reset on June 15, 1988, with its original coupon. It is slightly unusual, in that it has a floor and is non-callable. The next bond scheduled to reset is the 12.5% Knoll International issue on November 6, 1988. Investors may choose to put this bond after the reset is announced.

## II. EXTENDABLE RESET PROVISIONS

Among the 20 extendable reset bonds issued to date and the one issue pending, there are structural differences in several dimensions:

1. The reset structure of the bonds (the number of resets and the reset formula)
2. The call structure of the bonds
3. Provisions for caps on the reset bonds
4. Provisions for floors on the reset bonds
5. Put features
6. Deferred coupon features

---

[1]Theoretically, high yield investors could buy long-term high yield bonds and short Treasury bond futures against these instruments. In practice, however, high yield investors do not view Treasury futures as a viable hedging vehicle. Many high yield investors, particularly high yield funds, do not short futures because they are restricted by prospectus requirements. Other high yield investors feel that Treasury futures provide a relatively poor hedge for high yield bonds, as futures hedge only the base component and not the very substantial variations in spreads.

In the discussion that follows, we will examine these differences and their impact on the valuation of these securities.

### The Reset Structure

As Exhibit 1 indicates, there are many reset structures, ranging from annual resets (El Paso Products, CJI, and PA Holdings) to one reset over the life (SPI holdings, SCI Television, Knoll International 14.25, Brooke Partners, SSC Holdings 13 and 12.5, Viacom and Salant Corp.). Most of the bonds have a coupon reset formula requiring the issuer to reset the coupon so that the bond will have a market price of $101. The determination of the coupon is generally left up to the discretion of two investment banks.

Under the assumption that the reset is "fair"—i.e., that the reset fixes the coupon so that the security trades at the predetermined price—we can view a bond with a reset structure as having a maturity equal to the time until the next reset date. This is the case because if the firm's cost of funds declines, the coupon on the bond will also decline. If the firm's cost of funds rises, the coupon on the bond will rise to keep the bond priced as specified.

Thus, for pricing purposes, we can view a bond with a one-year reset as a one-year bond, and we can view a bond with a three-year bond.

### The Call Structure

Exhibit 2 shows the structural differences among the bonds other than the reset structure. As you can see, most of the extendable reset bonds give the issuer the option of calling the bond rather than extending the maturity. The bond is generally callable at the reset price on the reset date.

In the absence of floors, the call should not affect the value of the bonds. That is, investors should be indifferent between having a bond called at 101 and having the coupon reset to price the bond at 101. In the latter case, the investor can simply sell the bond at 101.

The call is important to the issuer for two reasons. First, it provides issuer protection, ensuring some recourse if the coupon is set too high. Second, it allows the firm greater flexibility in its managing its outstanding debt.[2] This is especially critical for highly leverage entities.[3]

---

[2]Conceptually, of course, firms can simply buy back their debt in the market. However, it is difficult to locate and buy back 100% of the debt. Moreover, without call provisions, the debt would be repurchased at a premium if credit quality has improved.

[3]Many of the extendable reset structures are the result of leveraged buyout (LBO) situations. In these situations, the firm often intends to sell off assets and reduce debt. The timing of the asset sales will, of course, depend on market conditions. Thus, flexibility is important to the issuers.

**EXHIBIT 1**
**EXTENDABLE RESET BONDS ISSUED TO DATE: RESET STRUCTURES**

| Issue Date | Issuer | Initial Coupon (%) | Issue Size (million) | Rank | Final Maturity | Years Until First Reset | Resets | Formula |
|---|---|---|---|---|---|---|---|---|
| 29-Sep-87 | GACC | 13 | $125 | Senior subordinated | 01-Jan-97 | 2 years | 2, 3, and 5 years | Mkt. value of $101 determined by Drexel |
| 29-Sep-87 | Seminole Kraft | 11.75 | $70 | Senior ext. notes | 01-Oct-99 | 3 years | Reset 9/30/90 then every 1, 2, or 3 years | Rate established by company |
| 01-Oct-87 | SPI Holdings | 14.875 | $125 | Senior sub. ext. reset notes | 01-Oct-99 | 4 to 5 yrs. ext. opt. | One reset, 10/1/91 to 9/1/92 | Mkt. value of $102 determined by two I-banks as reset advs. |
| 21-Oct-87 | SCI Television | 15.5 | $200 | Senior extend. reset notes | 15-Oct-95 | 3 years | One reset/ext. on 10/15/90 | Mkt. value of $102 determined by Drexel & one I-bank |
| 06-Nov-87 | Knoll International | 12.5 | $150 | Senior extendable | 15-Nov-94 | 1 year | 1 year, then every 1, 2, or 3 years until maturity | None |
| 06-Nov-87 | Knoll International | 14.25 | $100 | Senior subord. ext. | 15-Nov-94 | 3 years | One reset on 11/15/90 | None |
| 16-Dec-88 | Western Union | 16.5 | $500 | Senior secured reset notes | 15-Dec-92 | 6 months | Two resets 6/15/88 and 6/15/89 | Mkt. value of $101 determined by Drexel & one I-bank |
| 09-Feb-88 | Farley Inc. | 14.625 | $250 | Senior sub. ext. reset notes | 15-Feb-95 | 3 years | 2 reset dates/ extensions on 1/21/91, 1/21/93 | Mkt. value of $102 determined by Drexel & one I-bank |

| Issue Date | Issuer | Initial Coupon (%) | Issue Size (million) | Rank | Final Maturity | Years Until First Reset | Resets | Formula |
|---|---|---|---|---|---|---|---|---|
| 31-Mar-88 | Brooke Partners | 13.5 | $160 | Senior subordinated reset notes | 01-Apr-97 | 1 year or 90 days after $300mm acquis. | One reset on 4/1/89 | Mkt. value of $101 determined by Drexel & one I-bank |
| 12-Apr-88 | R-C Holdings | 12.875 | $160 | Senior extendable notes | 15-Apr-00 | 4 years, 4/15/92 | 4 years then every 1, 2, or 3 years until maturity | Spread off applic. Treas. rate |
| 13-Apr-88 | El Paso Products | 12.75 | $100 | Senior sub. extend. reset notes | 15-Apr-95 | 1 year | Every year | Mkt. value of $101 determined by Drexel & one I-bank |
| 29-Apr-88 | CJI | 13.5 | $350 | Senior extendable reset notes | 01-May-93 | 1 year | Every year | Mkt. value of $101 determined by Drexel & one I-bank |
| 30-Jun-88 | Community Newspapers | 13 | $125 | Senior subordinated reset notes | 01-Jul-97 | 2 yrs. and 5 yrs. | 2 yrs., 3 yrs. | Mkt. value of $101 determined by Drexel & one I-bank |
| 07-Jul-88 | Service Control | 14 | $100 | Senior subordinated | 15-Jul-98 | 1 year | 1 yr., 2 yrs., and 3 yrs. | Mkt. value of $101 determined by Drexel & one I-bank |
| 21-Jul-88 | SSC Holdings Ser. I | 13 | $200 | Senior sub. extend. reset notes | 15-Jul-98 | 2 years | One reset/ext. on 7/15/90 | Bid value of $101 determined by Drexel & one I-bank |
| 21-Jul-88 | SSC Holdings Ser. II | 12.5 | $125 | Senior sub. extend. reset notes | 15-Jul-98 | 3 years | One reset/ext. 7/15/91 by Drexel & one I-bank | Bid value of $101 determined |

**EXHIBIT 1 (CONTINUED)**
**EXTENDABLE RESET BONDS ISSUED TO DATE: RESET STRUCTURES**

| Issue Date | Issuer | Initial Coupon (%) | Issue Size (million) | Rank | Final Maturity | Years Until First Reset | Resets | Formula |
|---|---|---|---|---|---|---|---|---|
| 22-Jul-88 | Viacom | 11.5 | $200 | Senior sub. extend. reset notes | 15-Jul-98 | 3 years | 3 years, 1 reset | Mkt. value of $100 determined by Drexel & Bear, Stearns |
| 04-Aug-88 | Salant Corp | 13.375 | $75 | Senior subordinated reset notes | 15-Aug-95 | 1 year | One reset on 8-15-89 | Mkt. value of $101 determined by Drexel & one I-bank |
| 23-Aug-88 | PA Holdings | 12.5 | $235 | Senior sub. reset notes | 1998 | 1 year | Every year/ext. opt. | Mkt. value of $101 determined by F.B.C. & one I-bank |
| 21-Sep-88 | FF Acquisition | 14 | $40 | Senior sub. reset notes | 1998 | 2½ years | 2½ years, 1 reset | Mkt. val $102 set by DBL +1 other, or by a third bank |
| RED | Griffin Resorts Notes | ——— | $125 | Senior secured reset | 01-Aug-95 | 2 years | 2 years then 1, 2, or 5 years | Mkt. value of $101 determined by two I-banks |

**EXHIBIT 2**
**EXTENDABLE RESET BONDS ISSUED TO DATE: OTHER STRUCTURAL FEATURES**

| Issue Date | Issuer | Calls | Cap (%) | Floor (%) | Other | Concurrent Issues |
|---|---|---|---|---|---|---|
| 29-Sep-87 | GACC | Callable at $102, $101, and $101, for each reset date resp. | None | 13 | | None |
| 29-Sep-87 | Seminole Kraft | Callable at each reset date at par | None | None | Putable at each reset | None |
| 01-Oct-87 | SPI Holdings | Callable on 10/1/90 at 105, 10/1/98 at par | None | None | | $75mm. 14.75% sub. deb. due 10/1/02 callable 10/1/92 at 109.077, 10/100 at par |
| 21-Oct-87 | SCI Television | Callable at 102 if ext. not exercised; future call prices to be established | None | 15.5 | | $100mm. 16.5% sr. sub. deb. due 10/15/97, callable 10/15/92 at 107.33, 10/15/96 at par; $100mm. 17.5% sub. deb. due 10/15/99, callable 10/15/90 at 112.73, 10/15/98 at par |
| 06-Nov-87 | Knoll International | Callable at each reset Date at par | None | None | Putable at each reset | |
| 06-Nov-87 | Knoll International | Callable on 11/15/90 at par | None | None | Putable on reset date | $100mm 16% sub. deb. due 11/15/97, callable 11/15/90 at 110.00, 11/15/95 at par |
| 16-Dec-88 | Western Union | Non-Callable | None | 16.5 | | None |

**EXHIBIT 2 (CONTINUED)**
**EXTENDABLE RESET BONDS ISSUED TO DATE: OTHER STRUCTURAL FEATURES**

| Issue Date | Issuer | Calls | Cap (%) | Floor (%) | Other | Concurrent Issues |
|---|---|---|---|---|---|---|
| 09-Feb-88 | Farley Inc. | Not callable if extensions not exercised, 105% of principal due | 17.625 | 14.625 | | $125mm. 16.626 jr. sub. deb. due 4/15/08, callable 4/15/04 at 116.63, 4/15/04 at par; 250,000 warrants commencing 9/1/88 expiring 9/15/88, at $500 each for jr. sub. deb.; $250 mm. 15.625% sub. notes due 2/15/98, callable 2/15/93 at 106.94, 2/15/97 at par; 250,000 warrants commencing 9/1/88 expiring 9/15/88, at $500 each for jr. sub. deb. |
| 31-Mar-88 | Brooke Partners | Callable on reset date at $102 if Adj. I-rate > Initial I-rate; or 4/1/91 at 108.44, 4/1/96 at par | None | 13.5 | | $140mm. 14.5% sub. deb. due 4/1/98, callable 4/1/91 at 109.67, 4/1/97 at par; $140 mm. 15.50% jr. sub. deb due 6/1/08, callable 6/1/88 at 115.50, 6/1/04 at par; 140,000 warrants commencing 4/15/89, expiring 3/31/89 |
| 12-Apr-88 | R-C Holdings | Callable from 4/15/91 to 4/14/92 at $105; callable at each reset date at par | None | None | | $90mm. 7.5% sr. sub. deb. from 4/15/88 to 4/14/91, then 13.75% until maturity, callable 4/15/91 at $109.167, 4/15/97 at par |
| 13-Apr-88 | El Paso Products | Future call prices to be established | 14.75 | 12.75 | | $75mm. 13.75% sr. sub. notes due 5/15/98, callable 5/15/91 at 106.875 |

**EXHIBIT 2 (CONTINUED)**
**EXTENDABLE RESET BONDS ISSUED TO DATE: OTHER STRUCTURAL FEATURES**

| Issue Date | Issuer | Calls | Cap (%) | Floor (%) | Other | Concurrent Issues |
|---|---|---|---|---|---|---|
| 29-Apr-88 | CJI | Each reset at $101 | 16.5 | 13.5 | | $100mm. 14.5% sr. notes due 11/1/95, callable 5/1/92 at 106.214, 5/1/94 at 102.071; $250mm. 15.5% sr. sub notes due 11/1/97, callable 5/1/93 at 106.889, 5/1/96 at 101.722 |
| 30-Jun-88 | Community Newspapers | Callable on each reset date at $102, $101, & $101, respectively; after last reset date, callable for 12 months, 7/1/93 at 104.88, 7/1/96 at par | None | 13 | | None |
| 07-Jul-88 | Service Control | Each reset at $101, then $104 on 7/15/91, declining to par 7/15/95 | 16.25 | 14 | | None |
| 21-Jul-88 | SSC Holdings Ser. I | Callable on ext. date at $101 | 15.5 | 13 | P.I.K for 5 years | |
| 21-Jul-88 | SSC Holdigns Ser. II | Callable on ext. date at $101 | 15 | 12.5 | | $175mm. 13.25% sub. deb due 7/15/00, callable 7/15/88 at 113.250, 7/15/98 at par |
| 22-Jul-88 | Viacom | Callable 7/15/91 at 101 at bank's option; if reset occurs, future call provisions will be determined | None | 11.5 | | $300mm. 11.8% sr. sub. due 7/15/98, callable 7/15/91 at 106.24, 7/15/95 at par |

**EXHIBIT 2 (CONTINUED)**
**EXTENDABLE RESET BONDS ISSUED TO DATE: OTHER STRUCTURAL FEATURES**

| Issue Date | Issuer | Calls | Cap (%) | Floor (%) | Other | Concurrent Issues |
|---|---|---|---|---|---|---|
| 04-Aug-88 | Salant Corp | Callable on reset date at $102 or 8/15/91 at 106.687, 8/15/94 at par, 4/1/96 at par | 15.875 | 13.375 | | None |
| 23-Aug-88 | PA Holdings | Callable on reset date at $101 | 15 | 12.5 I-rate | | $100mm. 13.25% P.I.K. deb. due 8/15/00, callable 8/15/88 at $107.5, 8/15/93 at par |
| 21-Sep-88 | FF Acquisition | Callable 2/15/90 to 4/15/90 at $103; future calls to be determined | 18 | 14 | | |
| RED | Griffin Resorts | Callable on each reset date at $101 | None | Initial I-rate | | $200mm. ___% 1st mortg. notes due 2/1/98, callable 8/1/91 at ___, 8/1/97 at par |

### Caps on the Reset Rate

We cannot view issues with caps on the reset rate as having a maturity equal to the next reset date. For example, assume that a bond has an initial coupon of 12.5% and a maximum coupon (cap) of 15.0% coupon. Consequently, the bond would sell at a price of less than 101.

We can value the cap explicitly. Assume that a bond has one reset date. If the reset is expected to be "fair," we can think of the bond plus the cap as a short bond maturing on the reset date, plus the value of the issuer's option to extend the bond. That is, if rates rise, the issuer has the right to put the bond to investors at the cap rate.

Consider a 10-year bond with an initial coupon of 12.5%. Exhibit 3 shows values of the reset cap for different numbers of years to reset and different cap rates. For example, a 10-year bond with three years to reset and a 15.0% cap has a value of $0.82.

**EXHIBIT 3**
**CAP VALUES ON A 10-YEAR BOND (12.5% BOND, 90% VOLATILITY, 1 RESET)**
**(DOLLARS PER $100 PAR)**

| Cap Rate (%) | Years to Reset | | | | | | |
|---|---|---|---|---|---|---|---|
|  | 1 | 2 | 3 | 4 | 5 | 6 | 7 |
| 13.5 | 1.10 | 1.79 | 2.17 | 2.37 | 2.42 | 2.41 | 2.40 |
| 14.0 | .58 | 1.19 | 1.59 | 1.87 | 2.00 | 2.05 | 2.10 |
| 14.5 | .28 | .76 | 1.15 | 1.45 | 1.61 | 1.71 | 1.83 |
| 15.0 | .11 | .48 | .82 | 1.10 | 1.29 | 1.44 | 1.59 |
| 15.5 | 04 | .29 | .57 | .83 | 1.03 | 1.19 | 1.37 |
| 16.0 | .02 | .17 | .38 | .63 | .81 | 1.01 | 1.18 |
| 16.5 | .01 | .09 | .26 | .45 | .64 | .82 | 1.03 |
| 17.0 | .00 | .05 | .17 | .34 | .50 | .68 | .88 |

Thus, the value of the issuer put should affect both the initial coupon and the subsequent pricing of the bond. At issuance, the value of the issuer put will affect the initial coupon. That is, the coupon will be set such that:

$$P_S - O_I = 100$$

where: $P_S$ is the price of a short-maturity bond (a bond that matures on the reset date).

$O_I$ is the value of the issuer put option.

The initial coupon must be higher than that of a short-maturity bond without a cap, so that an investor will be compensated for writing the option.

For secondary market trading, the value of the issuer put will affect the price. Thus, we have:

$$P_S - O_I = P_{RB}$$

where: $P_{RB}$ is the price of the reset bond with caps.

If the bond has multiple resets with a cap at each reset date, we can view this structure as a series of put options. For example, assume that a 10-year bond has two resets, one after three years and one after six years. Each is capped at 15.5%. We can view the first option as the issuer's right, three years from now, to put a 15.5% bond for three years. We can view the second option as the issuer's right, six years from now, to extend a 15.5% bond for four years, Exhibit 4 portrays this structure.

**EXHIBIT 4**
**EXTENDABLE RESET BONDS WITH TWO RESETS AND CAPS**

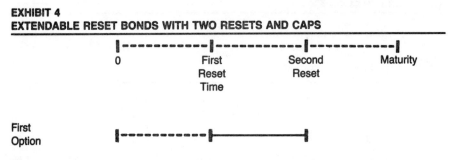

First
Option

Begins at Time 0, expires at first reset, issuer option (solid line) to extend bond from first reset to second reset.

Second
Option

Begins at Time 0, expires at second reset, issuer option (solid line) to extend bond from second reset to final maturity.

Note that the issuer can exercise the two options independently. That is, if the firm does not exercise the cap on the first reset (the coupon has simply been reset to a level less than the cap rate), it can still exercise the second cap. Similarly, if the firm exercises the cap on the first reset and rates subsequently decline, it need not exercise the second cap.

When two options are present, we can approximate the total value of the options by evaluating them separately and adding up the values.[4] For the hypothetical bond described earlier, our estimated value is $0.42 on the first option and $1.19 on the second option, for a total of $1.61. Note that this is larger than the option values in the one-reset case, where the reset after three years is worth $0.57 and the reset after six years is worth $1.19, as shown in Exhibit 3.

We can view three resets with a cap at each one as a series of three puts. In general, the number of resets will be equal to the number of puts.

### Comparing Structures

It is important for investors to realize the asymmetric nature of the payoff for a reset bond with caps. If rates go up and the cap is invoked, the coupon will not reset to price the bond at 101; the bond will trade lower. If rates go down, however, the bond will not appreciate because it will be called. Thus, the bond has limited upside (because of the call structure) and unlimited downside (because of the cap). Although a conventional callable bond also has an asymmetric payoff, there are two differences between the extendable bond with caps and an ordinary callable bond:

- The extendable bond provides less upside for investors if rates fall. In a conventional high yield bond, there is normally a premium call after five years and a par call after seven to ten years. The extendable bond is generally callable on the reset dates at par or 101.
- The extendable bond allows the coupon to reset up to the cap. The investor thus has some amount of protection if rates rise.

Exhibit 5 compares the price sensitivities (modified durations) of a callable bond, an extendable bond, and an extendable bond with a cap. All bonds have a 10-year final maturity. The conventional bond is callable after five years at $105 and after seven years at par. The extendable reset bond has a coupon reset in three years. As you can see, the extendable bond has a short duration—the duration of a three-year bond. That is, it is relatively insensitive to changes in yield. The capped resettable bond behaves like a short instrument at low interest rates. At high interest rates, it behaves like a conventional bond.

Note that at low interest rates, the callable bond will be more sensitive to changes in interest rates than a reset bond. That is, at very low interest rates the duration of

---

[4] In theory, the two options are not independent and cannot be valued independently. To see this, assume that the second option is valuable to issuers. For the bond to reset at a price of 101 on the first reset date, the coupon on the reset must be slightly higher than it would otherwise be. This would slightly increase the value of the first option to issuers. Thus, by adding option values, we are slightly understating the total option value on the bond.

**EXHIBIT 5**
**PRICE SENSITIVITY OF EXTENDABLE RESET BONDS VERSUS CONVENTIONAL
BONDS**

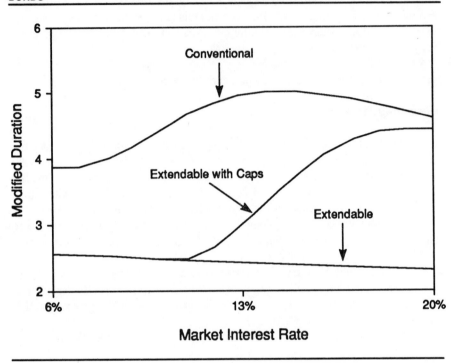

the callable bond is the duration of a bond with five years to maturity (the first call date), while the duration of the reset bond is the duration of a bond with three years to maturity. At higher interest rates the conventional bond will behave like a 10-year fixed rate bond.

### Floors on the Reset Rate

Most of the issues that have caps on the reset rate have floors as well. The floors tend to be set at the original coupon rate. Because of the call structure, the presence of a floor does not greatly affect the valuation of the bond. With an issuer call option on the reset date, the floor does not add much value. If the firm's borrowing rate declines below the floor, it could call the debt and reissue. In the absence of a call provision, a floor on the reset rate would make an issue more attractive to investors.

With a call, a floor adds value for investors only if the new issue costs including the new underwriting spread are greater than the floor, while these costs excluding the new underwriting spread are less than the floor. In this case, issuers would select a reset at the floor rate instead of the call.

## Put Features

As Exhibit 2 shows, there are three issues that are putable at each reset: Seminole Kraft 11.75%. Knoll International 14.5%. In each of these, the issuer establishes the reset rate, with no formula. The investor has the right to put the bond if he is unhappy with the rate.

A put ensures a fair repricing of the security. If rates change and the coupon is reset too low, the investor can put the bond. For example, if interest rates rise to 15.5% and the coupon is reset at 15%, putting the bond would make sense for investors. Similarly, if rates fall to 11.5% and the coupon is reset at 11.3%, putting the bond would again be the rational action. Thus, the put guarantees the integrity of the reset.

We can also view the put as an issuer call. By setting the coupon unrealistically low, the issuer would in essence be calling the bond. In the case of all three extendable bonds with puts, the bond is callable at par at each reset. Given the put structure, the par call neither reduces the value of the bond to investors nor increases it for the issuer.

Note that none of the bonds with put provisions have caps. This is because the investor would exercise the put precisely when the cap became binding.

The put structure in this reset bond differs markedly from that often found in high grade bonds. High grade put bonds typically have a European put feature but no call provision. These bonds are generally putable by the investor after 5-10 years. The investor will exercise the put if rates have risen and better investment opportunities are therefore available. Where call provisions are present, the call is exercisable after the put.

The extendable reset structure with puts is most similar to the put, call, and reset provisions found in floating rate note issues, in which the issuer can call the floater or reset the spread. If the spread is reset, the investor can then choose to put the floating rate issue.

## Deferred Coupon Features

Only one of the extendable reset bonds issued thus far—SSC Holdings Series I—has a pay-in-kind feature (PIK) for the initial five-year period. In an ordinary PIK bond, the coupon is fixed and the issuer has the right to choose whether to make the coupon payments in cash or in kind. Borrowers will pay the coupon in kind when rates have risen. Consider, for example, a 13% PIK bond. If the credit quality of this issuer has declined and its cost of funds has risen to 15%, the issuer is essentially able to put more of the bonds to investors at the 13% rate.[5]

---

[5]For a more complete treatment of PIK bonds, see Laurie S. Goodman and Alan H. Cohen, "PIK Debentures: Structure and Valuation," *Journal of Portfolio Management* (Winter 1989).

Let us now consider the PIK in a reset structure. In the SSC issue, the reset occurs after two years. Thus, the PIK feature is a combination of an option for two years plus an option for three years, rather than a five-year option. The first option has little value, as restrictive bank covenants will generally obligate the firm to pay in kind for the first year or year and a half. The second option, for three years, is more relevant. This 13% resettable PIK issue was accompanied by a 12.5% resettable issue with no PIK provisions. The 12.5% issue resets after three years. Since both issues were marketed at par, the 50 basis point coupon premium on the 13.0% SSC issue seems generous relative to the 12.5% SSC issue. That is, it is unlikely the PIK provisions are worth 50 basis points plus the give-up from a bond that is one year shorter.

## III. THE ISSUER'S PERSPECTIVE

If the firm substitutes resettable debt for fixed rate debt, the issuer will be assured of the availability of funds while being able to take advantage initially of an upward sloping yield curve. Thus, in exchange for lower issuing rates now, the firm is willing to pay a higher rate if market conditions warrant. This structure will be particularly attractive to firms that believe Treasury rates will decline or that expect their own creditworthiness to improve. A firm choosing this structure may be signaling that it anticipates an improvement in credit quality.

Resettable debt is ideally suited to LBOs. Many LBOs tend to be characterized by an initially highly leveraged structure with an anticipation of a great deal of asset sales. The firm is concerned with obtaining call flexibility and achieving a reasonably priced capital structure after the asset sales. Consider a world without resettable debt. The typical LBO structure has bank debt, which is paid off quickly, and various classes of fixed rate high yield bonds. After the bank debt is paid off, the capital market debt is relatively high cost.

With reset provisions, the picture is different. The resettable bonds, with their short call protection, could be called first. This would leave the firm with more bank debt, which is both cheaper and more easily renegotiable if credit improves.

Issuers have expressed two concerns about this debt when contemplating including it in their capital structure. One concern is that if it is short debt, the underwriting fees—typically 2.75% or 3.0%—are hard to justify. But issuers must realize that the debt is really long debt, in that the availability of funds is guaranteed. It becomes short debt only if it is called at the option of the issuer. This is similar to features in other high yield bond structures, such as PIK debentures of deferred coupon bonds with low call protection. Furthermore, in a number of cases (e.g., Stop and Shop), the indenture allows fractional amounts of the issue to be called. This provides the firm with greater flexibility to retire borrowings as asset sales or other considerations permit, without calling the whole issue. This gives resettable bond issuers flexibility similar to that accorded issuers of bank debt and medium term notes.

The second issuer concern is that coupon rates may rise when the firm is least able to absorb an increase. Coupon rates on resettable high yield bonds can rise either because Treasury rates have risen or because credit spreads have widened. While the latter possibility is a legitimate concern, rising Treasury rates should not be. As we explain below, using an extendable structure does not necessarily imply that the firm is substituting floating rate debt for fixed rate debt. Firms can increase the amount of fixed rate bank debt they undertake.

### Substituting Resettable Bonds for Bank Debt

A firm can substitute resettable rate debt for floating rate bank debt, leaving its debt structure unchanged. To illustrate how this can be done, we will consider the typical capital structure of a firm that has just undergone a leveraged buyout. In a representative LBO, 60% of the debt will be floating bank debt and the remaining 40% will be high yield bonds. Generally 50-70% of the floating rate bank debt will be swapped or capped. Firms can obtain floating rate bank debt via the reset structure. This necessitates swapping more floating rate bank debt into fixed rate bank debt. We can consider two debt structures as follows:

| Conventional Structure | Versus | Capital Structure Equivalent Using Resettable Structure |
|---|---|---|
| 30% fixed bank debt (fixed via a swap) | | 60% fixed bank debt (fixed via a swap) |
| 30% floating bank debt | | 30% resettable high yield debt |
| 40% fixed rate high yield | | 10% fixed rate high yield |

We illustrate these structures in Exhibit 6. Note that both of these structures have the same amount of floating or variable rate debt—30%.

Let us assume costs are as follows:[6]

| | |
|---|---|
| floating rate bank debt | LIBOR + 250 basis points |
| fixed rate high yield debt | $T_{10}$ + 500 basis points |
| fixed rate bank debt | $T_{10}$ + 330 basis points |

The fixed rate bank debt is obtained by swapping LIBOR for a fixed rate—in this example $T_{10}$ + 80. Thus, the all-in cost of fixed rate debt is $T_{10}$ + 80 + 250 = $T_{10}$ + 330 basis points.

We can now compute the break-even cost (X) on the extendable debt:

---

[6]LIBOR = London Interbank Offered Rate. $T_{10}$ = 10-year Treasury Rate.

**EXHIBIT 6**
**CAPITAL STRUCTURE COMPARISON FOR LBOs**

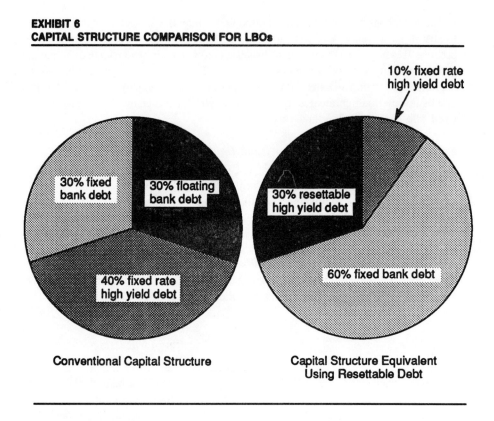

10% fixed rate
high yield debt

30% fixed
bank debt

30% floating
bank debt

30% resettable
high yield debt

40% fixed rate
high yield debt

60% fixed bank debt

**Conventional Capital Structure**

**Capital Structure Equivalent
Using Resettable Debt**

$$(.3)(\text{LIBOR} + 250) + (.3)(T_{10} + 330) + .4\,(T_{10} + 500)$$

$$= .6(T_{10} + 330) + .3\,(\text{LIBOR} + X) + .1(T_{10} + 500)$$

or $(.3)(\text{LIBOR} + 250) + (.3)(T_{10} + 500)$

$$= (.3)(T_{10} + 330) + (.3)(\text{LIBOR} + X)$$

or $X = 420$

Thus, if a firm can issue the resettable high yield debt for less than LIBOR + 420 basis points, it makes economic sense to consider this alternative.[7]

*Some Complications*

The simple analysis above ignores several complications. First, bank debt generally has a shorter maturity than the high yield subordinated debt. The bank debt may

---

[7]The difference between bank debt at LIBOR + 250 basis points and the resettable bonds at LIBOR + 420 basis points is that the former is usually secured. Foreign banks, which are permitted to purchase the debt, may want to view it as an alternative to extending a bank loan.

have a maximum term of five years, whereas the high yield reset debt typically has a maximum maturity of 10 years. Thus, in the conventional structure, after the fifth year all outstanding debt will be fixed and the remaining 30% of the debt will be floating for the last five years.

Second, and perhaps of more consequence, the resettable debt depends on both the credit spread and the base level of interest rates. Thus, the bonds do not reset at a market related rate plus a fixed spread. Rather, they reset at a market-related rate and a market-related spread. With a resettable structure, the firm is sending an important signal to the market, one that is not sent with the conventional structure.

The structure of this debt is highly favorable to some issuers. It affords them long-term rates, with a great deal of call flexibility. It is especially appropriate for issuers that expect their credit to improve. For issuers that believe their credit could deteriorate, this debt is less attractive, as the coupon will rise as the reset warrants. Moreover, there is no way to protect against the coupon rising because of an increase in the firm-specific credit spread or high yield credit spread. By fixing more of the bank debt, an issuer can protect against the coupon rising as a result of rising Treasury interest rates.

## IV. THE INVESTOR'S PERSPECTIVE

The structure of this instrument is well suited to high yield investors who anticipate an increase in high yield rates. In the face of expectations that interest rates will rise, any investor would want to hold paper that is not very interest rate sensitive—i.e., short paper. However, investors such as high yield money funds, which are constrained to purchase primarily high yield assets, face a particular dilemma. There are no short-term high yield instruments available except high yield commercial paper. But it is extremely costly for such a money manager to either hold cash or hold high yield commercial paper. The high yield commercial paper market is small, and yields are on the order of 50 basis points above high grade commercial paper. This represents a yield of 400-650 basis points less than that obtainable on high yield bonds.

While extendable bonds tend to have lower yields than longer-term conventional bonds, as a result of the reset feature, they provide protection against a rise in rates. For a short-term instrument, the yields are quite attractive. Exhibit 7 shows the yields at initial issuance for the five extendable reset bond issues that had current conventional issues with equal subordination. Thus, we compare senior subordinated reset notes only with senior subordinated conventional structures. We compare option adjusted yields in all cases. That is, we "correct" for the value of the option on both the conventional bond and the extendable reset bond. We do not perform a comparison if the reset notes are senior subordinated and the conventional bond, issued concurrently, is junior subordinated.

Note that in most of the cases the credit spreads are slightly higher on the extendable reset notes than on the conventional bond. This is very much in keeping

**EXHIBIT 7**
**CREDIT SPREADS ON RESET NOTES VERSUS CONVENTIONAL BONDS**
**(BASIS POINTS)**

| Date | Issuer | Spread on Option Free Reset Note | Spread on Option Free Conventional Bond | Spread Between Base Rates |
|------|--------|----------------------------------|------------------------------------------|---------------------------|
| 4/12/88 | R-C Holdings | +495/4 year | +510/10 year | 64 |
| 4/13/88 | El Paso Products | +529/1 year | +504/10 year | 172 |
| 4/29/88 | CJI | +601/1 year | +559/10 year | 176 |
| 7/21/88 | SSC Series II | +389/3 year | +403/10 year | 62 |
| 7/22/88 | Viacom | +297/3 year | +244/10 year | 62 |

with the idea that—in the absence of a significant amount of deferred coupon debt—the riskiest time for an LBO is in the early years. Thus, the credit spread curve is generally expected to be slightly downward sloping.

Because the extendable notes, particularly those without cap, can be viewed as short bonds, it may be somewhat less necessary to do a careful credit assessment than in the case of a fixed rate bond. If the company's credit deteriorates modestly but does not become impaired, it will be possible to find a coupon such that the bond will reset at 101. Moreover, the signal being sent to the market is that the issuer expects its credit to improve.

While the extendable structure somewhat reduces the need to look at the underlying creditworthiness of the issuer, it does not completely eliminate that need. If there is a severe credit deterioration, it would imply an even higher probability of bankruptcy, in turn causing the cost of funds to rise to a level that would imperil the company's viability.

In addition to the attractive yields when viewed as short-term investments, the resettable issue has a regulatory advantage for savings and loan (S&L) investors. Incremental Capital Requirements regulations imposed on August 15, 1986, placed a premium on asset/liability (or gap) management. These regulations raised capital requirements to 6% of liabilities by 1992, from the then-current level of 3%. However, savings institutions can reduce overall capital requirements to 3% prior to 1990 and 4% thereafter by matching assets and liabilities. Essentially, S&Ls receive a credit for matching assets and liabilities. If the interest rate gap is greater than 25% of assets at one and three years, the credit is eliminated entirely. For a gap between 15% and 25%, a partial credit is given.[8]

---

[8]If the one-year or three-year gap was between 15% and 25% of assets, the formula for computing the credit is:

net credit = .02005 - (.067 × GAP)
where GAP = gap as a percent of total assets.

For example, if the gap is 18% at one year, the net credit is .02005 - (.067 × 18) = .8%. Note that this credit is slightly higher than a pro rata would be.

For gap management purposes, reset bonds have a maturity equal to the time until the next reset. Since the profitability of most S&Ls is weakened by rising interest rates (i.e., they have a net short gap position), the reset of one to three years improves the interest rate gap position of these institutions vis-a-vis a long-term fixed rate bond.

Since most of these bonds are not accompanied by puts, there is some investor concern that the resets will not be "fair." Most of the resets are based on the opinion of two investment banks. The generally wide bid-asked spreads and the high cost of recourse provide sufficient scope for investor concern. However, the reset cannot be widely out of line, as there is the possibility of an investor lawsuit if the reset is bogus. As more resets come due—assuming that they are done fairly—investor fears will be alleviated.

## V. SUMMARY

Extendable reset bonds constitute a useful addition to the high yield landscape. A pure reset bond with no caps represents an instrument with the price action of a short bond. There are no other high yield instruments with this characteristic. In this article, we have also examined variations on the basic reset structure and have discussed how to value these variations.

We have examined the appeal of this instrument to issuers and investors. For issuers, the bonds provide the ability to fund at initially lower rates, while guaranteeing the long-term availability of funds. For investors, the instruments offer a short-term high yield investment alternative, providing protection against large increases in high yield interest rates. Investors, however, should be concerned about how the reset would work if a large credit deterioration occurred. Since only one issue in the current crop of resettable bonds has reset so far, investors should also be concerned with the integrity of the resets.

# Valuing Deferred Coupon Debentures

LAURIE S. GOODMAN, PH.D.
VICE PRESIDENT
FINANCIAL STRATEGIES GROUP
GOLDMAN, SACHS & CO.

ALAN H. COHEN
ASSOCIATE
HIGH YIELD GROUP
GOLDMAN, SACHS & CO.

## I. FINANCING LBOs

Leveraged buyout transactions have become increasingly common in recent years. In these transactions, investors take a public firm private by purchasing the company from existing shareholders, relying heavily on borrowed funds. Similar in spirit to LBOs are recapitalizations, in which the firm remains public but debt replaces equity. The leverage in LBO situations is very high, and the resulting debt is virtually always rated below investment grade.

The authors would like to thank Jonathan Kolatch, David Tepper, and Jack Walton for their help in establishing the analytic framework for this article; Eric Kades for his programming support; Jeff Zajkowski for his invaluable research assistance; and Bob Kopprasch and José Scheinkman for their helpful comments on several technical points.

139

### Deferred Coupon Bonds

Cash flows in the initial years of an LBO will often be insufficient to meet the interest payments of the highly levered firm. In general, any class of debt holders can force acceleration of principal payments when the company has missed an interest payment. Once a firm seeks protection from creditors via a bankruptcy, priority rules become compromises—junior subordinated debt holders may get paid something in situations where senior debt holders are not paid in full.

To avoid such early cash flow problems, firms involved in leveraged buyouts and recapitalizations have issued a sizable amount of high yield deferred interest securities. As of May 1, 1988, approximately $16 billion (face amount) of deferred coupon bonds had been sold or distributed. Deferred coupon debentures are the most common of these instruments, with more than 30 issues to date.[1] These debentures (often called "zeroes") sell at a deep discount, and no interest is paid for an initial period, generally three to seven years. The bond then trades with accrued interest six months before the first coupon is to be paid.

### Historical Spreads

Potential investors in deferred coupon securities should be interested in purchasing securities that represent "good value" relative to the universe of high yield investments. In order to make that assessment, investors generally look at two historical measures:

- How is the zero priced relative to a coupon bond of the same issuer? Is this spread wider than it has historically been?
- How has the zero traded relative to zeroes of other issuers of a similar credit quality across time? Is it currently "rich" or "cheap" in relation to other zeroes?

High yield deferred coupon securites tend to trade at yields 90-200 basis points higher than the same issuer's coupon bonds with similar maturities. For example, an Owens-Illinois deferred coupon bond, maturing on June 1, 2003, with a first accrual date of June 1, 1993, was priced to yield 13.72% (on a yield-to-worst-case basis) as of March 31, 1988, for settlement April 7, 1988. An Owens-Illinois 12.75% coupon bond maturing on June 1, 1999, was selling to yield 12.19% on the same date—a

---

[1]There are two other types of deferred interest securities: step-up bonds and pay-in-kind (PIK) debentures. In a step-up coupon debenture, the bonds pay a low coupon for an initial period and a higher coupon thereafter. PIK debentures give issuers the option of paying in cash or in kind for an initial period. The valuation method used in this article can also be applied to step-up bonds. We discuss the valuation of PIK debentures in depth in Laurie S. Goodman and Alan H. Cohen, *Pay-In-Kind Debentures: Structure and Valuation*, Financial Strategies Group, Goldman, Sachs & Co., November 1987.

difference of 153 basis points. Similarly, a deferred coupon issue of National Gypsum maturing in 2004 was yielding 15.50%—a 127 basis point difference vis-à-vis the conventional bond—on March 31, 1988. Exhibit 1 shows a number of pairwise comparisons as of that date. As the exhibit indicates, spreads to coupon bonds can be very different for different issuers.

Substantial variations occur not only between zeroes and coupon bonds of the same issuers at a given time, but also between zeroes of different issuers across time. Exhibit 2 shows the yields over the seven-month period covering October 1987 to April 1988 on the zeroes of three different issuers (based on "bid" prices). Yield differences between the Borg 0/13% and the Macy's 0/16.5% have ranged from a high of 579 basis points to a low of 10 basis points over the period.

### Relative Value

Using historical spreads as a guide can give misleading impressions of relative value. A wider-than-normal spread could indicate either a cheap zero, a change in the slope of the yield curve, or a credit deterioration that now justifies the higher spread. In this article we propose a fundamental—rather than an historical—approach to valuing deferred coupon bonds. In Section III we identify the fundamental ingredients that determine the value of deferred coupon bonds. Section IV explains how to use these ingredients to assess relative value. Before turning to this approach, however, we will first describe, in Section II, an alternative way to look at the relative value of these bonds. We will show that on occasion, zeroes can become so cheap that an arbitrage is possible.[2]

## II. THE ARBITRAGE APPROACH

Conventional bonds tend to be more liquid than deferred coupon bonds. Consequently, conventional bonds tend to react more quickly to market information. Situations occasionally can arise where deferred coupon bonds become so cheap relative to a conventional bond of the same issuer that a pure arbitrage may result. That is, *it is possible from time to time to buy Treasury zeroes and pair them with a deferred coupon bond to approximately duplicate the cash flow from the conventional bonds of the same issuer for a lower price.*

---

[2]We define "arbitrage" broadly, to encompass a replicating strategy involving similar as well as identical instruments.

**EXHIBIT 1**
**PAIRWISE COMPARISONS—YIELD ON DEFERRED COUPON VS. CONVENTIONAL BOND**
**(AS OF MARCH 31, 1988, FOR SETTLEMENT ON APRIL 7, 1988)**

| | Deferred Coupon Bond | | | | Conventional Bond | | | |
|---|---|---|---|---|---|---|---|---|
| Company | Maturity | Accrual Date | Coupon | Yield to Worst | Maturity | Coupon | Yield to Worst | Difference |
| Borg 13 | 7/1/07 | 7/15/92 | 0/13 | 15.16 | 7/15/97 | 12.75 | 13.12 | 2.49 |
| Borg 14 | 7/15/99 | 7/15/92 | 0/14.0 | 14.82 | 7/15/97 | 12.75 | 13.12 | 1.70 |
| Burlington | 10/03/03 | 10/1/93 | 0/16 | 14.73 | 10/01/99 | 14.25 | 13.02 | 1.71 |
| Container | 9/30/06 | 9/30/91 | 0/16.75 | 12.00 | 9/30/98 | 12.375 | 11.43 | .57 |
| Eckerd | 5/01/06 | 5.01/91 | 0/13 | 13.31 | 5/01/01 | 11.125 | 12.21 | 1.10 |
| HBJ | 9/15/02 | 9/15/92 | 0/14.75 | 13.71 | 9/15/99 | 13.75 | 12/31 | 1.40 |
| Macy's | 11/15/06 | 7/15/93 | 0/16.50 | 15.51 | 11/15/01 | 14.5 | 14.63 | .88 |
| Nat Gypsum | 6/30/04 | 6/30/91 | 0/15 | 15.50 | 4/29/01 | 14.5 | 14.23 | 1.27 |
| Owens-Corning | 12/01/06 | 12/01/91 | 0/15.0 | 11.39 | 11/15/01 | 11.75 | 11.22 | .17 |
| Owens-Illinois | 6/01/03 | 6/11/93 | 0/15 | 13.72 | 6/01/99 | 12.75 | 12.19 | 1.53 |
| Southland Sr. | 12/15/97 | 12/15/90 | 0/16.5 | 16.75 | 12/15/97 | 15.75 | 14.77 | 1.98 |
| Southland Jr. | 12/15/07 | 12/15/92 | 0/18.0 | 18.14 | 12/15/02 | 16.75 | 15.77 | 2.37 |
| Super General | 10/05/03 | 10/05/92 | 0/13.125 | 14.70 | 9/15/97 | 14.50 | 12.80 | 1.90 |

**EXHIBIT 2**
**HISTORICAL YIELDS OF SELECTED ZEROES (1987-88)**

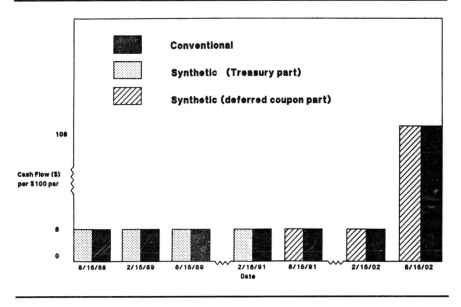

The deferred coupon part of the combination will, of course, have less liquidity than the conventional bond. However, since the front part of the synthetic consists of Treasury zeroes, the combination may well have more favorable credit characteristics. This strategy would appeal both to "buy and hold" investors and to others who believe the alignment will disappear in a short time.

### Creating the Arbitrage

As an example, consider a 16% deferred coupon bond and a 16% conventional bond of the same issuer. Both bonds are non-callable, rank *pari passu* in the capital structure, and have the same maturity date—August 15, 2002. The deferred coupon bond accrues no coupon until August 15, 1991. The conventional bond is currently selling at a price of 102.79 to yield 15.5%. The accured interest (as of April 7, 1988) is 2.31. The present value of the bond is 105.10. The deferred coupon bond is currently selling at a price of 57.26 to yield 16.5% (internal rate of return). We will combine the deferred coupon bond with Treasury zeroes to duplicate the cash flows of the conventional bond. That is, we will purchase enough Treasury zeroes to produce $8 of cash flow every six months until the deferred coupon bond begins paying interest.

To match the front-end coupon payments, we purchase Treasury zeroes as follows:

| Date | Yield on Treasury Zero as of Date Shown | Cost per $100 par of Treasury Zero | Cost of $8 of Treasury Zero |
|------|------|------|------|
| 8/15/88 | 6.90% | $97.595 | $7.808 |
| 2/15/89 | 7.20 | 94.117 | 7.529 |
| 8/15/89 | 7.45 | 90.550 | 7.244 |
| 2/15/90 | 7.62 | 87.038 | 6.963 |
| 8/15/90 | 7.75 | 83.591 | 6.687 |
| 2/15/91 | 7.85 | 80.252 | 6.420 |

**Total Cost   $42.65**

The cost of the synthetic combination is $99.91—$42.65 from the zeroes and $57.26 from the deferred coupon. This compares with a cost of $105.10 for the conventional bond. Thus, the cash flows of the synthetic are identical to those of the

**EXHIBIT 3**
**CONVENTIONAL BOND VERSUS SYNTHETIC COMBINATION**

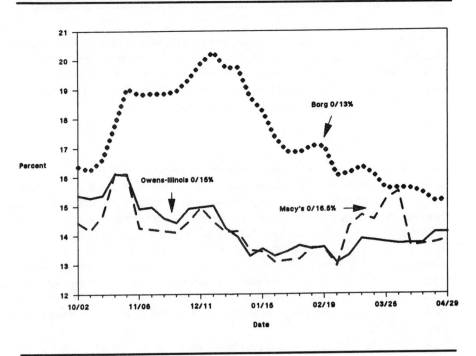

conventional bond, but the synthetic is far cheaper than the conventional. We depict the cash flows in Exhibit 3.

### Making the Arbitrage More Realistic

To highlight the salient points of the comparisons, we set up the previous example with a number of features rarely attainable in the real world. Both bonds were non-callable, had the same coupon and maturity dates, and ranked *pari passu* in the capital structure; the coupon payment dates coincided exactly with those of Treasury zeroes.

In reality, it is likely that both the deferred coupon and the conventional bonds will be callable, the bonds will have different coupons, they will often have slightly different maturity dates, the coupon payment dates will not coincide exactly with those of Treasury zeroes, and the bonds will not rank *pari passu* (the conventional bond will usually have a higher standing than the deferred coupon bond).

Essentially, we handle the structural and temporal differences by "adjusting" the conventional bond wherever necessary so that it has the same maturity date and coupon as the deferred coupon bond. Consider two Southland issues: the 15.75% conventional bond and the 16.50% deferred coupon bond. In this case, the bonds have identical maturity dates (December 15, 1997) and identical coupon payment dates, but we will have to adjust the coupons of the conventional bond. Both bonds are callable; the conventional bond is callable at 105 on December 15, 1992, at 102.5 on December 15, 1993, and at par on December 15, 1994, and thereafter. The deferred coupon bond is callable at par at any time. Since the cost to the issuer of an early call on the deferred coupon is prohibitively expensive, the call date effectively becomes December 15, 1990, the end of the deferral period. The two bonds rank *pari passu*.

The conventional bond has a present value of 108.90 (a price of 104.00 and accrued interest of 4.90 as of March 31, 1988, for settlement on April 7, 1988). We impute the yield to maturity consistent with the pricing of this bond to a bond with a 16.5% coupon, and obtain a present value of 113.04.[3] We wish to fill in the front end of the cash flows with Treasury zeroes. The problem is that Treasury zeroes mature only on February 15, May 15, August 15, and November 15. Thus, the closest zeroes are due May 15 and November 15. We use the yield on these zeroes to calculate the cost of a zero maturity on the desired dates—June 15, 1988; December 15, 1988; June 15, 1989; December 15, 1989; June 15, 1990; and December 15, 1990. We can calculate the cost of the zeroes as follows:

---

[3]We must look at the present value (price + accrued interest) of the conventional bond rather than the price. This is because the synthetic will not have an explicit accrued interest component at the time of purchase.

| Date | Yield on Treasury Zero as of Nearest Date | Cost per $100 Par of Treasury Zero | Cost of $8.25 of Treasury Zero |
|---|---|---|---|
| 06/15/88 | 6.80% | $98.739 | $8.146 |
| 12/15/88 | 7.00 | 95.370 | 7.868 |
| 06/15/89 | 7.35 | 91.782 | 7.572 |
| 12/15/89 | 7.55 | 88.230 | 7.279 |
| 06/15/90 | 7.70 | 84.752 | 6.992 |
| 12/15/90 | 7.80 | 81.406 | 6.716 |

**Total Cost  $44.57**

We must add this $44.57 cost of Treasury zeroes to the $64.25 cost of the deferred coupon bond. Thus, neglecting the call features, we can assemble the synthetic combination for a cost of $108.82 versus $113.04 for the adjusted conventional bond.

The call protection is somewhat different between the conventional bond and the deferred coupon bond. The deferred coupon bond has a shorter period of call protection, but the "strike yield"—i.e., the compensation paid by the issuer for the privilege of retiring the bond earlier than its stated maturity—is higher: 16.5% versus 15.75% for the par call in 1994. We can adjust the price for the difference in option value. In this case the option on the deferred coupon bond is worth $.44 per $100 bond. The option on the conventional bond is worth $2.89. The original bond has a present value of $108.90, and the cost of the "adjusted" bond is $113.04, so the option is worth $(113.04/108.90 \times 2.89) = \$3.00$. The option-adjusted cost of the synthetic package is $109.26, versus a price of $116.04 for a conventional bond of the same coupon.

Comparisons are more difficult if the conventional bond and the deferred coupon bond do not rank *pari passu*. If the deferred coupon bond is subordinated to the conventional bond, the resulting synthetic package will have a higher credit quality at the front end and a lower credit quality at the back end. We can handle this in two ways. The first is to determine (in basis points), how cheap the synthetic is relative to the conventional. We simply calculate the yield on a conventional bond selling at the synthetic price and compare this with the actual yield on the conventional. If the yield difference is larger than an appropriate subordinate correction, we may safely conclude that the deferred coupon bond is cheap.

We could also adjust the price of the conventional bond for credit quality by assuming a yield equal to the true yeld plus a subordination correction. Thus, the "fully" adjusted conventional bond—adjusted for both coupon and subordination—would have a higher yield than the actual conventional bond. However, offsetting this is the fact that approximately 40% of the present value of the synthetic security has *no* credit risk.

Exhibit 4 shows the prices of the adjusted conventional bond and the synthetic bond for the most actively traded deferred coupon bonds, with and without an option correction. This option correction is somewhat *ad hoc*, as we are unsure of the volatility of the embedded options. As illustrated, most of the deferred coupon bonds are cheap relative to the conventional bonds. These numbers, however, do not include a subordination correction. An asterisk marks those deferred coupon issues that are not subordinated. Assuming a subordination correction of 50 basis points—approximately \$3.00 on a 14%, 15-year bond—we see that many of these deferred coupon bonds still appear cheap.

Rather than make an option correction, we can look at the comparison between the deferred coupon and the conventional bond on a yield-to-worst basis. Yield-to-worst calculations ignore the time value of the options. Nonetheless, market participants use them extensively. If both bonds are trading to call, we can make a comparison to call. If both bonds are trading to maturity, we can make a comparison on that basis. However, if one bond is trading to call and the other to maturity, we generally cannot make a comparison. We provide a case-by-case analysis in Appendix A.

Note that the methodology described in the preceding paragraphs only highlights arbitrages. That is, if we can create a cheaper synthetic bond with the same cash flows as a conventional bond using Treasury zeroes, we have an arbitrage. If the *synthetic bond* is more expensive than the conventional bond, however, it does not necessarily mean the *deferred coupon bond* is expensive relative to the conventional bond. Since the Treasury zeroes are far more expensive than the conventional bond, the deferred coupon bond itself could be cheap, expensive, or fairly priced relative to the conventional bond.

## III. THE FUNDAMENTAL APPROACH

As the above discussion indicates, we can use the arbitrage approach to pricing deferred coupon bonds only to assess whether a deferred coupon bond is *cheap* relative to the conventional bond. We cannot use it to determine whether a deferred coupon bond is relatively *expensive*. To make a full comparison, we must first develop a comprehensive approach to pricing deferred coupon bonds. We do so below. In Section IV, we show how to use this approach to produce relative value pricing.

We can identify four fundamental influences on the pricing of deferred coupon bonds relative to conventional bonds of the same issuer: (1) differences in subordination, (2) differences in call protection, (3) the term structure of interest rates, and (4) the term structure of credit spreads. We will discuss each of these in turn.

**EXHIBIT 4**
**SYNTHETIC VS. CONVENTIONAL BOND ARBITRAGE COMPARISON (BASED ON APRIL 7, 1988 SETTLEMENT)**

| Company | Synthetic Callable Price | + Deferred Call Value | = Non-call Synthetic PV | Conventional Callable PV | + Adjusted Call Value | = Conventional Non-call PV | Amount Undervalued (Overvalued) | Without Option Adjustment |
|---|---|---|---|---|---|---|---|---|
| Borg 13 | $94.15 | $0.06 | $94.21 | $102.07 | $ 0.13 | $102.20 | $7.99 | $ 7.92 |
| Borg 14 | 105.95 | 0.13 | 106.08 | 108.24 | 0.13 | 108.37 | 2.29 * | 2.29 * |
| Burlington | 116.17 | 0.84 | 117.01 | 117.51 | 5.29 | 122.80 | 5.79 | 1.34 |
| Container | 126.83 | 14.53 | 141.36 | 137.85 | 11.71 | 149.56 | 8.20 ** | 11.02 ** |
| Eckerd | 106.56 | .1.22 | 107.78 | 111.34 | 5.37 | 116.71 | 8.93 * | 4.78 * |
| HBJ | 111.86 | 0.34 | 112.20 | 114.32 | 4.20 | 118.52 | 6.32 | 2.46 |
| Macy's | 125.26 | 0.31 | 125.57 | 118.38 | 8.05 | 126.43 | 0.86 | (6.88) |
| Nat Gypsum | 115.31 | 0.59 | 115.90 | 111.75 | 1.09 | 112.84 | (3.06) | (3.56) |
| Owens-Corning | 118.89 | 6.63 | 125.52 | 131.62 | 9.19 | 140.81 | 15.29 ** | 12.73 ** |
| Owens-Illinois | 118.08 | 0.25 | 118.33 | 121.74 | 3.95 | 125.69 | 7.36 | 3.66 |
| Southland Sr. | 108.82 | 0.44 | 109.26 | 113.04 | 3.00 | 116.04 | 6.78 * | 4.22 * |
| Southalnd Jr. | 118.98 | 0.25 | 119.23 | 117.84 | 2.69 | 120.53 | 1.30 | (1.14) |
| Super Gen'l | 97.56 | 0.22 | 97.78 | 100.76 | 2.37 | 103.13 | 5.35 | 3.20 |

* Denotes no subordination.
** These large undervaluations may not be meaningful. With the underlying bonds trading to call and the options very deep in the money, results may be more meaningful if these bonds are looked at as having a maturity equal to the call date, with an issuer option to extend (an issuer put).

### Subordination

High yield zeroes tend to have a lower status in the capital structure than conventional bonds, although this is not universally the case. If a conventional bond of an issuer is considered "senior subordinated debt," the zero is generally "subordinated debt." If the conventional bond is "subordinated debt," the zero is generally "junior subordinated." There are, of course, exceptions to this. The Southland 16.5% zeroes maturing December 15, 1997 rank *pari passu* with the 15.75% coupon bond maturing on the same date. The Eckerd 0/13% deferred coupon bond maturing May 1, 2006, actually has a higher standing in bankruptcy than the conventional bond maturity five years earlier.

We would not expect two coupon bonds from the same issuer to be valued identically if they had a different standing in bankruptcy. The credit spread should be higher for the lower status issue. Thus, we must make a "subordination correction" on the bond. The way to do this is to ask what yield premium the market would demand for the lower status issue vis-à-vis the higher status issue, assuming the two issues were equivalent in all other respects. The subordination correction is generally on the order of 25-50 basis points. It is approximately 25 basis points for the higher quality issues in the high yield market and closer to 50 basis points for other issuers in that market. For firms with serious problems, the differential could be much wider.

### Call Protection

Most deferred coupon bonds are callable by the accrual date, and more than half of the deferred coupon bonds are callable at par on that date. Some of these bonds have considerably lower call protection than their conventional counterparts. This low call protection is a logical extension of their lower standing in bankruptcy. Junior debt is the most expensive debt, and it is desirable from the point of view of shareholders to retire it as soon as possible. That is, holders of junior debt should be paid off as early as is consistent with the debt convenants agreed to by senior claimants.

We can think of a callable bond as a bond minus a call option. We may write this as:

$$P_{CB} = P_{NCB} - P_O \tag{1}$$

where:   $P_{CB}$ is the price of the callable bond
$P_{NCB}$ is the price of the non-callable bond
$P_O$ is the price of the option

In comparing two bonds, we must "correct" for the price of the call option on each of the bonds before the comparison is made. That is, we would add the price of the option to the price of a callable bond to obtain the price of a non-callable bond. We can then make the appropriate comparisons between the two non-callable bonds. The yield calculated after we make an adjustment for the price of the option is known as the "option-adjusted yield."

Exhibit 5 provides information on call protection for the deferred coupon nd conventional bonds listed in Exhibit 1. It also gives our estimate of the value of the call options. The call values on the zeroes range between $0.06 and $14.53 per $100 face amount of the bond. The call values on conventional bonds range between $0.13 and $8.84. The calls on the conventional bonds are currently more valuable than the calls on the zeroes, because zeroes have appreciated less than conventional bonds in the latest market rally. A call value of 1.00 means about 8 basis points in yield on a 15-year, 14% issue. Thus, if two bonds have different call protection, we must correct for these differences before trying to value the bonds. This allows us to compare the relative yields on identical non-callable bonds.

## The Term Structure of Interest Rates

Investors tend to focus on yield to maturity as a measure of relative value. They are, of course, aware that yield to maturity implicitly assumes a flat discount rate and an ability to reinvest at this discount rate. Nevertheless, it is a good measure of the relative value of two bonds with similar cash flows and maturities. If the cash flows are substantially different, an investor should evaluate the spread off a risk-free zero coupon yield curve rather than the simple yield-to-maturity measure. The zero coupon yield curve measures the yield on a risk-free bond with no interim payments and with a final payment on the maturity date. Thus, the two-year zero coupon rate is based on a bond paying $100 at the end of Year Two with no intermediate cash flows.

We can make this point most easily with a simple example. Let us consider three different bonds—each having a three-year maturity and paying an annual coupon. One pays a 12.5% coupon, one pays a 13.5% coupon, and one pays a zero coupon. The risk-free rates are 7% for one year, 8% for two years, and 9% for three years. All three of these bonds have a 400 basis point spread to the risk-free rate. We can calculate the price of each of these bonds and use this information to calculate the yield to maturity in each case.

Treasury (risk-free) bond (9% coupon)

$$\frac{9}{1.07} + \frac{9}{(1.08)^2} + \frac{109}{(1.09)^3} = 100.30$$

Yield to maturity = 8.88%

**EXHIBIT 5**
**CALL PROVISIONS ON DEFERRED COUPON VERSUS CONVENTIONAL BONDS (BASED ON APRIL 7, 1988 SETTLEMENT)**

| Company | Deferred Coupon Bond | | | | Conventional Bond | | | |
|---|---|---|---|---|---|---|---|---|
| | Maturity | 1st Call | Par Call | Call Value | Maturity | 1st Call | Par Call | Call Value |
| Borg 13 | 7/15/07 | Current/105 | 94 | .06 | 7/15/97 | 90/107.96 | 95 | .13 |
| Borg 14 | 7/15/99 | Current/105 | 94 | .13 | 7/15/97 | 90/107.96 | 95 | .13 |
| Burlington | 10/01/03 | 93/100 | | .84 | 10/01/99 | 92/105 | 94 | 4.75 |
| Container | 9/30/06 | 91/105 | 93 | 14.53 | 9/30/98 | 91/105 | 93 | 8.84 |
| Eckerd | 5/01/06 | Current/100 | | 1.22 | 05/01/06 | 91/100 | | 4.49 |
| HBJ | 9/15/02 | Current/105 | 94 | .31 | 9/15/99 | 92/103.93 | | 3.94 |
| Macy's | 11/15/06 | Current/100 | | .31 | 11/15/01 | 91/105 | 93 | 7.22 |
| Nat Gypsum | 06/30/04 | Current/105 | 96 | .59 | 4/29/01 | 91/107.25 | 96 | 1.03 |
| Owens-Corning | 12/01/06 | Current/100 | | 6.63 | 11/15/01 | 91/100 | | 7.38 |
| Owens-Illinois | 6/01/03 | Peculiar | 93 | .25 | 6/01/99 | 88/111.48 | 97 | 3.49 |
| Southland Sr. | 12/15/97 | Current/100 | | .44 | 12/15/97 | 92/105 | 94 | 2.89 |
| Southland Jr. | 12/15/07 | Current/100 | | .25 | 12/15/02 | 92/106 | 96 | 2.49 |
| Super Gen'l | 10/05/03 | 92/105 | 94 | .22 | 9/15/97 | 90/109.06 | 95 | 2.49 |

12.5% coupon

$$\frac{12.5}{1.11} + \frac{12.5}{(1.12)^2} + \frac{112.5}{(1.13)^3} = 99.19$$

Yield to maturity = 12.84%
Spread to risk-free bond = 396 basis points

13.5% coupon

$$\frac{13.5}{1.11} + \frac{13.5}{(1.12)^2} + \frac{113.5}{(1.13)^3} = 101.59$$

Yield to maturity = 12.83%
Spread to risk-free bond = 395 basis points

0% coupon

$$\frac{0}{1.11} + \frac{0}{(1.12)^2} + \frac{100}{(1.13)^3} = 69.31$$

Yield to maturity = 13%
Spread to risk-free bond = 412 basis points

When we compare the 12.5% and 13.5% coupon bonds on a yield-to-maturity basis, we find the difference insignificant: 12.84% versus 12.83%. In terms of yield spreads, the 12.5% bond has a spread of 396 basis points to the risk-free bond, the 13.5% bond a spread of 395 basis points. The zero has a measured yield of 13%, 17 basis points more than the measured yield on the 13.5% coupon. Its yield spread to the risk-free bond is 412 basis points. Remember, however, that all three bonds have the same true spread of 400 basis points.

We can make several points from this simple example:

- Comparing the yield to maturity of two bonds with similar coupons gives a good approximation of their *relative* spreads. In this example, the measured difference in spreads was 1 basis point. The true difference was 0 basis points.
- Comparing the yield spread on a high yield conventional bond selling near or above par will understate the true spread over Treasuries in an upward sloping yield curve environment. In this case, the true spread was 400 basis points and the measured spreads were 395 and 396 basis points. For a bond selling well above par, the understatement would have been larger.
- Using the yield-to-maturity measure on a high yield deferred coupon bond will considerably overstate its "true" spread in an upward sloping yield curve environment. In this case the overstatement is by 12 basis points.
- The yield-to-maturity measure on a zero or deferred coupon bond should be higher than on an otherwise identical conventional bond, in order to take

account of the shape of the yield curve. One way of understanding why this result occurs is to regard the yield to maturity of each bond as some type of cash-flow-weighted average of the individual discount rates applied to each cash flow. The conventional high yield securities have higher coupons than the risk-free bond and thus weighted the early period discount rates slightly more. In an upward sloping yield curve environment, this will reduce the "weighted average," or yield to maturity, relative to the yield on the risk-free bond. Conversely, the zero weights the third-year discount rate 100% and thus returns a signficantly higher yield than the risk-free asset.

These examples were based on a particular yield curve. The distortions would, of course, be larger if the yield curve were steeper. This can be seen from another simple example. Consider the following steep yield curve—5% base rate for one year, 7% for two years, and 9% for three years. We continue to assume a 400 basis point spread. We calculate the yield to maturity on each of the bonds we considered earlier:

Treasury (risk-free) bond (9% coupon)

$$\frac{9}{1.05} + \frac{9}{(1.07)^2} + \frac{109}{(1.09)^3} = 100.60$$

Yield to maturity = 8.76%

12.5% coupon

$$\frac{12.5}{1.09} + \frac{12.5}{(1.11)^2} + \frac{112.5}{(1.13)^3} = 99.58$$

Yield to maturity = 12.68%
Spread to risk-free bond = 392 basis points

13.5% coupon

$$\frac{13.5}{1.09} + \frac{13.5}{(1.11)^2} + \frac{113.5}{(1.13)^3} = 102.00$$

Yield to maturity = 12.66%
Spread to risk-free bond = 390 basis points

0% coupon

$$\frac{0}{1.09} + \frac{0}{(1.11)^2} + \frac{100}{(1.13)^3} = 69.31$$

Yield to maturity = 13%
Spread to risk-free bond = 424 basis points

Note that the measured spread is more distorted in this example; the 13.5% coupon has a spread of 390 basis points over Treasuries versus 424 basis points for the zero—a 34 basis-point distortion.

A longer maturity would worsen the distortion. However, this problem is somewhat mitigated by the fact that deferred coupons are not true zeroes—they do pay coupons beginning at a certain date. Exhibit 6 shows the distortion in the yield-to-maturity measure caused by the shape of the Treasury yield curve. (Yields assume April 7, 1988 settlement.) These computations are for a 15-year, 14% conventional bond versus a 14% deferred coupon bond. All bonds have a true credit spread of 500 basis points. As you can see, distortions in the measured spread are 41 basis points with a deferral period of five years and 48 basis points with a seven-year deferral. The distortions would, of course, be greater with a steeper yield curve. Clearly the shape of the yield curve is too important to be ignored in valuing deferred coupon securities.

### The Term Structure of the Credit Spread

In the examples of the previous section, we assumed that the credit spread was flat—400 basis points for all maturities. If we assume the term structure of credit spreads is flat when it is not, we can obtain distorted measures of the relative attractiveness of deferred coupon and conventional bonds.

Take, for example, a three-year bond with a "true" credit spread at 50 basis points for the first two years and 400 basis points for the last year. This structure could result from uncertainty over an expected event in Year Three that could drive the firm out of business or impair its ability to borrow to pay off existing debtholders. Using the zero yield curve from the first example of Section III—with risk-free rates at 7% for one year, 8% for two years, and 9% for three years—we have:

Treasury (risk-free) bond (9% coupon)

$$\frac{9}{1.07} + \frac{9}{(1.08)^2} + \frac{109}{(1.09)^3} = 100.30$$

Yield to maturity = 8.88%

12.5% coupon

$$\frac{12.5}{1.075} + \frac{12.5}{(1.085)^2} + \frac{112.5}{(1.13)^3} = 100.21$$

Yield to maturity = 12.41%
Spread to risk-free bond = 353 basis points

**EXHIBIT 6**
**EFFECT OF THE SHAPE OF THE YIELD CURVE ON A 14%, 15-YEAR BOND**

| Zero Yield Curve (years) for settlement 4/7/88 | 1 7.32% | 3 7.95% | 5 8.20% | 7 8.75% | 10 9.05% | 20 9.26% |
|---|---|---|---|---|---|---|

Yield to maturity on 10-year Treasury = 8.61%

| Deferral Period | Price | Yield | Measured Spread | True Spread | Distortion |
|---|---|---|---|---|---|
| 0 years | 101.06 | 13.83% | 522 bp | 500 bp | 22 bp |
| 1 year | 88.25 | 13.85 | 524 | 500 | 24 |
| 2 years | 76.94 | 13.89 | 528 | 500 | 28 |
| 3 years | 67.00 | 13.94 | 533 | 500 | 33 |
| 4 years | 58.30 | 13.98 | 537 | 500 | 37 |
| 5 years | 50.72 | 14.02 | 541 | 500 | 41 |
| 7 years | 38.40 | 14.09 | 548 | 500 | 48 |

13.5% coupon

$$\frac{13.5}{1.075} + \frac{13.5}{(1.085)^2} + \frac{113.5}{(1.13)^3} = 102.68$$

Yield to maturity = 12.37%
Spread to risk-free bond = 349 basis points

0% coupon

$$\frac{0}{1.075} - \frac{0}{(1.085)^2} + \frac{100}{(1.13)^3} = 69.31$$

Yield to maturity = 13%
Spread to risk-free bond = 412 basis points

Clearly, if the credit spread curve is upward sloping, the yield spread on a zero will be higher than on a conventional bond. The steeper the credit spread curve, the greater the discrepancy. Again, we can think of lower yields on the coupons of the conventional bond bringing down the "average" yield to maturity.

Exhibit 7 shows this effect, in basis points, for a conventional versus a deferred coupon bond. We assume there is a differential between the credit spread for the earlier years (the frontspread) and the credit spread for the later years (the backspread). The frontspread applies through the end of the deferral period. The exhibit assumes the Treasury curve yields 8.5% for all maturities and the backspread is 600 basis points. Thus, the deferred coupon bond yields 14.5%. The yield on the conventional bond depends on the backspread-frontspread differential and the length of the deferral period.

We calculate the yield on the conventional bond as follows: Assume that the backspread-frontspread differential is 300 basis points. The frontspread will therefore be 300 basis points (600 − 300). To compare the conventional bond with a bond having a three-year deferral period, we assume that the frontspread is in effect for the first three years and the backspread is in effect for the remaining 12 years. Thus, we discount the first six cash flows by 11.5% (8.5 + 3.0) and the next 24 cash flows by 14.5%. We then calculate the yield on this bond from the price. The yield is 14.238%, a difference of .262% (14.5−14.238) or 26.2 basis points (see Exhibit 7).

As the exhibit shows, the effect of the credit spread is greater as the backspread-frontspread differential is larger and the deferral period is longer. For example, for a 100 basis-point differential and a three-year deferral period, the yield difference between the deferral coupon and conventional bond is 8.6 basis points. For a 400 basis-point differential and a three-year deferral period, the difference is 35.3 basis points If the credit spread differential is held constant at 400 basis points and the deferral period is lengthened to five years, the difference grows to 77.5 basis points.

In terms of the analysis, the true shape of the term structure of credit spreads is

**EXHIBIT 7**
**EFFECT OF THE TERM STRUCTURE OF CREDIT SPREADS ON A 14%, 15-YEAR BOND—YIELD DIFFERENCE BETWEEN DEFERRED COUPON AND CONVENTIONAL BOND (*BASIS POINTS*)**

|  |  | Backspread Minus Frontspread = | | | | |
|---|---|---|---|---|---|---|
|  |  | *100* | *200* | *300* | *400* | *500* |
|  | 0 | 0 | 0 | 0 | 0 | 0 |
|  | 1 | 1.5 | 3.0 | 4.5 | 6.0 | 7.5 |
|  | 2 | 4.5 | 9.0 | 13.6 | 18.3 | 23.1 |
| Deferral Period | 3 | 8.6 | 17.4 | 26.2 | 35.3 | 44.4 |
|  | 4 | 13.5 | 27.2 | 41.2 | 55.4 | 69.8 |
|  | 5 | 18.9 | 38.1 | 57.6 | 77.5 | 97.6 |
|  | 7 | 30.4 | 61.2 | 92.4 | 124.2 | 156.4 |

Assumptions:
The jump date is the end of the deferral period. The backspread is 600 basis points and the Treasury rate is 8.5% for all maturities. Thus, the deferred coupon bond always yields 14.5%.

important. Like the subordination adjustment, however, it is a "soft" number. It will vary from firm to firm. Moreover, not enough issues exist from a single borrower to establish the complete term structure. Nonetheless, by careful credit analysis, we can assess whether the term structure of credit spreads is upward or downward sloping, and thus determine approximately what the differential should be between extremely short-term bonds and extremely long-term bonds.

In a leveraged buyout or recapitalization without deferred interest liabilities, we would expect credit spreads to be *downward* sloping. This is because the riskiest period for a highly leveraged company is the first couple of years, when leverage is highest and bank amortization and bank covenants are the most aggressive. In the case of a company with deferred coupon bonds or PIKs, we would expect an *upward* sloping credit spread. This is because of the relatively low cash requirements in the first couple of years (resulting from high non-cash interest payments) and because of the much higher cash interest requirements once the interest deferral periods ends. As this moment approaches, the credit risk increases.

## IV. ASSESSING RELATIVE VALUE

In this section, we show how to compare the relative values of a deferred coupon bond and a conventional bond. Our procedure is to first determine the price of the conventional bond, correct it for the four influences discussed in the previous section, and finally compute the "fair value" of the deferred coupon bond, which we can then compare with the actual value. This procedure assumes that the conventional bond is priced "fairly" and that the deferred coupon bond may be mispriced.

## Computing the Fair Value of the Deferred Coupon Bond

To compute the fair value of the deferred coupon bond, we begin with the conventional bond. We then make each of the four corrections.

*Step 1:* *Create a non-callable conventional bond.*
We do this by adding the value of the call option to the price of the bond, using equation (1).

*Step 2:* *Specify the shape of the credit spread curve.*
One simplification we often use is to assume there are only two credit spreads: a frontspread $S_F$, which applies for the first X years, and a backspread $S_B$, which applies thereafter. The frontspread can, but need not, coincide with the zero period. We must specify the relation between the spreads (e.g., the backspread is 200 basis points greater than the frontspread). The analyst determines the number of years during which the frontspread is applicable. It should be based on a firm-specific credit analysis.

*Step 3:* *Calculate the frontspread and the backspread.*
To compute these, we use the relationship specified in Step 2, along with the price of a non-callable bond and the zero coupon yield curve. We show the calculation in Appendix B.

*Step 4:* *Define the subordination correction.*
If the deferred coupon bond does not have the same standing in bankruptcy as the conventional bond, we must figure out the appropriate subordination correction (in basis points).

*Step 5:* *Price a non-callable deferred coupon bond.*
Using the backspread, the subordination correction, and the Treasury zero coupon yield curve, we can easily price a non-callable deferred coupon bond. See the calculation in Appendix B.

*Step 6:* *Find the fair value of the callable deferred coupon bond.*
To do this, we must value the option on the non-callable deferred coupon bond, based on the fair value of the non-callable bond. We then subtract the option value from the fair value calculated in Step 5.

*Step 7:* *Compare the fair value of the callable deferred coupon bond with the actual price.*
If the fair value is less than the actual price, the bond is expensive relative to the conventional bond. If the fair value is greater than the actual price, the bond is cheap relative to the conventional bond.

Note that our computation of the fair value of the callable deferred bond takes into account the four determinants discussed in Section III: subordination, call protection, the shape of the Treasury yield curve, and the term structure of credit spreads.

### An Illustration

We can demonstrate this procedure with an actual example. Consider two Southland issues:

Conventional Bond:

> 15.75%            Matures 12/15/97   Price = 104.00
> First call 12/15/92 @ 105   Par call 12/15/94
> Call value 2.89

Zero:

> 16.5%            Matures 12/15/97   Price = 64.0
> Par call anytime
> Call value .44

We have designed a program that, given a backspread-frontspread differential, calculates the frontspread and the backspread to match the price of the non-callable conventional bond. Using the zero yield curve and the calculated backspread, we can easily compute the price of an optionless zero. To arrive at the fair price of the callable deferred bond, we simply subtract the value of the option from the price of the zero.

Using this program, we assume alternative credit spread differentials and compute the fair price of the zero.

| Backspread minus Frontspread | Fair Price of Zero |
|:---:|:---:|
| 200 | 69.98 |
| 300 | 69.79 |
| 400 | 69.61 |
| 500 | 69.37 |

*Note that even at a 500 basis point difference between the backspread and the frontspread, the zero is still worth 69.37—5.37 more than its actual cost of 64.00. Thus, the zero appears to be underpriced relative to the conventional bond.*

Prices in this instance are insensitive to the backspread-frontspread differential. This is because the differential is in effect only until the end of the deferral period in 2½ years. If the deferral period were longer, the effect would be more pronounced. In addition, the higher the fair price of a non-callable zero, the more valuable the call option. This further narrows the difference between the fair price of callable zeroes at different backspread-frontspread differentials.

An alternative method for relative value calculations, developed in Appendix C, allows us to calculate the yield over the deferral period. This yield is based on today's zero prices and the forward price at the end of the deferral period. We calculate the forward price to equate the deferred coupon bond with the conventional bond. This method is mathematically equivalent to the method discussed in the text.

Exhibit 8 shows the actual price of zeroes vis-à-vis the fair price. As you can see, the fair prices for zeroes are much higher than the market prices for most of these issues. To some participants in the market, the vaues may seem so high as to be counter-intuitive. For example, the Southland Sr. at a fair price of 69.98 yields 13.73% to call. Remember that based on the pricing of the conventional bond, this bond would almost surely be called and would trade like a very short bond maturing on December 15, 1990. The 13.73% yield is roughly the appropriate Treasury zero rate plus the backspread of 579 basis points. Our analysis indicates that these zeroes are currently undervalued by the market and thus may represent good value for buy-and-hold investors. Of course, this analysis does not imply that a market realignment will occur over a short holding period.

## V. SUMMARY

We have argued in this article that simply looking at yields and yield spreads on deferred coupon bonds can give investors a misleading impression of the relative attractiveness of these securities. For example, if the yield curve is steeper than it has been historically, yield spreads will be wider than normal. This does not necessarily represent a good buying opportunity.

The article presents two different ways to look at the relative value of deferred coupon bonds. An arbitrage approach allows investors to establish whether a deferred coupon bond is so cheap that it can be combined with Treasury zeroes to create a cheap synthetic bond with cash flows similar to those of the conventional bond. This approach, while appealing, is not always applicable. The synthetic bond may be less attractive than the conventional bond, as Treasuries are expensive relative to high yield instruments.

An alternative approach is more generally applicable. We show that a full evaluation of relative value in deferred coupon bonds explicitly takes into account four fundamental influences on the pricing of deferred coupon bonds—the term structure of Treasury rates, the term structure of credit spreads, the differential value of the call protection, and the value of the subordination. We show how to compute the "fair value" of these securities, given a "fairly priced" conventional bond and knowledge of the four determinants. We can then compare this fair value with the actual market price.

**EXHIBIT 8**
**ACTUAL VERSUS FAIR PRICE OF SELECTED ZEROES (BASED ON APRIL 7, 1988 SETTLEMENT)**

| Issuer | $S_B - S_F$ | Sub. Cor. | Actual Price of Zero | Fair Price of Zero | Excess of Fair Price Over Actual Price |
|---|---|---|---|---|---|
| Borg 13 | 150 | 50 | 44.38 | 50.79 | 6.41 |
| Borg 14 | 150 | 0 | 52.38 | 57.29 | 4.91 |
| Burlington | 150 | 50 | 44.75 | 50.48 | 5.73 |
| Container | 100 | 0 | 69.25 | 73.34 | 4.09 |
| Eckerd | 150 | 0 | 66.50 | 71.39 | 4.89 |
| HBJ | 150 | 50 | 56.75 | 61.19 | 4.44 |
| Macy's | 150 | 50 | 47.00 | 53.41 | 6.41 |
| Nat Gypsum | 200 | 50 | 62.25 | 62.95 | .70 |
| Owens-Corning | 100 | 50 | 66.50 | 72.94 | 6.44 |
| Owens-Illinois | 150 | 50 | 50.25 | 54.82 | 4.57 |
| Southland Sr. | 200 | 0 | 64.00 | 69.98 | 5.98 |
| Southland Jr. | 200 | 50 | 44.75 | 52.18 | 7.43 |
| Super Gen'l | 150 | 50 | 48.25 | 52.38 | 4.13 |

## APPENDIX A—ANALYSIS OF ARBITRAGE OPPORTUNITIES

Elaborating on the discussion in Section II, we provide here an in-depth analysis of arbitrage opportunities for the high yield bonds listed in Exhibits 1, 4, 5 and 8. The prices are as of March 31, 1988, for settlement on April 7, 1988.

### 1. Borg Warner

| Rank | Coupon | Worst Case | Yield to Worst |
|------|--------|------------|----------------|
| SR SUB | 12.75% | Yield to Maturity | 13.12% |
| SR SUB | 0/14% | YTM | 14.82% |
| SUB | 0/13% | YTM | 15.61% |

The yield to '99 maturity on the 0/14% synthetic is 13.71%. The yield to maturity for a conventional bond is 13.12%. Thus, an arbitrage exists to pick up 59 basis points for a synthetic *pari passu* bond between the 12.75%'s and the 0/14%'s. The 0/13% is more heavily subordinated. The junior bond can be created synthetically for a 13.87% YTM, and the investor is rewarded with only 16 basis points for a longer junior bond.

### 2. Burlington

| Rank | Coupon | Worst Case | Yield to Worst |
|------|--------|------------|----------------|
| SUB | 14.25% | Yield to Call '94 | 13.02% |
| JR SUB | 0/16% | YTC '93 | 14.73% |

The yield to call on the synthetic is 11.97%. The yield to call on the conventional bond is 13.02%. No arbitrage exists.

### 3. Container Corp.

| Rank | Coupon | Worst Case | Yield to Worst |
|------|--------|------------|----------------|
| SR SUB | 12.375% | YTC '93 | 11.43% |
| SUB | 0/16.75% | YTC '91 | 12.00% |

The synthetic bond has an 8.98% yield to call in 1991, versus an 11.43% yield to a '93 call on the conventional. No arbitrage exists.

### 4. Jack Eckerd

| Rank | Coupon | Worst Case | Yield to Worst |
|------|--------|------------|----------------|
| SUB | 11.125% | YTM | 12.21% |
| SR SUB | 0/13% | YTM | 13.31% |

The synthetic 0/13% has a 12.86% YTM versus 12.21% on the underlying bond. The investor can pick up 65 basis points and gain seniority on all cash flows through 1996. An arbitrage exists.

### 5. Harcourt Brace Jovanovich

| Rank | Coupon | Worst Case | Yield to Worst |
|------|--------|------------|----------------|
| SUB | 13.75% | YTC '94 | 12.31% |
| JR SUB | 0/14.75% | YTC '94 | 13.71% |

Yields are 12.31% for the coupon bond versus 10.94% for the synthetic to the same call date. No arbitrage exists.

### 6. Macy's

| Rank | Coupon | Worst Case | Yield to Worst |
|------|--------|------------|----------------|
| SUB | 14.5%–'01 | YTM | 14.63% |
| JR SUB | 0/16.5% | YTM | 15.51% |

The yield on the synthetic is 11.64% versus 14.63% on the conventional bond to maturity. No arbitrage exists.

### 7. National Gypsum

| Rank | Coupon | Worst Case | Yield to Worst |
|------|--------|------------|----------------|
| SR SUB | 14.50% | YTC '96 | 14.23% |
| SUB | 0/15.5% | YTC '96 | 15.50% |

The deferred coupon bond is trading at par—15.5% on both a yield-to-call and a yield-to-maturity basis. The synthetic bond can be created for a yield of 11.29% to the 1996 call and 13.24% to maturity. The 14.5% coupon bond, which is senior, trades at a yield of 14.23% to maturity, so there is no arbitrage.

### 8. Owens-Corning

| Rank | Coupon | Worst Case | Yield to Worst |
|------|--------|------------|----------------|
| SR SUB | 11.75% | YTC '91 | 11.22% |
| SUB | 0/15% | YTC '91 | 11.39% |

The synthetic can be created for a 10.41% yield to 1991 call. The yield to call on the conventional is 11.22%. Thus, there is no arbitrage.

### 9. Owens-Illinois

| Rank | Coupon | Worst Case | Yield to Worst |
|------|--------|------------|----------------|
| SUB | 12.75% | YTC '97 | 12.19% |
| JR SUB | 0/15% | YTC '93 | 13.72% |

The synthetic yields 11.62% to 1993 call versus 12.19% to 1997 call for the coupon bond. No arbitrage exists.

### 10. Southland Sr.

| Rank | Coupon | Worst Case | Yield to Worst |
|------|--------|------------|----------------|
| SR SUB | 15¾% | YTC '94 | 14.77% |
| SR SUB | 0/16½% | YTM | 16.75% |

The yield is 14.58% to maturity for synthetic senior 0/16.5% versus 14.77% to par call for the conventional bond. It is irrational to assume that the 15.75% bond would be called and the 16.5% deferred coupon would not. That is, at the call date the issuer would buy 16½%'s in the market—driving the price up to par. Thus, an arbitrage exists.

## 11. Southland Jr.

| Rank | Coupon | Worst Case | Yield to Worst |
|------|--------|------------|----------------|
| SUB | 16¾% | YTC '96 | 15.77% |
| JR SUB | 0/18% | YTM | 18.14% |

The yield is 15.77% to maturity for the synthetic bond versus 15.77% to call for the coupon bond. A subordination adjustment is required. No arbitrage exists.

## 12. Supermarket General

| Rank | Coupon | Worst Case | Yield to Worst |
|------|--------|------------|----------------|
| SUB | 14% | YTC '95 | 12.80% |
| JR SUB | 0/13.125% | YTM | 14.70% |

The yield is 13.52% for the synthetic to '03 versus 12.80% to call on the conventional bond. The pickup is 72 basis points for the longer, subordinated bond.

### APPENDIX B—CALCULATING THE FAIR VALUE OF THE DEFERRED COUPON BOND

To calculate the frontspread and the backspread, we proceed as follows:

Given the price of a non-callable bond, the Treasury zero yield curve, and the relationship between the frontspread and the backspread, we would use the following equation:

Present value of option less bond =

$$
\sum_{i=1}^{2k} \frac{c/2}{\left(1+r_i/2+S_F/2\right)^i} + \sum_{i=2k+1}^{m} \frac{c/2}{\left(1+r_i/2+S_B/2\right)^i}
$$

$$
+ \frac{100}{\left(1+r_m/2+S_B/2\right)^m}
$$

where:  $r_i$ is the risk-free rate at time i.
       c is the coupon rate.
       2k is the date accrual begins.
       m is the maturity date.

This equation assumes that the frontspread coincides with the accrual period, but it need not.

Once we specify $q$—the difference between the backspread and the frontspread—we need to calculate only one of these in solving for the yield to maturity, as $S_F + q = S_B$. That is, we have one non-linear equation with one unknown.

To price a non-callable deferred coupon bond, we need to know the backspread, the subordination correction, and the risk-free zero coupon yield curve. We can obtain the price from the following equation:

Fair value of non-callable zero =

$$\sum_{i=2k+1}^{m} \frac{c_z/2}{\left(1 + r_i/2 + S_B/2 + w/2\right)^i} + \frac{100}{\left(1 + r_m/2 + S_B/2 + w/2\right)^m}$$

where:  w is the subordination correction in basis points per annum.
      $c_z$ is the coupon on the zero.
      2k + 1 is the semi-annual period in which the first coupon is paid (the first coupon begins to accrue on day 2k and is paid on 2k + 1).

## APPENDIX C—COMPUTING THE IMPLIED YIELD OVER THE ZERO PERIOD

In Section IV, we showed how to calculate the relative value of a deferred coupon bond vis-à-vis a conventional bond in price terms. We can also calculate relative value in yield terms.

We must first compute a forward price of the bond at the end of the deferral period. Given today's price, we can calculate the yield that will equal the forward price. This methodology assumes that by the first accrual date, the deferred bond will be trading at fair value. That is, as of that date, there is no difference between the deferred coupon bond and the conventional bonds; the deferred coupon bond will be paying coupons, just like a conventional bond. This calculation, then, front loads the relative differences between these instruments into the deferral period.

Steps 1-4 are exactly the same as those described in Section IV.

Step 5: Calculate the forward price of the deferred coupon bond, assuming no call provisions. This is simply equal to:

(Fair value of non-callable zero) $\times (1 + r_{2k}/2 + S_B/2 + w/2)^{2k}$

The first part of this expression is today's value of a non-callable deferred coupon bond today. The second part is the compounded value of \$1 at the end of the deferral period.[4]

Step 6: Calculate the value of the option on the deferred coupon bond. Add this to the actual price of the bond to price a non-callable bond today.

Step 7: Calculate the implied yield over the deferred coupon period:

$P_{znc} (1 + y/2)^{2k} =$ Forward price of non-callable deferred coupon bond

where: $P_{znc}$ is the current price of the bond, net of the call provisions. We can say a deferred coupon bond is cheap relative to a conventional bond if the calculated yield is greater than the sum of the yield on a Treasury zero of the appropriate maturity, the backspread, and the subordination correction.

That is:

If $y > (r_{2k} + S_B + w)$, then the zero is "cheap."

We can also express this yield, $y$, as a spread over the Treasury rate. It can be interpreted as the spread that is consistent with the pricing of the conventional bond.

To illustrate this point, we can again use the example of the Southland 15.75% conventional bond versus the 16.5% zero. We assume a 300 basis-point difference between the frontspread and the backspread. The fair yield for the deferral period is the yield on the appropriate Treasury zero plus the backspread, or 14.03%. If we assume that the forward price of the deferred coupon bond is appropriate, the actual yield for the zero period is 19.42%. Thus, the fair yield is much lower than the actual yield, again indicating that the Southland zeroes are cheap.

We can think about relative value in either price or yield terms. In price terms, we compute the fair price relative to the actual price. In yield terms, we compute the implied yield over the zero period. The two methods are mathematically equivalent; the deferred coupon bond will be cheap by both measures or expensive by both measures. The choice should depend on whether the user is more comfortable thinking in yield or price terms.

---

[4]This expression is equivalent to the discounting of future cash flows at the forward rate back to the beginning of the accrual period.

# PART III

# Agency, Eurobond and Foreign Bond Markets

# Trading and Investment Opportunities with Agency Securities

LAURIE S. GOODMAN, PH.D
VICE PRESIDENT
FINANCIAL STRATEGIES GROUP
GOLDMAN, SACHS & COMPANY

JUDITH JONSON
PRODUCT SPECIALIST
CITICORP

ANDREW SILVER, PH.D
SENIOR ANALYST
MOODY'S INVESTORS SERVICE

## I. INTRODUCTION

Agency securities have long been popular among buy-and-hold investors because of their yield premium over Treasury securities. However, for portfolio managers who trade more actively, there are also some good trading opportunities available in the agency market. Consider the following:

- The agency yield curve looked very steep in late October 1987, relative to the Treasury yield curve. If you had "gone short" the agency curve by buying a 10-year agency and selling a 7-year agency and "gone long" the Treasury curve by

171

buying a 7-year and selling the 10-year to take advantage of this, you could have made over $150,000 on a $10 million trade for eight days.

- Farm Credit securities traded very cheaply to other agencies and to Treasuries during their crisis period in 1985. If you had purchased certain Farm Credit securities and sold Treasuries in the 5-year area you could have made more than 1½ points in a six-week period. This type of opportunity arises from time to time.

- Agency securities that are just outside of "preferred maturity" ranges often appreciate in value relative to securities that are already in those ranges. For example, in December 1987 you could have earned more than two points in less than two months by buying a 5½-year agency (the 11.70 FHLB of 7/26/93) and selling a 5-year (the 11.10 FHLB of 11/25/92), profiting as the 5½-year security "slid" closer to the preferred 5-year range.

Each of these profit opportunities represents a different type of trade—what we call "yield curve," "agency credit," and "individual issue" trades, respectively. In Section III of this article we more fully analyze each of these trading strategies. However, before proceeding to that analysis, we provide some background information on agency securities in Section II: the characteristics of the securities and how they trade.

## II. BACKGROUND

For a variety of policy reasons, the Federal government has deemed it desirable to reduce the cost of capital for some of its more politically sensitive constituencies. For the most part, these have included farmers, homeowners, and students. To aid these relatively small borrowers, a series of legislative acts has created a network of Federally-sponsored financial intermediaries which provide credit to these borrowers at a lower cost than would otherwise be available to them.

The Federally-sponsored agencies issue securities in large blocks in the open market. The proceeds are then lent once again to intermediaries who distribute loans to targeted borrowers.

Though there are no explicit or implicit Federal guarantees of the securities issued by the Federally-sponsored agencies, the general market perception that the government would ultimately "cover" any defaults causes these securities to come to market at yields which are below those on most corporate securities, though slightly above the Treasury's cost of funding.

In this article, we make a distinction between Federal agencies and Federally-*sponsored* agencies. Federal agencies are direct arms of the U.S. government. Since 1973, they have not issued debt; their funds have been raised by the Treasury and passed through the Federal Financing Bank.[1] The amounts they owed at the end of June 1988 were (in millions of dollars):

| | |
|---|---:|
| Defense Department | $    11 |
| Export-Import Bank | 11,232 |
| Federal Housing Administration | 116 |
| Government National Mortgage Assn. | 830 |
| Postal Service | 5,842 |
| Tennessee Valley Authority | 18,330 |
| U.S. Railway Association | 0 |
| Federal Agency Total | $36,361 |

Since the federal agencies currently do not issue debt, we will not discuss them further in this article.

The Federally-sponsored agencies are privately owned, publicly chartered entities which raise funds in the market place. Their outstanding debt is:[2]

| | |
|---|---:|
| Financing Corporation | $  2,900 |
| Federal Home Loan Banks | 117,773 |
| Federal Home Loan Mortgage Corp. | 17,619 |
| Federal National Mortgage Assoc. | 104,757 |
| Farm Credit Banks | 55,779 |
| Student Loan Marketing Assoc. | 19,257 |
| Federally Sponsored Agency Total | $318,085 |

We will next examine the structure of the major Federally-sponsored agencies and look at the characteristics of their securities. As mentioned earlier, agriculture and home-ownership have been the largest beneficiaries of the Federally-sponsored agency system. Therefore, we will examine them by those classifications.

### Agricultural Agencies (the Federal Farm Credit Bank System)

There are three parts of the Federal Farm Credit Bank System (FFCBS), each created by a separate piece of Federal legislation. In 1916, the Federal Farm Loan Act created the Federal Land Banks (FLBs). The Federal Intermediate Credit Banks (FICBs) were organized under the Agricultural Credit Act of 1923, and finally, the Banks for Cooperatives (BCoops) were created by passage of the Farm Credit Act of

---

[1]Prior to 1973, each of the Federal agencies did issue its own debt securities. Since these issues were generally small and illiquid, they commanded a significant spread over Treasury securities. The Federal Financing Bank was organized in 1973 to address this problem.

[2]All amounts are as of June 1988. Data was obtained from the *Federal Reserve Bulletin*, November 1988.

1933. Originally, there was an FLB, an FICB, and a BCoop in each of twelve U.S. districts plus a Central Bank for Cooperatives, which together comprised the 37 Farm Credit Banks in the System. (In 1988, eight of the 12 district BCoops merged into a single institution called the National Bank for Cooperatives.)

The three networks were formed to serve different needs of the country's agricultural system, although some overlap exists. The FLBs extend first mortgage loans on agricultural properties, while the FICBs' main directive is to make available short term loans, usually for activities which tend to be seasonal in nature, such as the harvesting of crops. The Banks for Cooperatives were formed to provide loans to cooperative associations which are owned by farmers, as well as to assist farmers in obtaining operating capital and fixed assets.

The FICBs, BCoops and FLBs originally issued their own individual debt securities. In 1979, they began to issue debt on a consolidated basis as "joint and several obligations" of the entire Federal Farm Credit Bank system. (Their other functions were maintained separately.[3]) There are three types of securities issued by the System. They are:

- discount notes, with maturities from 5 to 270 days, auctioned daily;
- short-term bonds, with maturies of 3-9 months, auctioned monthly; and
- longer-term bonds, with maturities of 1-10 years.

These agencies were all originally Federally-owned, but subsequently converted to private ownership. Their securities are not guaranteed officially or unofficially by the United States government, but, given the banks' origin and other links to the Federal government,[4] it is generally considered highly unlikely that they would be permitted to default. They are fully Federally taxed, but no state or local taxes are collected on income received from the securities.

### Home Mortgage Intermediaries

The first residential mortgage agency was the Federal Home Loan Bank (FHLB) System, created in 1932. One of its main functions is to regulate the country's savings and loan associations (S&Ls, or "thrifts"), much as the Federal Reserve Bank does the nation's commercial banks. Its home office is in Washington, DC with regional banks in 12 cities. It is privately owned by the S&Ls that it regulates, but also operates under a Federal charter and is subject to Congressional legislative regulation.

---

[3]All FICB and BCoop debt issued prior to 1979 has matured. There is still some pre-1979 FLB debt outstanding, but it rarely trades.

[4]As a result of the Food Security Act of 1985, the FFCB System was provided with a mechanism for accessing Treasury funds after utilizing its own resources. Also, legislation passed in 1987 authorized the issuance of Government backed bonds to recapitalize the Farm Credit System and provided for Treasury assistance on some of those interest payments.

The main tasks of the FHLBs are to supervise thrift associations and to lend to them so they can supply mortgages at low rates. To obtain the funding for this purpose, the FHLB System issues securities in the open market. These are backed by collateral of government securities, insured mortgages, or secured advances to the S&Ls, but are not guaranteed by the Federal government. (The FHLB System does have a $4.0 billion credit line with the U.S. Treasury.) As in the case of Farm Credit securities, interest earned on the securities is taxed at the Federal, but not state or local levels. Types of securities issued include: discount notes (with less than one year to maturity) and non-callable bonds (with maturities of one to ten years).

The FHLB System also oversees the Federal Savings and Loan Insurance Corporation (FSLIC), which provides insurance on deposits up to $100,000 for the nation's S&Ls. In recent years, as a number of thrifts have run into solvency problems, there has been concern because the FSLIC does not have enough of an asset base to resolve the financial problems of the institutions that it insures. The U.S. Congress provided a plan to recapitalize the FSLIC as a part of the Competitive Equality Banking Act of 1987 (CEBA). A central part of CEBA was the creation of the Financing Corporation (FICO) as the newest Federally-sponsored agency. The purpose of FICO is to issue debt (up to a limit of $10.8 billion as of this writing) for the recapitalization of the FSLIC. To date, FICO has issued about $3 billion to non-callable 30-year bonds.[5]

In 1938, the Federal government created the Federal National Mortgage Association (commonly referred to as FNMA or Fannie Mae), the first Federally-sponsored agency whose primary purpose is to encourage the maintenance of an active secondary market for mortgages. A second agency with a similar purpose, the Federal Home Loan Mortgage Corporation (FHLMC or Freddie Mac), was created in 1970.[6] Fannie Mae and Freddie Mac purchase mortgages for sale to the secondary market and issue securities.

Both are privately owned (Fannie Mae by private stockholders and Freddie Mac by the thrift associations which belong to the Federal Home Loan Bank System) but have credit lines with the U.S. Treasury of $2.25 billion and $4 billion, respectively. Fannie Mae issues short-term discount notes, as well as coupon-bearing securities as far out as thirty years, some of which are callable.

Though Freddie Mac still issues discount notes to fund its day-to-day operations, it has issued very few longer term securities since late 1986, instead concentrating its term activities in the pass-through market.

Like the other Federally-sponsored agencies we have discussed so far, Freddie Mac securities are exempt from state and local taxation. However, Fannie Mae issues are taxed at the Federal, state, and local levels.

---

[5]Additional information concerning FICO and CEBA can be found in the next article.

[6]The Government National Mortgage Association (GNMA or Ginnie Mae) is a full Federal agency, does not issue debt, and will not be included in our discussion. A discussion of securities guaranteed by GNMA is given in several articles in this book.

The only Federally-sponsored agency that issues securities and does not serve the agricultural or housing areas is the Student Loan Marketing Association (SLMA or Sallie Mae). It is smaller than those discussed earlier but still has a noticeable market presence. SLMA issues short-term floating rate notes on a monthly basis and longer-term bonds several times per year.[7]

Agencies come to the market continuously to issue short-term discount notes for their day-to-day operational needs. They set the rates on those notes daily to reflect market conditions and their maturity preferences.

Intermediate and long-term coupon-bearing securities are sold through subscription offerings, i.e., through a syndicate of commercial banks and broker-dealers. The agencies do not issue longer-term securities on as regular a schedule as does the Treasury, and the maturities are considerably more flexible. Intermediate-term bonds are offered on a more or less monthly basis, and longer-term bonds several

**EXHIBIT 1**
**FEDERALLY-SPONSORED AGENCY COUPON-BEARING SECURITY ISSUANCE IN 1988 (IN MILLIONS OF DOLLARS)**

|  | *Maturity* | *Amount* |
|---|---|---|
| FFCB | 3 month | $10,534 |
|  | 6 month | 15,191 |
|  | 1 year | 4,585 |
|  | 2 year | 1,270 |
|  | 3 year | 550 |
| FHLB | 3 month | 1,000 |
|  | 1 year | 15,797 |
|  | 2 year | 5,820 |
|  | 3 year | 6,996 |
|  | 4 year | 1,550 |
|  | 5 year | 5,155 |
|  | 7 year | 1,530 |
|  | 10 year | 500 |
| FHLMC | 6 month | 1,500 |
| FICO | 30 year | 2,250 |
| FNMA | 3 year | 1,600 |
|  | 4 year | 2,300 |
|  | 5 year | 2,800 |
|  | 7 year | 1,200 |
|  | 10 year | 2,400 |
|  | 30 year | 200 |
| SLMA | 6 month | 4,350 |
|  | 3 year | 800 |
|  | 4 year | 300 |
|  | 5 year | 500 |
|  | 10 year | 250 |
|  | 12 year | 200 |

[7]Until late 1981, SLMA was a Federal agency which got its funding from the Federal Financing Bank.

times per year. Exhibit 1 lists, by agency, the approximate maturities and amounts of coupon-bearing debt issued in 1988.

Agency securities, like the rest of the fixed income market, generally trade at a yield spread above Treasuries. Though Federal sponsorship assures fairly low credit spreads, agency liquidity is not as high as in the Treasury market. The total amount of agency debt is currently about $350 billion, compared to about $1.8 trillion in the Treasury market. An average-sized agency debt issue is $500 million, while Treasury issues are often as large as $8-10 billion. Because the lesser liquidity of the agency market causes larger transaction costs, investors require a yield premium to invest in this market.

The yields on agency securities are generally highly correlated with yields on Treasuries. This is illustrated in Exhibits 2 and 3. Exhibit 2 shows the yield on a 5-year Farm Credit Bank security compared to that of a comparable Treasury. The correlation during the period shown was .95. Exhibit 3 plots the yields on a 10-year FNMA issue and Treasury, where the correlation is .99.

The agency yield curve is usually more steeply sloped than the Treasury yield curve. To see this, consider Exhibit 4, showing active issues on both yield curves on February 1, 1988. In the Treasury market, the total spread between the 2-year and

**EXHIBIT 2**
**YIELD LEVELS: 5 YR TREASURY VS FFCB 7.55 OF 4/22/91**
**(DAILY YIELDS, 4/20/87 TO 2/1/88)**

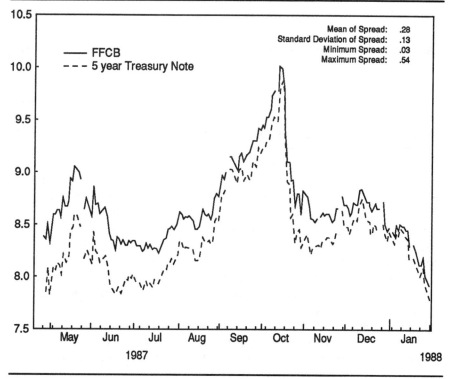

| | |
|---|---|
| Mean of Spread: | .28 |
| Standard Deviation of Spread: | .13 |
| Minimum Spread: | .03 |
| Maximum Spread: | .54 |

**EXHIBIT 3**
**YIELD LEVELS: 10 YR ACTIVE TREASURY VS FNMA 8s OF 7/10/96**
**(DAILY YIELDS, 4/20/87 TO 2/1/88)**

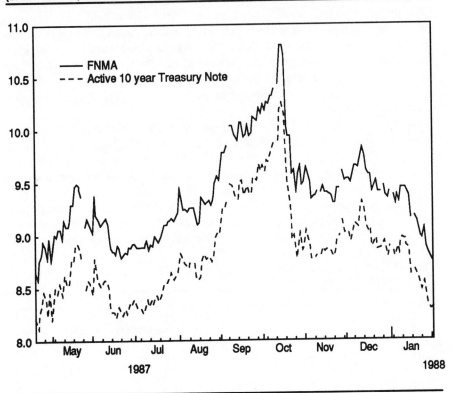

10-year active issues is 81 basis points. For the agency market it is 130 basis points. The difference between the two is compensation for less liquidity and slightly higher credit risk.

Computation of yield to maturity and accrued interest on agency securities is similar to the method used for Treasuries, but there are some important differences. These are explained and illustrated in the appendix to this article.

Within the agency market, spreads between different issues of the same agency seem to be based on factors like those in the Treasury market under normal circumstances. The most recently issued securities are the most active and therefore trade at lower yields than their more seasoned counterparts. Different agencies tend to trade at similar yields unless there is concern about the financial health of a particular agency. In this case, yields move upward to reflect concern about the possibility of default. It should be noted that though Fannie Mae securities are taxed at the state and local levels, these securities do generally have lower yields than other comparable-maturity agencies. This is probably because: 1) Fannie Mae is currently

**EXHIBIT 4**
**YIELD TO CURVE OF ACTIVE ISSUES. DATE: 2/1/88**

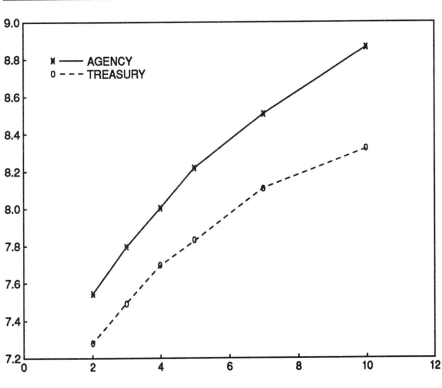

perceived to have slightly stronger quality than most other agencies, and 2) there are enough states without state and local taxes, and enough bondholders who are non-taxable, that these investors set the price.

## III. TRADING STRATEGIES

### Yield Curve Strategies

Many trades involving agency securities arise from anticipated movements in the agency yield curve. For those expected agency movements that simply reflect shifts similar to those in the Treasury yield curve, you are probably better off positioning yourself in the more liquid Treasury market, where bid-ask spreads are lower. (See Exhibit 5 for a parallel steepening of both curves.) However, the spreads between agencies and Treasuries of similar maturities are quite variable. As a result, profits can be made if you correctly anticipate these shifts and position yourself accordingly.

**EXHIBIT 5**
**PARALLEL STEEPENING IN AGENCY AND TREASURY YIELD CURVES**

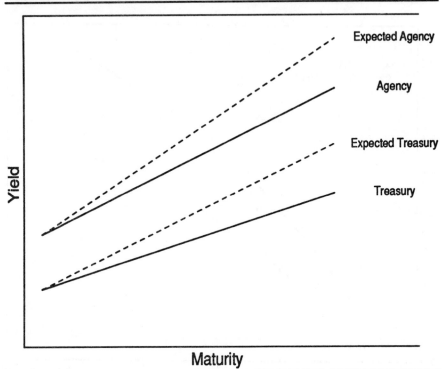

The particular positions that you should establish depend on whether you antici-pate a change in the agency-Treasury spread in a particular sector of the yield curve or whether you expect a general steepening or flattening of the agency yield curve relative to the Treasury curve, without a view about which end of the curve is going to move. In addition, the positions depend on whether you expect both curves to shift, or just the agency curve, as illustrated in the following examples.

*Trade #1: Anticipating changes in the agency-Treasury spread in a particular sector of the yield curve.*

Suppose that you thought the spread between agency and Treasury securities of a particular maturity was out of line and you expected it to realign in the near future. However, you did not know if the realignment would occur through a change in the yield on the agency security or on the Treasury security. (See Exhibit 6.)

To illustrate the point, consider that in late October 1987 the spread between 10-year agencies and Treasuries was considerably wider than it had been in the prior

**EXHIBIT 6**
**CHANGE IN AGENCY-TREASURY SPREAD IN PARTICULAR MATURITY**

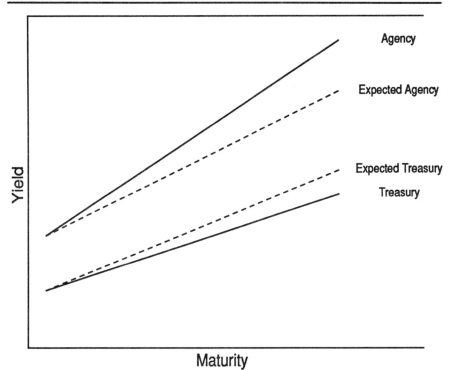

few weeks. For example, the spread between the FHLB 9.20 of 8/25/97 and the 8⅝ Treasury of 8/15/97 was 67 basis points on October 22, compared to roughly 50-55 basis points in September and the first half of October. Suppose at that time you had expected the spread to narrow.

To position yourself to take advantage of the anticipated movement, you could have bought the FHLB 9.20, financing it in the repurchase agreement (RP) market, and sold short the Treasury 8 5/8, purchasing it for forward sale in the RP market. The profitability of this trade depends on two factors. The first and most important factor is how the yield spread between the two securities behaves. Suppose you decided to unwind the trade on October 30, 1987, when the yield spread had narrowed to 50 basis points. As shown in Exhibit 7, this narrowing of 17 basis points in eight days would have represented a $110,708 profit on a $10 million trade. The second factor is the net financing costs of the transaction, that is, the difference between the rate at which you can finance the agency security and the rate at which you can "reverse in" the Treasury security. Generally, the RP financing rate is about ⅜ of 1% higher than the "reverse" rate, or about $104 per day on a $10 million trade. Factoring in the net financing costs reduces the net profit to $109,667.

**EXHIBIT 7**
**TEN-YEAR SPREAD NARROWS**

| | October 22, 1987 (Settlement October 23, 1987) | | | October 30, 1987 (Settlement November 2, 1987) | | |
|---|---|---|---|---|---|---|
| | Yield | Price plus Accrued Interest | Value of Position | Yield | Price plus Accrued Interest | Value of Position |
| 9.20 FNMA of 8/25/97 (buy) | 9.60 | $98.92 | $10,000,000 | 9.35 | $100.71 | $10,180,954 |
| 8 5/8 Treasury of 8/15/97 (sell) | 8.93 | 99.65 | −10,000,000 | 8.85 | 100.35 | −10,070,246 |
| | .67 | $ .73 | $ 0 | .50 | $ .36 | $ 110,708 |
| | | | | Net financing cost (3/8% for 10 days*) | | 1,041 |
| | | | | Net Profit | | $ 109,667 |

*Although the trade is unwound after eight days, 10/30/87 was a Friday; therefore financing costs must be paid through the following Monday.

*Trade #2: Anticipating changes in the slope of the agency curve with no change in the Treasury curve.*

Suppose you thought that the agency yield curve was "too steep" in a particular maturity range and would subsequently flatten, either through an increase in the yield on the shorter-term security or a decrease in the yield on the longer-term security. At the same time, you expected the Treasury yield curve to remain unchanged. (See Exhibit 8.) For example, suppose that, again on October 22, you expected the 40 basis point spread between the FHLB 9.20 of 8/25/97 (the 10-year) and the FHLB 8.50 of 4/15/94 (the 7-year) to narrow, but felt that the Treasury curve in that range would remain unchanged. (On that date, the 10- and 7-year Treasuries were yielding 8.93 and 8.83, respectively, for a spread of 10 basis points.) Then you could have positioned yourself by buying the 9.20s FHLB and selling short the 8.50s FHLB. However, note that the size of the 10-year trade should be smaller than that of the 7-year trade to account for the larger price-sensitivity (duration) of the 10-year issue. (If you used equal-sized trades, then you would lose money even if the agency yield curve flattened, but the general level of rates increased.)

**EXHIBIT 8**
**CHANGE IN SLOPE OF AGENCY CURVE: NO CHANGE IN TREASURY CURVE**

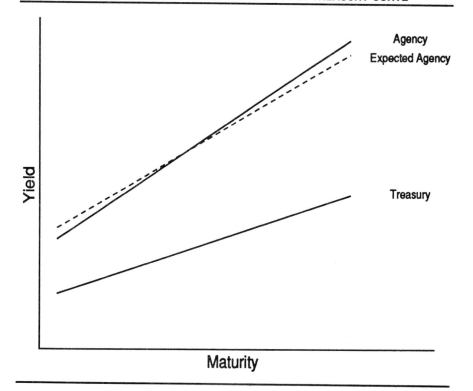

**EXHIBIT 9**
**FLATTENING OF THE AGENCY YIELD CURVE**

| | October 22, 1987 (Settlement October 23, 1987) | | | October 30, 1987 (Settlement November 2, 1987) | | | |
|---|---|---|---|---|---|---|---|
| | Yield | Price plus Accrued Interest | Value of Position | Yield | Accrued Interest | Value of Position | Change In Value of Position |
| 9.20 FNMA of 8/25/97 (buy) | 9.60 | $ 98.92 | $10,000,000 | 9.35 | $100.71 | $10,180,954 | $180,954 |
| 8.5 FNMA of 4/25/94 (sell) | 9.20 | $100.78 | −$13,341,176 | 9.09 | 101.57* | −13,445,756 | 104,580 |
| | .40 | −$ 1.86 | −$ 3,341,176 | .26 | −$ .86 | −$ 3,264,802 | $ 76,374 |
| | | | | Net financing cost (3/8% for 10 days) | | | 1,041 |
| | | | | Net Profit | | | $ 75,333 |

*Includes coupon drop on 10/25/87 which must be paid.

Exhibit 9 indicates that if you had bought $10 million of the 9.20s and sold the correct amount of the 8.50s (approximately $13.3 billion) to protect yourself against general interest rate increases and then you unwound the trades on October 30, you would have made $75,333. This would have been your net profit, after accounting for bid-ask spreads and net financing costs.

As a general strategy, if you had expected the agency spread to *widen* and the Treasury curve to remain unchanged, you should have *bought* the 8.50s FHLB and *shorted* the 9.20s FHLB. In this particular case, of course, that strategy would have resulted in a large loss.

*Trade #3: Anticipating changes in the relative slopes of the agency and Treasury yield curves.*

Now suppose that on October 22, 1987 you were not sure that the spread between 7- and 10-year agencies would narrow, but you did think that the slope of the agency yield curve between 7 and 10 years was too steep relative to the Treasury curve. In other words, you thought that *either* the agency curve would flatten or the Treasury curve would steepen in that range. (See Exhibit 10.) How should you have positioned yourself to take advantage of this expected movement?

This would have required four positions. You should have bought the 10-year agency and sold short the 7-year agency to take advantage of any flattening of the agency curve, and sold short the 10-year Treasury and bought the 7-year Treasury to gain from a steepening of the Treasury curve. Note, again, that the size of both 10-year trades should have been smaller than that of the 7-year trades to account for the larger price-sensitivity of the 10-year issues.

As Exhibit 11 indicates, if you unwound these positions on October 30, 1987, this would have been somewhat more profitable than the simpler Trade #2. This is because you were correct on both counts; the agency curve flattened (as in Trade #2), and the Treasury curve steepened.

We have described this four-position trade as a pair of two-position trades. One trade involved the agency yield curve, trading a 7-year agency versus a 10-year agency, while the other involved the Treasury yield curve, trading a 7-year Treasury versus a 10-year Treasury. However, we could have alternatively described it as a pair of trades across markets, where one involved a 7-year agency and a 7-year Treasury and the other involved a 10-year agency and a 10-year Treasury. Looked at this way, we expected the 7-year spread to widen and/or the 10-year spread to narrow. But whichever way you look at it, it involves the same four positons: short the 7-year agency, long the 7-year Treasury, long the 10-year agency, and short the 10-year Treasury.

In fact, any trade involving agencies can be put into this framework. For example, Trade #1 can be thought of as a special case of the "inter-market" second view, where only the 10-year agency-Treasury trade was implemented because the 7-year spread, implicitly at least, was expected to remain unchanged. In other words, you

**EXHIBIT 10**
**CHANGE IN RELATIVE SLOPE OF AGENCIES AND TREASURIES**

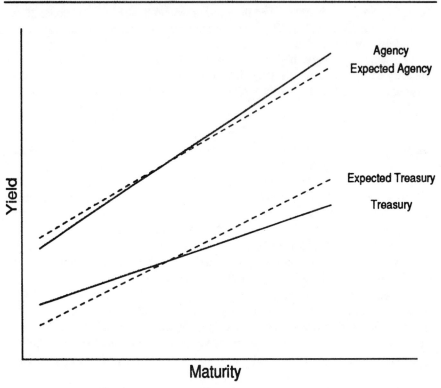

expected that executing the 7-year trade would have just resulted in additional transactions and financing costs. (In fact, you would have *lost* money on the trade.) On the other hand, Trade #2 is a special case of the first view in which the trades are looked at as yield curve plays. Here, only the agency yield curve was expected to shift, so it was unnecessary to put on a trade involving the Treasury curve, which again would have just added unnecessary transactions and financing costs.

### Agency Credit Quality Trade

Experienced players in the agency market have found that some of their best trading has involved taking advantage of the market's perception of the credit quality of a particular agency. In general, the market does not seem to react to the deteriorating financial condition of an agency until it receives extensive attention (by, for example, a newspaper article). Therefore, it has been possible to profit by acting on a judgment about an agency's underlying economic condition before media attention

# EXHIBIT 11
## RELATIVE FLATTENING OF THE AGENCY YIELD CURVE

| | October 22, 1987 (Settlement October 23, 1987) | | | October 30, 1987 (Settlement November 2, 1987) | | | |
|---|---|---|---|---|---|---|---|
| | Yield | Price plus Accrued Interest | Value of Position | Yield | Price Plus Accrued Interest | Change In Value of Position | Value of Position |
| 9.20 FNMA of 8/25/97 (buy) | 9.60 | $ 98.92 | $10,000,000 | 9.35 | $100.71 | $10,180,954 | $180,954 |
| 8.5 FHLB of 4/25/94 (sell) | 9.20 | $100.78 | -$13,341,176 | 9.09 | 101.57* | -13,445,756 | 104,580 |
| | .40 | -$ 1.86 | -$ 3,341,176 | .26 | -$ .86 | -$ 3,264,802 | $ 76,374 |
| | | | | Net financing cost (3/8% for 10 days) | | | 1,041 |
| | | | | Net Profit | | | $ 75,333 |
| Treasury 8⅝ of 8/15/97 (sell) | 8.93 | $ 99.65 | -$10,000,000 | 8.85 | $100.35 | -$10,070,246 | -$ 70,246 |
| Treasury 9½ of 10/15/94 (buy) | 8.83 | $103.65 | 12,604,826 | 8.64 | 104.88 | 12,754,406 | 149,580 |
| | .10 | -$ 4.00 | $ 2,604,826 | .21 | -$ 4.53 | $ 2,684,160 | $ 79,334 |
| | | | | Net financing cost (3/8% for 10 days) | | | 1,041 |
| | | | | Net Profit | | | $ 78,293 |
| | | | | Total Net Profit | | | $153,626 |

*Includes coupon paid out on 10/25/87.

was focused on it. Furthermore, once this "crisis" has become the center of attention, additional opportunities exist for outguessing the market on the resolution of the problem. In the past, the market has tended to overreact to negative publicity, at least in retrospect; recent crises have been resolved in such a way that spreads soon returned to more "normal" levels. In addition, it is interesting to note that when a particular agency is perceived as weak, the credit spreads for other agencies widen as well, offering additional trading opportunities. The case histories of the Farm Credit and Fannie Mae crises will illustrate these points.

**The Farm Credit Crisis.** The Farm Credit System has experienced great financial difficulties over the past few years. It has been necessary to pass legislation on two occasions to aid the System—the first bailout was in October 1985, while additional legislation was passed in late 1987. During the first half of 1985, two of the Intermediate Credit Banks, Spokane and Omaha, which are part of the Farm Credit System, sought long-term credit assistance. The assistance plans were worked out by mid-July 1985. An analysis of the Farm Credit System at that point would have revealed that the two Intermediate Credit Banks were only the tip of the iceberg—it was the first problem area to surface only because the Intermediate Credit Banks made shorter term loans (all were under five years, most were under 18 months) than the other banks in the system. The conditions of the Federal Land Banks, whose loans make up two-thirds of the loans outstanding of the Farm Credit System, were of much more serious concern. Federal Land Bank loans have maturities between 5 and 40 years. These loans were made for a high percentage of the value of the land at the time. Given the substantial drop in land values from an average of $825 per acre in 1982 to an average of $679 per acre in 1985, the collateral was inadequate. Moreover, the outlook for the cash flow of the borrowers was grim. Nonetheless, Farm Credit securities did not trade substantially differently from FNMA or FHLBB securities.

On July 22, 1985 the *Wall Street Journal* ran an article entitled "Farm Credit System Could Collapse Unless it Reorganizes . . ." which discussed the results of a study conducted during the spring. The study painted a darker picture of the System that had previously been brought to the public's attention. Spreads on the 5-year Farm Credit security—the 11.35 of 4/20/90—widened from 28 to 39 basis points over the 5-year Treasury (11⅜ of 5/15/90) on that day, and widened further to 45 basis points over the next two weeks. Although the article contained no new information, the market reacted strongly. Thereafter, despite no new development to change the basic outlook, the spread returned to 33 basis points over the 5-year Treasury by September 3.

During the period from September 3 to September 9, 1985 there was a barrage of unfavorable press. These articles contained a recognition on the part of the Farm Credit officials that the Farm Credit System was not in good shape, and could need Federal assistance within the next two years. There was no formal request for Federal assistance. The spread widened to 83 basis points. At this point, many buy-and-hold investors and portfolio managers began to sell off their holdings of Farm

Credit securities. There were relatively few non-dealers who were increasing their purchases of Farm Credit securities. As a result of this and the widely anticipated announcement of a third-quarter loss, spreads widened to 105 basis points on October 23. Note that the condition of the Farm Credit system was not fundamentally different than in mid-July, 1985. Press coverage had merely increased public awareness of the problems and spreads increased from 28 basis points to 105 basis points. (See Exhibit 12.)

In late October, Farm Credit officials formally sought Federal assistance. The reception by the House of Representatives was initially cool. On October 30, 1985 the press revealed that top Administration officials agreed to recommend support for a credit line for the system. The spread narrowed to 80 basis points that day. The support bill, as expected, easily cleared the Senate. The House Agriculture Committee recommended a bail-out bill on December 5 which was close to the Senate bill. It looked as if the bill would pass the House. As a result, the spread dropped from 70 basis points to 55 basis points. From the market's point of view, the crisis was now over, although the bill was not signed until late in the month. Spreads narrowed further to a level of 40-45 basis points over the next year.

**EXHIBIT 12**
**YIELD SPREAD: FFCB 11.35 OF 4/20/90 LESS TREASURY 11% OF 5/15/90**
**(WEEKLY AVERAGES MAY 10, 1985 TO JANUARY 29, 1988)**

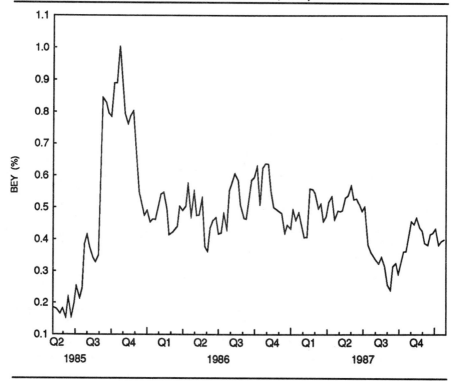

It is also useful to examine what happened to other agencies during this crisis. Exhibit 13 shows the spread between the FNMA 11.15 maturing 5/10/90 and the Treasury 11⅜ maturing 5/15/90. It is interesting that despite no change in the financial status of Fannie Mae, its spreads widened to Treasuries. (Indeed, as interest rates declined dramatically over this period, FNMA should have looked even stronger from a credit point of view.)

Of course, FNMA and FHLB spreads did not rise nearly as much as those on Farm Credit securities. Exhibit 14 shows the spread between the FFCB 11.35 of 4/20/90 and the FNMA 11.15 maturing 5/10/90. This spread widened considerably during the Farm Credit crisis.

The Farm Credit crisis in 1985 illustrates the market's typical pattern of a delayed reaction and then a very strong reaction as the news becomes known. If you had anticipated the public response and the subsequent correction, you could have easily taken advantage of it in the market.

**EXHIBIT 13**
**YIELD SPREAD: FNMA 11.15 OF 5/10/90 LESS TREASURY 11⅜ OF 5/15/90**
**(WEEKLY AVERAGES MAY 10, 1985 TO JANUARY 29, 1988)**

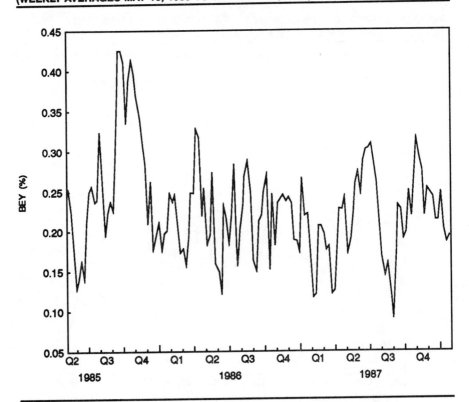

Assume, for example, that an investor had purchased the 5-year Farm Credit security, and shorted the 5-year Treasury note on October 24, 1985 at a spread of 105 basis points. Furthermore, assume the trade had been unwound on December 7, 1985 at a 55 basis point spread. The trade would have been as follows:

October 24, 1985 (for settlement October 25, 1985)

| | | | |
|---|---|---|---|
| Buy FFCB 11.35 | maturing 4/20/90 | price 101:28 | yield 10.81 |
| Sell treasury 11.375 | maturing 5/15/90 | price 105:26 | yield  9.76 |

Price spread 3:30 Yield spread 105 b.p.

December 7, 1985 (for settlement December 10, 1985)

| | | | |
|---|---|---|---|
| Sell FFCB 11.35 | maturing 4/20/90 | price 105:12 | yield 9.80 |
| Buy treasury 11.375 | maturing 5/15/90 | price 107:18 | yield 9.25 |

Price spread 2:06 Yield spread 55 b.p.

**EXHIBIT 14**
**YIELD SPREAD: FFCB 11.35 OF 4/20/90 LESS FNMA 11.15 OF 5/10/90 (WEEKLY AVERAGES MAY 10, 1985 TO JANUARY 29, 1988)**

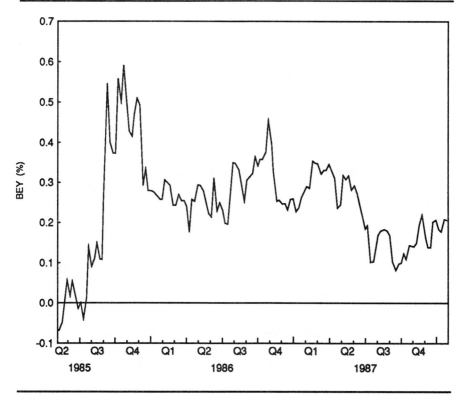

The gross profit on this trade would be 1:24. The financing costs of ⅜% per day would be roughly .003750 × 46/360 or 4.8 basis points. This is equivalent to 5/32. Since the coupons on these securities are nearly identical, the interest paid and received would be virtually the same and can be excluded from the calculations. Thus, the net profit on the trade would be a very hefty 5/32.

This trade also could have been put on by purchasing the Farm Credit securities and shorting another agency of the same maturity—for example, the FNMA 11.15 maturing 5/10/90. The trade would have been as follows:

October 24, 1985 (for settlement October 25, 1985)

| | | | |
|---|---|---|---|
| Buy FFCB 11.35 | maturing 4/20/90 | price 101:28 | yield 10.81 |
| Sell FNMA 11.15 | maturing 5/10/90 | price 103:16 | yield 10.17 |

Price spread—1:20 Yield spread 64 b.p.

December 7, 1985 (for settlement December 10, 1985)

| | | | |
|---|---|---|---|
| Sell FFCB 11.35 | maturing 4/20/90 | price 105:12 | yield 9.80 |
| Buy FNMA 11.15 | maturing 5/10/90 | price 106:00 | yield 9.45 |

Price spread 0:20 Yield spread 35 b.p.

This trade would not have been quite as profitable, as the FNMA spread to Treasuries opened up as well. It would, however, have provided protection against a general widening of agency spreads.

From the end of 1985 through the first half of 1987, spreads between Farm Credit issues and Treasuries remained fairly constant—lower than during the crisis period in 1985, but considerably higher than for other agencies. For example, as shown in Exhibits 12 and 13, the spread on the FFCB 11.35 of 4/90 ranged roughly from 40-55 basis points in the period, while the spread on a comparable FNMA issue was only 15-30 basis points. This additional credit premium on FFCB securities was because of continuing problems in the agricultural sector and losses suffered by the Farm Credit System. In response to these problems, Congress began considering legislation to assist the System in mid-1987, passing the Agricultural Credit Act of 1987 in December of that year. The law provided for a bond-financed capital infusion to the System, as well as for the merging of a number of BCoops, FICBs, and FLBs. During 1988, these provisions began to go into effect; spreads of Farm Credit System securities to Treasuries gradually narrowed as the market perception became that the Farm Credit System problem would be satisfactorily resolved over time.

**The FNMA Crisis.** In 1981, FNMA securities came under a great deal of pressure in the financial markets. Exhibit 15 shows a FNMA security vis-à-vis a comparable Treasury security. Essentially, this was a reaction to the sharp rise in interest rates in 1980 and 1981. Three-month LIBOR, which stood at 11.24% in January 1979 rose

**EXHIBIT 15**
**YIELD SPREAD: FNMA 9.30 OF 6/12/89 LESS TREASURY 10¾ OF 11/15/89**
**(MONTHLY AVERAGES, JANUARY 1980 TO JANUARY 1988)**

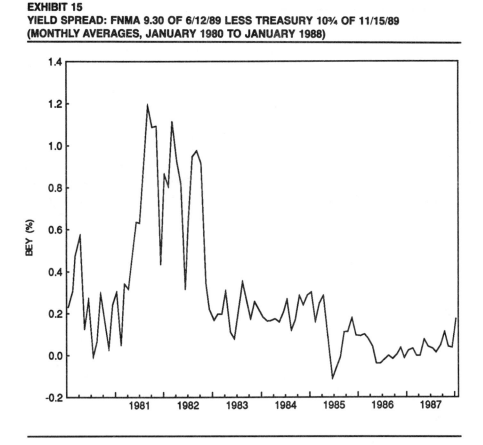

to 19.11% by May of 1981. The 10-year Treasury rate, which stood at 9.10% at the beginning of 1979, rose to 15.32% by September 1981. The problem for FNMA was that, at the time, it held a large portfolio of fixed-rate mortgages. By January of 1980, with the rise in interest rates, the average cost spread of outstanding debt rose above the average yield on the portfolio. This negative spread persisted through 1980 and resulted in a portfolio loss of $41.7 million for the year. In 1981, the negative spread between average yield and average borrowing cost worsened. By September 30, it had reached a negative 1.90%. It improved to negative 1.57% by year-end 1981. The portfolio loss for the four quarters totalled $484.8 million.

Note in Exhibit 15 we see the same pattern as in the Farm Credit case—a delayed reaction and then what turned out to be an overreaction. Despite FNMA's substantially widening negative margins throughout 1980 and the first part of 1981, the market did not demand a large premium for holding the securities until the summer of 1981. At that point, the market reacted strongly, with spreads to a comparable

Treasury reaching 150 basis points. As the market became aware of the situation and began to react, spreads widened a great deal. Buy-and-hold portfolio managers then began to dump their holdings, and the spread widened even more. As the panic cleared and interest rates fell, spreads between FNMAs and Treasuries narrowed.

**The FSLIC Recapitalization Plan.** In both of the instances discussed above, we saw a market overreaction to the credit condition of a particular agency. The same thing may happen to FHLB and perhaps FICO securities due to the FSLIC recapitalization, as the savings and loan crisis is resolved.

As was mentioned earlier, the FSLIC, the insurance fund for the savings and loan industry, is in deep financial trouble. There are potential problems in over 200 institutions, and the system is reportedly losing about $1 billion per month. Estimates of the total cost of resolution of the problem are on the order of $50 to $100 billion—the FSLIC has only a few billion dollars in reserves, which come from industry assessments from the institutions which it insures.

The first attempt to address the shortfall—the FSLIC recapitalization plan—was passed in the summer of 1987 as Title III of the Competitive Equality Banking Act of 1987 (CEBA). It created the Financing Corporation (FICO), which is a separate legal entity with sponsored-agency status in terms of tax treatment, collateral eligibility, and SEC exemption.

FICO was authorized to issue up to $11 billion of debt by 1991; the proceeds would be transferred to FSLIC in order to resolve the caseload of troubled thrifts.

This solution was regarded by most market observers as a temporary one, and in fact, since the passage of CEBA, the thrift crisis has continued to worsen. As this article is going to press in early 1989, a proposal for overhauling the industry has just been put forward by the current Administration. The plan calls for the issuance of $50 billion in bonds by a new entity called the Resolution Funding Corporation (REFCO), as well as transferrence of much regulatory control of thrifts from the FHLB to the FDIC.

As the resolution of the problem proceeds, the financial condition of the nation's savings and loan associations will continue to be under close scrutiny. Yields on FHLB, FICO and REFCO (if the Administration's plan is adopted) issues are likely to be quite sensitive to "news" regarding the thrift industry. Participants in the agency market will want to watch the situation closely. If past "crises" provide guidance, this may provide for some profitable trading opportunities.

### Individual Security Trades

The agency market does not quite have the depth that characterizes the Treasury market. As a result, there are often opportunities for trades involving individual securities. However, these opportunities tend to be transitory and require active involvement in the market in order to take advantage of them.

A type of trade that appears on a more regular basis is one that takes advantage of "hills and valleys" in the agency yield curve that are produced by investors' maturity preferences. The agency market is less efficient than the Treasury market in that agency investors are generally less willing to move out of certain preferred maturity ranges to pick up yield. As a result, there are often opportunities for other investors who are less constrained in their maturity preferences to take advantage of these yield differentials. Furthermore, as time passes and the securities "slide down the yield curve" into the preferred maturity ranges, demand picks up and prices rise. Thus, if you can identify a security that is just outside of a preferred maturity range, you can put on a trade to take advantage of the expected relative appreciation of that security as it slides into the preferred range.

For example, many investors prefer to invest in securities with maturities of less than five years. Thus the yield differential between securities with less than 5 years to maturity and those with more than, say, 5½ years to maturity is often much larger than that implied by the general slope of the yield curve. For example, in mid-December of 1987, the FHLB 11.10s of 11/25/92 had almost 5 years to maturity and was yielding 9.02%. At the same time, the FHLB 11.70 of 7/26/93 was yielding 9.42%. Therefore, by extending maturity by 7 months past five years in securities of the same agency with similar coupons, you could have picked up 40 basis points. Thus, if you were a buy-and-hold investor holding the 11.10s you could have sold the 11.10s, bought the 11.70s, paid a round-trip bid-ask spread of, say, 4/32nds (which is equivalent to about 3 basis points per year on a 5-year security) and picked up a net 37 basis points (i.e., 40-3) per year.

Alternatively, if you had been looking for a trading opportunity, you could have positioned yourself to take advantage of relative price changes as the 11.70s approached the 5-year maturity range and started to trade more like other securities within the 5-year range. For example, by early February 1988, the spread between the 11.10s and the 11.70s had narrowed to 8 basis points. If you had bought $10 million of the 11.70s and sold short the 11.10s in mid-December and unwound the positions in early February, you would have earned a net $143,615, as Exhibit 16 indicates.

## IV. CONCLUSION

The agency market presents many trading opportunities for astute market participants. Yield curve plays and individual securities trades can often be found. Credit quality trades are rarer, but can be extremely profitable. A thorough understanding of the agency market and the normal relationship between agency and Treasury securities will hold market participants in good stead, as it will allow for positioning on abnormalities.

**EXHIBIT 16**
**SLIDING DOWN THE YIELD CURVE**

| | December 15, 1987 (Settlement December 16, 1987) | | | February 2, 1988 (Settlement February 3, 1988) | | | |
| --- | --- | --- | --- | --- | --- | --- | --- |
| | Yield | Price plus Accrued Interest | Value of Position | Yield | Price Plus Accrued Interest | Value of Position | Change In Value of Position |
| 11.70 FHLB of 7/26/93 (buy) | 9.42 | $114.30 | $10,000,000 | 8.22 | $121.17* | $10,601,050 | $601,050 |
| 11.10 FHLB of 11/25/92 (sell) | 9.02 | $108.77 | −$10,000,000 | 8.13 | 113.69 | −10,452,331 | −452,331 |
| | .40 | −$ 5.53 | −$ 0 | .09 | $ 7.48 | $ 148,719 | $148,719 |
| $154,260 | | | | | | | |
| | | | | Net financing cost (3/8% for 49 days) | | | $ 5,104 |
| | | | | Net Profit | | | $143,615 |

*Includes receipt of coupon on 1/26/88.

## APPENDIX: CALCULATING YIELD AND ACCRUED INTEREST ON AGENCY SECURITIES

Yield to maturity calculation is an iterative process which gives the rate of discounting (r) necessary to arrive at the market price:

$$P = \sum_{k=1}^{N} \frac{C/2}{(1 + r/2)^{k-1+(t_{sc}/B)}} + \frac{100}{(1 + r/2)^{N-1+(t_{sc}/B)}}$$

where
$P$ = Price
$N$ = Number of remaining coupons
$C$ = Coupon
$B$ = Basis (number of days in coupon period in which settlement occurs)
$t_{sc}$ = Days from settlement to next coupon
$k$ = Number of whole coupon periods

The yields of agencies are calculated on what is known as a "30/360 basis," that is, assuming there are 30 days in each month and (therefore) 360 days per year. Treasuries, on the other hand, use an "actual/actual" method, that is, the actual number of days per month is counted, giving a 365-day year (or 366 in leap years). This affects the calculation of yield to maturity and the accrued interest on a security.

For example, consider an agency security, the FHLB 11¾ of 9/25/91. Its price for settlement on January 9, 1987 was 118:10, its yield was 7.102, and the accrued interest was 3.394 on a coupon of 5.875. If this had been calculated by the method used for Treasuries with the same price, the yield would have been 7.099, with accrued interest of 3.441. This is because of the day-count difference in calculating the partial semiannual period between settlement and the next coupon date, or $(t_{sc}/B)$ in the given equation.

Using a 30/360 method there are always 180 days between each coupon while the actual method result ranges from 181 to 184 (this is known as the "basis"). So, in our example, the basis would be 180 for the FHLB security and for a comparable Treasury it would be 181 (the number of days between 9/25/86 and 3/25/87. Further, in computing the number of days between the settlement date of a transaction and the next coupon date, we find that the agency method produces 76 days and the Treasury method 75 days, as shown below.

| Agency Method (Assuming 30 Days in Every Month) | | Treasury Method (Counting Actual Days) | |
|---|---|---|---|
| Jan. 9-end of Jan. | 21 | Jan. 9-Jan. 31 | 22 |
| Feb. | 30 | Feb. | 28 |
| Mar. 1-Mar. 25 | 25 | Mar. 1-Mar. 25 | 25 |
| TOTAL | 76 | TOTAL | 75 |

Therefore there is 76/180 (.4222) of a partial period when using the agency method and 75/181 (.4144) when using the Treasury method. The difference in the size of the fraction is small but enough to cause differences in yields.

A similar situation exists in calculating accrued interest. This time we need to look at the day-count difference in computing the number of days between the previous coupon and settlement:

| Agency Method (Assuming 30 Days in Every Month) | | Treasury Method (Counting Actual Days) | |
|---|---|---|---|
| September 25-30 | 5 | September 25-30 | 5 |
| October | 30 | October | 31 |
| November | 30 | November | 30 |
| December | 30 | December | 31 |
| January 1-9 | 9 | January 1-9 | 9 |
| TOTAL | 104 | TOTAL | 106 |

The basis remains the same—180 for the agency and 181 for a comparable Treasury. This means that 104/180 (.5778) of a 5.875 coupon is due if calculating with the agency method and 106/181 (.5856) if using the Treasury method.

# NADCO, NASBIC, HUD, PEFCO and FICO: High Quality Investment Opportunities Worth Investigating

JUDITH JONSON
PRODUCT SPECIALIST
CITICORP

ANDREW SILVER, PH.D.
SENIOR ANALYST
MOODY'S INVESTORS SERVICE

## I. INTRODUCTION

Most fixed income investors who are interested in high quality securities are well aware of those issued by the major Federally-sponsored agencies such as the Federal National Mortgage Association (FNMA), Federal Home Loan Mortgage Corporation (FHLMC), Federal Home Loan Banks (FHLBs), Farm Credit Banks (FCBs) and Student Loan Marketing Association (SLMA).[1] However, recently there has been a spate of issues by other entities that offer significant yield pickups over

---

[1] See the previous article for a fuller discussion of sponsored agency securities.

standard agency issues and yet provide at least comparable credit quality. These lesser-known securities are issued by:

1. The Small Business Administration (SBA), guarantor of National Association of Development Companies (NADCO) Participation Certificates and National Association of Small Business Investment Companies (NASBIC) Participation Certificates;
2. The Department of Housing and Urban Development, issuers of U.S. Government Guaranteed Notes;
3. The Private Export Funding Corporation (PEFCO), which obtains the explicit guarantee of the Export-Import Bank (a Federal agency) for the interest of its own Secured Notes and the *de facto* guarantee of the U.S. Government for the principal;
4. The Financing Corporation (FICO), a fully Federally-sponsored agency created in 1987 as part of the recapitalization plan for the Federal Savings and Loan Insurance Corporation (FSLIC).

This article describes these securities and shows how they often offer very attractive investment alternatives to the standard agency issues, as well as to Treasuries, mortgage-backed securities and high-quality corporate bonds.

## II. SBA PARTICIPATION CERTIFICATES: NADCO AND NASBIC

The Small Business Administration, an independent agency of the United States, runs two programs in which securities backed by the SBA's guarantee are sold to the public on a fairly regular basis. In both programs, which were begun in 1986, the SBA's guarantee is backed by the full faith and credit pledge of the United States.

### Characteristics of the Programs

The National Association of Development Companies (NADCO) program issues 10- and 20-year fully amortizing participation certificates. As of this writing (March 1988) the 10-year issues have been running about $5 million in size and usually have been issued quarterly. The last 10-year issue was sold on January 13, 1988 at a yield of 104 basis points above the 5-year Treasury. The 20-year issues have been larger, about $20 million, and are issued monthly. The last 20-year NADCO issue was priced on March 1, 1988 at 105 basis points over the active 10-year U.S. government issue.[2]

---

[2]Because of amortization and prepayment of principal, the 10-year NADCO issue had an average life comparable to the 5-year Treasury, and the 20-year NADCO had an average life comparable to the 10-year Treasury.

The National Association of Small Business Investment Companies (NASBIC) program also issues participation certificates, usually with maturities of 10 years, although the terms may be as long as 15 years. These securities are non-amortizing, and generally are issued quarterly in amounts of roughly $50-$70 million. The last issue, on February 1, 1988, was sold at about 70 basis points over the 10-year Treasury.

In both programs, the participation certificates (PCs) represent undivided fractional interests in a pool of debentures. In the case of the NADCO program, the debentures are issued by SBA-certified State and Local Development Companies, while in the NASBIC program, they are issued by SBA-licensed Small Business Investment Companies. Both the Development Companies and the Investment Companies use the proceeds of the debentures to make loans to small businesses. Prior to the enactment of the Consolidated Omnibus Budget Reconciliation Act of 1985 (COBRA), the debentures had been sold to the Federal Financing Bank (FFB) and hence were indirectly funded by the Treasury. COBRA prohibited continued purchases by the FFB and authorized the debentures to be pooled and sold to the public.

The PC principal loan can be prepaid to investors either because of optional loan prepayments by the small business borrower or because of defaults on the loan, in which case the SBA would prepay the outstanding principal. However, prepayments are low and as likely to occur when rates go up as when they go down. Therefore investors do not face the same type of prepayment risk as on mortgage-backed securities; the PCs do not have the negative convexity characteristics of some mortgage-backed securities. That is, when rates go down, NADCO and NASBIC investors are not likely to face accelerating prepayments which could then only be reinvested at lower rates, reducing the investor's return.

One reason why NADCO and NASBIC borrowers will be reluctant to opt to prepay if rates fall is that there is a large prepayment premium (on a declining scale over the first half of the security's life) on the underlying debentures. In the case of NADCO, another disincentive for prepayment exists. Here, an SBA requirement that NADCO securities be used to back only new loans effectively prohibits firms from refinancing within the program. Since there is little chance that the borrower could find comparable financing at a lower cost outside the program, under reasonable future interest rate scenarios, the borrower is unlikely to prepay simply because rates decline. Consequently, optional prepayments are minimal and not likely to reduce the investor's return.

Furthermore, the second way in which principal can be prepaid, through default, is more likely to be beneficial than harmful to investors. Default seems more probable when rates go up, which would be favorable to the PC investor, who could then reinvest at a higher rate. In any case, the effect to date has not been large. Since the NADCO loan program's inception in 1981 through December 31, 1987, only 3.5% of the total loans made in the first four years have defaulted; the default rate experience for the NASBIC program since 1975 averages 4-5% per year.

*Comparisons to Alternative Investments*

As noted earlier, both the NADCO and NASBIC PCs are guaranteed by the Small Business Administration, which brings with it the full faith and credit pledge of the United States. As a result the PCs are of equal credit quality to Treasuries and GNMAs and higher quality than the debt and mortgage-backed securities of Federally-sponsored agencies, as well as all corporate debt. Nevertheless, as shown in Exhibit 1, the PCs have offered significant yield pickups over comparable Treasuries, agencies and corporates. Furthermore, the negative yield spread to comparable mortgage-backed securities, can be viewed as the yield sacrifice for avoiding the prepayment risk inherent in mortgage-backed securities, as discussed earlier.

Two aspects of the NADCO and NASBIC securities might be viewed as disadvantages to some investors, however. First, there is only a limited secondary market in the issues. Second, the tax treatment of the PCs at the state and local level is uncertain at present. Investors should consult their tax counsel. At worst, the PC interest would be taxed at the state and local level, unlike Treasuries and most agencies. At best, interest would be tax-exempt at the state and local level, placing PCs at an additional advantage over corporates, GNMAs, and FNMAs.

Despite these potential disadvantages, the higher credit quality and yields on NADCO and NASBIC securites make them attractive investment alternatives for intermediate- and long-term investors.

## III.  HUD-GUARANTEED NOTES

In June 1987 the Department of Housing and Urban Development (HUD) began a program in which $53 million of 1- to 6-year notes, guaranteed by HUD, were sold to the public in a serial offering. The notes are the obligations of state and local governments, secured by the local government's current and future receipts of Community Development Block grants from HUD. The full faith and credit pledge of the United States is behind the HUD guarantee.

Prior to July 1, 1987, the guaranteed notes had been bought by the Federal Financing Bank (FFB). The Consolidated Omnibus Budget Reconciliation Act of 1985 prohibited future purchases by the FFB and directed HUD to have the notes sold to the public. We expect future public offerings, perhaps on a semi-annual basis.

The notes are "plain vanilla" securities; they have semi-annual coupons, no amortization, and are not subject to prepayments or acceleration of principal prior to maturity. These features, along with the full faith and credit pledge of the United States, make them very similar to Treasury securities. However, as with the SBA-guaranteed participation certificates, the state and local tax status of the Guaranteed Notes is not clear (investors should consult their tax counsel) and the issues do not

**EXHIBIT 1**
**SAMPLE YIELD SPREADS: NADCO AND NASBIC SECURITIES VS.**
**ALTERNATIVE INVESTMENTS**

I.  NADCO 20-year: March 1, 1988
    NADCO Yield: 9.40

| Yield Spread to: | Yield Spread (basis points) |
|---|---|
| 10-year Treasury 8⅛ of 2/15/98 | 105 |
| 10-year Agency FNMA 8.65 of 2/10/98 | 50 |
| AAA-Corp. (Moody's index) | 30 |
| 30-year GNMA (9.50 coupon) | −9 |

II. NADCO 10-year: January 13, 1988
    NADCO Yield: 9.25

| Yield Spread to: | Yield Spread |
|---|---|
| 5-year Treasury 8¼ of 2/15/98 | 104 |
| 5-year Agency (FNMA 9s of 12/10/92) | 40 |
| AAA-Corp. (GE 8¾ of 11/92) | 12 |
| 15-year GNMA (9.00 coupon) | −13 |

III. NASBIC 10-year: February 1, 1988
     NASBIC Yield: 8.85

| Yield Spread to: | Yield Spread (basis points) |
|---|---|
| 10-year Treasury 8⅞ of 11/15/97 | 70 |
| 10-year Agency (FNMA 9.55 of 12/10/97) | 51 |
| AAA-Corp. (Moody's index) | 20 |
| 30-year GNMA (9.5% coupon) | −12 |

**EXHIBIT 2**
**HUD-GUARANTEED NOTES—YIELD SPREADS IN OCTOBER, 1987**

| Maturity | Spread to Comparable Active Treasury Security (basis points) |
|:---:|:---:|
| 1-year | 20 |
| 2-year | 20 |
| 3-year | 25 |
| 4-year | 34 |
| 5-year | 43 |
| 6-year | 56 |

have an active secondary market. As a result they yield more than comparable Treasuries, as shown in Exhibit 2. Therefore, the Notes are best suited for buy-and-hold investors interested in a predetermined cash flow of Treasury quality.


## IV. PEFCO

The Private Export Funding Corporation (PEFCO) issues fixed rate notes (Secured Notes) whose interest is guaranteed by the Export-Import Bank of the United States (Eximbank, a Federal agency) and whose principal is secured by either cash, securities backed by the full faith and credit of the United States, or Guaranteed Importer Notes, which, as described below, are guaranteed by the Eximbank. The Secured Notes, which are rated AAA, have been issued periodically in amounts ranging up to $200 million. The most recent issue was a 7-year note, sold in June 1987 at 50 basis points above the 7-year Treasury. This was the 25th issue since the program's inception in the early 1970's. To date, PEFCO has had a perfect payment record. Furthermore, the size and standard specifications of the securities have enabled a secondary market to develop.

PEFCO is a private corporation owned by 49 commercial banks, seven manufacturing companies and one investment banking firm. With the approval of the Eximbank, PEFCO makes loans to foreign importers to finance purchases of U.S. goods and services. The principal and interest (except in some limited cases) of the Guaranteed Importer Notes that evidence these loans are guaranteed by the Eximbank. One of the ways that PEFCO funds its loan program is by issuing the Secured Notes.

Exhibits 3 and 4 show that PEFCO yields are considerably higher than comparable Treasuries. Given the direct Federal guarantee on interest and indirect guarantee on principal, this yield pickup on PEFCO securities can be obtained with little, if any, sacrifice in credit quality. The main sacrifice would be in terms of liquidity; although there is a secondary market in PEFCO securities, bid-offer spreads are wider than for Treasuries (roughly 8/32nds on PEFCO issues versus 1/32 or 2/32nds on Treasuries). Thus, PEFCO securities would appeal especially to buy-and-hold investors.

**EXHIBIT 3**
**PEFCO 8.60% OF 6/30/94 LESS TREASURY 8.00% OF 7/15/94**
**(DAILY, 10 JULY 1987 TO 1 FEBRUARY 1988)**

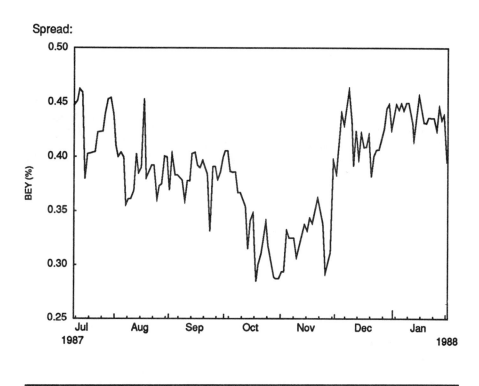

The liqudity of PEFCO issues is probably closer to Federally-sponsored agency issues, such as those of FNMA. As Exhibits 5 and 6 indicate, the direct and indirect Federal guarantees behind the PEFCO securities (which are not available on FNMAs) can be obtained by sacrificing relatively little yield—the 7-year and 10-year PEFCOs have yielded, on average, 4 basis points less than comparable FNMAs.

## V. FICO

On September 30, 1987 the Financing Corporation (FICO) sold its first bond, a 30-year $500 million issue, priced to yield 10.73%, 90 basis points over the 30-year Treasury. FICO was created by the Competitive Equality Banking Act of 1987 (CEBA) to recapitalize the Federal Savings and Loan Insurance Corporation (FSLIC). (See the appendix to this article, The Competitive Equality Banking Act

**EXHIBIT 4**
**PEFCO 7.70% OF 1/31/97 LESS TREASURY 7 1/4% OF 11/15/96**
**(DAILY, 2 OCTOBER 1987 TO 1 FEBRUARY 1988)**

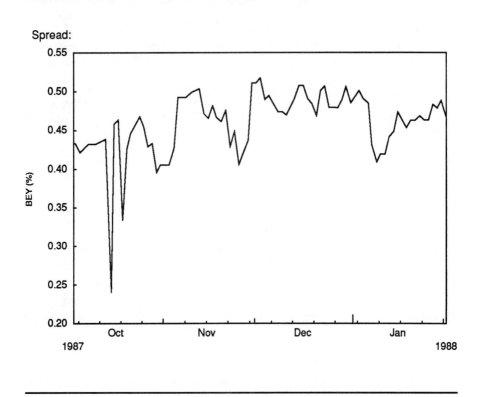

and FICO.) The law allows FICO to issue up to $10.825 billion of securities, and no more than $3.75 billion in any one year. FICO is expected to issue $400-$600 million of 20- to 30-year debt on a quarterly basis for the next few years. As of this writing, $1.75 billion has come to market.

### Pros and Cons of FICO Securities

FICO was granted full Federally-sponsored agency status by the legislation which created it. This means that its securities, though not guaranteed by the Federal government, may be perceived, as are those of other agencies, to have its *de facto* backing. Many market participants consider it inconceivable that the United States government would allow securities issued by any of the Federally-sponsored agencies to default on interest or principal payments. Moreover, the fact that funds are

**EXHIBIT 5**
**PEFCO 8.60% OF 6/30/94 LESS FNMA 8.90% OF 8/10/94**
**(DAILY, 10 AUGUST 1987 TO 1 FEBRUARY 1988)**

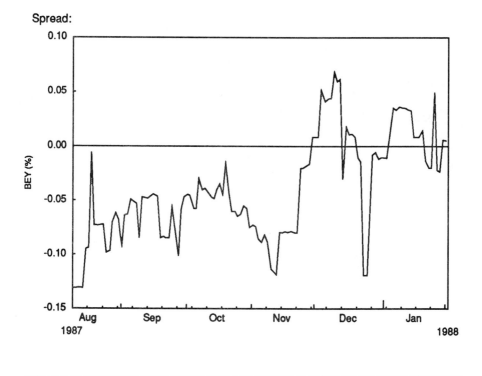

being set aside to pay the securities' principal—a new wrinkle for agency securities—should add to the attractiveness of FICO issues. (See the appendix to this article, The Competitive Equality Banking Act and FICO.)

CEBA provides that securities issued by FICO will be exempt from state and local taxes, as are most Federally-sponsored agency securities. This places FICO bonds at an advantage over corporate bonds, those issued by FNMA, and those guaranteed by GNMA.

Further, FICO is planning to issue its securities in the 20- to 30-year range. This will be an attractive maturity range for some investors (index funds, for example) since there is not a large supply of high-credit long-term debt other than Treasuries. (Much long-term corporate debt is callable, while FICO issues to date are not.)

Still, the creation of FICO and its projected debt issuance raises some questions which should be understood and considered by potential investors and by current holders of outstanding FHLB debt.

**EXHIBIT 6**
**PEFCO 7.70% OF 1/31/97 LESS FNMA 7.70% OF 12/10/96**
**(DAILY, 2 OCTOBER 1987 TO 1 FEBRUARY 1988)**

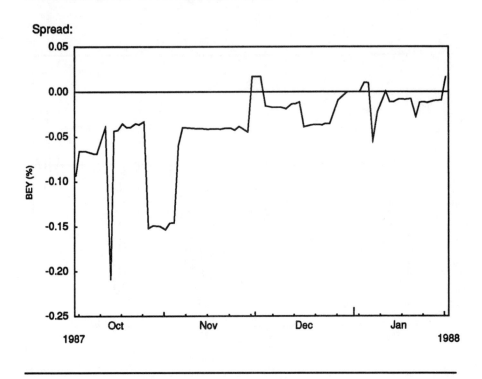

**Coverage of interest payments.** Since the current S&L crisis is largely a regional phenomenon, there is some concern that, in order to avoid the assessments (see the appendix), the healthier thrift institutions will elect to leave the System and instead become insured by the FDIC. A moratorium has been placed on exits from the System; after it is lifted, it is not certain how many S&Ls will actually qualify to join the FDIC insurance system and, of those, how many will apply. A large exodus would of course cause a lower deposit level and, therefore, lower assessments available to FICO.

A savings and loans institution that is eligible for FDIC insurance must consider a number of factors when making the decision of whether or not to leave the Federal Home Loan Bank (FHLB) System. The main attraction of FDIC insurance is that the premiums are lower than for FSLIC insurance. However, banks regulated by the FDIC are restricted as to their involvement in some types of investments, such as real estate and insurance. An S&L which has large holdings in such areas might not be willing to give up a large part of them in order to comply with FDIC regulations. Further, termination fees of two years worth of insurance premiums and supplemental assessments will be collected by FICO from institutions leaving the FHL Bank System.

To help assess the adequacy of interest coverage under different interest rate and FSLIC membership assumptions, we have included, as Exhibit 7, a table from FICO's "Preliminary Information Statement" entitled "Estimated Interest Coverage Analysis." This examines interest rate scenarios (weighted average coupon of outstanding debt) ranging from 7-17% and aggregate deposit reductions of 0-25%. We have added to the table the last two columns, showing interest coverage with deposit reductions of 30% and 35%. These are simple extrapolations of FICO's numbers.

Coverage as shown here will not be a problem if the average coupon paid is 13% or less and if no more than 25% of deposits leave the FHLB System. However, there are some estimates (including one by a former head of the FHLB System quoted in the *Wall Street Journal* in June of 1987) that thrift institutions holding up to ⅓ of the System's assets could, with some effort, be eligible to leave FSLIC. If those institutions hold deposits in a similar proportion, and if they elect to leave the System, the interest coverage ratio could conceivably go below 1.0 at interest levels lower than 13%.

Also, it is possible that the average coupon rate on the FICO debt issues will exceed 13%, which also would increase the likelihood of insufficient interest coverage. Although it is unlikely that interest rates would increase sharply enough over the issuance period so that the average rate would exceed 13%, such an occurrence is not without precedent. If interest rates rise during the years in which FICO debt will be issued, and/or if deposit reductions from the FHLB System are high, there will be a significantly greater chance of interest coverage which is less than 1.0.

**EXHIBIT 7**
**ESTIMATED INTEREST COVERAGE ANALYSIS (RATIO OF ESTIMATED FICO ASSESSMENTS TO INTEREST)**

| Average Interest Rate Per Annum | Percentage Reduction in Aggregate Deposits | | | | | | | |
|---|---|---|---|---|---|---|---|---|
| % | 0 | 5 | 10 | 15 | 20 | 25 | 30 | 35 |
| 17 | 1.02 | .97 | .92 | .86 | .81 | .76 | .71 | .66 |
| 16 | 1.08 | 1.03 | .97 | .92 | .86 | .81 | .76 | .70 |
| 15 | 1.15 | 1.09 | 1.04 | .98 | .92 | .86 | .81 | .75 |
| 14 | 1.23 | 1.17 | 1.11 | 1.05 | .99 | .93 | .87 | .80 |
| 13 | 1.33 | 1.26 | 1.20 | 1.13 | 1.06 | 1.00 | .93 | .87 |
| 12 | 1.44 | 1.37 | 1.30 | 1.22 | 1.15 | 1.08 | 1.01 | .94 |
| 11 | 1.57 | 1.49 | 1.41 | 1.34 | 1.26 | 1.18 | 1.10 | 1.02 |
| 10 | 1.73 | 1.64 | 1.56 | 1.47 | 1.38 | 1.30 | 1.21 | 1.13 |
| 9 | 1.92 | 1.82 | 1.73 | 1.63 | 1.54 | 1.44 | 1.35 | 1.25 |
| 8 | 2.16 | 2.05 | 1.94 | 1.84 | 1.73 | 1.62 | 1.52 | 1.41 |
| 7 | 2.47 | 2.35 | 2.22 | 2.10 | 1.98 | 1.85 | 1.73 | 1.61 |

We do not think it is likely that deposit withdrawals from the System or interest rate increases will cause interest coverage from assessments to fall below 1.0. Furthermore, if this did occur, it seems probable that a supplemental rescue package would be assembled. However, as with other Federally-sponsored agency securities, investors should remember that there is no explicit Treasury guarantee behind FICO's debt. As a result, prices of FICO securities, especially in the short run, will be sensitive to "news" about the health of the savings and loan industry.

**Will $10.8 billion solve the problem?** Market estimates of the amount of money needed to solve completely the problems of the thrift industry range from $50 to $100 billion, making it likely that the amount of currently authorized debt will not be enough.[3] The Preliminary Information Statement does not rule out the possibility of authorization of more debt, stating that "it may be necessary in the future for Congress to consider amending the Act to expand FICO's financing authority or change its capital structure or authorize other measures." Pursuant to this, concern has been expressed about whether additional debt will adversely affect interest coverage or the value of already-outstanding FICO debt. At a meeting of market transactors and analysts at the Federal Reserve Bank of New York on September 9, 1987, a spokesperson for FICO asserted that Congress had no intent to disadvantage any FHLB or FICO bondholders, but it was not made clear exactly how Congress would seek to avoid such an occurrence. The Preliminary Information Statement is even less comforting, stating: "It is not possible to predict whether any such future legislative action would be taken or how such action, if taken, might affect holders of the Obligations."

*Other Market Effects*

**Effect of capital transfers on the regional FHLBs.** Because CEBA provides that the 12 regional FHLBs will be required to purchase stock in the Financing Corporation when so directed, in proportions as prescribed in the law, concern has been voiced regarding what this reallocation of FHLB capital will do to the health of the FHLBs and to the value of the securities already issued by them.

While the Act provides for redemption of FICO stock purchased by the FHLBs if money is available after FICO's dissolution, it is not certain how much, if any, of the capital will finally be returned to the FHLBs. For instance, if the full $10.825 billion of bonds are issued, approximately $1 billion will be needed to purchase zeroes to fund the principal as required by the Act. The proceeds from the additional $2 billion of stock which can be issued to the FHLBs can either be invested or used to meet interest payments in the event that industry assessments are not sufficient. Therefore, some level of loss between $1 billion and $3 billion seems to be in store for the FHLBs, representing an erosion of the FHLB System's current capital base of between 8% and 23%.

---

[3] Recent newspaper reports estimate that $7 billion in aid will be dispensed by the FSLIC in 1988 alone.

A loss to the FHLBs would create an increase in the System's debt-to-equity ratio, though it would still remain well within the 12:1 ratio imposed by regulation. However, it is not clear whether a weakened FHLB System capital base would represent a sufficient cushion to support the narrow spreads above Treasuries that FHLB debt traditionally has enjoyed.

**Funding of principal with zero-coupon securities** A final issue is the potential effect of the refinancing on the zero-coupon market. The law provides that the principal repayment of FICO securities shall be provided for by the purchase of zero-coupon securities whose face value is approximately equal to the principal issued. This added demand for zeroes should increase the prices of long-dated STRIPs and could possibly again make it profitable for dealers to strip Treasury long-dated securities.[4] However, this effect will be limited by the extent to which FICO chooses to arrange for a private placement of zero-coupon agency or Treasury debt, which is also permitted under the CEBA legislation.

### Comparison to Alternative Investments

As with other agency securities, FICO's obligations will trade at some yield spread above Treasury obligations of a similar maturity. Few coupon-bearing agency securities currently exist in as long a maturity range as the FICO issues. However, the World Bank, which is viewed by the market similarly to Federally-sponsored agencies, issues 30-year debt that trades about 80-85 basis points above the 30-year Treasury. Therefore, the FICO securities offer an additional 5-10 basis point yield pickup. This, combined with the long maturity range, the zero coupon funding of principal, the insurance premium coverage of interest payments, and the Federally-sponsored status of the agency, should make the securities attractive to many investors.

## APPENDIX
## THE COMPETITIVE EQUALITY BANKING ACT AND FICO

The thrift industry in the United States has been undergoing this latest crisis for about two years. The problems are, for the most part, concentrated in the energy and agricultural belts. For example, many loans made for oil-producing and related purposes have defaulted since the prices of oil and land associated with it have dropped. Congress had been trying to pass legislation to aid the thrift industry for well over a year.

Title III of CEBA authorizes and outlines a recapitalization of the FSLIC under

---

[4]Prior to September 1987 it had not been profitable to strip any Treasury bonds maturing after 2015. However, since the time of the first FICO issuance, stripping of these issues has occurred.

FICO. (Title IV has other provisions intended to help effect a recovery of the thrift industry, but this discussion will largely be confined to the refinancing.)

FICO will be recapitalized by non-voting stock purchases made by the twelve regional Federal Home Loan Banks (FHLBs). On August 28, 1987 $1 billion of stock purchases were authorized, allocating a percentage to each regional bank as listed in the Act. Further stock purchases are limited by formula to a portion of each FHLB's legal reserves and undivided profits up to a maximum of an additional $2 billion. As of June 30, 1987, under the formula provided, this extra amount would have been about $2.5 billion, $500 million above the allowable amount.

After issuing securities, FICO will transfer the proceeds by buying capital stock and certificates in FSLIC. FICO is to be dismantled in 2026 or after all securities have matured, whichever comes sooner, and the stock which is originally purchased by the FHLBs will at that time be redeemed if there are funds available to do so. In the interim, no dividends are scheduled to be paid to the FHLBs.

The infusions of capital are to be used partly to buy zero-coupon securities which will be placed in a segregated account to pay the principal of securities issued by FICO. Amounts not placed in this separate account can be used for "eligible investments" as defined by CEBA.

In addition to providing that FHLBs are to purchase stock for the financing of FICO, the act authorizes FICO to levy a regular annual assessment (maximum of 1/12 of 1% of aggregate deposits) on all FSLIC-insured institutions in order to provide funds for the payment of interest and related costs on securities issued by FICO. FICO can also impose special assessments (to an annual maximum of $\frac{1}{8}$ of 1%) if they are needed to meet interest payments. These percentages are about equal to the amounts FSLIC is currently authorized to collect in 1988 from the savings and loans which it regulates; any assessments collected by FICO will reduce the insurance premiums and special assessments that S&Ls would be required to pay to FSLIC. This means that, on a net basis, S&Ls will continue to pay about the same premiums, but that they may go partly or fully to FICO instead of to FSLIC. Between 1988 and 1991, the special FSLIC assessments are scheduled to decline gradually, but FICO can still collect the full $\frac{1}{8}$% of 1% if it is needed for interest or related costs.

# Invoice Prices, Special Redemption Features, Cash Flows, and Yields on Eurobonds

KENNETH D. GARBADE, PH.D.
MANAGING DIRECTOR
BANKERS TRUST COMPANY

## I. INTRODUCTION

This article has two objectives. The first is to describe carefully the calculation of invoice prices, future cash flows, and yields on Eurobonds with no special redemption features. The second objective is to describe some of the special redemption features which can be incorporated in a Eurobond. These features are important, because they can alter the amount of interest, and the timing of principal, paid on a Eurobond, and hence may alter the yield on the bond. The most important include options for an issuer to "call" his bonds for retirement in advance of the stated maturity date, and options for an investor to "put" bonds back to an issuer for early redemption. We will also examine retractable and extendible bonds which carry both put and call options. Finally, we will describe a sinking fund, or provision for one or more *partial* redemptions of a bond before its final maturity.

This article focuses on the fixed-rate, United States dollar sector of the Eurobond market. We will not examine securities which pay, or which may pay, in other currencies; we will not examine floating rate notes; and we will not examine bonds convertible into other securities such as common stock.

---

Copyright 1987 Bankers Trust Company. Reprinted with permission.

## II. PLAIN VANILLA: EUROBONDS WITH NO SPECIAL REDEMPTION FEATURES

The easiest way to begin examining Eurobonds is with a bond which unconditionally promises (1) to pay interest periodically until and including its final maturity date, and (2) to repay principal on that date. This section describes cash flows, invoice prices, and yields on such "plain vanilla" bonds. The following sections examine more complicated cases of bonds with special redemption features.

Defining the yield on a plain vanilla Eurobond proceeds along the following lines. We first specify the future cash flows from the bond—what and when we get paid. Next, we compute the invoice price of the bond. Finally, we calculate the yield on the bond as the discount rate which equates the present value of the bond's future cash flows to the invoice price.

### Cash Flows

The cash flows from a plain vanilla Eurobond are unambiguous and simple to construct. Consider, for example, the 5-year issue of the International Bank for Reconstruction and Development (IBRD, or the World Bank) carrying a 7% coupon, dated January 28, 1987, and maturing January 28, 1992. Interest on the bond is paid annually, so the future cash flows are:

| Date | Payment* |
|---|---|
| January 28, 1988 | 7. (interest) |
| January 28, 1989 | 7. (interest) |
| January 28, 1990 | 7. (interest) |
| January 28, 1991 | 7. (interest) |
| January 28, 1992 | 7. (interest) |
| | + 100. (principal) |

*Expressed as a percent of principal.

Almost all Eurobonds pay interest annually, but a few pay semi-annually.

### Prices

Bids and offers for the purchase and sale of Eurobonds are quoted in terms of percent of principal value. Prices finer than one percent may be quoted either in decimal terms, e.g., 98.55, or as a fraction, e.g., 98⅝ = 98.625.

The invoice price on a transaction is the quoted price plus accrued interest on the next coupon, where interest accrues from the issue date or last coupon payment date to the settlement date of the trade.

**Accrued Interest.** Calculation of accrued interest on a Eurobond uses a "30/360 calendar," meaning a calendar with 30-day months and 360-day years. The appendix explains day counts using such a calender.

Exhibit 1 illustrates the computation of accrued interest for a settlement date of March 5, 1987 on the 7% World Bank bond described above. As shown in the exhibit, 37 days elapsed between the January 28, 1987 issue date of the bond and the March 5 settlement date (2 days remaining in January, plus 30 days in February, plus 5 days in March). There are 360 days in the January 28, 1987 to January 28, 1988 interest period (12 calendar months at 30 days per month). Thus, on the settlement date a fraction equal to .102778 of the full interest period had elapsed (.102778 = 37/360), and the accrued interest on the bond was .71944 percent of principal (.71944% = .102778 • 7% coupon rate).

**EXHIBIT 1**
**CALCULATING ACCRUED INTEREST ON THE WORLD BANK 7.00% BOND OF JANUARY 28, 1992, FOR SETTLEMENT ON MARCH 5, 1987**

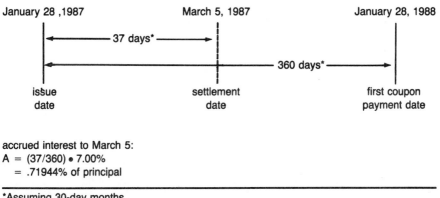

accrued interest to March 5:
A = (37/360) • 7.00%
  = .71944% of principal

*Assuming 30-day months.

## Yields

The yield on a Eurobond is conventionally computed with the assumption of annual compounding if the bond pays interest annually. However, if there is only a single payment remaining on the bond, the yield is figured using simple interest. (Yield is conventionally computed with the assumption of semi-annual compounding if the bond pays interest semi-annually and has more than one payment remaining.)

**Yield on a Eurobond with Multiple Remaining Coupons.** When a Eurobond has more than one payment remaining, the yield on the bond is computed using annually compounded interest, including compound interest over any fractional part of a year remaining to the next coupon payment.

To construct the yield, consider a Eurobond quoted at price P, with accrued interest A, an annual coupon of Rcp, and with n coupons remaining to be paid. The yield on the bond is the value of Ra which solves the equation:

$$P+A = \frac{Rcp}{(1+Ra)^v} + \frac{Rcp}{(1+Ra)^{1+v}} + \cdots + \frac{Rcp}{(1+Ra)^{n-1+v}}$$

$$+ \frac{100}{(1+Ra)^{n-1+v}} \tag{1}$$

where v is the fraction of a year remaining to the next coupon payment, computed using a 30/360 calendar.

For a concrete example of equation (1), consider the yield on the 7% World Bank bond described above, quoted at 99½ for settlement on March 5, 1987. Equation (1) becomes:

$$99.5 + .71944 = \frac{7}{(1+Ra)^{.89722}} + \frac{7}{(1+Ra)^{1.89722}}$$

$$+ \frac{7}{(1+Ra)^{2.89722}} + \frac{7}{(1+Ra)^{3.89722}} \tag{2}$$

$$+ \frac{7}{(1+Ra)^{4.89722}} + \frac{100}{(1+Ra)^{4.89722}}$$

This implies a value of Ra = .0712, or 7.12% per annum, compounded annually. The value of v is computed as v = 323/360 = .89722, where there are 323 days between settlement on March 5, 1987 and the next, January 28, 1988, coupon payment (323 = 25 days remaining in March, plus 30 days in each of the next nine months, plus 28 days in January).

**Conversion to Semi-Annual Compounding.** Since yields on a wide variety of fixed income securities (including Treasury, Federal agency, and U.S. domestic corporate bonds) are conventionally computed using semi-annual compounding, market participants often convert the annually compounded yield on a Eurobond to its equivalent semi-annually compounded value. The equivalent semi-annually compounded yield is the value of Rs which solves the equation:

$$(1 + \tfrac{1}{2}Rs)^2 = 1 + Ra \tag{3}$$

Thus, Rs = 7.00% is equivalent to an annually compounded yield of Ra = 7.12%

**Yield on a Bond with One Coupon Remaining.** When a Eurobond has only one payment remaining, the yield on the bond is computed with simple (rather than compound) interest.

To derive the yield, consider a Eurobond quoted at price P, with accrued interest A, an annual coupon of Rcp, and with one coupon remaining to be paid. The yield on the bond is the value of R which solves the equation:

$$P + A \quad = \quad \frac{100 + Rcp}{(1 + v \bullet R)} \tag{4}$$

where v is the fraction of a year remaining to the last payment, computed using a 30/360 calendar.

For a concrete example of equation (4), consider the yield on the 7% World Bank bond quoted at 99½ for settlement on March 5, 1991. Equation (4) becomes:

$$99.5 + .71944 \quad = \quad \frac{100 + 7}{(1 + .89722 \bullet R)} \tag{5}$$

This implies a value of R = .0754, or 7.54% per annum.

**A Simple Interest Money-Market Yield.** It should be noted that some market participants prefer to define the yield on a Eurobond using a money-market yield convention when there is only one payment remaining. In this case the yield is the value of Rmm which solves the equation:

$$P + A \quad = \quad \frac{100 + Rcp}{(1 + v \bullet Rmm)} \tag{6}$$

where v is the fraction of a year remaining to the last payment; computed as the *actual* number of days to the payment, divided by 360.

Finally, it is also possible to define the yield on a Eurobond with one payment remaining using annual compounding instead of simple interest, although such a yield is not commonly encountered in the market. With annual compounding, the definition of yield becomes:

$$P + A \quad = \quad \frac{100 + Rcp}{(1 + Ra)^v} \tag{7}$$

This expression can be compared to equation (4). The only difference is whether v, the fraction of a year remaining on the life of the bond, multiplies the annual rate (as in equation (4)) or whether it appears as an exponent to the annual compounding term (as in equation (7)).

## Bonds with Odd First Coupons

Up to this point we have examined Eurobonds which mature on an anniversary of their issue date. The 7% World Bank bond, for example, was issued on January 28, 1987 and matures exactly five years later, on January 28, 1992. However, some Eurobonds mature on a date which is *not* an anniversary of their issue date. The first interest payment on such a bond is different from subsequent payments, and the bond is known as an "odd-first-coupon" bond.

Cash flows and yields on odd-first-coupon bonds are computed differently from ordinary bonds. We will illustrate the differences with the 7⅛% bond issued by the Kingdom of Denmark on February 5, 1987 which matures on March 5, 1992.

**Cash Flows.** The cash flows on the Danish bond include five interest payments and a return of principal at maturity:

| Date | Payment* |
|------|----------|
| March 5, 1988 | 7.71875 (interest) |
| March 5, 1989 | 7.125    (interest) |
| March 5, 1990 | 7.125    (interest) |
| March 5, 1991 | 7.125    (interest) |
| March 5, 1992 | 7.125    (interest) |
|               | + 100.   (principal) |

*Expressed as a percent of principal.

The only unusual aspect of these payments is the larger amount of the first coupon. Since the bond was issued on February 5, 1987, it will be outstanding for 13 months before the March 5, 1988 interest payment. Investors get a larger first coupon, because the first interest period is longer than one year. If the interval were less than a year, the first coupon would be smaller than subsequent interest payments.

The amount of the first interest payment on an odd-first-coupon bond is computed with a 30/360 calendar. In the case of the Danish bond, there are 13 full months, or 390 days, between issue and the first coupon. The size of that coupon is, therefore, $(390/360) \cdot 7.125\%$, or 7.71875% of principal, where 7.125% is the stated annual coupon rate on the bond.

**Accrued Interest.** Interest on an odd-first-coupon Eurobond accrues at the stated coupon rate on a 30/360 calendar, just like an ordinary Eurobond. Thus, the accrued interest on the 7⅛% Denmark bond for settlement on March 15, 1987 is .791667% of principal ($.791667\% = (40/360) \cdot 7.125\%$, where there are 40 days from issue on February 5, 1987 to settlement on March 15, 1987).

**Yield.** The yield on an odd-first-coupon Eurobond is defined essentially the same way as the yield on a regular Eurobond. The only difference is that we have to recognize the unusual size of the first interest payment.

To construct the yield, consider a Eurobond priced at P, with accrued interest A, a first coupon payment Q, subsequent coupon payments Rcp, and with a total of n coupons remaining to be paid. The annually compounded yield on the bond is the value of Ra which solves the equation:

$$P + A = \frac{Q}{(1+Ra)^v} + \frac{Rcp}{(1+Ra)^{1+v}} + \cdots + \frac{Rcp}{(1+Ra)^{n-1+v}}$$

$$+ \frac{100}{(1+Ra)^{n-1+v}} \tag{8}$$

where v is the fraction of a year remaining to the first coupon, computed with a 30/360 calendar. This expression may be compared to the definition of the yield on a regular bond shown in equation (1).

For a concrete example of equation (8), consider the 7⅛% Kingdom of Denmark bond described above, priced at 99⅝ for settlement on March 15, 1987. Equation (8) becomes:

$$99.625 + .791667 = \frac{7.71875}{(1+Ra)^{.97222}} + \frac{7.125}{(1+Ra)^{1.9722}}$$

$$+ \frac{7.125}{(1+Ra)^{2.97222}} + \frac{7.125}{(1+Ra)^{3.97222}} \tag{9}$$

$$+ \frac{7.125}{(1+Ra)^{4.97222}} + \frac{100.}{(1+Ra)^{4.97222}}$$

This implies a value of Ra = .0721, or 7.21% per annum, compounded annually. The value of v was computed as v = 350/360 = .97222, where there are 350 days between settlement on March 15, 1987 and the March 5, 1988 coupon payment (350 = 15 days remaining in March, 1987, plus 30 days in each of the next eleven months, plus 5 days in March, 1988).

It should be noted that an odd-first-coupon feature is irrelevant on any bond which has passed its first interest date. In particular, equations (1) and (4) define the yield on any plain vanilla Eurobond with equal remaining interest payments, regardless of whether the bond initially had an odd first coupon.

## III. EUROBONDS WITH OPTIONS FOR EARLY REDEMPTION

Plain vanilla Eurobonds with no put or call options and with no sinking fund provisions account for about one-half of all Eurobond issues. The remaining bonds have one or more features providing for early redemption, or repayment of principal before maturity. This section describes the two most important early redemption features: options for an issuer to call his bonds back from an investor, and options for an investor to put his bonds back to the issuer. The next section describes sinking fund redemptions.

### Call Options[1]

Broadly stated, call options provide that an issuer may redeem his bonds before maturity by paying investors a designated call or option exercise price. The easiest way to appreciate call options is to examine a series of examples.

Example 1 shown in Exhibit 2 shows the call provisions on a 12-year Campbell Soup Company issue. The provisions illustrate several common aspects of Eurobond call options. First, the bond is not callable for seven years following issue. It is, consequently, said to have seven years of "call protection." Second, the bond is callable pursuant to a *declining* schedule of call prices during the next four years. The issuer can, for example, call back his bonds at a redemption price of 102% of principal, plus accrued interest, on any date between April 30, 1993 and April 29, 1994. Similarly, he can redeem his bonds at 101.5% of principal, plus accrued interest, on any date between April 30, 1994 and April 29, 1995. Third, the bond is callable at principal value, plus accrued interest, i.e., with no "call premium," during the last year of the bond's life.

These three features (call protection, premium call options, and a par call option) represent the basic components of a Eurobond call provision. It should be noted, however, that there are cases where a bond does not carry any premium call options (see Example 2 in Exhibit 2), and cases where a bond does not carry any par call option (see Example 3 in Exhibit 2). There are also cases where a Eurobond can be called only on its interest payment dates, and can not be called on other dates (see Example 4 in Exhibit 2).

**Value of a Call Option.** The rights to call a bond for early redemption are valuable rights, because they give the issuer an opportunity to refinance his principal borrowing should interest rates fall. From an investor's perspective, call options impose a burden if money received from exercise of a call has to be reinvested at lower interest rates. Issuers can, consequently, expect to "pay" for their call options, either by increasing the coupon rate on a bond or by selling the bond at a lower price.

---

[1]A framework for valuing callable Eurobonds is given in Kenneth D. Garbade and Richard Tanenbaum, "Assessing the Value of a Callable Eurobond," Chapter 17 in Frank J. Fabozzi (ed.), *The Handbook of Fixed Income Options* (Chicago, IL: Probus Publishing, 1989).

EXHIBIT 2

## Example 1.
## Call Options on the Campbell Soup Company 7½% Eurobond of April 30, 1998

Issued:    April 30, 1986

Matures:    April 30, 1998

Callable:    April 30, 1993* at 102**
April 30, 1994* at 101½**
April 30, 1995* at 101**
April 30, 1996* at 100½**
April 30, 1997* at 100**

*Or later.
** Plus accured interest.

## Example 2.
## Call Options on the GMAC Overseas Finance Corporation NV (Curacao) 10½% Eurobond of February 1, 1990

Issued:    February 1, 1983

Matures:    February 1, 1990

Callable:    February 1, 1988 or later at 100, plus accrued interest.

## Example 3.
## Call Options on the European Economic Community 9⅝% Eurobond of July 27, 1990

Issued:    July 27, 1985

Matures:    July 27, 1990

Callable:    July 27, 1988* at 102**
July 27, 1989* at 101**

* Or later.
** Plus accured interest.

## Example 4.
## Call Options on the European Investment Bank 10¾% Eurobond of May 19, 1993

Issued:    May 19, 1983

Matures:    May 19, 1993

Callable:    May 19, 1990 at 101
May 19, 1991 at 100½
May 19, 1992 at 100
(This issue is not callable on any other dates)

To appreciate this claim, consider again the 12-year Campbell Soup bond shown in Example 1. In April, 1986, Campbell Soup might have been able to sell a plain vanilla 12-year bond with a 7¼% coupon at par. As the price of attaching the call provisions in Example 1, however, it had to advance the coupon rate to 7½%. Alternatively, it might have kept the 7¼% copuon and sold the callable bond at a discount from its principal value.

**Yield on a Callable Bond.** Computing the yield on a callable Eurobond is a tricky proposition. Recall, from Section II, that the yield on a plain vanilla bond is defined as the interest rate at which the present value of the bond's future cash flows is equal to the bond's invoice price.

The problem with defining a yield for a callable Eurobond is that the future cash flows from the bond are not known with certainty. Example 5 in Exhibit 3 shows three possible "scenarios" for the cash flows from the Campbell Soup issue described in Example 1. Scenario A shows the bond being called at 102% of principal immediately upon termination of the call protection period. Scenario B shows the bond being called at 100.5 on April 30, 1996. Scenario C shows the bond maturing as scheduled, or where the issuer never exercises any of his call options. Since each of these scenarios, as well as many others, is possible, there is no basis for identifying any one of them as "the" correct scenario of future cash flows.

**EXHIBIT 3**

**Example 5.**
**Three Possible Scenarios for the Future Cash Flows on the**
**Campbell Soup Company 7½% Eurobond of April 30, 1998**

| | Payment* | | |
|---|---|---|---|
| Date | A | B | C |
| April 30, 1987 | 7.5 | 7.5 | 7.5 |
| April 30, 1988 | 7.5 | 7.5 | 7.5 |
| April 30, 1989 | 7.5 | 7.5 | 7.5 |
| April 30, 1990 | 7.5 | 7.5 | 7.5 |
| April 30, 1991 | 7.5 | 7.5 | 7.5 |
| April 30, 1992 | 7.5 | 7.5 | 7.5 |
| April 30, 1993 | 109.5 | 7.5 | 7.5 |
| April 30, 1994 | — | 7.5 | 7.5 |
| April 30, 1995 | — | 7.5 | 7.5 |
| April 30, 1996 | — | 108.0 | 7.5 |
| April 30, 1997 | — | — | 7.5 |
| April 30, 1998 | — | — | 107.5 |

*Expressed as a percent of principal.

As a matter of convention, many market participants arbitrarily define the yield on a callable Eurobond in terms of a "most likely" outcome. More specifically, they identify the highest call price which is *below* the *current* market quote on the bond, and assume the bond will be called at that price. If the Campbell Soup issue is priced above 102, they would assume Scenario A will occur. If the issue is priced above 100.5, but not above 101, they would assume Scenario B will occur. Finally, if the issue is priced at or below 100, they assume the issue will not be called, and that Scenario C will occur. Thus, for any given market quote they can compute a "yield to currently most likely call" or, more simply, "yield to call."

It should be clear that yield to call is an *ad hoc* measure of rate of return. In particular, it can not be compared in any simple way to the yield on an issue with fixed future cash flows.[2]

## *Put Options[3]*

Put options are a mirror image of call options. They provide that a bondholder can force an issuer to redeem his bonds before maturity at a designated put or option exercise price. Such options can become quite valuable if interest rates rise and investors can reinvest principal at higher yields.

Example 6 in Exhibit 4 exhibits the put provisions on a 10-year Eurobond issued by the French railway, Societe Nationale des Chemins de Fer Francais (SNCF). A holder of the bond can, at his option, force SNCF to redeem it at its principal value on March 15, 1990, March 15, 1991, or March 15, 1992. In the alternative, he can hold the bond until its final maturity in 1993.

Most of the comments made above with respect to call provisions also apply to puts. Thus, for example, the SNCF issue has seven years of put protection and three par put option exercise opportunities. As with a callable issue, market participants compute "yield to put" on a Eurobond with put options when the bond is trading below a put option exercise price. Again, however, such a yield is *ad hoc,* and not directly comparable to the yield on a plain vanilla Eurobond.

## *Retractable and Extendible Eurobonds*

In some cases a Eurobond will carry both call *and* put options. If these options are exercisable at par on the same date, the bond is usually called either a "retractable" or "extendible" security.

---

[2]For a general exposition of the meaning of the yield on a fixed income security, see Kenneth D. Garbade, "Rate of Return and Futurity of Cash Flow from a Bond—Are Yield and Duration Good Measures?" *Topics in Money and Securities Markets* (Bankers Trust Company, December, 1984).

[3]For framework for valuing Eurobonds with both put and call options, see Kenneth D. Garbade, "Assessing the Value of a Eurobond with Issuer Call and Holder Put Options," Chapter 18 in *The Handbook of Fixed Income Options.*

**EXHIBIT 4**

---

### Example 6.
### Put Options on the Societe Nationale des Chemins de Fer Francais 11½% Eurobond of March 15, 1993

| | |
|---|---|
| Issued: | March 15, 1983 |
| Matures: | March 15, 1993 |
| Putable: | March 15, 1990 at 100 |
| | March 15, 1991 at 100 |
| | March 15, 1992 at 100 |
| | (This issue is not putable on any other dates.) |

---

### Example 7.
### Options on the General Electric Company 7% Eurobond of May 22, 1998

| | |
|---|---|
| Issued: | May 22, 1986 |
| Matures: | May 22, 1998 |
| Callable: | May 22, 1989 or later at 100, plus accrued interest. |
| Putable: | Annually from May 22, 1989 to May 22, 1997 at 100. |
| | (This issue is not putable on any other dates.) |

---

### Example 8.
### Options on the General Electric Company 7⅜% Eurobond of May 1, 2006

| | |
|---|---|
| Issued: | May 1, 1986 |
| Matures: | May 1, 2006 |
| Callable: | May 1, 1991 or later at 100, plus accured interest. |
| Putable: | Annually from May 1, 1991 to May 1, 2005 at 100. |
| | (This issue is not putable on any other dates.) |

Interest rate on this issue will be reset by the issuer on May 1, 1991, and annually thereafter.

---

Example 7 in Exhibit 4 shows the put and call option provisions on a 12-year Eurobond issued by the General Electric Company (GE). Observe that the bond is callable at par on and after May 22, 1989, and is putable at par on every interest payment date on and after May 22, 1989.

This conjunction of options implies that the bond will trade at, or close to, par on May 22, 1989 and on every subsequent payment date. If the bond were to trade significantly above par, the issuer would have an incentive to call his bonds at par and issue an identical security at a higher price. Conversely, if the bond were to trade significantly below par, investors would have an incentive to put their bonds back to GE and reinvest the proceeds in some other comparable security at a lower price.

Since the GE issue can be expected to trade at (or near) par on May 22, 1989, most market participants treat it as if it had a May 22, 1989 maturity date. This is justified in view of the essentially known market value of the issue on that date.

**Interest Rate Reset Options.** In many cases a retractable or extendible Eurobond will provide for resetting the rate of interest on dates at which the bond is both putable and callable at par. Example 8 in Exhibit 4 shows a General Electric bond retractable in 1991 which pays a 7⅜% coupon until the retraction date and on which the issuer can reset the coupon annually thereafter. These reset options do not materially affect the market value of the bond before the retraction date, because the bond will then be trading as if it were to mature on the retraction date.

## IV. EUROBONDS WITH SINKING FUND REDEMPTIONS

We observed in Section II that a plain vanilla Eurobond provides for payment of periodic interest and return of principal at maturity. This structure is commonly called a "bullet" redemption, because principal is repaid in one lump sum.

In some cases, however, a borrower may not need the entire principal to the final maturity of his bond, and might prefer to repay a portion of the principal periodically before maturity. Similarly, a lender might feel more comfortable with a borrower's credit-worthiness if the borrower agrees to amortize his loan periodically, rather than attempt to make a single repayment of principal. (This is the basis for the payment structure on a conventional American residential mortgage.)

Sinking funds provide for periodic partial repayments of principal before the final maturity of a bond. As an illustration, Example 9 in Exhibit 5 shows the sinking fund redemption schedule on a $175 million 10½-year Eurobond issue of the French utility Gaz de France (GDF). The schedule shows that $87.5 million of the bonds will be redeemed one year before maturity, and the other $87.5 million will be redeemed at maturity. Example 10 in Exhibit 5 shows a sinking fund schedule where the redemptions are at quite different dates. Example 11 in Exhibit 5 shows a schedule where the redemptions are spread out over six consecutive years.

Perhaps the most interesting aspect of a sinking fund provision is whether it allows the issuer to retire bonds with market purchases, or whether it requires him to redeem bonds at their principal value. The latter is true for the GDF bonds in Example 9 and the European Investment Bank (EIB) bonds in Example 10. However, the Swedish Export Credit bonds in Example 11 may be retired either by redemption at par or by market purchase. The issuer will choose the latter option if the bonds can be purchased at a discount from principal value. Note also that the EIB sinking fund clause provides for a partial, *pro-rata* redemption of *all* bonds, while the GDF clause provides for *complete* redemption of a *randomly selected* lot of bonds.

This section examines the value of sinking fund provisions generally, and focuses especially on the difference between mandatory par redemptions and sinking funds with market purchase options. Within the former category we will also examine the difference between pro-rata redemption and random selection redemption. We begin by analyzing several financing strategies which might be pursued by a borrower who wants to repay principal in installments without a market purchase option.

EXHIBIT 5

## Example 9.
### Sinking Fund Redemptions on the Gaz de France 12¼% Eurobond of May 3, 1993

Issued: November 3, 1982

Matures: May 3, 1993

Redemptions:

| Date | Principal |
|------|-----------|
| May 3, 1992 | $ 87,500,000 |
| May 3, 1993 | $ 87,500,000 |
| Total Principal | $175,000,000 |

Bonds for early redemption selected by drawing and retired at principal value.

## Example 10.
### Sinking Fund Redemptions on the European Investment Bank 15½% Eurobond of March 15, 1989

Issued: March 15, 1982

Matures: March 15, 1989

Redemptions:

| Date | Principal |
|------|-----------|
| March 15, 1985 | $ 75,000,000 |
| March 15, 1989 | $ 75,000,000 |
| Total Principal | $150,000,000 |

One half of the principal amount of every bond will be repaid in 1985, and the remaining principal on the bond reduced commensurately.

## Example 11.
### Sinking Fund Redemptions on the Swedish Export Credit 9¼% Eurobond of October 10, 1993

Issued: February 10, 1986

Matures: October 10, 1993

Redemptions:

| Date | Principal |
|------|-----------|
| October 10, 1988 | $ 16,665,000 |
| October 10, 1989 | $ 16,665,000 |
| October 10, 1990 | $ 16,665,000 |
| October 10, 1991 | $ 16,665,000 |
| October 10, 1992 | $ 16,665,000 |
| October 10, 1993 | $ 16,675,000 |
| Total Principal | $100,000,000 |

Bonds for early redemption may be either (a) bought in secondary market transactions, or (b) selected by drawing and retired at principal value.

## Financing Strategies with Mandatory Par Redemption

Consider a corporation which wants to borrow $50 million for 2 years and $50 million for 3 years. There are several different ways the corporation can structure a bond offering which meets these requirements.

The simplest way to effect the desired borrowing is to sell two plain vanilla, bullet redemption, bonds: a two-year issue of $50 million principal and a three-year issue of $50 million principal. This strategy is common in the American municipal securities market, and is called a "serial" bond offering.

Panel a of Exhibit 6 shows the payments which result from a serial offering. Assuming a 10% coupon rate, Bond A, the 2-year issue, will pay $5 million interest at the end of years 1 and 2, and will repay $50 million principal at the end of year 2. Bond B, the 3-year issue, will pay $5 million interest at the end of years 1, 2, 3, and will repay principal at the end of year 3.

A second strategy available to the corporation is to issue $100 million of a 3-year bond with a sinking fund providing for retirement of half the principal at the end of two years, and with the further proviso that the sinking fund redemption will be effected by a pro-rata reduction of the principal of every bond. Panel b of Exhibit 6 shows that this offering, denoted as Bond C, will pay $10 million interest at the end of years 1 and 2, $5 million interest at the end of year 3, and $50 million principal at the end of years 2 and 3.

Comparing in Exhibit 6 the serial offering (panel a) and the pro-rata sinking fund offering (panel b) shows that the payments by the issuer are identical. The issuer's

**EXHIBIT 6**
**PAYMENTS ON ALTERNATIVE FINANCING STRATEGIES ASSUMING A 10% COUPON**

| | Payment of Interest and Principal ($ Millions) | | |
|---|---|---|---|
| | Year 1 | Year 2 | Year 3 |
| **a) Serial bond offering** | | | |
| Bond A | $ 5 | $5 + 50 | |
| Bond B | 5 | 5 | $5 + 50 |
| Total | 10 | 10 + 50 | 5 + 50 |
| **b) Sinking fund with pro-rata redemption** | | | |
| Bond C | 10 | 10 + 50 | 5 + 50 |
| **c) Sinking fund with redemption by drawing** | | | |
| Bond D | 10 | 10 + 50 | 5 + 50 |

choice of offering will, therefore, depend on which package is valued more highly by investors.

It appears that a clear decision is impossible on this question of value. On the one hand, an investor could always assemble a position identical to Bond C by buying equal amounts of Bonds A and B. Thus, the serial offering would appear to be at least as advantageous as the sinking fund bond. Moreover, the serial offering would be more attractive to investors who prefer only 2-year issues or only 3-year issues. The serial offering would, therefore, appear to be more valuable. On the other hand, the serial offering is split between two distinct bonds. Since investors generally value liquidity, and since a larger issue is usually more liquid than a smaller issue, the sinking fund bond may be more valuable.

One of the drawbacks to the sinking fund offering is the bookkeeping associated with tracking the declining principal value of Bond C. To avoid this problem, we might consider a sinking fund where the issuer selects at random half of the outstanding bonds for full redemption at the end of two years, rather than redeeming half of the principal on all of the bonds. The resulting cash flows, shown in panel c of Exhibit 6, are identical to those from the pro-rata sinking fund.

Whether bonds issued with a random selection sinking fund are more or less valuable than serial bonds or pro-rata sinking fund bonds can be analyzed by examining the implications of random selection. The issuer of the random selection sinking fund bonds is really offering the package of serial bonds in panel a of Exhibit 6, but without telling an investor whether he bought Bond A, which matures in two years, or Bond B, which matures in three years. The identification of who owns which bonds is determined at the time of the sinking fund selection.

Viewed from this perspective, a random selection sinking fund is seen to create uncertainty in the future cash flows from a bond. It would seem, therefore, that investors will not value such bonds higher than either serial bonds or pro-rata sinking fund bonds. On the other hand, a random selection bond has lower bookkeeping costs than a pro-rata bond, and it may have more liquidity than several different serial bonds.

### Yield on a Sinking Fund Bond with Mandatory Par Redemption

We have thus far described two categories of mandatory par redemption sinking fund bonds—one with pro-rata redemption and the other with random selection redemption. Yields on bonds in the former category can be computed easily. Yields on bonds in the latter category are more difficult.

To construct the yield on a bond with a pro-rata sinking fund, consider a bond priced at P, with accrued interest A, and whose $i^{th}$ future payment of interest and partial principal is $F_i$ for $i = 1, 2, \ldots, n$, where there are a total of n payments remaining. (Note that the value of each $F_i$ is known with certainty, because the sinking fund does not have a random selection feature.) The annually compounded yield on the bond is the value of Ra which solves the equation:

$$P+A \quad = \quad \frac{F_1}{(1+Ra)^v} \quad + \quad \frac{F_2}{(1+Ra)^{1+v}} \quad + \bullet\bullet\bullet + \quad \frac{F_n}{(1+Ra)^{n-1+v}} \tag{10}$$

where v is the fraction of a year remaining to the next payment, computed using a 30/360 calendar. This definition of yield follows the same form as equations (1) and (8), except that it provides for partial repayments of principal prior to final maturity.

As a practical matter, we might also use equation (10) to define the yield on a bond with a random selection sinking fund. In that case, however, the $F_i$ terms would represent the *expected* future payments from the bond. The actual payments can not be determined until the sinking fund selections are made. This implies that the computed yield is a "certainty-equivalent" yield. As such, it can not be compared directly to the yield on a plain vanilla, bullet redemption bond, or to the yield on a pro-rata sinking fund bond.

### Sinking Funds with a Market Purchase Option

The second major class of sinking fund bonds are those which allow the issuer to retire bonds either by par redemption or by market purchase. A casual inspection might suggest that the option for market purchase is only a minor modification of the sinking fund structures described above. We argue, however, that this is not the case, and that bonds with market option sinking funds are quite different from bonds with mandatory par redemption sinking funds.

To begin the analysis, we will consider two bond offerings roughly similar to those in Exhibit 6:

Offering d: $100 million principal value of a 10%, 3-year bond with a market option sinking fund on $50 million at the end of two years. Denote this as Bond E.

Offering e: $50 million principal value of a 10%, 3-year plain vanilla bond (Bond F), and $50 million principal value of a 10%, 3-year bond with a conventional call option at an exercise price of par exercisable at the end of the two years (Bond G).

The structure of these two offerings are roughly similar. The primary difference is that if the issuer declines to exercise the par call option on Bond G he simply lets the bond mature as scheduled one year later. If, however, he declines to exercise his right to purchase $50 million principal amount of Bond E at par pursuant to the sinking fund on the bond, then he *must* purchase $50 million principal amount of the bonds in secondary market transactions.

From this analysis we conjecture that investors will value the market option sinking fund bonds (offering d) at least as highly as they value the split issue (offering e). In particular, the issuer has more flexibility with offering e (because he can leave all of the bonds with investors for the full term), so he can not sell that offering for more than he can sell the sinking fund bonds.

**Sinking Fund Corners.** Another way to appreciate the claim that the sinking fund offering is more valuable than the split issue is to examine a special, but quite important, case. Suppose that two years have elapsed since issuance, and that interest rates have risen dramatically in the interim, so that Bond F (the 3-year plain vanilla bond) is trading at a price of 92. What can we say about the values of Bond E (the sinking fund bond) and Bond G (the callable bond)?

It should be clear that Bond G will trade at the same price as Bond F, or 92. In particular, the issuer has no incentive to exercise his par call option, because interest rates are well above the coupon on the bond.

Valuing the sinking fund bond is more difficult. The bond can not be worth less than 92, because it is no worse an investment than Bond G in an environment of high interest rates. However, it may be worth more than Bond G, because the issuer must purchase $50 million of Bond E pursuant to the sinking fund. This can create some peculiar results.

If, for example, a small group of investors owned all of Bond E, they could bargain with the issuer over the price at which they would sell bonds to satisfy the sinking fund obligation. The negotiated price will not exceed par, because the issuer can unilaterally choose to redeem the bonds at par, but it can easily exceed 92.

The situation where a small number of investors own a large fraction of a market option sinking fund bond priced at a substantial discount from face value is commonly known as a "sinking fund corner." Valuing a bond caught in a sinking fund corner is notoriously difficult, because the value will depend, *inter alia*, on the bargaining power of the major holders and on the willingness of small holders to sell their bonds in the secondary market.

## V. CONCLUSIONS

This article has analyzed the payment characteristics of several important classes of Eurobonds, including plain vanilla Eurobonds, bonds with optional redemption features, and sinking fund bonds.

We suggested that there are only two cases where the yield on a Eurobond can be computed unambiguously: plain vanilla bonds, and sinking fund bonds with a provision for pro-rata mandatory par redemption. These are the only cases where the future cash flows are known with certainty.

A yield can also be computed for a sinking fund bond with a provision for par redemption of randomly selected bonds. In this case, however, the yield is computed for the expected, rather than known, future cash flows. The procedure may be justified by noting that the early redemption of any particular bond does not depend on movements in interest rates.

The most difficult cases are those where either the issuer or investors have a right to compel early redemption. These cases include bonds with put and call options, and sinking fund bonds with market purchase options. These options create uncertainty in future cash flows which is inextricably linked to changes in interest rates.

## APPENDIX—COUNTING DAYS WITH A 30/360 CALENDAR

This appendix describes the method used in the Eurobond market for counting the number of days in the interval between two dates. In the United States Treasury market the practice is: compute the actual number of days. In the Eurobond market, however, the number of days is calculated with an assumption that all months have 30 days.

Consider the problem of counting the number of days between May 14 and September 17. Assuming all months have 30 days implies there are 16 days remaining in May, and 30 days each in June, July, and August. Adding the 17 days in September gives a total count of 123 days ($123 = 16 + 30 + 30 + 30 + 17$).

Looking at a calendar, however, shows the actual day count between May 14 and September 17 is 126 days. The discrepancy between the counts arises because May, July, and August have 31 days, and not 30 days. Assuming months of 30 days each thus leads to a short count of the number of days between May 14 and September 17.

When an interval includes the end of February, assuming a 30-day month can produce a long day-count. For example, there are actually 16 days between February 22 and March 10 (17 days in a leap year). Assuming a 30-day month gives a day-count of 18 days (8 days remaining in February, plus 10 days in March).

Counting days with a 30-day month thus far seems reasonably straight-forward. There is, however, one unusual case: when an interval begins or ends on the 31st day of a month.

If the beginning or ending date of an interval is on the 31st, that date is replaced by the 30th of the month. Applying this convention, we find there are 10 days between August 31 and September 10. That is, the August 31 date is moved back to August 30, and the number of days between August 30 and September 10 is 10 days.

The day-count convention for intervals which begin on the 30th of a month leads to a particularly unusual result when the interval ends on the 31st of the same month. The convention then implies that there are zero days in the interval. There are, for example, zero days between March 30 and March 31. This follows because March 31 is replaced by March 30, so the interval becomes March 30 to March 30.

# Institutional Characteristics of the Gilt-Edged Securities Market

THOMAS J. URICH, PH.D.
VICE PRESIDENT
BANKERS TRUST COMPANY

## I. INTRODUCTION

Gilt-edged stock, or "gilts," are the British equivalent of U.S. Treasury securities. The origins of gilt-edged stock date to 1694, when the Bank of England was established to help finance a war against France. The name "gilt-edged" comes from the gilt (gold)-colored edges of the certificates, which signified they were of the highest quality.

Standard gilt stock are very similar to U.S. Treasury securities. They have a fixed maturity or "redemption" date, carry a fixed annual coupon (known as a dividend) paid in semi-annual installments, and are quoted as a percent of principal or "redemption" value. Maturities extend out to almost 30 years and there are a wide range of coupon rates in every maturity segment. Some issues also carry a call provision which allows the Treasury to redeem the stock prior to maturity. For example, the Treasury 9% of March 15, 1992/96 matures on March 15, 1996, but the Treasury can redeem the bond any time after March 15, 1992.

Gilts are bonds which are issued or guaranteed by the British government. They go by a variety of names, such as Exchequer 12% of November 20, 1998, but the names have no significance for investment purposes other than as a means of identification. For example, the Treasury 10% of April 15, 1993, Exchequer 13¼% of May 15, 1996 and Funding 6% of September 15, 1993 are gilts issued by the British government, while Gas 3% of May 1, 1990/1995 is guaranteed by the British government. Some issues are less marketable than others, but this is due to the underlying characteristics of the particular security (such as issue size and age) rather than creditworthiness. In general, however, most of the stock guaranteed by the British government are small in size and were issued some time ago. Consequently, they tend to be relatively illiquid.

In addition to the standard gilts, there are several types of special gilt stock, including index-linked, convertible, and undated stock. Index-linked stock have their coupon payments and principal indexed to the UK Retail Price Index (RPI), which is the British equivalent of the Consumer Price Index in the United States. Index-linked stock are meant to protect the investor against inflation.

Convertible gilts carry an option for the holder of the security to convert into one or more other gilts at specific dates and conversion ratios. The underlying or "conversion" stock usually have longer maturities, e.g., Treasury 10½% of May 7, 1992 is convertible into Conversion 9¾% of May 7, 2003. When interest rates fall, the holder of the gilt can convert into the longer maturity stock, thereby locking in the yield.

Undated or "irredeemable" gilts have no final maturity dates but are redeemable at par after specified dates at the option of the Treasury. For example, War 3½% is redeemable at the Treasury's option any time after December 1, 1952. The U.K. government has no obligation to redeem these issues and will probably not do so. At the present time there are six undated stock with coupons ranging from 2½% to 4%. The stock all sell at a substantial discount to par value. Redemption would, therefore, be quite expensive.

This article describes practices in the gilt-edged securities market and how these practices differ from the U.S. Treasury market. Procedures for issuing new stock are discussed in the next section. Section III examines the characteristics of the standard or conventional gilt stock. Specifically, we describe how accrued interest, invoice prices, and yields are calculated. Section IV examines gilts with special characteristics.

## II. NEW ISSUE PROCEDURES

Unlike the U.S. Treasury market, there is no regular issue schedule in the gilt market. The size and number of new issues which come to the market are determined by the funding requirements of the British government. However, the government is presently moving to a partially standardized issue schedule. There are three main systems for issuing new stock: tender offer, direct issue, and competitive price auction. The price auction system was introduced in May 1987, and supplements the tender offer and direct issue procedures.

### Competitive Price Auction

Under the price auction system, the terms of the auction are announced at least one week in advance. The announcement specifies maturity, coupon rate, and amount of the stock to be sold. The securities may be a completely new issue or a new tranche of an existing stock. In the case of a new tranche, the issue is designated as an "A" or "B" version of the stock to denote a different first coupon. The first time a new tranche is opened on a particular stock, it is denoted as the "A" version. The second time a new tranche is opened, it is denoted as the "B" version of the stock since the "A" version refers to the old tranche. After the stock goes ex-dividend, it is absorbed into the existing issue.

The Bank of England, acting as agent for the British treasury, accepts both competitive price bids and non-competitive bids. Non-competitive bids are for the benefit of relatively small investors and are limited to 100,000 pounds per bidder. Non-competitive bids are charged the average of the accepted competitive bids.

An auction is conducted in the following manner. The Bank of England announces the upcoming auction and solicits bids. Bids are accepted going from the highest price to the lowest price until the Bank exhausts the amount of stock it wishes to sell. All allotments, or accepted bids, are charged their bid price. If the quantity of bids at the lowest accepted price is greater than the amount remaining to be sold, bids accepted at that price may be scaled down. The Bank of England reserves the right not to sell the full amount of the issue under extraordinary circumstances. Price auctions are only used for conventional, current coupon stock.

### Tender Offer

The tender offer system is similar to the price auction system, except that a minimum application price is specified. No bids are considered below this price. In addition, all accepted bids are charged the lowest accepted bid price, which is known as the "allocation" price. In the case where the amount of bids is larger than the amount to be sold, bids at the allocation price may be scaled back. On the other hand, when the amount of bids is less than the amount to be auctioned, there is stock left over.

Stock which remain unsold after the tender is completed are sold by the Bank of England on a "tap" basis. The Bank adjusts the price of the stock to regulate the amount of sales. That is, the offering price (or "tap price") of the stock is raised or lowered to adjust the amount of sales in the same manner that a water tap is opened or closed to increase or decrease the flow of water. These stock are normally called "tap stock." Several tap stocks may exist at the same time.

### Direct Issue

The third method of issuing gilts is where the stock are sold directly by the Bank of England at the prevailing market price in the same manner as tap stock. These issues are usually a relatively small offering of existing stock. They are commonly known as "taplets." Taplets may be offered in a variety of different maturities at the same time. For the year ending March 31, 1986, the Bank of England offered over thirty additional tranches of existing stock directly to the public.

### Partially-paid Gilts

The Treasury issues stock on a partially-paid as well as a fully-paid basis. The issue price for partially-paid gilts is paid to the Treasury in installments over the first few months of the issue. The amount of the first coupon payment and the market price reflect the partially-paid status of the stock. After the installment payments have been completed, the partially-paid distinction disappears.

The Treasury issues stock on a partially-paid basis to make the timing of its cash inflows match its cash needs. This is a Treasury decision, and investors do not have the option to choose between partially-paid and fully-paid. Partially-paid gilts have been offered by all three issue systems.

### Taxes

U.K. tax law requires a withholding tax on gilt dividends. However, this tax can be avoided by U.S. investors by buying the specific issues which are free of taxation to non-U.K. residents (and completing the appropriate paperwork). Exhibit 1 shows the stock which are free of tax for non-U.K. residents. Withholding tax can also be avoided by buying and selling securities between ex-dividend dates.

## III. ACCRUED INTEREST AND YIELD ON STANDARD GILT-EDGED STOCK

Gilts are quoted in terms of percent of principal value, with fractions of a percent in 32nds. For example, a price of 94-16 means 94 and $16/32\%$. The gilt market is divided into three segments according to maturity: "shorts" with a maturity under 5 years, "mediums" or "medium longs" with a maturity ranging from 5 to 10 years, and "longs" with a maturity over 10 years. All gilts are quoted on a "clean price" basis, excluding accrued interest. Accrued interest must be added to the quoted price to arrive at the "dirty price" or invoice price. (U.S. Treasury bond conventions are similar.)

This section describes how the gilt-edged market calculates accrued interest and yield to maturity for standard gilt stock. It should be noted that these calculations are made using scheduled payment dates and not actual payment dates, i.e., no adjustment is made when a scheduled payment falls on a holiday or weekend.

**EXHIBIT 1**
**STOCKS WHICH ARE EXEMPT FROM U.K. TAXATION TO NON-RESIDENTS OF THE UNITED KINGDOM**

Treasury 7¾% of January 26, 1985/88
Treasury 13% of January 15, 1990
Exchequer 11% of February 12, 1990
Treasury 8¼% of June 15, 1987/90
Funding 5¾% of April 5, 1987/91
Treasury convertible 10% of July 12, 1991
Treasury 12¾% of January 22, 1992
Treasury 8% of April 13, 1992
Treasury convertible 10½% of May 7, 1992
Treasury 10% of April 15, 1993
Treasury 12½% of July 14, 1993
Funding 6% of September 15, 1993
Treasury 13¾% of November 23, 1993
Treasury 14½% of March 1, 1994
Treasury 10% of June 9, 1994
Treasury 9% of November 17, 1994
Treasury 12¾% of November 15, 1995
Treasury 9% of March 15, 1992/96
Treasury 15¼% of May 3, 1996
Exchequer 13¼% of May 15, 1996
Treasury 13¼% of January 22, 1997
Treasury 8¾% of September 1, 1997
Treasury 8¾% "A" of September 1, 1997
Treasury 6¾% of May 1995/98
Treasury 15½% of September 30, 1998
Treasury 9½% of January 15, 1999
Treasury 8½% of January 28, 2000
Conversion 9% of March 3, 2000
Treasury 8% of October 5, 2002/06
Treasury 8% "A" of October 5, 2002/06
Treasury 8½% of July 16, 2007
Treasury 9% of October 13, 2008
Treasury 5½% of September 10, 2008/12
Treasury 7¾% of January 26, 2012/15
War 3½% after December 1, 1952
Treasury Index-linked 2½% of July 17, 2024

*Accrued Interest*

Gilts normally make coupon payments semi-annually, with the semi-annual anniversary dates on the same day of the month six months apart, e.g., February 15th and August 15th or January 22nd and July 22nd. (The exception is the Consolidated 2½% stock redeemable at the Treasury's option after April 5, 1923 which makes quarterly coupon payments.) Each coupon payment is one-half the annual coupon rate, regardless of the number of days between payments. (The exception is when there is an odd first coupon. This point is discussed later.)

For the greatest part of a coupon period, a stock will be quoted on a cum dividend (CD) basis, i.e., the purchaser of the security is entitled to the forthcoming coupon payment. However, several weeks prior to the coupon payment, the stock begins to trade on an ex-dividend (XD) basis. Entitlement to the dividend remains with the owner of record when the stock goes ex-dividend. The ex-dividend date normally occurs 37 calendar days before the coupon payment date. If this date is a weekend or a holiday, the XD date occurs on the next business day.

An exception to this rule is Consolidated 2½% redeemable after April 5, 1923 (which is referred to as Consols 2½%) and other stock that pay dividends on the 5th, 6th, 7th, and 8th of January, April, July, and October. The Consols 2½% pays dividends quarterly on the 5th of January, April, July, and October and has historically gone ex-dividend on the first business day of the month preceding the payment month, e.g., September 1st for an October 5th payment. Under normal rules, stock which pay dividends on the 5th, 6th, 7th, and 8th of these months would go ex-dividend before Consols 2½%, but pay the coupon afterwards. To remedy this anomaly, these stock also go ex-dividend on the first business day of the month preceding the coupon payment month.

**Cum Dividend (CD) Accrued Interest.** When a stock trades on a cum dividend basis, interest accrues from the last coupon date (or issue date) to the settlement date. Accrued interest is calculated using an "actual/365" day count method.

For example, consider the 12% Treasury stock of November 3, 1987, which pays a 6% coupon payment on May 3 and November 3 each year. If this bond is bought for settlement on July 31, 1987, there are 89 days since the last coupon payment date on May 3, 1987. As shown in Exhibit 2, accrued interest is 2.926%, which is 89/365ths of the annual coupon ($2.926\% = 89/365 \times 12.00\%$).

**Ex-dividend (XD) Accrued Interest.** When a stock trades XD, accrued interest is calculated back from the next semi-annual anniversary date to the installment date. In this case, accrued interest is negative and represents the fact that the stock does not start accruing coupon interest until after the next semi-annual anniversary date.

As shown in Exhibit 3, if the Treasury 8¾% of September 1, 1997 is purchased for settlement on July 31, 1987, it has 32 days until the next coupon payment date on September 1 and is thus sold on an XD basis. (The stock went XD on Monday, July 27th—36 days before the next coupon payment date. Since 37 days prior to the payment date is a Sunday, the XD date fell on the next business day.) Accrued interest is therefore negative and is $-.767\%$ ($-.767\% = -32/365 \times 8.75\%$).

**Special Ex-dividend (SXD) Period.** At the present time, stock with a maturity over five years may trade on either an ex-dividend or cum dividend basis during the three

**EXHIBIT 2**
**CALCULATING ACCRUED INTEREST ON THE TREASURY 12% GILT OF NOVEMBER 3, 1987 FOR SETTLEMENT ON JULY 31, 1987**

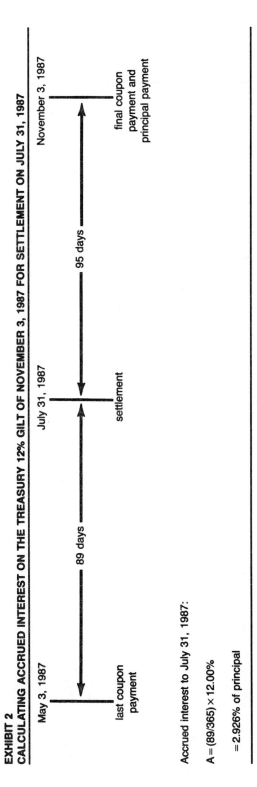

Accrued interest to July 31, 1987:

$A = (89/365) \times 12.00\%$

$= 2.926\%$ of principal

# EXHIBIT 3
## CALCULATING XD ACCRUED INTEREST ON THE TREASURY 8¾% GILT OF SEPTEMBER 1, 1997 FOR SETTLEMENT ON JULY 31, 1987

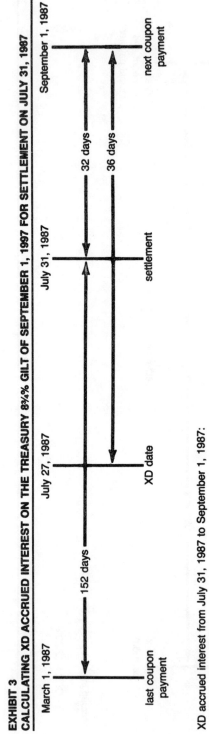

XD accrued interest from July 31, 1987 to September 1, 1987:

$A = -(32/365) \times 8.75\%$

$= -.767\%$

week interval prior to the ex-dividend date. This is known as the "special ex-dividend period." The significance of this provision is mainly historical, i.e., it was used by U.K. investors to avoid tax under a tax code which is no longer applicable. However, it may be used by investors (who may be subject to withholding tax) to extend the period between coupon payments.

If the Exchequer 13½% stock of September 22, 1992 was purchased for settlement on July 31, 1987, it would be trading special XD (see Exhibit 4). The stock becomes XD on Monday, August 17th, 36 days prior to the September 22nd coupon payment date. Commencing three weeks prior to the XD date, on July 27th, the stock would trade special XD. Thus, if the stock was purchased on a cum dividend basis for settlement on July 31st, it would have accrued interest of 4.845% (4.845% = 131/365 × 13.5%). At the same time, the stock could be purchased on an XD basis with accrued interest of −1.960% (−1.960% = −53/365 × 13.5%).

It is interesting to note that the sum of the CD and XD accrued interest (neglecting the negative sign on the XD term), which is 6.805% (6.805% = 4.845% + 1.960%), is greater than the coupon payment which is 6.75% (6.75% = 13.5%/2). This is because market convention assumes a coupon period of 182.5 days, while there are actually 184 days in this period. When the actual number of days in a coupon period exceeds 182 days, total accrued interest, CD plus XD, will be greater than the actual coupon.

The converse will also be true. Between March 22 and September 22, 1987 there are 184 days, while from September 22, 1987 to March 22, 1988 there are 182 days (1988 is a leap year). In the March to September period, total accrued interest is 6.805% (6.805% = 184/365 × 13.5%). In the September to March period, total accrued interest is 6.732% (6.732% = 182/365 × 13.5%).

**Odd First Coupons.** New stock, and new tranches of existing stock, are generally not issued on a semi-annual anniversary date. As a result, the first coupon payment is generally different from the following payments. The size of an odd first coupon is the interest that would accrue during the first coupon period.

Consider the Treasury 3% of June 11, 1992 issued on July 15, 1987. As shown in Exhibit 5, the issue date is 149 days before the first coupon payment date on December 11, 1987. The first coupon payment is 1.2247%. The Bank of England always specifies the size of the first coupon in the prospectus, but it can also be easily calculated. In the present case, the first coupon equals the 149 days of interest that would accrue between the issue date and the first coupon payment date, i.e., 1.2247% = 149/365 × 3%.

Accrued interest on an odd first coupon is calculated in the same manner as on a regular coupon, i.e., 1/365th of the annual coupon would accrue each day. For example, if the Treasury 3% stock of June 11, 1992 was purchased for settlement on July 31, 1987 (which is 16 days after issue), accrued interest would be .132% (.132% = 16/365 × 3%).

**EXHIBIT 4**
**CALCULATING SPECIAL XD ACCRUED INTEREST ON THE EXCHEQUER 13½% GILT OF SEPTEMBER 22, 1992**
**FOR SETTLEMENT ON JULY 31, 1987**

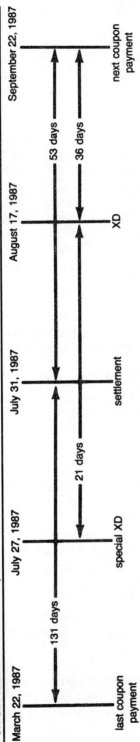

CD accrued interest from March 22, 1987 to July 31, 1987:

$A = (131/365) \times 13.5\%$

$= 4.845\%$ of principal

XD accrued interest from July 31, 1987 to September 22, 1987:

$A = -(53/365) \times 13.5\%$

$= -1.960\%$ of principal

**EXHIBIT 5**
**CALCULATING THE ODD FIRST COUPON AND ACCRUED INTEREST ON THE TREASURY 3% GILT OF JUNE 11, 1992**
**FOR SETTLEMENT ON JULY 31, 1987**

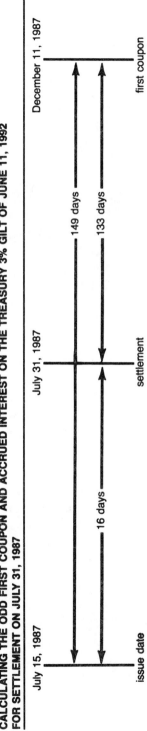

Odd first coupon payable on December 11, 1987:

$Q = (149/365) \times 3\%$

   $= 1.2247\%$ of principal

Accrued interest to July 31, 1987:

$A = (16/365) \times 3\%$

   $= .132\%$ of principal

**Partially-paid Stock Sold by Tender Offer.** An odd first coupon will also occur when a stock is issued in a partially-paid form, i.e., the issue price of the stock is paid to the Treasury in installments known as "calls." In this case, the size of the first coupon, and accrued interest on the first coupon, depend on the size and timing of the installment payments.

For example, the Treasury 8% of December 10, 1991 was issued by tender on July 22, 1987 with a minimum tender price of 97.25% and the following installment payment schedule:

| Date | | Amount Paid |
|------|---|-------------|
| July 22, 1987 | Deposit with Tender | 20% |
| August 24, 1987 | Call | Balance |

While the first coupon is specified in the prospectus as 2.5159%, it can easily be calculated. For a partially-paid stock, the first coupon is the interest that accrues between issue and the first coupon payment date on the fraction of the total investment paid in at any time. Since the actual price is not known prior to issue, the minimum tender price is the investment base normally used to calculate the percent of the investment paid-in at any time. The minimum tender price is also used as the investment base after issue, even if the issue price is different from the minimum tender price.

As shown in Exhibit 6, for the first 33 days the stock accrues interest at $20/97.25$ths of the coupon rate, since only $20/97.25$ths of the total investment has been paid in during this period. On August 24th, the remainder of the purchase price is paid to the Treasury and the stock becomes fully-paid. The stock then begins to accrue interest at the full daily rate, i.e., $1/365$th of the annual coupon per day. Thus, the first coupon is 2.5159% ($2.5159\% = 20/97.25 \times 33/365 \times 8\% + 108/365 \times 8\%$).

Accrued interest on the first coupon is calculated in a similar manner. For the first 33 days, the stock accrues interest at $20/97.25$ths of the coupon rate. It accrues interest at the full coupon rate thereafter. Thus, if the stock was purchased for settlement on July 31, 1987, which is 9 days after issue, it would have accrued interest of .041% ($.041\% = 9/365 \times 20/97.25 \times 8\%$).

**Partially-paid Stock Sold by Price Auction.** In the case of a partially-paid stock issued by tender, the last payment is the allocation price (which is the same for everyone) minus the previous installment(s). However, for a stock issued in partially-paid form through a price auction, accepted bids pay their bid price. Therefore, a different installment procedure is used for the price auction system. Auction participants must submit a check with their bid for their bid price minus what is to be paid in subsequent installments. For example, the Treasury 8% of April 13, 1992 issued by price auction on May 13, 1987 had the following installment payment schedule:

| Date | | Amount Paid |
|------|---|-------------|
| May 13, 1987 | Deposit on Application | Price Bid less 50% |
| June 29, 1987 | Call | 50% |

**EXHIBIT 6**

**CALCULATING ODD FIRST COUPON AND ACCRUED INTEREST ON THE PARTIALLY-PAID TREASURY 8% GILT OF DECEMBER 10, 1991 FOR SETTLEMENT ON JULY 31, 1987**

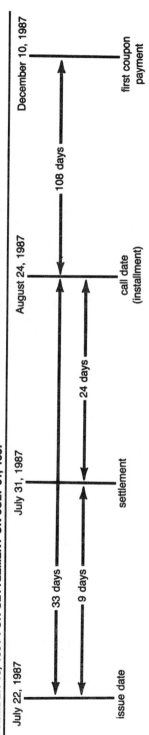

Odd first coupon payable December 10, 1987:

$Q = (33/365) \times (20/97.25) \times 8\% + (97.25/97.25) \times (108/365) \times 8\%$

$= 2.5159\%$ of principal

Accrued interest to July 31, 1987:

$A = (9/365) \times (20/97.25) \times 8\%$

$= .041\%$ of principal

Thus, the last installment payment is the same for everyone.

Partially-paid stock sold in a price auction accrue interest in the same manner as partially-paid stock sold by tender offer. However, par value is used as the investment base rather than minimum tender price. Similarly, stock which are directly issued in partially-paid form accrue interest in the same manner, except that issue price is used as the investment base.

### Yield To Maturity

Yield to maturity, or redemption yield, is the discount rate which makes the present value of the future cash flows on a stock equal to the invoice price. The gilt market generally uses semi-annual compounding on an actual/182.5 basis. This is similar to the U.S. Treasury market convention, which uses semi-annual compounding on an actual/actual basis.

**Yield on a Stock with One Remaining Coupon Payment.** When a stock has one coupon payment remaining, it is market convention to calculate yield with simple interest over the fractional semi-annual period. The yield to maturity in this case is the value of Rm which solves the equation:

$$P + A = \frac{\frac{1}{2}Rcp + 100}{\left(1 + W \times \frac{1}{2}Rm\right)}$$

where $P$ is the quoted market price, $A$ is accrued interest. $Rcp$ is the annual coupon rate, and $W$ is the fraction of the last coupon period remaining before maturity. $W$ is calculated by dividing the number of days to maturity by 182.5

Turning to the example in Exhibit 2, we can calculate the yield for the 12% Treasury of November 3, 1987 quoted at a price of 100-20 ($100^{20}/32$ or 100.625) for settlement on July 31, 1987. Using the information in Exhibit 2, Rm is calculated as:

$$100.625 + 2.926 = \frac{\frac{1}{2}(12) + 100}{\left(1 + (95/182.5) \times \frac{1}{2}Rm\right)}$$

$$Rm = .09087, \text{ or } 9.087\%$$

**Yield on a Stock with More than One Coupon Remaining.** When more than one period remains before maturity, the gilt market uses semi-annual compounding. In the case when yield is calculated on a coupon payment date, yield to maturity is the value of Rm that solves:

$$P = \frac{\frac{1}{2}Rcp}{\left(1 + \frac{1}{2}Rm\right)^1} + \frac{\frac{1}{2}Rcp}{\left(1 + \frac{1}{2}Rm\right)^2} + \ldots + \frac{\frac{1}{2}Rcp + 100}{\left(1 + \frac{1}{2}Rm\right)^N}$$

where there are exactly N semi-annual periods left prior to maturity. Note that accrued interest is zero in the case where yield is calculated on a coupon payment date.

In the case where the stock is valued between coupon payment dates, the above expression must be adjusted to reflect the shorter time before the first coupon payment. The yield to maturity formula becomes:

$$P + A = \frac{\frac{1}{2}Rcp}{\left(1 + \frac{1}{2}Rm\right)^W} + \frac{\frac{1}{2}Rcp}{\left(1 + \frac{1}{2}Rm\right)^{1+W}} + \dots + \frac{\frac{1}{2}Rcp + 100}{\left(1 + \frac{1}{2}Rm\right)^{N-1+W}}$$

where W is the length of the first period in semi-annual periods. It is the number of days to the first coupon payment date divided by 182.5

Consider the Exchequer 13½% of September 22, 1992 described in Exhibit 4. If the stock was purchased on a CD basis for settlement on July 31, 1987, its market price was 115-06 (115⁶/₃₂ or 115.1875). The purchaser of the stock would be entitled to the remaining 11 coupon payments over the next 5 years and 53 days. The yield on this stock would be the value of Rm that solved:

$$115.1875 + 4.845 = \frac{6.75}{\left(1 + \frac{1}{2}Rm\right)^{.2904}} + \frac{6.75}{\left(1 + \frac{1}{2}Rm\right)^{1.2904}} + \dots$$

$$+ \frac{106.75}{\left(1 + \frac{1}{2}Rm\right)^{10.2904}}$$

$$Rm = .09662, \text{ or } 9.662\%$$

where $W = {}^{53}/_{182.5} = .2904$.

On the other hand, if the stock was purchased on an XD basis for settlement on July 31st, the purchaser would be entitled to 10 coupon payments. The first coupon payment to be received would be on March 22, 1988, 235 days or 1.2877 $(1.2877 = {}^{235}/_{182.5})$ periods in the future. The quoted market price for XD trading in this stock was 115-10 (115¹⁰/₃₂ or 115.3125) and yield would be calculated as:

$$115.3125 - 1.96 = \frac{6.75}{\left(1 + \frac{1}{2}Rm\right)^{1.2877}} + \frac{6.75}{\left(1 + \frac{1}{2}Rm\right)^{2.2877}} + \dots$$

$$+ \frac{106.75}{\left(1 + \frac{1}{2}Rm\right)^{10.2877}}$$

$$Rm = .09671, \text{ or } 9.671\%$$

where $W = {}^{235}/_{182.5} = 1.2877$.

Some market participants use a slightly different method for calculating the size of the first period when its length is greater than six months. They assume that the time between coupon payment dates is always one period. The length of the first period is equal to the fraction of the coupon period remaining until the next coupon payment date, .2904 (.2904 = $^{53}/_{182.5}$), plus 1 (the time between payment dates). Thus the length of the first period is 1.2904 semi-annual periods.

**Yield on a Stock with an Odd First Coupon.** The yield on a stock with an odd first coupon would be calculated in the same manner as the yield on a stock between coupon payment dates except that the first coupon is different. The Treasury 3% of June 11, 1992, which is shown in Exhibit 5, is an example of this case. This stock had a market price of 85-14 (85$^{14}/_{32}$ or 85.4375) on July 30, 1987 for settlement on July 31, 1987. On the settlement date, the stock had 10 coupon payments remaining, the first coming 133 days after settlement. The size of the first coupon was 1.2247% compared to the regular coupon of 1.5%. Yield to maturity would be calculated as the value of Rm that solved the equation:

$$85.4375 + .132 = \frac{1.2247}{\left(1 + \frac{1}{2}Rm\right)^{.7288}} + \frac{1.50}{\left(1 + \frac{1}{2}Rm\right)^{1.7288}} + \cdots$$

$$+ \frac{101.50}{\left(1 + \frac{1}{2}Rm\right)^{9.7288}}$$

$$Rm = .06544, \ or \ 6.544\%$$

where $W = {}^{133}/_{182.5} = .7288$.

**Yield on a Partially-paid Stock.** Yield on a partially-paid stock is calculated in the same manner as for a stock with an odd first coupon, except that the value of the time delay in the installment payments must be taken into account. For the Treasury 8% of December 10, 1991 described in Exhibit 6, the quoted market price for settlement on July 31, 1987 was 18-09 (18$^9/_{32}$ or 18.28125). The first coupon was 2.5159% payable on December 10, 1987, 132 days after settlement. The low price reflects the fact that as of July 31st, only 20% of par value has been paid to the Treasury. The remaining balance of 77.25% (the allocation price in the auction minus the 20% that was submitted with the tender) must be paid to the Treasury on August 24, 1987, 24 days after settlement ($^{24}/_{182.5}$ths or .1315 of a semi-annual period). The yield to maturity on this stock is the value of Rm that solves:

$$18.28125 + .041 + \frac{77.25}{\left(1 + \frac{1}{2}Rm\right)^{.1315}}$$

$$= \frac{2.5159}{\left(1 + \frac{1}{2}Rm\right)^{.7233}} + \frac{4.0}{\left(1 + \frac{1}{2}Rm\right)^{1.7233}} + \cdots + \frac{104.0}{\left(1 + \frac{1}{2}Rm\right)^{8.7233}}$$

$$Rm = .09290, \text{ or } 9.290\%$$

where $W = {}^{132}/_{182.5} = .7233$. Note that the allocation price and the minimum tender price were both 97.25% in this example.

## IV. GILTS WITH SPECIAL FEATURES

### Convertible Gilts

Convertible gilts are normally short maturity stock which carry an option for the holder to convert into one or more gilts with a longer maturity. The underlying gilt or conversion stock may be either a new issue, which would be known as Conversion, or it may be an existing stock. Exhibit 7 shows the convertible gilts and their conversion stock that were outstanding on July 31, 1987. Conversion can usually be made only on specific dates (usually the coupon payment dates) and at specific conversion ratios. The conversion values typically decline with time to conversion. For example, 100 pounds par value of the 9¾% Treasury of June 14, 1988 was convertible into 100 pounds par value of Conversion 9¼% of June 14, 2002 on June 14, 1984 but only 92 pounds par value of Conversion 9¼% of June 14, 2002 on June 14, 1986.

### Indexed-linked Stock

Index-linked stock have their principal and coupon payments linked to the UK Retail Price Index (RPI). These stock are meant to offer a hedge against inflation. They were first issued in 1981 when there was a great deal of investor concern about inflation.

Index-linked stock are quoted on a "real" yield basis, i.e., yield over the inflation rate. The amount of each coupon payment is determined by the percent change in the RPI measured from the base month (which is eight calendar months prior to the issue month) to eight months prior to the payment month. Payment of principal at maturity is calculated in the same way. There is an eight month lag in the RPI figures so that the size of the coupon payment is known before the coupon period starts.

**EXHIBIT 7**
**CONVERTIBLE STOCK**

100 £ par value of Treasury 9¾% of June 14, 1988 is convertible into:

| Date | Conversion 9½% of Jun 14, 2002 |
| --- | --- |
| | £ par value |
| Jun 14, 1984 | 100 |
| Dec 14, 1984 | 98 |
| Jun 14, 1985 | 96 |
| Dec 14, 1985 | 94 |
| Jun 14, 1986 | 92 |

100 £ par value of Treasury 10% of October 25, 1990 is convertible into:

| Date | Conversion 9½% of Oct 25, 2004 |
| --- | --- |
| | £ par value |
| Oct 25, 1984 | 98 |
| Apr 25, 1985 | 96 |
| Oct 25, 1985 | 94 |
| Apr 25, 1986 | 92 |
| Oct 25, 1986 | 90 |

100 £ par value of Treasury 9½% of April 18, 1989 is convertible into:

| Date | Conversion 9½% of Apr 18, 2002 |
| --- | --- |
| | £ par value |
| Apr 18, 1985 | 99 |
| Oct 18, 1985 | 97 |
| Apr 18, 1986 | 95 |
| Oct 18, 1986 | 93 |
| Apr 18, 1987 | 91 |

100 £ par value of Treasury 10% of July 12, 1991 is convertible into:

| Date | Conversion 9¼% of Jul 12, 2001 | or | Conversion 9% of Jul 12, 2011 |
| --- | --- | --- | --- |
| | £ par value | | £ par value |
| Jan 12, 1988 | 101 | | 103 |
| Jul 12, 1988 | 100 | | 101 |
| Jan 12, 1989 | 99 | | 99 |
| Jul 12, 1989 | 98 | | 97 |

100 £ par value of Exchequer 10¼% of November 15, 1989 is convertible

| Date | Conversion 10% of Nov 15, 1996 | or | Conversion 9¾% Nov 15, 2006 |
| --- | --- | --- | --- |
| | £ par value | | £ par value |
| May 15, 1986 | 101 | | 100 |
| Nov 15, 1986 | 100 | | 99 |
| May 15, 1987 | 99 | | 98 |
| Nov 15, 1987 | 98 | | 97 |
| May 15, 1988 | 97 | | 96 |
| Nov 15, 1988 | 96 | | 95 |

100 £ par value of Treasury 10½% of May 7, 1992 is convertible into:

| Date | Conversion 9¾% of May 7, 2003 |
| --- | --- |
| | £ par value |
| Nov 7, 1985 | 98 |
| May 7, 1986 | 96 |
| Nov 7, 1986 | 94 |
| May 7, 1987 | 92 |
| Nov 7, 1987 | 90 |

Consider the Treasury 2% Index-linked of January 25, 1990 issued on January 5, 1984 (shown in Exhibit 8). The RPI base for this stock is the RPI number for May 1983, 333.9, which is eight calendar months prior to the issue month. If this stock was purchased for settlement on July 31, 1987, the next coupon would be paid on January 25, 1988. The size of the coupon would be calculated by multiplying ½ the coupon rate by the ratio of the RPI for May 1987, eight months prior to the payment month, to the RPI for May 1983, the base month. The January 1988 coupon would be:

$$\text{January } 25, 1988 \text{ coupon} = \frac{1}{2} \times 2\% \times 402.0/333.9 = 1.2040\%$$

where 402.0 is the RPI value for May 1987.

Accrued interest is calculated in the same manner as the standard gilt. However, since each coupon will be different, $1/182.5$th of the semi-annual coupon accrues each day instead of $1/365$th of the annual coupon. Referring to the above example, there are six days from the last coupon payment (on July 25, 1987) to the July 31, 1987 settlement date. Accrued interest would be $6/182.5$ths of the coupon or .040% of principal (.040% $= 6/182.5 \times 1.2040\%$).

Yield on an index-linked stock depends on one's assumption about the future rate of inflation which will occur over the life of the stock, since future inflation will determine the size of future payments. This is true for both "nominal" yield and "real" yield. Index-linked stock are generally quoted on a real yield basis. However, it is necessary to calculate nominal yield before real yield can be calculated.

The first step is to calculate the size of the future cash flows for the stock. A widely used method is to assume that the RPI grows at a fixed (inflation) rate from its last reported value. For example, assume that the future rate of inflation will be 5%. In the present case, we would project RPI growth at 5% per year for the last reported RPI number 402.0, which was for the month of June 1987 (and was reported in July).

The first cash flow which we must project is the July 25, 1988 coupon since the size of the January 25, 1988 coupon is already known. Therefore, we need an estimate of the RPI number for November 1987, 8 months before this July 25, 1988 coupon payment date. In order to calculate this November estimate, the June 1987 RPI number would be projected forward at a 5% rate (compounded annually) for 5 months. The remaining cash flows are assumed to grow at a 5% rate compounded annually from July 1988. Calculations of these payments are shown in Exhibit 9 where 1.2040 is one plus the percentage change in the RPI from the base period until June 1987. Note that the RPI for May and June 1987 were both 402.0; thus the percent change in the RPI was the same for both months, 20.4% (.204 $= (402.0/333.9) - 1$). The size of each payment would be one plus the percent change in the index times the coupon and the principal.

Given the payment schedules, it is possible to calculate nominal yield and then the real yield assuming a 5% inflation rate. Noting that the first payment is made 178

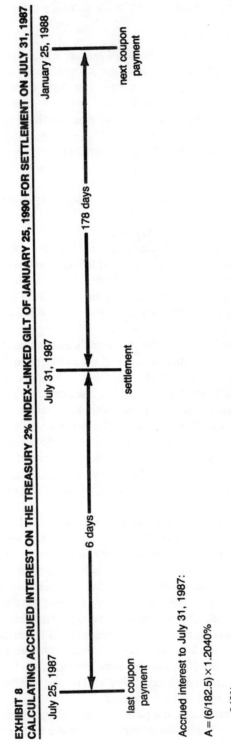

EXHIBIT 8
CALCULATING ACCRUED INTEREST ON THE TREASURY 2% INDEX-LINKED GILT OF JANUARY 25, 1990 FOR SETTLEMENT ON JULY 31, 1987

July 25, 1987          July 31, 1987                              January 25, 1988

last coupon              settlement                              next coupon
payment                                                           payment

← 6 days →         ←——— 178 days ———→

Accrued interest to July 31, 1987:

A = (6/182.5) × 1.2040%

= .040%

days after settlement, and that the quoted price was 116-26 ($116^{26}/_{32}$ or 116.8125), the nominal yield, Rn, is the rate that makes the forecasted future cash flows equal to the invoice price:

$$116.8125 + .040 = \frac{1.204}{\left(1 + \frac{1}{2}Rn\right)^{.9753}} + \frac{1.2287}{\left(1 + \frac{1}{2}Rn\right)^{1.9753}} +$$

$$\frac{1.2591}{\left(1 + \frac{1}{2}Rn\right)^{2.9753}} + \frac{1.2902}{\left(1 + \frac{1}{2}Rn\right)^{3.9753}} +$$

$$\frac{145.9753}{\left(1 + \frac{1}{2}Rn\right)^{4.9753}}$$

$$Rn = .0709, \ or \ 7.09\%$$

where $W = {}^{178}/_{182.5} = .97534$.

Real yield can be calculated once we have the nominal yield by noting the relationship between real yield, nominal yield and inflation:

$$(1 + \tfrac{1}{2}Rn)^2 = (1 + \tfrac{1}{2}Rr)^2(1 + I)$$

where $Rr$ is the real rate of return compounded semi-anually, and $I$ is the inflation rate compounded annually. While it is somewhat unusual to mix annual and semi-annual compounding together, this is the convention that is used. Given the nominal rate and the inflation rate, the real rate of return is equal to 2.10%. If the assumption about the inflation rate is changed from 5% to 10%, the nominal yield becomes 10.81% and the real yield declines to 1.00%. As the inflation rate increases, the size of the future coupons increases. However, the real return due to capital appreciation decreases.

### Low Coupon Stock

The Treasury issues low coupon stock as well as current coupon stock. Low coupon stock are gilts which are issued with coupon rates substantially below current market interest rates and which therefore sell at a substantial discount to par value at issue. They are usually issued in short maturities.

Low coupon stock, however, are not actively traded in the secondary market. They typically have a small issue size and are purchased at issue and held by individuals in high tax brackets to reduce their income tax liability. (For gilts, individuals in the U.K. pay income tax on coupon income but not on capital gain.)

**EXHIBIT 9**
**PAYMENTS OF THE 2% TREASURY INDEX-LINKED OF JANUARY 25, 1990 ASSUMING A 5% INFLATION RATE (CALCULATED ON JULY 31, 1987)**

| Payment Date | Real Payment | × | Inflation Factor | = | Nominal Payment |
|---|---|---|---|---|---|
| Jan 25, 1988 | 1% | | 1.2040 | | 1.2040 |
| Jul 25, 1988 | 1% | | $1.2040(1.05)^{9/12}$ | | 1.2287 |
| Jan 25, 1989 | 1% | | $1.2040(1.05)^{11/12}$ | | 1.2591 |
| Jul 25, 1989 | 1% | | $1.2040(1.05)^{17/12}$ | | 1.2902 |
| Jan 25, 1990 | 101% | | $1.2040(1.05)^{23/12}$ | | 145.9753 |

For example, 400 million pounds of Treasury 3% maturing June 11, 1992 was issued on July 16, 1987 at a price of 85½% in fully paid form. The yield to maturity of this stock at issue was 6.5%.

### Undated or Irredeemable Stock

Undated or irredeemable gilts have no final maturity date. The UK government has the option (but not the obligation) to redeem these gilts. They have low coupon rates, 2½% to 4%, and sell at a substantial discount to par value. Redemption, which would take place at par value, would therefore be expensive and the government is unlikely to exercise its redemption option. However, Conversion 3½% after April 1, 1961 has a 1% semi-annual sinking fund on the amount outstanding. The sinking fund operates when the average daily price during the preceding six months has not exceeded 90. Exhibit 10 shows the six undated stocks which exist at this time.

Undated stock accrue interest in the same manner as standard gilts, but calculation of yield is somewhat different. For example, consider War Loan 3½% redeemable after December 1, 1952 which makes coupon payments on June 1st and December 1st. If this gilt was purchased for settlement on July 29, 1987, there would be 58 days from the last coupon payment (on June 1) to settlement and 125 days from settlement to the next coupon payment (on December 1). Accrued interest would be .556% ($.556\%^{58}/_{365} \times 3\frac{1}{2}\%$).

Yield on an undated stock is the valaue of Rm that solves

$$P + A = \frac{\frac{1}{2}Rcp}{\left(1 + \frac{1}{2}Rm\right)^{W}} + \frac{\frac{1}{2}Rcp}{\left(1 + \frac{1}{2}Rm\right)^{1+W}} + \ldots + \frac{\frac{1}{2}Rcp}{\left(1 + \frac{1}{2}Rm\right)^{\infty}}$$

This equation simplifies to:

$$P + A = \frac{\frac{1}{2}Rcp}{\frac{1}{2}Rm \times \left(1 + \frac{1}{2}Rm\right)^{W-1}}$$

where $W$ is the number of days from settlement to the next coupon payment divided by 182.5. However, $W$ is assumed to be 1 on a coupon payment date regardless of the number of days until the next coupon payment date. Given that the market price for settlement on July 29, 1987 was 37-16 ($37^{16}/_{32}$ or 37.5), the yield is the value of Rm that solves:

$$37.5 + .556 = \frac{1.75}{\frac{1}{2}Rm \times \left(1 + \frac{1}{2}Rm\right)^{-315}}$$

$$Rm = .09330, \text{ or } 9.330\%$$

where $(W - 1) = -.315 = (^{125}/_{182.5}) - 1.$

Some market participants use a slightly different measure of yield for undated stock. They use current yield which is the value of Rc that solves:

$$Rc = \frac{Rcp}{P}$$

In the above example, current yield on War Loan 3½% for settlement on July 19, 1987 is:

$$Rc = \frac{3.5}{37.5}$$
$$Rc = .09333, \; or \; 9.333\%$$

Actual return on undated stock, however, is solely due to the receipt of coupon payments and any price appreciation between purchase and sale.

**EXHIBIT 10**
**UNDATED OR IRREDEEMABLE STOCK**

| Stock | Issue Date |
| --- | --- |
| Consols 2½% redeemable after Apr 5, 1923 | 1889 to 1902 |
| War 3½% redeemable after Dec 1, 1952 | 1932 |
| Consols 4% redeemable after Feb 1, 1957 | 1926 to 1932 |
| Conversion 3½% redeemable after Apr 1, 1961 | 1922 to 1925 |
| Treasury 3% redeemable after Apr 5, 1966 | 1946 |
| Treasury 2½% redeemable after Apr 1, 1975 | 1946 to 1947 |

## V. CONCLUSIONS

This article discussed the institutional characteristics of the gilt-edged securities market. Procedures for issuing new stock (tender offer, direct issue, and competitive price auction) were discussed. How accrued interest and yield to maturity are calculated for standard or conventional gilt stock was examined. Finally, characteristics of convertible, index-linked, low coupon, and undated stock were described.

# PART IV

# Mortgage-Backed and Asset-Backed Securities Markets

# Mortgage Pass-Through Securities

LAKHBIR S. HAYRE, D.PHIL.
VICE PRESIDENT AND MANAGER
FINANCIAL STRATEGIES GROUP
PRUDENTIAL-BACHE CAPITAL FUNDING

CYRUS MOHEBBI, PH.D.
ASSOCIATE
FINANCIAL STRATEGIES GROUP
PRUDENTIAL-BACHE CAPITAL FUNDING
AND
ASSISTANT PROFESSOR OF FINANCE
LASALLE UNIVERSITY

## I. INTRODUCTION

Few markets in recent years have experienced the rapid growth and innovations of the secondary mortgage markets. Issuance of mortgage-backed securities (MBSs) reached record levels in 1986, with about $262 billion of new pass-through securities being issued. There also has been a rapid expansion in the issuance of derivative mortgage securities, such as Collateralized Mortgage Obligations (CMOs)[1] and

The authors would like to thank Valerie Kubisiak and Joe Reel for preparing the graphs; Gladys Torres for preparation of the manuscript; and Patricia Brehm and Lisa Pendergast for the editing and final production of the paper.

[1]For a discussion of CMOs, see Lakhbir Hayre and Lisa Pendergast, "Floating-Rate CMOs," Financial Strategies Group, Prudential-Bache Capital Funding, July 1987; and Lakhbir Hayre, "A CMO Primer," Financial Strategies Group, Prudential-Bache Capital Funding, October 1987.

259

stripped MBSs (strips), which have broadened the range of investors in MBSs. The secondary mortgage market is now comparable to the corporate bond market in terms of size and constitutes a major segment of the fixed-income markets. It also has potential for substantial continued growth; mortgage debt in the United States currently exceeds $2.6 trillion, of which only about one-quarter has been securitized.[2]

However, the mortgage market can present challenges to the investor. The typical fixed-income investor has developed valuation standards based on the relatively simple cash-flow patterns of standard bond investments, such as Treasury or corporate securities. The cash-flow patterns of mortgage securities are more complex. Mortgage securities are self-amortizing—principal is returned gradually over the term of the security, rather than in one lump sum at maturity. A more fundamental complexity arises from the homeowners' right to prepay part or all of a mortgage at any time. Prepayment levels, which fluctuate with interest rates and a number of other economic and mortgage variables, play a major role in determining the size and timing of cash flows. In evaluating the characteristics of an MBS, it is necessary to project prepayment rates for the remaining term of the security. This introduces an element of subjectivity into MBS analysis.

### Why Mortgage-Backed Securities?

Although mortgage securities are relatively complex, they should be seriously considered by fixed-income investors who seek both high credit quality and high yields. The benefits of mortgage securities include:

**High Returns.** The complexity and uncertainty associated with MBSs have resulted in pricing at significantly higher yields than other comparable-quality securities. Consequently, in the last 15 years pass-throughs have consistently performed better than comparable Treasuries and corporates.[3] Recent yields on MBSs have been between 100 to 200 basis points higher than yields on comparable-maturity Treasuries. The recent yield spread for AAA-rated corporates over Treasuries has averaged between 30 to 90 basis points.

**Wide Range of Product.** The mortgage pass-through markets include 15- and 30-year securities with a wide range of coupons, as well as adjustable-rate mortgage (ARM) securities and graduated payment mortgage (GPM) securities. Recent innovations have expanded the type of MBSs that are available. CMOs have created

---

[2]Data in this article have been obtained from GNMA, FNMA, FHLMC and the *Bulletin of the Federal Reserve Board*.

[3]M. Waldman and S. Guterman, "The Historical Performance of Mortgage Securities: 1972-1985," in Frank J. Fabozzi (ed), *The Handbook of Mortgage-Backed Securities* (Chicago: Probus Publishing, 1985).

short-, intermediate- and long-maturity securities by sequentially segmenting mortgage cash flows. Strips separate the interest and principal components of mortgage cash flows to create synthetic securities with a wide range of investment profiles as interest rates change.

**High Credit Quality.** Agency pass-throughs have a government or quasi-government guarantee as to payment of interest and principal and therefore can be considered to be of higher credit quality than corporate AAA-rated bonds. Non-agency pass-throughs typically have the same rating as the issuer.

**Liquidity.** There is an active and liquid market in pass-throughs. The major agency pass-through coupons are as liquid as Treasuries and more liquid than most corporates.

**Monthly Income.** An important consideration for the retail investor may be the regular monthly income from pass-through securities.

### Overview of the Article

This article attempts to provide a comprehensive introduction to the investment characteristics of pass-throughs. Section II provides an overview of the pass-through market, discussing its history and growth and the three agency pass-through programs. Section III discusses prepayments and their effect on pass-through cash flows, and Section IV discusses methods of measuring the investment life of a pass-through. Section V describes the effect of interest rate and hence prepayment rate changes on the price and yield of a pass-through security.

The final two sections cover more advanced topics. Section VI discusses holding-period returns, while Section VII provides an introduction to duration and convexity and their calculation and interpretation for MBSs.

## II. OVERVIEW OF THE MARKET

### The Advent of the Secondary Mortgage Market

A secondary market for whole loans, or unsecuritized mortgages, existed long before the creation of mortgage pass-through securities. The secondary whole-loan market helped to reduce imbalances between lenders in capital-deficit areas and lenders in capital-surplus areas. Even though the servicing often remained with the originator of the mortgage, buyers of whole loans faced many of the legal complications and paperwork of mortgage ownership. More importantly, there was little liquidity in the whole-loan market, and buyers ran the risk of potential losses if forced to sell their mortgages quickly. The extensive details, paperwork and cost involved in these types of transactions prevented many small buyers from entering the market.

The introduction of the mortgage pass-through created a means of buying and selling mortgages that was more convenient and in many ways more efficient than the whole-loan market. Pass-through certificates are shares issued against pools of specified mortgages. The cash flows from the mortgages are "passed through," after subtraction of a service fee, to the holders of the pass-through securities on a monthly basis, typically with a delay. The payments made to the investor consist of scheduled principal and interest and any unscheduled payments of principal (resulting from prepayments and defaults) that may occur.

The great majority of pass-throughs have been issued by three agencies that were created by Congress to increase liquidity in the secondary mortgage markets and thus increase the supply of capital available for residential housing loans. The Federal National Mortgage Association (FNMA or "Fannie Mae"), the oldest of these agencies, was established by the federal government in 1938 to help solve some of the housing finance problems brought on by the Depression. FNMA's original mandate allowed it to buy Federal Housing Administration (FHA) and Veterans Administration (VA) loans from lenders. In 1968, Congress divided the original FNMA into two organizations: the current FNMA and the Government National Mortgage Association (GNMA or "Ginnie Mae"). GNMA remains a government agency within the Department of Housing and Urban Development (HUD), helping to finance government-assisted housing programs. FNMA became a private corporation rechartered by Congress with a mandate to establish a secondary market for conventional mortgages; that is, loans not FHA insured or VA guaranteed. Established in 1970, the Federal Home Loan Mortgage Corporation (FHLMC or "Freddie Mac") is a government-chartered corporation owned by the 12 Federal Home Loan Banks and the federally-insured savings institutions, which in turn own stock in the Federal Home Loan Banks. Like FNMA, FHLMC seeks to enhance liquidity for residential mortgage investments, primarily by assisting in the development of secondary markets for conventional mortgages.

### Growth in Pass-Through Issuance

The first pass-throughs were issued by GNMA in 1970. FHLMC issued its first pass-throughs in 1971. FNMA, which traditionally financed its mortgage purchases through debenture offerings, began issuing pass-throughs at the end of 1981. In recent years, a small fraction of the total pass-through volume has been comprised of non-agency pass-throughs from private issuers. Exhibit 1 shows the yearly volume of pass-through issuance from 1970 through August 1987; notice the dramatic growth in pass-through issuance in the last few years, and especially in 1986.

This growth can be attributed partly to the surge in mortgage originations after the high rates of the early 1980s, with issuance reaching record levels in 1986. A related

**EXHIBIT 1**
**PASS-THROUGH ISSUANCE FROM 1970 THROUGH AUGUST 1987***

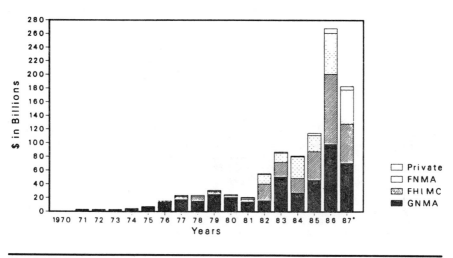

*As of 8/31/87.

factor is the larger proportion of mortgage issuance that is now securitized. Mortgage lenders, after their experiences of the early 1980s, are now more likely to sell their fixed-rate mortgages in order to avoid losses if rates rise. The increased participation of agency and private issuers in this market has facilitated the increase in mortgage securitization.

The growth in pass-through issuance has occurred not only in absolute terms, but also relative to other sectors of the fixed-income market. Exhibit 2 shows the sizes of the pass-through, Treasury, corporate and agency markets from year-end 1980 through June 1987.

As Exhibit 2 shows, the pass-through market is now comparable to the corporate market and is substantially larger than the agency market.

A striking aspect of the secondary mortgage markets is their potential for growth. Residential debt alone is about $2 trillion in the U.S., a figure greater than the total Treasury market. When commercial debt, farm mortgage debt and home-equity loans are considered, the potential for growth appears substantial.

## Comparisons of GNMA, FNMA and FHLMC Pass-Throughs

Although all pass-throughs basically have the same structure—cash flows from the mortgages in the pool are passed through to the security holders after subtraction of a servicing fee—there are a number of generally minor differences among the pass-throughs issued by the three agencies. Exhibit 3 gives basic information about the GNMA, FNMA and FHLMC pass-through programs.

**EXHIBIT 2**
**SIZES OF THE PASS-THROUGH, TREASURY, CORPORATE AND AGENCY MARKETS:**
**YEAR-END 1980 THROUGH JUNE 1987***

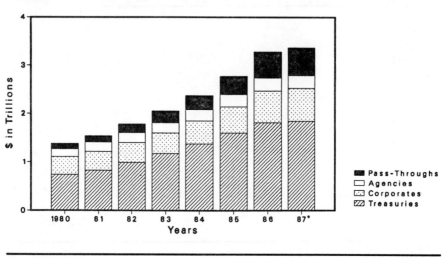

*As of 6/30/87.

Among the important features of the agency pass-through programs are:

**Guarantees.** GNMA pass-throughs are guaranteed directly by the U.S. government as to timely payment of interest and principal. FNMA and FHLMC pass-throughs carry agency guarantees only; however, both agencies can borrow from the U.S. Treasury, and it is not likely that the U.S. government would allow the agencies to default. While FNMA guarantees the timely payment of interest and principal, FHLMC generally guarantees the timely payment of interest and the ultimate (within one year) payment of principal. From the investor's point of view, because of the guarantees, a default is essentially equivalent to a prepayment.

**Payment Delay.** Pass-throughs pay interest after a specified delay. For example, interest for the month of August would be paid on September 15 for GNMAs (September 20 for GNMA II pass-throughs), on September 25 for FNMAs and on October 15 for FHLMCs. On these dates, the security holder would also receive any principal payments made by the mortgage holders during the month of August. The delay is said to be 45, 55 and 75 days for GNMAs, FNMAs and FHLMCs, respectively. However, since interest for the month of August would be paid on September 1 if there were no delay, the actual delays are 14, 24 and 44 days, respectively.

**EXHIBIT 3**
**COMPARISON OF GNMAs, FNMAs AND FHLMCs**

| | GNMA | FNMA | FHLMC |
|---|---|---|---|
| **Types of Mortgage** | FHA/VA | Conventional (Some FHA/VA) | Conventional (Some FHA/VA) |
| **Main Payment Types** | Level Payment Graduated Payment ARM | Level Payment ARM | Level Payment ARM |
| **Maximum Mortgage Balance** | $153,100* | $168,700* | $168,700* |
| **Age** | New Origination | New or Seasoned | New or Seasoned |
| **Term** | 30- and 15-Year (Some 40-Year Project Loans) | 30- and 15-Year (Some 40-Year ARMs) | 30- and 15-Year |
| **Minimum Pool Size ($mm)** | GNMA I: 1.0 GNMA II: 0.25 | 1.0 | Guarantor: 1.0** Cash: 10.0 or 50.0 |
| **Number of Pools:** | | | |
| Issued | GNMA I: 159,543 GNMA II: 9,043 | 45,811 | 59,730 |
| Outstanding | GNMA I: 157,756 GNMA II: 8,853 | 45,549 | 59,593 |
| **Amount ($bb):** | | | |
| Issued | 405.83 | 149.29 | 283.54 |
| Outstanding | 277.91 | 111.44 | 201.04 |

**EXHIBIT 3**
**COMPARISON OF GNMAs, FNMAs AND FHLMCs**

| | GNMA | FNMA | FHLMC |
|---|---|---|---|
| **Mortgage Coupon Allowed (%)** | 0.5 over Pass-Through Rate (GNMA II: 0.5-1.5 over Pass-Through Rate) | 0.5-2.5 over Pass-Through Rate | 0.5-2.5 over Pass-Through Rate |
| **Delays (Days):** | | | |
| Stated | 45 (GNMA II: 50) | 55 | 75 |
| Actual | 14 (GNMA II: 19) | 24 | 44 |
| **Range of Coupons (%)** | 5.25-17.00 | 4.25-16.50 | 4.00-17.00 |
| **Denominations** | $25,000 Minimum with Increments of $5,000 | $25,000 Minimum | $25,000 Minimum with Increments of $5,000 |
| **Method of Payment** | Multiple Monthly Checks from Issuers (GNMA II: One Check Monthly) | One Check Monthly | One Check Monthly |

* Stated maximum mortgage balances are for single-family structures. Maximums are higher for multi-family dwellings, as well as for single- and multi-family structures in Alaska and Hawaii.
** Some mini-pools of $0.25 million.

**Pool Composition.** GNMA pools consist of VA- and FHA-insured mortgages that are assumable, while FNMA and FHLMC pools generally consist of conventional loans that are not assumable. FNMA and FHLMC pools also tend to be much larger than GNMA pools and hence are less regionally concentrated.

**Liquidity.** The growth in the size of the pass-through markets has led to greater liquidity, with FNMAs and FHLMCs now generally as liquid as GNMAs. Bid/ask spreads for the major coupons (currently in the 7% to 12.5% range) are generally about 1/8 of a point, which is similar to Treasuries and less than most corporates. Thus, liquidity for the major coupons is comparable to that for Treasuries and greater than that for most corporates.

Exhibit 4 shows total pass-through issuance by the three agencies for coupons from 7% to 15% (only 30-year securities are included). Also shown is the amount outstanding. Two points are clearly indicated by Exhibit 4. First, the market for high-premium securities (with coupons of 13% or higher) has virtually disappeared because of the massive refinancings of high-coupon mortgages in 1986 and early 1987. Second, although recent issuance by FHLMC and FNMA has increased substantially, GNMA still remains by far the largest presence in the secondary mortgage markets.

## III. PREPAYMENTS AND CASH-FLOW BEHAVIOR

The timing and amounts of the cash flows received from a pass-through are greatly affected by the prepayment rates of the mortgages in the underlying pool. This makes the choice of a projected prepayment rate critical in evaluating and pricing an MBS. Prepayment rates tend to fluctuate with interest rates and other economic variables and depend on mortgage characteristics, such as coupon and age. There is also a strong seasonal effect on prepayment, which reflects the well-known seasonal variations in housing turnover. A more detailed discussion of the determinants of prepayment behavior is given in a separate article.[4] This section addresses the prepayment conventions and models used in pricing and trading MBSs, as well as the effect of prepayments on pass-through cash flows.

### Prepayment Models and Conventions

**Twelve-Year Prepaid Life.** At one time the standard approach to prepayments was 12-year prepaid life, which assumes no prepayments for the first 12 years of the pass-through's life and then full prepayment at the end of the twelfth year. This was based on FHA data that showed that on the average mortgages terminated in their twelfth year. It is now generally realized that the 12-year prepaid life assumption can

---

[4]*See* Lakhbir S. Hayre, Kenneth Lauterbach and Cyrus Mohebbi, "Prepayment Models and Methodologies," in this book.

**EXHIBIT 4**
**TOTAL PASS-THROUGH ISSUANCE FOR MAJOR 30-YEAR COUPONS**

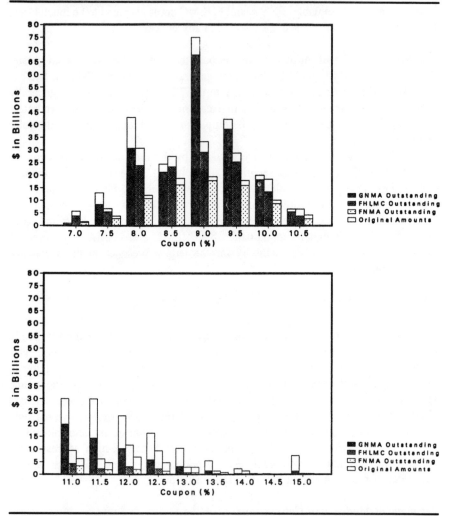

often give misleading results; prepayment rates tend to vary with interest rates and mortgage characteristics and are higher for premium coupons than for discounts. This method is now rarely used in the pricing and trading of MBSs, although quoted mortgage yields are sometimes based on it.

**Constant Prepayment Rate (CPR).** A commonly used method is to assume a constant prepayment rate (CPR) for a pool of mortgages. If one thinks of the pool as consisting of a large number of $1 mortgages, then the CPR for a period is the percentage of mortgages outstanding at the beginning of the period that terminate during that period. The CPR is usually expressed on an annualized basis, while the terms *single monthly mortality (SMM)* or *constant monthly prepayment (CMP)* refer to monthly prepayment rates.

For example, if a pool of mortgages is prepaying at a constant rate of 1% per month, than 1% of the outstanding balance, after subtraction of the scheduled principal, will be prepaid in each month. Thus, if the outstanding principal balance at the beginning of the month is $100,000 and the scheduled principal payment is $1,000, then an SMM of 1% means that 1% of $99,000 (the remaining balance after the scheduled principal payment), or $990, will be prepaid that month. (Since the scheduled principal payments for a 30-year mortgage are generally small until the latter part of the mortgage term, one can, as a good approximation, multiply the outstanding balance by the SMM to obtain the amount of principal prepayment.)

The effective annual prepayment rate, or CPR, corresponding to a given monthly prepayment rate is almost, but not quite, equal to 12 times the monthly rate. For a 1% monthly rate, the CPR is 11.36%. The reason that the annual rate is less than 12% is that the monthly prepayment rate of 1% is being applied to a decreasing principal balance each month. Hence, a 1% SMM in month ten, say, means less principal prepayment in dollar terms than a 1% SMM in month one. (See the Appendix for a formula for converting a monthly rate to an annual rate, and vice versa.)

**FHA Experience.** At one time, FHA experience was a widely used prepayment model. However, it is not often used today. FHA experience projects the prepayment rate of a mortgage pool relative to the historical prepayment and default experience of FHA-insured, 30-year mortgage loans. FHA periodically publishes a table of 30 numbers that represent the annual survivorship rates of FHA-insured mortgages. The table indicates the probability for survival of a mortgage and reports the percentage of mortgages expected to terminate for any given policy year.

A mortgage pool's prepayment rates are expressed as a percentage of FHA experience. For example, if a pool of mortgages prepays at 100% FHA, then in each mortgage year the loans in the pool will terminate at the rate given by FHA statistics. A rate of 200% FHA means that the mortgages terminate twice as fast as 100% FHA experience would predict, and 50% FHA means that the mortgages terminate half as fast as 100% FHA experience would predict.

The major advantage of FHA experience over CPR is that it reflects the effect of age on prepayments and, in particular, the low prepayment levels typical of newer mortgages. Its major disadvantages are its complexity and the fact that periodic updates of the FHA data mean that the prepayment rates implied by a given percentage of FHA experience also change periodically.

**Public Securities Association (PSA) Model.** The current industry standard is the Public Securities Association (PSA) prepayment model, which was developed to

**EXHIBIT 5**
**FHA AND PSA PREPAYMENT MODELS**

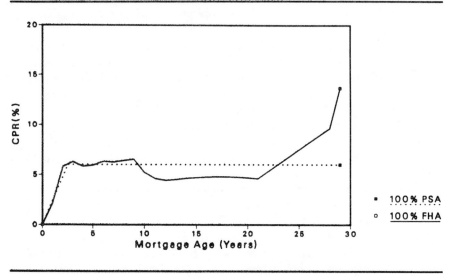

describe mortgage prepayment behavior by combining the information in the FHA survivorship schedules with the simplicity of the CPR method. The PSA benchmark (denoted 100% PSA) assumes a series of CPRs that begin at 0.2% in the first month and increase by 0.2% thereafter, until leveling 30 months after mortgage origination, when the CPR is 6%, as shown in Exhibit 5. Also shown in Exhibit 5 is the FHA curve on which the PSA model is based.

Interpreting multiples of PSA is simpler than interpreting multiples of FHA. For example, a projected prepayment rate of 200% PSA means that the CPR in any month will be twice the CPR corresponding to 100% PSA; thus, for 200% PSA the CPR will be 0.4% in month one, 0.8% in month two and so on, until it levels off at 12% in month 30. Exhibit 6 illustrates this for 50% PSA, 100% PSA and 150% PSA.

**Econometric Prepayment Models.** Many major Wall Street firms have developed econometric models that project prepayment rates as a function of specified economic and mortgage variables. In the most general case, an econometric prepayment model will project SMMs for each remaining month of the mortgage security. This vector of monthly prepayment rates will reflect seasonal and age variation in prepayments, as well as changing patterns of housing turnover and refinancing over time for a given pool of mortgages.

For trading and sales purposes, however, using a vector of monthly prepayments is generally impractical, since it is necessary to be able to quote a prepayment rate

**EXHIBIT 6**
**MULTIPLES OF PSA**

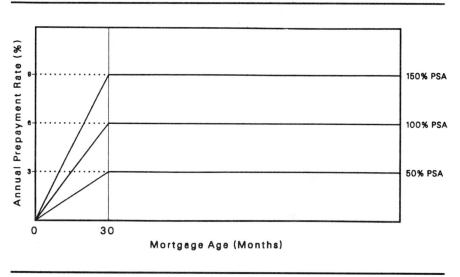

used in pricing or in yield calculations. Hence, the vector is usually converted to an equivalent averaged CPR or percentage of PSA. For example, the Prudential-Bache Prepayment Model calculates the PSA rate that for a given price produces the same yield as the vector of monthly prepayment rates. Using econometric models is often preferable to using recent prepayment levels as a means of choosing a projected CPR or PSA rate, since changing economic factors may have made recent prepayment levels an unreliable indicator of future prepayments.

### *Effect of Prepayments on Cash Flows*

Exhibit 7 shows the cash flows generated by the pool of mortgages backing a new GNMA 9 at various prepayment rates. At a zero prepayment level, the monthly dollar cash flows from the mortgage loans are constant. Notice, however, that the composition of principal, interest and servicing that comprise each of the monthly cash flows changes as the mortgages amortize. As principal payments increase and the remaining principal balance declines, the dollar amount of interest due declines proportionally. Servicing fees, like interest payments, are calculated based on the remaining principal balance of the mortgage loan. For the GNMA 9 in Exhibit 7, the servicing fee is 50 basis points of interest. Pass-through investors will experience the effect of a decrease in servicing fees (as the remaining principal balance declines) in terms of slightly increasing monthly dollar cash flows.

At more realistic prepayment levels, the cash flows are more concentrated early in the pass-through term. The second diagram in Exhibit 7 shows the cash flows at a

**EXHIBIT 7**
**GNMA 9 CASH FLOWS AT VARIOUS PREPAYMENT RATES**

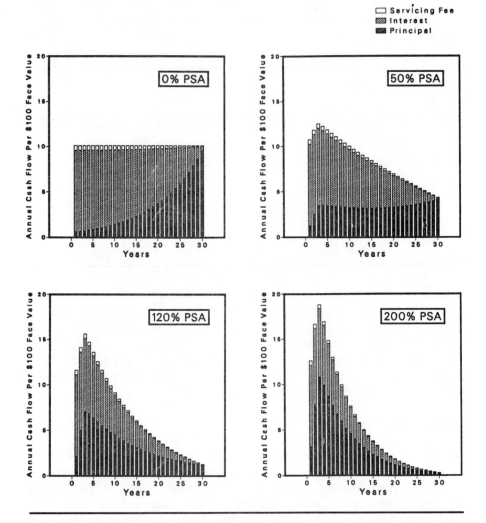

prepayment rate of 50% PSA—historically a slow speed for GNMA 9 prepayment levels. The principal paydowns increase for the first two and one-half years, as the prepayment rate increases according to the PSA pattern until month 30. The prepayment rate then remains constant at 3% per year. Note that the total amount of principal received by the pass-through investor is fairly constant after the first two years. At an assumed prepayment rate of 50% PSA, the increase in the scheduled principal payment each period offsets the decline in prepaid principal, which is approximately a constant percentage of the remaining principal balance.

The third diagram in Exhibit 7 shows the cash flows at a prepayment rate of 120% PSA. Again, the amount of principal increases for the first two and one-half years, as the prepayment rate increases for 30 months before leveling off at 7.2% (1.20 x 6%) per year after month 30. The total principal payments gradually decrease after month 30, since at 120% PSA the principal balance has declined to the point at which the scheduled principal payments are much less significant than they are at 50% PSA.

The final diagram in Exhibit 7 shows the cash flows at a prepayment rate of 200% PSA, which is considered to be fast by historical standards for a GNMA 9. The prepayment rate levels off at 12% per annum after month 30, and the principal paydown is concentrated in the early years.

The outstanding principal balances at 0%, 50%, 120% and 200% PSA are shown in Exhibit 8. These reflect the principal payment patterns shown in Exhibit 7.

## IV. MEASURES OF PASS-THROUGH LIFE

A pass-through is a self-amortizing security that returns principal throughout its term. In comparing pass-throughs (or any MBS) with other bonds, such as a Treasury that returns all its principal at maturity, it is necessary to determine some reasonable measure of the investment life of the pass-through.

The selection of a reasonable measure of mortgage life is important. Measures of investment life are used in several ways when assessing the investment's value. The measure of investment life:

**EXHIBIT 8**
**OUTSTANDING BALANCES OF A GNMA 9 AT VARIOUS PREPAYMENT RATES**

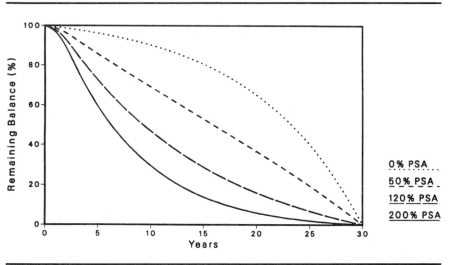

- Suggests the effective span of time during which a mortgage security provides a stated yield or return.
- Suggests how to compare the mortgage security to other, more familiar bond investments—in particular, it suggests the maturity on the Treasury yield curve against which to compare a pass-through.
- Can indicate the pass-through's volatility in a shifting interest-rate environment.

### Average Life

Average life or weighted-average life (WAL) is defined as the weighted-average time to the return of a dollar of principal. It is calculated by multiplying each portion of principal received by the time at which it is received, then summing and dividing by the total amount of principal. (See the Appendix for the mathematical formula for average life.) For example, consider a simple annual-pay, four-year bond with a face value of $100 and principal payments as in Exhibit 9.

**EXHIBIT 9**
**CALCULATION OF AVERAGE LIFE**

| Time | Principal Received | Time x Principal |
|------|--------------------|------------------|
| 1 Yr. | $ 40 | 1 year  x $40 =  40 |
| 2 | 30 | 2 years x  30 =  60 |
| 3 | 20 | 3 years x  20 =  60 |
| 4 | 10 | 4 years x  10 =  40 |
|   | $100 | 200 |

$$\text{Average Life} = \frac{\text{Sum of (Time x Principal)}}{\text{Total Principal}} = \frac{200}{100} = 2 \text{ years}$$

As Exhibit 9 illustrates, each time point at which principal is returned is weighted by the percentage of principal returned at that time point, so that the average life in this example could be calculated as

Average Life = .4 * 1 year + .3 * 2 years + .2 * 3 years + .1 * 4 years = 2 years

Average life is commonly used as the measure of investment life for MBSs, and the yield of an MBS is typically compared against a Treasury with maturity close to the average life of the MBS.

**EXHIBIT 10**
**AVERAGE LIFE OF A NEW GNMA 9 AT 50%, 120% AND 200% PSA**

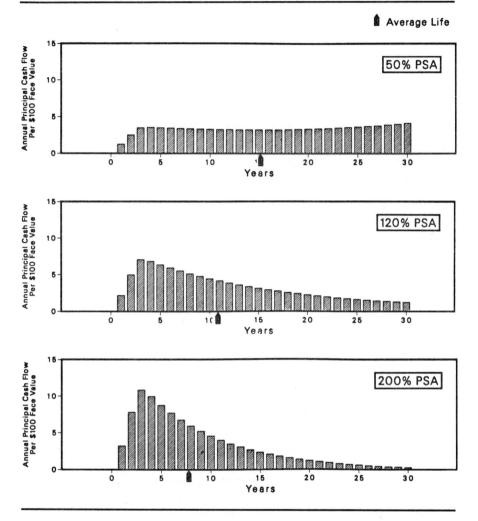

Exhibit 10 plots the average life of a new GNMA 9 at prepayment speeds of 50% PSA, 120% PSA and 200% PSA. As Exhibit 10 demonstrates, the average life of an MBS depends heavily on the prepayment rate. An interesting graphical interpretation of average life is obtained if one thinks of the principal payments as weights, with each weight equal to the amount of principal. The average life is the point at which the weights on each side of the point are exactly balanced. In other words, if in Exhibit 10 the horizontal axis were a seesaw, then the seesaw would have to be balanced at the average life for it not to tilt to one side.

**EXHIBIT 11**
**AVERAGE LIFE OF NEW GNMA 6s, 9s AND 14s**

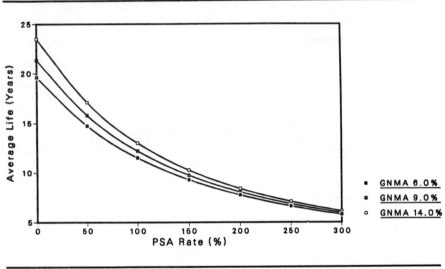

Exhibit 11 shows the variation of average life with respect to coupon and prepayment rate. Specifically, it indicates that, for a given remaining term and prepayment rate, the average life of an MBS increases with the coupon. This is because a higher coupon means that the interest portion is a higher percentage of the monthly payments in the early years of the mortgage term, with the principal payments being more concentrated toward the later years.

### Macaulay Duration

An alternative to average life as a measure of investment life is duration. Duration, or Macaulay duration (named after Frederick Macaulay, who introduced the concept in 1938), is defined as the weighted-average time to return of a dollar of price. It is calculated by multiplying the present value of each cash flow by the time at which it is received, summing and then dividing by the price. (See the Appendix for the mathematical formula for Macaulay duration.) Exhibit 12 demonstrates the calculation of Macaulay duration for an annual-pay, four-year bond with cash flows of $30 each year and an assumed discount rate of 10%.

This example shows that one can obtain Macaulay duration, if, in the formula for average life, the total principal is replaced by the price and the principal payments at each point in time are replaced by the present values of the cash flows. *Thus, Macaulay duration can be thought of as the average life of a dollar of price of the security.*

**EXHIBIT 12**
**CALCULATION OF MACAULAY DURATION**

| Time | Cash Flow | Present Value at 10% | Present Value x Time |
|------|-----------|----------------------|----------------------|
| 1 Yr. | $30 | $27.27 | 27.27 |
| 2 | 30 | 24.79 | 49.58 |
| 3 | 30 | 22.54 | 67.62 |
| 4 | 30 | 20.49 | 81.96 |
| | | Price =$95.09 | 226.43 |

$$\text{Duration} = \frac{\text{Sum of (Present Values x Time)}}{\text{Price}} = \frac{226.43}{95.09} = 2.38 \text{ years}$$

Macaulay duration is often considered to be a superior measure of investment life than average life. It considers the total cash flow, not just the principal component. Thus, it can be applied to derivative MBSs, such as CMO residuals and interest-only strips, that have no principal payments. It also recognizes the time value of money by giving greater weight to earlier cash flows.

Exhibit 13 shows the Macaulay durations of a new GNMA 9 at prepayment rates of 50% PSA, 120% PSA and 200% PSA. A comparison of Exhibit 10 and Exhibit 13 shows that the later cash flows are less significant in the calculation of duration than in the calculation of average life. Consequently, the duration tends to be less than the average life.

Macaulay duration (or a slight variation on it called modified duration, which is defined in Section VII) is often used as a measure of the volatility of price with respect to changes in yield. This is appropriate as long as the cash flows are not a function of interest rates. However, the cash flows of an MBS depend on prepayments, which are driven to a large extent by interest rates. In the case of interest-rate-dependent cash flows, great care must be taken in using Macaulay duration as a measure of price volatility. This is discussed further in Section VII.

## V. PRICE AND YIELD BEHAVIOR

This section will examine how the price and yield-to-maturity of pass-through securities vary as interest rates vary. As discussed in Section III, the cash flows from an MBS are affected by changes in interest rates, due to the resulting changes in prepayment levels. This makes the price and yield characteristics of an MBS more complex than those of a standard fixed-income security such as a Treasury.

**EXHIBIT 13**
**MACAULAY DURATION FOR A NEW GNMA 9\* at 50%, 120% and 200% PSA**

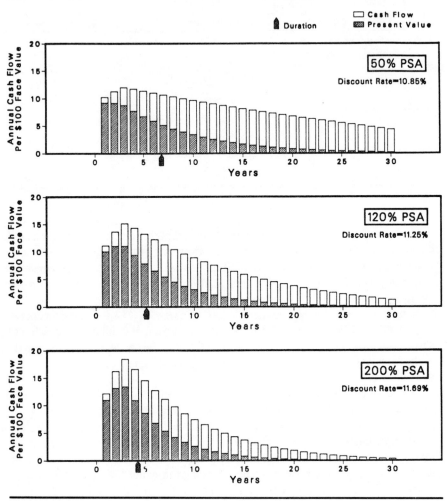

\*Priced at 88-21.

## Calculation of Yield-to-Maturity

The yield-to-maturity, or simply yield, of a security is defined as the discount rate that makes the present value of the security's cash flows equal to its current price. (See the Appendix for a mathematical formula for calculating yield.)

For a non-callable bond, the calculation of yield is straightforward, given the price, coupon and timing of cash flows. Even for a standard callable bond, one can calculate a yield-to-call or estimate the probability of calls at different points in time.

However, for an MBS there is a separate call option on each dollar of mortgage, since in general a homeowner can prepay part or all of a mortgage at any time. Furthermore, since mortgages are self-amortizing, the amount redeemed if a homeowner "exercises a call" will depend on the original term, coupon and age of the mortgage.

To calculate a yield for an MBS, a prepayment rate must be specified for each remaining month of the MBS's term. Once the prepayment rate has been chosen, cash flows can then be obtained for each month, and the yield (and other security characteristics, such as average life) can be calculated. The necessity of specifying a prepayment rate introduces an element of subjectivity into the calculation of an MBS's yield; there is generally no consensus on the projected prepayment rate of an MBS and hence no consensus on the yield.

The traditional approach to prepayments has been to assume a 12-year prepaid life, but this is generally recognized as inadequate. MBSs are now usually priced at a specified CPR or percentage of PSA. The CPR or percentage of PSA to be used for a given MBS should be chosen using relevant mortgage characteristics and economic variables.

Exhibit 14 shows the projected yields-to-maturity of various seasoned GNMAs plotted against average lives. These are calculated using prepayment projections from the Prudential-Bache Prepayment Model. This graph can be thought of as a GNMA yield curve. For comparison, the graph also shows the Treasury curve and an agency yield curve based on the averages of the yields of selected agencies of varying maturities. Pass-throughs have essentially the same credit quality and liquidity as agencies, so the pass-through spread over the agencies can be thought of as compensation for prepayment uncertainty and for the relative complexity of pass-throughs compared with agencies.

**Mortgage Yield and Bond-Equivalent Yield.** Mortgage pass-through cash flows typically are paid monthly. The yield calculated from these monthly cash flows is called the mortgage yield; it implicitly assumes monthly compounding of interest. To make the yield of an MBS comparable to semi-annual-pay Treasuries or corporates, the mortgage yield must be converted to a semi-annual compounding basis, or bond-equivalent yield. (See the Appendix for the mathematical formula for bond-equivalent yield.) The bond-equivalent yield is higher than the mortgage yield, since monthly compounding generates a higher annual yield than semi-annual compounding. Hence, to be equivalent to the mortgage yield, the semi-annual yield must be higher.

### Price Behavior as Interest Rates Vary

The prepayment of principal affects price in different ways for different coupon mortgage securities. Discount coupon securities—those with coupon rates lower than the current coupon rate—trading below par benefit from the early return of principal at par. On the other hand, premium securities trading above par experience

**EXHIBIT 14**
**GNMA, AGENCY AND TREASURY YIELD CURVES***

| GNMA Coupon | 7.5 | 8 | 8.5 | 9 | 9.5 | 10 | 10.5 | 11 | 11.5 | 12 | 12.5 | 13 |
|---|---|---|---|---|---|---|---|---|---|---|---|---|
| Rem. Term (Yrs.-Mos.) | 19-04 | 19-05 | 19-06 | 21-04 | 22-02 | 27-10 | 28-02 | 26-06 | 26-00 | 26-11 | 25-10 | 25-08 |
| Price | 89-31 | 92-07 | 94-10 | 96-17 | 98-27 | 100-29 | 103-29 | 106-08 | 107-28 | 109-00 | 109-30 | 110-30 |
| Projected Prepayment Rate (% PSA) | 109 | 113 | 118 | 123 | 128 | 140 | 181 | 246 | 325 | 416 | 475 | 533 |
| Average Life (Yrs.) | 7.9 | 7.9 | 7.8 | 8.2 | 8.3 | 9.1 | 7.7 | 5.8 | 4.4 | 3.5 | 3.0 | 2.6 |
| Yield-to-Maturity (Bond Equivalent) | 9.68 | 9.72 | 9.80 | 9.83 | 9.86 | 9.95 | 9.75 | 9.44 | 9.08 | 8.64 | 8.33 | 7.91 |

*Data are based on closing prices and projected prepayments from the Prudential-Bache Prepayment Model on August 18, 1987.
The base mortgage rate is 10.34%.

a negative effect from early principal prepayment. As an extreme example, if a premium MBS is bought for a price of 105 and a full prepayment of principal is made the next month, 100 is received for 105 paid a month earlier.

Exhibit 15 shows closing prices on August 18, 1987, for seasoned GNMA, FNMA and FHLMC pass-throughs. The most striking aspect of the graph is the price compression that occurs at the higher coupons. For FNMAs and FHLMCs, the prices level off and are the same for 13% and higher coupons; for GNMAs, the price compression is not as drastic, but prices still begin to level off for the higher coupons.

The price compression in premium coupon mortgage securities can be explained by the fact that prepayments tend to increase the further the coupon is above the current coupon. The higher the coupon rate on the underlying security, the greater is the likelihood that the homeowner will refinance at the lower prevailing mortgage rates. Exhibit 15 indicates that in the opinion of the market, the extra coupon income earned from the FNMAs and FHLMCs with coupons of 13% and higher is canceled exactly by higher expected prepayment levels.

Changes in the prevailing level of interest rates affect the prepayment rates of mortgage securities. As interest rates increase, prepayments tend to slow down, and as interest rates decrease, prepayments tend to increase. The interaction of interest-rate and prepayment-rate changes on the price of an MBS can be illustrated by looking at projected price paths if interest rates change. Exhibit 16 shows the projected prices of GNMA 9s and 11s as interest rates change.

**EXHIBIT 15**
**PRICES OF PASS-THROUGH SECURITIES**

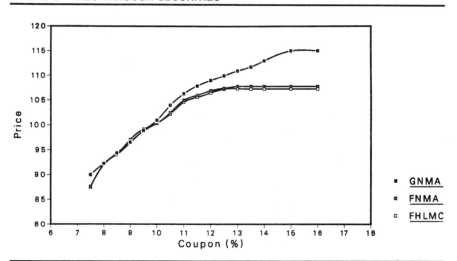

*Data are based on closing prices on August 18, 1987. The base mortgage rate is 10.34%

**EXHIBIT 16**
**PROJECTED PRICE PATHS OF GNMA 9s AND 11s***

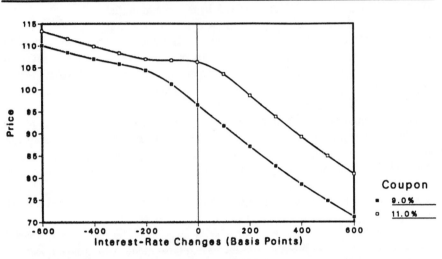

*Data are based on assumptions of a parallel shift in interest rates. Projected prices are calculated using prepayment projections from the Prudential-Bache Prepayment Model. The no-change prices are the closing prices on August 18, 1987, and the base mortgage rate is 10.34%.

As interest rates increase, the slowdown in prepayments has an adverse price effect on the GNMA 9, which is priced below par. As interest rates continue to increase, prepayments on the GNMA 9 bottom out and become relatively insensitive to interest rates, and its price behavior is similar to that of a Treasury or corporate security. For the GNMA 11, which is priced above par, the slowdown in prepayments is beneficial. It reduces the size of the price decline if rates increase 100 basis points. If rates continue to increase, any further slowdown in the prepayment rate for the GNMA 11 is minor, and the GNMA 11, like the GNMA 9, behaves like a Treasury or corporate security.

If interest rates decline, there is a sharp increase in projected prepayment rates for the GNMA 11 and consequently very little price appreciation for interest-rate declines of up to 200 basis points. However, if rates decline further, prepayments level off, and there is more price appreciation. For the GNMA 9, the drag on price appreciation does not occur unless interest rates decline by 200 or more basis points. The GNMA 9 then becomes a premium security, and there is a sharp increase in prepayments. If interest rates continue to decline, prepayments on the GNMA 9 begin to level off, and its price behavior is like that of the GNMA 11.

### Yield Behavior as Interest Rates Vary

Exhibit 17 illustrates the effect of various interest-rate changes on the yields-to-maturity of GNMA 9s and GNMA 11s.

**EXHIBIT 17**
**PROJECTED YIELDS-TO-MATURITY FOR GNMA 9s AND 11s\***

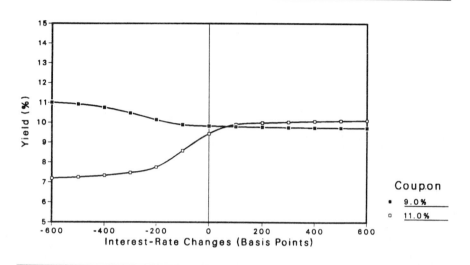

\*The GNMA 9 was bought at a price of 96-17 and the GNMA 11 at a price of 106-08. Yields are calculated using projections from the Prudential-Bache Prepayment Model. The base mortgage rate is 10.34%.

As interest rates increase and prepayments slow down, the yield on the discount GNMA 9 decreases slightly, while the yield on the premium GNMA 11 increases slightly. The effect is more pronounced if interest rates decline. As interest rates decrease and prepayments accelerate, there is a sharp drop in the yield of the GNMA 11 and an appreciable rise in the yield of the GNMA 9.

### Prepayment Volatility

In general, prepayment volatility is greatest for MBSs whose underlying mortgages have coupons between 100 to 300 basis points above current mortgage rates. At the lower end of this range, a decrease in interest rates may trigger a surge in refinancings, while at the upper end, an increase in interest rates may slow down prepayments substantially. The effect of prepayments on yield will depend on the magnitude of the MBS price discount or premium; for an MBS priced at par with no payment delay, the yield-to-maturity does not depend on the level of prepayments. Exhibit 18 illustrates the yield and average-life volatility of several GNMA coupons if interest rates decline or increase by 50 basis points.

For all four coupons in Exhibit 18, average life increases with interest rates. The GNMA 11.5 has the highest prepayment volatility and thus experiences the largest increase in average life as mortgage rates rise. The GNMA 11.5 also has the highest

**EXHIBIT 18**
**YIELD AND AVERAGE-LIFE VOLATILITY OF GNMAs***

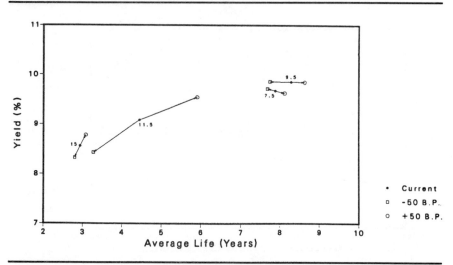

*Data are based on closing prices and projected prepayments from the Prudential-Bache Pre-payment Model on August 18, 1987. The base mortgage rate is 10.34%.

yield volatility, with its higher prepayment volatility outweighing the greater differ-ences from par of the GNMA 7.5 and the GNMA 15. The yield change of the GNMA 9.5 is slight since it is priced close to par.

**Breakeven Prepayment Rates.** A useful way of measuring the amount of "cush-ion" in the yield spread of an MBS over another security is to calculate, for a given price, the minimum (for a discount) or maximum (for a premium) prepayment rate for which the MBS's yield still exceeds that of the other security. This prepayment rate is often called a "breakeven" prepayment rate.

Exhibit 19 gives breakeven prepayment rates for four GNMA coupons against comparable-maturity Treasuries.

For the discount securities (the 7.5 and 9.5 coupons), the yield decreases as prepayments decrease. For both securities, the worst case is no prepayments, and their yields still exceed the yield of the benchmark Treasury in this case. For the GNMA 11.5, the breakeven prepayment rate is 482% PSA; a higher prepayment rate will reduce the yield below 8.15%, the yield of the benchmark Treasury. The GNMA 15 has the least prepayment cushion; an increase in prepayments from the projected 485% to 538% reduces the yield to the benchmark Treasury's yield of 7.96%.

**EXHIBIT 19**
**BREAKEVEN PREPAYMENT RATES***

| Coupon | Price | Projected Prepayment Rate | Bond Equivalent Yield | WAL | Spread/ Treasury | Benchmark Treasury Yield | Breakeven Prepayment Rate |
|---|---|---|---|---|---|---|---|
| GNMA 7.5 | 89-31 | 109% PSA | 9.68 | 7.9 | 100 | 8.68 | (1) |
| GNMA 9.5 | 98-27 | 128 | 9.86 | 8.3 | 118 | 8.68 | (2) |
| GNMA 11.5 | 107-28 | 325 | 9.08 | 4.4 | 93 | 8.15 | 482% PSA |
| GNMA 15 | 115-00 | 485 | 8.56 | 2.9 | 60 | 7.96 | 538% PSA |

*Data are based on closing prices and projected prepayments from the Prudential-Bache Prepayment Model on August 18, 1987. The base mortgage rate is 10.34%.
(1) Lowest yield, at 0% PSA, is 9.07.
(2) Lowest yield, at 0% PSA, is 9.80.

The calculation of breakeven prepayment rates assumes the benchmark Treasury as the one with maturity closest to the WAL of the MBS at the projected prepayment rate. An increase or decrease in prepayments will change the WAL; hence, an alternative approach to determining the benchmark Treasury is to use the new WAL as the prepayment rate is decreased or increased.

## VI. TOTAL HOLDING-PERIOD RETURNS

Fixed-income securities are generally priced and traded by yield-to-maturity. However, from the investor's point of view, yield-to-maturity can be an unsatisfactory measure of the likely return from the security for two important reasons:

- The yield-to-maturity assumes that all cash flows are reinvested at a rate equal to the yield; and
- It assumes that the security is held until maturity, thus ignoring the capital gain or loss from selling the security at the end of a holding period.

The total return (or the horizon or holding-period return) measures the actual return over a specified holding period. This return is composed of three elements:

- The cash flows from the security during the holding period;
- The reinvestment income from the cash flows from the time each cash flow is received to the end of the holding period for specified levels of reinvestment rates that prevailed during the holding period; and
- The gain or loss from selling the security at the end of the period. The proceeds from the sale are equal to the price at the end of the period multiplied by the amount of principal still outstanding at the time, plus any accrued interest.

## Calculation of Total Return

Exhibit 20 illustrates the calculation of the total return from holding a three-year-old GNMA 9 for five months. The security is purchased on January 12 at a price of 96-08, i.e., $96 8/32 or $96.25 is paid for each $100 of face value, with settlement on January 20. The security is sold on June 17 for a price of 97-00, with settlement on June 20. Since the security is actually transferred between the buyer and seller and cash is exchanged on the settlement dates, these dates should be used as the beginning and end of the holding period.

The first cash flow is received on February 15 and constitutes interest and principal for the month of January. The fifth and final cash flow is received on June 15. All cash flows (including reinvestment income) are assumed to be reinvested each month at a reinvestment rate of 6%. A prepayment rate of 120% PSA is assumed.

With these assumptions, the actual return from holding the security over the five months is 4.767% or, stated as an annual rate, 11.441%. The effective annual return, with a five-month compounding frequency, is 11.825%. The corresponding bond-equivalent (semi-annual compounding) rate of return is 11.495%.

## Assumptions Used in Calculating Total Returns

The calculation of a projected rate of return over a holding period requires assumptions about the values of three major determinants of the holding-period return: prepayment rates, reinvestment rates and the selling price at the end of the holding period. The question of prepayment assumptions was addressed in Section III. Here the other two assumptions are discussed.

**Reinvestment Rates.** There are several approaches for determining appropriate reinvestment rates. The calculation in Exhibit 20 uses a constant reinvestment rate of 6% with monthly roll-over of accumulated cash flows. This method is similar to assuming that all cash flows are deposited in a short-term cash or money-market account. Under this method, the money-market reinvestment rate can be allowed to change over the course of the holding period in line with projected changes in the yield level used in calculating the selling price of the security. For example, if the initial reinvestment rate is 6%, and it is assumed that yield levels will increase by 100 basis points over the holding period, then the reinvestment rate could be allowed to increase gradually to 7% over the holding period.

A second approach that is sometimes used is to reinvest each cash flow from the time it is received to the end of the holding period at a rate chosen according to the length of the reinvestment period. For example, if a cash flow is received one year before the end of the holding period, it may be reinvested at the one-year Treasury rate, rather than at a short-term money-market rate. However, this assumes that the end of the holding period is known from the start. In practice, an investor does not generally know the exact time at which the security will be sold.

**EXHIBIT 20**
**CALCULATION OF TOTAL RETURN FOR A GNMA 9**

**Buy:**  $1 million face value of GNMA 9s, with a remaining term of 27 years on January 12 at 96-08. Settlement is January 20.

**Amount Paid:**

$$\$1MM \times 96\text{-}08 = \$962,500.00$$
$$+ \ 19 \text{ days of accrued interest } = \$4,750.00$$
$$\text{Total} \quad \$967,250.00$$

*Cash Flows*

| Date | Remaining Balance | Interest | Scheduled Principal | Prepaid* Principal | Reinvestment** Income | Total Cash Flow |
|------|-------------------|----------|---------------------|--------------------|-----------------------|-----------------|
| 2/15 | 993,129.58 | 7,500,00 | 666.95 | 6,203.47 | 0.00 | 14,370.42 |
| 3/15 | 986,300.71 | 7,448,47 | 668.05 | 6,160.82 | 71.85 | 14,349.19 |
| 4/15 | 979,513.12 | 7,397.26 | 669.16 | 6,118.42 | 143.60 | 14,328.44 |
| 5/15 | 972,766.57 | 7,346.35 | 670.27 | 6,076.28 | 215.24 | 14,308.14 |
| 6/15 | 966,060.79 | 7,295.75 | 671.39 | 6,034.39 | 286.78 | 14,288.31 |
| 6/20 | 966,060.79 | 0.00 | 0.00 | 0.00 | 47.76 | 47.76 |
| Totals: | | 36,987.83 | 3,345.82 | 30,593.38 | 765.23 | 71,692.26 |

**Sell:**  Remaining $966,060.79 face value of GNMA 9s on June 17 at 97-00 for settlement on June 20.

**Sale Proceeds:**

$$\text{Remaining Balance} \times \text{Price} = \$937,078.97$$
$$+ 19 \text{ days of accrued interest } = \$4,588,79$$
$$\text{Total} \quad \$941,667.76$$

**Total Return over Holding Period**

$$= \frac{\text{Sale Proceeds} - \text{Price Paid} + \text{Total Cash Flows}}{\text{Price Paid}'}$$

$$= \frac{\$941,667.76 - \$967,250.00 + \$71,692.26}{\$967,250.00}$$

$$= .04767 \text{ or } 4.767\%.$$

**Total return on an annualized basis** $= 4.767\% \times (12/5) = 11.441\%$.

**Effective annual return with five-month compounding frequency =**
$$[1 + (.11441/(12/5))]^{12/5} - 1 = 11.825\%$$

**Total return on a semi-annual compounding basis** $= 2[(1 + 11.825/100)^{1/2} - 1] = 11.495\%$

*Constant prepayment rate of 120% PSA is assumed.
**Assumed reinvestment rate is 6%.

A third approach is to assume that all cash flows are reinvested in securities of the same type and to assume a reinvestment rate close to the yield of the security. However, this approach raises questions about the meaning of the holding-period return, since at the end of the period some of the cash flow received is tied up in new securities.

**Selling Price at End of the Holding Period.** Choosing the price of an MBS at the end of the holding period is perhaps the assumption most open to question. In the example in Exhibit 20, a known horizon selling price was assumed for illustrative simplicity. The standard approach in calculating projected returns is to assume a given change in yield levels and then calculate the price at the end of the holding period by discounting future cash flows at the assumed horizon yield. However, in projecting prepayment and reinvestment rates and in comparing the total return of an MBS with a Treasury, assumptions must be made about the relationship between changes in the yield levels of MBSs and changes in interest rates in general. A common assumption is a parallel shift in interest rates, so that short-term, MBS and Treasury yields all change by the same amount. It is important to realize that this is just an assumption, and that yield spreads of MBSs to Treasuries may widen or narrow.

As this discussion suggests, the calculation of a holding-period return requires important assumptions about reinvestment rates and the yields used to calculate the redemption value at the end of the period. This is true for all securities, not just MBSs. However, for MBSs there is the additional assumption concerning prepayment levels. These assumptions can have a strong impact on the value of the projected return, so it is important that these assumptions be understood when evaluating securities on a total-return basis over a holding period.

## Variation of Total Returns with Holding Period and Rate Changes

Exhibit 21 shows the total returns for one-year and five-year holding periods under various interest-rate changes for a GNMA 9 and a GNMA 11. A parallel shift in interest rates and the yield spreads of mortgages to Treasuries is assumed. The initial reinvestment rate is assumed to be 7% with all cash flows reinvested monthly. Interest rates are assumed to change uniformly over the year for the one-year horizon and at a rate of 100 basis points per year for the five-year horizon.

As indicated in Exhibit 21, the one-year returns depend on interest-rate changes to a greater degree than do the five-year returns. There are two reasons for this:

- The coupon and reinvestment income constitutes a much larger proportion of the total return over the five-year holding period, thus reducing the importance of the change in price of the security due to changes in interest rates.

**EXHIBIT 21**
**ONE-YEAR AND FIVE-YEAR HOLDING-PERIOD RETURNS FOR GNMA 9s and 11s\***

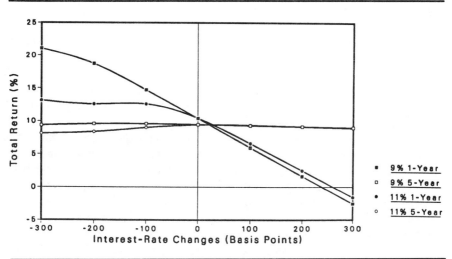

\* The GNMA 9 is bought at a price of 96-08 and the GNMA 11 at a price of 105-16 with the base mortgage rate equal to 10.34%. The following assumptions are made: (1) a parallel shift in interest rates and yield spreads; (2) initial reinvestment rate is 7% with all cash flows reinvested monthly; (3) interest rates change uniformly over the year for the one-year horizon and at a rate of 100 basis points per year for the five-year horizon.

- A larger proportion of the principal will pay down over the five-year period, due both to scheduled payments and prepayments. This also reduces the importance of price changes, particularly in a declining interest-rate environment when prepayments will be high.

The lackluster performance of both securities over the five-year period in the declining interest-rate scenarios is explained by the second point. The high prepayment levels result in a low remaining balance at the time of sale. This reduces the benefits from price appreciation, which in any case has become compressed by the high prepayments (as illustrated in Exhibit 16).

Over the one-year holding period, the GNMA 9, like other fixed-income securities, performs poorly if interest rates increase and performs well if interest rates decline (although there is some effect of price compression and high prepayments if interest rates decline by 300 basis points). The GNMA 11 does slightly better than the GNMA 9 if rates increase, due to the benefits of a slowdown in prepayments for the premium GNMA 11. In the declining interest-rate scenarios, the high prepayments and the resulting price compression cause the GNMA 11 return to level off after interest rates have declined by more than 100 basis points.

## VII. DURATION AND CONVEXITY

### Modified and Effective Durations

In Section IV, Macaulay duration was defined as a commonly used measure of maturity for MBSs. Macaulay duration, or a slightly adjusted version known as modified duration,[5] is often used as a measure of the sensitivity of price to small changes in yields. This is based on the fact that if cash flows are not dependent on interest rates, then modified duration is equal to the rate of percentage change of price with respect to changes in yield.

For an MBS, however, a key characteristic is the dependence of cash flows, via prepayments, on interest rates. This can make Macaulay or modified duration an inadequate or even misleading measure of price sensitivity. To examine the price effect for changes in interest rates, an "effective duration" is often calculated as an alternative measurement of price sensitivity. Effective duration incorporates the changes in prepayment levels that may occur as a result of interest-rate changes. (See the Appendix for a mathematical definition of effective duration.)

Exhibit 22 illustrates the calculation of effective duration for a FNMA 12, using the closing price on September 24, 1987. The FNMA 12 had underlying mortgages with coupons 150 to 200 basis points above prevailing mortgage rates, and hence had very high prepayment volatility.

Exhibit 22 shows that for small changes in interest rates, the change in prepayments for a high prepayment volatility premium coupon can counterbalance the effects on price of a change in yield; if interest rates increase, the resulting slowdown in prepayments will benefit the premium MBS and reduce the price decline, while if interest rates decrease, the increase in prepayment speeds will reduce the price appreciation of the security. In the example in Exhibit 22, the FNMA 12 is projected to have an effective duration, or price volatility, of 1.36% per 100 basis points. This means that at current interest-rate levels, a one-basis-point change in yield will lead to a percentage change in price of 0.0136%. This is much lower than the price volatility of 3.07% per 100 basis points given by the traditional modified duration calculation, which does not take into account changes in prepayments.

The example in Exhibit 22 indicates that while the usual duration calculation may be adequate for discount or high-premium MBSs whose prepayment levels are unlikely to change much for small changes in interest rates, it can be inadequate or

---

[5]Formally,

$$\text{Modified duration} = \frac{\text{Macaulay duration}}{\left(1 + \dfrac{y}{1200}\right)}$$

where $y$ is the mortgage yield.

**EXHIBIT 22**
**CALCULATION OF EFFECTIVE DURATION FOR A FNMA 12***

| | Interest-Rate Change (Basis Points) | | |
| --- | --- | --- | --- |
| | -25 | 0 | 25 |
| Pricing Yield (%) | 10.23 | 10.48 | 10.73 |
| Projected Prepayment Rate (% PSA) | 355 | 313 | 281 |
| Price at 313% PSA | 105.5620 | 104.7520 | 103.9547 |
| Price at Projected Prepayment Rate | 105.0172 | 104.7520 | 104.3042 |

Modified Duration = Price volatility assuming no change in prepayments

$$\approx \frac{-100}{Price} \times \frac{Change\ in\ price}{Change\ in\ yield} = \frac{-100}{104.7520} \times \frac{(103.9547 - 105.5620)}{0.50}$$

= 3.07% per 100 b.p. change in yield.

Effective Duration = Price volatility assuming change in prepayments

$$\approx \frac{-100}{Price} \times \frac{Change\ in\ price}{Change\ in\ yield} = \frac{-100}{104.7520} \times \frac{(104.3042 - 105.0172)}{0.50}$$

= 1.36% per 100 b.p. change in yield.

*Data are based on FNMA 12s priced at 104-24 on September 24, 1987. Underlying mortgage coupons were 150 to 200 basis points above prevailing mortgage rates.

**EXHIBIT 23**
**MODIFIED AND EFFECTIVE DURATIONS FOR FNMAs\***

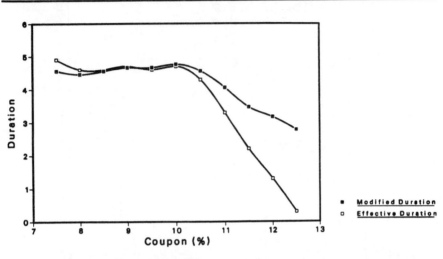

---

\*Data are based on closing prices and prepayment projections on September 24, 1987. Effective durations are calculated using 25-basis-point moves in interest rates in each direction, with the base mortgage rate equal to 10.99%.

even misleading for low-premium coupons, which have high prepayment volatility. An effective duration calculation is more appropriate in such cases. This is borne out by historical studies that have shown that price volatilities do tend to follow the pattern suggested by effective durations.[6]

Exhibit 23 shows modified and effective durations for several seasoned FNMA securities. The effective durations are calculated by using 25-basis-point moves in interest rates in each direction.

Exhibit 23 indicates that modified duration overestimates the price volatility of low-premium coupons. This has important implications for hedging strategies. Hedge ratios based on the use of Macaulay or modified duration to estimate price volatility will fail for mortgage coupons with high prepayment volatility. (This has been a painful lesson for many participants in the MBS markets.) It is important to look at changes in both yield and prepayment rates when calculating price volatility. Effective duration provides a means for doing this. Another useful analytic tool in this context is convexity, which measures the rate of change of price volatility.

---

[6] Scott M. Pinkus and Marie A. Chandoha, "The Relative Price Volatility of Mortgage Securities," Frank Fabozzi (ed.) *Mortgage-Backed Securities: New Strategies, Applications and Research,* (Chicago: Probus Publishing, 1987).

## Convexity

Considerable attention has been focused recently on the concept of convexity and in particular on the so-called "negative convexity" of MBSs. Convexity refers to the curvature of the price/yield curve. (See the Appendix for a mathematical definition of convexity.) In other words, convexity is the rate of change of duration, i.e., price volatility. If one considers duration to be the speed of price changes, then convexity can be thought of as acceleration. The projected price paths shown in Exhibit 16 illustrate positive, zero and negative convexity.

A straight line has zero convexity. Thus, since the price/yield curve of the GNMA 9 in Exhibit 16 is essentially a straight line at the no-change point on the horizontal axis, then the GNMA 9 has almost zero convexity at prevailing interest rates. This means that for small equal changes in interest rates the price of the GNMA 9 will increase or decrease approximately the same amount.

Discount MBSs, like Treasuries, tend to have positive convexity. Positive convexity implies that for small, equal and opposite changes in interest rates, the price increase if rates decline will be more than the price decrease if rates increase. This means that the rate of decrease in price slows down as interest rates increase, i.e., the curve has a downward "bulge" in the middle. When interest rates rise by several hundred basis points, the GNMA 9 becomes a deep-discount coupon and has positive convexity, as indicated in Exhibit 16.

Negative convexity means that the price/yield curve flattens as interest rates decline. This is characteristic of premium MBSs for which increasing prepayments place a drag on price increases as interest rates decline. Thus, for small equal changes in rates, the price is likely to decline more than it will increase. Referring again to Exhibit 16, it can be seen that at prevailing interest rates the GNMA 11 has a high degree of negative convexity, while the GNMA 9 has negative convexity if interest rates decline by between 100 to 200 basis points. If rates decline by several hundred basis points, both the GNMA 9 and the GNMA 11 become high-premium coupons and will have almost zero or even positive convexity. *Hence, negative convexity is a characteristic of low-premium MBSs.*

**Calculation of Convexity.** Convexity can be estimated by considering small positive and negative changes in yields and calculating the changes in price in both cases. The prepayment rate used in calculating the new prices should reflect the changes in yield levels. Exhibit 24 illustrates the calculation of the convexities of a FNMA 8 and a FNMA 11 using 25-basis-point changes in interest rates.

The discount FNMA 8 has positive convexity, while the low-premium FNMA 11 has negative convexity. This can be explained by considering the likely magnitudes and effects of prepayment changes for the two coupons. For the FNMA 8, prepayments do not change very much for small changes in interest rates; thus, its price behavior for small interest-rate changes is like that of a standard non-callable instrument, such as a Treasury. However, the FNMA 11 has high prepayment

**EXHIBIT 24**
**CALCULATION OF CONVEXITY***

| | FNMA 8 | | | FNMA 11 | | |
|---|---|---|---|---|---|---|
| | *Projected* | | | *Projected* | | |
| *Change in Rates* | *Prepayment* | | | *Prepayment* | | |
| *(Basis Points)* | *Rate* | *Yield* | *Price* | *Rate* | *Yield* | *Price* |
| -25 bp | 135% PSA | 10.32% | 90.35 | 233% PSA | 10.42% | 102.34 |
| 0 | 132 | 10.57 | 89.33 | 206 | 10.67 | 101.56 |
| 25 | 129 | 10.82 | 88.32 | 181 | 10.92 | 100.65 |

$$*\text{Convexity} = \frac{100}{\text{Price}} \times \frac{\text{Change in price if rates go down} - \text{Change in price if rates go up}}{(\text{Change in rates})^2}$$

$$= \frac{100}{89.33} \times \frac{(90.35\text{-}89.33) - (89.33\text{-}88.32)}{(.25)^2} = 0.180 \text{ for the FNMA 8.}$$

$$= \frac{100}{101.56} \times \frac{(102.34\text{-}101.56) - (101.56\text{-}100.65)}{(.25)^2} = \text{-}2.048 \text{ for the FNMA 11.}$$

volatility; the increasing prepayments as interest rates decline put a drag on price increases. The benefits of a slowdown in prepayments if interest rates increase are not sufficient to offset this price compression.

Exhibit 25 shows the convexities of various FNMA pass-throughs based on prices and prepayment projections on September 24, 1987. It can be seen that convexity reaches a low at the 11% to 12% coupons, and then starts increasing again. This is because high-premium coupons, like deep-discounts, have low prepayment volatility and, hence, positive convexity.

**Investment Implications of Convexity.** Positive convexity is generally a desirable characteristic in a fixed-income security. However, this does not mean that securities with negative convexity, such as low-premium pass-throughs, should be avoided. The market may have adjusted the prices of such securities to compensate investors for the negative convexity, making their yields sufficiently high so that they offer better value than many securities with positive convexity.

Another point that should be kept in mind is that for a given security convexity changes with interest rates. In other words, negative convexity is a "local" property of low-premium pass-throughs; if there are substantial changes in interest rates, the low-premium pass-through will become a discount or high-premium pass-through

**EXHIBIT 25**
**CONVEXITIES OF FNMA PASS-THROUGHS***

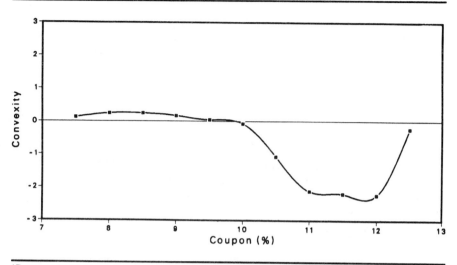

*Data are based on prices and prepayment projections from the Prudential-Bache Prepayment Model on September 24, 1987, with the base mortgage rate equal to 10.99%.

and may then have positive convexity. This is a relevant consideration if one plans to hold the security for a year or more, when the length of the holding period makes large interest-rate changes possible. In general, securities should be evaluated and compared by calculating total holding-period returns under a range of projected interest-rate changes. The total return incorporates such factors as initial price and convexity (through the change in the price over the period) and hence will give a good indication of the value of the security.

### A Comment on the Units Used to Measure Duration and Convexity

Traditionally, duration has been measured in units of years, and convexity in (years)$^2$. This is because Macaulay duration, which is a measure of investment life, is measured in years. Modified duration, which is used as a measure of price volatility, is closely related to Macaulay duration and therefore is also measured in years. The units of convexity result from the fact that it has been defined as a weighted (the weights being the present values of the cash flows) average of the squares of the times-to-receipt of all cash flows.

However, years and (years)$^2$ are not appropriate measures of price volatility and convexity. As discussed previously, duration (or effective duration) is the percentage change in price for a given change in yield. In the example in Exhibit 22, the price volatility of the FNMA 12 was 1.36% per 100 basis points, or 0.0136% per basis point. The appropriate units for duration when it is used as a measure of price volatility are change per basis point or 100 basis points.

Convexity is the rate of change of price volatility. The convexity of the FNMA 8 in Exhibit 24 was 0.180. Analysis of the calculation in Exhibit 24 shows that this can be expressed as 0.180% per 100 basis points per 100 basis points. In other words, the price volatility, expressed as a percentage price change per 100 basis points, increases by 0.180 for each 100-basis-point change in yield.

## VIII. SUMMARY

The secondary mortgage market has grown tremendously in recent years, and now constitutes a major sector of the fixed-income market, comparable in size to the corporate market and greater than the agency market. The huge amount of mortgage debt in the United States and the fact that only one-quarter of this debt has been securitized to date indicate substantial potential for growth.

This article has attempted to provide a modern treatment of mortgage-backed pass-throughs, which constitute the largest sector of the secondary mortgage markets. Pass-throughs, like all MBSs, are more complex in their investment characteristics and behavior than standard Treasury or corporate securities. Their cash flows are unpredictable; they are self-amortizing; their price/yield relationship is complicated by prepayments; and consequently, the usual interpretations of duration and convexity may be misleading.

Despite their complexity, or rather because of it, the mortgage markets provide opportunities for astute fixed-income investors seeking high yields without sacrificing high quality. The complexity of pass-throughs has resulted in pricing at significantly higher yields than comparable-quality securities. Recent yields have been between 100 to 200 basis points higher than comparable-maturity Treasuries, compared with yield spreads of 30 to 90 basis points over Treasuries for AAA-rated corporates. The credit quality of agency pass-throughs is clearly higher, however, than even AAA-rated corporates, due to U.S. government or quasi-government guarantees concerning payment of interest and principal. Historical studies have shown that, as a result of their higher yields, pass-throughs have provided consistently higher returns than Treasuries or high-quality corporates.

In sum, pass-throughs provide investors with a large and liquid market in securities that combine very high credit quality with yields that are substantially higher than other comparable-quality securities. Mortgage securities have complex investment characteristics and require a more careful analysis than a plain-vanilla Treasury or corporate security. The higher potential returns of mortgage pass-through securities, however, suggest that the extra effort may be well worthwhile for fixed-income investors.

## APPENDIX: MORTGAGE MATHEMATICS

### Mortgage Cash Flow without Prepayments

**Monthly Payment.** For a level-payment mortgage, the constant monthly payment is

$$M_n = \frac{B_0\left(\frac{G}{1200}\right)\left(1 + \frac{G}{1200}\right)^N}{\left[\left(1 + \frac{G}{1200}\right)^N - 1\right]}$$

where $M_n$ = Monthly payment for month $n$;
  $B_0$ = Original balance;
  $G$  = Gross coupon rate (percent);
  $N$  = Original term in months (e.g., 360).

**Remaining Balance.** The remaining balance after $n$ months is

$$B_n = \frac{B_0\left[\left(1 + \frac{G}{1200}\right)^N - \left(1 + \frac{G}{1200}\right)^n\right]}{\left[\left(1 + \frac{G}{1200}\right)^N - 1\right]}$$

where $B_n$ = Remaining balance at the end of month $n$.

**Principal Payment.** The amount of principal paid in month $n$ is given by

$$P_n = \frac{B_0\left(\frac{G}{1200}\right)\left(1 + \frac{G}{1200}\right)^{n-1}}{\left[\left(1 + \frac{G}{1200}\right)^N - 1\right]}$$

where $P_n$ = Principal paid in month $n$.

**Interest Payment.** The amount of interest paid in month $n$ can be written as

$$I_n = \frac{B_0\left(\frac{G}{1200}\right)\left[\left(1+\frac{G}{1200}\right)^N - \left(1+\frac{G}{1200}\right)^{n-1}\right]}{\left[\left(1+\frac{G}{1200}\right)^N - 1\right]} = B_{n-1}\left(\frac{G}{1200}\right)$$

where $I_n$ = Interest paid in month $n$.

It should be noted that

$$G = S + C$$

where $S$ = Service fee (%)
and  $C$ = Security coupon rate (%),

so  *Servicing Amount* $= \left(\frac{S}{C+S}\right)I_n.$

Therefore, the cash flow to the security holder in month $n$ is given by

$$CF_n = P_n + I_n - \textit{Servicing Amount} = P_n + \left(\frac{C}{C+S}\right)I_n$$

## *Prepayment Measuring Conventions*

For a given pool of mortgages, let

$B_n$ = Remaining principal balance per dollar of mortgage at the end of month $n$ if there are no prepayments.
$C_n$ = Pool factor (i.e., actual remaining principal balance per dollar of mortgage) at the end of month $n$.

Let $Q_n = C_n / B_n$. If one thinks of the pool as consisting of a very large number of $1 mortgages, each of which can terminate separately, then $Q_n$ represents the percentages of mortgages still remaining at the end of month $n$. Then

Percentage of initial balance has been prepaid $= 1 - Q_n$.

For month $n$, the single monthly mortality, or *SMM*, stated as a decimal, is given by

SMM = Proportion of $1 mortgages outstanding at the beginning of the month that are prepaid during the month

$$\frac{Q_{n-1} - Q_n}{Q_{n-1}} = 1 - \frac{Q_n}{Q_{n-1}}.$$

For the period from month $m$ to month $n$, the constant SMM rate that is equivalent to the actual prepayments experienced is given by

$$(1 - SMM)^{n-m} = \frac{Q_n}{Q_m},$$

i.e.,
$$SMM = 1 - \left(\frac{Q_n}{Q_m}\right)^{\frac{1}{n-m}}$$

The conditional prepayment rate, or CPR (also expressed as a decimal), is the SMM expressed as an annual rate and is given by

$$1 - CPR = (1 - SMM)^{12},$$

i.e.,
$$CPR = 1 - (1 - SMM)^{12}.$$

Inverting,
$$SMM = 1 - (1 - CPR)^{\frac{1}{12}}.$$

**Percentage of PSA.** If a mortgage prepays at a rate of 100% PSA, then the CPR for the month when the mortgage is $n$ months old is

$$CPR = 6\% \times \frac{n}{30} \qquad\qquad \text{if } n \leq 30$$

$$= 6\% \qquad\qquad \text{if } n > 30$$

$$= 6\% \times Min\left(1, \frac{n}{30}\right) \qquad\qquad \text{for any } n.$$

For a general prepayment rate of $x\%$ PSA, for age $n$,

$$CPR = 6\% \times \frac{x}{100} \times \frac{n}{30} \qquad\qquad \text{if } n \leq 30$$

$$= 6\% \times \frac{x}{100} \qquad\qquad \text{if } n > 30$$

$$= 6\% \times \frac{x}{100} \times Min\left(1, \frac{n}{30}\right) \qquad\qquad \text{for any } n.$$

Conversely, if a mortgage of age $n$ months prepays at a given CPR, the PSA rate for that month is given by

$$\% \text{ of } PSA = CPR \times \frac{100}{6} \times \frac{30}{n} \qquad\qquad \text{if } n \leq 30$$

$$= CPR \times \frac{100}{6} \qquad\qquad \text{if } n > 30$$

$$= CPR \times \frac{100}{6} \times Max\left(1, \frac{30}{n}\right) \qquad\qquad \text{for any } n.$$

### Mortgage Cash Flow with Prepayments

Let $\hat{M}_n$, $\hat{P}_n$, $\hat{I}_n$ and $\hat{B}_n$ denote the actual monthly scheduled payment, scheduled principal, interest and remaining (end-of-month) balance for month $n$. Let $SMM_n$ be the prepayment rate in month $n$, stated as a decimal, and let

$$Q_n = \left(1 - SMM_n\right)\left(1 - SMM_{n-1}\right) \cdots \left(1 - SMM_1\right).$$

The *total monthly payment* in month $n$ is given by

$$\hat{M}_n = \frac{\hat{B}_{n-1}\left(\dfrac{G}{1200}\right)\left(1 + \dfrac{G}{1200}\right)^{N-n+1}}{\left[\left(1 + \dfrac{G}{1200}\right)^{N-n+1} - 1\right]} = M_n Q_{n-1}$$

The *scheduled principal* portion of this payment is given by

$$\hat{P}_n = \frac{\hat{B}_{n-1}\left(\dfrac{G}{1200}\right)}{\left[\left(1 + \dfrac{G}{1200}\right)^{N-n+1} - 1\right]} = P_n Q_{n-1}.$$

The *interest* portion is given by

$$\hat{I}_n = \hat{B}_{n-1}\left(\frac{G}{1200}\right) = I_n Q_{n-1}.$$

The *unscheduled principal payment* in month $n$ is written as

$$PR_n = \left(\hat{B}_{n-1} - \hat{P}_n\right) SMM_n.$$

The *remaining balance* is given by

$$\hat{B}_n = \hat{B}_{n-1} - \hat{P}_n - PR_n = B_n Q_n.$$

The total cash flow to the investor is

$$\widehat{CF}_n = \hat{P} + PR_n + \left(\frac{C}{C+S}\right)\hat{I}_n.$$

## Average Life

Average life assigns weights to principal paydowns according to their arrival dates.

$$Average\,Life\;(in\;years\,)=\frac{1}{12}\sum_{t=1}^{N}\frac{(t+\alpha-1)(Principal_t)}{\sum_{t=1}^{N}Principal_t}$$

where $t$        = Time subscript, $t=1,...N$.
  $Principal_t$  = Principal arriving at time $t$.
  $N$        = Number of months until last principal cash flow comes in.
  $\alpha$        = Days between settlement date and first cash flow date, divided by 30 (i.e., the fraction of a month between settlement date and first cash-flow date).

## Macaulay Duration

Duration assigns time weights to the present values of all cash flows.

$$Macaulay\;Duration\;(in\;years\,)=\frac{1}{12}\sum_{t=1}^{N}\frac{\dfrac{(t+\alpha-1)C(t)}{(1+r/1200)^{t+\alpha-1}}}{\sum_{t=1}^{N}\dfrac{C(t)}{(1+r/1200)^{t+\alpha-1}}}$$

where $C(t)$ = Cash flow at time $t$.
  $r$    = Yield of mortgage (percent).

## Cash-Flow Yield

To obtain the cash-flow yield, the present value of the security's cash flows on the settlement date is equated to its initial price $P$ plus its accrued interest $I$.

$$P+I=\sum_{t=1}^{N}\frac{C(t)}{(1+r/1200)^{t+\alpha-1}}.$$

This equation is solved iteratively for $r$. The solution is called the mortgage yield.

### Bond-Equivalent Yield

The interest on a mortgage security is compounded monthly, while the interest on bonds such as Treasuries and corporates is compounded semi-annually. The compounding frequency is reflected in the yield of a security. Therefore, to make mortgage yields and bond yields comparable, the yield of a mortgage is normally converted to a bond-equivalent yield, i.e., a yield based on semi-annual compounding of the mortgage's interest payments.

A yield based on monthly compounding can be converted to a bond-equivalent yield and vice versa as follows:

$r$ = Mortgage yield based on monthly compounding (percent).
$y$ = Bond-equivalent yield (percent).

$$y = 200\left[\left(1 + \frac{r}{1200}\right)^6 - 1\right],$$

$$r = 1200\left[\left(1 + \frac{y}{200}\right)^{1/6} - 1\right].$$

### Total Return

$$Y_h = \text{Total return over a holding period } h \text{ (percent)} = \frac{\substack{\text{Sales} \\ \text{proceeds}} - \substack{\text{Total} \\ \text{price} \\ \text{paid}} + \substack{\text{Total net cash flow} \\ \text{received during} \\ \text{the holding period}} + \substack{\text{Total reinvestment} \\ \text{income during} \\ \text{the holding period}}}{\text{Total price paid}} \times 100.$$

The bond-equivalent total return rate $y_{BE}$ is given by

$$\left(1 + \frac{Y_h}{100}\right)^{12/h} = \left(1 + \frac{y_{BE}}{200}\right)^2.$$

### Duration and Convexity

Modified duration is given by

$$Modified\,Duration = \frac{Macaulay\ Duration}{1 + y\,/\,(k \times 100)}$$

where $y$ = Periodic yield.
$k$ = Number of coupon payments per year.

If the cash flows do not change with interest rates,

$$Modified\ Duration = Percentage\ Price\ Volatility = -\frac{1}{P}\frac{dP}{dy}.$$

In general, price volatility is approximated by

$$Effective\ Duration = -\frac{1}{P}\left[\frac{P\left(y_0 + \Delta y_0\right) - P\left(y_0 - \Delta y_0\right)}{2\Delta y_0}\right] \approx -\frac{1}{P}\frac{dP}{dy}.$$

Convexity is calculated using

$$Convexity = \frac{1}{P}\frac{d^2P}{dy^2} \approx \frac{1}{P}\left[\frac{P\left(y_o + \Delta y_o\right) + P\left(y_o - \Delta y_o\right) - 2P\left(y_o\right)}{\Delta y_o^2}\right].$$

# Analyzing MBS:
# A Comparison of Methods
# For Analyzing Mortgage-
# Backed Securities

ANDREW S. DAVIDSON
DIRECTOR
MORTGAGE-BACKED SECURITIES RESEARCH
MERRILL LYNCH CAPITAL MARKETS

MICHAEL D. HERSKOVITZ
VICE PRESIDENT
MORTGAGE-BACKED SECURITIES RESEARCH
MERRILL LYNCH CAPITAL MARKETS

## I. INTRODUCTION

The central issue in all mortgage-backed security (MBS) valuation methods is the treatment of prepayment uncertainty. The home owners' right to prepay their loans introduces a significant degree of uncertainty to the cash flows, and consequently the value, of mortgage-backed securities.

The relationship between interest rates and MBS prepayment rates directly influences MBS pricing. In a bond market rally prepayment rates rise, reducing the price

The authors thank H. Halperin, K. Rogers, J. Van Lang, B. Starr, and N. Perrotis for their assistance. In addition, the authors acknowledge the contributions of R. Kulason and L. Murakami.

gains of mortgage-backed securities. In a bear market, however, prepayment rates slow, resulting in increased price losses. This price movement pattern is commonly referred to as "negative convexity."

The dependence of prepayment rates on interest rates affects not only MBS returns but also their interest rate risk. A traditional measure of the price sensitivity of fixed income securities, modified duration, gives the percent change in price caused by a 100 basis point shift in the yield curve. Modified duration is a reasonable price sensitivity measure for securities with constant cash flows. It is often inadequate for MBS, however, because prepayment rates, and consequently cash flows, vary as interest rates change.

The inadequacy of traditional fixed-income analytical tools for valuing MBS has led to the development of alternative methods. This article reviews four approaches to quantifying MBS return and risk characteristics. The methods discussed are: (1) static cash flow yield (SCFY) analysis, (2) total rate of return scenario analysis (SA), (3) option-adjusted spread (OAS) Monte Carlo models and, (4) the Refinancing Threshold Pricing (RTP) model. The first three methods constitute the currently accepted set of valuation techniques. The final method, Refinancing Threshold Pricing, is an approach pioneered recently at Merrill Lynch.

Multiple approaches to valuing MBS exist because no single methodology has been shown to completely explain the price performance of these securities. Each of the methods listed has its strengths and weaknesses. SCFY analysis is the simplest approach; however, it ignores a number of factors critical to the valuation of MBS by assuming constant future interest rates. SA improves on the SCFY methodology by projecting MBS performance in a limited set of interest rate scenarios. OAS Monte Carlo models extend SA by simulating MBS performance over numerous interest rate paths. Critical to the SA and OAS approaches is the manner in which the future interest rate paths are selected and the specification of the relationship between interest rates and MBS prepayment rates. RTP is a binomial option-pricing-based methodology which differs fundamentally from the SA and OAS approaches. RTP directly models the refinancing decision of the individual mortgagor instead of attempting to specify aggregate MBS prepayment rates as a function of interest rates.

The article is divided into five sections. One section is devoted to each of the valuation methodologies and a final section outlines our conclusions and recommendations. Each methodology section contains a description of the technique, the value and risk measures provided, the sensitivity of the results to input parameters, and a summary of the advantages and disadvantages of the approach. Throughout the article 30-year GNMA Single Family (SF) 8.0%, 9.5%, and 11.0% pass-throughs are used as examples to allow the comparison of results across methodologies. At the time the analyses were conducted, the GNMA 9.5% pass-through was the current coupon. The GNMA 8% and 11% pass-throughs were selected to represent the characteristics of discount and premium MBS, respectively.

## II. STATIC CASH FLOW YIELD

The static cash flow yield (SCFY) is the discount rate which equates the value of future MBS cash flows with their market price. The future cash flows are projected based on the prepayment rate that is anticipated if interest rates remain stable for the life of the security.

SCFY is the basic measure of value in the mortgage market. Its primary advantage is its simplicity; the only required assumption is a prepayment projection. After a prepayment rate has been specified, cash flows can be generated and a yield calculated based on the security's market price. The tradeoff for simplicity is that SCFY analysis ignores a number of factors critical to the valuation of MBS including the shape of the yield curve, the distribution and volatility of future interest rates, and the relationship between interest rates and MBS prepayment rates.

### *Required Assumptions*

*The only assumption required to compute the SCFY of MBS is the projected prepayment rate assuming static interest rates.* Typically, prepayment projections are made based on the results of a statistical analysis of historical prepayment data and are generally quoted as Conditional Prepayment Rates (CPR) or percentages of the Public Securities Association (PSA) prepayment model. Investors should be aware that prepayment forecasts based on statistical models imply a confidence interval which in turn implies a range of possible values for MBS.

Exhibit 1 illustrates the average prepayment forecast and the forecast range for seasoned GNMA pass-throughs made available by 13 firms through Telerate on March 15, 1988. Using the width of the range as a proxy for forecast uncertainty, it is clear that the level of uncertainty is significant for all coupons and is greatest for premium MBS.[1]

### *Value Measures*

Given a prepayment forecast for an MBS and its market price, its cash flow yield is uniquely determined. *The spread between the MBS static cash flow yield and either its average life or duration-matched Treasury issue has traditionally been used as a measure of value in the mortgage market.*

One way to interpret MBS static cash flow yield spreads to Treasuries is in an historical context. Based on current yield spreads, an evaluation can be made as to whether the mortgage market is historically rich or cheap relative to Treasuries.

---

[1]For more information on prepayments refer to *Understanding MBS Prepayments*, Merrill Lynch Mortgage-Backed Securities Research, October 1987.

**EXHIBIT 1**
**AVERAGE PREPAYMENT FORECAST AND FORECAST RANGE FOR SEASONED GNMA PASS-THROUGHS**

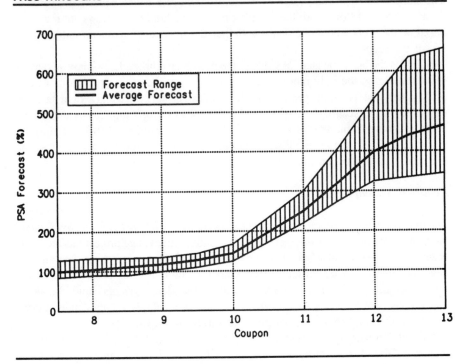

Further, spread differentials between discounts, currents, and premiums can be compared to determine intra-MBS market relative sector values.

Exhibit 2 shows GNMA MBS yield spreads to the ten-year Treasury bond as a function of the distance of the MBS coupon from the current coupon for selected historical dates.

Premium MBS spreads decline relative to the current coupon spread because the shorter durations of these securities cause them to trade off of the short end of the yield curve. In order to adjust for the distortion introduced by mismatched durations, Exhibit 3 displays MBS spreads to duration-matched Treasury issues.

Exhibits 2 and 3 demonstrate that MBS spread levels have varied significantly over time. Spread level variation can be related to changes in interest rates and corresponding changes in the option value of mortgage securities. In general, increases in interest rate volatility will raise the value of the short option positions embedded in MBS, which in turn reduces the prices (widens the spreads) of the securities. Conversely, lower volatility reduces the value of the short option components, thereby increasing the prices (reducing the spreads) of MBS.

**EXHIBIT 2**
**GNMA YIELD SPREADS TO THE TEN-YEAR TREASURY BOND FOR SELECTED
HISTORICAL DATES**

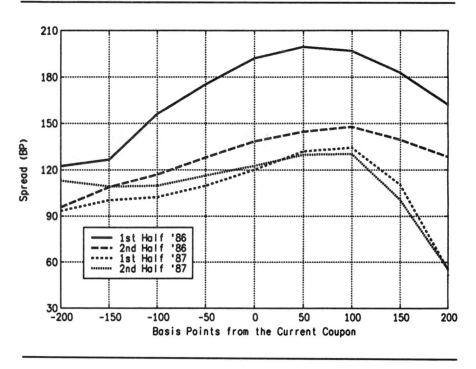

The relationship between spreads and volatility is demonstrated in Exhibit 4 which shows a high degree of correlation between the yield volatility of the ten-year Treasury and the spread between the current coupon GNMA and the ten-year Treasury between January 1985 and January 1988. This is strong evidence that the market uses its assessment of interest rate volatility in pricing MBS.

In addition to interest rate volatility, SCFY spreads are also affected by the state of the housing market. A robust housing market will generally increase MBS supply, leading to wider MBS yield spreads.

Consequently, an evaluation of MBS based on SCFY spreads to Treasuries should incorporate current interest rate volatility levels and housing market conditions, and investors' beliefs about the future directions of these factors.

## *Interest Rate Risk Measures*

The *weighted average life* (WAL) of a MBS is the average time to receipt of the principal of the security. It is used as a measure of the effective maturity of MBS in

**EXHIBIT 3**
**GNMA YIELD SPREADS TO DURATION-MATCHED TREASURY ISSUES FOR SELECTED HISTORICAL DATES**

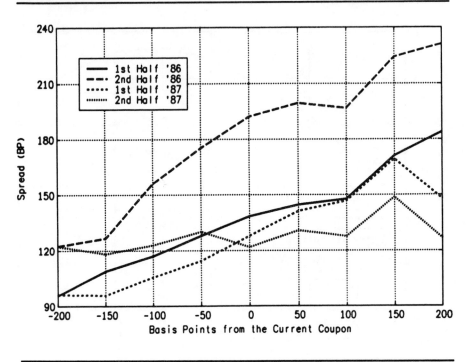

the place of stated maturity. Stated maturity is a poor measure of effective maturity for MBS because most principal is amortized or prepaid well before this date. Although an exact relationship between MBS WAL and MBS price sensitivity to interest rates does not exist, it is generally true that the longer the WAL, the greater the interest rate sensitivity. Consequently, WAL can be employed as an indicator of the price risk of MBS.

Another risk measure that can be obtained from SCFY analysis is *Macaulay duration*. The Macaulay duration of a security is the present value weighted average time to receipt of its cash flows. For true fixed-income instruments this measure can be shown to be equivalent to the price elasticity of the security with respect to interest rates. However, for MBS, where cash flows are dependent on interest rates, Macaulay duration is often a poor measure of price sensitivity.

In the sections of this article dealing with option-adjusted spread Monte Carlo models and the Refinancing Threshold Pricing model, MBS WALs and Macaulay durations will be compared to effective durations estimated by models which account for the dependence of MBS cash flows on interest rates.

**EXHIBIT 4**
**YIELD VOLATILITY OF THE TEN-YEAR TREASURY BOND AND THE SPREAD BETWEEN
THE CURRENT COUPON GNMA AND THE TEN-YEAR TREASURY BOND**

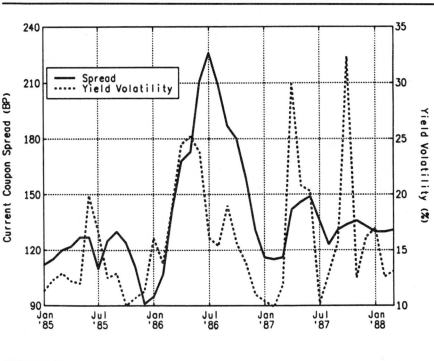

*Parameter Sensitivity*

Changing the prepayment assumption can materially alter the yield, weighted average life, and duration of MBS. Exhibit 5 demonstrates this sensitivity, displaying static cash flow yields, weighted average lives, and Macaulay durations for GNMA 8.0%, 9.5%, and 11.0% pass-throughs at constant prices at three different prepayment rates: the minimum, average, and maximum forecasts depicted in Exhibit 1.

**EXHIBIT 5**
**EFFECT OF PREPAYMENT RATE SPECIFICATION ON SCFY RISK AND RETURN
MEASURES**

| GNMA | Price | SCFY(%) | | | WAL (YRS) | | | Macaulay Duration | | |
|------|-------|---------|-----|-----|-----------|-----|-----|-------------------|-----|-----|
| | | *MIN* | *AVG* | *MAX* | *MIN* | *AVG* | *MAX* | *MIN* | *AVG* | *MAX* |
| 8.0% | 90-20 | 9.59 | 9.64 | 9.79 | 12.9 | 12.2 | 10.6 | 6.6 | 6.4 | 5.8 |
| 9.5% | 99-10 | 9.74 | 9.75 | 9.75 | 12.8 | 10.9 | 9.2 | 6.5 | 5.9 | 5.3 |
| 11.0% | 107-00 | 9.36 | 9.17 | 8.97 | 6.2 | 5.4 | 4.7 | 4.1 | 3.7 | 3.4 |

As prepayment rates increase, the yield on the discount increases and the yield on the premium decreases. The yield on the current coupon is insensitive to the projected prepayment rate since it is priced close to par. Weighted average lives and durations for all the pass-throughs decrease with increasing prepayment rates. Because MBS duration is dependent on the projected prepayment rate, the calculated yield spread to duration-matched Treasury is also dependent on this assumption. This is true even for the current coupon for which the SCFY is nearly independent of the assumed prepayment rate.

### Summary

The major attractions of the SCFY methodology are its simplicity and its acceptance by the market as the standard measure of MBS value. The only assumption required is a prepayment projection. After specifying a prepayment rate and generating cash flows, a yield can be calculated based on the security's market price. The tradeoff for simplicity is that by assuming constant future interest rates the approach ignores a number of factors critical to the valuation of MBS including the shape of the yield curve, the distribution and volatility of future interest rates, and the relationship between interest rates and MBS prepayment rates. Consequently, investors who rely on this methodology must subjectively decide how much spread is required to compensate them for the uncertainty introduced by these factors.

Despite these problems, an historical analysis of SCFY spreads is a useful adjunct to the other valuation methodologies presented in this article. In particular, the SCFY approach is most useful for the high premium and deep discount MBS having cash flows with little sensitivity to interest rates.

## III. SCENARIO ANALYSIS

Scenario analysis (SA) can be used to supplement SCFY analysis by examining the dynamic nature of MBS. It consists of calculating MBS holding period returns for a variety of possible future interest rate scenarios. For each scenario, cash flows are generated based on coupon, scheduled principal amortization, and prepayments. Cash flows that occur prior to the horizon are reinvested to the end of the holding period. At the horizon, the value of the remaining principal balance is calculated. The rate of growth necessary to equate the initial investment with the sum of the reinvested cash flows and the value of the remaining principal balance at the horizon is the total return for the scenario. The total scenario return is then converted to an annualized rate of return based on the length of the holding period.

Scenario analysis differs from the other approaches presented because it requires the use of a separate valuation model in order to arrive at the security's horizon price. Consequently, it can be employed in conjunction with OAS models or the RTP model to assess the implications of these pricing models for the dynamic performance of MBS in a holding period return context.

A simple but useful alternative horizon pricing model values the MBS based on SCFY spreads and projected horizon prepayment rates. The scenario horizon prepayment rate determines MBS WAL at the horizon. A MBS is then priced at a spread to its WAL-matched Treasury issue. Scenario spreads are determined by the SCFY spreads at which the same relative coupon MBS are currently trading. This approach has the advantage of investigating the implications of existing spread relationships on holding period returns. It determines the scenario holding period returns of MBS assuming current spread relationships are maintained. Using this pricing methodology, SA can be used in conjunction with an historical analysis of SCFY spreads to make assessments of MBS relative sector values. For example, if the expected returns of discount MBS are inordinately large relative to premium MBS using this approach, an argument can be made that discount MBS spreads are too large relative to premium MBS spreads. Consequently, discount MBS would be the better value.

### Required Assumptions

**(1) Holding Period:** The length of the holding period affects the shape of the total rate of return profile. Assuming monotonic parallel yield curve shifts, the effect of the reinvestment rate for interim cash flows will tend to offset the effect of the change in the value of the remaining principal balance at the end of the holding period. Higher interest rates imply greater reinvestment income but lower horizon prices for the remaining principal balance. For short holding periods, the price change of the security will dominate the reinvestment effect; the total scenario rate of return will decrease as interest rates increase. For sufficiently long holding periods, the reinvestment effect will dominate the impact of the horizon price, and total scenario rate of return will increase as interest rates rise.

When employing SA, the conventional practice is to evaluate MBS based on a one-year holding period. Most investors have an opportunity to rebalance their portfolios at least this often. Further, a one-year holding period limits the effect of the reinvestment rate assumption. A short holding period, however, increases the importance of the horizon pricing model.

**(2) Prepayment Rate Function:** The specification of the relationship between scenario interest rates and prepayment rates is critical. This relationship defines the embedded option in MBS and is what differentiates MBS from true fixed-income securities. As noted in the SCFY analysis section, the uncertainty of prepayment forecasts for MBS assuming static interest rates is substantial. The level of difficulty associated with forecasting prepayment rates assuming non-constant paths of future interest rates is much greater, implying even wider confidence intervals for such projections. Consequently, it is important that investors assess the sensitivity of SA risk and return measures to the prepayment rate function specification.

**(3) Interest Rate Distribution and Volatility:** The type of interest rate probability distribution and volatility level determine the weights that are assigned to each scenario. This is important when calculating the expected return and the variance of returns across all scenarios. The most popular distributions are the bell-shaped normal and the right-skewed lognormal. Normal implies equal probability of equal absolute changes while lognormal implies equal probability of equal percentage changes. At low levels of volatility the two assumptions give similar results.

Instead of selecting a probability distribution and a volatility assumption, an investor can subjectively assign probabilities to each of the scenarios. This is only feasible if a small number of scenarios are run.

Generally, the lower the volatility assumption, or for subjective probability distributions, the more heavily weighted the scenarios near the central scenario, the higher the expected return and the lower the variance of returns. The increase in expected return results from the negative convexity of MBS.

**(4) Central Scenario:** The interest rate scenarios must be centered on a base case. Two conventional central scenarios are the unchanged market and the implied forward rate scenarios. In the unchanged market scenario, interest rates remain unchanged over the holding period. For the implied forward scenario, interest rates follow paths described by the implied forward rates. Generally, the other scenarios selected assume parallel yield curve shifts about the central scenario. It is also possible to specify scenarios in which yield curve rotations occur. However, the added complexity of specifying such scenarios and assigning probabilities limits their usefulness.

The implied forward scenario is generally considered to be the more theoretically sound central scenario. It also has the advantage of simplifying comparisons between different duration securities; for example, the expected returns on all Treasury bonds are equal under this scenario, independent of maturity.

**(5) Horizon Pricing Model:** The horizon pricing model is another critical aspect of scenario analysis. It determines the value of the remaining principal balance of MBS at the horizon. The shorter the horizon the greater the impact of horizon prices on holding period returns.

**(6) Number of Scenarios Simulated:** The number of scenarios simulated can also affect calculated expected returns and variances of returns. Generally for MBS pass-throughs these values converge to their asymptotic values when scenarios are run at 50 basis point intervals between −400 and +400 basis point shifts in the yield curve, assuming a one-year horizon.

**(7) Reinvestment Rate:** The impact of the reinvestment rate is proportional to the length of the holding period. For short holding periods its effect is negligible. Since the standard approach is to assume a one-year holding period, the reinvestment rate assumption is relatively unimportant. If analyses are conducted employing longer holding periods the sensitivity of the results to this assumption increases.

*Value Measures*

The expected return is the weighted average of the total rates of return of all the scenarios where each scenario is weighted by its probability. The scenario weights are dependent on the assumed level of interest rate volatility and the probability distribution employed.

A more complete value measure is a graph of total returns versus interest rate scenarios (it could also be deemed a risk measure because the dispersion of the returns is evident). This approach has the advantage of visually displaying the dynamic performance characteristics of MBS. However, comparisons between securities can be difficult since it is unlikely that one security will completely dominate another.

*Interest Rate Risk Measures*

One of the most widely used statistical measures of dispersion is variance. The square root of variance is called standard deviation. This measure is particularly useful when dealing with normally distributed data. In this case approximately 68% of the observations can be expected to lie within one standard deviation of the mean and 95% within two standard deviations. The greater the variance and standard deviation, the wider the dispersion of scenario returns, and consequently the riskier the security.

*Parameter Sensitivity*

Exhibit 6 demonstrates the effect of the length of the holding period on the total return profile of a GNMA 9.5% pass-through. As the length of the holding period increases, the profile rotates counter-clockwise due to the increasing effect of the reinvestment rate and the reduced impact of the horizon price on scenario returns.

Due to their shorter durations, the corresponding return profiles for premium MBS would be flatter for the one-year holding period and rotate further counter-clockwise as the length of the holding period increased. Discount MBS would display the opposite behavior.

Exhibit 7 shows the effect of the specification of the prepayment rate function on the total return profile of a GNMA 11% pass-through. The underlying prepayment model was shifted up and down 15%. A faster prepayment rate specification results in reduced holding period returns in falling interest rate scenarios and increased returns in rising interest rate scenarios due to the reduction in the duration of MBS cash flows. Current and discount MBS would behave similarly.

Exhibit 8 displays the effect of interest rate volatility on the expected returns and the standard deviations of returns of GNMA 8%, 9.5%, and 11% pass-throughs assuming future changes in interest rates are lognormally distributed. The base volatility level was shifted up and down 40%. Increased interest rate volatility results

316    Davidson/Herskovitz

**EXHIBIT 6**
**EFFECT OF HOLDING PERIOD ON THE TOTAL RETURN PROFILE OF A GNMA 9.5% PASS-THROUGH**

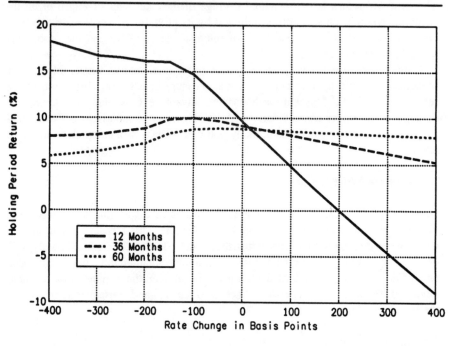

in reduced expected returns and increased standard deviations of returns. The normal distribution would result in slightly higher expected returns due to its symmetry.

The expected return of the GNMA 8.0% pass-through displays little sensitivity to interest rate volatility because its embedded prepayment option is far out of the money. The interest rate volatility assumption is more important for current coupon and premium MBS.

Exhibit 9 demonstrates the effect of the central scenario yield curve on the expected returns and the standard deviations of returns for GNMA 8%, 9.5%, and 11% pass-throughs. The implied forward scenario shifts the return profiles downward relative to the unchanged market scenario and consequently results in lower expected returns. This effect is due to the rising implied forward rates embedded in an upward sloping yield curve. An inverted yield curve would cause the opposite effect. Although the choice of the central scenario yield curve has a large effect on the absolute levels of MBS expected returns, it has little impact on their relative levels.

**EXHIBIT 7**
**EFFECT OF PREPAYMENT RATE SPECIFICATION ON THE TOTAL RETURN PROFILE OF A GNMA 11.0% PASS-THROUGH**

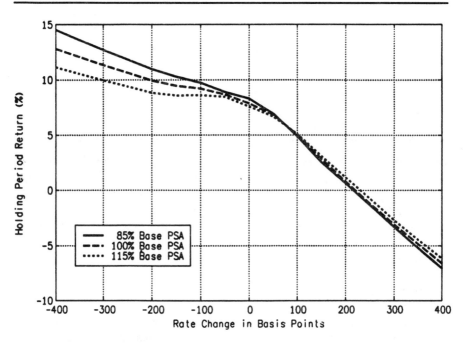

**EXHIBIT 8**
**EFFECT OF INTEREST RATE VOLATILITY ON SA RISK AND RETURN MEASURES**

| GNMA | Expected Return (%) | | | Standard Deviation of Returns (%) | | |
|---|---|---|---|---|---|---|
| | LOW | MID | HIGH | LOW | MID | HIGH |
| 8.0% | 8.16 | 8.01 | 7.85 | 3.97 | 6.30 | 8.29 |
| 9.5% | 8.32 | 7.95 | 7.47 | 3.55 | 5.39 | 6.88 |
| 11.0% | 7.43 | 6.81 | 6.22 | 1.75 | 3.10 | 4.25 |

## Summary

The SA approach extends the SCFY methodology by examining the dynamic nature of MBS. It can be used in conjunction with other MBS pricing models to assess their implications for the dynamic performance of MBS in a holding period return context. If the SCFY spread-based pricing approach described in this section is

**EXHIBIT 9**
**EFFECT OF CENTRAL YIELD CURVE SCENARIO ON SA RISK AND RETURN MEASURES**

| GNMA | Expected Return (%) | | Standard Deviation of Returns (%) | |
| --- | --- | --- | --- | --- |
| | Implied Forward | Unchanged Market | Implied Forward | Unchanged Market |
| 8.0% | 8.01 | 9.07 | 6.30 | 6.41 |
| 9.5% | 7.95 | 9.00 | 5.39 | 5.50 |
| 11.0% | 6.81 | 7.74 | 3.10 | 3.15 |

employed, SA investigates the impact of existing spread relationships on MBS holding period returns. This approach can be very useful when used in conjunction with an historical analysis of SCFY spreads. Relative value between MBS market sectors can be evaluated by reviewing existing spread levels in an historical context and by assessing their impact on MBS expected returns and variances of returns. MBS value relative to other fixed income markets can be evaluated in a similar fashion through a comparison of these values to those calculated for the alternative markets. Further, the historical analysis of SCFY spreads can be used to assess likely future spread movements. This information can in turn be used when evaluating the spread sensitivity of SA results.

Ideally, an investor would like to select the security with the highest expected return and the lowest variance of returns. Usually this is not possible, since it would probably indicate that the security was mispriced. Under normal circumstances an investor must accept additional risk in order to obtain a higher expected return. SA has the advantage of delineating the available sets of MBS risk/return profiles for specific holding periods.

An additional advantage of SA is that the limited number of scenarios allows the investor to review the assumptions and results of each scenario. A relatively small set of scenarios, however, may not adequately model the effect on value of the complete distribution of future interest rate paths.

## IV. OPTION-ADJUSTED SPREADS

In an attempt to improve upon the static cash flow yield and scenario analysis measures of MBS value, mortgage market participants have begun to rely on option-adjusted spread simulation models. The OAS simulation approach generates numerous interest rate paths which then determine future MBS cash flows. These cash flows are discounted by the simulated interest rates plus the option-adjusted spread. The model solves for the spread which equates the market price to the average simulated price. The simulation approach provides a method for estimating MBS yields and spreads to the Treasury yield curve that are adjusted for the embedded options in these securities. In addition, these models can provide estimates of MBS option cost and effective MBS duration and convexity.[2]

### Required Assumptions

**(1) Prepayment Rate Function:** One of the two critical assumptions in the OAS simulation methodology is the link between interest rates and prepayment rates. If the relationship between interest rates, time, and MBS prepayments is misspecified, the calculated value and risk measures will be biased. The sensitivity of OAS model results to different prepayment function specifications is explored in the parameter sensitivity section.

**(2) Interest Rate Diffusion Process:** The second critical assumption in the OAS simulation approach is the specification of the interest rate diffusion process. Most models assume that interest rates evolve as a lognormal random walk with a drift that centers the distribution on the implied forward rates. If the yield curve is upward sloping, the implied forward rates will indicate an upward bias to short term interest rates. This may not reflect investors' rate expectations. However, the use of implied forward rates with the typical positively sloped yield curve builds in the requirement that longer duration securities must yield more than shorter duration securities in order to be fairly priced. This is necessary to price non-callable bonds correctly and is consistent with option pricing theory.

Most models diffuse a single short term rate. In these models the current MBS coupon, which drives the prepayment function, is assumed to shift deterministically based on the change in the short term rate. At least one model seeks to introduce a greater amount of realism into the interest rate process by diffusing both a short and long term rate. In this model the short and long term rate changes are less than perfectly correlated, thereby allowing for the possibility of yield curve inversions. The long term rate is used to drive the prepayment function, while MBS cash flows are discounted back along the short term rate paths.

**(3) Interest Rate Volatility:** In addition to specifying an interest rate process, an assumption about interest rate volatility must be made. Higher volatility assumptions increase the dispersion of the simulated interest rate paths. Since MBS are effectively short a call option, increasing interest rate volatility will increase calculated option cost and decrease option-adjusted spread. The sensitivity of these results to this parameter is discussed in the sensitivity section.

---

[2]Michael D. Herskovitz, "Option-Adjusted Spread Analysis for Mortgage-Backed Securities," Chapter 21 in Frank J. Fabozzi (ed.) *The Handbook of Fixed-Income Options* (Chicago, IL: Probus Publishing, 1989).

**(4) Number of Scenarios Simulated:** The reliance of the OAS approach on a set of randomly generated interest rate paths introduces additional uncertainty into the results of these models. The magnitude of the additional uncertainty is inversely proportional to the number of interest rate paths simulated. Consequently, there is a tradeoff between computational efficiency and the confidence intervals of the results.

**(5) Averaging Methodology:** OAS values are also sensitive to the method used to aggregate the information from the individual interest rate paths. For example, the cash flows for the paths could be averaged first, and then the OAS calculated as the spread that equates this average cash flow vector with the market price of the security. Alternatively, OAS could be defined as the spread which equates the mean of the individual prices for each of the simulated interest rate paths to the market price. Each of these methods will produce different OAS values.

The Merrill Lynch OAS model employs the latter averaging methodology. Under this approach OAS values can be interpreted as the expected yield spreads of MBS to Treasuries over the full range of probable interest rate scenarios. The alternative methodology does not fully account for the relationship between scenario interest rates, prepayment rates, and MBS value.

### Value Measures

**(1) Option-Adjusted Spread:** Option-adjusted spread is the primary value measure produced by OAS models. Most models define OAS as the spread which equates the average simulated price to the market price. Implicit in this methodology is the assumption that the fair option-adjusted yield curve for mortgages is a fixed spread over the Treasury yield curve.

When the interest rate diffusion process is centered on the implied forward rates, the OAS has embedded in it the requirement that different duration securities must have different yields in order to be fairly priced. Consequently, OAS values for different duration MBS should be directly comparable.

**(2) Option Cost:** Spread to Treasury alone may not be a good indicator of MBS relative value. In order to compare various MBS, the yield spreads should be benchmarked to an appropriate level, namely, the static cash flow yield. The static cash flow yield spread minus the OAS equals the implied option cost.

### Interest Rate Risk Measures

**(1) Effective Duration and Convexity:** By shifting the simulated interest rate paths up and down slightly and holding the OAS fixed, estimates of MBS price sensitivity can be calculated. The average percentage price change can be used to calculate a security's OAS effective duration. OAS effective convexity can be computed by observing the rate of change of the OAS effective duration. These price sensitivity measures can be useful for hedging since they incorporate the effect of the prepayment option. However, OAS effective durations are measures of price sensitivity and not of maturity.

**(2) OAS Macaulay Duration:** A measure of MBS maturity that is adjusted for the prepayment option is the OAS Macaulay duration. This duration measure represents the present value weighted average time to receipt of MBS cash flow averaged across all simulation trials. Exhibit 10 shows the SCFY WAL, SCFY Macaulay duration, OAS Macaulay duration, and OAS effective duration of GNMA 8%, 9.5%, and 11% pass-throughs.

**EXHIBIT 10**
**A COMPARISON OF SCFY AND OAS RISK MEASURES**

| GNMA | SCFY WAL (YRS) | SCFY Macaulay Duration | OAS Macaulay Duration | OAS Effective Duration |
|---|---|---|---|---|
| 8.0% | 11.5 | 6.1 | 5.5 | 5.8 |
| 9.5% | 10.2 | 5.6 | 4.8 | 4.1 |
| 11.0% | 5.8 | 3.9 | 3.9 | 2.3 |

The OAS Macaulay durations of the GNMA 8.0% and 9.5% pass-throughs are shorter than their SCFY Macaulay durations. This result is consistent with expectations. Using the simulation approach, discount and current coupon securities are likely to experience an increase in prepayments relative to the static forecast, as prepayments are near their minimum based on the assumed prepayment model. The OAS effective durations of all the pass-throughs are below their SCFY Macaulay durations, reflecting the negative convexity of MBS. On a relative basis, the OAS effective duration of the GNMA 11.0% pass-through is depressed the most below its SCFY Macaulay duration, while the OAS effective duration of the GNMA 8.0% pass-through is depressed the least.

*Parameter Sensitivity*

Exhibit 11 demonstrates the effect of the specification of the prepayment rate function on the OAS, option cost, OAS Macaulay duration, and OAS effective duration of GNMA 8%, 9.5%, and 11% pass-throughs. The underlying prepayment model was shifted up and down 15%. A faster prepayment rate specification results in a reduction in both the OAS Macaulay and OAS effective durations of MBS. A faster prepayment rate specification will generally also increase the OAS of discount MBS and reduce the OAS of premium MBS.

**EXHIBIT 11**
**EFFECT OF PREPAYMENT RATE SPECIFICATION ON OAS RISK AND RETURN MEASURES**

| GNMA | OAS (BP) | | | Option Cost (BP) | | | OAS Macaulay Duration | | | OAS Effective Duration | | |
|---|---|---|---|---|---|---|---|---|---|---|---|---|
| | Low | Mid | High | Low | Mid | High | Low | Mid | High | Low | Mid | High |
| 8.0% | 66 | 79 | 108 | 48 | 35 | 6 | 5.8 | 5.5 | 5.2 | 6.0 | 5.8 | 5.7 |
| 9.5% | 51 | 60 | 56 | 67 | 58 | 62 | 5.1 | 4.8 | 4.6 | 4.3 | 4.1 | 3.9 |
| 11.0% | 16 | 4 | -13 | 102 | 114 | 131 | 4.3 | 3.9 | 3.6 | 2.9 | 2.3 | 1.9 |

Exhibit 12 displays the effect of interest rate volatility on the OAS, option cost, OAS Macaulay duration, and OAS effective duration of GNMA 8%, 9.5%, and 11% pass-throughs. The base volatility level was shifted up and down 40%. Increased interest rate volatility results in higher option costs and lower OAS. The OAS effective duration of premium MBS and discount MBS is increased and decreased respectively as volatility increases.

**EXHIBIT 12**
**EFFECT OF INTEREST RATE VOLATILITY ON OAS RISK AND RETURN MEASURES**

| GNMA | OAS (BP) | | | Option Cost (BP) | | | OAS Macaulay Duration | | | OAS Effective Duration | | |
|---|---|---|---|---|---|---|---|---|---|---|---|---|
| | Low | Mid | High | Low | Mid | High | Low | Mid | High | Low | Mid | High |
| 8.0% | 104 | 79 | 74 | 10 | 35 | 40 | 5.8 | 5.5 | 5.0 | 6.2 | 5.8 | 5.3 |
| 9.5% | 102 | 60 | 24 | 16 | 58 | 94 | 5.1 | 4.8 | 4.4 | 4.5 | 4.1 | 3.7 |
| 11.0% | 56 | 4 | -41 | 62 | 114 | 160 | 3.9 | 3.9 | 3.7 | 2.2 | 2.3 | 2.5 |

## Summary

The OAS methodology has a number of advantages over both the SCFY and SA approaches. The large number of simulated future interest rate paths may better model the complete distribution of future rate paths and improve the statistical significance of the risk and return measures. Further, the risk measures account for the dependence of MBS prepayments on interest rates. If the interest rate diffusion process and the relationship between interest rates and prepayment rates are correctly specified, these price sensitivity measures should be more useful for hedging than their SCFY counterparts.

The major drawback to the OAS approach is that it is basically a black box into which an investor puts assumptions and out of which comes risk and return measures. The prepayment functions and term structure models embedded in OAS models are generally proprietary, precluding the possibility of an investor inspecting these key aspects of the model. Even if the model specifications are available, it may be difficult to evaluate them. This makes it imperative that the investor which employs these models determine their sensitivity to the required assumptions.

Because of the sensitivity of OAS results to model specification and assumptions, these values are difficult to compare on an absolute basis between models. OAS results are best employed as indicators of relative value between similar securities run under identical assumptions using a consistent methodology.

## V. REFINANCING THRESHOLD PRICING MODEL

The Refinancing Threshold Pricing (RTP) model is a binomial option-pricing-based methodology that differs fundamentally from the SA and OAS approaches. RTP directly models the refinancing decision of the individual mortgagor instead of attempting to specify aggregate MBS prepayment rates as a function of interest rates. This approach is based on three main concepts:

- An options approach is effective in modeling mortgage prepayments, as the mortgagor's ability to prepay the mortgage constitutes an option.

- The costs a mortgagor incurs when refinancing are not paid to the holder of the MBS.

- Mortgagors have different interest rate levels, or thresholds, at which they prepay their mortgages. That is, different homeowners face different levels of refinancing costs.

The concept of heterogeneous mortgagors provides a fundamental and innovative insight into analyzing MBS value and serves as the starting point for the Refinancing Threshold Pricing model. The RTP models the underlying economics of MBS by focusing on the refinancing decision of the individual mortgagor. These individual refinancing decisions are observed as prepayments. Models which estimate prepayments based on interest rate levels, however, reverse this process. They examine the effect rather than the cause. The RTP provides the potential for robust results and additional insights into MBS valuation because RTP models the underlying process.

The process of valuing a mortgage pool begins with modeling a single mortgage loan. The RTP values individual mortgagor cash flows, given their refinancing costs. This procedure, however, is not repeated for each mortgage in the pool. Instead, the pool is divided into groups of borrowers who share similar refinancing costs. Using market data, the RTP endogenously determines both the costs that mortgagors face, as well as the proportion of the pool in each refinancing cost class. This division into mortgage groups is termed pool composition.[3]

---

[3]For a more detailed discussion of the RTP approach refer to *The Refinancing Threshold Pricing Model: An Economic Approach to Valuing MBS*, Merrill Lynch Mortgage-Backed Securities Research, November 1987.

### Required Assumptions

**(1) Interest Rate Diffusion Process:** The first assumption required is the specification of the interest rate diffusion process. A term structure model generates a binomial interest rate tree. The rates at the successive branches of the tree, as well as probabilities of interest rates increasing and decreasing are selected in a manner that is consistent with the observed prices on the current Treasury securities.

The interest rate tree is used by a binomial option pricing model to value each of the endogenously determined refinancing classes in MBS. When the present value of the mortgagor's cash flows exceeds the remaining principal plus refinancing costs, the mortgage is assumed to be refinanced and the market value of the mortgage is set equal to the principal amount of the mortgage. Refinancing is not economic when the remaining principal plus refinancing costs is greater than the present value of the cash flows to be paid by the mortgagor.

**(2) Interest Rate Volatility:** In addition to specifying an interest rate process, an assumption about interest volatility is required. Higher assumed interest rate volatility generally results in a reduction in MBS price due to the increase in the value of the embedded short option position.

**(3) Pool Composition:** The third required assumption is the pool composition and the associated thresholds. Mortgages in a pool are divided into three classes according to interest rate sensitivity: very sensitive, moderately sensitive, and not interest rate sensitive. The degree of interest rate sensitivity depends on the mortgagors' refinancing costs. Mortgagors considered very interest rate sensitive face low refinancing costs, while mortgagors with less interest rate sensitivity have correspondingly higher refinancing costs. While the pool could be divided into any number of classes, three capture the major implications of heterogeneous borrowers for descriptive purposes.

The model assumes that non-refinancing prepayments occur at a constant rate over the life of the mortgage pool and are proportionally drawn from the three refinancing cost classes. At origination, the distribution of mortgagors in refinancing cost classes is assumed to be identical across all pools. This does not imply that each seasoned pool contains an equal number of high, medium, and low interest rate sensitive borrowers, but rather, the proportion of highly interest rate sensitive individuals in a GNMA 8% pool at origination equals the proportion of highly interest rate sensitive individuals in a GNMA 10% pool at origination. Over time, the proportions will shift as mortgagors refinance or move. Consequently, one would expect seasoned GNMA 14s to have very few highly and moderately interest sensitive borrowers remaining in the pool, while seasoned GNMA 7s may have proportions which have not changed much since origination.

After assuming an initial pool distribution, pool composition and refinancing cost levels at origination are determined by recursively comparing market prices with model results until the difference between the two is minimized. These implied pool compositions generally remain stable over time and are consistent with prepayment expectations. Once the value of each of the refinancing classes has been determined, a weighted average is calculated based on the pool composition to determine MBS value.

## Value Measures

**(1) Price:** The RTP directly computes the theoretical price of MBS. Comparisons between theoretical values and actual market prices may help investors determine MBS relative value.

**(2) Implied Spread and Implied Volatility:** The term structure model within the RTP model creates a binomial tree of future Treasury rates based on the prices of the current Treasury securities. The RTP model discounts MBS cash flows back through this binomial lattice at the Treasury rate plus some constant spread. This spread reflects the yield premium of MBS securities after accounting for the prepayment option held by the mortgagor. The implied spread and volatility are calculated by varying the respective parameter, holding the other constant and finding the level at which the model price equals the market price. In general, the larger the implied volatility and spread, the cheaper the security.

## Interest Rate Risk Measures

By shifting the yield curve up and down slightly, estimates of MBS price sensitivity can be calculated in a manner analogous to that described in the OAS section. In addition, the price sensitivity of MBS to changes in interest rate volatility can be computed. Exhibit 13 shows the SCFY WAL, SCFY Macaulay duration, RTP effective duration, RTP effective convexity, and RTP dP/dVol[4] of GNMA 8%, 9.5%, and 11% pass-throughs.

**EXHIBIT 13**
**A COMPARISON OF SCFY AND RTP RISK MEASURES**

| GNMA | SCFY WAL (YRS) | SCFY Macaulay Duration | RTP Effective Duration | RTP Effective Convexity | RTP dP/dVol |
|------|------|------|------|------|------|
| 8.0% | 11.5 | 6.1 | 6.0 | 0.37 | -0.02 |
| 9.5% | 10.2 | 5.6 | 5.1 | -0.94 | 0.16 |
| 11.0% | 5.8 | 3.9 | 2.8 | -2.48 | 0.62 |

---

[4]dP/dVol is defined as the price change of MBS resulting from a 1% reduction in interest rate volatility.

Consistent with expectations, the RTP effective durations of the pass-throughs are all below their SCFY Macaulay durations due to the negative convexity of MBS. The convexities of the current coupon and premium pass-throughs are negative while that of the discount is slightly positive. The dP/dVol estimates are consistent with the convexity estimates; the more negatively convex a security, the faster its price increases as volatility falls.

## Parameter Sensitivity

Exhibit 14 demonstrates the effect of the refinancing cost specification on the RTP price, RTP effective duration, and RTP convexity of GNMA 8%, 9.5%, and 11% pass-throughs. Refinancing costs were shifted up and down 25%. Higher refinancing costs reduce the value of the short option position embedded in MBS which result in higher model prices. Higher refinancing costs also extend the duration of MBS due to the reduction in the incentive for mortgagors to prepay their loans.

**EXHIBIT 14**
**EFFECT OF REFINANCING COST SPECIFICATION ON RTP RISK AND RETURN MEASURES**

| GNMA | RTP Price | | | RTP Effective Duration | | | RTP Effective Convexity | | |
|------|------|------|------|-----|-----|------|-------|-------|-------|
|      | Low | Mid | High | Low | Mid | High | Low | Mid | High |
| 8.0% | 90-25 | 90-26 | 90-27 | 5.9 | 6.0 | 6.1 | 0.34 | 0.37 | 0.38 |
| 9.5% | 99-00 | 99-10 | 99-15 | 4.8 | 5.1 | 5.4 | -0.70 | -0.94 | -0.22 |
| 11.0% | 105-12 | 106-29 | 107-27 | 0.9 | 2.8 | 3.2 | -1.57 | -2.48 | -0.86 |

Exhibit 15 displays the effect of interest rate volatility on the RTP price, RTP effective duration, and RTP effective convexity of GNMA 8%, 9.5%, and 11% pass-throughs. The base volatility level was shifted up and down 40%. Increased interest rate volatility generally results in lower prices and shorter effective durations. The largest effects occur for the current coupon and premium pass-throughs. Discount pass-throughs are less affected by interest rate volatility because their embedded prepayment options are far out of the money.

## Summary

As with the OAS approach, the RTP model provides risk and return measures that account for the dependence of MBS prepayments on interest rates. The major attraction of the RTP methodology is its independence from an exogenous prepayment function. By directly modeling the refinancing decision of mortgagors the method provides the potential for more robust results.

Despite its conceptual relevance, RTP is still essentially a black box into which

**EXHIBIT 15**
**EFFECT OF INTEREST RATE VOLATILITY ON RTP RISK AND RETURN MEASURES**

| GNMA | RTP Price | | | RTP Effective Duration | | | RTP Effective Convexity | | |
|---|---|---|---|---|---|---|---|---|---|
| | Low | Mid | High | Low | Mid | High | Low | Mid | High |
| 8.0% | 90-22 | 90-26 | 90-27 | 6.1 | 6.0 | 5.6 | 0.53 | 0.37 | -0.01 |
| 9.5% | 99-15 | 99-10 | 98-18 | 5.4 | 5.1 | 4.5 | -0.89 | -0.94 | -0.66 |
| 11.0% | 107-31 | 106-29 | 105-09 | 3.9 | 2.8 | 2.0 | -0.89 | -2.48 | 0.57 |

the investor puts assumptions and out of which comes risk and return measures. The endogenously determined pool compositions are available for inspection as are the parameters defining the interest rate process. However, it may be difficult for the typical investor to assess the reasonableness of these values. As with the OAS approach, this makes it imperative that the investor assess the sensitivity of RTP results to the required assumptions.

## VI. CONCLUSIONS

Multiple approaches to valuing MBS exist because no single methodology has been shown to completely explain the price performance of these securities. All of the valuation methods discussed in this article are useful. However, it is critical that the results of each methodology be assessed in terms of their sensitivity to the specification of, and assumptions required for, each model. Investors should examine not only point estimates of MBS risk and return, but also the confidence intervals associated with these point estimates.

SCFY analysis was the simplest approach reviewed. Although it ignores a number of factors critical to the valuation of MBS, historical analysis of SCFY spreads is a useful check on the results of other methodologies and can provide an historical perspective on the MBS market.

SA is a valuable extension of the SCFY approach, examining the dynamic nature of MBS in a holding period return context. If the spread-based horizon pricing model described in the SA section is used, SA investigates the implications of existing spread relationships for holding period returns. Used in conjunction with an historical analysis of SCFY spreads, this can be an important tool in assessing the relative attractiveness of different MBS coupons.

OAS Monte Carlo models extend SA by simulating MBS performance over a large number of interest rate paths. If the interest rate diffusion process and the relationship between interest rates and prepayment rates are correctly specified, this class of model has the potential to provide MBS risk and return measures superior to those available from SCFY analysis.

The RTP model is a binomial option-pricing-based methodology that differs fundamentally from the OAS approach. RTP directly models the refinancing decision of the individual mortgagor instead of attempting to specify aggregate MBS prepayment rates as a function of interest rates. As with the OAS approach, RTP provides risk and return measures that account for the dependence of MBS prepayments on interest rates. A major attraction of the RTP methodology is that it does not depend on the specification of an exogenous prepayment function. By directly modeling the refinancing decision of mortgagors RTP provides the potential for more robust results.

The major drawback of both the OAS and RTP approaches is that they are essentially black boxes into which an investor puts assumptions and out of which comes risk and return measures. Even if model specifications are available for inspection it may be difficult to evaluate them. Consequently, it is imperative that investors determine the sensitivity of the results of these models to the assumptions employed. OAS and RTP results should not be used in isolation, but only in conjunction with the results of SCFY analysis and SA. The simpler approaches can be used as checks on the reasonableness of the results of the more sophisticated models.

The proper use of these tools can reduce the difficulties created by prepayment uncertainty and should enable investors to make portfolio decisions with greater confidence.

# Prepayment Models and Methodologies

LAKHBIR S. HAYRE, D. PHIL.
VICE PRESIDENT AND MANAGER
FINANCIAL STRATEGIES GROUP
PRUDENTIAL-BACHE CAPITAL FUNDING

KENNETH LAUTERBACH
SENIOR ASSOCIATE
FINANCIAL STRATEGIES GROUP
PRUDENTIAL-BACHE CAPITAL FUNDING

CYRUS MOHEBBI, PH.D.
ASSOCIATE
FINANCIAL STRATEGIES GROUP
PRUDENTIAL-BACHE CAPITAL FUNDING
AND
ASSISTANT PROFESSOR OF FINANCE
LASALLE UNIVERSITY

## I. INTRODUCTION

It is generally recognized that prepayment rates are a critical variable in determining the value of a mortgage-backed security (MBS). The prepayments experienced by the security over its remaining term will determine the stream of cash flows from the

The authors would like to thank Joe Reel for preparing the graphs; Gladys Torres for preparing the manuscript; and Lisa Pendergast and Joe Reel for the editing and final production of the article.

security and hence security characteristics, such as yield, average life and duration. Prepayments are especially critical for derivative mortgage securities, such as CMO residuals and STRIPs, which tend to be very sensitive to changes in prepayment levels.

The growth of the MBS markets and the proliferation of CMOs and STRIPs have focused increased attention on methods of projecting prepayment rates. Both investors and securities firms have become more sophisticated in their approach to prepayments. The 12-year prepaid life convention, which assumes no prepayments for the first 12 years of a mortgage's life, has been generally discarded. Instead, attention has shifted to the relationship of prepayment levels to economic factors, such as interest rates, and to mortgage characteristics, such as coupon and age. Econometric models, which provide a mathematical means of projecting prepayment rates as a function of relevant economic and mortgage variables, have been developed by many firms. Such models can be valuable tools in obtaining an investment profile of an MBS. Prepayment models are also an essential tool for calculating "option-adjusted" spreads for MBSs.

This article discusses the economic factors and mortgage characteristics that influence prepayment behavior. Econometric prepayment models and their applications are also discussed, with the Prudential-Bache Prepayment Model *used as an example*.

## II. DETERMINANTS OF PREPAYMENT BEHAVIOR

In general, there are two main causes of prepayments on mortgages:

- *Turnover*—or the sale of property. This can be viewed as an "uneconomic" prepayment, since the mortgage coupon may be lower than prevailing mortgage rates.
- *Refinancing*—or "economic" prepayments. This is caused by the mortgage holder deciding to obtain a new mortgage in order to take advantage of prevailing mortgage rates significantly lower than the mortgage coupon.

In addition, partial prepayments can occur should the mortgage holder decide in a particular month to pay more than the scheduled amount of interest and principal. A variety of factors influence prepayments in varying degrees. Among these are:

- Mortgage rates.
- Seasonal variation.
- Mortgage security characteristics, such as the coupon, security type, age and pool factor.

● General economic factors.

These variables are discussed below in greater detail.

## Mortgage Rates

Mortgage rates affect prepayment levels according to the spread between mortgage coupons and mortgage rates, which determines whether refinancing is economically worthwhile, and through their influence on housing turnover.

**Coupon Spread.** The spread or difference between the coupon on a mortgage and current mortgage rates determines the economic gain to be obtained from refinancing and is probably the single most important variable for projecting prepayment rates. Because of the cost (and time) involved in obtaining a new mortgage, homeowners will generally not refinance unless the new mortgage rate is between 100 to 200 basis points below the old rate, and in fact, prepayments on a given mortgage coupon do tend to surge when mortgage rates fall 200 basis points or more below the mortgage coupon. This is illustrated in Exhibit 1, which shows the monthly prepayment rates for GNMA 13s, expressed as an annualized constant prepayment rate (CPR), and the spread between the underlying mortgage coupons (13.5%) and mortgage rates in recent years.

As Exhibit 1 shows, prepayment rates for GNMA 13s first increased significantly in the late summer of 1985, after mortgage rates had declined from approximately 13.30% in March 1985 to just over 12% by June, increasing the coupon spread to approximately 150 basis points. GNMA 13s experienced really extensive refinancings, however, in the spring of 1986 after mortgage rates fell to the 10% level, and the coupon spread increased to over 250 basis points.

**Influence on Housing Turnover.** In addition to being an important determinant of refinancing levels, mortgage rates also influence housing turnover. Lower rates mean a greater number of people can afford to move (the so called "affordability index" rises); this results in higher housing turnover and in turn higher prepayments. This is illustrated in Exhibit 2, which shows the prepayment rates of GNMA 8.5s and estimated national average mortgage rates (with a three-month lag), from January 1982 to November 1987. The mortgages underlying GNMA 8.5s generally have coupons of 9.0%, and over the period shown, the mortgage rate exceeded 9.0%. Thus, prepayments on GNMA 8.5s during this period were attributed primarily to housing turnover. There was a significant increase in prepayments in the spring of 1986, after mortgage rates declined to about 10%, the lowest level in many years.

The effect of lower mortgage rates on prepayments is particularly pronounced after a period of high mortgage rates. The high prepayment levels, even for discount

**EXHIBIT 1**
**PREPAYMENT RATES AND COUPON SPREADS FOR GNMA 13s**

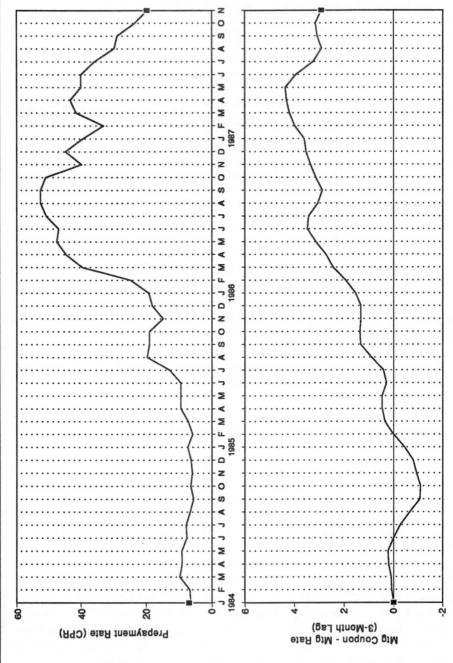

**EXHIBIT 2**
**PREPAYMENT RATES FOR GNMA 8.5s AND MORTGAGE RATES**

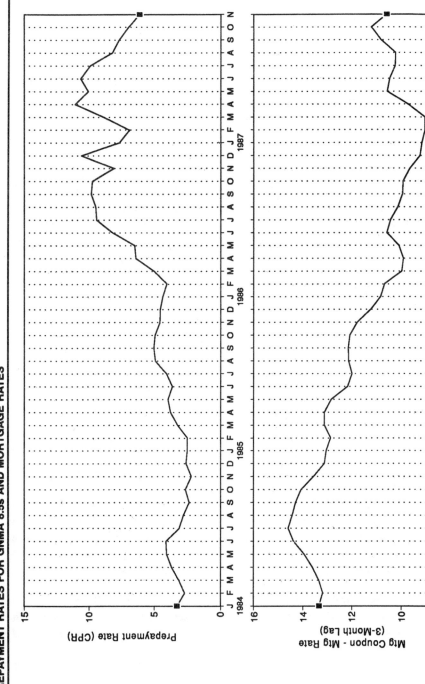

coupons, in the summer of 1986 following several years of high mortgage rates is an example of this effect. However, if rates remain low, the effect on housing turnover will decrease with time, since most homeowners who were previously discouraged from moving by high rates will have already done so.

Conversely, if there has been a sharp increase in mortgage rates, there will be an initial decline in prepayments. However, if rates remain high, the housing markets will adjust to the high rates to some extent and turnover should gradually pick up.

### Seasonal Variation

Housing turnover follows an established and well-known seasonal pattern, with a high in the summer and a low in the winter. This is illustrated in Exhibit 3, which shows U.S. Census Bureau seasonality adjustment factors for monthly sales of existing single-family homes in recent years.

Although the seasonal pattern in the housing market clearly affects the turnover components of prepayments directly, there is no clear reason to expect refinancings to follow such a pattern. The main determinants of the seasonal variation in housing turnover (such as the school-year calendar) are not likely to affect the timing of refinancing decisions. Some analysts have cited evidence of a seasonal pattern in refinancings; however, this assertion may be due to the fact that much of the refinancing activity in recent years occurred in the summer of 1986 after a sharp drop in mortgage rates and coincided with the usual seasonal high in turnover, thus giving a statistical impression of seasonality in refinancing activity.

### Mortgage Security Characteristics

The characteristics of individual mortgage securities are obviously important determinants of prepayment levels. Among the most salient characteristics are:

**Coupon.** As discussed previously, the difference or spread between the coupons on the underlying mortgages and current mortgage rates is probably the single most important influence on prepayments. The absolute value of the coupon can also be a factor, since because of the higher monthly payments, there may be more incentive to refinance a high-coupon mortgage.

**Security Type.** Differences in the mortgages underlying GNMA securities and those underlying FNMA and FHLMC securities account for the disparities in their prepayment levels. The mortgages underlying GNMAs are insured by the Federal Housing Administration (FHA) or the Veterans' Administration (VA), while FNMA and FHLMC pools are typically composed of conventional mortgages. Consequently:

- The mortgages in GNMA pools are assumable, implying lower prepayments if the mortgage coupons are below current rates;

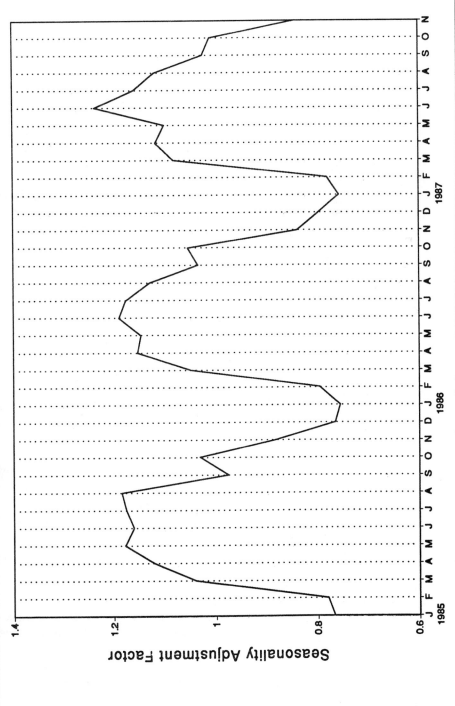

- GNMA mortgage holders tend to have lower incomes, which is thought to make them less mobile, again lowering prepayment levels;
- The mortgages underlying GNMAs tend to be smaller, giving the mortgage holder less incentive to refinance.

Another difference between GNMAs and FNMAs or FHLMCs is that the underlying mortgages in the GNMA pools generally have coupons that are 50 basis points higher than the pass-through coupon, while for FNMAs and FHLMCs the underlying mortgages may have coupons that are several hundred basis points higher than the security coupon (on average, the mortgage coupons are approximately 70 to 80 basis points higher).

As a result of these differences, FNMA and FHLMC prepayment levels tend to be higher than GNMA prepayment levels. In addition, if the gross coupons on the mortgages backing a FNMA or FHLMC security are not known (as is generally the case, for example, with CMO collateral at the time a CMO is priced), there is an extra degree of uncertainty in projecting prepayment levels.

**Age of Mortgages.** The prepayment data collected by the FHA after 1957 showed that prepayment rates on new mortgages gradually increased with the age of the mortgages until they were two to three years old and then leveled off. The Public Securities Association (PSA) benchmark prepayment curve, now widely used in the industry, captures this pattern.

However, there has been some debate concerning the degree to which mortgage age affects refinancings. The FHA data pertain mostly to the period preceding the very high mortgage rates of the 1980s and the subsequent high levels of refinancing after mortgage rates declined in 1986. Although refinancing involves a certain amount of time and cost, it is not the major upheaval that moving can be. Thus, homeowners may be just as likely to refinance a 15-month-old mortgage as they are a 30-month-old mortgage if rates were to drop dramatically. Hence, it is possible that while the age effect on the turnover component of prepayments follows the FHA/PSA pattern, the refinancing component could have an accelerated age effect. However, there is no definitive study or consensus on this, and the PSA model (and hence the age effect implied by the PSA curve) seems to be gaining increased acceptance in the industry.

**Pool Factors.** One important variable that is sometimes overlooked when projecting prepayments is the security's pool factor, i.e., its current outstanding principal balance relative to the initial balance. The pool factor can suggest the amount of potential refinancing that remains in the given security or collateral. If a given security's prepayments have been high for several years and, consequently, its pool factor is low, it is not likely to experience the same surge in refinancing after a drop in mortgage rates as a security that has been experiencing moderate or low prepayments but whose underlying mortgages now provide economic incentive to refinance. This was illustrated by prepayment levels in 1986 and 1987, when securities

**EXHIBIT 4**
**PREPAYMENT RATES FROM MARCH TO MAY 1987**

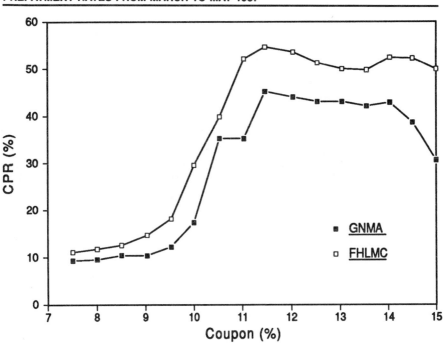

with coupons in the 12% to 14% range generally prepaid at a faster rate than the 15% to 16% coupons. For example, from spring 1986 to spring 1987, FNMA 13s prepaid at an annual prepayment rate of almost 60%, while FNMA 16s, whose underlying mortgages provided significantly greater incentive to refinance, prepaid at a rate of about 49%. Unlike FNMA 13s, the FNMA 16s had been prepaying at a high level for several years, and many of the mortgage holders most able or anxious to refinance had already done so.

This point is further illustrated in Exhibit 4, which shows the prepayment rates for the three-month period from March to May 1987, for seasoned 30-year GNMAs and FHLMCs. This was a period when refinancing activity was at a high level. The prepayment rates actually decline for the very high-coupon securities, due to the fact that the higher coupons have been prepaying at a higher level for a longer period of time, and consequently, have lower pool factors. (If the mortgages in a pool were already well seasoned when the pool was formed, it may be necessary to make adjustments to the pool factors.)

### General Economic Factors

A number of economic variables can influence housing turnover and refinancing activity, and hence prepayments. Among these are:

- Housing costs.
- Construction activity.
- Demographic trends.
- The general health of the economy: for example, there is less housing turnover in periods of recession.
- Regional factors (if a particular pool is known to be concentrated in a specific area of the country).
- Incentives offered by mortgage originators to attract customers.

While these variables could be included for specialized analyses or to improve the accuracy of short-term projections, there are practical considerations that limit the inclusion of numerous variables in a general prepayment model. Mortgage prepayment models are used to price mortgage securities, and a reasonably quick response time is often essential. However, a more fundamental difficulty arises in that prepayments have to be projected over the remaining term of a mortgage security, a period often in the 25- to 30-year range. If factors such as demographic trends and the general state of the economy were to be included in a prepayment model, they similarly would have to be projected for the next 25 to 30 years.

One practical way of capturing the effects of general economic factors is to include housing turnover as a variable. This is the approach used in the Prudential-Bache Prepayment Model. In practice, prepayment rates are projected for a specified path of future interest rates. Housing sales can be modeled as a function of interest rates, and the effects of other economic influences can be captured by specifying for a given level of interest rates either a low, average or high level for housing turnover.

## III. PREPAYMENT MODELS

Mathematical models provide a means for projecting prepayment levels as a function of economic and mortgage variables. In the statistical literature, such models are referred to as econometric or multiple regression models. The model used in our discussion is a non-linear multiple regression model that calculates projected prepayment rates for specified values of the economic and mortgage characteristics discussed in Section II. This section gives a description of the model and its operation.

### Functional Form of the Model

The functional form of the model expressing prepayments in terms of the variables discussed in Section II is important, as it will determine the accuracy and effectiveness with which the relationship between prepayments and those variables is captured.

In choosing the model, two important considerations have to be kept in mind:
(1) Prepayment rates, by definition, are between 0% and 100%. Hence, the

functional form of the model should preferably be one whose value cannot be less than zero or exceed one, regardless of the value of interest rates and other variables in the model. Otherwise arbitrary restrictions or cutoffs may have to be imposed to ensure that the projected prepayment rate is not negative or greater than one.

(2) As Exhibit 4 in Section II illustrates, the prepayment rate has a distinctively non-linear S-shape with respect to the spread between the mortgage coupon and the current mortgage rate, which as stated previously is perhaps the most important single variable influencing prepayments. Prepayment rates tend to be fairly constant for discount coupons; they start increasing very sharply as the coupon goes "into-the-money" at 1% to 2% above current mortgage rates, and then level off for high coupons. The functional form of the model should capture this S-shape.

The Prudential-Bache Prepayment Model is a non-linear multiple regression model with a functional form that is consistent with (1) and (2) above and that incorporates the variables discussed in Section II. The core of the model is a modified Arc-Tangent function, which captures the S-shape of prepayments across coupons. This generates a "raw" prepayment projection for a given month. The raw prepayment rate is then divided into turnover and refinancing components, and adjustments are made to each part to incorporate seasonality, aging factors, housing turnover and refinancing patterns over time. The two parts are then summed to obtain the projected prepayment rate for the month.

Model parameters were estimated using historical prepayment data and are periodically updated. Although the parameters for FNMAs and FHLMCs are essentially the same, the projections for the same coupon tend to differ slightly, for two reasons:

- The pool factors are generally different.
- For a given month, FNMA and FHLMC prepayments typically tend to represent principal received during different periods. FNMA prepayments are for the preceding calendar month, while FHLMC prepayments are for the one-month period ending on the fifteenth of the preceding month. This affects the values of the interest rates and other variables used in the model and can mean slightly differing projections for the next few months.

The model was fitted using historical prepayment data from 1979 to the present. Correlations between actual and fitted prepayments are very high—about 96% for GNMAs and 95% for FNMAs and FHLMCs. Exhibit 5 shows actual and fitted (i.e., calculated using the model) prepayments for GNMA 9s and 13s, while Exhibit 6 shows these for FNMA 10s and FHLMC 12s.

## Projections from the Model

For given security characteristics and a mortgage-rate path, the model gives a projected monthly prepayment rate (single monthly mortality or "SMM") for each

**EXHIBIT 5**
**ACTUAL AND FITTED PREPAYMENTS FOR GNMA 9s and 13s**

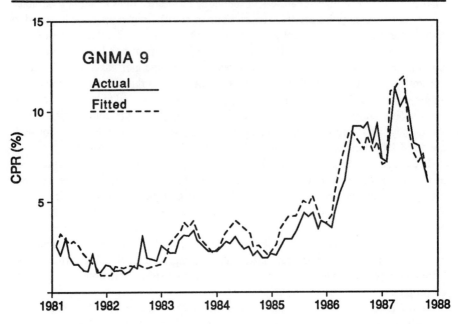

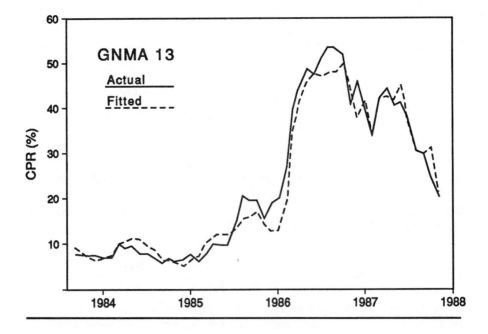

**EXHIBIT 6**
**ACTUAL AND FITTED PREPAYMENTS FOR FNMA 10s AND FHLMC 12s**

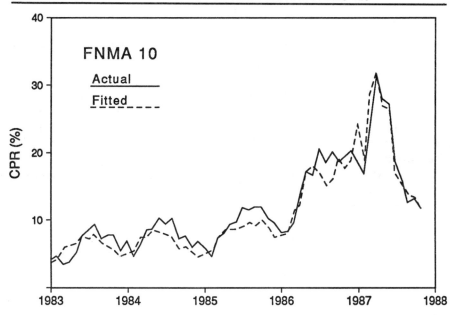

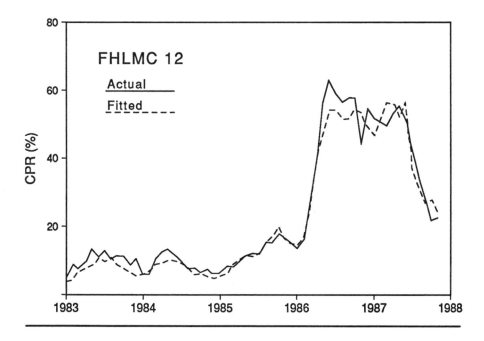

remaining month of the security's term. The security characteristics generally input-
ted are the agency type, net and gross coupons and age. The pool factor used is the
generic value for the security, given its coupon and age, but can be changed if
necessary.

The interest-rate information specified is the projected changes in short-term
rates. Changes in mortgage rates are computed from the changes in short-term rates,
with the relationship between short-term and mortgage-rate changes reflecting the
lower volatility of mortgage rates and the time lag generally seen between these
changes. It is important to realize that the Prudential-Bache Prepayment Model, like
most such models is a *conditional model;* that is, *the prepayment projections are
conditional on the specified path of interest rates.* No attempt is made to forecast
interest rates.

Exhibit 7 shows the monthly projections from the model for a seasoned GNMA 10
for the next 24 months under three projected interest-rate environments: rates remain
at current levels, and rates increase and decrease by 200 basis points over the next
year and then remain constant for the following 12 months.

Exhibit 8 shows long-term projected prepayment rates for several FHLMC coupons. The projections are given for interest-rate moves of 0, ± 50, ± 100, ± 200,
± 300 and ± 400 basis points, and three speeds of interest-rate change: instantaneous, over a year and at a maximum rate of 100 basis points per year.

**EXHIBIT 7**
**MONTH-BY-MONTH PREPAYMENT PROJECTIONS FOR A GNMA 10**

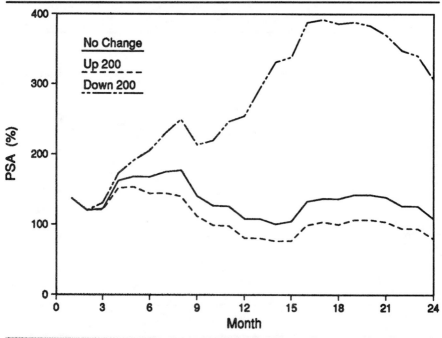

Note: Projections are as of January 25, 1988, when the base mortgage rate was 10.34%.

# EXHIBIT 8
## LONG-TERM PREPAYMENT PROJECTIONS FOR SEASONED FHLMCs

| Coupon | Price | Rem Term | | Interest Rate Changes | | | | | | | | | | |
|--------|-------|----------|---|------|------|------|------|-----|-----|-----|------|------|------|------|
| | | | | −400 | −300 | −200 | −100 | −50 | 0 | +50 | +100 | +200 | +300 | +400 |
| 8.000 | 93- 4 | 19- 4 | Immediately: | 648 | 456 | 218 | 150 | 132 | 118 | 107 | 99 | 92 | 85 | 80 |
| | | | Over 1 Year: | 502 | 361 | 198 | 145 | 130 | 118 | 108 | 101 | 94 | 88 | 83 |
| | | | 100 bp/Year: | 298 | 257 | 183 | 145 | 131 | 118 | 108 | 101 | 96 | 93 | 90 |
| 9.000 | 97-16 | 21- 1 | Immediately: | 670 | 626 | 426 | 204 | 162 | 141 | 125 | 112 | 95 | 88 | 82 |
| | | | Over 1 Year: | 561 | 505 | 348 | 191 | 159 | 141 | 127 | 116 | 100 | 93 | 87 |
| | | | 100 bp/Year: | 377 | 367 | 299 | 191 | 161 | 141 | 126 | 116 | 104 | 100 | 98 |
| 10.000 | 100-30 | 23- 0 | Immediately: | 665 | 633 | 583 | 376 | 258 | 189 | 153 | 135 | 109 | 93 | 87 |
| | | | Over 1 Year: | 600 | 561 | 502 | 329 | 242 | 189 | 158 | 142 | 118 | 103 | 96 |
| | | | 100 bp/Year: | 466 | 460 | 441 | 329 | 249 | 189 | 156 | 142 | 124 | 115 | 112 |
| 11.000 | 104-26 | 24- 6 | Immediately: | 638 | 603 | 567 | 509 | 429 | 311 | 225 | 175 | 133 | 110 | 96 |
| | | | Over 1 Year: | 605 | 573 | 537 | 476 | 406 | 311 | 244 | 201 | 158 | 134 | 118 |
| | | | 100 bp/Year: | 532 | 525 | 512 | 476 | 416 | 311 | 236 | 201 | 174 | 162 | 156 |
| 12.000 | 107- 4 | 24- 4 | Immediately: | 597 | 561 | 522 | 483 | 463 | 423 | 350 | 259 | 166 | 135 | 115 |
| | | | Over 1 Year: | 577 | 545 | 512 | 477 | 459 | 423 | 362 | 293 | 215 | 180 | 155 |
| | | | 100 bp/Year: | 520 | 513 | 500 | 477 | 461 | 423 | 357 | 293 | 240 | 224 | 215 |
| 13.000 | 108- 0 | 24- 3 | Immediately: | 592 | 557 | 520 | 482 | 463 | 444 | 426 | 387 | 242 | 162 | 134 |
| | | | Over 1 Year: | 574 | 543 | 511 | 478 | 461 | 444 | 427 | 396 | 286 | 221 | 190 |
| | | | 100 bp/Year: | 518 | 512 | 499 | 478 | 462 | 444 | 426 | 396 | 312 | 275 | 263 |
| 14.000 | 108- 0 | 24- 3 | Immediately: | 567 | 533 | 498 | 461 | 443 | 425 | 408 | 391 | 339 | 214 | 149 |
| | | | Over 1 Year: | 549 | 519 | 489 | 457 | 441 | 425 | 409 | 394 | 350 | 256 | 202 |
| | | | 100 bp/Year: | 495 | 489 | 478 | 457 | 442 | 425 | 408 | 394 | 363 | 308 | 283 |
| 16.000 | 108- 0 | 24- 0 | Immediately: | 577 | 546 | 513 | 479 | 462 | 445 | 428 | 412 | 380 | 349 | 304 |
| | | | Over 1 year: | 560 | 532 | 504 | 475 | 460 | 445 | 430 | 415 | 386 | 359 | 322 |
| | | | 100 bp/Year: | 509 | 503 | 493 | 475 | 461 | 445 | 429 | 415 | 395 | 383 | 370 |

Immediately: Interest rates move the indicated amount immediately.
Over 1 Year: Interest rates move the indicated amount linearly over one year.
100 bp/Year: Interest rates move the indicated amount gradually (by a maximum of 100 basis points per year).

Note: Prepayment projections are based on seasoned 30-year mortgages and on closing prices on February 9, 1988. The base mortgage rate is 9.94%.

For the no-change case, month-to-month changes are caused primarily by seasonality. For the case of increasing interest rates, there is a gradual decrease in prepayment levels. The decline begins to take effect after two to three months, reflecting the typical time lag between changes in interest rates and changes in prepayment levels. In the second year prepayment rates begin to stabilize, reflecting interest-rate stability and hence relatively stable housing turnover.

If interest rates decline, there is an appreciable increase during the second year in the prepayment rates of the GNMA 10s. Prepayments reach a peak around months 16 to 18, several months after rates have declined to their lowest point, reflecting the time lag between mortgage-rate changes and their effect on prepayments, and the usual summer seasonal high in housing turnover (in the example, month 1 corresponds to February). The coupons on the mortgages underlying the GNMA 10s are 10.50%. A 200-basis-point drop in mortgage rates, to 8.34%, means that the underlying mortgages are in the range in which refinancing is worthwhile. The drop in mortgage rates also leads to higher housing turnover and hence higher prepayments.

### Converting Monthly Prepayment Projections to a Single Rate

As described previously, the Prudential-Bache Prepayment Model generates month-by-month prepayment projections for the remaining term of a mortgage security. These projected monthly prepayment rates can be used to obtain the security's cash flows, from which security characteristics, such as yield, average life and duration, can be calculated. However, the use of prepayment projections in their month-by-month form is often impractical in the mortgage markets. Securities are generally priced at an assumed single prepayment rate, e.g., 9% CPR, 150% PSA, making it necessary to calculate a single CPR or PSA rate that is "equivalent" in some sense to the set of month-by-month prepayment projections.

One method for converting a set of month-by-month prepayment projections into an equivalent CPR or PSA rate is to calculate a simple average of the monthly projections, for example, a geometric average. However, this can be misleading since prepayments in the earlier years of a mortgage term are much more important than later ones, due to the greater outstanding principal balance and hence larger cash flows in the early part of the security's term.

A preferable method is weighted averaging, with the weights for each month reflecting the relative size of the cash flows in that month. Weighted-averaging methods that do this include:

(i) Equating average lives, i.e., finding the single prepayment rate that gives the same average life as the set of monthly prepayment rates;

(ii) Equating yields, i.e., finding the single rate that for a given price leads to the yield as the set of monthly projections.

Method (ii) is the method used in the Prudential-Bache model. Thus, the model's operation is as follows:

(1) For specified mortgage-security and interest rate information, month-by-month prepayment projections are generated for each remaining month of a security's term;

(2) These monthly projections are used to calculate the monthly cash flows for the security;

(3) For a given price, the model then calculates the yield from the cash flows;

(4) Finally, the model calculates the single prepayment rate, expressed as a percentage of the Public Securities Association (PSA) benchmark curve, that for the specified price gives the same yield for the security as the vector of month-by-month projections.

This yield-equivalent PSA rate is labeled the *long-term projected prepayment rate*. A similar technique, applied only to the next 12 monthly prepayment projections, gives a short-term projected prepayment rate.[1]

The exhibit illustrates a number of facets of prepayment behavior and of the Prudential-Bache Prepayment Model.

- For a given interest-rate movement, an immediate change has greater impact on prepayments, as might be expected.
- The securities with the greatest prepayment volatility are those with coupons between 0.5% to 1.5% above current mortgage rates. These are on the steep section or cusp of the S-shape of prepayments shown in Exhibit 4. An increase in interest rates means a sharp decline in prepayments for coupons at the upper end of this range, while a decrease in interest rates leads to a surge of refinancings for coupons at the lower end of this range, as their underlying mortgages come "into-the-money," i.e., there is economic incentive to refinance. In Exhibit 8, the projections are based on a prevailing mortgage rate of 9.94%, so the FHLMC 11s display the highest prepayment volatility.
- As interest rates continue to increase or decrease, prepayments tend to level off, again reflecting the S-shape shown in Exhibit 4. Once the mortgage coupon is several hundred basis points above prevailing mortgage rates, substantial economic incentive to refinance already exists; further declines in mortgage rates tend to have only a marginal effect on the rate of refinancings. Conversely, if prevailing mortgage rates are above the mortgage coupon, prepayments will be caused by normal housing turnover, so that further increases in mortgage rates will affect prepayment rates only in so far as they affect housing turnover. Although there will be some negative impact on

---

[1]There has been some discussion as to the applicability of the long-term projected prepayment rate to derivative securities such as STRIPs or CMOs, since the rate is yield-equivalent for the underlying pass-through, not for the derivative. However, the magnitude of the statistical errors and assumptions inherent in projecting prepayments 30 years into the future dwarfs the differences between using the vector of monthly projections and the single averaged rate, so that not using the single averaged rate seems an unnecessary complication. One application, however, where the monthly projections should be used is in calculating short-term total returns, as discussed later in this article.

housing sales, these tend to pick up eventually as the market adjusts to the higher rates (via, for example, lower house prices), and this reduces the long-term effect on prepayments.

- The very high coupons, such as the FHLMC 16s, have been experiencing high levels of refinancing for several years and, consequently, have low pool factors. This reduces their prepayment levels since, as discussed in Section II, many of the homeowners most able or anxious to refinance have already done so, leaving a smaller pool of potential refinancings. This is reflected in the projections in Exhibit 8. The very high coupons also display less sensitivity to interest-rate declines.

### Applications of the Model

A good prepayment model can be an invaluable tool in evaluating MBSs. This section illustrates some applications of a prepayment model.

**Return Profiles Across a Range of Rate Changes.** A prepayment model can be used to obtain the return profile of an MBS across a range of specified interest-rate movements. (This is often referred to as "scenario analysis.") For each movement of interest rates an appropriate level of prepayments can be estimated to reflect more accurately the yield impact. This gives an indication of the security's sensitivity to interest-rate movements and can thus help investors to determine whether the risk/reward profile of the security is suitable for them.

As an example, consider a FNMA 11 that has been stripped into interest-only (IO) and principal-only (PO) pieces.[2] The FNMA 11 has a remaining term of 306 months and is priced at 105-00. The IO and the PO are priced at 34-16 and 71-16, respectively. Exhibit 9 gives the yields of the FNMA 10, the IO and the PO across a range of interest-rate movements.

Exhibit 9 illustrates the differing responses of the three securities to changes in interest rates and thus gives a return profile for each security. If the investor is thinking of buying the IO, for example, he can examine the return profile shown in Exhibit 9, combine this with his own expectations about the direction of interest rates and make an informed decision about whether to buy the IO.[3]

---

[2]In other words, two separate securities, the IO and the PO, are created from the FNMA pass-through security. Each month the interest portion of the cash flow from the FNMA is allocated to the IO while the principal (scheduled and prepaid) component is given to the PO.

[3]For more detailed applications of scenario analysis to CMOs and pass-throughs, see Lakhbir S. Hayre, David Foulds and Lisa A. Pendergast, "An Introduction to Collateralized Mortgage Obligations," Chapter 14 in Frank J. Fabozzi (ed.), *The Handbook of Mortgage-Backed Securities* (Chicago, IL: Probus Publishing, 1988, Second Edition); Ravi E Dattatreya and Lakhbir S. Hayre, "Floating-Rate CMOs," Chapter 15, in *The Handbook of Mortgage-Backed Securities;* and Lakhbir S. Hayre and Cyrus Mohebbi, "Mortgage Pass-Through Securities," in this book.

**EXHIBIT 9**
**YIELDS OF A FNMA 10, AN IO AND A PO**

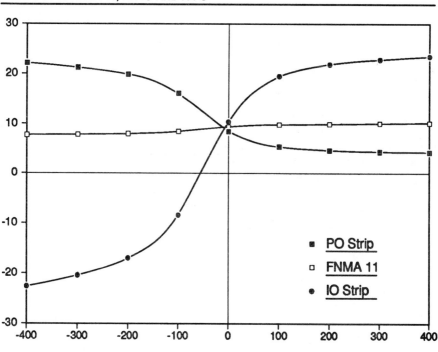

**Total Horizon Returns.** While an MBS is generally a long-term security, an investor may plan to hold it for a shorter period of time, for example, six months or one year. In this case the investor will want to know what his return over the holding period is likely to be under various interest-rate scenarios.

For an MBS an important determinant of the projected total return will be the amount of principal paydown over the holding period. The monthly prepayment projections from the model allow investors to obtain objective estimates of the month-by-month principal paydowns. For a short holding period, using the monthly projections is preferable to using an averaged long-term projected prepayment rate.

As an example, suppose an investor buys a seasoned GNMA 9 on January 8, for settlement on January 20, at a price of 95-12. The investor has a six month horizon, and is bullish, expecting interest rates to decrease by 100 basis points over the holding period. Exhibit 10 illustrates the calculation of the projected total return over the six-month holding period. The GNMA 9 has a remaining term of 21 years and, at the time of purchase, a projected long-term prepayment rate of 109% PSA, giving a yield of 10.05%. A parallel shift in yields is assumed, with rates decreasing by equal amounts over the six months for a total decrease of 100 basis points. The initial reinvestment rate is 6.5%.

Exhibit 10 shows a projected annualized return of 20.4% if rates decline by 100 basis points over the next six months. Note that the projected monthly prepayments take into account not only the declining interest rates, but also other factors, such as seasonality. This gives a more realistic calculation than one made assuming a single constant prepayment rate.

**Option-Adjusted Analysis.** This is a recent development in MBS analysis. Option-adjusted analysis deals with the uncertainty of mortgage cash flows due to possible changes in interest rates and hence prepayment rates, by using computer-generated random numbers to simulate possible interest-rate behavior over the life of the security. For each generated path of interest rates, the prepayment model is used to obtain monthly prepayment projections. The prepayment projections give the cash flows from the security along each path. These cash flows are then used to obtain averaged or "option-adjusted" security characteristics, such as yield spreads. A more detailed explanation of option-adjusted analysis is given elsewhere.[4]

The preceding examples illustrate the value of a prepayment model in evaluating MBSs. There are numerous other applications, such as calculating projected price paths and effective durations and convexities.[5] In sum, prepayment models allow MBSs to be analyzed in an accurate, consistent and meaningful way.

## IV. SUMMARY

An understanding of prepayments—their underlying causes, how they vary with fluctuations in interest rates and with changes in other economic and mortgage characteristics and how they affect investment returns—is essential for participants in the MBS markets. Prepayment rates are especially important for derivative mortgage securities, such as CMO residuals and STRIPs, which tend to be very sensitive to changes in prepayment rates.

This article has discussed the variables that influence prepayments and the basics of econometric prepayment models, using the Prudential-Bache Prepayment Model as an example. It seems clear that these mathematical models provide an effective way of projecting prepayments as a function of known or specified economic and mortgage characteristics. Proper use of these models can provide a very powerful tool to investors seeking to determine the investment characteristics of MBSs across a range of possible interest-rate movements. However, it is important to remember

---

[4]See the "Option-Adjusted Mortgage Value Report," Financial Strategies Group, Prudential-Bache Capital Funding, December 1987.

[5]See Lakhbir S. Hayre and Cyrus Mohebbi, "Mortgage Pass-Through Securities."

# EXHIBIT 10
## CALCULATION OF TOTAL RETURN

**Buy:** $1 million face value of GNMA 9s, with a remaining term of 21 years on January 8 at 95-12 (corresponding yield is 10.05% at a projected prepayment rate of 109% PSA). Settlement is January 20.

**Amount paid:**

$1MM × 95-12 = $953,750.00  
+ 19 days of accrued interest = $4,750.00  
Total $958,500.00

|  |  |  | | Cash Flows | | | | | |
| Date | Reinv. Rate (%) | Projected SMM (%) | Interest | Scheduled Principal | Prepaid Principal | Total Cash Flow | Remaining Balance | Reinv. Income | Cumulative Cash Flow |
|---|---|---|---|---|---|---|---|---|---|
| 1/20 | 6.50 | | | | | | 1,000,000.00 | | |
| 2/15 | 6.33 | 0.4773 | 7,500.00 | 1,257.68 | 4,767.34 | 13,525.02 | 993,974.98 | | 13,525.02 |
| 3/15 | 6.16 | 0.4039 | 7,454.81 | 1,261.58 | 4,009.08 | 12,725.47 | 988,704.32 | 70.42 | 26,320.91 |
| 4/15 | 5.99 | 0.4405 | 7,415.28 | 1,266.43 | 4,349.85 | 13,031.56 | 983,088.04 | 133.41 | 38,485.89 |
| 5/15 | 5.82 | 0.5461 | 7,373.16 | 1,270.84 | 5,361.78 | 14,005.78 | 976,455.42 | 194.68 | 53,686.35 |
| 6/15 | 5.65 | 0.6047 | 7,323.42 | 1,273.90 | 5,897.05 | 14,494.37 | 969,284.47 | 257.28 | 68,438.00 |
| 7/15 | 5.50 | 0.6315 | 7,269.63 | 1,276.22 | 6,112.75 | 14,658.60 | 961,895.50 | 318.50 | 83,415.10 |
| 7/20 | | | | | | | | 50.40 | 83,465.50 |

**Sell:** Remaining $961,895.50 face value of GNMA 9s on July 8 at 100-21 (based on a yield of 9.05% and a projected prepayment rate of 135% PSA) for settlement on July 20.

**Sale Proceeds:**

Remaining Balance × Price = $968,207.94  
+ 19 days of accrued interest = $4,569.00  
Total $972,776.94

**Total Return over Holding Period** = $\dfrac{\text{Sale Proceeds} - \text{Price Paid} + \text{Total Cash Flows}}{\text{Price Paid}}$

$$= \frac{\$972,776.94 - \$958,500.00 + \$83,465.50}{\$958,500.00}$$

$$= .10197 \text{ or } 10.197\%.$$

Bond-equivalent total return on an **annualized basis** = 20.395%.

that econometric prepayment models are *conditional* models in that they give projected prepayments for a *specified* future path of interest rates. Actual prepayments in a period will depend on prevailing interest rates, and trying to forecast interest rates is commonly acknowledged as a notoriously difficult task.

It is often noted that there are wide differences in the prepayment projections from the major Wall Street firms, both in CMO pricings and on the Telerate numbers collected by the PSA. This reflects the large role of subjective judgment in the construction of a complex, non-linear econometric regression model. There are simply not enough prepayment data available to estimate accurately the effects of changing patterns of interest rates, economic activity and demographic trends on prepayment levels. In many cases, this means having to extrapolate or make assumptions. Unless the major Wall Street houses agree to pool resources and construct a single prepayment model, different firms will have different projections.

# Relative Prepayment Rates on Thirty-Year FNMA, FHLMC and GNMA Fixed Rate Mortgage-Backed Securities

SCOTT F. RICHARD, D.B.A.
VICE PRESIDENT
MORTGAGE SECURITIES RESEARCH
GOLDMAN, SACHS & CO.

## I. INTRODUCTION

In a recent article we presented a new model for forecasting prepayments on fixed rate mortgage-backed securities (MBSs).[1] The results reported in that article are estimates of the model for 30-year GNMA MBSs. Since accurate predictions of mortgage prepayment rates are vital in determining relative values of MBSs and their derivatives, in this article we extend our analysis to FNMA and FHLMC 30-year MBSs. We will emphasize the important difference in prepayments between these major sectors of the MBS market. Because we see no compelling economic reason to distinguish between FNMA and FHLMC pools, we have combined the data from these two sectors in estimating our prepayment model.

Our main result is that FNMA and FHLMC pools prepay faster than GNMA pools in equivalent interest rate environments. While it is well known that FNMA and

---

[1] Scott F. Richard and Richard Roll, "Modeling Prepayments on Fixed Rate Mortgage-Backed Securities", *Journal of Portfolio Management*, Spring 1989.

351

FHLMC pools are qualitatively faster than GNMA, we are able to quantify this differential. The biggest surprise (to us) are the speeds of the FNMA and FHLMC coupons in the 9% to 10.5% range. We find that pools with these coupons have prepaid at faster rates than commonly believed.

In our previous article we establish that the seasoning for GNMA pools differs from the PSA standard in two important ways. First, discount pools take much longer to season fully than do premium pools. Second, the seasoning process is nonlinear. We find similar results for FNMA and FHLMC. Furthermore, we find that FNMA and FHLMC pools season somewhat faster than do equivalent coupon GNMA pools.

Finally, in our earlier article we examined the tendency of premium GNMA mortgages to slow or "burnout" over time. We introduced a measure of premium burnout which depends on the entire history of interest rates since the mortgage was issued. Using the same measure for FNMA and FHLMC pools we find that they tend to burnout faster than GNMA pools.

As we did for GNMA, we try to provide sufficient detail about our results for FNMA and FHLMC so that readers can understand the differences. A series of charts compare and contrast GNMA with FNMA/FHLMC. Again, we report a detailed summary of our model's prediction in relation to actual prepayment data, but we now report separate results for the 30-year GNMA and FNMA/FHLMC sectors.

## II. A COMPARISON OF THE GOLDMAN SACHS PREPAYMENT MODEL FOR GNMA VS. FNMA AND FHLMC

Our empirical prepayment model is based on four important economic effects.[2] These effects are:

1. the refinancing incentive.
2. seasoning or age of the mortgage.
3. the month of the year.
4. premium burnout.

These effects combine in a multiplicative function to determine prepayment rates:

Monthly Prepayment Rate =
(Refinancing Incentive) x (Seasoning Multiplier) x
(Month Multiplier) x (Burnout Multiplier)

The multiplicative formulation makes the effects interact proportionally.

---

[2]See Richard and Roll, *ibid*. Our model is based on an economic analysis of the mortgagor's prepayment decision.

To use the model we first determine the basic refinancing incentive. This quantity is then multiplied by the seasoning multiplier, so that if the bond is not fully seasoned the predicted prepayment rate is reduced. The result of combining the first two effects is then multiplied by the monthly multiplier, which raises or lowers the estimate depending on the time of year. Finally, the cumulative result of the first three effects is multiplied by the burnout multiplier which may reduce the estimate if the pool has previously experienced any premium burnout. We will discuss in turn the form and empirical measurement of each of these effects.

### The Refinancing Incentive

We measure the refinancing incentive as the weighted average of the values of C/R, the weighted average coupon (WAC) divided by the refinancing rate, in each of five recent months. The homeowner's monthly savings from refinancing at the current market rate is C-R per dollar of principal. Capitalizing the monthly savings at the appropriate long-term rate, R, give an approximate value of C/R-1. Hence the higher the value of C/R, the greater will be the homeowner's incentive to refinance.

We use a weighted average of recent values of C/R to capture the fact that homeowners face varying delays in responding to refinancing incentives due to differences in processing times by mortgage lenders and, perhaps, due to differences in the time needed to react to a favorable interest rate environment.[3] For convenience we will call this weighted average C/R. The lower recent interest rates have been, the higher will be the value of C/R and therefore the higher prepayment rates will be.

We model the relationship between prepayments and C/R by using a curve-fitting technique. Exhibit 1 shows monthly prepayment rates (expressed in % CPR) for seasoned 30-year FNMA/FHLMC and GNMA single family pools. The curves in Exhibit 1 reflect only the pure refinancing incentive for seasoned pools without adjustment for path-dependent burnout. Notice that there is a highly non-linear relationship, typical of option-pricing models, between the prepayment rate and C/R.

For values of C/R below one, the homeowner's prepayment option is out-of-the-money and the refinancing incentive is relatively small. For example, if C/R is 0.825, corresponding to a seasoned 8.25% conventional mortgage (with a pass-through rate of 7.5%) in a current mortgage refinancing rate environment of 10%, then the prepayment rate is approximately 9% CPR. Conversely, when C/R exceeds one, the mortgage is a premium and the refinancing incentive increases dramatically. For example, a seasoned 13% conventional mortgage in a 10% refinancing rate environment (C/R = 1.3) has a base prepayment rate of about 60% CPR without adjusting for premium burnout.

Because the refinancing incentive is very sensitive to C/R, it is important to use

---

[3]For GNMA and FNMA we use a weighted average of C/R in the past five months beginning with last month. Because of the extra month pass-through delay, for the FHLMC program we use a weighted average of C/R in the past five months, but beginning two months previously.

**EXHIBIT 1**
**GNMA VS. FNMA/FHLMC REFINANCING INCENTIVE**
**(WITHOUT PATH DEPENDENCY)**

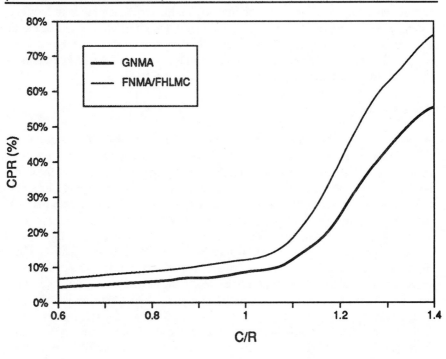

the proper pool WAC when calculating C/R for conventional MBSs. For example, the estimated WAC for generic, 30-year FNMA 7.5s is currently 8.88% (with a WAM of 345). This WAC is significantly greater than the standard assumption, which is the coupon plus 75 basis points. This issue is not vital for GNMAs because the WAC is always 50 basis points greater than the coupon.

It is well known that conventional MBSs prepay at a faster rate than do GNMA MBSs. The curves in Exhibit 1 quantify this differential. Notice that the refinancing inventive is greater for conventional pools for all values of C/R. This can be easily understood for discount pools, with C/R less than one, because FHA/VA mortgages (the type collateralizing GNMA pools) are all assumable. The increasing differences in basic prepayment incentives for premium pools with C/R greater than one is somewhat surprising. We think it is evidence that the population of individuals who take conventional mortgages is different than the population who take FHA/VA loans. Evidently, conventional mortgagors are more sensitive to refinancing incentives than mortgagors in FHA/VA pools.

## *Seasoning*

It is well known that mortgage prepayment rates rise from very low to much higher levels as the mortgages ages. This is the rationale for the PSA Standard Prepayment Model which, in its base case, models mortgage prepayment rates as increasing linearly from 0% CPR at issue to 6% CPR at 30 months and then remaining constant.

What is not as well known is that the mortgage seasoning process differs markedly depending on the coupon rate relative to current refinancing rates. Slight premium FNMA/FHLMC pools, for example, are typically fully seasoned in about 30 months, as suggested by the PSA standard. Current coupon pools, on the other hand, take nearer to four years to season fully and discount pools can take considerably longer.

Our model captures the interaction between seasoning and coupon by making the seasoning effect a function of the mortgage's current C/R. In Exhibit 2 we show the relative seasoning effects for a discount pool with C/R equal to 0.8, a par pool with C/R equal to 1.0 and a premium pool with C/R equal to 1.2 for both FNMA/FHLMC and GNMA pools. Our model shows that these pools season at remarkably different rates.

**EXHIBIT 2**
**GNMA VS. FNMA/FHLMC SEASONING**

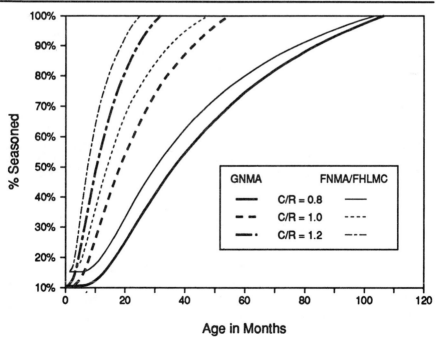

For GNMA a discount pool (C/R=0.8) takes about 9 years to season fully, although it is 75% seasoned in about 5 years; conventional discount pools season faster but follow a similar qualitative pattern. This is not hard to understand in terms of the homeowner's disincentive to move when his mortgage rate is low compared to rates currently available. Additionally, the seasoning process for discount GNMA pools is further slowed by the fact that FHA/VA mortgages are assumable and that the incentive to assume is greater, the smaller is C/R. The par pool with C/R equal to 1.0 typically takes nearly five years to season fully for GNMAs, but only four years for FNMAs/FHLMCs.

Even faster to season fully are premium pools; at a C/R value of 1.2, a GNMA pool typically seasons in just over 30 months, as prescribed by PSA, and in about 20 months for FNMA/FHLMC pools. Unfortunately, the seasoning process is decidedly nonlinear and PSA is a poor approximation throughout. Again it is not difficult to understand the fact that premiums season relatively quickly in terms of the homeowner's incentives: A homeowner will not be deterred from moving because he holds a premium mortgage and it is implausible that anyone will want to assume a high premium mortgage.

After seasoning fully, we assume that aging has no further effect on mortgage prepayment rates since we have no data on the end-of-life prepayment behavior of mortgage-backed security pools. Furthermore, economic theory gives little guidance to whether prepayments should increase or decrease as a mortgage nears maturity. Hence in the absence of theory and data, we have made the neutral choice to assume no further aging effect.

### Month of the Year

The seasonal pattern of mortgage prepayments is both important and somewhat surprising. It is commonly believed that prepayments peak in the summer months and trough in the winter because household moves follow this seasonal pattern. Exhibit 3 shows our model's estimate of the relative month-of-the-year effect for FNMA/FHLMC and GNMA 30-year Single Family MBSs. While the winter trough is evident in February-March, the peak occurs in the autumn in October-November. This is perhaps due to lags in passing through prepayments.

### Premium Burnout

Premium burnout is the tendency for the prepayment rates on premium coupon mortgages to slow over time.[4] There are two important manifestations of premium burnout, the first is cross-sectional and the second is dynamic. In any given month the highest coupon pool will not necessarily display the fastest prepayment rate. In fact in 1988 the FNMA 15.5% coupon MBS prepaid faster than higher coupon FNMAs, while the GNMA 14s were fastest in 1988.

---

[4]See Richard and Roll, *op. cit.*, for a discussion of the economic causes of premium burnout.

**EXHIBIT 3**
**GNMA VS. FNMA/FHLMC MONTHLY MULTIPLIERS**

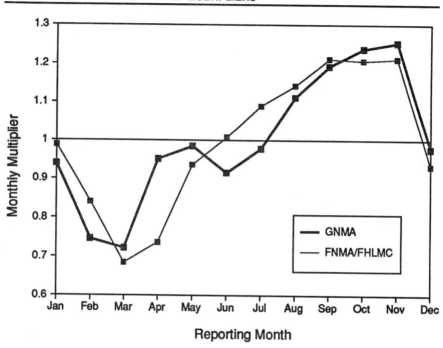

The dynamic manifestation of premium burnout can be seen in an environment in which mortgage rates fall, then rise and then fall again. In this scenario the prepayment rates on high coupon mortgages will surge in the first rally, decline when rates rise, and finally surge again when rates fall for the second time. The prepayment rate in the second surge will not be typically as high as the prepayment rate in the first surge because of premium burnout.

In the Goldman Sachs empirical prepayment model we capture the effect of premium burnout through a complicated nonlinear function. This function depends on the entire history of C/R since the mortgage was issued. Roughly we try to measure how much the option to prepay has been deep in-the-money since the pool was issued. The more that the prepayment option has been deep in-the-money, the more burned-out the pool is and the smaller prepayments are, all other things being equal. Exhibit 4 illustrates the effect of the adjustment for premium burnout. Exhibit 4 shows the burnout multiplier as a function of time for hypothetical, newly issued 11.5%, 12%, 12.5% and 13% coupon GNMA pools (with underlying gross mortgage rates of 12%, 12.5%, 13% and 13.5%, respectively) and for hypothetical, newly issued 12%, 12.5%, and 13% coupon FNMA or FHLMC pools (with underlying gross mortgage rates of 12.75%, 13.25% and 13.75%, respectively) in a constant 10% mortgage refinancing rate environment.

**EXHIBIT 4**
**GNMA VS. FNMA/FHLMC BURNOUT FOR NEW ISSUES**
**(REFINANCING RATE = 10.0%)**

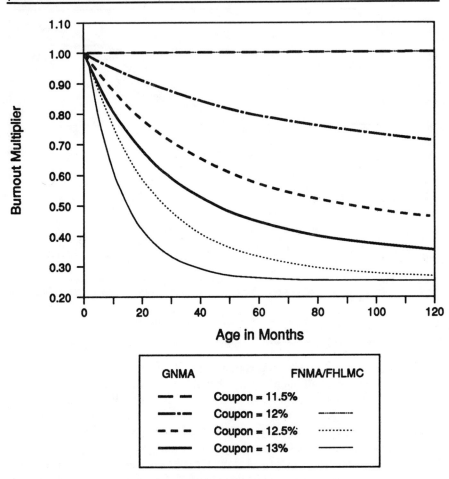

To understand the effect of premium burnout examine Exhibit 4. We see that in a constant 10% mortgage refinancing rate environment, *newly issued* GNMA pools with 13%, 12.5% and 12% coupons will all experience premium burnout, but at decreasing rates, and that an 11.5% pool will not. The prepayment options for the higher coupon pools are more in-the-money than for the lower coupon pools. From Exhibit 1 we find that the higher coupon pools have a higher refinancing effect. But over time, the more interest rate sensitive households in the 13% pool choose to prepay, leaving only the households which are less interest rate sensitive remaining in the pool. A similar effect is found among households comprising 12.5% and 12%

coupon pools. The 11.5% pool experiences no premium burnout because this group of homeowners' options are not as deeply in-the-money. After 40 months in a constant 10% refinancing rate environment, the 13% pool has burned out to the point that prepayments are about half of what they would otherwise have been. Of course, this decline in prepayments is somewhat offset by the seasoning of the pool as shown in Exhibit 2. Similarly, the 12.5% pool will have a burnout multiplier of about 0.65 and the 12% pool will have a multiplier of about 0.85.

Turning now to FNMA and FHLMC pools, we see from Exhibit 4 that they burnout even faster than do GNMA pools. For example, after 40 months in a constant 10% refinancing rate environment, the 13% FNMA/FHLMC pool has burned out to the point that prepayments are about 30% of what they would otherwise have been. The faster burnout experienced by FNMA/FHLMC pools is consistent with our previous findings that conventional mortgagors are more interest sensitive than are FHA/VA mortgagors.

### Combined Effects

We can see how the effects combine by calculating prepayment rates for GNMA and FNMA/FHLMC pools with various coupons in a constant refinancing rate environment. This is illustrated in Exhibit 5, which shows seasonally adjusted CPRs for hypothetical, newly issued GNMA pools with 9%, 11% and 13% coupons in a constant 10.55% mortgage refinancing rate environment (i.e., a GNMA coupon of 10% priced at its parity price) and for hypothetical, newly issued FNMA/FHLMC pools with the same coupons, but in a constant 10.78% mortgage refinancing rate environment. Notice that speeds increase for all coupons due to seasoning, but that the 13% coupon experiences burnout which eventually slows its prepayment rate. In actuality, prepayment rates over time are much less smooth due to monthly multipliers and to interest rate fluctuations, as we discuss in the next section.

## III. ESTIMATION AND EMPIRICAL RESULTS

The model is estimated using nonlinear least-squares. Data for each sector is taken from the Goldman Sachs Mortgage Database and is aggregated into cohorts each month. For purposes of estimation, cohorts are formed by taking the weighted average of all pools in a sector with equal coupons and remaining terms (WAMs). The weights are the outstanding pool balances. In each case, all cohort-months are included in the nonlinear regression estimation.

Consider first the results for the GNMA single family 30-year MBSs for the period May, 1979 through May, 1988, inclusive. During this sample period there is a total of 103,694 observations in the Goldman Sachs database. The coefficient of determination (R-squared) is 94.6%, which is the proportion of cross-cohort and cross-month variability in prepayment rates explained by the four effects in the

**EXHIBIT 5**
**PREPAYMENTS OF SELECTED GNMA VS. FNMA/FHLMC COUPONS**
**(ALL ASSUMED TO BE NEWLY ISSUED. MORTGAGE REFINANCING RATE = 10.55%**
**FOR GNMA AND 10.75% FOR FNMA/FHLMC.)**

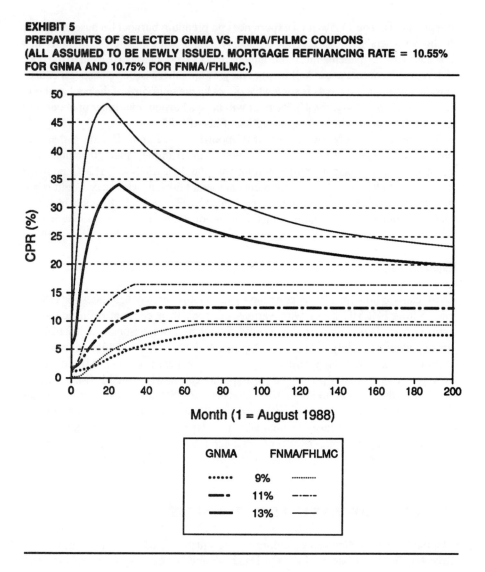

| GNMA | FNMA/FHLMC |
|---|---|
| ······ 9% ·········· |
| ▬▬· 11% ▬·▬· |
| ▬▬ 13% ▬▬ |

regression. Thus, in the GNMA 30-year sector, roughly 95% of the prepayment differences over time and across coupons can be attributed to refinancing incentives, seasoning, seasonality, and premium burnout.

Now consider the results for the FNMA/FHLMC single family 30-year MBSs for the same period. During this sample period there is a total of 446,468 observations in the Goldman Sachs database. The R-squared is 70.2%. This lower level of explanatory power in comparison to the GNMA regression is due, we think, to the method by which FNMA and FHLMC pools are formed. Conventional mortgage pools can include underlying mortgages which have gross coupons differing by up to 200 basis points and there are almost no restrictions on underlying WAMs. So, for example, a FNMA 10% coupon MBS pool might contain mortgages with gross coupons between 10% and 12.75%. Since prepayments are very sensitive to the actual WAC and WAM of a mortgage, the relatively looser pooling criterion for conventional mortgages induces much more variation in observed prepayments for FNMA/FHLMC pools than for GNMA pools with the same coupon and WAM.

Our model's high degree of explanatory power was obtained in a sample that included *all* coupons and *all* maturities of 30-year GNMA single family pools. The procedure of combining all mortgages in a single estimation should be contrasted with estimating a *separate* model for each coupon and for each maturity year, a procedure apparently followed by some other investigators. We have examined the differences and found that explanatory power can be increased to as much as 99% if a separate model is estimated for each coupon and maturity year. These separate models, however, have different coefficients in each case and we suspect they would fit poorly out-of-sample. Furthermore, estimating separate models ignores much useful information because pools with equal C/R, age and burnout should behave similarly. (Our high R-squared shows that they, in fact, do behave similarly.) Hence there is important information about the prepayment characteristics of a 12% pass-through in a 10% refinancing rate environment that can be inferred from the prepayment behavior of a 10% pass-through in an 8.25% refinancing rate environment.

This cross-coupon information is particularly important when using a prepayment model for valuation purposes. In valuation models, prepayments in many different interest rate scenarios are considered (usually through Monte Carlo simulations). In many of these scenarios, the prepayment model is forced to forecast out-of-sample because the simulated interest rate scenario lies outside the bounds of observed interest rates. For example we have no observations on 7.5% GNMA pools in a 6.5% refinancing rate environment, (C/R = 8/6.5 = 1.23) although these are frequently observed in simulation models. We have, however, many observations of 11.5% coupons with a 9.75% refinancing rate or a 12% coupon with a 10.2% refinancing rate (both also have C/R = 1.23). Guided by our analysis of the homeowner's prepayment option and lacking data to the contrary, we anticipate that the 7.5% coupon pool in a 6.5% mortgage refinancing rate environment will behave much as an 11.5% coupon pool does in a 9.75% mortgage refinancing rate environment.

Exhibits 6 and 7 contain a comparison of our model's in-sample predictions to the actual prepayment rates for GNMA MBSs from May 1979 through May 1988 and for FNMA/FHLMC MBSs from June 1982 through May 1988, respectively. For each coupon and each range of mortgage refinancing rates we show five statistics: our prediction of the weighted average prepayment rate (weighted by the outstanding principal balance in the cohort), the actual weighted average prepayment rate, the standard deviation of the actual prepayments in the cell, the number of observations, and the weight of each observation.

**EXHIBIT 6**
**PREPAYMENTS OF GNMAs IN YEARS 1979-1988**

| Coupon | Refinancing Rate Range | 8.5% – 9.5% | 9.5% – 10.5% | 10.5% – 11.5% | 11.5% – 12.5% | 12.5% – 13.5% |
|--------|------------------------|-------------|--------------|---------------|---------------|---------------|
| 7.5% | Predicted CPR (%) | 5.1 | 4.2 | 3.3 | 4.1 | 2.4 |
| | Actual Average CPR (%) | 6.9 | 4.9 | 3.2 | 4.3 | 2.8 |
| | Standard Deviation of CPR (%) | 4.5 | 3.8 | 2.9 | 1.9 | 1.4 |
| | Number of Observations | 826 | 2583 | 975 | 1074 | 2811 |
| | Weight | 12702 | 11976 | 14401 | 2947 | 1446 |
| 8% | Predicted CPR (%) | 4.1 | 3.6 | 2.6 | 4.8 | 2.9 |
| | Actual Average CPR (%) | 5.1 | 3.9 | 2.6 | 4.4 | 3.0 |
| | Standard Deviation of CPR (%) | 4.6 | 3.6 | 2.6 | 1.4 | 1.4 |
| | Number of Observations | 1164 | 3585 | 1361 | 1510 | 3919 |
| | Weight | 36001 | 34813 | 43274 | 5966 | 2953 |
| 8.5% | Predicted CPR (%) | 2.0 | 2.0 | 1.5 | 5.5 | 3.4 |
| | Actual Average CPR (%) | 1.9 | 2.3 | 1.6 | 4.7 | 3.3 |
| | Standard Deviation of CPR (%) | 3.4 | 2.5 | 1.8 | 2.5 | 2.1 |
| | Number of Observations | 741 | 2043 | 790 | 837 | 2159 |
| | Weight | 38266 | 41967 | 52320 | 1884 | 938 |
| 9% | Predicted CPR (%) | 2.6 | 2.9 | 2.3 | 5.5 | 3.3 |
| | Actual Average CPR (%) | 2.3 | 3.0 | 2.2 | 3.9 | 2.6 |
| | Standard Deviation of CPR (%) | 2.9 | 2.3 | 1.6 | 1.2 | 1.1 |
| | Number of Observations | 676 | 1761 | 683 | 677 | 1526 |
| | Weight | 192096 | 164202 | 194260 | 9418 | 5296 |
| 9.5% | Predicted CPR (%) | 5.4 | 3.5 | 2.8 | 6.2 | 3.5 |
| | Actual Average CPR (%) | 4.5 | 3.7 | 2.9 | 3.6 | 2.5 |
| | Standard Deviation of CPR (%) | 4.1 | 3.0 | 2.0 | 1.0 | 0.8 |
| | Number of Observations | 482 | 1172 | 463 | 417 | 850 |
| | Weight | 107511 | 150647 | 151852 | 12909 | 8014 |
| 10% | Predicted CPR (%) | 9.5 | 4.1 | 3.5 | 6.1 | 3.5 |
| | Actual Average CPR (%) | 7.5 | 4.3 | 3.7 | 3.4 | 2.3 |
| | Standard Deviation of CPR (%) | 4.6 | 3.4 | 2.3 | 2.3 | 1.5 |
| | Number of Observations | 608 | 1412 | 606 | 577 | 1034 |
| | Weight | 50041 | 71933 | 66226 | 2905 | 1892 |

**EXHIBIT 6 (continued)**
**PREPAYMENTS OF GNMAs IN YEARS 1979-1988**

| Coupon | Refinancing Rate Range | 8.5% – 9.5% | 9.5% – 10.5% | 10.5% – 11.5% | 11.5% – 12.5% | 12.5% – 13.5% |
|--------|------------------------|-------------|--------------|---------------|---------------|---------------|
| 10.5%  | Predicted CPR (%)              | 17.8  | 6.2   | 3.9   | 3.9   | 2.0   |
|        | Actual Average CPR (%)         | 18.8  | 7.0   | 4.4   | 2.4   | 1.7   |
|        | Standard Deviation of CPR (%)  | 11.2  | 5.3   | 3.7   | 3.7   | 3.2   |
|        | Number of Observations         | 487   | 1106  | 488   | 434   | 695   |
|        | Weight                         | 22731 | 30837 | 32939 | 1146  | 617   |
| 11%    | Predicted CPR (%)              | 29.6  | 13.5  | 7.0   | 5.2   | 4.2   |
|        | Actual Average CPR (%)         | 27.2  | 13.4  | 7.6   | 3.5   | 3.2   |
|        | Standard Deviation of CPR (%)  | 9.0   | 5.5   | 3.7   | 2.6   | 1.6   |
|        | Number of Observations         | 614   | 1395  | 549   | 619   | 1056  |
|        | Weight                         | 71564 | 76453 | 79997 | 15852 | 7594  |
| 11.5%  | Predicted CPR (%)              | 38.0  | 23.3  | 10.9  | 6.0   | 2.7   |
|        | Actual Average CPR (%)         | 38.3  | 25.3  | 12.5  | 5.0   | 2.8   |
|        | Standard Deviation of CPR (%)  | 8.0   | 10.0  | 4.7   | 2.6   | 1.6   |
|        | Number of Observations         | 546   | 1268  | 491   | 573   | 1003  |
|        | Weight                         | 56271 | 58748 | 57620 | 26256 | 14612 |
| 12%    | Predicted CPR (%)              | 41.2  | 29.8  | 13.4  | 4.7   | 2.1   |
|        | Actual Average CPR (%)         | 41.1  | 30.6  | 15.4  | 4.2   | 2.4   |
|        | Standard Deviation of CPR (%)  | 6.4   | 10.4  | 5.4   | 3.1   | 2.0   |
|        | Number of Observations         | 490   | 1139  | 425   | 483   | 900   |
|        | Weight                         | 47550 | 50026 | 50371 | 25533 | 9564  |
| 12.5%  | Predicted CPR (%)              | 41.8  | 35.7  | 18.3  | 8.2   | 4.1   |
|        | Actual Average CPR (%)         | 41.4  | 34.8  | 18.9  | 7.8   | 4.2   |
|        | Standard Deviation of CPR (%)  | 6.8   | 11.7  | 5.6   | 3.9   | 3.1   |
|        | Number of Observations         | 511   | 1177  | 436   | 516   | 1003  |
|        | Weight                         | 25628 | 27430 | 27827 | 15108 | 7244  |
| 13%    | Predicted CPR (%)              | 41.1  | 39.2  | 22.5  | 12.2  | 4.7   |
|        | Actual Average CPR (%)         | 41.9  | 37.5  | 22.0  | 12.9  | 5.3   |
|        | Standard Deviation of CPR (%)  | 7.8   | 12.8  | 7.3   | 5.8   | 3.8   |
|        | Number of Observations         | 441   | 1013  | 380   | 440   | 847   |
|        | Weight                         | 15146 | 16288 | 16313 | 10041 | 5530  |

**EXHIBIT 7**
**PREPAYMENTS OF FNMAs/FHLMs IN YEARS 1982-1988**

| Coupon | Refinancing Rate Range | 8.5%–9.5% | 9.5%–10.5% | 10.5%–11.5% | 11.5%–12.5% | 12.5%–13.5% |
|---|---|---|---|---|---|---|
| 7.5% | Predicted CPR (%) | 8.8 | 8.8 | 6.6 | 5.9 | 5.5 |
| | Actual Average CPR (%) | 8.3 | 8.5 | 6.0 | 5.6 | 6.6 |
| | Standard Deviation of CPR (%) | 6.9 | 6.7 | 4.8 | 4.8 | 5.1 |
| | Number of Observations | 2319 | 8116 | 5612 | 2364 | 4769 |
| | Weight | 4021 | 3565 | 6010 | 2062 | 685 |
| 8% | Predicted CPR (%) | 9.3 | 8.8 | 6.8 | 5.4 | 5.4 |
| | Actual Average CPR (%) | 8.9 | 8.6 | 6.3 | 5.6 | 6.9 |
| | Standard Deviation of CPR (%) | 5.7 | 5.2 | 4.0 | 3.5 | 3.6 |
| | Number of Observations | 2891 | 10178 | 7140 | 2991 | 5784 |
| | Weight | 9799 | 9464 | 14862 | 8051 | 1894 |
| 8.5% | Predicted CPR (%) | 9.1 | 8.6 | 6.5 | 6.7 | 6.8 |
| | Actual Average CPR (%) | 9.1 | 8.8 | 6.2 | 6.2 | 7.4 |
| | Standard Deviation of CPR (%) | 6.8 | 5.9 | 4.1 | 3.9 | 4.2 |
| | Number of Observations | 2797 | 10094 | 7119 | 2972 | 5777 |
| | Weight | 8062 | 8474 | 14623 | 6250 | 1339 |
| 9% | Predicted CPR (%) | 9.0 | 8.4 | 6.9 | 7.6 | 6.8 |
| | Actual Average CPR (%) | 8.6 | 7.7 | 6.4 | 6.4 | 7.4 |
| | Standard Deviation of CPR (%) | 7.5 | 6.0 | 4.1 | 3.8 | 4.7 |
| | Number of Observations | 2711 | 10033 | 6519 | 2572 | 4819 |
| | Weight | 9532 | 10569 | 18135 | 6593 | 1135 |
| 9.5% | Predicted CPR (%) | 12.9 | 9.2 | 7.9 | 8.7 | 7.3 |
| | Actual Average CPR (%) | 11.7 | 8.4 | 6.8 | 7.2 | 7.0 |
| | Standard Deviation of CPR (%) | 9.2 | 7.0 | 4.6 | 3.9 | 4.4 |
| | Number of Observations | 2271 | 8505 | 5661 | 2141 | 3685 |
| | Weight | 8379 | 10403 | 17722 | 9144 | 1770 |
| 10% | Predicted CPR (%) | 23.9 | 13.5 | 9.6 | 10.0 | 7.9 |
| | Actual Average CPR (%) | 22.9 | 13.5 | 8.9 | 9.3 | 8.1 |
| | Standard Deviation of CPR (%) | 11.4 | 9.8 | 6.5 | 4.8 | 5.6 |
| | Number of Observations | 2102 | 7928 | 5527 | 2417 | 3818 |
| | Weight | 6556 | 7532 | 10979 | 6488 | 1007 |

**EXHIBIT 7 (continued)**
**PREPAYMENTS OF FNMAs/FHLMs IN YEARS 1982-1988**

| Coupon | Refinancing Rate Range | 8.5% – 9.5% | 9.5% – 10.5% | 10.5% – 11.5% | 11.5% – 12.5% | 12.5% – 13.5% |
|--------|------------------------|------|------|------|------|------|
| 10.5% | Predicted CPR (%) | 40.0 | 22.3 | 13.6 | 11.2 | 9.4 |
| | Actual Average CPR (%) | 37.7 | 21.8 | 13.4 | 10.9 | 8.3 |
| | Standard Deviation of CPR (%) | 15.5 | 14.8 | 10.3 | 8.7 | 7.8 |
| | Number of Observations | 2105 | 7625 | 5207 | 2393 | 3773 |
| | Weight | 3497 | 3527 | 4475 | 1886 | 549 |
| 11% | Predicted CPR (%) | 50.0 | 31.1 | 17.7 | 11.0 | 9.0 |
| | Actual Average CPR (%) | 47.6 | 29.7 | 16.8 | 9.4 | 8.2 |
| | Standard Deviation of CPR (%) | 15.5 | 16.3 | 12.0 | 8.7 | 7.7 |
| | Number of Observations | 2337 | 8367 | 5458 | 2824 | 4149 |
| | Weight | 3627 | 3669 | 4463 | 2115 | 642 |
| 11.5% | Predicted CPR (%) | 53.6 | 39.3 | 21.4 | 11.6 | 9.9 |
| | Actual Average CPR (%) | 49.6 | 37.4 | 20.6 | 10.1 | 7.4 |
| | Standard Deviation of CPR (%) | 16.4 | 17.5 | 14.8 | 9.8 | 7.8 |
| | Number of Observations | 2330 | 8321 | 5350 | 2784 | 4366 |
| | Weight | 2440 | 2611 | 3045 | 1630 | 642 |
| 12% | Predicted CPR (%) | 53.6 | 47.8 | 25.9 | 13.5 | 10.1 |
| | Actual Average CPR (%) | 51.6 | 45.6 | 24.2 | 11.9 | 8.4 |
| | Standard Deviation of CPR (%) | 14.3 | 17.6 | 14.8 | 8.4 | 6.9 |
| | Number of Observations | 2270 | 8554 | 5733 | 2930 | 5387 |
| | Weight | 2878 | 3102 | 3536 | 2470 | 1057 |
| 12.5% | Predicted CPR (%) | 51.7 | 50.6 | 30.5 | 17.6 | 11.0 |
| | Actual Average CPR (%) | 49.3 | 47.6 | 28.3 | 16.1 | 9.4 |
| | Standard Deviation of CPR (%) | 17.9 | 20.9 | 18.0 | 10.2 | 8.9 |
| | Number of Observations | 2138 | 8102 | 5234 | 2647 | 4690 |
| | Weight | 1549 | 1737 | 2022 | 1548 | 741 |
| 13% | Predicted CPR (%) | 49.2 | 51.1 | 32.2 | 24.3 | 12.3 |
| | Actual Average CPR (%) | 46.8 | 46.3 | 28.5 | 22.8 | 11.1 |
| | Standard Deviation of CPR (%) | 20.5 | 23.5 | 20.4 | 13.1 | 11.0 |
| | Number of Observations | 1795 | 6794 | 4237 | 2225 | 3898 |
| | Weight | 980 | 1094 | 1189 | 990 | 556 |

For GNMA pools, our predictions are close to the actual observed prepayment rates in each cell. Our prediction is within two standard deviations of the actual prepayment rate in all but two cells and is within one standard deviation in all but four of the cells.

The model also does very well for FNMA/FHLMC pools. Our model's predictions are within one standard deviation of the actual prepayment rate in all cells.

## IV. USING THE RESULTS TO PREDICT PREPAYMENTS

To predict prepayments over the remaining life of an MBS, the model requires two sets of inputs, (1) the characteristics of the MBS itself, i.e., its sector, WAC, and WAM; and (2) the actual historical path of the mortgage refinancing rate since origination and its assumed path from now to maturity. The actual path since origination is a matter of public record, but, of course, the assumed path could take any desired shape.

One commonly used assumption in generating prepayment forecasts is that the refinancing rate will remain constant at its current level. This is called a static scenario. In Exhibit 8 we show the static scenario forecasts for selected generic GNMA coupons in a constant 10.55% mortgage refinancing rate and for selected generic FNMA coupons in a constant 10.78% mortgage refinancing rate environment. (These forecasts are seasonally adjusted by removing the effect of the monthly multiplier.) The assumed remaining terms are 350, 296, and 282 months for the 9%, 11%, and 13% GNMA generic coupons, respectively, and 355, 296, and 280 months for the FNMA generic coupons.

Because conventional current coupon MBSs are frequently used as collateral in Collateralized Mortgage Obligations (CMOs),[5] the prepayment behavior of 9.5% and 10% coupon FNMA and FHLMC MBSs is of particular interest. In Exhibit 9 we show our projected (seasonally adjusted) prepayment rates for generic FNMA MBSs with these coupons in a constant 10.75% mortgage refinancing rate environment. The generic FNMA 9.5s are assumed to have a WAC of·10.12% and a WAM of 355 months and the generic FNMA 10s have a WAC of 10.59% and a WAM of 352 months. Notice that the long-run prepayment rates are 11.4% and 12.1% CPR for the 9.5s and 10s, respectively. These projected prepayment rates are somewhat higher than the common consensus. Nevertheless, we believe these rates are accurate since seasoned FNMA 9.5s and 10s have prepaid at 12.1% CPR and 12.4% CPR, respectively, over the past year.

---

[5]See Richard Roll, "Collateralized Mortgage Obligations: Characteristics, History, Analysis," in Frank J. Fabozzi (ed.), *Mortgage-Backed Securities: Strategies, Applications and Research* (Chicago: Probus Publishing, 1987), and; Richard Roll, "Recent Innovations in Collateralized Mortgage Obligations," Goldman, Sachs & Co., 1987.

**EXHIBIT 8**
**PREPAYMENTS OF GENERIC GNMA VS. FNMA COUPONS**
**(MORTGAGE REFINANCING RATE = 10.55% FOR GNMA AND 10.78% FOR FNMA)**

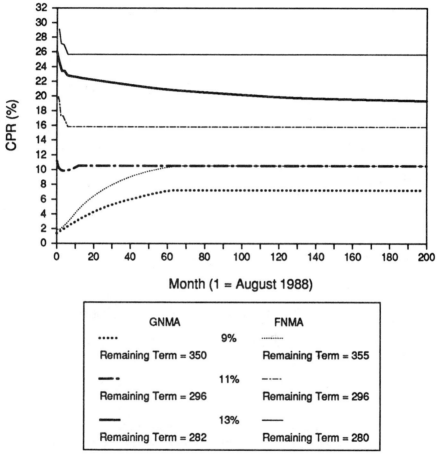

Month (1 = August 1988)

**EXHIBIT 9**
**PREPAYMENTS OF GENERIC FNMA COUPONS (REFI RATE = 10.75%)**

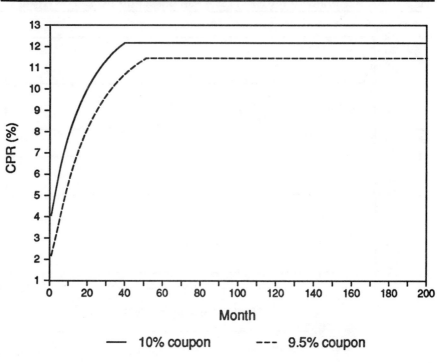

— 10% coupon      --- 9.5% coupon

## V. CONCLUSION

We have presented a model of prepayments for mortgage-backed securities which has many unique features and a high level of explanatory power. Among these novel features, three are key in understanding mortgage prepayments.

First, we have shown that option pricing theory suggests that the homeowner's refinancing incentive is best measured in our sample by the ratio of the mortgage coupon rate to the mortgage refinancing rate. By measuring properly the refinancing incentive, we find that the empirically measured effect of the refinancing incentive corresponds well with the type of effect predicted by option pricing theory.

The other two key effects modify the pure refinancing incentive. We have shown that the rate of seasoning of a mortgage pool depends importantly on whether it is a premium, par or discount pool. In particular, premium pools season quickly, typically in 30-months or less. Current coupon pools take longer to season, about 4 to 5 years. Finally, discount pools can take substantially more time to season fully, even as much as 10 years.

The third key effect is premium burnout, and it is the most difficult to measure empirically. This effect is measured by the cumulative refinancing incentive experienced by the mortgage pool when the homeowners' prepayment options were deep in-the-money. Proper measurement and use of premium burnout are vital for explaining mortgage prepayments accurately.

The prepayment model has a good fit to the data available over the last 10 years. Nevertheless, a note of caution is in order. There is no reliable data available on some aspects of mortgage-backed security prepayments, such as end-of-life prepayment rates or burnout on slight premium mortgages over longer time periods. To forecast these effects, for example in our valuation model, we must extrapolate out-of-sample. While we feel that our extrapolations are sensible, the passing of time will produce further data which we will use to revise our model.

# Analysis of Adjustable Rate Mortgages

ANDREW S. DAVIDSON
DIRECTOR
MORTGAGE-BACKED SECURITIES RESEARCH
MERRILL LYNCH CAPITAL MARKETS

YUNG C. LIM
ASSOCIATE
MORTGAGE-BACKED SECURITIES RESEARCH
MERRILL LYNCH CAPITAL MARKETS

## I. OVERVIEW OF ARM MARKET

Responding to rising interest rates in 1988 and a more competitive lending environment, adjustable rate mortgage (ARM) originations have begun to rise significantly, accounting for over half the overall originations from August 1987 to December 1988. This latest increase in the supply of existing ARMs has focused attention once again on the need for standard measures to evaluate the performance of ARM-backed securities. This article presents and compares alternative methods for assessing the performance of ARM-backed securities.

In 1983 when the ARM market was relatively new, there were many ARM programs with diverse payment characteristics. During this time, ARMs were primarily traded in whole loan form. Since late 1984, ARMs have been securitized in the secondary markets into agency and AA-rated securities. The agency issues outstanding have grown to the current size of over $30 billion. The major agency ARMs outstanding are FNMA ARMs indexed to the 11th District Cost of Funds (COF) and FHLMC and GNMA ARMs indexed to the one-year Constant Maturity Treasury.

The performance of ARM securitites under different interest rate environments is significantly influenced by the base index used and the ARMs' cap and floor levels. The two most commonly used indices for setting the ARM coupon rate are the 11th District Cost of Funds and the one-year Treasury rate. The COF reflects the average liability cost for thrifts in the 11th District (members of the Federal Home Loan Bank (FHLB) of San Francisco). The COF is a composite index that exhibits less volatility than the one-year Treasury rate and tends to lag movements in market rates. In addition to differences in the index, ARMs have varying cap and floor levels that limit the periodic adjustment of the coupon. Since these adjustment limitations have a significant impact on the performance of ARMs, they have to be properly accounted for in the valuation of ARM-backed securities.

A measure often used in the secondary markets for indicating value in ARM securities is the effective margin (EM) or discount margin. The EM measures the average yield spread over the base index that the security provides in a stable interest rate environment. The EM, however, does not fully capture the risks associated with the adjustment limitations and the differences in index behavior. The options and Monte Carlo simulation approaches discussed in this article incorporate the effects of various interest rate environments on the performance of ARM securities and derive option-adjusted margins that reflect fundamental value in ARMs. These evaluation methods are used to compare different types of ARMs and to analyze price volatility.

## II. SECONDARY MARKET

*Fannie Mae* began the first agency ARM program in late 1984 with its COF ARM program. Fannie Mae COF ARMs currently represent the largest market among agency ARMs with approximately $16 billion outstanding. Under the Fannie Mae COF ARM swap program, ARM originators swap mortgages for Fannie Mae securities. These securities are subsequently sold in the secondary markets by the originating institutions. Fannie Mae COF ARMs are often used by thrifts for asset-liability gap management since they offer rates that more closely track the thrifts' average cost of funds.

The Treasury-indexed ARM market is dominated by Freddie Mac and *GNMA* ARMs with $7 billion and $2 billion outstanding, respectively. Freddie Mac began purchasing ARMs for its portfolio in 1985 under the ARM Cash program. Beginning in early 1986, these mortgages were pooled and auctioned in the form of ARM Participation Certificates (PCs). Total auction volume increased from $1.6 billion in 1986 to $3.9 billion in 1987. In October 1987, Freddie Mac began the ARM Guarantor program under which ARM originators swap mortgages for ARM PCs.

Despite the increased volume of securitization, the agency market for ARMs is still in its early stages of development, with only about 15% of ARM originations being sold to agencies. A major reason for this may be the small number of standardized agency programs available for the wide variety of ARM characteristics existing in the primary market. The size of loan balances and different underwriting standards are the main reasons many loans are non-conforming to agency standards. This has spawned the development of credit-enhanced ARMs that offer a higher yield than agency ARMs. Credit enhancements such as a senior-subordinate structure have been used to obtain Aaa and AA ratings, respectively, from Moody's and Standard and Poor's.

## III. ARM CHARACTERISTICS

The ARM coupon resets periodically to a specified index rate subject to caps and floors which limit the adjustments.

The *index* is the base rate used to determine the coupon level on every adjustment date. The two most commonly used indices are the 11th District Cost of Funds published monthly by the FHLB of San Francisco and the one-year Constant Maturity Treasury. The one-year Constant Maturity Treasury is the weekly average yield of U.S. Treasury securities adjusted to a constant maturity of one year as published by the Federal Reserve. Other indices which have also been used include the National Cost of Funds Index, the six-month Treasury rate and the five-year Treasury rate.

*Security margin* is the spread that is added to the base index to arrive at the reset level of the coupon. The spread typically ranges from 100 to 200 basis points.

*Frequency of adjustment* determines how often the coupon resets to the prevailing index rate. For one-year Treasury-indexed ARMs, the coupon resets once a year and the monthly payment changes accordingly on the reset date. On many COF-indexed ARMs, the coupon resets monthly while the monthly payment which the borrower makes adjusts annually.

*Periodic rate cap* limits the periodic increase or decrease in the coupon to a specified amount. Periodic caps are usually semi-annual or annual caps in the 1% to 2% range.

*Lifetime cap* is the maximum rate for the coupon at any time. ARMs typically have a lifetime cap at 500-600 basis points above the initial coupon.

*Lifetime floor* is the minimum rate for the coupon. COF-indexed ARMs have a floor at a spread below the initial coupon while most Treasury-indexed ARMs do not have a floor.

*Teaser rate* is the relatively low initial coupon on the security. The teaser rate is lower than the fully-indexed rate (current index rate plus security margin) and stays in effect until the first reset date.

*Payment cap* limits the periodic increase or decrease in the monthly payment on the underlying mortgage to a specified percentage of the previous monthly payment. Fannie Mae COF ARMs typically have an annual payment cap of 7.5%. Based on current interest rate levels, the 7.5% payment cap is reached if the coupon rate changes by approximately 100 basis points.

*Negative amortization limit* is the maximum percentage of the initial principal balance to which the current outstanding balance can grow. Negative amortization, or growth in the outstanding principal, is possible because the coupon rate on most Fannie Mae COF ARMs adjusts monthly, while the payment resets annually. If the coupon rate rises sharply before the next payment adjustment date, the monthly payment may not be sufficient to cover the accrued interest. In this case, the shortfall in interest is added to the outstanding principal. A typical negative amortization limit is 125% of the original balance.

*Reamortization period* refers to the periodic waiving of the payment cap (usually every five or ten years) in order to reset the payment such that the mortgage will fully amortize over the remaining term of the loan. If the payment cap limits the adjustment of the payment to a higher coupon rate, the mortgage will not fully amortize over the original term of the mortgage.

## IV.  THE INDEX

The behavior of the ARM index relative to market rates has a significant impact on the performance of the ARM security. The two most frequently used indices for ARMs have been the 11th District Cost of Funds and the one-year Treasury rate. Other less frequently used indices such as the National Cost of Funds Index and the six-month Treasury rate can be classified as being either a Cost of Funds-based or Treasury-based index.

The one-year Treasury rate represents a market rate while the COF index is an average of various interest rates. The following section describes the COF index and its relationship to the one-year Treasury.

### The 11th District Cost of Funds Index

The COF is a monthly weighted average interest cost for liabilities of thrifts in the 11th District. The 11th District thrifts are members of the FHLB in California, Arizona and Nevada. The COF is computed monthly and published on the last business day of the following month. For example, the COF for January is published at the end of February. In the calculation, the monthly interest expenses for all 11th District thrifts are summed and divided by the average of beginning and ending month liability balances.

$$\text{Annualized COF} \quad = \quad \frac{\text{Total Interest}}{\text{Avg. Liab. Bal.}} \quad \times \quad \frac{365}{\text{Actual Days in Month}}$$

where Avg. Liab. Bal. = (Beginning Balance + Ending Balance)/2

The liabilities used in the COF calculation can be broken down into three main categories: fixed maturity deposits, other deposits and borrowings.

*Fixed maturity deposits* include fixed rate certificates of deposit (CDs) with maturities ranging from less than six months to more than three years and a small percentage of variable rate deposits. Typically, over half of total liabilities have been in fixed maturity deposits. Over 50% of these deposits have an original maturity of less than one year.

*Other deposits* are money market deposit accounts, transaction accounts and passbook savings accounts. Approximately 10% of total liabilities have been in interest rate sensitive money market accounts, while another 10% have been in transaction and passbook accounts which are usually less responsive to changes in market rates.

*Borrowings* consist primarily of FHLB advances and reverse repurchase agreements. FHLB advances represent approximately 10% of total liabilities and range in maturity from a few months to over four years.

A detailed breakdown of the liability structure as of September 1987 is provided below.

| *Liability Component* | *Percent of Liabilities* |
|---|---|
| Fixed Maturity Deposits | |
|     Less than 6 months | 19.6% |
|     6-12 months | 14.0 |
|     1-3 years | 13.2 |
|     More than 3 years | 8.0 |
|     Variable rate | 1.3 |
| Total Fixed Maturity Deposits | 56.1% |
| Other Deposits | |
|     Money Market Deposit Accounts | 9.4 |
|     Transaction Accounts | 4.2 |
|     Passbook Saving | 4.5 |
| Total Other Deposits | 18.1 |
| Borrowing | |
|     FHLB Advances | 9.5 |
|     Reverse Repurchase Agreements | 10.1 |
|     Mortgage-backed Bonds Issued | 1.5 |
|     Commercial Bank Loans | 0.2 |
|     Other Borrowing | 4.6 |
| Total Borrowings | 25.9 |

The COF is a composite index which reflects both short and long term liability costs. Furthermore, old liabilities reflect past rates while new funds represent current interest costs. Since the COF is an average of these varied rates, it exhibits two distinctive qualities:

*Low volatility:* The COF is less volatile than market rates such as the one-year Treasury. While market rates fluctuate constantly in response to changes in market conditions, the COF is less responsive because old liabilities continue to reflect past rates.

*Lag:* The COF generally lags movements in market rates because old liabilities reflect past interest costs until they are rolled over at current rates.

Exhibit 1 illustrates the low volatility of the COF relative to the one-year Treasury and three-month LIBOR, as well as the tendency of the COF to lag changes in market rates.

**EXHIBIT 1**

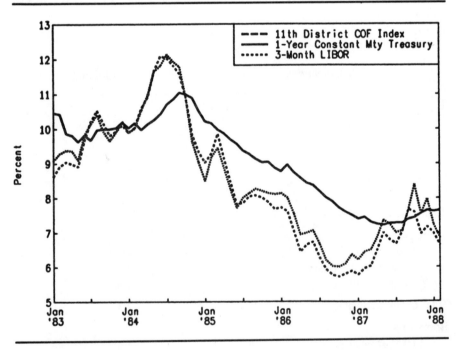

## COF Projection Model

A model which relates movements in the COF index to changes in the one-year Treasury rate was developed using regression techniques. The simulated COF rates based on the regression model are compared to the actual COF rates in Exhibit 2.

**EXHIBIT 2**

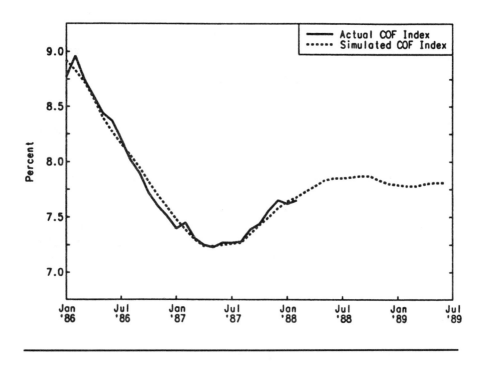

The model's estimates match actual data well, with an average estimation error of seven basis points. In a stable interest rate environment, the model predicts that the COF will continue to rise for a few months and stabilize at a level of approximately 80 basis points over the current one-year Treasury.

The two-year period beginning January 1986 was used to develop the model. Using data from over a longer period of time to estimate the model would not accurately reflect the current liability composition since the composition of 11th District liabilities has changed over the years. The resulting regression equation was estimated to be:

Projected $COF = 2.64 + 0.75 \times T14$

where T14 = 14-month moving average of one-year Treasury

The two main components of the model are:

1.  A 14-month moving average of the one-year Treasury (T14) is used to project the COF. The moving average is simply the average one-year Treasury rate

over the past 14 months. Various moving average lengths were tested and the 14 month period produced the best results. The moving average reflects both past and current rates and is consistent with the 11th District's liability structure in which the average maturity is between one and two years.

2. An adjustability factor (0.75 in the model) indicates the responsiveness of the COF to changes in the one-year Treasury. Since a percentage of the liabilities such as passbook savings are less sensitive to fluctuations in market rates, the COF does not adjust fully to changes in general interest rates. The 0.75 adjustability factor implies that the COF adjusts only 75% to changes in market rates. In other words, a 100 basis point drop in the one-year Treasury will cause a drop of approximately 75 basis points in the COF over a period of 14 months.

Exhibits 3 and 4 demonstrate the behavior of the COF in relation to the one-year Treasury rate based on the regression model. Exhibit 3 shows the effect of two different adjustability factors on the COF projections under rising and falling interest rate scenarios. For a 100 basis point rise in the one-year Treasury over a one year period, the COF rises by 85 basis points with high adjustability and by 65 basis points with low adjustability. The adjustability factor reflects the percentage

**EXHIBIT 3a**

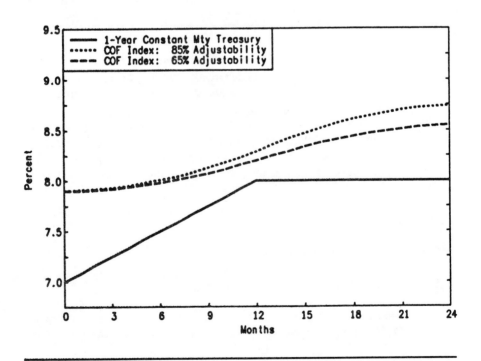

**EXHIBIT 3b**

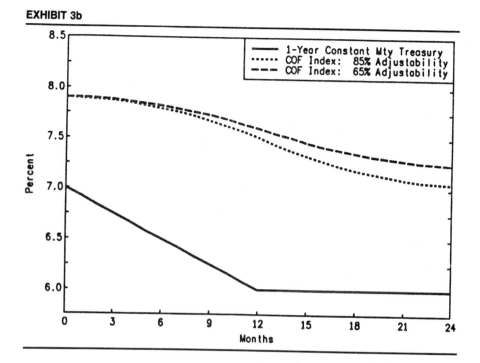

**EXHIBIT 4a**

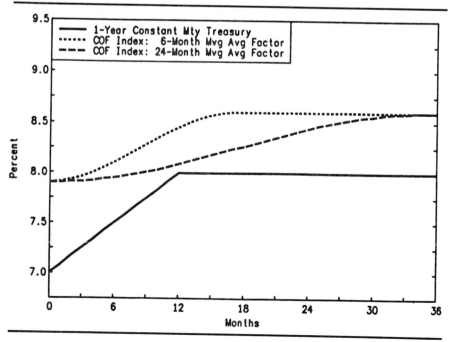

**EXHIBIT 4b**

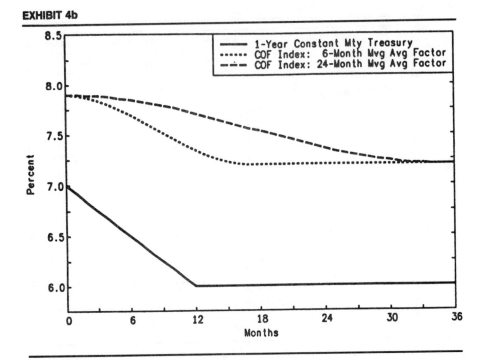

of COF liabilities that are interest rate sensitive. If a greater proportion of liabilities are in interest rate sensitive instruments, such as CDs, the COF becomes more responsive to movements in market rates.

Exhibit 4 illustrates the effect of varying the moving average term. The long term level at which the COF projections stabilize is independent of the length of moving average in both interest rate environments. However, a longer moving average slows down the rise of the COF to the long term level. The moving average term is related to the average maturity of the interest rate sensitive liabilities. If the average maturity is longer, it will take longer for the liabilities to reprice to current market rates.

The spread between the COF and the one-year Treasury tightens in a rising rate environment and widens in a falling rate environment. This is due to the presence of liabilities such as passbook savings, which do not respond to moderate changes in market rates.

In order to improve the accuracy of the projection model, several market rates of varying maturities may be used as independent variables. The COF may exhibit a closer relationship to a basket of market rates. For purposes of security valuation, however, a simple model based on the one-year Treasury rate is more appropriate for making comparisons with Treasury-indexed ARMs.

## V. PREPAYMENTS ANALYSIS

Many factors affect the rate at which ARMs prepay: general interest rate levels, the spread between the ARM coupon rate and alternative mortgage financing rates, pool seasoning, caps and floors, seasonality and expectations of future rates.

Since the spread between the rate on 30-year fixed rate mortgages and the ARM coupon is not constant, borrowers may see an opportunity to refinance into a fixed rate mortgage as spreads change. Additionally, even if spreads are unchanged, borrowers may feel that rates have generally reached a low point and will begin to rise. When this occurs, borrowers may wish to lock in what they perceive to be a low fixed rate.

Whenever caps and floors limit the coupon adjustment, prepayments will be affected. If a cap limits the upward adjustment of the coupon, prepayments will tend to decline since the borrower's interest is being kept artificially low. Prepayments will increase, however, if a floor is reached. As with fixed rate mortgages, seasoned pools tend to prepay faster.

### Freddie Mac

Sixty-six pools of Freddie Mac ARMs with 2% annual caps were analyzed. Monthly Conditional Prepayment Rates (CPRs) were calculated for each pool and aggregated for each month from April 1986 to January 1988. The following summarizes the main characteristics of the pools:

| | |
|---|---|
| WAM at origination | 330 to 359 months |
| WAC at origination | 7.1% to 9.945% |
| Original balance | $1.5 to $290 million |
| Weighted avg. lifetime cap | 13.1% to 15.95% |

Despite the limited sample size and short time period examined, some general observations can be made. Prepayments on ARMs are less variable than prepayments on fixed rate mortgages. In declining interest rate environments, prepayment rates on ARMs varied roughly between 6% and 12% CPR (see Exhibit 5), while some fixed rate mortgage-backed securities experienced prepayment rates as high as 40% CPR.

Prepayment rates on ARMs may actually increase in response to a rise in rates if investors perceive that rates have "bottomed out". During a period in which rates increased after a steady decline of about 400 basis points, several pools prepaid at rates of nearly 12%. This occurred shortly after origination when prepayments might have been expected to be low because of the lack of seasoning. A similar pattern is observed when rates increased dramatically in 1987 after a period of steady decline.

**EXHIBIT 5**

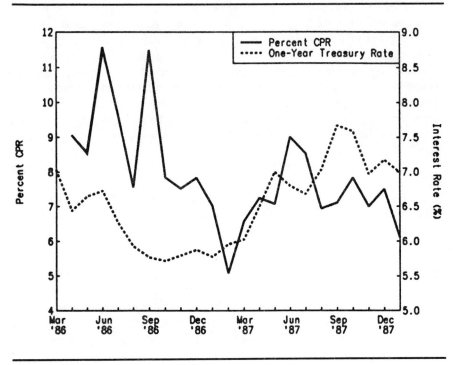

## Fannie Mae ARMs

Thirty-one pools of Fannie Mae COF ARMs which adjust monthly with life caps 500 basis points above the initial coupon were analyzed. The mortgages were originated in 1983 and 1984 and the total balance outstanding at origination was over $1 billion. The CPRs were calculated from July 1985 to January 1988.

| | |
|---|---|
| WAM at origination | 378 to 438 months |
| WAC at origination | 10.8% to 12.5% |
| Original balance | $1.3 to $148 million |
| Weighted avg. lifetime cap | 14.7% to 16.2% |

Exhibit 6 shows the Fannie Mae ARM CPRs relative to the spread between the average rates on the FNMA ARM pools and 30-year fixed rate mortgages. The exhibit indicates that there is some correlation between COF ARM prepayment rates and the spread between rates on COF and fixed rate mortgages. As the spread widens

**EXHIBIT 6**

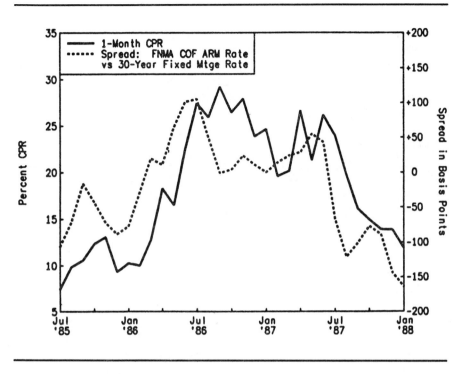

in a falling rate environment, borrowers find it more attractive to refinance into a fixed rate mortgage (as in the period from mid-1986 to early 1987). In a rising rate environment, the lag in the COF has the effect of lowering prepayments. In addition to the spread between the COF rate and the fixed rate, the absolute level of interest rates influences prepayments just as it affects prepayments on fixed rate mortgages.

Prepayments on COF ARMs appear to be more variable than prepayments on Treasury-indexed ARMs. In comparison to fixed rate mortgages, however, COF ARMs generally display more stable prepayment behavior.

The evaluation methods presented in this article for the most part assume constant prepayment rates. Although this may ignore the additional risk due to varying prepayments, the evaluation methods capture the major risk elements associated with the cap structure and the behavior of the index. In addition, ARMs trade closer to par than fixed rate instruments and varying prepayments have a smaller impact on adjustables than on fixed rates. As more data on ARM prepayments become available, a prepayment model can be developed and incorporated into the analysis.

## VI.  EVALUATION METHODS

The performance of Treasury-indexed ARMs is mainly influenced by the securities' cap structure. For COF-indexed ARMs, however, there is an additional element of risk present in the behavior of the COF index relative to market rates. The effect of caps and floors on ARM value is less significant in COF ARMs. Because of this basic difference between Treasury and COF ARMs, the option-adjusted margin approach is presented separately for each type of ARM. First, the conventional measures of ARM value are discussed.

### Effective Margin

Since the coupon on ARMs resets periodically to changes in market rates, the yield does not accurately indicate their investment performance. The yield assumes a constant reinvestment rate and does not reflect the variable nature of the coupons on ARMs. An alternative measure which is commonly used in the secondary markets is the effective margin (EM). The effective margin measures the average yield spread over the underlying index that the security holder expects to earn in a given interest rate environment. If the ARM cash flows are discounted by the index rate plus the constant EM, the resulting present value of the discounted cash flows equals the price of the security.

The EM is useful for analyzing the performance of ARMs in specific interest rate environments. Moreover, the EM can be averaged over several representative scenarios to obtain a measure of expected performance. Exhibit 7 illustrates the relationship between the ARM coupon and the index under three interest rate scenarios. For a fully-indexed par security under a constant rate assumption, the EM is the security margin adjusted for bond equivalent yield conversion. A rising rate assumption lowers the EM due to the adjustment limitations imposed by the adjustment caps. A falling rate scenario increases the EM. Changes in the price and delay days also affect the EM just as they would affect the yield on fixed rate securities. The table below compares the EMs under the scenarios presented in Exhibit 7.

| Scenario | Effective Margin (bp) |
|----------|-----------------------|
| Stable   | 191 |
| Rising   | 173 |
| Falling  | 206 |

For COF-indexed ARMs, the COF projection model can also be used to derive the EM relative to the one-year Treasury. This EM can then be directly compared with the EM of Treasury-indexed ARMs. The effective margins of Fannie Mae + 125 and Freddie Mac 7.25% ARMs are compared below.

**EXHIBIT 7a**

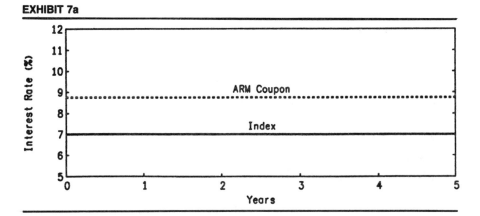

**EXHIBIT 7b**

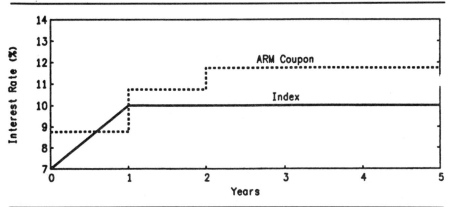

**EXHIBIT 7c**

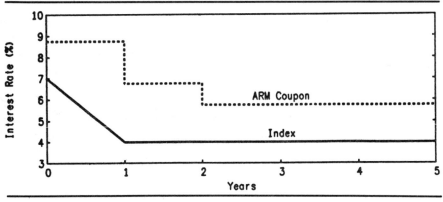

| | Fannie Mae + 125 | Freddie Mac 7.25% |
|---|---|---|
| Index | COF | One-year Treasury |
| Security Margin | 1.25% | 1.75% |
| Annual Rate Cap | — | 2.00% |
| Annual Payment Cap | 7.5% | — |
| Life Cap | 13.0% | 13.25% |
| Life Floor | 4.0% | — |
| Price | 101-4 | 98-24 |
| EM to COF | 103 bp | — |
| EM to One-year Treasury | 185 bp | 165 bp |

In a stable interest rate environment, the Fannie Mae ARM offers an average yield spread of 103 bases points over the COF index. The margin over the one-year Treasury, 185 basic points, is computed by using the projected COF rates to determine the coupon cash flows in the future, assuming stable rates for the one-year Treasury. These cash flows are then discounted at a constant spread over the current one-year Treasury. Although the EM approach may provide some indication of relative value, it does not fully account for the effects of the cap structure and index behavior.

### Option-Adjusted Margin - Treasury ARMs

The option-adjusted margin (OAM) is the margin the investor would earn if he purchased caps and sold floors to create an uncapped ARM. In other words, the OAM is the spread over a specified index that one would expect to earn on a similar floater without caps, floors and teaser rate. It is a measure of intrinsic value in ARMs and can be used as a basis of comparison against alternative investments. The OAM is derived by adjusting the price of the ARM to account for the values of the various caps and floors built into the ARM. The effective margin based on the adjusted price is the OAM.

The simplest example of this method is an ARM floater with a life cap and no periodic adjustment caps. The life cap is analogous to the caps traded in the swap market. These caps have varying strike rates and maturities. For example, if an investor sells a 13% cap, he would make a payment if the index rate were to rise above 13% (the cap holder receives the difference between between the index rate and the cap rate on settlement date). These caps can also be viewed as a series of put options. The price of the cap is equal to the sum of the values of the put options. An ARM with a life cap, therefore, can be viewed as a long position in a pure floater and a short position in a cap or series of put options. The purchaser of the floater is in effect buying a pure floater and selling a cap. Exhibit 8 shows the decomposition of the ARM into a put floater and a cap. In order to remove the risk of the coupon

**EXHIBIT 8a**

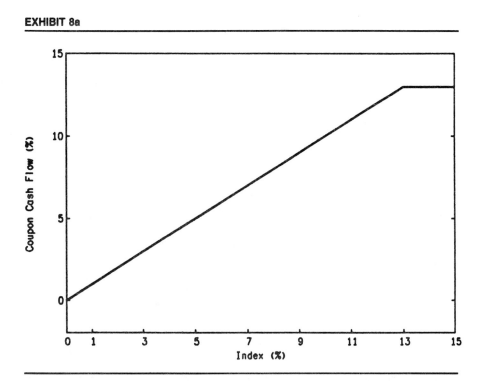

capping out, the security holder would have to buy a cap with the same maturity and strike rate as the ARM's life cap.

The pricing of an ARM with a life cap can thus be broken down into the price of a pure floater and the price of a cap.

Price of Pure Floater  = Price of ARM + Price of Life Cap
        104.0        =       100.5     +        3.5

For example, consider a hypothetical ARM with an 8.5% coupon, 13% life cap, security margin of 150 basis points and a market price of 100.5. If the life cap is worth 3.5 points, the adjusted price or price of a comparable pure floater is the sum of the market price of the ARM and the price of the cap. The effective margin in a stable interest rate scenario is calculated for the pure floater and the original ARM.

|  | *Price* | *Effective Margin (bp)* |
|---|---|---|
| Pure Floater | 104.0 | 110 |
| ARM | 100.5 | 175 |

**EXHIBIT 8b**

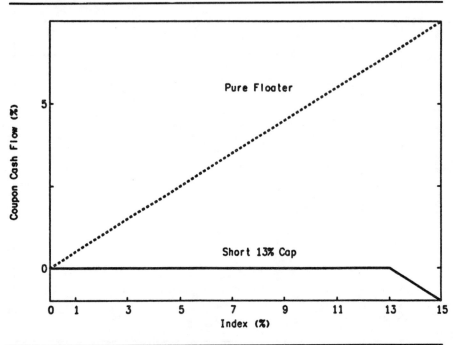

The effective margin of the pure floater is the OAM for the ARM security. The OAM of 110 basis points is significantly lower than the effective margin of 175 basis points for the ARM because the EM does not capture the burden of the life cap which is valued at 3.5 points.

The basic approach described above is used to value the major caps and floors in ARMs. The main components of the option valuation are the life cap and adjustment limits (adjustment caps).

*Adjustment Limits (Adjustment Caps):* The valuation of the periodic adjustment limits is not as straightforward as the life cap valuation. Although they can be treated as call and put options, the difficulty in valuation lies in trying to determine the level to which the coupon will reset every year. This is important because the adjustment limits are based on the prior period's coupon rate. For the first year, the adjustment limit levels can easily be determined since the initial coupon rate is known. A Freddie Mac 7% ARM with a 200 basis point adjustment limit and one year remaining to the next reset has a cap at 9% and a floor at 5%. These can be treated as put and call options. However, the second year's adjustment cap and floor are not known with certainty, since they depend on the actual reset level of the coupon. For later years' adjustment limits, it becomes increasingly difficult to determine the limit levels because they depend on the interest rate path taken.

The valuation of the adjustment limits can be simplified because of the low initial rate on most ARMs. Under these circumstances, the first year's cap is much more restrictive than the first year's floor. Consequently, the security holder must be compensated for the extra burden of the cap relative to the benefit of the floor. In subsequent years, when the effect of the teaser rate diminishes, the price of the floor approximately offsets the price of the cap. In view of this, our options approach only values the first two years' adjustment limits as an approximation for the value of all the adjustment limits.

In order to value the second year's adjustment limit, the cap and floor levels must be determined. The simplest approach would use a constant interest rate assumption. However, this assumption overlooks the shape of the current yield curve and the forward rate implied by the yield curve. Implied forward rates are used for pricing caps in the swap market and the same approach is adopted here.

*Interaction Between Adjustment Limits and Life Cap:* The periodic adjustment limits and the life cap are not independent. The adjustment caps may limit the coupon in certain interest rate environments, while the life cap may supersede the adjustment cap in other environments. Their effects overlap and may have to be considered in tandem. For most securities, however, the adjustment cap limits the coupon adjustment to a level well below the life cap during the first two years. Thus, only the adjustment limits have a significant impact on the security's value for the first two years. For the remaining period, only the effect of the life cap is taken into account. The interaction between the later years' adjustment limits and the life cap is considered insignificant and not considered. Despite these simplifications, this method values the most important caps and floors and provides a reasonably good measure of option-adjusted margins.

**Example: Freddie Mac ARM Valuation**  The methodology outlined above is used to explicitly price the various components of the Freddie Mac 7.25%ARM PC and arrive at the OAM. Because of the illiquidity of the Treasury-based cap market, a modified Black-Scholes option pricing formula is used to value the various caps and floors. Two important inputs to this model are the volatility assumption and implied forward rates for the one-year Treasury. The volatility of the Treasury rate has a direct impact on option values. An increase in volatility increases option prices because of the higher likelihood that the caps and floors will be hit. The model's volatility assumptions are based on historical and implied volatility levels.

The option pricing method produces an OAM of 81 basis points for the FHLMC 7.25% ARM which is lower than the effective margin of 176 basis points. The valuation assumes a level of 7.05% for the one-year Treasury with 26% annual volatility. The price adjustments in the option valuation reflect the values of the teaser rate, adjustment limits and life cap.

Freddie Mac 7.25% ARM PC

| | |
|---|---|
| Initial Coupon | 7.25% |
| Annual Cap | 2.00% |
| Life Cap | 13.25% |
| Security Margin | 1.75% |
| Market Price | 98.00 |
| **Effective Margin** | **176 bp** |

Option Valuation

| | |
|---|---|
| Teaser | 1.55 |
| 1st year's Adjust. Limit | 1.25 |
| 2nd year's Adjust. Limit | 0.61 |
| Life Cap | 2.96 |
| Total Price Adjustments | 6.37 |
| Market Price | 98.00 |
| Adjusted Price | 104.37 |
| **Option-Adjusted Margin** | **81 bp** |

*Teaser:* The value of the teaser is the present value of the difference between the teaser rate and the fully-indexed rate. For the Freddie Mac 7.25% ARM, the current fully-indexed level is 8.80% (7.05 + 1.75) and the value of earning 155 basis points less (8.80 − 7.25) for one year is approximately equivalent to 1.55 points in price.

*1st Year's Adjustment Limit:* The first year's adjustment cap is 9.25%, 200 basis points above the current coupon rate. This cap is hit if the one-year Treasury is at or above 7.50% (9.25 − 1.75). The cap is equivalent to writing a one-year put option with a strike rate of 7.50%. The value that the security holder receives for writing this one-year put is 1.25 points. Hence, the value of the ARM, adjusted for the value of the one-year cap, is 1.25 points higher. The security also has an adjustment floor at 3.5% for the first year, which is equivalent to purchasing a call option. The call is way out of the money in the current market and has negligible value. Therefore, the net price compensation for taking on the first year's adjustment limit is the value of the cap minus the value of the floor (1.25 − 0 = 1.25).

*2nd Year's Adjustment Limit:* The valuation of the second year's adjustment cap considers the one-year Treasury forward rate a year from now and assumes that the index resets to this forward rate, if this indexed rate is within the adjustment cap. In this example, the second year's cap and floor are at 9.5% (11.25 − 1.75) and 5.5%, respectively. The value of a two-year put option with a strike at 9.5% is 0.71 points, while the value of a two-year call option at 5.5% is 0.10 points. Since the security holder is writing the put and buying the call, the net value of the second year's adjustment limit is 0.61 (0.71 − 0.10).

*Life Cap:* Using a 10% CPR assumption, the Freddie Mac 7.25% ARM has an average life of approximately eight years. This indicates that the life cap on the security is roughly equivalent to writing an eight-year cap in the swap market. This cap price must be adjusted for the first two years because during this period the adjustment caps limit the coupon below the life cap. Therefore, the value of the life cap is the price of an eight-year cap minus the price of a two-year cap $(3.41 - 0.45 = 2.96)$.

*Option-Adjusted Margin:* The prices of all the adjustments are added to the current market price of the Freddie Mac 7.25% ARM to derive the price of a hypothetical pure floater. Based on this adjusted price, the Freddie Mac ARM has an OAM of 81 basis points over the one-year Treasury. An equivalent interpretation is that a pure floater with no caps indexed to the one-year Treasury should have a comparable effective margin if the market is pricing the Freddie Mac ARM correctly. The OAM is significantly less than the effective margin of 176 basis points because the effective margin does not fully account for the effects of the caps and floors.

**Monte Carlo Simulation - Treasury ARMs** An alternative way of deriving an option-adjusted margin is through the use of Monte Carlo simulations. The objective of a Monte Carlo simulation is to determine the effects of various interest rate environments on the value of the security. Thousands of different interest rate paths are generated and cash flow analysis is performed for each scenario. The results are then averaged over all scenarios.

In the Monte Carlo simulator, the interest rate paths for the one-year Treasury are generated assuming that the average scenario follows a path given by the one-year Treasury forward rates implied by the current yield curve. The dispersion of the rate paths around this base path depends on the volatility assumption used.

An ARM model was used to perform a Monte Carlo simulation on the Freddie Mac 7.25% ARM. The resulting average margin is compared to the previously derived OAM.

| Monte Carlo Margin: | 93 basis points |
|---|---|
| Option-Adjusted Margin: | 81 basis points |

The Monte Carlo margin is slightly different from the OAM because the OAM approach makes some simplifications. One major source of difference may be in the valuation of the later years' adjustment limits. While the Monte Carlo approach takes these adjustment limits into account, the options approach assumes that the adjustment caps and floors offset each other in the later years and only values the life cap. However, due to the interaction of the adjustment limits and life cap, the options approach may tend to slightly undervalue the adjustment floors. This is because the addition of a periodic adjustment cap to a life cap adds little incremental risk to the security holder, while the addition of an adjustment floor provides a relatively greater benefit which more than offsets the risk of the adjustment cap. Despite these differences, both approaches should provide consistent measures of relative value.

## Option-Adjusted Margin: COF ARMs

For COF-indexed ARMs, an option-adjusted margin relative to the COF index does not fully reflect their investment performance because of the unique behavior of the COF. In order to make valid comparisons with Treasury-indexed ARMs, an OAM measure relative to Treasury rates is necessary. The approach taken in this article is to use the COF projection model discussed above in conjunction with a cap model or Monte Carlo simulator to derive meaningful option-adjusted margins.

In the options approach the major caps and floors on the COF ARM are valued. The market price of the security is then adjusted to account for the values of the adjustment limitations. Finally, the effective margin relative to the implied forward rates of the one-year Treasury is computed based on the adjusted price. This is accomplished by using the COF projection model to determine the corresponding forward rates for the COF index. The coupon cash flows are determined from the COF projections and discounted at a spread over the one-year Treasury implied forward rates. The analysis is shown for the Fannie Mae +125 COF ARM:

| | |
|---|---|
| Market Price | 101.13 |
| Price of Life Cap | 0.88 |
| Adjusted Price | 102.01 |
| OAM | 132 bp |

On the Fannie Mae COF ARM, the life cap is the only major adjustment limitation that has significant value. The life floor, payment caps and negative amortization have negligible effects on the security yield. The value of the life cap can be estimated using a Monte Carlo simulator by comparing the margin on the actual security with that of a security without the life cap. Alternatively, the life cap can be valued by using option pricing methods similar to the way caps are valued in the swap market. The cap prices would be based on a volatility assumption lower than that used to price Treasury-based caps because of the lower volatility of the COF index.

The life cap on the Fannie Mae ARM is worth approximately 0.88 points. The OAM of 132 basis points accounts for the cost of removing the effect of the life cap and is the margin that one would expect to earn on a COF ARM without a life cap.

**Monte Carlo Simulation - COF ARMs** For evaluating COF ARMs, the COF projection model discussed above is used to project the COF index for each interest rate path of the one-year Treasury. The security's coupon cash flows are determined from the COF projections. The cash flows are then discounted at a spread over the corresponding Treasury rates to derive the margin relative to the one-year Treasury. The margin averaged over all the scenarios is the Monte Carlo margin.

The Monte Carlo simulation results for the Fannie Mae +125 COF ARM are presented below. The Fannie ARM offers a spread of 139 basis points over the one-year Treasury after accounting for the effects of the adjustment limitations and the lagged response of the COF to movements in market rates.

### Fannie Mae +125 COF ARM

| | |
|---|---|
| *Price* | *101.13* |
| *EM to COF.* | *103 bp* |
| *OAM to 1-yr Tsy.* | *139 bp* |

**Sensitivity Analysis** The results of the Monte Carlo margin calculation for COF ARMs are dependent on the model used for projecting the COF. Although the regression model presented above produces COF values that closely match actual COF rates, it will be useful to determine how sensitive the Monte Carlo simulation results are to the specifications of the COF model. The two main components of the COF model, as mentioned above, are the adjustability factor and the moving average term. The sensitivity of the Monte Carlo margin to these two variables is discussed below. In order to demonstrate clearly the effects of the two factors, the time periods are chosen such that rates are either generally rising or falling.

*Adjustability Factor:* Three levels of adjustability to the one-year Treasury are used to perform Monte Carlo simulations on the generic Fannie Mae COF ARM. The time period analyzed is September 1987, when interest rates were generally rising.

### Rising Rate Environment

| Adjustability Factor | OAM | Change from Base Case |
|---|---|---|
| High | 96 bp | + 17 bp |
| Base | 79 bp | — |
| Low | 66 bp | − 13 bp |

For high adjustability, an 85% adjustability to market rates was assumed, while a 65% factor was assumed for low adjustability. The effects of the high and low adjustability factors were presented above in Exhibits 3 and 4. Given greater responsiveness to market rates, the OAM is higher. This occurs because in September 1987, the COF had not fully adjusted to the rise in market rates over the prior months. Therefore, an increase in the adjustability causes the COF to stabilize at a wider spread over the one-year Treasury and increases the security's yield. The reverse is true with a low adjustability factor.

Historically, the adjustability factor has varied by less than 10%. Regressions performed on the COF index using different time periods produced adjustability factors in the 70% to 80% range. Thus, the sensitivity analysis presented above represents a significant change in the COF liability structure.

In a falling interest rate environment, the adjustability factor has an opposite effect on the margin. If the COF has not adjusted fully to a decline in interest rates, an increase in its responsiveness will lead to a steeper drop in the COF. To illustrate this point, the sensitivity analysis is performed based on prices in July 1986, during a period of prolonged declining rates. In contrast to the results in a rising rate environment, the margin is lower with a higher adjustability factor.

### Falling Rate Environment

| Adjustability Factor | OAM | Change from Base Case |
|---|---|---|
| High | 94 bp | −7 bp |
| Base | 101 bp | — |
| Low | 110 bp | +9 bp |

The composition of the COF has the greatest impact on the adjustability of the index to market rates. An increase in the proportion of interest rate sensitive liabilities will tend to increase the responsiveness of the COF, as will a shortening of the average liabililty maturity. A change in the COF composition can thus affect the security's value, even if general interest rates remain constant.

*Moving Average:* The Monte Carlo simulation is performed for three different moving averages of the one-year Treasury in the COF projection model and their effects on the OAM are shown below for two different time periods:

### Rising Rate Environment

| Moving Average | OAM | Change from Base Case |
|---|---|---|
| 6 mos. | 81 bp | +2 bp |
| 14 mos. | 79 bp | — |
| 24 mos. | 76 bp | −3 bp |

### Rising Rate Environment

| Moving Average | OAM | Change from Base Case |
|---|---|---|
| 6 mos. | 98 bp | −3 bp |
| 14 mos. | 101 bp | — |
| 24 mos. | 108 bp | +7 bp |

The effect of these moving average terms was shown above in Exhibit 4. The moving average factor has a less significant impact on security value than the adjustability factor discussed above. A longer moving average in the COF model implies a longer average maturity of the interest rate sensitive COF liabilities. This will inhibit the short term responsiveness of the COF, but will not affect the long term spread between the COF and the one-year Treasury.

As with the adjustability factor, the history of market rates has an impact on the relationship between yield and length of moving average. In a falling rate environment, a longer moving average will boost the yield due to the slower drop in the COF, while a shorter moving average will have the opposite effect.

The moving average term reflects the mix of short term and long term liabilities in the COF which are interest rate sensitive. A short moving average implies a shorter average maturity on the COF liabilities and a more frequent repricing of the liabilities to current market rates. The adjustability factor, however, also accounts for a change in the percentage of liabilities insensitive to market rates such as passbook savings. If there is an increase in the percentage of passbook savings, the COF will be less responsive to fluctuations in market rates. This will be reflected in a lower adjustability factor.

## VII. APPLICATIONS OF THE EVALUATION METHODS

### Historical Performance

Exhibit 9 shows the semi-monthly measures of the effective margin, the option-adjusted margin and the Monte Carlo margin for the Freddie Mac 7.25% ARM and the corresponding one-year Treasury rates. As expected, the fluctuations in the effective margin have often deviated from the changes in the OAM and Monte Carlo margin. During the first half of September, the effective margin increased by over 20 basis points while the OAM and Monte Carlo margin were relatively stable. The stock market crash in mid-October and the subsequent volatility in the bond market caused the effective margin to rise to 217 basis points before coming down to 190 basis points, while the OAM and Monte Carlo margin widened by about 15 basis points and have not returned to their earlier levels.

Although the OAM and Monte Carlo margin have been consistent in showing relative value, the Monte Carlo margin has typically been higher by approximately 15 basis points. This is due to the differences in assumptions made in the two methods. One source of discrepancy may be the interaction effects between the adjustment limits and the life cap mentioned above. Nevertheless, the differences between the two methods are small and these approaches provide consistent measures of relative value.

Exhibit 10 presents the effective and Monte Carlo margins for the Fannie Mae + 125 ARM in relation to the TED spread (spread between prices on Treasury-bill futures and Eurodollar futures). The EM has tracked the TED spread reasonably well. This is because the TED spread widens (LIBOR rates rise relative to Treasury rates) when Treasury-based securities are in higher demand relative to non-Treasury products. A widening TED spread thus implies softening in demand for securities

**EXHIBIT 9a**

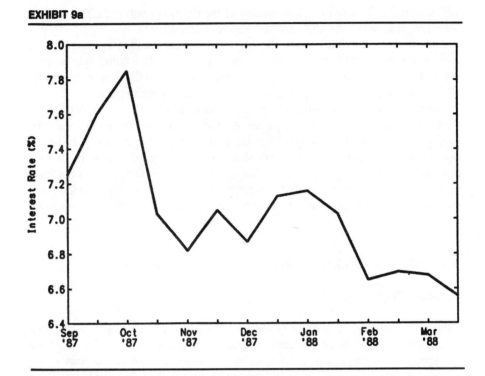

such as COF-indexed ARMs. This drives down prices of COF ARMs and increases margins. The EM, however, does not fully account for the lag in the COF or the effect of the life cap. The historical measures of the Monte Carlo margin suggest that Fannie Mae COF ARM spreads have generally widened since October 1987.

### Relative Valuation

Performance of COF ARMs can be compared with Treasury-indexed ARMs using margins derived from Monte Carlo simulations. The margins on the Fannie Mae +125 ARM and the Freddie Mac 7.25% ARM are compared below.

|                      | Fannie Mae + 125 | Freddie Mac 7.25% |
| -------------------- | ---------------- | ----------------- |
| Index                | COF              | 1-yr Tsy          |
| Price                | 101.13           | 98.75             |
| Monte Carlo Margin   | 139 bp           | 102 bp            |

The Monte Carlo margin measure should account for the differences in the cap structure in the two securities, as well as the discrepancy in the behavior of the two

**EXHIBIT 9b**

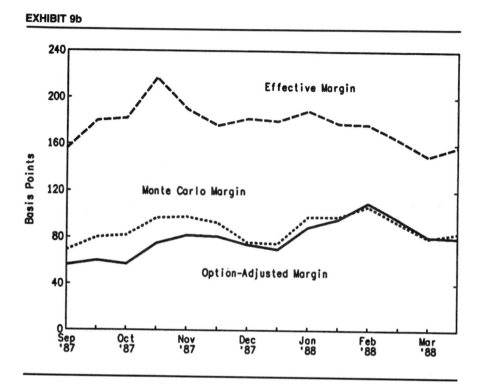

indices. The Fannie Mae ARM offers a significantly higher margin over the one-year Treasury than the Freddie Mac ARM.

## Scenario Analysis

The Fannie Mae and Freddie Mac ARMs are evaluated under three different interest rate environments to gain insight into their price volatility. The Monte Carlo margin or OAM can be used to determine the prices in the different scenarios.

| *Freddie Mac 7.25%* | | | |
|---|---|---|---|
| | *Rising* | *Stable* | *Falling* |
| CPR | 8% | 10% | 12% |
| Monte Carlo Margin | 94 bp | 94 bp | 94 bp |
| Price | 95.38 | 97.63 | 99.42 |
| Risk (dP/dY) | 2.25 | — | 1.79 |

**EXHIBIT 10**

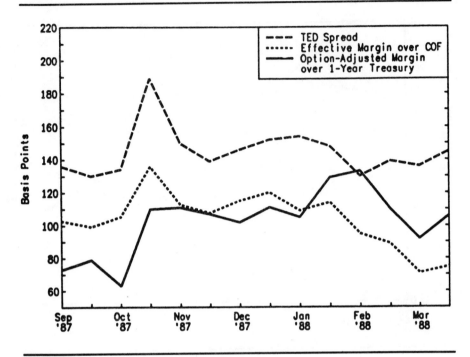

| | Rising | Stable | Falling |
|---|---|---|---|
| | *Fannie Mae +125* | | |
| CPR | 10% | 10% | 12% |
| Monte Carlo Margin | 139 bp | 139 bp | 139 bp |
| Price | 98.25 | 101.13 | 102.66 |
| Risk (dP/dY) | 1.88 | — | 1.53 |

The rising rate scenario assumes an immediate 100 basis point upward shift in the yield curve while a falling rate scenario assumes a 100 basis point drop. The Monte Carlo margins are derived from the current market prices. These margins are then assumed to remain constant in computing the prices in the rising and falling rate environments using the Monte Carlo simulator. The risk measure is the ratio of the price change to the yield change. The price volatility of the two ARMs is approximately equal to that of a two-year Treasury security. Although the coupon resets monthly on the Fannie Mae ARM, the slow adjustment of the index to changes in market rates causes the security to behave like a longer term instrument.

The price volatility of the Fannie Mae ARM is also examined for differing adjustability factors and moving averages in the COF projection model. With increased responsiveness, either due to higher adjustability or shorter moving average, the security behaves like a shorter term instrument.

| | *Risk (dP/dY)* | |
|---|---|---|
| *Adjustability* | *Rising* | *Falling* |
| High | 1.75 | 1.33 |
| Base | 1.87 | 1.53 |
| Low | 2.23 | 1.82 |
| *Moving Average* | | |
| 6 mos. | 1.52 | 1.49 |
| 14 mos. | 1.87 | 1.53 |
| 24 mos. | 2.31 | 1.79 |

## VIII. CONCLUSION

The growth in ARM originations has sparked increased securitization in recent years. In evaluating the performance of ARM securities, one must consider the effects of the caps and floors which limit the coupon adjustments on the security, as well as the behavior of the ARM index relative to market rates. The options and Monte Carlo approaches produce option-adjusted margins that account for both the values of the adjustment limitations and the behavior of the index. Prepayment risk in ARMs may be secondary to the cap and index risk. The use of evaluation methods that analyze fundamental value in ARMs should improve liquidity and efficiency in the secondary markets.

# Interest Only and Principal Only STRIPs

MICHAEL WALDMAN
SALOMON BROTHERS INC

MARK GORDON, CFA
SALOMON BROTHERS INC

K. JEANNE PERSON
SALOMON BROTHERS INC

## I. INTRODUCTION

Interest Only and Principal Only (IO/PO) STRIPs are an important development in the evolution of the mortgage market. These instruments have broadened the range of mortgage-backed securities—PO STRIPs are now the most bullish investments available and IO STRIPs are the most bearish. Furthermore, certain of these STRIPs are among the few mortgage securities with positive convexity.

In general, IO/PO STRIPs are ideal securities for investors who wish to take a position on prepayment rates. They can also be used to hedge movements in interest rates. Finally, IO/PO STRIPs can be mixed with other STRIPs or pass-throughs to produce hybrid securities with superior performance characteristics.

The authors would like to express their appreciation to Mark Schlawin, Angela Liu and Dawn Byrnes for their assistance with this article.

At the same time, a high degree of prepayment rate sensitivity makes IO/PO STRIPs more volatile than other mortgage securities and places a premium on accurate prepayment projections. These attributes make it essential that investors fully understand the risks as well as the benefits of the investments. In this article, we describe the basic characteristics of IO/PO STRIPs and examine a variety of portfolio applications.

## II. STRUCTURE

IO/PO STRIPs are created in much the same manner as other STRIPs: The cash flows from a pool of mortgages or mortgage securities are divided, with specified proportions of the monthly interest and principal allocated to two (or more) STRIP securities. In the case of IO/PO STRIPs, the IO class receives 100% of the interest payments and the PO class receives 100% of the principal payments.

The IO/PO format has proved quite popular. As of year-end 1988, roughly $18 billion of IO/PO STRIPs had been issued by the Federal National Mortgage Association (FNMA), the Federal Home Loan Mortgage Corporation (FHLMC) and investment banks.[1] The majority are backed by FNMA and FHLMC pass-throughs, although Government National Mortgage Association (GNMA) collateral also has been used.

## III. PRICE PERFORMANCE

IO/PO STRIPs have investment features that differ markedly from those of other mortgage securities. These special characteristics are illustrated by their price movement patterns under shifting interest rates. In Exhibit 1, we use the Salomon Brothers Prepayment and Mortgage Option Pricing Models[2] to project the price paths of IO and PO STRIPs backed by FNMA 9s. The most striking aspect of the exhibit is that when interest rates rise, the projected IO STRIP prices increase sharply while the projected PO STRIP prices fall sharply—that is, the IO STRIPs have a large negative duration and the PO STRIPs have a large positive duration.[3] This feature of STRIPs can be explained largely in terms of the response of prepayments to interest rate movements.

---

[1]FNMA's Mortgage STRIPs are known as Stripped Mortgage-Backed Securities (SMBS). In FHLMC's version, they are called Strip Mortgage Participation Certificates (PCs).

[2]See Michael Waldman, Mark Gordon, and Steven Guterman, *The Salomon Brothers Prepayment Model: Impact of the Market Rally on Mortgage Prepayments and Yields,* Salomon Brothers Inc, September 4, 1985 and Michael Waldman and Mark Gordon, *Evaluating the Option Features of Mortgage Securities: The Salomon Brothers Mortgage Pricing Model,* Salomon Brothers Inc, September 1986.

[3]For purposes of this article, duration means the "effective duration"—the percentage price move per 100-basis-point movement in interest rates.

**EXHIBIT 1**
**PROJECTED PRICE PATHS—FNMA 9% IOs AND POs (APRIL 16, 1987)**

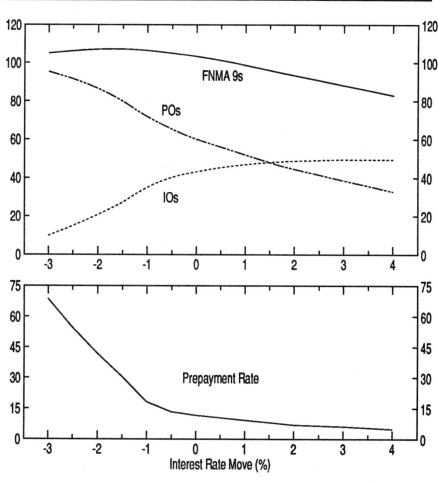

For an IO STRIP, the amount of interest received varies directly with the principal balance outstanding at the end of each month, which in turn depends on the prepayment rate of the underlying mortgages. Faster prepayments reduce the principal balance more quickly, leading to smaller interest payments in future periods. Slower prepayments diminish the outstanding balance more slowly and result in larger interest payments. Because prepayments accelerate when interest rates fall, and vice versa, the size of the payments from an IO will vary in the same direction as interest rates. Thus, the value of this STRIP falls when interest rates fall and rises when interest rates rise—that is, IO STRIPs have negative durations.

The PO STRIP is also sensitive to prepayments, but its price response is opposite that of the IO piece. Because a principal only STRIP is a discount instrument, its value increases when principal is returned (at par) at a faster rate. This occurs when interest rates fall and prepayments accelerate. When interest rates rise and prepayments slow, the value of a PO STRIP decreases. Thus, PO STRIPs have positive durations.

The total of the payments received by investors in a PO STRIP is fixed—only their timing varies with the prepayment rate. For an IO STRIP, both the amount of interest received and its timing depend on the prepayment rate.

One way to interpret the price behavior of IOs and POs is by viewing a pass-through, such as a FNMA 9%, as the sum of an IO and a PO STRIP. Thus, if all three instruments were priced as the same yield, the prices of the IO and PO STRIPs would add up to the price of the FNMA 9%. For this reason, the effective duration of the pass-through is (roughly) the weighted average of the effective durations of the IO and PO STRIPs.

## IV. CONVEXITY

The price patterns in Exhibit 1 illustrate an additional feature of the FNMA 9% IO and PO STRIPs. For a region around the current market price, the PO price path is curved in the investor's favor. That is, for interest rate movements of similar magnitude, the prices rise more rapidly under market rallies than they fall when the market declines. This represents positive convexity. The IO, on the other hand, has negative convexity. Prices fall more rapidly than they rise.

These properties can also be explained in terms of the response of prepayments to interest rate movements. The projected long-term average prepayment rate for FNMA 9s for various market levels is displayed in the bottom panel of Exhibit 1. This prepayment rate is projected to rise substantially under a market rally but to fall only moderately under a market decline. Consequently, the price gain on the PO in a rally will be greater than the price loss in a decline, given comparable movements in interest rates. In a similar fashion, the price loss on the IO in a rally will be greater than the price gain in a decline. This pattern holds in general for lower coupon securities—that is, issues with coupons no more than about 2% above the current rate. For such collateral, the PO STRIPs display positive convexity and the IO STRIPs exhibit negative convexity.

For higher coupon securities undergoing rapid financing—those with coupons approximately 3% or more above the current rate—the relationship is reversed. Within a range of the current market price, the IO STRIP displays positive convexity and the PO STRIP shows negative convexity. These characteristics are illustrated by the projected price paths shown in Exhibit 2 for IO and PO STRIPs backed by GNMA 13s.

In the case of these high-coupon securities, the convexity pattern is explained by

**EXHIBIT 2**
**PROJECTED PRICE PATHS—GNMA 13% IOs and POs (APRIL 16, 1987)**

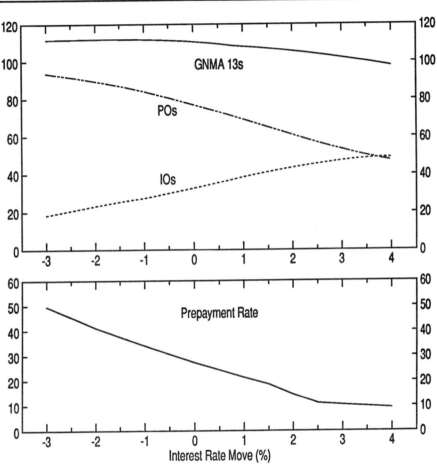

the price levels of the IO and PO STRIPs. The expected rapid prepayment rate of the underlying GNMA 13s reduces the value of the IO STRIP and raises the value of the PO STRIP, so that these issues trade at relatively high and low price levels— representative prices for GNMA 13% IOs and POs are 33 and 77, respectively.[4] At these levels, the IO STRIP price has much more room to expand than to decline further. On the other hand, the value of the PO STRIP has more room to fall than to rise. (At the extreme limits, the PO price could rise at most 23 points, but could fall 77 points.)

---

[4]At the present time, STRIPs backed by GNMA 13s have not been created.

**EXHIBIT 3**
**PROJECTED PRICE PATHS—GNMA 11% IOs and POs (APRIL 16, 1987)**

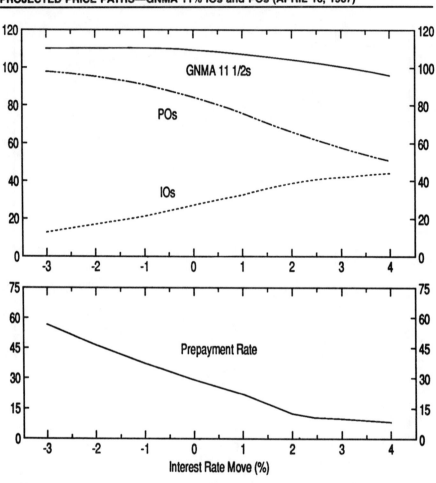

There is a third class of IO and PO STRIPs to consider—those backed by securities with coupons roughly 2%-3% above the current coupon rate. For these "midrange" securities, both the IOs and POs exhibit negative convexity. An example is given in Exhibit 3, which shows the projected price paths for IO and PO STRIPs backed by GNMA 11½s.

It should be understood that the positive and negative convexity regions discussed above depend on several factors, including the type of collateral, the level of market interest rates and the prepayment rates and prices of the various STRIPs. Exhibit 4 summarizes the approximate ranges for the current market.

**EXHIBIT 4**
**APPROXIMATE CONVEXITY RANGES (APRIL 16, 1987)**

| | Convexity | |
|---|---|---|
| Coupon minus<br>Current Coupon | PO | IO |
| Less than 2% | + | − |
| 2% - 3% | − | − |
| More than 3% | − | + |

## V. INVESTMENT CHARACTERISTICS

The Salomon Brothers Prepayment and Mortgage Option Pricing Models, used to determine option-adjusted spreads and effective durations of mortgage pass-through securities, can also be helpful in analyzing the investment characteristics of IO and PO STRIPs.

Exhibit 5 illustrates the basic properties of three of the STRIPs we have just considered: the FNMA 9% POs, GNMA 11½% IOs and GNMA 13% IOs. The effective duration of the FNMA 9% PO STRIP is 14.4 years, which is longer than the duration of the 30-year Treasury. On the other hand, the IO STRIPs have large negative effective durations of − 17.8 years and − 16.0 years. All three STRIPs are very sensitive to changes in interest rates and prepayment rates.

The FNMA 9% POs and GNMA 13% IOs have positive convexity values of 32 and 22 basis points, respectively. In contrast, the GNMA 11½% IOs have a large negative convexity value of 214 basis points. The option-adjusted spreads are 109 basis points for the FNMA 9% POs and a massive 399 basis points for the GNMA 11½% IOs and 334 basis points for the GNMA 13% IOs.

The yields and option-adjusted spreads in Exhibit 5 are based on projected prepayment rates. If the actual prepayment rates differ from these projections, the IO/PO STRIPs will react quite strongly. We give an indication of this prepayment sensitivity in the last row of the exhibit. For a 10% change in the projected prepayment rate, the yield on the FNMA 9% POs would change by 82 basis points. For the GNMA 11% IOs, the yield would change by a substantial 263 basis points and for the GNMA 13% IOs by an even larger 371 basis points.

## VI. APPLICATIONS

Because of their unusual return characteristics, IO and PO STRIPs can be used to meet a wide variety of investment objectives. Some of these applications are outlined below.

**EXHIBIT 5**
**INVESTMENT CHARACTERISTICS—FNMA 9% POs, GNMA 11½% IOs AND GNMA 13% IOs (APRIL 16, 1987)**

|  | FNMA 9% PO | GNMA 11½% IO | GNMA 13% IO |
|---|---|---|---|
| Price[a] | 53-24 | 35-16 | 33-0 |
| Remaining Term (Yrs.) | 29.1 | 26.2 | 26.0 |
| *Projected[b]* | | | |
| Prepayment Rate | | | |
| ● One Year | 4.2% | 27.5% | 34.7% |
| ● Long Term | 9.9 | 20.7 | 27.4 |
| Yield | 10.18% | 8.89% | 7.59% |
| *Option-Adjusted Results[c,d]* | | | |
| Convexity Value | +32 bp | −214 bp | +22 bp |
| Option-Adjusted Spread | 109 | 399 | 334 |
| Effective Duration (Yrs.) | 14.4 | −17.8 | −16.0 |
| Prepayment Sensitivity[e] | 82 bp | 263 bp | 371 bp |

Treasury Yield Curve:

| Maturity (Years) | 1 | 2 | 3 | 5 | 7 | 10 | 30 |
|---|---|---|---|---|---|---|---|
| Yield | 6.39% | 6.86% | 7.19% | 7.51% | 7.80% | 7.99% | 8.21% |

Current-Coupon Mortgage Rates: GNMA 9.53%, FHLMC 9.56%.

[a] In 32nds.
[b] Projected prepayment rate and yield assuming interest rates remain at current levels.
[c] The option pricing model evaluates the STRIPs for a probability distribution of potential future interest rate levels. Given today's positively sloped Treasury yield curve, the base case for this distribution comprises a set of rising future interest rates. Consequently, the prepayment rates for this base case scenario are slower than the projections assuming an unchanged market. This yield curve effect increases the option-adjusted spreads of IOs and decreases the option-adjusted spreads of POs. For a detailed discussion of the option pricing model, see *Evaluating the Option Features of Mortgage Securities: The Salomon Brothers Mortgage Pricing Model.*
[d] Assuming 16.0% one-year Treasury rate volatility and 12.8% mortgage rate volatility.
[e] Yield change for a 10% prepayment rate change.

## POs as Alternatives to Treasury STRIPs

A PO STRIP can be used as an outright investment as a long-duration security. For example, the long effective duration and positive convexity of FNMA 9% POs make them logical alternatives to long Treasury STRIPs. Exhibit 6 compares the projected one-year returns of the FNMA 9% POs and 15½-year Treasury STRIPS for various interest rate moves. For each scenario, we use the Salomon Brothers Prepayment Model to project the cash flows of the POs and the Salomon Brothers Mortgage Pricing Model to estimate their price at the end of the one-year period.[5] This analysis

---

[5]The PO STRIPs horizon price is calculated assuming the same option-adjusted spread as at the beginning of the period.

**EXHIBIT 6**
**FNMA 9% POs VERSUS 15½-YEAR TREASURY STRIPS**
**(ONE-YEAR TOTAL RETURN, APRIL 16, 1987)**

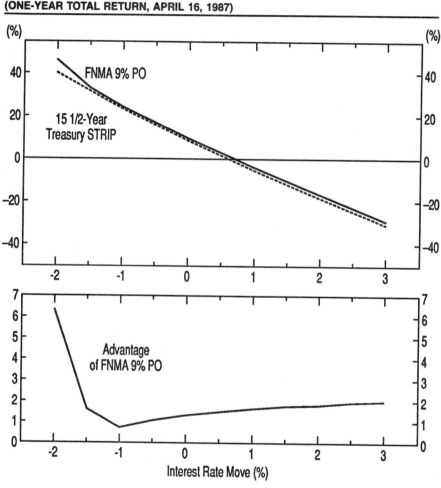

indicates that the PO STRIPs outperform the Treasury STRIPS for a wide range of market moves. Furthermore, because of the positive convexity of the PO STRIPs, this advantage largely expands as rates shift away from current levels.

It should be emphasized that the returns from IO/PO STRIPs, in general, depend significantly on the assumed prepayment rates. To examine the sensitivity of the results, total returns for the PO STRIPs have also been calculated for prepayment rates that are 10% faster and 10% slower than our projections. Exhibit 7 indicates that within this range of prepayment variability, the PO STRIPs continue to outperform the Treasury STRIPS.

**EXHIBIT 7**
**ADVANTAGE OF FNMA 9% PO STRIPS—PREPAYMENT SENSITIVITY**
**(ONE-YEAR TOTAL RETURN)**

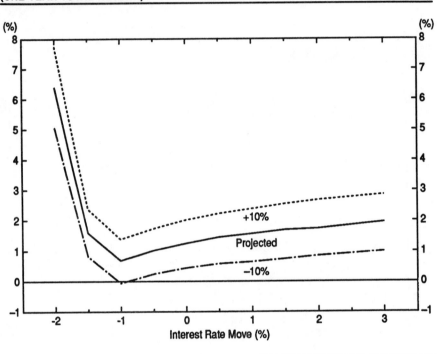

## Hedging Interest Rate Risk

Although IO and PO STRIPs can serve as investments in their own right, the best way to make use of these instruments is to combine them with other securities to alter their return characteristics.

For example, GNMA 11½% IOs have a large negative duration. Their defensive response to interest rate movements can be used to stabilize the pattern of an existing security's return.

Exhibit 8 shows how this strategy might be applied in an example which mixes GNMA 11½% IOs with GNMA 8s. The exhibit illustrates the moderately bullish performance pattern of the GNMA 8s, with greater returns under falling rates than under rising rates. By combining a 73% market value weighting of the GNMA 8s with a 27% market value weighting of the IOs, we create a synthetic security with a relatively flat return pattern.

**EXHIBIT 8**
**GNMA 8s, GNMA 11½% IOs AND SYNTHETIC**
**(ONE-YEAR TOTAL RETURN, APRIL 16, 1987)**

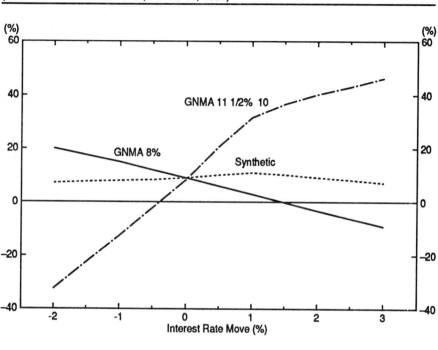

Note: Synthetic Market Value Weights—GNMA 8s (73%) and GNMA 11½% IOs (27%).

Exhibit 9 compares the total return of this synthetic with short-term financing at a fixed rate of 7%. As shown here, the synthetic has a projected return advantage across a 500-basis-point range of rate shifts.

Exhibit 10 examines the prepayment sensitivity of these results by assuming prepayment rates alternately 10% higher and 10% lower than our base case projections (for both the GNMA 11½% IOs and the GNMA 8s). As the exhibit indicates, a significant advantage remains for a substantial band of rate movements.

## Combining IO and PO STRIPs

Another type of synthetic is created by combining two STRIPs. Exhibit 11 illustrates a synthetic comprising two STRIPs with wide option-adjusted spreads—GNMA 11½% IOs and FNMA 9% POs. Once again, the proportions of IOs and POs (45% and 55%, respectively) have been chosen to balance the returns against short-term

**EXHIBIT 9**
**GNMA 8%—GNMA 11½% IO SYNTHETIC VERSUS SHORT-TERM FINANCING**
**(ONE-YEAR TOTAL RETURN, APRIL 16, 1987)**

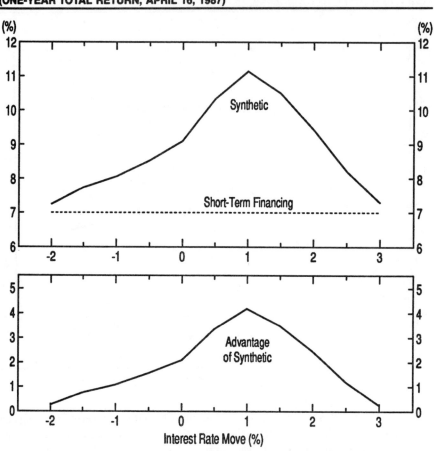

Interest Rate Move (%)

Note: Synthetic Market Value Weights—GNMA 8s (73%) and GNMA 11½% IOs (27%).

financing. By varying these weights, various other effective duration targets could be met.

As indicated in Exhibit 11, this synthetic produces a performance advantage across a wide range of scenarios. This advantage is greatest for a significant market rally or a moderate market decline. A variation of this strategy involves selling caps and floors and/or options to augment the returns for those scenarios with smaller advantages.

Prepayment sensitivity analysis is particularly important for this synthetic strategy because it is exposed to two independent prepayment risks. Less favorable returns will result from slower prepayment rates on the PO's FNMA 9% collateral and/or

**EXHIBIT 10**
**ADVANTAGE OF SYNTHETIC—PREPAYMENT SENSITIVITY**
**(ONE-YEAR TOTAL RETURN)**

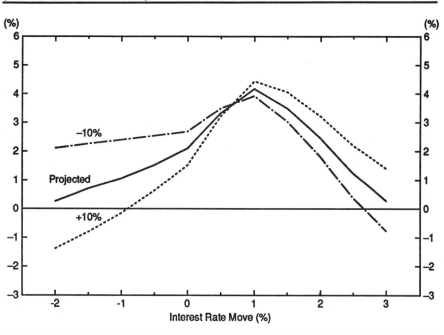

Note: Synthetic Market Value Weights—GNMA 8s (73%) and GNMA 11½% IOs (27%).

faster prepayment rates on the IO's GNMA 11½% collateral. To examine this risk, in Exhibit 12 we assume prepayment rates 10% slower than our base case projection for the FNMA 9s and 10% faster than our projections for GNMA 11½s. For the most part, the synthetic still provides a significant advantage.

This IO-PO mix forms the basis for an attractive risk-controlled arbitrage strategy. The long-term earnings improvement projected for this arbitrage exceeds that for arbitrages using standard mortgage securities. Furthermore, because the interest rate sensitivities of the IO and PO pieces, when appropriately weighted, offset one another, the position's exposure to interest rate movements is hedged. As with any risk-controlled arbitrage, it is important to rebalance the position over time and for each significant movement in interest rates.

### Hedging Prepayment Risk

IO and PO STRIPs can also be used to hedge other mortgage securities against prepayment risk. For example, one way to protect high-coupon mortgage portfolios against rising prepayments is to purchase high-coupon PO STRIPs such as GNMA

**EXHIBIT 11**
**GNMA 11½% IO—FNMA 9% PO SYNTHETIC VERSUS SHORT-TERM FINANCING**
**(ONE-YEAR TOTAL RETURN, APRIL 16, 1987)**

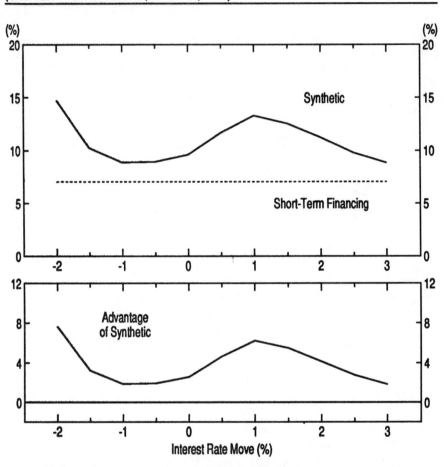

Note: Synthetic Market Value Weights—GNMA 11½% IOs (45%) and FNMA 9% POs (55%).

11½% POs. If prepayments accelerate, the gain on the POs will tend to offset the loss on the pass-throughs.

Exhibit 13 illustrates such a strategy, which combines a 19% market value weighting of GNMA 11½% POs with an 81% market value weighting of GNMA 11½s to create a synthetic 8.66% GNMA coupon, priced at 99 ²¹⁄₃₂.

**EXHIBIT 12**
**ADVANTAGE OF SYNTHETIC AT PESSIMISTIC PREPAYMENT RATES**
**(ONE_YEAR TOTAL RETURN)**

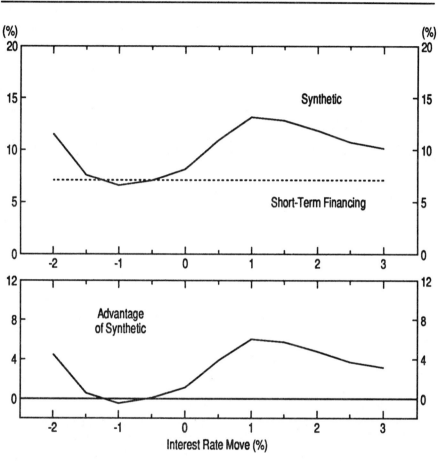

Assumed Prepayment Rates: FNMA 9% POs—Projected  −10%,
GNMA 11½% IOs—Projected  +10%.

As the exhibit indicates, for a prepayment rate range of 0%-50%, the yield on the 11½s varies from 10.74% to 5.94%, while the yield of the synthetic is essentially fixed. It should be understood that, although the synthetic's yield is immune to prepayment changes, its average life and duration are affected by prepayment rate shifts.

**EXHIBIT 13**
**HEDGING PREPAYMENT RISK WITH POs**

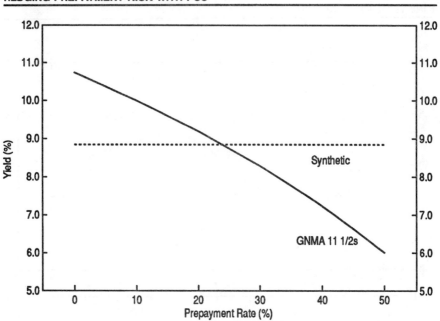

Note: Synthetic Market Value Weights—GNMA 11½s (81%) and GNMA 11½% POs (19%).

## VII. CONCLUSION

The creation of IO STRIPs, with their large negative durations, and PO STRIPs, with their large positive durations, has dramatically increased the range of mortgage securities. IOs and POs, alone or in combination with other securities, have given market participants many new mortgage products from which to choose. The new IOs and POs enable investors to construct positions in accordance with their prepayment viewpoints, and some of these STRIPs provide mortgage instruments with positively convex return characteristics.

The very sensitivity to prepayments that makes IOs and POs useful as hedging devices also constitutes a risk. Evaluation of these securities depends critically on the prepayment projections used. Even with that caveat, based on recent price levels, GNMA 11½% IOs appear to be undervalued. Combinations made from these STRIPs are projected to outperform alternative investments substantially for market moves in either direction over a significant range of prepayment assumptions.

# Collateralized Mortgage Obligations: The Impact of Structure on Value

Scot D. Perlman
Vice President
Mortgage Securities Research
Goldman, Sachs & Co.

## I. INTRODUCTION

Since CMOs were first introduced in June 1983, the market has evolved considerably. The first CMOs, which segmented cash flows across time, were revolutionary in concept but relatively straightforward in design. Over the past two years, the structures of CMOs have become far more complex. To accommodate PAC and floating rate classes, issuers have employed various combinations of stripping and tranching.

In these newer structures, a class cannot be analyzed sufficiently by knowing only the coupon, expected average life, and underlying collateral. Additional information, including an understanding of the relationships between all bonds in the issue, is often necessary to evaluate the performance characteristics of a particular class.

To this end, this article will examine the ways in which the performance of a tranche is affected by the structure of the entire CMO. First, we will describe the

The author would like to thank Hal Hinkle, Debbie Kemp, Richard Loggins, Scott Pinkus, and Arbella Salik for their assistance and Larry Weiman for the development of the principal allocation structure diagram.

characteristics of the more traditional (or classic) CMO structures, i.e., those that contain only the more basic CMO bond classes. Next, we will examine two recent CMOs that contain a variety of bonds. Here, we will show how the various bonds are created fom the underlying collateral and determine how the interaction of the tranches impacts value.

## II. PRINCIPAL ALLOCATION STRUCTURES

### The "Classic" CMO

CMOs were developed in response to investor demands for mortgage-backed securities that were targeted to different segments of the yield curve.[1] A summary of terms for the first CMO, FHLMC Series 1983-A, appears in Exhibit 1. The tranches receive principal payments sequentially; that is, no principal payment is made to class A-2 until class A-1 has been retired. Although the bonds are supported by mortgages having approximately 30 years remaining, principal is allocated in such a way as to create bonds with shorter maturities. Class A-1, with a 3.2-year average life, was targeted to investors seeking relatively short-term assets. On the other hand, class A-3 was created for investors seeking longer-term assets.

**EXHIBIT 1**
**SUMMARY OF TERMS—FHLMC SERIES 1983-A**

| Tranche | Original Balance ($MM) | Coupon | Stated Maturity | Expected Average Life |
|---------|----------|--------|-----------------|----------------------|
| A-1 | 215 | 10.625% | 06/15/88 | 3.2 yr. |
| A-2 | 350 | 11.250% | 12/15/95 | 8.6 yr. |
| A-3 | 435 | 11.875% | 06/15/13 | 20.4 yr. |

Collateral: FHLMC whole loans

While a summary of terms, such as the one shown in Exhibit 1, provides important information about the CMO, it does not clearly identify the interaction between the various classes. A visual aid, the *principal allocation structure diagram*, will be introduced to highlight the relationships between the tranches. The principal allocation structure for FHLMC Series 1983-A, depicted in Exhibit 2, illustrates how principal payments are allocated among the classes over time.

In the structure diagrams, time is plotted along the horizontal axis and the percent of principal allocated to each tranche is plotted along the vertical axis. A caveat

---

[1]For a complete analysis of the payment characteristics of CMOs, see Richard Roll, "Collateralized Mortgage Obligations: Characteristics, History, Analysis," in Frank J. Fabozzi (ed.), *Mortgage-Backed Securities* (Chicago, IL: Probus Publishing, 1987).

**EXHIBIT 2**
**PRINCIPAL ALLOCATION STRUCTURE—FHLMC SERIES 1983-A**

Principal
Allocation

| A-1 | A-2 | A-3 |

Time

about the diagrams: both the size of the tranches and the relationship between them are *not drawn to scale*. Unless the diagrams were large, it would be difficult to preserve scale for small classes or for those that were outstanding only a short time. Furthermore, the scale of the diagram would be different for every interest rate and prepayment scenario. The purpose of the principal allocation structure diagram is merely to provide the investor with a visual representation of the relationships between the classes.

The "classic" CMO, three or four sequential-pay tranches (possibly with an accrual bond), results in a simple principal allocation structure diagram. As in Exhibit 2, the structure diagram for a classic CMO shows that the current class receives 100% of the principal payments from the underlying collateral until the class is retired. The diagram helps to identify which bonds are subject to extension risk (i.e., an increase in average life resulting from a slowing of prepayments), or conversely, call risk (i.e., a reduction in average life due to an acceleration of prepayments). Even if prepayments were too slow, class A-1 is somewhat protected from an extension in its life since classes A-2 and A-3 succeed it. On the other hand, class A-3 has call resistance; if prepayments were to speed up, it would still not receive any principal payments until the earlier classes had been retired.

To avoid drawing incorrect conclusions, one should not view the diagrams in isolation. For example, even though the principal balance for class A-3 is twice as large as class A-1, the tranches have the same width in Exhibit 2. Although the principal balances differ, the time they are receiving principal payments *may be* similar. Since the CMO is backed by level pay mortgages, the amount of principal available during the initial years (when class A-1 receives payments) will be less than the amount of principal available in later years (for class A-3) when principal is the main component of the homeowners' mortgage payments. The combination of a summary of terms (e.g., Exhibit 1) and the principal allocation structure diagram should provide investors with a more complete understanding of the structural aspects of the issue.

The characteristics of the underlying collateral are also crucial to determining the expected performance of the tranches in a CMO. For every CMO, it is essential that the investor be familiar with the type of collateral supporting the issue. While the prepayment history of the collateral may be helpful, it is more important to develop a sense of how the collateral might prepay in the future in different interest rate environments. Each CMO issue should be analyzed under different scenarios in order to evaluate its performance characteristics.

An accrual bond is represented in the principal allocation structure diagrams in the same way as a current interest-paying bond. Since the accrual refers only to the interest component of the bond, once payments begin, principal is allocated in the same way as for an interest-paying bond. Compared to an interest-paying bond, however, an accrual bond more effectively limits the extension risk of the prior classes because its interest cash flow is allocated to earlier tranches as principal payments.

Until mid-1986, most CMOs were structured like the classic CMO. For these issues, the structure diagrams are not necessary to understand the structure of the issue. However, with the introduction of PAC bonds, floaters, and strips, the complexity of CMOs, increased dramatically. For these more complex issues, the principal allocation structure diagrams impart a further understanding of the relationship between tranches and the impact of prepayments.

### PAC Bonds

Planned amortization class (PAC) bonds offer investors a mortgage-backed security with substantially reduced prepayment risk.[2] When prepayments on the underlying collateral occur within a designated range (referred to as the PAC band), the PAC will receive the principal payments specified in the sinking fund schedule in the prospectus. The PAC band is often wide (e.g., 75% PSA to 300% PSA), providing investors with a stable cash flow over a wide range of interest rate scenarios. In order to preserve the PAC schedule, the non-PAC classes must absorb the prepayment risk. Therefore, investors in the non-PAC classes should know when a PAC bond may affect the cash flow allocated to their class. The principal allocation structure diagram identifies the classes that may be affected by the PAC.

A summary of terms for the first CMO containing a PAC class, M.D.C. Mortgage Funding Corp. Series O, appears in Exhibit 3. Unlike the classic CMO, it is not apparent from the summary of terms how the PAC impacts the other classes. What is the relationship of the PAC to the other classes? Is it significant that the PAC has the same stated maturity as class O-4?

The principal allocation structure for M.D.C. Series O can be seen clearly in

---

[2]For a detailed discussion of PAC and floating rate tranches of CMO, see Richard Roll, "Recent Innovations in Collateralized Mortgage Obligations," Mortgage Securities Research, Goldman Sachs & Co., January 1987.

**EXHIBIT 3**
**SUMMARY OF TERMS—M.D.C MORTGAGE FUNDING CORP. SERIES O**

| Tranche | Original Balance ($MM) | Coupon | Stated Maturity | Expected Average Life |
|---|---|---|---|---|
| O-1 | 87.325 | 7.75% | 05/20/10 | 3.3 yr. |
| O-2 (PAC Bond) | 46.975 | 8.45% | 11/20/17 | 7.8 yr. |
| O-3 | 57.700 | 9.00% | 05/20/13 | 10.9 yr. |
| O-4 | 8.000 | 9.00% | 11/20/17 | 20.8 yr. |
| (Accural Bond) | | | | |

Collateral: FHLMC 9s

**EXHIBIT 4**
**PRINCIPAL ALLOCATION STRUCTURE—M.D.C. MORTGAGE FUNDING CORP. SERIES O**

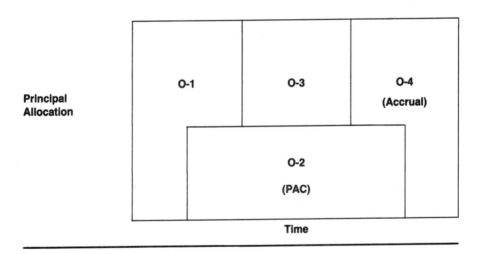

Exhibit 4. Payments to the PAC, class O-2, span those of the other classes. Inititally, class O-1 receives 100% of the principal payments from the underlying collateral. When payments to the PAC begin, it will receive a portion of the principal payments, with the remainder going to class O-1. Payments from the collateral will continue to be divided between the PAC and non-PAC classes throughout the life of class O-3 and the inititalal years that class O-4 receives principal payments. Once the PAC is retired, class O-4 will receive 100% of the principal payments. Thus, the fact that classes O-2 and O-4 have the same stated maturity date is misleading.

As in the classic CMO, the structure is not drawn to scale. Since each of the non-PAC classes may have its principal payment schedule modified to meet the PAC schedule, the PAC is shown to pay concurrently with all other classes.

The amount of extension (or call) risk each non-PAC class faces is a function not only of the prepayment sensitivity of the underlying collateral but also of the size of the tranche compared to the PAC schedule. Under the pricing assumption for M.D.C. Series O, the prospectus indicates that roughly 30% of class O-1 will be retired before the first PAC payment is scheduled to be made. For this PAC, the initial principal payments, $1,050,000 per quarter, are higher than the principal payments scheduled in the tenth year (approximately $500,000). If prepayments are slow, class O-1 faces extension risk because its principal balance will still be large at the time that payments on the PAC are scheduled to begin. Furthermore, the PAC obligation itself is also large. Compared to other non-PAC CMO classes that have lower outstanding balances when the PAC payments begin and a smaller PAC obligation in the early years, class O-1 would be judged a riskier bond. The non-PAC classes are also subject to a greater amount of call risk than classes in a CMO that does not contain a PAC. The indenture requires the PAC sinking fund schedule to be maintained as well as possible. Therefore, after meeting the PAC obligation for the current period, all remaining money will be used to make principal payments on the non-PAC classes. Under high prepayment scenarios, this will result in a quick retirement of the non-PAC classes.

The stated maturity of a PAC often matches that of the underlying collateral. If prepayments are rapid and the non-PAC tranches are retired, principal payments will be made to the PAC until the underlying collateral amortizes completely. However, unless prepayments fall outside of the PAC band (or are extremely erratic within the band), the PAC will pay according to schedule and the final maturity date can be determined from the sinking fund schedule.

### Floating Rate Tranches

The structure of the early CMOs containing floating rate tranches resembles the classic CMO. When the floater is the current-pay class, it receives 100% of the principal allocation. Extension risk for a "tranched" floater can be evaluated in the same way as if the bonds had a fixed coupon. In many of these early issues, excess cash flow is retained in a reserve account to allow the interest rate cap to rise over time (these are known as stepped caps). Therefore, if interest rates increase, prepayments slow and the bonds extend, the cap on the floater will rise over time. The increased cap serves to minimize the negative impact associated with the bonds extending; since the bonds are most likely to extend when interest rates rise, the higher cap reduces the chance that the coupon will be restricted below the market level.

Only a dozen or so tranched floaters with stepped caps were offered before issuers developed a more efficient structure: the "stripped" floater. In this structure, principal and interest payments are divided between tranches with discount coupons and tranches with a floating interest rate. Floaters created by stripping offer two benefits compared to floaters created by tranching. First, the coupon has a single cap, effective immediately, that is higher than the initial caps available with a tranched floater. Proceeds from issuance are likely to be higher than for a floater with stepped caps since the risk of having the coupon reach the cap in the early years is reduced. A second benefit with the stripped floater is that the reserve fund can be eliminated. This will enhance the issuer's return, since excess cash flow will be available sooner.

A summary of terms for Ryland Series 33, an issue containing a stripped floater backed by FHLMC 9.5s, appears in Exhibit 5. On each payment date, 6% interest is due on the fixed rate tranches that constitute approximately 50% of the outstanding principal balance of the bonds. The surplus of 350 basis points from the fixed rate tranches combined with the 9.5% interest from the remaining 50% of the FHLMC collateral permits interest up to 13% to be paid on the floater. The technique of stripping the 9.5% coupon into 6% and 13% components is identical to the methodology used to create stripped mortgage-backed securities.[3]

The principal allocation structure of Ryland Series 33 is depicted in Exhibit 6. The diagram indicates that the floater portion of the strip (top), class 33-A, is outstanding until the underlying collateral has been retired. The bottom portion of the strip is tranched; class 33-C will not receive any principal payments until class 33-B has been retired.

When stripping has been employed to structure a CMO, the tranches in each portion of the strip should be viewed independently. During each payment period, a fixed percentage of principal is allocated to each portion of the strip; the amount of money available to pay bonds is solely a function of prepayments on the underlying

**EXHIBIT 5**
**SUMMARY OF TERMS—RYLAND SERIES 33**

| Tranche | Original Balance ($MM) | Coupon | Stated Maturity | Expected Average Life |
|---|---|---|---|---|
| 33-A (Floating Rate Bond) | 197.2 | LIBOR + 70 | 06/20/18 | 8.5 yr. |
| 33-B | 95.2 | 6.0% | 06/20/12 | 3.2 yr. |
| 33-C | 37.6 | 6.0% | 03/20/15 | 7.8 yr. |
| 33-D | 19.4 | 6.0% | 03/20/16 | 10.8 yr. |
| 33-E | 50.6 | 6.0% | 06/20/18 | 18.0 yr. |

Collateral: FHLMC 9.5s

---

[3]For an in-depth discussion of the creation of strips, see Michael R. Asay and Timothy D. Sears, "Stripped Mortgage-Backed Securities, Part I: Basic Concepts and Pricing Theory," Mortgage Securities Research, Goldman Sachs & Co., January 1988.

collateral. As a result, investors considering the floating rate tranche can disregard the other classes. When valuing the floater, they should focus on the effect of prepayments, margin over the index, and the cap. Investors examining the discount tranches should use the same methodology as when examining a classic CMO.

Inverse floating rate tranches can also be created by stripping, and are issued in conjunction with a floating rate tranche. Interest for the inverse floater represents the difference between the interest rate cap on the floater and the floater coupon. The floater is designed for the bearish investor or those seeking an asset which pays at a spread above LIBOR. The inverse floater, on the other hand, will produce higher coupon income in a falling interest rate environment, providing a hedge against lower interest rates.

**EXHIBIT 6**
**PRINCIPAL ALLOCATION STRUCTURE—RYLAND SERIES 33**

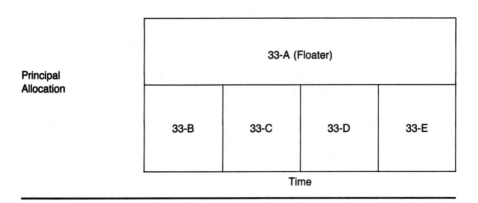

Principal Allocation

33-A (Floater)

| 33-B | 33-C | 33-D | 33-E |

Time

**EXHIBIT 7**
**SUMMARY OF TERMS—CMO TRUST 14**

| Tranche | Original Balance ($MM) | Coupon | Stated Maturity | Expected Average Life |
|---|---|---|---|---|
| A-1 (Floating Rate Bond) | 779 | LIBOR + 45 | 04/01/09 | 5.9 yr. |
| A-2 (Inverse Floating Rate Bond) | 280 | FORMULA | 04/01/09 | 5.9 yr. |
| A-3 | 130 | 5.0% | 04/01/09 | 5.9 yr. |
| Z (Accrual Bond) | 111 | 8.0% | 01/01/17 | 18.1 yr. |

Collateral: FNMA 9s

**EXHIBIT 8**
**PRINCIPAL ALLOCATION STRUCTURE—CMO TRUST 14**

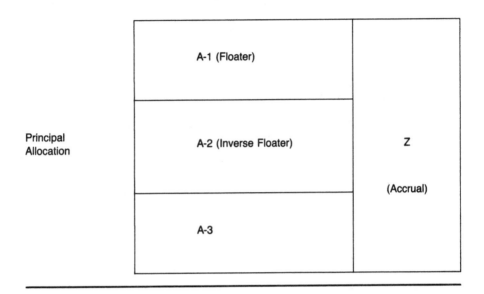

Principal
Allocation

The summary of terms and the principal allocation structure diagram for CMO Trust 14, an issue with an inverse floater, are presented in Exhibits 7 and 8, respectively. Here, the first three tranches, a floater, inverse floater, and discount bond are stripped over time. As a result, there is no interaction between the first three tranches and each may be viewed in isolation. The accrual bond, class Z, helps to reduce extension risk on the prior classes.

### Residuals

The final type of bond to be discussed here, the residual, has been created by a diverse set of structures.[4] For the most part, the residual is a minor component of the CMO, with less than 1% of principal allocated to it every period. Investors not purchasing residuals can generally ignore their effects without introducing much error to the analysis. Residual buyers, on the other hand, should be very interested in the way payments will be made. The timing of the residual cash flows is critical to the value of these leveraged instruments.

A principal allocation structure diagram can be created for CMOs that include residual tranches. Although the scaling of the diagrams tends to magnify the residual, the diagrams can be utilized to show how the residual and non-residual tranches

---

[4]For a complete analysis of residuals, see Howard Altarescu et al. "Mortgage Residuals," Mortgage Securities Research, Goldman Sachs & Co., May 1987.

impact one another. In most CMOs, principal is allocated to residuals in one of two ways. In the first example, the residual class (A-2) in GS Trust 7 Series A is stripped from the other tranches (see Exhibit 9). Each month, approximately 3.5% of the total principal payments is allocated to class A-2. The second common residual structure, used in PaineWebber CMO Trust I (shown in Exhibit 10), resembles the classic CMO. The residual, class I-4, receives principal payments only after all other

**EXHIBIT 9**
**PRINCIPAL ALLOCATION STRUCTURE—GS TRUST 7 SERIES A**

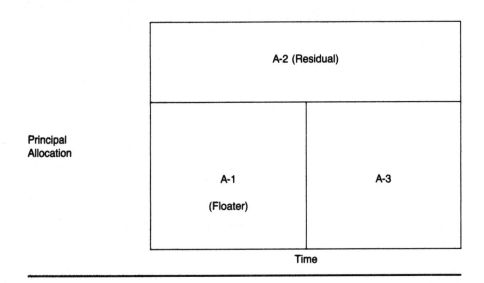

**EXHIBIT 10**
**PRINCIPAL ALLOCATION STRUCTURE—PAINEWEBBER CMO TRUST SERIES I**

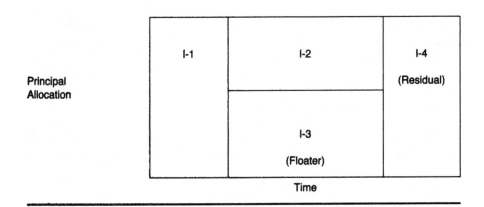

classes have been retired. For this issue, as in many, the residual class also receives any excess cash flow remaining after the bond obligations have been paid each period. Since excess cash flow does not constitute a principal payment, it is not represented in the principal allocation structure diagrams.

## III. COMPOUND STRUCTURES

While investor demand led to the development of PAC and floating rate bonds, the quest by issuers for the most efficient use of collateral (i.e., the structure that produces the greatest proceeds) often fuels the market today. Recent offerings have contained something for everyone: PACs, floaters, and principal-only tranches, in addition to current interest-paying and accrual bonds. To accommodate bonds with such diverse payment characteristics, the structures have become more complex, with multiple layers of stripping and tranching.

Now more than ever, investors must comprehend the relationships among all tranches in a CMO to determine their potential impact on the tranche they want to purchase. Below, we will examine how two compound structures are created and the interaction among the tranches. We will see that the same techniques used to evaluate tranches in the basic structures also apply when the tranches are part of compound structures. Although the relationshps are not as readily apparent, they become clearer when the structure is analyzed in stages.

### GS Trust 5 Series A

The first example, GS Trust 5 Series A, is collateralized by GNMA 11s and contains a floater, a PAC, two accrual bonds and two current interest-paying bonds. The summary of terms and the principal allocation structure diagram appear in Exhibit 11 and 12, respectively.

One way to highlight the structural features of this issue is to demonstrate how the principal allocation structure in Exhibit 12 was constructed. To begin, the collateral cash flow can be viewed as supporting a one tranche CMO, as shown in Exhibit 13a. Class A-6 is the only tranche with a stated maturity after January 2015 (see Exhibit 11). It is the final tranche and it will not begin receiving principal payments until all other classes have been retired. Exhibit 13b depicts the relationship between class A-6 and the other classes. Note that it can be considered the equivalent of the second tranche of a classic CMO. The crucial factors determining its performance will be the rate of prepayments on the underlying collateral and the amount of call protection provided by the prior classes. Call protection can be measured by comparing the principal balance of class A-6 ($3 million) to the size of the entire issue ($150 million). In addition to being the final class, the accrual feature of class A-6 minimizes the extension risk for all other tranches.

Next, the floater (class A-2) is created by stripping principal and interest payments from the "first class" of Exhibit 13b (see Exhibit 13c). Aside from the reduced

**EXHIBIT 11**
**SUMMARY OF TERMS—GS TRUST 5 SERIES A**

| Tranche | Original Balance ($MM) | Coupon | Stated Maturity | Expected Average Life |
|---------|------------------------|--------|-----------------|-----------------------|
| A-1 | 28.650 | 9.0% | 06/07/08 | 3.3 yr. |
| A-2 (Floating Rate Bond) | 71.250 | LIBOR + 85 | 01/07/15 | 7.1 yr. |
| A-3 (PAC Bond) | 35.625 | 9.0% | 01/07/15 | 5.8 yr. |
| A-4 | 5.625 | 9.0% | 03/07/09 | 10.9 yr. |
| A-5 (Accrual Bond) | 5.850 | 9.0% | 01/07/15 | 14.9 yr. |
| A-6 (Accrual Bond) | 3.000 | 9.0% | 12/07/16 | 22.5 yr. |

Collateral: GNMA 11s

**EXHIBIT 12**
**PRINCIPAL ALLOCATION STRUCTURE—GS TRUST 5 SERIES A**

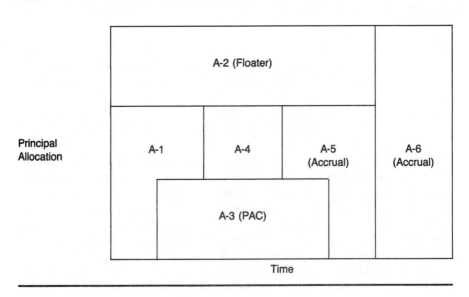

extension risk provided by class A-6, the floater's performance can be measured by its coupon formula and cap, and the prepayments associated with the underlying collateral.

The second portion of the strip contains all of the remaining classes: two current interest-paying bonds, a PAC, and an accrual bond. Their relationship, depicted in Exhibit 13d, is similar to the bonds in M.D.C. Series O, discussed earlier (Exhibit 4). Only classes A-1, A-4, and A-5, which were constructed from the strip that produced the PAC bond (class A-3) can have their payment schedules modified in order to preserve the PAC schedule. While the accrual feature of class A-6 helps to reduce the extension risk for all of the other bonds in this strip, the fact that class A-5 is an accrual bond provides further protection for classes A-1, A-3, and A-4. In addition, the two accrual bonds reduce the extent to which principal payments to class A-1 might be delayed in order to preserve the PAC schedule.

One way to measure the performance characteristic of a CMO tranche is to examine its behavior in different interest rate environments. A prepayment forecast for GNMA 11s under different interest rate scenarios is shown in Exhibit 14. At the

**EXHIBIT 13**
**PRINCIPAL ALLOCATION STRUCTURE—GS TRUST 5 SERIES A**

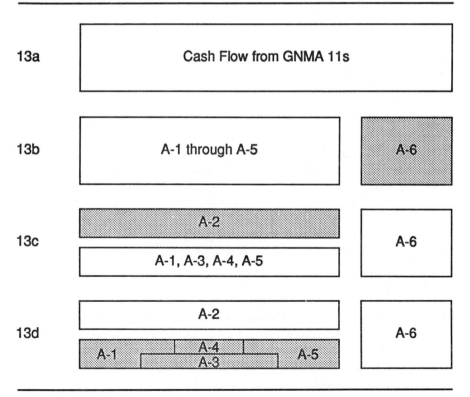

**EXHIBIT 14**
**PREPAYMENT FORECAST FOR GNMA 11s**

| Change in Interest Rates (b.p.) | Prepayment Rate (% PSA) |
|:---:|:---:|
| −300 | 453 |
| −200 | 423 |
| −100 | 332 |
| 0 | 175 |
| 100 | 113 |
| 200 | 91 |
| 300 | 80 |

Assuming the current coupon GNMA is the 10% coupon priced at 99-26 (May 9, 1988).

time of the analysis, 10s were the current coupon, so the slight premium nature of GNMA 11s causes their prepayments to be very sensitive to changes in interest rates. If interest rates were to decline, prepayments would be expected to accelerate rapidly. Although prepayments would likely decline if interest rates were to rise, the change would probably not be as dramatic as when interest rates were assumed to fall.

The average life profiles for each tranche are shown in Exhibit 15. The profiles assume prepayments on the underlying collateral change immediately to the levels shown in Exhibit 14.

As expected, when interest rates decline, the average lives shorten significantly for the non-PAC classes (A-1, A-4, and A-5) that are part of the strip containing the PAC (class A-3). In these scenarios, payments are accelerated to the non-PAC classes in order to preserve the PAC schedule. On the other hand, when interest rates increase, their average lives lengthen, especially for class A-1. The profile for the PAC, class A-3, shows stability in all but the −200 and −300 basis point scenarios. Here, the average life shortens slightly since all non-PAC classes would be quickly retired. The average life profiles for the floater, class A-2, and the final tranche, class A-6, are similar to profiles for the tranches in a classic CMO. For both classes, the paydowns are largely a function of the prepayment rate on the underlying collateral and the size and placement of the tranches.

## FHLMC Series 7

The second example of a compound structure which will be reviewed here is FHLMC Series 7. This is collateralized by FHLMC 9.5s and contains six PACs (one with a floating interest rate), a floating rate class, a zero coupon bond, one accrual bond, and a residual. The summary of terms and the principal allocation structure diagram appear in Exhibits 16 and 17, respectively.

**EXHIBIT 15**
**AVERAGE LIFE SENSITIVITY—GS TRUST 5 SERIES A**

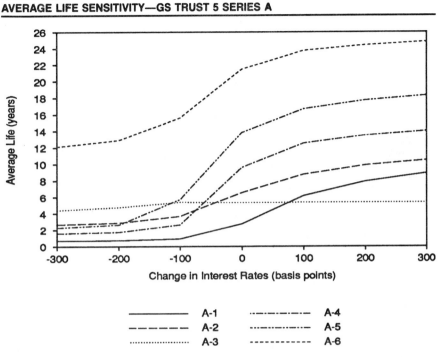

| | A-1 | | A-4 |
|---|---|---|---|
| | A-2 | | A-5 |
| | A-3 | | A-6 |

Once again, in an issue that has so many tranches with different payment characteristics, it will be helpful to show how the principal allocation structure diagram is constructed. Exhibit 18a depicts the structure before any tranches are created. First, the residual, class 7-R, is stripped from all other tranches, as shown in Exhibit 18b. The residual will receive a small portion of principal throughout the life of the issue and its principal allocation will not be materially impacted by the PAC bonds.

In contrast, the principal for the non-PAC classes (7-A, 7-B, and 7-Z) is segregated, not stripped, from the remaining classes (see Exhibit 18c). Unlike a strip, which was used to create the residual, principal payments to these classes can be accelerated or deferred to preserve the various PAC schedules. Note that the principal allocation structure diagram of FHLMC Series 7 shown in Exhibit 17 does not distinguish between the horizontal line used to indicate the strip that created class 7-R and the segregation of cash flow used to create the other non-PAC classes.

The relationship among the non-PAC classes is shown in Exhibit 18d. The second strip in this issue is used to create classes 7-A (the floater) and 7-B (the principal-only bond). After classes 7-A and 7-B have been retired, the accrual bond, class 7-Z, begins to receive principal payments. The tranching will cause the non-PAC classes to bear some resemblance to the tranches in a classic CMO.

**EXHIBIT 16**
**SUMMARY OF TERMS—FHLMC SERIES 7**

| Tranche | Original Balance ($MM) | Coupon | Stated Maturity | Expected Average Life |
|---|---|---|---|---|
| 7-A (Floating Rate Bond) | 160.80 | LIBOR + 80 | 12/15/16 | 8.9 yr. |
| 7-B | 88.50 | 0.00% | 12/15/16 | 8.9 yr. |
| 7-C (PAC Bond) | 10.15 | 7.60% | 11/15/01 | 1.0 yr. |
| 7-D (Floating Rate PAC Bond) | 69.94 | LIBOR + 40 | 7/15/14 | 3.2 yr. |
| 7-E (PAC Bond) | 42.51 | 7.75% | 8/15/13 | 3.3 yr. |
| 7-F (PAC Bond) | 7.50 | 8.00% | 7/15/14 | 5.6 yr. |
| 7-G (PAC Bond) | 87.60 | 8.50% | 9/15/18 | 7.9 yr. |
| 7-H (PAC Bond) | 22.90 | 8.50% | 6/15/19 | 10.9 yr. |
| 7-R (REMIC Residual Interest) | 0.10 | FORMULA | 6/15/19 | 8.6 yr. |
| 7-Z (Accrual Bond) | 10.00 | 9.50% | 6/15/19 | 22.8 yr. |

Collateral: FHLMC 9.5s

The behavior of class 7-A, the floater, will depend on prepayments on the underlying collateral, the floater formula and cap, and the requirements to service the PAC bonds. The extension risk for the floater, however, will be diminished somewhat since it is succeeded by an accrual bond.

The payment characteristics of the other tranches have a major impact on the performance of class 7-B. Unlike most principal-only bonds, whose returns are based solely on the price and prepayments on the underlying collateral, class 7-B has additional leverage caused by the PAC bonds. If prepayments are rapid, class 7-B may be retired quickly to preserve the PAC schedules. On the other hand, if prepayments slow, principal payments to class 7-B may be deferred in order to maintain the PAC schedules.

In contrast to class A-6 in GS Trust 5 Series A, the accrual bond in FHLMC Series 7 (class 7-Z) is not always the final tranche to be retired. However, it limits extension risk on the other classes in the same way as class A-6. In low prepayment rate environments, the deferred interest from the accrual bond will be available to limit

**EXHIBIT 17**
**PRINCIPAL ALLOCATION STRUCTURE—FHLMC SERIES 7**

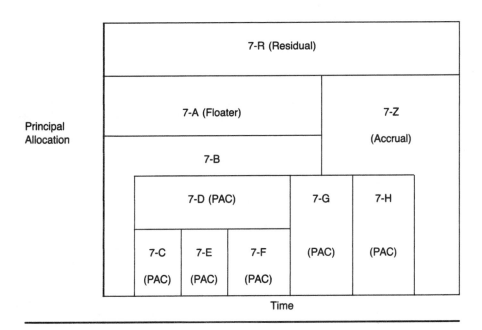

extension risk for classes 7-A and 7-B, unless it is required to preserve the PAC schedules. When prepayments are rapid, class 7-Z may be retired quickly in order to preserve the PAC schedules. In this scenario, the PACs will be the last classes outstanding.

Exhibit 18e highlights how the PAC classes are related. Class 7-D is a floating rate PAC; it is stripped from classes 7-C, 7-E, and 7-F. Since classes 7-D and 7-F mature on the same date, classes 7-C, 7-D, 7-E, and 7-F can be considered as one tranche. When viewed this way, the combined tranche and classes 7-G and 7-H resemble a three tranche classic CMO consisting entirely of PACs. Classes 7-C, 7-D, 7-E, and 7-F have extension protection due to classes 7-G and 7-H, while classes 7-G and 7-H have call protection as a result of the preceding classes.

When structuring a CMO with PAC classes, an issuer must consider two competing demands by investors. If the PAC contains a short payment schedule (e.g., class 7-F has only 9 payments), the average life will be very stable under a wide range of prepayment rates. However, since the PAC receives only a small portion of the total cash flow generated by the underlying collateral, it will have a small principal balance and, therefore, limited liquidity. For FHLMC Series 7, the six PACs total approximately $240 million, yet only two tranches are larger than $50 million. Like issuers, investors considering a PAC must determine which is more valuable: increased cash flow certainty or better liquidity.

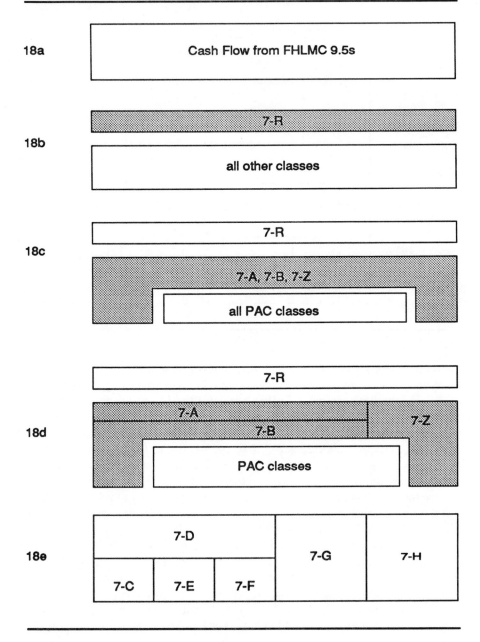

A prepayment forecast for FHLMC 9.5s under different interest rate scenarios is presented in Exhibit 19. Since 10s were the current coupon at the time of the analysis, prepayments on 9.5s would be expected to be relatively sensitive to changes in interest rates. If interest rates were to fall by 300 basis points, prepayments would be expected to climb from the current level of 149% PSA to above 500% PSA, yet they would only be expected to fall to 103% PSA if interest rates were to rise 300 basis points. Once again, changes in interest rates and, consequently, prepayment rates, are assumed to occur instantaneously.

The average life sensitivities for each tranche are shown in Exhibit 20. For the non-PAC classes (7-A, 7-B, and 7-Z), the average lives drop sharply in the −200 and −300 basis point scenarios. These classes all pay down quickly in an attempt to preserve the PAC schedules. On the other hand, their average lives increase to a lesser extent when interest rates rise. In these scenarios, prepayments are still within the PAC band (75% to 300% PSA); the bulk of the extension is due to the reduced prepayments on the underlying collateral.

For the PAC classes, the variability in average life is based on the class's position in the structure. Class 7-C, the first PAC, has a constant average life under all scenarios. The PAC schedule is preserved for the next PAC, class 7-E, except when interest rates fall 300 basis points. For classes 7-F, 7-G, and 7-H, the PAC schedules are not preserved in the scenarios where interest rates decrease 200 and 300 basis points. Declining interest rates have their greatest impact on the longer PACs. The PAC with the greatest average life variability is class 7-H. Its average life shortens to 10.7 years (versus 11.0 if the PAC schedule is preserved) when interest rates decline 300 basis points, while its average life extends to 14.3 years in the −200 basis points scenario.

**EXHIBIT 19**
**PREPAYMENT FORECAST FOR FHLMC 9.5s**

| Changte in Interest Rates (b.p.) | Prepayment Rate (% PSA) |
|:---:|:---:|
| −300 | 527 |
| −200 | 399 |
| −100 | 215 |
| 0 | 149 |
| 100 | 123 |
| 200 | 111 |
| 300 | 103 |

Assuming the current coupon FHLMC is the 10% coupon priced at 99-28 (May 9, 1988).

**EXHIBIT 20**
**AVERAGE LIFE SENSITIVITY—FHLMC SERIES 7**

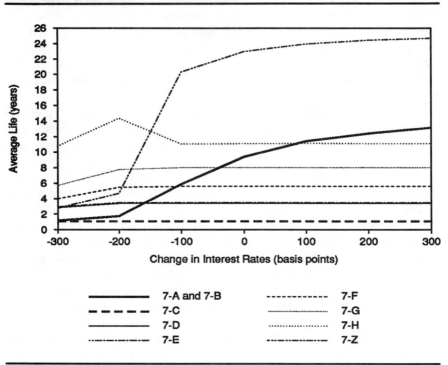

## IV.  CONCLUSION

As CMOs have evolved, their complexity has increased dramatically. A review of
the principal balance, coupon, and expected average life is no longer sufficient to
determine the payment characteristics of the bonds. Unlike the early CMOs, the
various classes of a CMO in today's structures often interact with one another. To
fully comprehend the performance characteristics of a tranche, it is necessary to
understand the structure of the entire issue and the relationship between the tranches,
as well as the prepayment characteristics of the underlying collateral. This article has
examined the fundamental CMO structures and provided two examples where compound structures were shown to merely be combinations of these fundamental
structures. Generally speaking, the methodology used in the two examples can be
extended to other compound structures. In this way, investors can more easily
determine the relationships among the tranches and better predict their behavior in
different interest rate environments.

# Advances and Innovations in the CMO Market

BLAINE ROBERTS, PH.D.
SENIOR MANAGING DIRECTOR
BEAR, STEARNS & CO. INC.

SARAH KEIL WOLF
SENIOR ANALYST
BEAR, STEARNS & CO. INC.

NANCY WILT
SENIOR ANALYST
BEAR, STEARNS & CO. INC.

## I. DYNAMICS OF CURRENT MARKET

Three attractive innovations have emerged in the CMO marketplace in response to the continued flattening of the Treasury yield curve and the relatively high level of LIBOR—the index on which most earlier floating rate CMO classes were based:

- Targeted Amortization Class Bonds (TACs)
- "Super" Principal Only (PO) Bonds
- Cost of Funds Index (COFI) Floaters

In the three months from June to August, 1988, $16.3 billion CMOs were issued. The face value of TAC classes was $4.1 billion and the face value of COFI floaters amounted to $.5 billion. Most of these deals also contained zero coupon bonds as one of the classes; the face value of these "Super POs" was $.5 billion.

This article explains the characteristics of these new securities and demonstrates the sensitivity of the bonds to changes in assumptions and structure. More and more, the complexity and sensitivity of mortgage-related derivative securities requires valuation techniques that capture the sensitivity or the option-like characteristics of these securities to compare relative value. These techniques include option adjusted spreads and net expected return. Astute investors, however, should understand the sources of variation and the risk that are summarized by one statistic.

## II. TAC BONDS

### Definition

TAC bonds evolved from Planned Amortization Class Bonds (PACs). Whereas PAC bonds maintain an amortization schedule within a specified range of prepayment speeds *above and below* the pricing speed, TACs are "targeted" to a narrower range of speeds and have the pricing speed as one of the boundaries. In the simplest case, a TAC bond's amortization schedule may be based on a single prepayment assumption, the pricing speed. PAC and TAC classes are designed to have a constant average life and yield within a specified prepayment range assuming that the prepayment rate remains constant over time. The schedule is only guaranteed to be maintained when prepayment rates remain constant over time. Therefore, if a PAC is guaranteed between a specific range, and prepayments are extremely volatile within the range, the schedule will not necessarily be maintained.

### Cashflow Pattern

As with PACs, incoming cashflow is first directed towards meeting the scheduled principal payment due on the TAC bonds. Excess cashflows resulting from higher prepayment speeds are absorbed by the non-PAC/non-TAC classes. If prepayments increase, the TAC bond will not fall off its TAC schedule until all non-PAC/non-TAC classes are retired.

When a structure contains more than one PAC/TAC class, a priority must be given to each PAC/TAC class within the structure. If a PAC/TAC bond has first priority, after necessary bond interest payments are made, cashflows are allocated to meet its schedule. If there is a cash shortfall (i.e., slow prepayments), then all available cashflows will be used to pay that class down, and the non-priority PAC/TAC classes will extend. On the other hand, if prepayment speeds become so high that all non-PAC/non-TAC classes are retired, any excess cashflow is directed first towards the lower priority PAC/TAC class.

The guaranteed range of the PAC/TAC has a direct correlation to the bonds' extension risk. The wider the guaranteed range, the lesser the amount of bonds in the PAC/TAC class, and therefore, the lower the extension risk for that class.

### Benefits

One of the benefits to the purchaser of a PAC/TAC bond is a certain measure of call protection. As prepayments increase, the PAC/TAC bonds are protected by the non-PAC/non-TAC classes which receive any excess cashflow. The call protection is directly related to the ratio of PAC/TAC bonds to non-PAC/non-TAC classes. The more PAC/TACs versus non-PAC/non-TACs, the less the call protection because there are fewer bonds to absorb the excess cashflows. Another factor that plays a role in the degree of call protection and extension risk is the priority of the class. Higher priority classes are much more stable and therefore should trade at a richer level.

While non-PAC/non-TAC classes have less certain average lives because these classes absorb excess prepayments, certain structures have been created to use prepayments advantageously. "Super" PO classes are the most typical of these structures, and are discussed later in this article.

### TACs versus PACs

To demonstrate the differences in the performance of the underlying bonds and respective residuals with structures containing TACs, a comparison was made among several different cases:

- CMO with a 3-year PAC and a 10-year PAC structured so as to hold between 60 and 300 PSA;
- CMO with a 3-year TAC and a 10-year TAC structured so as to hold between 140 and 220 PSA;
- CMO with a 3-year TAC and a 10-year TAC structured so as to hold at 140 PSA; and,
- Base Case CMO (no PACs, no TACs);

Each structure was modeled with four otherwise similar classes assuming the same pricing speed:

- One 3-year average life class;
- One 10-year average life class;
- One Principal Only (PO) class; and,
- One Floater class based over COFI.

The collateral supporting the bonds in each structure was FNMA 9% coupons with a weighted average coupon of 9.625% and a weighted average maturity of 348 months. (See Exhibits 1-A through 1-D.)

**EXHIBIT 1-A**
**PAC CLASSES STRUCTURED WITH 60% PSA—300% PSA RANGE**

| Class | Amount | Coupon | Price | WAL | Yield | Dur. | Mat. |
|---|---|---|---|---|---|---|---|
| 1-PAC | 49,391,000 | 9.000 | 98.73215 | 3.39 | 9.4190 | 2.8 | 6.6 |
| 2-PAC | 49,110,000 | 9.000 | 93.11841 | 10.93 | 10.1808 | 6.6 | 20.9 |
| 3-PO | 44,406,000 | 0.000 | 58.87441 | 11.59 | 5.4975 | 8.1 | 29.0 |
| 4-FLOAT | 57,093,000 | 8.868 | 100.03523 | 11.59 | 9.0442 | 6.1 | 29.0 |
| TOTAL | 200,000,000 | 6.964 | 88.87606 | 9.40 | | | 29.0 |
| RESIDUAL | | | 16,647,989 | | 17.7500 | | |

**EXHIBIT 1-B**
**TAC CLASSES STRUCTURED AT 140% PSA—220% PSA RANGE**

| Class | Amount | Coupon | Price | WAL | Yield | Dur. | Mat. |
|---|---|---|---|---|---|---|---|
| 1-TAC | 94,386,000 | 9.000 | 98.73215 | 3.39 | 9.4200 | 2.8 | 7.0 |
| 2-TAC | 60,581,000 | 9.000 | 93.11841 | 10.93 | 10.1730 | 6.6 | 17.3 |
| 3-PO | 19,702,000 | 0.000 | 35.10037 | 19.95 | 5.4975 | 18.6 | 29.0 |
| 4-FLOAT | 25,331,000 | 8.868 | 100.00000 | 19.95 | 9.0446 | 9.1 | 29.0 |
| TOTAL | 200,000,000 | 8.097 | 90.92393 | 9.40 | | | 29.0 |
| RESIDUAL | | | 10,065,238 | | 17.7500 | | |

**EXHIBIT 1-C**
**TAC CLASSES STRUCTURED WITH 140% PSA**

| Class | Amount | Coupon | Price | WAL | Yield | Dur. | Mat. |
|---|---|---|---|---|---|---|---|
| 1-TAC | 94,386,000 | 9.000 | 98.73215 | 3.39 | 9.4200 | 2.8 | 7.0 |
| 2-TAC | 66,693,000 | 9.000 | 93.11841 | 10.93 | 10.1700 | 6.7 | 16.0 |
| 3-PO | 17,028,000 | 0.000 | 32.00000 | 21.36 | 5.4976 | 20.6 | 29.0 |
| 4-FLOAT | 21,893,000 | 8.868 | 100.00000 | 21.36 | 9.0442 | 9.5 | 29.0 |
| TOTAL | 200,000,000 | 8.219 | 91.31737 | 9.40 | | | 29.0 |
| RESIDUAL | | | 8,842,692 | | 17.7500 | | |

**EXHIBIT 1-D**
**BASE CASE, NO TAC OR PAC CLASSES***

| Class | Amount | Coupon | Price | WAL | Yield | Dur. | Mat. |
|---|---|---|---|---|---|---|---|
| 1 | 94,386,000 | 9.000 | 98.73215 | 3.39 | 9.4200 | 2.8 | 7.0 |
| 2 | 66,693,000 | 9.000 | 93.11841 | 10.93 | 10.1700 | 6.7 | 16.0 |
| 3-PO | 17,028,000 | 0.000 | 32.00000 | 21.36 | 5.4976 | 20.6 | 29.0 |
| 4-FLOAT | 21,893,000 | 8.868 | 100.00000 | 21.36 | 9.0442 | 9.5 | 29.0 |
| TOTAL | 200,000,000 | 8.219 | 91.31737 | 9.40 | | | 29.0 |
| RESIDUAL | | | 8,842,756 | | 17.7500 | | |

*The Base Case structure and the simplest TAC structure with no range are sized identically. This is because there is only one speed that the TAC schedule is guaranteed for, that is, the pricing speed. However, these two structures do not behave identically, in that, with any change in speed, the TAC schedule must always take precedence over the other classes.

## Impact of PAC and TAC Ranges on Relative Bond Amounts

To maintain a planned amortization schedule, the assumptions under which the schedule is guaranteed must be adhered to. One consideration, in that regard, is the initial size of the classes. To guarantee cashflows within a range, one has to provide for a possible shortfall because of slower prepayments. Thus, the wider the range, the lower the amount of TAC/PAC bonds that can be originated.

### Relative Size of Class 1 and Class 2

| PAC Classes 60% PSA - 300% PSA (Exhibit 1A) | TAC Classes 140% PSA - 220% PSA (Exhibit 1B) | TAC Classes 140% PSA Only (Exhibit 1C) | Base Case (Exhibit 1D) |
|---|---|---|---|
| Small | Medium | Large | Large |

The greater the guaranteed prepayment range, the greater the possibility of a shortfall of cashflows that needs to be provided for; therefore, the size of the PAC/TAC classes must be smaller.

### Relative Size of PO Class and Floater Class

| PAC Classes 60% PSA - 300% PSA (Exhibit 1A) | TAC Classes 140% PSA - 220% PSA (Exhibit 1B) | TAC Classes 140% PSA Only (Exhibit 1C) | Base Case (Exhibit 1D) |
|---|---|---|---|
| Large | Medium | Small | Small |

The greater the guaranteed prepayment range, the greater the possibility of a shortfall of cashflows which needs to be provided for, therefore, the size of the non-PAC/non-TAC classes must be larger to provide for this possible shortfall.

### Weighted Average Lives of PO and Floater Classes

| PAC Classes 60% PSA - 300% PSA (Exhibit 1A) | TAC Classes 140% PSA - 220% PSA (Exhibit 1B) | TAC Classes 140% PSA Only (Exhibit 1C) | Base Case (Exhibit 1D) |
|---|---|---|---|
| Short | Medium | Long | Long |

Larger PAC/TAC classes result in more cashflow directed away from the PO and floater classes, in the early years. Therefore, the larger the size of the PAC/TAC classes, the longer the average lives of the non-PAC/non-TAC classes.

To demonstrate further the contrasts in performance among the different structures, sensitivity analyses were prepared reflecting projected changes in yields and average lives because of changes in prepayment speeds and COFI rates. The prepayment speeds selected ranged from 0 PSA to 400 PSA and the COFI rates selected ranged from 4.618 to 10.618.

### Sensitivity of Bond Classes to Changes in Prepayment Rates

The differences between the four structures are evident in the average life and yield sensitivities of the four classes. In the Base Case structure, the first class performs as expected; that is, as prepayment speeds rise, average lives decrease and as speeds fall, average lives extend. This is the expected performance for standard sequential pay structures. Alternatively, the average lives of the PAC/TAC classes in the other CMO structures are more stable because of their higher priority and the non-PAC/non-TAC classes ability to absorb excess cashflow.

The average life of a PAC class or TAC class always holds when prepayments remain constant within the PAC/TAC range. Outside the range, when PSAs increase, there is often enough of a cushion from the non-PAC/non-TAC classes and lower priority PAC/TAC classes, so that the average life is maintained. When PSAs decrease, the PAC is effected least because there are fewer bonds in the PAC class, which is mandated by the wider guaranteed prepayment range. (See Exhibits 2 and 3.)

The average life of a PAC class or a TAC class again holds when prepayment rates are within the PAC/TAC range. Outside the range, when PSAs increase, the amount of average life call protection is inversely related to the amount of bonds in the class. When PSAs decrease, the PAC is effected least because of the few PAC class bonds, caused by the wider guaranteed prepayment range.

The second class in the Base Case structure performs as expected: as speeds increase, the average lives decrease and vice versa. However, in examining the

**EXHIBIT 2**
**CLASS 1 YIELD AND AVERAGE LIFE SENSITIVITY**

| PSA | PAC Class CMO 60% - 300% PSA (Exhibit 1A) | | TAC Class CMO 140% - 220% PSA (Exhibit 1B) | | TAC Class CMO 140% PSA Only (Exhibit 1C) | | Base Case (Exhibit 1D) | |
|---|---|---|---|---|---|---|---|---|
| | Yield | AL | Yield | AL | Yield | AL | Yield | AL |
| 0 | 9.28 | 10.2 | 9.26 | 14.5 | 9.26 | 14.5 | 9.26 | 14.5 |
| 50 | 9.40 | 3.8 | 9.31 | 7.2 | 9.31 | 7.2 | 9.31 | 7.2 |
| 60 | 9.42 | 3.4 | 9.32 | 6.4 | 9.32 | 6.4 | 9.32 | 6.4 |
| 100 | 9.42 | 3.4 | 9.37 | 4.4 | 9.37 | 4.4 | 9.37 | 4.4 |
| 140 | 9.42 | 3.4 | 9.42 | 3.4 | 9.42 | 3.4 | 9.42 | 3.4 |
| 200 | 9.42 | 3.4 | 9.42 | 3.4 | 9.42 | 3.4 | 9.49 | 2.5 |
| 220 | 9.42 | 3.4 | 9.42 | 3.4 | 9.42 | 3.4 | 9.51 | 2.3 |
| 250 | 9.42 | 3.4 | 9.42 | 3.4 | 9.42 | 3.4 | 9.54 | 2.1 |
| 300 | 9.42 | 3.4 | 9.42 | 3.4 | 9.42 | 3.4 | 9.60 | 1.8 |
| 400 | 9.42 | 3.4 | 9.42 | 3.4 | 9.42 | 3.4 | 9.70 | 1.4 |
| PAC/TAC Priority | Highest | | Highest | | Highest | | N/A | |

**EXHIBIT 3**
**AVERAGE LIFE SENSITIVITY TO PREPAYMENTS (CLASS 1)**

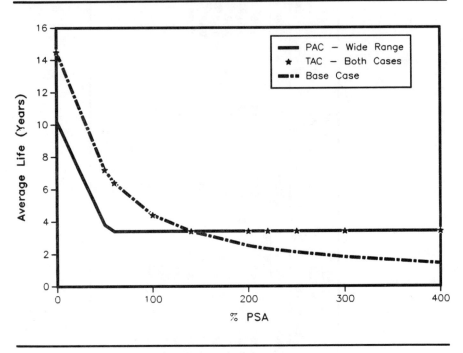

second class's performance in the three PAC/TAC structures, the differences are notable. In the simplest PAC/TAC case, the TAC structure guaranteed at only one speed, the second class maintains its average life at only that speed. Whereas, in the PAC and TAC structures with a range, the average life is maintained within the range. As speeds increase slightly, there is initially some extension and then, as speeds increase further, average lives drop. This movement may seem counterintuitive. However, the cashflows are paying down the non-PAC/non-TAC classes first and, over time, there is not enough cashflow in the amortization schedule to pay the bonds on schedule, so they extend. As speeds climb, the second class gets retired faster and the average lives begin to drop. (See Exhibits 4 and 5.)

## III. "SUPER" PO BONDS

The presence of a PAC class or a TAC class requires that some other class or classes absorb prepayments in excess of those expected at the pricing speed. Such classes, acting as prepayment absorbers, will have very volatile average lives. This volatility

**EXHIBIT 4**
**CLASS 2 YIELD AND AVERAGE LIFE SENSITIVITY**

| PSA | PAC Class CMO 60% - 300% PSA (Exhibit 1A) | | TAC Class CMO 140% - 220% PSA (Exhibit 1B) | | TAC Class CMO 140% PSA Only (Exhibit 1C) | | Base Case (Exhibit 1D) | |
|---|---|---|---|---|---|---|---|---|
| | Yield | AL | Yield | AL | Yield | AL | Yield | AL |
| 0 | 9.92 | 19.6 | 9.87 | 24.4 | 9.87 | 24.6 | 9.87 | 24.6 |
| 50 | 10.14 | 11.6 | 9.93 | 18.9 | 9.93 | 19.3 | 9.93 | 19.3 |
| 60 | 10.18 | 10.9 | 9.95 | 17.7 | 9.95 | 18.1 | 9.95 | 18.1 |
| 100 | 10.18 | 10.9 | 10.06 | 13.4 | 10.05 | 13.9 | 10.05 | 13.9 |
| 140 | 10.18 | 10.9 | 10.17 | 10.9 | 10.17 | 10.9 | 10.17 | 10.9 |
| 200 | 10.18 | 10.9 | 10.17 | 10.9 | 10.16 | 11.3 | 10.38 | 8.1 |
| 220 | 10.18 | 10.9 | 10.17 | 10.9 | 10.14 | 11.6 | 10.45 | 7.4 |
| 250 | 10.18 | 10.9 | 10.15 | 11.5 | 10.14 | 12.1 | 10.56 | 6.6 |
| 300 | 10.18 | 10.9 | 10.23 | 10.5 | 10.29 | 9.8 | 10.75 | 5.6 |
| 400 | 10.35 | 8.7 | 10.62 | 6.9 | 10.71 | 6.5 | 11.13 | 4.2 |
| PAC/TAC Priority | Lowest | | Lowest | | Lowest | | N/A | |

**EXHIBIT 5**
**AVERAGE LIFE SENSITIVITY TO PREPAYMENTS (CLASS 2)**

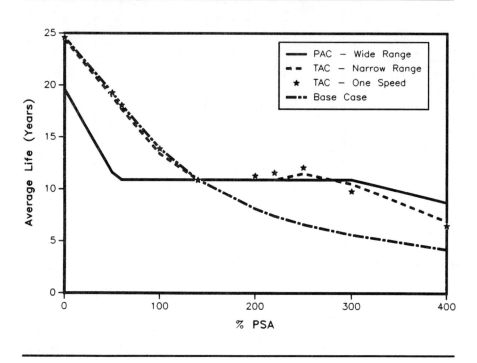

can be turned to advantage by making the class a principal-only class. Exhibit 6 displays the beneficial effect of prepayments on yields using this technique. (Also see Exhibit 7.)

Classes which absorb excess cashflows will have the most volatile average lives. The greater the size of the PAC/TAC classes, the greater the sensitivity of the non-PAC/non-TAC classes to prepayments. In the case of the PAC/TAC structure containing a zero coupon or principal only (PO) bond, the more PAC/TAC bonds, the more sensitive the PO becomes because it takes on more of the prepayment risk. This creates what has come to be known as a "Super PO."

The positive convexity of the super PO at the pricing speed is derived from the inclusion of the PAC or TAC classes. As prepayments increase, the non-PAC/non-TAC classes (i.e., PO) absorb all of the excess cashflows. This results in a marked decrease in average life and, since the PO is bought at an extremely discounted price, a highly increased yield. The greater the amount of PAC/TAC bonds, the greater the consequences to the other classes as prepayments increase. (See Exhibit 8.)

**EXHIBIT 6**
**"SUPER" PO YIELD AND AVERAGE LIFE SENSITIVITY**

| PSA | PAC Class CMO 60% - 300% PSA (Exhibit 1A) | | TAC Class CMO 140% - 220% PSA (Exhibit 1B) | | TAC Class CMO 140% PSA Only (Exhibit 1C) | | Base Case (Exhibit 1D) | |
|---|---|---|---|---|---|---|---|---|
| | Yield | AL | Yield | AL | Yield | AL | Yield | AL |
| 0 | 2.05 | 26.0 | 3.80 | 27.8 | 4.11 | 28.0 | 4.11 | 28.0 |
| 50 | 2.44 | 22.1 | 4.04 | 26.2 | 4.33 | 26.6 | 4.33 | 26.6 |
| 60 | 2.58 | 21.0 | 4.12 | 25.8 | 4.40 | 26.2 | 4.40 | 26.2 |
| 100 | 3.75 | 15.6 | 4.58 | 23.3 | 4.83 | 24.0 | 4.83 | 24.0 |
| 140 | 5.50 | 11.6 | 5.50 | 19.9 | 5.50 | 21.4 | 5.50 | 21.4 |
| 200 | 9.74 | 7.4 | 20.68 | 10.6 | 31.68 | 9.8 | 6.85 | 17.5 |
| 220 | 11.67 | 6.4 | 33.29 | 8.2 | 49.26 | 6.6 | 7.37 | 16.4 |
| 250 | 14.99 | 5.0 | 53.69 | 4.5 | 74.87 | 2.3 | 8.20 | 14.8 |
| 300 | 21.33 | 3.3 | 84.97 | 1.8 | 114.00 | 1.5 | 9.68 | 12.7 |
| 400 | 32.19 | 2.0 | 143.43 | 1.1 | 193.37 | 1.1 | 12.90 | 9.7 |

**EXHIBIT 7**
**AVERAGE LIFE SENSITIVITY TO PREPAYMENTS**
**(PO AND FLOATER CLASSES)**

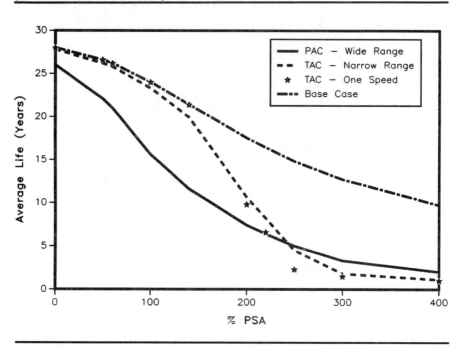

## IV. COST OF FUNDS INDEX (COFI) FLOATER BONDS

The Eleventh District Cost of Funds Index, sometimes referred to as COF and more recently, COFI, is the monthly weighted average interest cost of deposits and borrowings of the Federal Home Loan Bank (FHLB) member thrifts in California, Arizona, and Nevada. COFI is a composite index that reflects both short and long term costs as well as past and current interest rates.

The COF Index is computed by the FHLB of San Francisco for each month by dividing the cost of funds (interest paid during the month by Eleventh District savings institutions on saving, advances, other borrowings) by the average of the total amount of those funds outstanding at the end of that month and the prior month and annualizing and adjusting the result to reflect the actual number of days in the particular month. If necessary, before these calculations are made, the component figures are adjusted by the FHLB of San Francisco to neutralize the effect of events such as member institutions leaving the Eleventh District or acquiring institutions outside the Eleventh District. The COF Index has been reported each month since August 1981.

**EXHIBIT 8**
**YIELD OF "SUPER" PO**

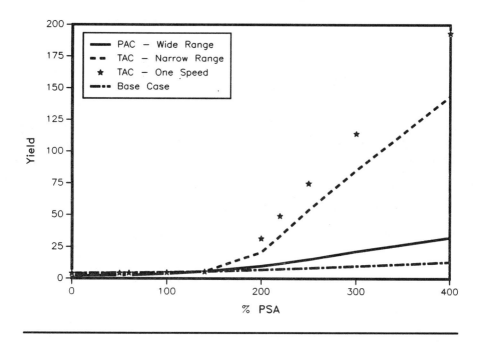

The COF Index reflects the interest costs paid on all types of funds held by Eleventh District member savings and loan associations and savings banks. The COF Index is weighted to reflect the relative amount of each type of funds held at the end of the relevant month. There are three major components of funds of Eleventh District member institutions: *(1) savings deposits; (2) Federal Home Loan Bank advances; (3) all other borrowings, such as reverse repurchase agreements and mortgage-backed bonds.*

Unlike many other short-term interest rate measures, the COF Index does not necessarily reflect current market rates. The component funds represent a variety of terms to maturity whose costs may react in different ways to changing market conditions. Since COFI depends upon past rates as well as member bank funding strategies, COFI exhibits less volatility than other short-term market rates and generally lags movements in rates. (See Exhibit 9.)

A statistical relationship between the COFI and Treasury rates is difficult to establish because the COFI reflects market conditions with a significant and complex time lag. Theoretically, one could use dimension reduction techniques to find a basket of Treasuries that would mirror the COFI over the business-interest rate

**EXHIBIT 9**
**INDEX COMPARISON**

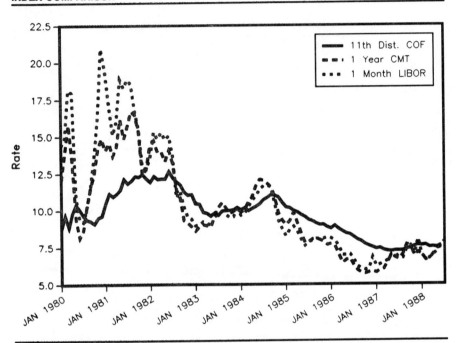

cycle. However, it is analytically useful and practical to relate the COFI to the one-year Treasury because these are the two most popular ARM indexes. One approach is to regress the COFI on a moving average of the one-year Treasury rates. (See Exhibit 10.)

This approach can be successful as Exhibit 10 illustrates. Because COFI is a lagging index, future COFI rates can be fairly well predicted.

Because the floater class is often used to keep PAC or TAC classes on schedule, as is the case in our analysis, it too will exhibit average life volatility. The shortening of average life can be beneficial in those instances in which it makes less likely a "capping-out" of the floater as short rates increase. As can be seen in Exhibit 11, in each CMO structured with a PAC or TAC class, the floater enjoys a shorter average life than in the base case.


## V. RESIDUAL SENSITIVITIES

In the four case structures, all of the residual cashflows result from the last two classes: the floater and the principal-only (PO) bonds. This is because the first two

**EXHIBIT 10**
**ACTUAL COFI VS. FITTED COFI**

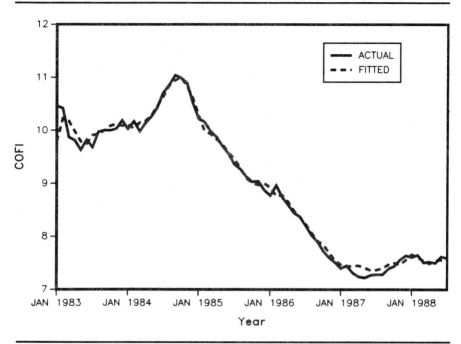

**EXHIBIT 11**
**FLOATER CLASS AVERAGE LIVES**

| PSA | PAC Class CMO 60% - 300% PSA (Exhibit 1A) Average Life | TAC Class CMO 140% - 220% PSA (Exhibit 1B) Average Life | TAC Class CMO 140% PSA Only (Exhibit 1C) Average Life | Base Case (Exhibit 1D) Average Life |
|---|---|---|---|---|
| 0 | 26.0 | 27.8 | 28.0 | 28.0 |
| 50 | 22.1 | 26.2 | 26.6 | 26.6 |
| 60 | 21.0 | 25.8 | 26.2 | 26.2 |
| 100 | 15.6 | 23.3 | 24.0 | 24.0 |
| 140 | 11.6 | 19.9 | 21.4 | 21.4 |
| 200 | 7.4 | 10.6 | 9.8 | 17.5 |
| 220 | 6.4 | 8.2 | 6.6 | 16.4 |
| 250 | 5.0 | 4.5 | 2.3 | 14.8 |
| 300 | 3.3 | 1.8 | 1.5 | 12.7 |
| 400 | 2.0 | 1.1 | 1.1 | 9.7 |

classes both have coupons of 9%, which equal the coupon of the collateral supporting the structures. This results in no excess cashflow to the residual from those two classes.

Since the residual cashflow is derived from the PO and the floater, their proportion relative to the PAC/TAC classes accounts for a great deal of the residual's sensitivity. When evaluating the sensitivity of a residual, it is common to view the diagonal of yields projected assuming that as rates rise, prepayment speeds fall and as rates fall, prepayment speeds rise. For residual sensitivities, the diagonal is the primary focus but the entire matrix should be considered to gauge the degree of risk. (See Exhibits 12-A–12-D.)

### Prepayments Below Pricing Speed

In comparing the Base Case structure with the TAC structured at one speed, as speeds slow down, the residual sensitivities remain the same. This is because they have been structured with the same initial balances and as speeds slow down, they pay down in the same manner.

In comparing the wide range PAC and narrow range TAC structures, however, slower prepayment speeds increase the residual yields. This is because there is a greater proportion of PO and Floater bonds in these two structures. As speeds decrease, there is more cashflow creating more residual.

### Prepayments Above Pricing Speed

As prepayment speeds increase, the residual yields vary substantially. In the Base Case structure, as prepayments increase and interest rates decline (referred to as the upper right or "northeast" corner of the sensitivity grid), residual yields increase. The reason is two-fold: as PSAs increase, the first two classes protect the PO and floater; in addition, there is an increased spread between the collateral coupon and the weighted average of the PO and the Floater because of the lower rate paid out on the Floater. The latter effects all cases but the effect is less pronounced in the case of the TAC and PAC structures because the PO and Floater are outstanding a shorter period of time.

In the PAC and TAC cases, there is a direct correlation between the prepayment range and the sensitivity of the residual to the PSA. Incoming cash is always directed to the PAC/TAC classes, and then any excess cashflow is directed to the non-PAC/non-TAC classes. Thus, the wider the guaranteed prepayment range, the less the initial size of the PAC/TAC classes and the less sensitive the residual. The most sensitive residual at the higher PSA speeds is that of the single speed TAC structure. In summary, the residual sensitivity of the Base Case structure is most stable and the single speed TAC is the most volatile. A portfolio containing this residual would benefit from being hedged by a Super PO that would offset negative residual returns should prepayment speeds climb and interest rates fall.

EXHIBIT 12-A
PAC CLASS WIDE RANGE BETWEEN 60 AND 330

| | Starting COFI: | 7.618 |
|---|---|---|
| | Starting Speed: | 140 |
| | Months to Change: | 0 |
| | Present Value: | $16,647,989 |

Residual Sensitivities

| COFI Rate | 0 | 50 | 60 | 100 | 140 | 200 | 220 | 250 | 300 | 400 |
|---|---|---|---|---|---|---|---|---|---|---|
| 4.618 | 37.14 | 37.08 | 37.02 | 33.01 | 28.72 | 21.47 | 18.73 | 14.14 | 3.83 | −24.58 |
| 5.618 | 33.31 | 33.23 | 33.15 | 29.23 | 25.03 | 17.94 | 15.25 | 10.73 | 0.55 | −29.86 |
| 6.618 | 29.52 | 29.40 | 29.29 | 25.47 | 21.38 | 14.46 | 11.84 | 7.43 | −2.46 | −35.34 |
| 7.618 | 25.74 | 25.56 | 25.43 | 21.72 | 17.75 | 11.04 | 8.50 | 4.24 | −5.21 | −41.09 |
| 8.618 | 21.97 | 21.71 | 21.54 | 17.96 | 14.12 | 7.66 | 5.22 | 1.14 | −7.74 | −47.18 |
| 9.618 | 18.18 | 17.81 | 17.59 | 14.15 | 10.47 | 4.29 | 1.97 | −1.90 | ..... | −53.73 |
| 10.618 | 14.31 | 13.80 | 13.53 | 10.23 | 6.72 | 0.87 | −1.32 | −4.94 | ..... | ..... |

EXHIBIT 12-B
TAC CLASS NARROW RANGE BETWEEN 140 AND 220

| | Starting COFI: | 7.618 |
|---|---|---|
| | Starting Speed: | 140 |
| | Months to Change: | 0 |
| | Present Value: | $10,065,238 |

Residual Sensitivities

| COFI Rate | 0 | 50 | 60 | 100 | 140 | 200 | 220 | 250 | 300 | 400 |
|---|---|---|---|---|---|---|---|---|---|---|
| 4.618 | 26.75 | 26.74 | 26.73 | 26.67 | 26.37 | 15.66 | 11.37 | 1.97 | −47.04 | ..... |
| 5.618 | 24.01 | 23.98 | 23.97 | 23.89 | 23.53 | 13.31 | 9.26 | 0.33 | −51.52 | ..... |
| 6.618 | 21.27 | 21.23 | 21.22 | 21.10 | 20.66 | 10.97 | 7.17 | −1.29 | −56.23 | ..... |
| 7.618 | 18.52 | 18.47 | 18.44 | 18.29 | 17.75 | 8.62 | 5.07 | −2.89 | −61.21 | ..... |
| 8.618 | 15.75 | 15.67 | 15.64 | 15.42 | 14.77 | 6.22 | 2.94 | −4.52 | ..... | ..... |
| 9.618 | 12.92 | 12.80 | 12.76 | 12.47 | 11.69 | 3.75 | 0.73 | −6.20 | ..... | ..... |
| 10.618 | 9.98 | 9.81 | 9.75 | 9.37 | 8.43 | 1.12 | −1.62 | ..... | ..... | ..... |

**EXHIBIT 12-C**
**TAC CLASS ONE SPEED AT 140**

Starting COFI: 7.618
Starting Speed: 140
Months to Change: 0
Present Value: $8,842,692

Residual Sensitivities

| COFI Rate | 0 | 50 | 60 | 100 | 140 | 200 | 220 | 250 | 300 | 400 |
|---|---|---|---|---|---|---|---|---|---|---|
| 4.618 | 26.29 | 26.28 | 26.28 | 26.23 | 26.12 | 13.38 | 7.29 | −26.69 | −63.59 | ...... |
| 5.618 | 23.60 | 23.58 | 23.57 | 23.51 | 23.35 | 11.23 | 5.45 | −30.71 | −68.20 | ...... |
| 6.618 | 20.91 | 20.87 | 20.86 | 20.77 | 20.57 | 9.10 | 3.63 | −34.92 | −73.03 | ...... |
| 7.618 | 18.20 | 18.16 | 18.14 | 18.01 | 17.75 | 6.95 | 1.82 | −29.36 | ...... | ...... |
| 8.618 | 15.47 | 15.41 | 15.38 | 15.21 | 14.86 | 4.78 | −0.02 | −44.11 | ...... | ...... |
| 9.618 | 12.69 | 12.59 | 12.55 | 12.32 | 11.87 | 2.53 | −1.92 | ...... | ...... | ...... |
| 10.618 | 9.79 | 9.65 | 9.60 | 9.28 | 8.71 | 0.13 | −3.96 | ...... | ...... | ...... |

**EXHIBIT 12-D**
**BASE CASE STRUCTURE**

Starting COFI: 7.618
Starting Speed: 140
Months to Change: 0
Present Value: $8,842,756

Residual Sensitivities

| COFI Rate | 0 | 50 | 60 | 100 | 140 | 200 | 220 | 250 | 300 | 400 |
|---|---|---|---|---|---|---|---|---|---|---|
| 4.618 | 26.29 | 26.28 | 26.28 | 26.23 | 26.12 | 25.72 | 25.52 | 25.14 | 24.32 | 21.99 |
| 5.618 | 23.60 | 23.58 | 23.57 | 23.51 | 23.35 | 22.87 | 22.63 | 22.19 | 21.25 | 18.68 |
| 6.618 | 20.91 | 20.87 | 20.86 | 20.77 | 20.57 | 19.97 | 19.68 | 19.17 | 18.11 | 15.27 |
| 7.618 | 18.20 | 18.16 | 18.14 | 18.01 | 17.75 | 17.01 | 16.67 | 16.08 | 14.87 | 11.73 |
| 8.618 | 15.47 | 15.41 | 15.38 | 15.21 | 14.86 | 13.97 | 13.56 | 12.87 | 11.50 | 8.04 |
| 9.618 | 12.69 | 12.59 | 12.55 | 12.32 | 11.87 | 10.78 | 10.31 | 9.50 | 7.95 | 4.13 |
| 10.618 | 9.79 | 9.65 | 9.60 | 9.28 | 8.71 | 7.38 | 6.83 | 5.90 | 4.13 | −0.09 |

## VI. THE IMPACT OF VOLATILE PREPAYMENTS WITHIN THE GUARANTEED RANGE/FALLING OFF SCHEDULE AND CATCHING-UP

PAC and TAC classes are structured to guarantee an average life and yield within a specified prepayment range assuming prepayments remain constant within the range. *However, it is possible that there will be periods where the next targeted principal payment will not be met because of the variability of mortgage principal prepayments.* This activity is referred to as "falling off schedule." In such a case, any subsequent excess principal will be directed to the missed payment. This is sometimes referred to as a "catch-up."

Since the issuance of the first PAC bond, most have maintained the expected schedule. Many that have fallen off schedule in the past have been able to return to schedule. One structure, for example, with the exception of the first month, has never met the projected schedule because the mortgages never prepaid within the guaranteed prepayment range of 600 to 800 PSA.

To illustrate the effect of varying prepayment speeds on a projected PAC/TAC schedule, an example has been prepared assuming several changes in prepayment speed. Using the three PAC/TAC case structures, a simulation of the varying prepayment rates was made. The simulation assumed that prepayments began at the pricing speed of 140 PSA gradually moving to 290 PSA in six months, remaining stable at 290 PSA for one year and then gradually shifting downward to 70 PSA; after remaining stable at 70 PSA for one year, the prepayment rate was moved over six months to the pricing speed of 140 PSA where it remained for the lifetime of the bonds.

For the TAC structure priced at one speed: the first class lenghtens because as speeds increase in the early years, the PO and Floater classes receive the excess cashflows and are paid down more quickly (their average lives shorten to 12.47 years). Then, suddenly, speeds decrease; there is a shortfall of cash when PSAs decrease to 70 PSA and the PAC schedule cannot be met. As a result, the first class and consequently, the second class, both fall off their respective PAC schedules and lengthen in average lives to 3.99 and 13.46 years.

The PAC has a much better resistance to the movements than the ranged TAC because of the wider guaranteed prepayment range. The effect is significant in that the ranged TAC classes extend to 3.99 and 12.83 whereas, the PAC class extends only to 3.40 and the second class doesn't even extend.

The wider the PAC/TAC range, the lesser the PAC/TAC bonds and therefore, the greater the protection. In a volatile market, the PAC bond did fall off schedule (albeit only a slight amount) even though prepayments remained within the range. As volatility increases, the chances of falling off the PAC/TAC schedule increase. As the ratio of PAC/TACs to non-PAC/non-TACs increase, the chances of falling off the PAC/TAC schedule increase.

# Mortgage-Backed Bonds

STAN AUGUST
VICE PRESIDENT
CORPORATE BOND RESEARCH DEPARTMENT
GOLDMAN, SACHS & CO.

JOHN SIPP
ASSOCIATE
MORTGAGE FINANCE DEPARTMENT
GOLDMAN, SACHS & CO.

## I. OVERVIEW

As of April, 1988, over $10 billion in principal amount of domestically-issued mortgage-backed bonds were outstanding. In addition, over $3.3 billion of mortgage-backed medium term note programs were in place. Partly as a result of a new structure which allows issuers of mortgage-backed bonds to post less collateral while maintaining a high level of credit protection for investors, the pace of issuance of mortgage-backed bonds has accelerated substantially in the past year. In 1987, nearly $3 billion of mortgage-backed bonds were issued, a sharp increase over the $1.4 billion issued in 1986. From January through May 1988, over $1.4 billion of these securities were issued.

The authors would like to thank Howard Altarescu, Larry Kochard, Chris Norton, Scott Pinkus, and Jon Winkelried for their comments and assistance in preparing this article. Special thanks to David Carlson for his work in preparing the appendixes. The information and comments contained in this article were developed and expressed as of May 1988.

Despite the fact that these securities bear "Aaa" ratings from Moody's and/or "AAA" ratings from Standard and Poor's (S&P), they have historically traded at spreads which are comparable to single A finance credits. We believe that this yield premium reflects investor uncertainty about the structure of mortgage-backed bonds and concerns about the level of credit protection afforded investors by these structures. In this article we describe the mechanics of mortgage-backed bonds and assess their value on both an absolute and relative basis.

A mortgage-backed bond is a general obligation debt security issued by a savings and loan institution or other mortgage related entity. Structurally, mortgage-backed bonds are similar to other corporate debt securities, providing periodic interest payments and bullet payments of principal at maturity. The key distinguishing feature of mortgage-backed bonds is that the obligation of the issuer to make interest and principal payments is collateralized, generally with agency guaranteed mortgage-backed securities such as GNMA, FNMA and FHLMC certificates. As a result of this collateralization, mortgage-backed bonds are typically rated triple-A.

Mortgage-backed bonds differ in several important respects from other types of mortgage securities like collateralized mortgage obligations. A mortgage-backed bond, as noted above, is a corporate debt security which provides for periodic interest and payment of principal at maturity. Collateralized mortgage obligations, or CMOs, are debt securities issued by a corporation or a trust and are secured by mortgage securities such as GNMA, FNMA, and FHLMC certificates. CMOs may also be structured to evidence ownership in a trust which owns mortgage securities. In either case, payments received on the underlying mortgage securities are allocated to the various classes of the CMO and passed through to investors as they are received. Thus, payments on CMOs are dependent on the rate of payments, including principal prepayments, on the underlying mortgage securities. The payment schedule for mortgage-backed bonds is established at issuance and is not related to the cash flows on the mortgage securities posted as collateral for the bonds.

## II. MORTGAGE-BACKED BOND STRUCTURES

The collateral structures of mortgage-backed bonds are primarily driven by rating agency criteria for triple-A ratings. The most important of these criteria is that the amount and quality of collateral posted by the issuer must be sufficient to assure that, in the event of a default, the collateral could be liquidated by the bond trustee to yield enough cash to make bondholders "whole." Depending on the structure of the transaction, bondholders may be made "whole" in one of two ways. In what we will call a traditional mortgage-backed bond structure, proceeds from the liquidation of the collateral are used to accelerate the bonds and pay off bondholders at par plus accrued interest. Under the newer structure, which we will call a defeasance structure, the proceeds from the liquidation of the collateral are used to purchase a portfolio of U.S. Treasury securities in appropriate quantities and with appropriate maturities sufficient to, in effect, defease the interest and principal payments remaining on the bonds until their maturity.

To assure that the liquidation of the collateral will yield sufficient cash proceeds to either call the bonds at par plus accrued interest (under the traditional structure) or to defease the bonds with U.S. Treasury securities (in the defeasance structure), the rating agencies require that the posted collateral be marked-to-market periodically. This mark-to-market, referred to as a collateral maintenance test, consists of the following steps:

1. A "basic maintenance amount" is calculated. In the traditional structure, this is equal to par plus accrued interest on the bonds, plus an additional number of days of accrued interest to cover the lag expected to occur between a default on the bonds and the date on which bondholders are repaid. In a defeasance structure, the basic maintenance amount is equal to the current market value (determined by taking the higher of two dealer offer prices) of a portfolio of U.S. Treasury securities which would defease the bonds.
2. The market value of the pledged collateral is determined, using the lower of two dealer bid prices.
3. The adjusted market value of the pledged collateral is calculated by dividing the market value of each item of collateral by an overcollaterialization factor. These overcollateralization factors vary by type of collateral and by the length of time between mark-to-markets, as discussed further below.

For both traditional and defeasance structures, the adjusted market value of the pledged collateral must exceed the basic maintenance amount each time the collateral maintenance test is performed. Defeasance structures include an additional requirement that the unadjusted market value of the pledged collateral must exceed par plus accrued interest on the bonds. There are two reasons for this additional test. First, it affords investors additional protection in the event that the bonds are accelerated and redeemed at par. Second, bonds issued by thrifts are generally exempt from SEC registration and avoid Federal Home Loan Bank Board (FHLBB) registration provided that they are issued in denominations of $100,000 or greater and are "fully collateralized" by certain types of securities, as described below. This means that the value of the collateral securing the bonds cannot be allowed to fall below par plus accrued interest.

If the above requirements are not met, the issuer must, within a given period (referred to as the "cure period"), either post additional collateral or repurchase bonds in the open market sufficient to meet the collateral maintenance test after such repurchases. If the issuer does not comply with the collateral maintenance test within the cure period specified in the bond indenture, generally three to five business days, the bonds will be in default.

The types of collateral which are eligible to be pledged vary from deal to deal. (See Appendix A for a description of eligible collateral.) The most common types of eligible collateral are cash, U.S. Treasury securities, GNMA, FNMA, and FHLMC certificates, and high quality short-term money market securities. Securities in this last category are usually pledged by issuers immediately prior to scheduled interest or principal payments to satisfy requirements of the rating agencies that short-term liquid securities be pledged to cover these payments. As discussed below, there are limitations on the amounts of these securities which can be posted as collateral.

Other types of collateral which may be permitted by the indentures of certain transactions include whole mortgage loans (either fixed-rate or adjustable-rate), "private label" mortgage pass-through securities, collateralized mortgage obligations, and corporate bonds (either investment grade or non-investment grade). However, as noted above, most mortgage-backed bonds avoid registration with the FHLBB by providing for minimum denominations of $100,000 and collateralization by cash, U.S. Treasury securities, whole mortgage loans, and GNMA, FNMA, and FHLMC certificates. Thus, for the bonds to remain exempt from FHLBB registration, the maximum amount of corporate bonds or money market securities which may be pledged is the amount of overcollateralization above par plus accrued interest on the bonds.

When the issuer pledges the collateral to secure the bonds, the trustee for the bondholders acquires a first priority perfected security interest in the collateral. In general, this means that the collateral will be available solely to satisfy bondholder claims, until such claims are satisfied in full. At the time the collateral is pledged, it is typically registered in the name of the trustee, and the trustee ordinarily receives all cash flows on the collateral.

An issuer may at any time substitute different types of collateral which are explicitly permitted in the bond indenture, provided that there is sufficient collateral after the substitution to meet the collateral maintenance test. Many investors are concerned that new securities which were not mentioned in the bond indenture may be introduced as collateral for certain bonds after issuance. Most mortgage-backed bond indentures provide for the introduction of "new eligible collateral" into the pledged collateral if the rating agency or agencies rating the bonds confirm in writing that inclusion of this collateral will not result in a downgrading of the bonds. In recognition of investor concerns about this indenture provision, most recent transactions have provided that new eligible collateral cannot include certain types of securities, ranging from corporate bonds to whole loans and mortgage pass-through securities. (See Appendix B for a table of outstanding mortgage-backed bond issues.) The exclusion of these types of securities can only be overridden by a vote of 100% of the bondholders. Investors can derive further comfort from statements by S&P and Moody's that they will not permit substitution of corporate bonds as collateral for mortgage-backed bonds issued prior to certain dates (January, 1987 for S&P; September, 1987 for Moody's). Finally, investors should note that neither Moody's nor S&P has published overcollateralization guidelines which would allow issuers to use corporate bonds or whole mortgage loans as collateral for defeasance mortgage-backed bonds, which are the primary type of securities now being issued in this sector.

As discussed above, the collateral maintenance test requires the application of an overcollateralization factor to the market value of the pledged property securing the bonds. A summary of the overcollateralization factors applicable to various types of collateral appears below:

|  | Traditional Structure | Defeasance Structure |
|---|---|---|
| GNMA Certificates | 124%-140% | 111%-120% |
| FNMA/FHLMC Certificates | 135-150 | 111-120 |
| U.S. Treasury strips | 105-180 | 105-180 |
| Other U.S. Treasury securities | 112-135 | 105-125 |
| Fixed rate whole loans | 150-170 | Cannot currently be used |
| Adjustable rate whole loans | 160-190 | Cannot currently be used |
| Mortgage pass-through securities | 140-155 | Cannot currently be used |
| Collateralized mortgage obligations | 135-150 | Cannot currently be used |
| Corporate bonds | 140-200 | Cannot currently be used |

The specific overcollateralization factors applicable to a particular transaction will depend on the frequency of collateral maintenance tests and on the period of time that the issuer has to cure a collateral shortfall.

The rating agencies have conducted extensive studies of price movements of each of the above types of collateral. The overcollateralization factors for traditional structures are designed to protect investors against absolute price declines in the collateral between collateral maintenance tests. The overcollateralization factors for defeasance structures are designed to protect investors against price declines in the collateral *relative to* the price of a portfolio of Treasury securities that would defease the bonds. There are two potential sources of these relative price declines. The first is a widening in the basis between the pledged collateral and Treasuries. The second is the duration mismatch between the pledged collateral and the portfolio of Treasuries that would defease the bonds. Based on their analysis, the rating agencies have concluded that the above overcollateralization factors provide investors with a level of protection against these risks which is consistent with a triple A rating.

## III. REMEDIES ON DEFAULT; CERTAIN REGULATORY CONSIDERATIONS

The question of exactly what would happen in the event of a default on a mortgage-backed bond is obviously of great interest to investors. Unfortunately (or fortunately!), there has never been a defaulted payment of principal or interest on a mortgage-backed bond. However, there have been situations in which thrift issuers of mortgage-backed bonds have become insolvent. An example of this is Eureka Federal Savings and Loan Association of San Francisco, which issued $45 million of 9.85% mortgage-backed bonds in August, 1979. Pursuant to their indenture, these bonds were scheduled to mature August 1, 1986 and were callable at par anytime after August 1, 1985. In June of 1985, Eureka was placed into the Federal Savings and Loan Insurance Corporation's (FSLIC) Management Consignment Program. While the indenture for Eureka's mortgage-backed bond provided for the acceleration of the bonds in the event of Eureka's insolvency, the FSLIC instead continued to make interest payments on the bonds and retired them via a call at par in August of 1985.

Because of a lack of a definitive precedent, and because the FSLIC is not bound to take the same steps in all cases, it is impossible to determine exactly what the FSLIC might do in the event of a future thrift issuer's insolvency. This question is further complicated by the fact that the insolvency of a thrift is not subject to the U.S. Bankruptcy Code. However, based on our consultations with counsel, we believe that several statements can be made regarding the FSLIC's actions in the event of a thrift insolvency.

First, it is clear that investors in mortgage-backed bonds would, at a minimum, be able to satisfy their claims out of the collateral securing the bonds in the event of a thrift issuer's insolvency. The FHLBB, which administers the FSLIC, has stated that the FSLIC, as receiver of an insolvent thrift, would generally respect the interests of bondholders in the collateral securing a mortgage-backed bond. This position was articulated in letters written by Norman H. Raiden, then General Counsel to the FHLBB, to counsel for S&P. These letters, known as the "Raiden letters," have given the rating agencies, as well as underwriters, comfort that the collateral securing the bonds will be available to bondholders in the event of insolvency.

Thus, bondholders are assured of receiving principal and accrued interest on a defaulted mortgage-backed bond. The issue then becomes exactly when and how the FSLIC, as receiver of an insolvent thrift, would choose to return bondholders' principal. Broadly speaking, the FSLIC could honor the provisions of the bond's indenture, either accelerating the bonds in the traditional structure or defeasing them in the defeasance structure, or act contrary to the indenture. Actions contrary to the indenture could take several forms, including leaving the bonds outstanding (as was the case with Eureka), defeasing the bonds in the traditional structure, or accelerating the bonds in the defeasance structure. The Raiden letters are silent as to exactly how the FSLIC would act with respect to the provisions of a particular indenture. Discussions with counsel lead us to believe that FSLIC would likely act in accordance with the indenture, but that under certain circumstances FSLIC may not. For example, it may be to the economic benefit of the FSLIC as receiver, and therefore to the benefit of the depositors and other creditors of the insolvent thrift, for the FSLIC to redeem the bonds issued under the defeasance structure at par rather than effect a defeasance. This would be more likely if interest rates have fallen substantially since the issuance of the bonds. It is important to note that the FSLIC would likely weigh this one-time benefit against the disruption that this action could cause in the market for mortgage-backed bonds, a market which is a significant source of term funding for the thrift industry. The Eureka precedent provides little insight into the way in which the FSLIC might view the tradeoff between a one time economic benefit and a market disruption because the Eureka bonds were, by their terms, subject to an óptional par call within two months of FSLIC assuming control of the institution.

## IV. THE UNRECOGNIZED VALUE OF MORTGAGE-BACKED BONDS

We feel that a combination of investor apprehension and incomplete understanding, along with a lack of depth in the mortgage-backed bond market, has created attractive investment opportunities (as often happens when the market does not fully understand a security). The two principal factors restraining investor appetite for mortgage-backed bonds and creating this undervaluation are: 1) a lingering concern that the mortgage-backed bond structure may not fully protect the investor's security interest in the collateral, and 2) the possibility of an extraordinary redemption at par due to an issuer's insolvency. Investor concerns about these issues are understandable given the lack of an issuer bankruptcy precedent. However, we contend that investors have focused excessively on these issues and have either overlooked or failed to adequately consider the following significant points:

1) **"AAA" Rated Securities at "A" Rated Finance Company Spreads**—Mortgage-backed bond spreads do not appropriately reflect their high quality. Currently, mortgage-backed bonds trade like "A" rated securities (approximately U.S. Treasuries + 80 bp in 5 years). This is considerably wider (30 bp +) than 5 year "AAA" rated finance paper (i.e., General Electric Credit), and is 10 bp wider than "AA" rated Ford Motor Credit. Thus, the mortgage-backed sector enables investors the unique opportunity to either *improve portfolio quality without sacrificing yield or increase yield without compromising credit quality.*

2) **Absence of Event Risk Enhances Relative Value**—The relative value of mortgage-backed bonds is enhanced because they are generally not subject to precipitous price declines and rating downgrades that stem from unforeseen events such as friendly or hostile takeovers or leveraged recapitalizations which have wreaked havoc in the unsecured corporate debt market. Corporate bond investors are justifiably sensitive to this risk. Because mortgage-backed bonds are devoid of this risk, they afford investors the best protection available against a high quality bond turning into a speculatively rated security overnight. Furthermore, investors gain protection against the adverse price reaction associated with rating downgrades resulting from a deterioration in the issuer's financial condition.

3) **Differentiation Among Underlying Issuer's Financial Condition**—Most investors do not, but unequivocally should, differentiate between the financial condition of issuers. The stronger the issuer, the lower the probability that the issuer bankruptcy problem arises. Therefore, within the mortgage-backed bond universe, a higher market value should be attached to mortgage-backed bonds issued by financially stronger than financially weaker thrifts. For example, mortgage-backed bonds issued by investment grade thrifts such as Bowery Savings Bank (now owned by H.F. Ahmanson & Co.), California Federal, Great Western Financial and Sears

Savings should trade at premiums over noninvestment grade rated thrifts. *This gives investors the opportunity to improve credit quality and maintain yield.*

**4) Relative Value of Defeasance versus Traditional Structure**—For a given level of interest rates and assuming all other characteristics are identical, the relative value of defeasance versus traditional mortgage-backed bonds changes as the issuer nears insolvency. When a thrift becomes insolvent, FSLIC, as receiver, can either act in accordance with the indenture, or take actions which are contrary to the indenture. Assuming that the FSLIC will strive to preserve the orderliness of the mortgage-backed bond market by adhering to the indenture's provisions, the following relationships should prevail:

**A defeasance bond should outperform a traditional bond when its yield drops below its coupon.** Defeasance bonds will trade at a higher premium over par because if the issuer becomes insolvent, the bonds will be defeased instead of redeemed at par, as would be the case for traditional bonds.

**A traditional bond should outperform a defeasance bond when its yield rises above its coupon.** Traditional bonds will not trade at as large a discount as the defeasance bonds because traditional bonds will be called at par instead of being defeased when the issuer becomes insolvent.

## V. SUMMARY

We believe that mortgage-backed bonds represent an excellent value in today's market. The combination of a triple-A level of credit protection with spreads which are comparable to single-A credits affords investors the opportunity to increase portfolio yields without sacrificing credit quality, or to increase credit quality without sacrificing yield. By differentiating between issuers and/or structures, investors can select issues which best meet their investment objectives.

## APPENDIX A

### Description of Eligible Collateral

**AMBS**—Agency Mortgage-Backed Securities. AMBS that currently qualify as eligible collateral must evidence proportional undivided interests in specified pools of level payment or graduated payment (if past the graduated payment period) fixed, variable or adjustable rate, fully amortizing mortgage loans secured by one- to four-family residences. Presently, there are three types of allowable agency mortgage-backed securities:

- GNMA "fully modified" mortgage pass-through certificates. The full and timely payment of principal and interest on each GNMA Certificate is backed by the full faith and credit of the United States.
- FNMA Guaranteed Mortgage-Backed Securities. FNMA Certificates represent fractional undivided interests in a pool of mortgage loans purchased by the Federal National Mortgage Association. FNMA guarantees that it will make timely distribution of scheduled principal and interest payments. The Certificates are guaranteed solely by FNMA and are not backed by, nor entitled to, the full faith and credit of the United States.
- FHLMC Mortgage Participation Certificates. FHLMC Certificates represent undivided interests or participation interests in specified pools of mortgage loans purchased by the Federal Home Loan Mortgage Corporation. FHLMC guarantees the timely payment of interest and the ultimate payment of principal (not backed by, nor entitled to, the full faith and credit of the United States).

MM—Money Market Securities, Government Securities and Cash

- Government Securities: must be direct obligations of the United States that are not callable by the U.S. Government at any time prior to the stated maturity of the bonds.
- Money Market Securities: short-term obligations of commercial banks with short-term ratings of A-1+/P-1 and long-term ratings of at least Aa3 (if the mortgage-backed bond has been rated by Moody's). Money Market Securities have remaining terms to maturity of 90 days or less when they are pledged as collateral and include certain demand deposits, Federal Funds, certificates of deposit and repurchase agreements.
- Cash: Coin or currency of the United States.

WL—Whole Loans and Eligible Mortgage Notes. Whole loans are mortgages which are not guaranteed or insured by any governmental body, agency or authority (conventional mortgages). Under Moody's and Standard & Poor's criteria, whole loans must conform to several standards, including the following characteristics: 1) must be level pay and fully amortizing; 2) properties must be owner occupied, detached homes, and should be well dispersed throughout a strong and diverse economic area; 3) primary residence; 4) no more than 5% zip code representation; 5) mortgage balance is less than the FHLMC limit, but greater than $10,000; 6) Loan to Value at origination is less than 80%; 7) mortgages originated after 1977 are on FNMA/FHLMC documents; 8) mortgages pledged are representative of the pledgor's portfolio; 9) each mortgage has a remaining term to maturity of at least one year, as of each valuation date; and 10) no mortgage is more than 30 days delinquent. Subject to certain limitations, some loans with loan to value ratios of 90% may be allowed if they have primary mortgage insurance and some loans may be over the FHLMC loan limit. Other characteristics may be permitted or excluded subject to the specific offerings.

**PT**—Private Pass-Through Certificates.  A Private or Conventional Mortgage Pass-Through Certificate evidences a proportional undivided interest in specified pools of mortgage loans that are secured by one-to-four-unit residences. Each Certificate must be rated "Aa2" or better by Moody's and/or "AA" or better by Standard & Poor's.

**C**—Corporate Bonds.   Consist of corporate debt obligations registered with the SEC or FHLBB. The Bonds must be rated "B3" or better by Moody's and "B-" or better by Standard & Poor's. In addition, there are restrictions on the concentration of the industry type of issuer, issue amount, and rating category.

**CMO**—Collateralized Mortgage Obligations.   Eligible CMOs must be bonds which pay interest currently and are collateralized by GNMA, FNMA or FHLMC Certificates. Eligible CMOs must be rated Aaa by Moody's or AAA by Standard & Poor's.

## APPENDIX B

### *Outstanding Mortgage-Backed Bond Issues*

The following table presents a list of outstanding mortgage-backed bond issues and their corresponding characteristics. The table separates the bonds by structure type, i.e. traditional or defeasance, and divides these into the following three types based on the types of collateral which are eligible. These categories are:

**Type A** The indentures permit only agency mortgage-backed securities and money market certificates and specifically *exclude* one or more of the following: whole loans, private pass-through certificates, CMOs or corporate securities.

**Type B** The indentures allow only agency mortgage-backed securities and money market certificates. Other types of collateral are not explicitly excluded and may be included as "new eligible collateral" subject to rating agency considerations.

**Type C** These indentures allow agency mortgage-backed securities, money market certificates and explicitly permit the inclusion of one or more of the following: whole loans, private pass-through certificates or CMOs.
   A table of collateralized medium-term note programs and their corresponding collateral characteristics is also included.

## APPENDIX B (continued)
## OUTSTANDING MORTGAGE-BACKED BOND ISSUES ($50 million or larger, as of 4/25/88)

| Issuer | Offer Date | Princip. $Mils | Coupon (%) | Years Mat. | Ratings Moody/S&P | Collateral Eligibility(1) Eligible: | Collateral Eligibility(1) Excluded: | Optional Call | Put Option Date | Collat. Valu-ation(2) | Mark Period | Cure (Days) | Trustee |
|---|---|---|---|---|---|---|---|---|---|---|---|---|---|
| *Traditional: Type A* | | | | | | | | | | | | | |
| Franklin Savings - KS (REALS) | 21-Jan-88 | 170 | Floats | 20 | Aaa/AAA | AMBS,MM | WL | NCL | | TST | Weekly | 2 | IBJ Schroder B&T |
| *Traditional: Type B* | | | | | | | | | | | | | |
| Florida Federal Int'l Fin | 03-Jun-79 | 100 | 12.375 | 5 | Aaa/AAA | AMBS,MM | CR | 6/15/88 (4) | | IS | Weekly | 5 | Citibank |
| Franklin Savings - KS (EURO) | 11-Apr-85 | 100 | 11.625 | 5 | Aaa/AAA | AMBS,MM | CR | (3) | | TST | Weekly | 1 | IBJ Schroder B&T |
| Franklin Savings - KS (EURO) | 31-Jul-87 | 250 | 8.125 | 2 | Aaa/— | AMBS,MM | CR | (3) | | TST | Weekly | 2 | IBJ Schroder B&T |
| Franklin Savings - KS | 15-Mar-85 | 100 | 12.250 | 7 | Aaa/AAA | AMBS,MM | CR | NCL | | TST | Weekly | 1 | IBJ Schroder B&T |
| Gibraltar Savings (EURO) | 12-Nov-85 | 115 | 10.875 | 7 | Aaa/AAA | AMBS,MM | CR | (3) | | IS | Monthly | 11 | Citibank |
| Guardian Savings & Loan Assoc | 19-Apr-85 | 100 | Floats | 10 | Aaa/AAA | AMBS,MM | CR | 6/28/90 | | IS | Monthly | 30 | Irving Trust |
| Home Owners Federal S&L | 08-Oct-87 | 100 | 10.250 | 5 | Aaa/— | AMBS,MM | | NCL | | IS | Weekly | 6 | F.N.B. Boston |
| Imperial Savings Association | 13-Aug-86 | 450 | 8.000 | 8 | Aaa/AAA | AMBS,MM | CR | NCL | 8/15/94 | TST | Monthly | 10 | Citibank |
| Imperial Savings Association | 31-Jul-86 | 300 | 8.500 | 10 | Aaa/AAA | AMBS,MM | CR | NCL | | TST | Monthly | 10 | Citibank |
| Leader Federal | 20-Dec-84 | 100 | 10.875 | 7 | Aaa/AAA | AMBS,MM | | NCL | 1/1/89 | IS | Bi-Monthly | 6 | Citibank |
| Roosevelt Federal S&L | 25-Feb-87 | 200 | 7.375 | 5 | —/AAA | AMBS,MM | | NCL | | IS | Weekly | 2 | Citibank |
| Santa Barbara Savings and Loan | 12-Feb-87 | 150 | 7.450 | 5 | Aaa/— | AMBS,MM | CR | NCL | | TST | Daily | 3 | Citibank |
| Santa Barbara Savings and Loan | 02-Dec-86 | 100 | 7.625 | 7.1 | Aaa/— | AMBS,MM | CR | NCL | 1/1/94 | TST | Daily | 6 | Citibank |
| Santa Barbara Savings and Loan | 17-Nov-86 | 100 | 7.750 | 10.1 | Aaa/— | AMBS,MM | CR | NCL | | TST | Daily | 8 | Citibank |
| Santa Barbara Savings and Loan | 05-Feb-87 | 300 | 8.000 | 10 | Aaa/— | AMBS,MM | CR | 6/30/92 | | TST | Daily | 3 | Citibank |

(1) Collateral Types:

AMBS - Agency Mortgage-Backed Securities i.e. GNMA, FNMA, FHLMC.

MM - Money Market Securities, Government Securities and Cash.

WL - Whole Loans and Eligible Mortgage Notes secured by conventional mortgages.

PT - Private Pass-Through Certificates, rated AA or better.

C - Corporate Bonds specifically excluded by indenture provision.

CR - Corporate Bonds effectively prohibited because of rating agency criteria prohibiting introduction of corporate bonds as collateral for bonds issued before certain dates (January, 1987 for S&P; September, 1987 for Moody's).

CMO - Collateralized Mortgage Obligations.

Unless specifically excluded, other collateral would be eligible subject to the rating agencies' determination that such collateral would not result in a rating downgrade.

See Appendix A for a more complete description of collateral types.

(2) Collateral Valuation Test conducted by Issuer (IS) subject to semi-annual reviews by independent auditor or Trustee (TST); information from trustee.

(3) Bonds may be optionally redeemed in whole at any time at par if issuer becomes subject to tax law changes.

(4) Issuer has announced its intention to call the bonds on May 15, 1988.

**APPENDIX B (continued)**

**OUTSTANDING MORTGAGE-BACKED BOND ISSUES ($50 million or larger, as of 4/25/88)**

*Traditional: Type C*

| Issuer | Offer Date | Princip. $Mills | Coupon (%) | Years Mat. | Ratings Moody/S&P | Collateral Eligibility(1) Eligible: | Excluded: | Optional Call | Put Option Date | Collat. Valuation(2) | Mark Period | Cure (Days) | Trustee |
|---|---|---|---|---|---|---|---|---|---|---|---|---|---|
| Bowery Savings Bank | 21-Apr-83 | 100 | 10.625 | 5 | —/AAA | AMBS,MM,WL,PT | CR | NCL | | IS | Quarterly | 45 | Bankers Trust |
| CenTrust Savings Bank | 11-Apr-88 | 100 | Floats | 3 | Aaa/— | AMBS,MM,PT,CMO | WL,C | 11/1/89 | | IS | Bi-Weekly | 3 | Wilmington Trust |
| Century Federal Savings & Loan | 10-Apr-85 | 50 | 11.750 | 7 | Aaa/AAA | AMBS,MM,WL | CR | NCL | 4/1/90 | IS | Monthly | 28 | Bank of America |
| City Federal | 15-Sep-86 | 100 | 7.750 | 5 | Aaa/AAA | AMBS,MM,PT | CR | NCL | | IS | Monthly | 28 | Citibank |
| Community Federal S&L | 06-Sep-79 | 65 | 10.000 | 10 | Aaa/AAA | AMBS,MM,WL | CR | 9/1/86 | | IS | Semi-annual | 90 | St. Louis Union TR |
| Ensign Bank | 14-Nov-86 | 100 | 7.625 | 5 | Aaa/AAA | AMBS,MM,PT,WL | CR | NCL | 11/15/91 | IS | Monthly | 10 | Citibank |
| Fidelity Federal S&L | 08-Apr-87 | 100 | 8.500 | 10 | Aaa/— | AMBS,MM,WL | CR | NCL | | IS | Monthly | 15 | Bankers Trust |
| Fidelity Federal S&L | 12-Mar-85 | 100 | Floats | 10 | Aaa/AAA | AMBS,MM,WL,PT | CR | 4/1/90 | | IS | Monthly | 20 | First Interstate |
| First Federal S&L - Arizona | 25-Jul-80 | 50 | 11.750 | 10 | —/AAA | AMBS,MM,WL | CR | 7/15/87 | | IS | Quarterly | 15 | Manufacturers HT, CA |
| Florida Federal (EURO) | 20-Jun-85 | 100 | Zero | 10 | Aaa/AAA | AMBS,WL | CR | (3) | | IS | Weekly | 5 | Citibank |
| Franklin Savings - KS | 04-Feb-85 | 200 | 8.000 | 9.9 | Aaa/— | AMBS,MM,CMO | CR | 6/30/92 | | TST | Weekly | 2 | IBJ Schroder B&T |
| Franklin Savings - KS | 08-Apr-88 | 100 | Floats | 15 | Aaa/AAA | AMBS,MM,CMO | WL,C(5) | NCL | 7/15/91 | TST | Weekly | 2 | IBJ Schroder B&T |
| Gibraltar Savings | 02-Aug-79 | 100 | 9.500 | 10 | Aaa/— | AMBS,WL | CR | NCL | 8/1/88 | IS | Semiannual | 5 | Union Bank, CA |
| Glendale Federal | 03-Jun-79 | 100 | 9.350 | 10 | Aaa/AAA | AMBS,WL | CR | NCL | | IS | Semiannual | 30 | Bank of America |
| Great Lakes Federal | 01-Jul-85 | 100 | 10.125 | 5 | Aaa/AAA | AMBS,MM,WL | CR | NCL | | IS | Monthly | 5 | N.B. of Detroit |
| Great Western Savings & Loan | 01-Oct-77 | 100 | 7.800 | 12 | —/AAA | AMBS,WL | CR | NCL | 1/11/88 | IS | Semiannual | 20 | Bank of America |
| HomeOwners Federal S&L | 14-Aug-87 | 50 | 8.750 | 5 | Aaa/— | AMBS,MM,WL | CR | NCL | | IS | Weekly | 8 | F.N.B. Boston |
| HomeOwners Federal S&L | 22-Oct-84 | 60 | 12.350 | 5 | —/AAA | AMBS,MM,WL,PT | CR | NCL | | IS | Weekly | 8 | F.N.B. Boston |
| HomeOwners Federal S&L | 23-Apr-87 | 75 | 8.625 | 5 | Aaa/— | AMBS,MM,WL | CR | NCL | | IS | Weekly | 8 | F.N.B. Boston |
| HomeOwners Federal S&L | 11-Feb-87 | 75 | 7.500 | 5 | Aaa/— | AMBS,MM,WL | CR | NCL | | IS | Weekly | 8 | F.N.B. Boston |
| HomeOwners Federal S&L | 13-Nov-86 | 80 | 7.750 | 5 | Aaa/— | AMBS,MM,WL | CR | NCL | | IS | Weekly | 8 | F.N.B. Boston |
| Imperial Savings Association | 24-Sep-87 | 100 | 9.375 | 3 | Aaa/AAA | AMBS,MM,C,PT | | NCL | | IS | Bi-Weekly | 5 | Chemical Bank |
| Metropolitan Federal Savings | 22-May-85 | 100 | 10.375 | 5 | Aaa/AAA | AMBS,MM,WL | CR | NCL | | IS | Monthly | 5 | F.N.B. Minneapolis |
| Nevada Savings & Loan | 11-Feb-87 | 100 | 8.125 | 9.9 | —/AAA | AMBS,MM,PT | | 6/30/92 | | IS | Monthly | 20 | Mellon Bank |
| Philadelphia Savings Fund | 08-Nov-84 | 225 | 12.000 | 6 | Aaa/AAA | AMBS,MM,WL,PT | CR | NCL | 11/15/90 | IS | Monthly | 5 | Bankers Trust |
| Pima Savings & Loan | 11-Dec-84 | 100 | Floats | 10 | Aaa/AAA | AMBS,MM,WL,PT | CR | 12/1/91 | | IS | Monthly | 20 | Valley Nat. Bk., Ariz. |
| Poughkeepsie Savings Bank | 17-Sep-85 | 75 | 10.500 | 5 | Aaa/AAA | AMBS,MM,WL | CR | NCL | 10/1/90 | IS | Monthly | 14 | IBJ Schroder B&T |
| Sears Savings Bank | 14-May-85 | 100 | 10.800 | 5 | Aaa/— | AMBS,MM,WL,PT,C | | NCL | | IS | Monthly | 30 | Union Bank |
| Sears Savings Bank | 12-Jun-85 | 50 | 10.000 | 5 | Aaa/— | AMBS,MM,WL,PT,C | | NCL | | IS | Weekly | 30 | Union Bank |
| Society for Savings (EURO) | 14-Feb-85 | 75 | 11.375 | 5 | Aaa/— | AMBS,MM,WL,PT | CR | (3) | | IS | Monthly | 15 | Citibank |
| Sun Savings & Loan Assoc-ME | 10-Jul-86 | 100 | 8.250 | 10 | Aaa/— | AMBS,MM,WL | CR | NCL | 2/1/91 | IS | Weekly | 8 | F.N.B. Boston |
| Transohio Savings Bank | 30-Jan-86 | 75 | 9.250 | 5 | Aaa/AAA | AMBS,MM,WL | CR | NCL | | IS | Monthly | 30 | AmeriTrust Co. |

| Transohio Savings Bank | 18-Jul-85 | 75 | 10.125 | 5 | Aaa/AAA | AMBS,MM,WL | CR | NCL | 8/1/90 | IS | Monthly | 30 | AmeriTrust Co. |
| Valley Federal Savings & Loan | 12-Jun-80 | 50 | 11.000 | 10 | —/AAA | AMBS,MM,WL | CR | 6/15/87 | | IS | Bi-Monthly | 30 | Valley & Union Bank |
| Washington Mutual Savings Bank | 16-Aug-79 | 50 | 9.700 | 10 | Aaa/AAA | AMBS,MM,WL | CR | 7/31/86 | | IS | Semiannual | 30 | Pacific N.B. of WA |

(1) Collateral Types:

AMBS - Agency Mortgage-Backed Securities i.e. GNMA, FNMA, FHLMC.

MM - Money Market Securities, Government Securities and Cash.

WL - Whole Loans and Eligible Mortgage Notes secured by conventional mortgages.

PT - Private Pass-Through Certificates, rated AA or better.

C - Corporate Bonds.

CR - Corporate Bonds effectively prohibited because of rating agency criteria prohibiting introduction of corporate bonds as collateral for bonds issued before certain dates (January, 1987 for S&P; September, 1987 for Moody's).

CMO - Collateralized Mortgage Obligations.

Unless specifically excluded, other collateral would be eligible subject to the rating agencies' determination that such collateral would not result in a rating downgrade. See Appendix A for a more complete description of collateral types.

(2) Collateral Valuation Test conducted by Issuer (IS) subject to semi-annual reviews by independent auditor or Trustee (TST); information from trustee.

(3) Bonds may be optionally redeemed in whole at any time at par if issuer becomes subject to tax law changes.

(5) Non-investment grade corporate bonds.

# APPENDIX B (continued)
## OUTSTANDING MORTGAGE-BACKED BOND ISSUES ($50 million or larger, as of 4/25/88)

| Issuer | Offer Date | Princip. $Mils | Coupon (%) | Years Mat. | Ratings Moody/S&P | Collateral Eligibility(1) Eligible: | Excluded: | Optional Call | Put Option Date | Collat. Valuation(2) | Mark Period | Cure (Days) | Trustee |
|---|---|---|---|---|---|---|---|---|---|---|---|---|---|
| **Defeasance (9): Type A** | | | | | | | | | | | | | |
| CenTrust Savings Bank | 16-Oct-87 | 100 | 10.000 | 10 | —/AAA | AMBS,MM | C,WL,PT | NCL | 10/27/92 | IS | Bi-Weekly | 2 | Wilmington Trust |
| East River Savings Bank | 29-Feb-88 | 100 | 8.375 | 5 | Aaa/— | AMBS,MM | C,WL,PT,CMO | NCL | | TST | Weekly | 5 | Bankers Trust |
| Franklin Savings - KS | 24-Feb-88 | 200 | 9.000 | 7 | Aaa/AAA | AMBS,MM | C,WL,PT | 3/15/92 | | TST | Weekly | 3 | IBJ Schroder B&T |
| Franklin Savings - KS | 05-Feb-88 | 150 | 9.500 | 30 | Aaa/— | AMBS,MM | C,WL,PT | 2/15/98 | | TST | Weekly | 3 | IBJ Schroder B&T |
| HomeOwners Federal S&L | 08-Oct-87 | 100 | 10.000 | 10 | Aaa/— | AMBS,MM | C,WL,PT | NCL | 10/27/92 | TST | Weekly | 6 | F.N.B. Boston |
| Roosevelt Federal | 06-Apr-88 | 100 | 10.125 | 30 | —/AAA | AMBS,MM | C,WL,PT,CMO | 4/15/98 | | TST | Weekly | 4 | Citibank |
| San Francisco Federal S&L | 10-Nov-87 | 100 | 10.375 | 10 | Aaa/— | AMBS,MM | C | 11/17/92 | | TST | Weekly | 3 | Security Pacific |
| Transohio Savings Bank | 28-Aug-87 | 75 | 9.200 | 5 | Aaa/— | AMBS,MM | WL,PT | 9/5/90 | | TST | Weekly | 4 | IBJ Schroder B&T |
| **Defeasance (9): Type B** | | | | | | | | | | | | | |
| Albuquerque Federal S&L | 02-Oct-87 | 100 | 9.375 | 3 | Aaa/— | AMBS,MM | | 10/15/89 | | TST | Weekly | 4 | Security Pacific |
| CenTrust Savings Bank | 05-Feb-88 | 100 | 8.500 | 30 | Aaa/AAA | AMBS,MM | | NCL | 2/15/93,98 | IS | Bi-Weekly | 3 | Wilmington Trust |
| Columbia Savings and Loan | 02-Nov-87 | 150 | 8.700 | 3 | Aaa/— | AMBS,MM | | NCL | | TST | Weekly | 3 | Security Pacific |
| Columbia Savings and Loan | 30-Sep-87 | 125 | 9.500 | 4 | Aaa/— | AMBS,MM | | 10/15/89 | | TST | Weekly | 3 | Security Pacific |
| Columbia Savings and Loan | 01-Sep-87 | 125 | 9.850 | 10 | —/AAA | AMBS,MM | | 9/15/92 | | TST | Weekly | 3 | Security Pacific |
| First Indiana Bank | 04-Aug-87 | 50 | 9.500 | 7 | Aaa/— | AMBS,MM | CR | NCL | | TST | Weekly | 1 | Citibank |
| Franklin Savings - KS | 14-Nov-84 | 500 | Zero | 40 | Aaa/AAA | AMBS,MM | CR | NCL | | TST | Weekly | 1 | IBJ Schroder B&T |
| Franklin Savings - KS | 14-Nov-84 | 1600 | Zero | 32 | Aaa/AAA | AMBS,MM | CR | NCL | | TST | Weekly | 1 | IBJ Schroder B&T |
| Franklin Savings - KS | 14-Nov-84 | 800 | Zero | 30 | Aaa/AAA | AMBS,MM | CR | NCL | | TST | Weekly | 1 | IBJ Schroder B&T |
| Franklin Savings - KS | 4-Jun-85 | 100 | 10.375 | 7 | Aaa/AAA | AMBS,MM | CR | NCL | | TST | Weekly | 1 | IBJ Schroder B&T |
| Roosevelt Federal S&L | 17-Jul-87 | 200 | 8.250 | 3 | Aaa/— | AMBS,MM | CR | NCL | | TST | Weekly | 4 | Citibank |
| Roosevelt Federal S&L | 26-Feb-88 | 100 | 9.000 | 10 | Aa2/AAA | AMBS,MM | | NCL | | TST | Weekly | 3 | Citibank |
| Santa Barbara Savings and Loan | 17-Jun-87 | 100 | 8.750 | 5 | Aaa/AAA | AMBS,MM | CR | NCL | | TST | Weekly | 3 | Citibank |
| Transohio Savings Bank | 01-Mar-88 | 100 | 8.350 | 5.2 | Aaa/— | AMBS,MM | | NCL | | TST | Weekly | 4 | IBJ Schroder B&T |

## Defeasance (6): Type C

| | | | | | | | | | | | | |
|---|---|---|---|---|---|---|---|---|---|---|---|---|
| ComFed Savings Bank | 30-Oct-87 | 100 | 9.350 | 5 | Aaa/— | AMBS,MM,WL,PT | C | NCL | IS | Weekly | 3 | Conn. Nat. Bank |
| Seaman's Mortgage Finance Inc. | 24-Sep-87 | 200 | 9.750 | 5 | Aaa/— | AMBS,MM,PT | | | TST | Weekly | 3 | Delaware Trust |
| Seaman's Mortgage Finance Inc. | 08-Apr-88 | 250 | 8.875 | 5 | Aaa/— | AMBS,MM,PT | C | NCL | TST | Weekly | 3 | Wilmington Trust |

(1) Collateral Types:

AMBS - Agency Mortgage-Backed Securities i.e. GNMA, FNMA, FHLMC.
MM - Money Market Securities, Government Securities and Cash.
WL - Whole Loans and Eligible Mortgage Notes secured by conventional mortgages.
PT - Private Pass-Through Certificates, rated AA or better.
C - Corporate Bonds.
CR - Corporate Bonds effectively prohibited because of rating agency criteria prohibiting introduction of corporate bonds as collateral for bonds issued before certain dates (January, 1987 for S&P; September, 1987 for Moody's).
CMO - Collateralized Mortgage Obligations.

Unless specifically excluded, other collateral would be eligible subject to the rating agencies' determination that such collateral would not result in a rating downgrade. See Appendix A for a more complete description of collateral types.

(2) Collateral Valuation Test conducted by Issuer (IS) subject to semi-annual reviews by independent auditor or Trustee (TST); information from trustee.

(3) Bonds may be optionally redeemed in whole at any time at par if issuer becomes subject to tax law changes.

(6) Defeasance type bonds also called TERMS (Top Efficiency Reliable Maturity Security) when underwritten by Salomon Brothers Inc.

## APPENDIX B (continued)
## SELECTED COLLATERALIZED MEDIUM-TERM NOTE PROGRAMS

| Issuer | Initial Offer Date | Amount $Mils | Ratings Moody/S&P | Dealers | Collateral Eligibility(1) Eligible: | Collateral Eligibility(1) Excluded: | Mark Period | Cure Days | Trustee |
|---|---|---|---|---|---|---|---|---|---|
| **Traditional:** | | | | | | | | | |
| Sears Savings Bank | 5/13/85 | 250 | Aaa/AAA | DWR,GS | AMBS,MM,WL,PT,C* | | Monthly | 30 | Union Bank |
| California Federal Savings | 11/1/85 | 500 | Aaa/AAA | MLCM | AMBS,MM,WL,PT | CR | Monthly | 20 | Citibank |
| Carteret Savings | 1/22/86 | 200 | Aaa/AAA | MLCM,FBC | AMBS,MM | WL,PT | Monthly | 15 | Citibank |
| Pacific First Federal | 5/28/86 | 250 | Aaa/AAA | MLCM, SAL | AMBS,MM | CR | Monthly | 20 | Citibank |
| Santa Barbara Savings | 7/22/86 | 500 | Aaa/AAA | FBC,BSC,GS | AMBS,MM | CR | Daily | 6 | Citibank |
| South Boston Savings Bank | 9/22/86 | 100 | Aaa/AAA | MLCM | AMBS,MM | CR | Quarterly | 20 | F.N.B. Boston |
| California Federal Savings | 10/30/86 | 500 | Aaa/AAA | MLCM, FBC | AMBS,MM,WL | CR | Monthly | 20 | Citibank |
| Alabama Federal Savings & Loan | 7/24/87 | 200 | Aaa/AAA | LBS,FBC | AMBS,MM,PT | CR | Monthly | 3 | Citibank |
| Imperial Savings Association | 11/13/87 | 500 | Aaa/AAA | DBL,GS,MLCM,MS | AMBS,MM,PT,C | | Semi-Monthly | 5 | Chemical |
| Citizens Federal Savings & Loan | 1/14/88 | 150 | Aaa/AAA | MLCM, DBL,GS | AMBS,MM,WL,C* | | Monthly | 20 | SoutheastBank |
| **Defeasance:** | | | | | | | | | |
| Leader Federal Savings & Loan | 8/5/87 | 200 | Aaa/AAA | GS,FBC | AMBS,MM | | Weekly | 6 | Citibank |

(1) Collateral Types:
- AMBS - Agency Mortgage-Backed Securities i.e. GNMA, FNMA, FHLMC.
- MM - Money Market Securities, Government Securities and Cash.
- WL - Whole Loans and Eligible Mortgage Notes secured by conventional mortgages.
- PT - Private Pass-Through Certificates, rated AA or better.
- C - Corporate Bonds.
- C - Corporate Bonds rated AA or better.
- CR - Corporate Bonds effectively prohibited because of rating agency criteria prohibiting introduction of corporate bonds as collateral for bonds issued before certain dates (January, 1987 for S&P; September, 1987 for Moody's).
- CMO - Collateralized Mortgage Obligations.

Unless specifically excluded, other collateral would be eligible subject to the rating agencies' determination that such collateral would not result in a rating downgrade. See Appendix A for a more complete description of collateral types.

# Senior-Subordinated Mortgage Pass-Throughs

Anand K. Bhattacharya, Ph.D.
Director of Financial Strategies
Security Pacific Merchant Bank

Peter J. Cannon
Rice University

## I. INTRODUCTION

One of the major financial innovations in the capital markets has been the securitization of assets. The process involves the transformation of assets into securities with appealing investment characteristics, such as creditworthiness, liquidity, and yields typically higher than comparable maturity Treasury securities. It provides the issuer with access to national and global capital markets. While the wave of securitization has permeated all sectors of the asset markets, such as mortgages, credit cards, automobile and mobile home loans, computer leases and home equity loans, the manifestation of the securitization process is most visible in the mortgage market. The need to attract investors traditionally committed to the Treasury and corporate markets has spawned a variety of new structures, such as stripped mortgage-backed securities, collateralized mortage obligations and mortgage-backed bonds which utilize a defeasance feature to reduce the level of over-collateralization.

Within the mortgage market, the thrust of securitization has centered on loans which meet underwriting criteria (the "conforming" loans) specified by the various programs of the Government National Mortgage Associaton (GNMA), Federal National Mortgage Association (FNMA) and Federal Home Loan Mortgage Corporation (FHLMC). The development of the secondary market for GNMA, FNMA, and FHLMC securities, combined with the explicit and implicit federal credit guarantees associated with these securities, has made them attractive candidates for inclusion in portfolios of traditional MBS investors. These include thrifts, as well as certain non-traditional investors such as pension funds, insurance companies and mutual funds. It is only recently that alternative structures have been developed which allow originators of mortgages which do not meet the underwriting criteria specified by these agencies (the "non-conforming" loans) to reap the advantages of securitization.

This article explores the mechanics of a popular vehicle for non-conforming mortgage loans, namely the senior-subordinated mortgage pass-through structure, where the subordinated portion of the structure is used to enhance the credit-worthiness of the senior portion. The senior-subordinated structure is also flexible enough to be utilized with other mortgage products, such as commercial mortgages, mobile home contracts and loans on multi-family housing, where credit enhancement may be required to improve investor appeal to the securities.

## II. CREDIT ENHANCEMENT ASSOCIATED WITH CONVENTIONAL PASS-THROUGHS

Mortgage pass-through securities are created when the lender pools mortgages and sells ownership interests in the pool. As payments from homeowners are received, the servicing institution "passes through" to security holders the interest portion as well as scheduled and unscheduled principal, less any servicing and guarantee fees.

Originators of conforming loans can choose from several alternatives in executing the securitization of mortgages.[1] Loans which are insured either by the Federal Housing Administration (FHA) or guaranteed by the Veterans Administration (VA) are eligible for pooling under the various programs of the Government National Mortgage Association (GNMA). FHA or VA fixed rate mortgages, graduated pay-

---

[1]See Kenneth H. Sullivan and Linda Lowell, "Mortgage Pass-Through Securities," Chapter 5 in *The Handbook of Mortgage-Backed Securites: Revised Edition*, Frank J. Fabozzi (ed.), (Chicago: Probus Publishing, 1988), for a complete description of the various alternatives for securitizing mortgages.

ment loans, growing equity mortgages, mobile home loans, as well as certain types of FHA/VA adjustable rate mortgages qualify for pooling under the GNMA guarantor programs. Since GNMA guarantees the full and timely payment of principal and interest, irrespective of the payment history of the underlying loans, the resultant securities are obligations of a U.S. government agency and hence appeal to credit quality-conscious investors.

Conventional loans which do not qualify for inclusion under GNMA programs can be securitized under the various programs of the Federal National Mortgage Association (FNMA) or the Federal Home Loan Mortgage Corporation (FHLMC). While these entities are not U.S. government-owned agencies, securities issued by both FNMA and FHLMC are perceived as negligible credit risks, mainly due to the presumed government guarantees associated with obligations of these agencies. The effect of the activities of these agencies has been to improve liquidity in the secondary mortgage market by providing credit enhancement for pools of mortgage loans. As a result, the intermediation function of the mortgage lenders has been tremendously facilitated since funds have been channelled from the capital markets to the primary mortgage market. These programs have also helped reduce mortgage rates.

However, for the originators of "non-conforming" loans, choices for accessing the capital markets are limited. At first blush, the nomenclature, "non-conforming" may indicate negative connotations associated with the credit quality of the loan. This is not always the case, as often mortgage loans may not conform to agency underwriting criteria because the original principal balance exceeds the government's prescribed limit, as exemplified by "jumbo" loans. Additionally, mortgages may not qualify for inclusion in the various GNMA, FNMA and FHLMC programs due to non-standard documentation or the nature of the underlying collateral. Previously, loans falling into this category were unable to be securitized or were securitized as conventional pass-through securities. The credit worthiness of these pass-throughs was often enhanced using external credit support devices, such as pool insurance or letters of credit. The more efficient senior-subordinated structure, however, now dominates the new issue market and is expected to account for a majority of the pass-throughs issued in the future. Usually, private label conventional mortgage pass-through securities are rated AA by Standard and Poor's and/or Aa by Moody's Investors Service.

Pool insurance has been a commonly used form of credit enhancement for securities backed by non-conforming loans. Note that this insurance is required in addition to the standard hazard insurance, flood insurance (if applicable) and private mortgage insurance on loans with high loan-to-value ratios. The credit protection provided by a pool insurance policy is heavily dependent on the rated claims paying capability of the insurer. Additionally, pool insurance may also have to be supplemented by additional hazard protection to include occurrences and disasters not covered by standard hazard insurance covenants. To meet these requirements, issuers of conventional mortgage pass-through securities have used either corporate guarantees from the parent company or obtained letters of credit from banks and insurance companies. However, as with pool insurance, the credit quality of the mortgage pass-throughs is directly related to the long-term credit rating of the issuing entity. When the credit rating of the mortgage pass-through is enhanced using a letter of credit from a financial institution, the cost may be prohibitive due to the limited number of providers of unconditional long-term letters of credit.

Although private label issuers have employed senior-subordinated participation as a means of credit enhancement for non-conforming loans, the tax status of trusts which issued such investments was in jeopardy in 1984, when the Internal Revenue Service (IRS) proposed taxation of trusts which actively managed investments. While several private entities have issued conventional pass-throughs, the size of this market is a fraction compared to the market for agency securities, perhaps due to thin secondary market trading, the prohibitive cost of credit enhancements, the unfamiliarity of investors with the product, and the lack of originators of nonconforming loans.[2]

However, recent regulatory pronouncements suggest that the size of this market can be expected to grow in the future, benefitting from the senior-subordinated structure as its most popular credit enhancement vehicle. In March 1986, the IRS clarified that senior-subordinated participations issued via a grantor trust would not be subject to double taxation. The Real Estate Mortgage Investment Conduit (REMIC) provision of the Tax Reform Act of 1986 added a further dimension of flexibility to senior-subordinated structures by permitting the subordinated interest to be sold instead of being retained by the issuer as a means of self insurance, as well as permitting greater flexibility in the issuance of multi-class transactions. The REMIC provision in the tax law also allows the issuing entity to be elected as a REMIC for tax purposes without sacrificing the tax advantages available to a grantor trust.

## III. THE SENIOR-SUBORDINATED STRUCTURE

The senior-subordinated structure is composed of two types of securities, namely, the senior pass-throughs (Class A) which are rated securities and the subordinated securities (Class B), which supply the credit enhancement for the senior pass-throughs. The size of the subordinated pass-through depends on the amount of credit support required to obtain an investment grade rating (usually AA) for the senior pass-throughs. The subordinate piece, which is not rated, is usually retained by the issuer. Recent AA rated pass-throughs issued as REMICs have also included a

---

[2]See Howard Altarescu, Erik Anderson, Michael Asay and Hal Hinkle, "The Conventional Mortgage Pass-Through Market," Chapter 8 in *The Handbook of Mortgage-Backed Securities: Revised Edition*, for a detailed description of the development of the conventional pass-through market.

residual class of securities. In the event a market develops for subordinated B class securities, they may be sold by the issuer and removed from the books.

These structures have also been labelled as "A/B Structures" or as an example "90/10", where the latter amount refers to the percentage of the mortgage pool which is subordinated to the interests of the holders of the senior pass-throughs. The issuer of the senior-subordinated structure has the option of either retaining or selling the subordinated portion of the structure. Payments are made to the holder(s) of the subordinated securities *only* if there is sufficient cash flow to make all senior pass-through payments.

## IV. DETERMINATION OF THE SUBORDINATED AMOUNT

Since the subordinated Class B securities serve as credit enhancement for the holders of the Class A certificates, the rating agencies determine the credit quality of the structure on the ability of the cash flows due to the holders of Class B certificates to meet Class A shortfalls arising on account of delinquencies and foreclosures. In this respect, the factors involved in determining the size of the subordinated piece are no different than determining the credit support required in a traditional pass-through utilizing an alternative credit enhancement vehicle, such as pool insurance.

The credit support for a senior-subordinated structure is determined by adjusting pre-established credit support guidelines for a representative sample of prime loans, labelled as benchmark pools for the attributes of the specific loan pools under consideration. A specific example provided in the appendix to this article determines the subordinated amount. In general, the process may be outlined as follows:[3]

1. The starting point for determining the level of the credit support required for a specific mortgage pool is to divide the pool among the six loan-to-value (LTV) groups listed below. Benchmark pools are as follows:

| Pool Number | LTV Range |
| --- | --- |
| Pool 1 | 91% to 95% |
| Pool 2 | 86% to 90% |
| Pool 3 | 81% to 85% |
| Pool 4 | 71% to 85% |
| Pool 5 | 61% to 70% |
| Pool 6 | 51% to 60% |

---

[3]This description relies heavily on the criteria used by Moody's Investor Services in rating mortgaged-backed securities collateralized by whole loans. The interested reader is referred to *Moody's Approach to Rating Whole Loan Mortgage-Backed Securities*, Moody's Investor Services, January 1987 for a more complete description of the process. While the approach used by Standard and Poor's is similar, see *Credit Review*, Standard and Poor's, October 19, 1987 for a description of S&P's approach to determining credit enhancement for non-conforming mortgage pools.

2. Each benchmark pool is composed of fixed rate, level payment, fully amortizing mortgages. The properties are owner occupied, single family residences and the weighted average coupon is 10%. Underwriting criteria of the mortgages conforms to FNMA/FHLMC guidelines and the mortgages are serviced by high quality servicers approved by these agencies. The residences securing these mortgages are well dispersed geographically in economically diverse communities. The mortgages also carry primary mortgage insurance (PMI) in the following amounts.

| LTV | PMI Level |
|-----|-----------|
| 95% | 20% |
| 90% | 15% |
| 85% | 10% |
| Below 80% | 0% |

3. The credit support for each benchmark pool is a function of the forecasted *foreclosure frequency* and the expected *severity of loss* percentage. The foreclosure frequency refers to the probability of default of the mortgages in the pool. The severity of loss measures the expected loss as a percentage of the loan balance and takes into account factors such as attributes of the loan (age, seasoning, LTV, adequacy of PMI, coupon rate), and delinquency and foreclosure costs. Benchmark credit support percentages are developed individually for different types of mortgage loans, such as 30-year loans, 15-year loans and bi-weekly mortgages.

4. The credit support for each banchmark loan pool is adjusted to reflect characteristics of the pools under consideration. In the case of adjustable rate mortgages, additional elements such as the volatility of the index and periodic and lifetime caps are also evaluated in addition to the following features of the mortgages.

**Size of the Pool:** The expected default ratio is adjusted for the size of the pool and the size of the mortgages composing the pool under the rationale that smaller pools of mortgages are more susceptible to losses than larger pools.

**Geographic Concentration:** The credit coverage is adjusted for skewed geographic concentration of the mortgages in the pool. This adjustment takes into account the vagaries of the economic base of the region(s) where the mortgages were originated. A similar adjustment is also made if there is undue concentration within certain postal zip codes.

**Quality of Servicing Agent:** Since the management of cash flows is a critical element in a senior-subordinated structure, the ability of the servicing agent to service the mortgages is also factored in the determination of the level of credit support required. The capabilities of the servicer with respect to collection and disbursement are specifically evaluated in determining the magnitude of this adjustment.

**Hazard Coverage:** In order to guard against hazards not specifically covered by standard insurance, adjustments are also made to the level of subordination in the event there is excessive concentration of mortgages in known hazard-prone geographic areas or zip codes.

**Mortgagor Delinquency:** In order to provide safeguards against short-term delinquencies, either cash must be deposited at the closing (the "initial deposit") of the transaction or a bankruptcy bond or a letter of credit may be obtained.

Given these guidelines, the process of determining the required level of subordination in a senior-subordinated structure requires stratification of the whole loan pool along various LTV categories. The "raw" benchmark credit support is determined as the weighted average of the credit support levels required for the various benchmark pools. If the actual pools exhibit variation along the attributes listed above, then the "raw" benchmark credit support should be adjusted to reflect these pool specific risks.

## V. ADDITIONAL LIQUIDITY SAFEGUARDS

While the credit protection provided by the subordinated piece may be considered sufficiently adequate, it is not a perfect substitute for other credit enhancement devices such as pool insurance or a letter of credit. In the event of default or foreclosure, other credit enhancement alternatives provide immediate coverage up to the limit protection. However, the ability of the subordinated cash flows to meet shortfalls in the senior class cash flow is limited by the balance in any fund created specifically for the purposes of such contingencies and any current cash flow due to the subordinated holders. In order to guard against such occurrences, liquidity safeguards in the form of a *reserve fund* or a *shifting interest* structure are used in senior-subordinated pass-through structures,

In a reserve fund structure, the holders of the subordinated securities give up the right to receive any cash flow until the reserve fund reaches a pre-specified balance. Once this level is attained, holders of the subordinated securities receive their prorata share of mortgage payments except in instances where such cash flow is required to make up shortfalls due to the senior security holders. The principal component of the cash flows due to the subordinated securities may also be interrupted to replenish the reserve fund when the reserve balance falls below a specified level. Alternatively, a shifting interest structure could also be used to cover contingencies in cash flow due to Class A security holders. Under this regime, holders of the subordinated class give up the right to receive future cash flow which is generated by mortgages having a current principal balance equal to the amount of the shortfall occurring in the senior cash flow. In other words, instead of subordinating their interests in current cash flow, holders of the subordinated securities give up the right to receive future cash flow. Not surprisingly, a majority of issuers of senior-subordinated structures have opted for the reserve fund alternative.

## VI. ACCOUNTING CONSIDERATIONS

The issuance of a senior-subordinated structure is considered a sale of assets, if the tenets specified in Statement of Financial Accounting Standards 77, *Transfer of Receivables with Recourses* are not violated. According to SFAS 77, an issuer may report the transaction as a sale if the following conditions are met.

- The issuer surrenders control of future economic benefits.
- The remaining obligations of the issuer to the buyer under recourse provisions can be reasonably estimated.
- The issuer cannot be required to repurchase the receivables from the buyer except in accordance with the provisions of the recourse arrangement. Additionally, the amount of such receivables to be repurchased pursuant to such provisions must be minimal.

Senior-subordinated transactions can be structured to meet all the tests specified in SFAS 77 since issuers do not have the option to repurchase the loans, losses can be estimated using historical evidence on foreclosure and loss severity, and repurchase obligations arise only due to technical deficiencies in the loans. Assuming that the requirements specified in SFAS 77 are not violated, the amount of Class A certificates is removed from the books of the issuer while the Class B amount is classified as an asset which bears the default risk of the senior class of the structure. In the event any excess servicing associated with the loans is part of the sale, the present value of the excess servicing stream, calculated at a realistic discount rate and prepayment expectation, is added to the sale price for the purposes of determining the total price on the sale of assets.

## VII. ADVANTAGES OF SENIOR-SUBORDINATE STRUCTURES

From the issuer's point of view, there are several advantages in using a senior-subordinated pass-through as a securitization vehicle.

**Disposition of Non-Conforming Whole Loans:** The retention of a subordinated interest in a pool of loans allows an issuer to create investment grade securities and access the capital markets by using collateral which otherwise would be sold in the whole loan market or as insured conventional pass-throughs. The issuer also obtains pricing advantages over unsecuritized whole loans. The senior class of certificates in the senior-subordinated structure is usually priced at lower spreads to corresponding Treasury securities, based on the average life of the mortgage pool, than unsecuritized whole loans.

**Efficient Credit Support:**  The "self-reliance" feature of senior-subordinated pass-throughs makes the vehicle an attractive alternative to credit enhancements obtained via pool insurance and letters of credit. In addition to insulating the senior class from vagaries in the credit rating of either the insurer or the provider of the letter of credit, the senior-subordinated structure also allows unrated entities to issue rated securities.

**Reduction of the Subordinated Amount:**  As the underlying mortgage pool becomes seasoned and exhibits a low frequency of foreclosures, the subordinated amount can be reduced. Currently, such reductions in the subordinated amount can be accomplished after the end of the fifth year for fixed rate collateral and after the end of the eleventh year for adjustable rate mortgage transactions.

## VIII. CONCLUDING COMMENTS

While the private label market has not exhibited the same level of growth as the market for agency mortgage-backed securities, there are indications that this market will expand in the future. Within this market, the senior-subordinated structure offers an efficient alternative to "self insuring" investment grade securities. Since these securities are not U.S. government obligations nor do they carry implicit federal guarantees, the yield associated with these securities is usually higher than agency securities. At the same time, investors are provided with a considerable degree of insulation from credit risk.

The sentiment that this market will grow considerably in the future is also echoed by industry observers. For instance, the share of the thrift industry in the market is expected to increase from 31% in 1987 to 65% in 1988.[4] The rationale for such deductions is based upon the belief that securitization of assets allows financial institutions to retain market share and generate fee income. Several other accounting and regulatory developments lend credence to this forecast. With the issuance of Statement of Financial Accounting Standards 91, *Accounting for Non-refundable Fees and Costs Associated with Originating or Acquiring Loans and Initial Direct Costs of Leases*, which requires financial institutions to defer loan fees over the life

---

[4]See "Moody's Finds Silver Lining in Nation's Thrift Woes," *Asset Sales Report*, June 27, 1988, page 5.

of the loan, securitization of loans, especially as a sale of assets, allows the institution to recognize income over a shorter period of time. Additionally, if risk-based capital guidelines currently under consideration are enacted for thrifts as well as banks, financial institutions may be able to reduce their capital requirements by improving the creditworthiness of their assets or expunging assets with lower credit quality from the balance sheet.

## APPENDIX
## SAMPLE CALCULATION OF THE LEVEL OF CREDIT SUPPORT REQUIRED TO OBTAIN DESIRED RATING FROM MOODY'S INVESTOR SERVICES

The whole loan pool contains 30-year original term, single family residences and resembles the prescribed benchmark pool except for the following LTV ratios:

| 95% LTV | 90% LTV | 85% LTV | 80% LTV | 70% LTV |
|---------|---------|---------|---------|---------|
| 10%     | 10%     | 30%     | 40%     | 10%     |

Deviations from the benchmark pools also include:

1. The pool contains 400 mortgages, 100 more than the benchmark.
2. 30% of the homes in the 80% LTV category exceeded Moody's prescribed state home value standard.
3. 10% of the homes in each LTV are valued above $700,000.
4. All of the homes are located in regions that rank strong in industry diversification.
5. 11.0% weighted average coupon, 1% higher than the benchmark.

Desired Rating: Aa
Calculations:
The Benchmark Weighted Average Level of Credit Support:

$$10\%(5.35) + 10\%(6.06) + 30\%(7.38) + 40\%(6.77) + 10\%(2.35) = 6.298\%$$

Adjustments:

1. 100 extra mortgages than benchmark pool:

$$10\% \ (-0.05) + 10\%(-0.05) + 30\%(-0.06) + 40\%(-0.08) + 10\%(-0.03) = -0.063\%$$

2. 30% of the homes in the 80% LTV category were above Moody's home standard:

$$30(40\%)(0.08) = +0.960\%$$

3. 10% of the homes in each LTV category exceeded \$700,000[5]:

$$10 [10\%(0.12) + 10\%(0.12) + 30\%(0.10) + 40\%(0.12) + \\ 10\%(0.09)] = +1.110\%$$

4. The loans in the pool are allocated in strong economic regions:

$$10\%(-0.62) + 10\% (-0.70) + 30\%(-0.75) + 40\%(-1.05) + \\ 10\%(-0.37) = -0.814\%$$

5. Pool has a 1% higher weighted average coupon than the benchmark pool:

$$10\%(0.69) + 10\%(0.70) + 30\%(0.68) + 40\%(0.73) + \\ 10\%(.50) = +0.616\%$$

Total Level of Credit Support structure, utilizing this pool of mortgages, the senior portion would be approximately 91.5% and the subordinated amount would be 8.5%.

---

[5]The adjustment coefficients are obtained from Moody's Investors Service, *Moody's Approach to Rating Whole Loan Mortgage-Backed Securities*, January 1987.

# Structured Arbitrage Transaction Analysis

STEVEN J. CARLSON
VICE PRESIDENT AND MANAGER
TRANSACTION STRATEGIES GROUP
SHEARSON LEHMAN HUTTON INC.

NIRMAL SINGH
VICE PRESIDENT
TRANSACTION STRATEGIES GROUP
SHEARSON LEHMAN HUTTON INC.

ERIC B. FIX
ASSOCIATE
TRANSACTION STRATEGIES GROUP
SHEARSON LEHMAN HUTTON INC.

## I. INTRODUCTION

The structured arbitrage transaction is by now a familiar asset/liability management strategy for banks and thrift institutions. These structured arbitrage transactions (SATs) constitute a balance sheet growth strategy whereby financial institutions

The authors wish to acknowledge the valuable comments and assistance of their colleagues: Jacques Rolfo, Joseph Hu, Ron Juster, Phil Erlanger, Ralph Schlosstein, Barrett Moore, Brent Anderson, Randy Stoller, and Phil Kim. Special thanks also go to Rob Appelbaum for his invaluable technical contribution, to Mary Parker and Suzanne Franks for painstaking editing, and to Tricia Brady for graphics work.

purchase assets in the capital markets with funding raised mainly through debt collateralized by the asset purchased. Then the assets are hedged using a combination of financial instruments. The assets are usually of superior credit quality, particularly mortgage security assets guaranteed by the U.S. Government (GNMAs) and other government-related agencies (FNMAs and FHLMCs). Because of low credit risk in SATs, investors need only manage their interest rate risk exposure.

Financial institutions are drawn to this type of growth activity as a way to leverage their capital base to generate additional income as net interest margin without incurring the overhead generally associated with traditional growth strategies. SATs also allow investors to control interest rate risk and limit additional credit risk exposure.[1] In broad terms, the goal of investing in SATs is to maximize return on the investment while maintaining acceptable levels of risk. Some investors, however, have based their decisions about SATs on incomplete performance measures and have failed to analyze the potential risks involved.

A review of SAT performance during 1986 and 1987 reveals less than satisfactory results, due in part to tight spreads between mortgage assets and financing costs, and to overhedging that resulted from that period's powerful market rally. The spread of the benchmark GNMA security to the 10-year swap and Treasury rates from January 1986 to December 1987 (see Exhibit 1) indicates the relative financing costs for SATs employing mortgage securities hedged by interest rate swaps. Spreads were relatively tight at the beginning of 1986 and in early 1987. However, the SAT's objective is not only to capture the initial spread available on any given trading day, but to devise a strategy that allows the investor to maintain an acceptable interest margin in spite of volatile interest rate environments.

This article describes an analytical framework for SAT simulation analysis. Section II provides an example of a SAT. For illustrative purposes, this section relies on a hypothetical SAT that roughly matches projected asset maturities with fixed-rate liabilities to explain the structured arbitrage concept.

Section III gives results for the sample SAT simulation. It also describes and evaluates performance measures employed in SAT simulation. The cash-based and effective margin spread measures are the most consistent indicators of performance. Book-based and some yield spread measures are more useful for accounting and regulatory purposes than for measuring financial performance.

Section IV uses a more complex transaction to describe the main pitfalls in simulating SATs, including performance sensitivity to prepayment rates, yield curve shape, margin calls, length of horizon, cyclical interest rate risk, and terminal asset value. In addition, it provides a brief discussion of rebalancing SATs, i.e., the regular adjustments to redress original errors in matching asset/liability (A/L) positions or to accommodate changes in originally well hedged positions.

---

[1]Thrift institutions are particularly drawn to the SAT analytical framework as a result of recent Federal Home Loan Bank Board proposals to change regulatory capital requirements. Increased emphasis on interest rate exposure and corresponding links between exposure and equity requirements imply the need for more systematic understanding and monitoring of asset/liability strategies.

**EXHIBIT 1**
**CURRENT COUPON GNMA, 10-YEAR SWAP AND 10-YEAR TREASURY YIELDS AND**
**SPREADS (WEEKLY DATA FROM JANUARY 1986 to DECEMBER 1987)**

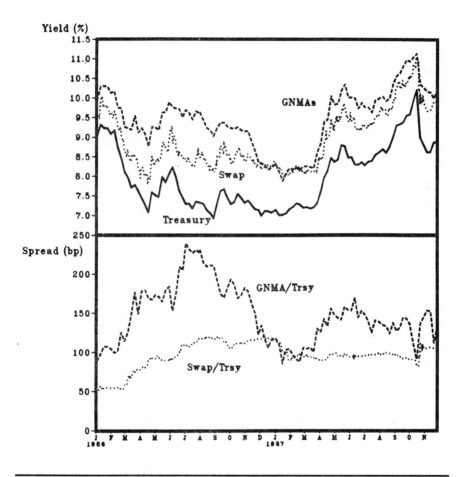

Source: Shearson Lehman Hutton Mortgage Securities.

Section V outlines seven achievable SAT performance profiles—long and short straddle positions, call- and put-like structures, straight bear and bull market plays, and stable returns. It also describes possible asset and liability combinations that can achieve these profiles. Conclusions and recommendations of the article constitute the final section. The article also has two appendixes: an overview of financial tools available for SATs, and a statement of the accounting conventions employed in the analysis.

## II. SAT BASICS

Structured arbitrage is a widely accepted growth strategy for leveraged financial institutions. Long-term assets are purchased through short-term borrowings which can then be converted to long-term financing at a fixed rate to lock in costs. Assets may also be used to hedge each other and assure stability in the transaction under a variety of interest rate scenarios. Arbitrage returns result from combining assets whose returns are higher than their borrowing costs. By entering into SATs, a thrift can earn the spread between the income on assets and the liability costs. Thus, the institutions's balance sheet grows significantly without the administrative costs normally associated with such expansion.

Exhibit 2 depicts a typical SAT. In step one, the hypothetical Leveraged Financial Institution (LFI) purchases $100 million of assets using funds made available by entering into a $94 million reverse repurchase (repo) agreement, and by adding the $6 million net investment required of the borrower. The repo agreement requires that the borrower overcollateralize the financing, in this case with $6 million. This overcollateralization (the haircut) is the net investment required to enter into a SAT (additional overcollateralization may be required in connection with interest rate swap agreements). In this context, the haircut can be viewed as an equity participation.[2] This strategy amounts to lending long (the mortgage asset) and borrowing short (the repos). In each period the reverse agreement is renewed (rolled over). The size of the renewed agreement is a function of market value and paydown of the asset. In a positive yield curve environment, high yielding assets are paid for with low cost, short-term floating rate liabilities (the reverse agreements). This investment strategy entails risk: if interest rates rise, the cost of funding can exceed the return on assets, resulting in poor performance.

Traditionally, investors have hedged this risk by synthetically extending the duration of their liabilities through interest rate swap agreements. In the swap, the borrower agrees to pay a fixed rate in return for a rate pegged to an index (usually 3-month LIBOR). LIBOR-based receipts over the horizon are expected to offset payments on the repos. Thus, the investor effectively extends the duration of his financing.

In the LFI example, a hypothetical structured arbitrage transaction begins on December 1, 1987 with LFI's purchase of a portfolio consisting of GNMA 10.5% pass-through securities. LFI's initial SAT balance sheet is shown in Exhibit 3. To hedge the interest rate risk in the mortgage portfolio, LFI matches the expected asset principal paydown with serially maturing interest rate swaps. The top of the exhibit lists assets of the GNMA portfolio. The bottom describes the liability structure,

---

[2]The required overcollateralization is the market-imposed leverage constraint. Investors may not wish to leverage as much as the market will allow and may maintain some lower leverage. If the financing does not require overcollateralization, the equity contribution is the allocation of capital, by the SAT investor, to the transaction. Equity is still the up-front cash infusion necessary to enter into the transaction. This equity is analogous to CMO equity.

**EXHIBIT 2**
**TYPICAL STRUCTURED ARBITRAGE TRANSACTION DYNAMICS FOR A LEVERAGED FINANCIAL INSTITUTION (LFI)**

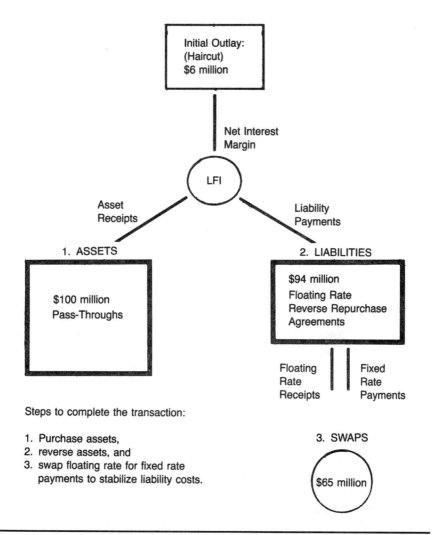

Steps to complete the transaction:

1. Purchase assets,
2. reverse assets, and
3. swap floating rate payments to stabilize liability costs.

Source: Shearson Lehman Hutton Mortgage Securities.

including the notional amount that has been swapped for fixed rates via medium- and long-term interest rate swap liabilities. Maturity matching in this context is an attempt to immunize spread income over the life of the transaction. The amount assigned to each swap maturity approximates the expected decline in the asset's principal value due to prepayments and principal amortization for that time horizon.[3]

**EXHIBIT 3**
**LFI SAT INITIAL BALANCE SHEET**

**Assets**

| Type | Coupon | Yield[a] | Mortgage Duration (Yrs.) | Price ($) | Face Amount ($000) | Market Value ($000) |
|---|---|---|---|---|---|---|
| GNMA | 10.50 | 10.17 | 4.32 | 102.25 | 97,800 | 100,000 |
| Avg/Total | | 10.17 | 4.32 | 102.25 | 97,800 | 100,000 |

**Liabilities**

| Type | Cost[b] | Maturity (Months) | Modified Duration[c] (Yrs.) | Swap Spread (BP) | Treasury Rate (%) | Notional Amount ($000)[d] |
|---|---|---|---|---|---|---|
| REPO | 8.00 | 3 | 0.25 | 0 | 0.00 | 29,132 |
| SWAP | 8.12 | 12 | 0.94 | 116 | 6.96 | 10,000 |
| SWAP | 8.67 | 24 | 1.80 | 93 | 7.74 | 10,000 |
| SWAP | 9.04 | 36 | 2.58 | 101 | 8.03 | 10,000 |
| SWAP | 9.32 | 48 | 3.28 | 101 | 8.31 | 5,000 |
| SWAP | 9.52 | 60 | 3.91 | 103 | 8.49 | 5,000 |
| SWAP | 9.82 | 84 | 4.98 | 104 | 8.78 | 10,000 |
| SWAP | 10.02 | 120 | 6.23 | 104 | 8.98 | 15,000 |
| Avg/Total | 8.86 | | 2.54 | | | 94,132 |

| *Initial Investment* | | | | | | 5,868 |
|---|---|---|---|---|---|---|

| Total Liabilities | | | | | | 100,000 |
|---|---|---|---|---|---|---|

[a] Semiannually compounded yield under projected prepayment rates.
[b] The fixed cost on the interest rate swaps excludes placement and credit intermediation fees that are typically paid by the fixed-rate payer.
[c] Swap duration computation assumes a hypothetical bond with a face amount equal to the notional amount and a coupon rate equal to the all-in cost.
[d] All assets are reversed with the notional repo amount representing the net quantity of liabilities not swapped.
Source: Shearson Lehman Hutton Mortgage Securities.

---

[3] The additional overcollateralization that is often required for interest rate swap agreements has been ignored in this example. However, interest rate swap agreement overcollateralization requirements can be included in the analysis.

**EXHIBIT 4**
**LFI MODIFIED MATURITY MATCHING WITH SWAPS UNDER THREE INTEREST RATE SCENARIOS**

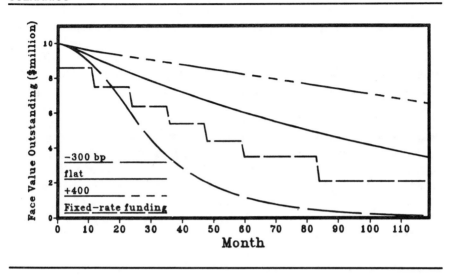

Exhibit 4 displays the A/L maturity structure of the sample transaction under alternative interest rate scenarios. Maturity matching techniques are widely used, but transactions can quickly become mismatched when SATs employ assets with embedded options, such as mortgage securities with valuable prepayment rights, especially current and premium mortgage pass-through securities. SATs with mortgage assets can become overhedged as rates fall and prepayments accelerate, decreasing the "duration" of the assets as the duration of the liabilities increases. Exhibit 4 shows this effect when interest rates drop 300 basis points. An asset with embedded options is often better hedged with financial instruments having option-like characteristics, or by duplicating the option characteristics through a dynamic hedging strategy. This would require frequent adjustments to the SAT throughout the investment horizon.

## III. SAT SIMULATION: PERFORMANCE MEASURES

This section describes and evaluates the simulation measures used to assess SAT performance characteristics. It also reports the SAT simulation performance measures for the LFI transaction. Finally, it provides performance statistics on an amended version of LFI's transaction—one that employs derivative mortgage assets to give greater stability to the simulation returns.

### *SAT Performance Measures*

Two types of performance measures can be used to evaluate structured arbitrage transactions, book-based and cash-based. Book-based measures are used principally for accounting and regulatory purposes (see Appendix B, "Accounting Fundamentals for MBS"); cash-based measures are better for evaluating the financial performance of a SAT. The two cash-based measures—return on investment (ROI) and internal rate of return (IRR)—and the yield spread measure of effective margin provide the best and most internally consistent indicators of investment performance.

**Book-Based Measures** Book-based profitability measures—return on assets (ROA), cumulative book income and book profit—do not provide SAT investors with sufficient information about the performance of the transaction. (ROA is the income booked each year divided by the average dollar-weighted annual book value of assets.) First, these measures do not recognize the time value of money; they ignore the fact that a dollar today is worth more than a dollar tomorrow. This defect can hamper comparisons of transactions, although time value is introduced to some degree in the reinvestment of cash proceeds over the horizon. Two transactions may be viewed as identical in absolute dollars earned, even though one has clearly superior cash flow timing.

A second difficulty is that the rigidity of accounting practices makes ROA, book profit, and some yield-based measures less valuable than their more comprehensive cash-based counterparts. For example, in cash-based analysis a premium paid for an option is recognized in the period it is purchased. Conversely, in book-based analysis, the premium cost is amortized over the life of the option.

A third limitation of book-based measures, particularly for ROA, is the failure to offer insight on the total return of the transaction; that is, the liquidation value of the remaining SAT asset/liability position is ignored.

**Cash-Based Measures** The cash-based measures, particularly ROI and IRR, are concerned with the true financial characteristics of the transaction. The IRR is the discount rate that equates net cash flows generated by the transaction with the initial SAT investment. Net cash flows are composed of dividends periodically doled out from net interest income, and a balloon payment at the end that values assets and liabilities at current market prices. Although conceptual kin, the ROI and IRR differ in their implicit reinvestment rates. Cash flows underlying the ROI are not paid out as dividends but accumulate at an explicit reinvestment rate. Theoretically, this rate should reflect the financial institution's investment opportunities in the given interest rate environment.

The ROI is similar to the conventional holding period return (HPR) measure.[4] As

---

[4]The HPR measure is often used in *ex post* analysis while the YTM is used in *ex ante* analysis. For present purposes, the HPR analysis is analogous to horizon analysis, an *ex ante* framework.

applied to security analysis used in modern portfolio theory, HPR incorporates returns from cash flows generated by the security, reinvestment of these interim cash flows to the horizon, and liquidation value at the sale of the security. On the other hand, IRR is similar to yield to maturity (YTM). The YTM measure does represent projections of total rate of return but under more restrictive assumptions. It assumes cash flows on the transaction are discounted without regard to actual reinvestment opportunities.

The future value orientation of the HPR/ROI measure, as opposed to the YTM/IRR's implied reinvestment, gives the ROI two positive features:

1. Reinvestments within an interest period occur at rates linked to the scenario, unlike IRR reinvestment. This feature is attractive for SAT strategies with a total return orientation.
2. The future value calculation implied by the ROI measure discounts cash flows as they are discounted in net present value (NPV) calculations. NPV allows for comparison of incremental opportunities by deriving a single number that can be ranked against all others. ROI inherits the robustness of this comparative approach.

**Yield Spread Measures** SAT scenario yield spread measures are perhaps the most widely used to judge performance. Though actual techniques vary, this type of measure should reflect the net effective interest margin over the scenario. Often SAT investors evaluate transactions based upon spread measures, e.g., asset yield less liability yield, and time- and dollar-weighted average spreads between asset income and liability costs. The spread measure employed here—the effective margin—goes beyond the other spread measures. For a given SAT, the scenario's effective margin is the yield spread that must be added to the financing cost in order to equal the asset return.[5] The effective margin can therefore be seen as the break-even asset financing spread of the SAT under the particular interest rate scenario. Viewed in this way, the effective margin is an extremely useful tool for assessing the relative merits of alternative A/L transactions.

**Cash- vs. Book-Based Measures** Publicly held financial institutions, particularly thrifts, often concentate on book-based ROA and certain spread-based measures.[6]

---

[5] The effective margin is the equivalent of the familiar yield-to-maturity (YTM) spread and discounted margin of the floating rate note (FRN) market. The two money market approaches—YTM spread and discounted margin—provide consistent results. The YTM spread is the standard relative value measure in the domestic-FRN market; the discounted margin is used in the Euro-FRN market. The same approach extends to the pricing of caps on floating rate securities, and underlies most industry models analyzing caps on adjustable rate mortgages and floating rate CMO bonds.

[6] Accounting principles influence financial decisions and income recognition because they are concerned with tax issues and tax-related arbitrage. Although the accountant's definition of earnings provides a standardized means of relaying information about a firm's profitability, these earnings may not always conform to real financial earnings.

This is motivated by the belief that stockholders focus on the difference between operating income and operating expenses, i.e., the spread, without regard for nonrecurring gains and losses. As a result, some investors argue that ROA measures give them all the information necessary to make an investment decision. Nonetheless, there are often assets and liabilities remaining on the books beyond the intended life of the transaction which are essentially ignored by the ROA approach.

Whether the investor plans to liquidate a position or carry it on the books, any remaining assets/liabilities have earnings implications. A reasonable indicator of the ongoing performance of an A/L position is its liquidation value. Failure to incorporate the terminal A/L impact in the analysis provides an incomplete evaluation of the transaction. The ROI, the IRR, and the effective margin together provide rigorous and internally consistent means of addressing the terminal A/L problem by giving a more complete picture of the simulated performance. Because spread measures (ROA and other yield spread measures) do not include this information, they leave out a critical component of thorough SAT analysis.

### The LFI Example

The performance of LFI's transaction under alternative interest rate scenarios is simulated under the following assumptions:

- interest rate phase-in of 100 basis points for each year;
- horizon of 120 months;
- prepayments at levels projected by a prepayment model;
- parallel yield curve shifts for interest rate movements;
- periodic reinvestment of cash in the transaction at the prevailing short-term interest rate (the reverse rate);
- pricing of remaining assets at the end of the horizon at yields consistent with the original spread to comparable weighted average life (WAL) Treasury securities under the scenario-specific prepayment projection; and
- no required additional overcollateralization as asset values decline, particularly in the rising interest rate scenarios, and vice versa (no margin calls).[7]

Exhibit 5 shows summary performance measures for the base case. These measures indicate that the transaction performs satisfactorily in the flat interest rate environment but deteriorates significantly in the rising and falling rate scenarios. This is primarily attributable to the call option embedded in the asset.

To achieve performance profiles that do not deteriorate, alternative hedging techniques must often be employed. LFI could reduce the variability of returns in the

---

[7]The analytical framework is a static one, i.e., the model examines the transaction's performance without requiring that the investor add collateral as asset values diminish or reduce collateral as asset values increase.

**EXHIBIT 5**
**LFI SAT SIMULATION RESULTS (BASE CASE ANALYSIS)**

| Interest Rate Chg. (bp) | Cash-Based Measures | | | Book-Based Measures | | | | Average Prepayment Assumptions (% PSA) |
|---|---|---|---|---|---|---|---|---|
| | ROI (%) | IRR (%) | Term. Net Position ($000) | Cumulative Book Income ($000) | ROA (%) | Profit ($000) | Effective Margin (%) | GNMA 10.5s |
| -300 | 2.09 | | 7,228 | 1,293 | 0.28 | 1,360 | 0.59 | 612 |
| -200 | 8.80 | | 13,889 | 7,723 | 1.55 | 8,021 | 0.80 | 426 |
| -100 | 13.56 | 27.91 | 21,797 | 15,221 | 2.51 | 15,929 | 1.24 | 265 |
| 0 | 15.62 | 29.27 | 26,405 | 20,195 | 2.67 | 20,537 | 1.28 | 157 |
| 100 | 14.83 | 25.63 | 24,537 | 20,396 | 2.40 | 18,669 | 0.90 | 100 |
| 200 | 11.90 | | 18,642 | 17,325 | 1.97 | 12,774 | 0.38 | 76 |
| 300 | 6.57 | | 11,203 | 13,025 | 1.47 | 5,335 | -0.17 | 63 |
| 400 | -9.15 | | 2,299 | 7,224 | 0.82 | -3,569 | -0.77 | 55 |

Common SAT Terms:

ROI = return on investment, the annual compounded growth rate of the initial net investment.

IRR = internal rate of return, the discount rate that equates the present value of the net future cash flow to the initial investment. Missing values result when mathematical computations provide either multiple-root or no solution due to sign changes in cash flows.

ROA = return on assets, the annual booked income divided by the average dollar-weighted annual book value of assets.

Effective margin = margin of assets over financing cost for the scenario.

Profit = spread income booked plus sale gain or loss.

Terminal net position = net position at the end of the horizon.

Note: Horizon period = 120 months.
Source: Shearson Lehman Hutton Mortgage Securities.

base case analysis by adding assets that enhance performance in falling and rising rate scenarios. Two such assets are principal only (PO) strips collateralized by current coupon GNMAs and interest only (IO) strips collateralized by high coupon pass-throughs (a more complete listing of available tools for SATs appears in Appendix A). The balance sheet for such a combination is displayed in Exhibit 6. As is shown in Exhibit 7, the variability in the performance measures across the interest

**EXHIBIT 6**
**AMENDED LFI SAT INITIAL BALANCE SHEET**

*Assets*

| Type | Coupon | Yield[a] | Mortgage Duration (Yrs.) | Price ($) | Face Amount ($000) | Market Value ($000) |
|------|--------|--------|--------|--------|--------|--------|
| GNMA | 10.50 | 10.17 | 4.32 | 102.25 | 73,350 | 75,000 |
| IO-strip | 11.00 | 9.78 | −25.44 | 47.00 | 21,277 | 10,000 |
| PO-strip | 10.00 | 8.17 | 22.22 | 52.50 | 28,571 | 15,000 |
| Avg/Total | | 9.83 | 4.03 | 81.17 | 123,198 | 100,000 |

*Liabilities*

| Type | Cost[b] | Maturity (Months) | Modified Duration[c] (Yrs.) | Swap Spread (BP) | Treasury Rate (%) | Notional Amount ($000)[d] |
|------|--------|--------|--------|--------|--------|--------|
| REPO | 8.00 | 3 | 0.25 | 0 | 0.00 | 27,885 |
| SWAP | 8.12 | 12 | 0.94 | 116 | 6.96 | 10,000 |
| SWAP | 8.67 | 24 | 1.80 | 93 | 7.74 | 10,000 |
| SWAP | 9.04 | 36 | 2.58 | 101 | 8.03 | 10,000 |
| SWAP | 9.32 | 48 | 3.28 | 101 | 8.31 | 5,000 |
| SWAP | 9.52 | 60 | 3.91 | 103 | 8.49 | 5,000 |
| SWAP | 9.82 | 84 | 4.98 | 104 | 8.78 | 10,000 |
| SWAP | 10.02 | 120 | 6.23 | 104 | 8.98 | 15,000 |
| Avg/Total | 8.87 | | 2.58 | | | 92,885 |

| | |
|---|---|
| Initial Investment | 7,115 |
| Total Liabilities | 100,000 |

[a] Semiannually compounded yield under projected prepayment rates.
[b] The fixed cost on the interest rate swaps excludes placement and credit intermediation fees that are typically paid by the fixed-rate payer.
[c] Swap duration computation assumes a hypothetical bond with a face amount equal to the notional amount and a coupon rate equal to the all-in cost.
[d] All assets are reversed with the notional repo amount representing the net quantity of liabilities not swapped.

Source: Shearson Lehman Hutton Mortgage Securities.

rate scenarios is reduced significantly. Balance sheets over time for selected scenarios are shown for this amended SAT in Exhibit 8. Exhibit 9 illustrates yearly net income earned on the transaction over its life for three interest rate scenarios.

This analysis provides a useful starting point for evaluating a prospective transaction. However, a more comprehensive understanding also involves analyzing the sensitivity of SAT performance to changes in the simulation assumptions and anticipating risks affecting the arbitrage and, therefore, the simulated performance.

## IV. KEY RISKS IN SAT EVALUATION

SAT investors face several risks. Volatility can significantly affect SATs that use securities with embedded options, particularly mortgage securities. Due to volatility, SAT investors must reexamine positions continuously and rebalance where and when appropriate. In the case of mortgage securities where investors implicitly write the call option to the borrower, volatility can have a negative impact. Credit is not a critical concern in SATs employing government-guaranteed assets, but it is important with corporate bonds and other unsecured assets, including interest rate caps and floors. Swaps, repos, and other financing instruments can also generate credit risk on the liability side of the balance sheet.

In addition to these risks, understanding the sensitivity of the simulated SAT performance to changes in the basic assumptions of the model is critical for assessing specific SAT transactions. Uncertainties in the simulated performance profile need to be quantified. Much of the traditional SAT analysis has relied on the assumption of parallel yield curve shifts. In addition, other important assumptions and economic events are often left untested. A comprehensive risk assessment of SAT performance must consider the effects of prepayment sensitivity, nonparallel shifts in the yield curve and other changes in yield basis relationships, terminal asset and liability values, reinvestment risk, margin calls, earlier or later than planned liquidation (horizon risk), and cyclical changes in interest rates.

SAT investors must assess all these risks in light of alternative investment opportunities and the institution's existing balance sheet. This section of the article describes some risks affecting SATs, and demonstrates approaches to quantifying the sensitivities. In addition, this section examines the rebalancing of existing SATs.

### Prepayment Sensitivity

Essential to any analysis of mortgage-backed securities is a prepayment model used to forecast prepayments in scenarios where market interest rates are assumed to vary. While the relationship between interest rates and prepayments cannot be known with certainty, an analysis of historical relationships provides the basis for modelling possible future outcomes. These SAT simulations rely on such a prepayment model.[8]

---

[8]See the SLH special report, *Projecting Prepayments with the Shearson Lehman Prepayment Model*, July 1987.

# EXHIBIT 7
## AMENDED LFI SAT SIMULATION RESULTS (BASE CASE ANALYSIS)

| Interest Rate Chg. (bp) | Cash-Based Measures | | Book-Based Measures | | | | | Average Scenario Prepayment Assumptions (%PSA) | | |
|---|---|---|---|---|---|---|---|---|---|---|
| | ROI (%) | IRR (%) | Term. Net Position ($000) | Cum. Book Income ($000) | ROA (%) | Profit ($000) | Effective Margin (%) | GNMA 10.5s | 11% IOs | 10% POs |
| -300 | 5.38 | | 12,102 | 4,914 | 1.01 | 4,987 | 1.09 | 612 | 708 | 525 |
| -200 | 8.64 | | 16,578 | 9,459 | 1.81 | 9,463 | 0.84 | 426 | 534 | 343 |
| -100 | 11.47 | 21.22 | 21,711 | 14,358 | 2.30 | 14,596 | 0.93 | 265 | 349 | 206 |
| 0 | 13.24 | 21.16 | 25,653 | 18,307 | 2.41 | 18,537 | 0.92 | 157 | 209 | 125 |
| 100 | 13.04 | 19.26 | 25,174 | 19,806 | 2.32 | 18,058 | 0.67 | 100 | 128 | 87 |
| 200 | 10.89 | | 20,545 | 18,184 | 2.05 | 13,430 | 0.25 | 76 | 91 | 71 |
| 300 | 6.50 | | 13,486 | 14,480 | 1.61 | 6,370 | -0.28 | 63 | 73 | 61 |
| 400 | -4.48 | | 4,525 | 8,761 | 0.98 | -2,591 | -0.88 | 55 | 63 | 52 |

Note: Horizon period = 120 months.
Source: Shearson Lehman Hutton Mortgage Securities.

# EXHIBIT 8
## AMENDED LFI SAT ANNUAL BALANCE SHEET (FLAT INTEREST RATE SCENARIO, $ THOUSAND)

| Year End | Assets | | | Liabilities | | Equity | |
|---|---|---|---|---|---|---|---|
| | Mortgage Balance | Book Value | Liquid Balance | Short-term | Long-term | Haircut | Cum. Retained Earnings |
| 1 | 112,380 | 91,116 | 1,739 | 29,633 | 55,000 | 7,115 | 1,107 |
| 2 | 101,550 | 82,845 | 4,276 | 31,950 | 45,000 | 7,115 | 3,055 |
| 3 | 91,649 | 74,917 | 6,433 | 34,586 | 35,000 | 7,115 | 4,648 |
| 4 | 82,599 | 67,654 | 8,620 | 32,841 | 30,000 | 7,115 | 6,318 |
| 5 | 74,328 | 61,007 | 10,829 | 31,666 | 25,000 | 7,115 | 8,054 |
| 6 | 66,773 | 54,924 | 13,092 | 26,016 | 25,000 | 7,115 | 9,884 |
| 7 | 59,873 | 49,359 | 15,356 | 30,847 | 15,000 | 7,115 | 11,753 |
| 8 | 53,573 | 44,271 | 17,817 | 26,121 | 15,000 | 7,115 | 13,852 |
| 9 | 47,826 | 39,619 | 20,328 | 21,800 | 15,000 | 7,115 | 16,031 |
| 10* | 42,583 | 35,369 | 22,905 | 32,852 | 0 | 7,115 | 18,307 |

* End figures for year 10 represent the balance sheet before liquidation of the transaction.
Source: Shearson Lehman Hutton Mortgage Securities.

# EXHIBIT 9
## AMENDED LFI SAT ANNUAL NET INCOME STATEMENT UNDER THREE INTEREST RATE SCENARIOS ($ THOUSAND)

| Year | Revenues | | | Expenses | | Net Income | ROA (%) |
|---|---|---|---|---|---|---|---|
| | Coupon | Reinvestment | Discount Accretion | Interest | Premium Amortized | | |
| **a. −300 basis points** | | | | | | | |
| 1 | 9,475 | 233 | 1,597 | 7,816 | 2,480 | 1,009 | 1.02 |
| 2 | 7,346 | 411 | 5,787 | 6,243 | 5,929 | 1,373 | 1.58 |
| 3 | 4,519 | 617 | 3,705 | 4,503 | 2,893 | 1,445 | 2.46 |
| 4 | 2,591 | 954 | 1,442 | 3,427 | 854 | 706 | 1.52 |
| 5 | 1,500 | 1,288 | 909 | 2,961 | 465 | 271 | 0.65 |
| 6 | 878 | 1,373 | 582 | 2,485 | 258 | 91 | 0.25 |
| 7 | 520 | 1,569 | 376 | 2,485 | 144 | −165 | −0.45 |
| 8 | 312 | 1,174 | 245 | 1,503 | 82 | 146 | 0.54 |
| 9 | 189 | 1,251 | 161 | 1,503 | 47 | 51 | 0.19 |
| 10 | 116 | 1,296 | 107 | 1,503 | 27 | −12 | −0.04 |
| **b. Flat** | | | | | | | |
| 1 | 9,631 | 234 | 1,150 | 8,018 | 1,890 | 1,107 | 1.12 |
| 2 | 8,673 | 390 | 1,417 | 7,345 | 1,187 | 1,948 | 2.11 |
| 3 | 7,777 | 556 | 1,033 | 6,665 | 1,109 | 1,593 | 1.85 |
| 4 | 6,965 | 712 | 969 | 5,991 | 984 | 1,670 | 2.08 |
| 5 | 6,228 | 874 | 903 | 5,402 | 867 | 1,736 | 2.30 |
| 6 | 5,560 | 1,041 | 840 | 4,848 | 763 | 1,830 | 2.57 |
| 7 | 4,956 | 1,215 | 779 | 3,411 | 671 | 1,869 | 2.76 |
| 8 | 4,408 | 1,386 | 722 | 3,828 | 589 | 2,099 | 3.25 |
| 9 | 3,913 | 1,579 | 667 | 3,462 | 517 | 2,179 | 3.51 |
| 10 | 3,465 | 1,777 | 615 | 3,128 | 454 | 2,275 | 3.79 |
| **c. +400 basis points** | | | | | | | |
| 1 | 9,767 | 243 | 844 | 8,277 | 1,196 | 1,380 | 1.39 |
| 2 | 9,343 | 929 | 213 | 8,640 | 200 | 1,644 | 1.71 |
| 3 | 9,008 | 659 | 447 | 9,049 | 324 | 741 | 0.78 |
| 4 | 8,683 | 756 | 784 | 8,999 | 529 | 696 | 0.75 |
| 5 | 8,356 | 855 | 776 | 8,792 | 531 | 665 | 0.73 |
| 6 | 8,027 | 950 | 761 | 8,570 | 530 | 638 | 0.72 |
| 7 | 7,696 | 1,055 | 744 | 8,219 | 528 | 748 | 0.87 |
| 8 | 7,363 | 1,149 | 726 | 8,082 | 526 | 630 | 0.75 |
| 9 | 7,029 | 1,254 | 707 | 7,722 | 524 | 744 | 0.91 |
| 10 | 6,693 | 1,374 | 686 | 7,357 | 521 | 874 | 1.10 |

Source: Shearson Lehman Hutton Mortgage Securities.

**EXHIBIT 10**
**PROJECTED PREPAYMENTS UNDER THREE INTEREST RATE SCENARIOS**

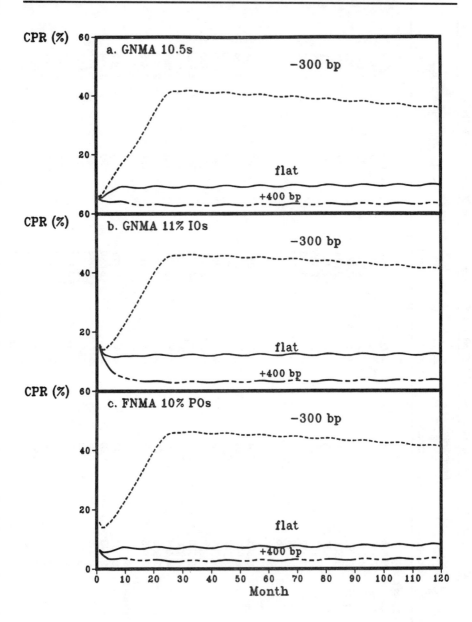

Prepayments for three interest rate scenarios are shown for assets in the amended LFI transaction in Exhibit 10. Investors need to understand the extent to which simulation results are affected by the prepayment assumptions of the model.

For small portfolios and pools with high geographical concentrations, examining the impact of adverse and favorable prepayment behavior can be critical. Exhibit 11 shows the effects of both adverse and advantageous prepayment stress tests on ROI. It illustrates the impact to the base case profile of (1) prepayments 20% faster than anticipated in the case of the IO strip and 20% slower in the case of the GNMA 10s and the PO strip—the adverse prepayment stress test; and of (2) prepayments 20% slower in the case of the IO strip and 20% faster in the case of the GNMA 10s and the PO strip—the advantageous prepayment stress test.

### Yield Basis Risk

Structured arbitrage transactions employ assets financed with liabilities that have various maturities and yield spread relationships. For example, fixed-rate mortgage assets may be financed with reverse repurchase agreements and interest rate swaps to lengthen the duration of liabilities. As a result, SATs are exposed to many kinds of basis risk, perhaps the greatest of which is an overall steepening or flattening of the yield curve. The shape of the yield curve has a dramatic impact on performance because a sizeable portion of SAT financing can be in short-term floating rate liabilities. In addition, for SATs that employ interest rate swaps, changes in the shape of the term structure influence performance. Changes in the basis between short- and long-term interest rates, therefore, strongly influence spread income.

**EXHIBIT 11**
**IMPACT OF CHANGES IN PREPAYMENTS AND YIELD CURVE SLOPE**

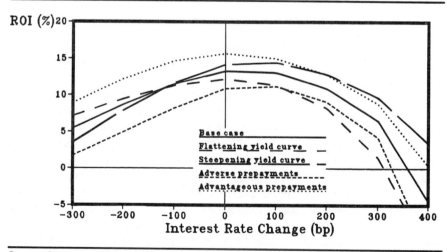

Source: Shearson Lehman Hutton Mortgage Securities.

For example, the short-term financing costs increase if the short end of the yield curve rises and decrease if it falls, all else equal. Exhibit 11 shows the impact of a 100-basis-point steepening or flattening over one year's time across all scenarios. This stress test indicates transaction sensitivity to yield basis changes. If the yield curve flattens, returns are reduced in rising interest rate scenarios. In the flat rate scenario, ROI is reduced by 111 basis points. Returns are enhanced as interest rates decline, primarily because higher short-term reinvestment opportunities become more important as a result of the rapid runoff of mortgage assets. If the yield curve steepens, returns are enhanced if rates remain stable or rise. This is attributable to lower financing costs.

Other types of yield basis risk can also influence the profitability of the transaction. For example, changes in the spread between the 3-month LIBOR payments received in the interest rate swap agreements and the GNMA 3-month repo rate paid add to the uncertainty of the transaction's performance (see Exhibit 12). Exhibit 13 shows the impact of a 30-basis-point reversal in the LIBOR/repo spread on the base case ROI performance measure (the repo rate rises 30 basis points and LIBOR stays constant). A rise in the reverse rate systematically reduces returns. Another example of the effect of changes in yield basis relationships on the transaction's profitability is the impact on the sale price of the securities remaining when the transaction is liquidated.

### Terminal Asset/Liability Analysis

For a given SAT horizon, there are likely to be assets and/or liabilities remaining on the books of the institution at the end of the intended investment period. Investors may also wish to modify their asset/liability mix over the life of the transaction. While the institution may not want to liquidate assets at that time, liquidation value is often a key indicator of future earnings. In the case of an institution financing a 5-year note with a 2-year liability, the income generated over the first two years could easily be lost if interest rates rise and the 5-year note is sold at a loss. This example shows that the liquidation value of the terminal asset/liability position may have a critical impact on the profitability of the transaction. Additionally, market liquidity can influence the resale value of assets and is of concern to SAT investors. The importance of this factor for SAT performance needs to be assessed.

In the LFI example, 35% of the initial face value of the mortgage assets remains at the end of the 10-year horizon in the flat interest rate scenario. The liquidation value plays an important role in determining the performance of the transaction. In the base case analysis, the terminal sale values are calculated by assuming that the assets were priced at a spread to the prevailing WAL Treasury yield comparable to the one at purchase. However, any number of market events could fundamentally alter the yield spread relationship between these assets and the Treasury yield curve. In addition, the bid/ask spread can reduce the proceeds of liquidating A/L positions.

**EXHIBIT 12**
**THREE-MONTH LIBOR VS. THREE-MONTH GNMA**
**REPO RATE\* AND SPREAD**
**(MONTHLY DATA FROM MAY 1981 to DECEMBER 1987)**

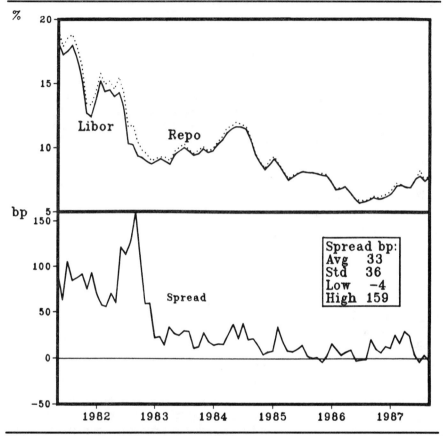

\*Calculated on an actual/360 simple interest basis.
Source: Shearson Lehman Hutton Mortgage Securities.

Investors need to evaluate the relative importance of terminal asset valuation for the overall profitability of the transaction.

Exhibit 14 shows such an evaluation for the sample transaction over a 10-year horizon. In the unchanged interest rate scenario, the terminal asset prices were assumed to be 102.63, 43.20, and 61.67 for the GNMA 10.5s, 11% IOs, and 10% POs, respectively. A terminal asset price of 96.30 for the GNMA 10.5s, or 13.43 for the 11% IOs, or 48.39 for the 10% POs, with all else equal, would reduce the scenario ROIs by one percentage point. Exhibit 14 describes the effect of the terminal asset values on the overall profitability of the transaction.

**EXHIBIT 13**
**IMPACT OF A 30-BASIS-POINT CHANGE IN THE LIBOR/REPO SPREAD**

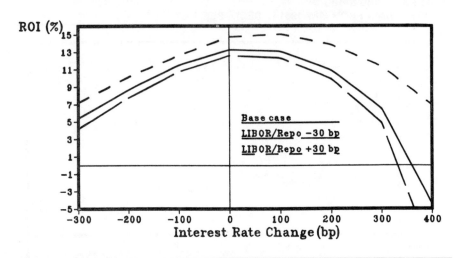

Source: Shearson Lehman Hutton Mortgage Securities.

### Reinvestment Risk

Nearly all of the measures used to quantify SAT scenario performance make an assumption about reinvestment of cash. Two types of cash accounts exist in SAT simulation and both are generally assumed to earn some level of return. These are retained earnings and asset paydown prior to liability maturity. In the base case analysis for LFI, all cash is reinvested at the same rate as the short-term borrowing costs, a conservative assumption. However, in the IRR calculation, cash on hand is assumed to earn a rate comparable to the short-term borrowing cost, and retained earnings are implicitly assumed to be reinvested at a rate identical to the calculated IRR. Depending on available reinvestment opportunities, any of these assumptions may prove inappropriate. Exhibit 15 compares the impact of increasing the investment rate from the base case assumption of short-term borrowing costs, to 200 and 400 basis points above the short-term rate. As is shown, the impact of higher reinvestment rates is more dramatic for falling interest rate scenarios where assets prepay rapidly.

### Impact of Margin Calls

A critical component in the evaluation of SATs is the impact of margin requirements. In the typical SAT, overcollateralization is necessray to secure the short-term reverse

**EXHIBIT 14**
**LFI SAT TERMINAL ASSET PRICING STRESS RESULTS**

| Interest Rate Change (bp) | Base Case Scenario - ROI (%) | Asset (%) | Ending Unpaid Balance ($000) | Base Case Ending Price ($) | What Terminal Asset Price Will Change ROI by . . . (in percentage pts.) | |
|---|---|---|---|---|---|---|
| | | | | | −1 | +1 |
| Ten-Year Horizon | | | | | | |
| −300 | 5.38 | GNMA 10.5s | 747 | 108.23 | −36.64 | 288.33 |
| | | IO 11s | 97 | 52.37 | −1067.14 | 1444.21 |
| | | PO 10s | 632 | 63.84 | −107.47 | 276.83 |
| −200 | 8.64 | GNMA 10.5s | 3,649 | 107.75 | 71.04 | 162.76 |
| | | IO 11s | 477 | 53.29 | −227.80 | 474.35 |
| | | PO 10s | 2.687 | 59.91 | 10.05 | 134.61 |
| −100 | 11.47 | GNMA 10.5s | 12,147 | 105.92 | 93.36 | 129.77 |
| | | IO 11s | 2,028 | 47.53 | −27.68 | 190.39 |
| | | PO 10s | 7,056 | 60.43 | 38.81 | 101.49 |
| 0 | 13.24 | GNMA 10.5s | 25,217 | 102.63 | 96.30 | 117.17 |
| | | IO 11s | 5,358 | 43.20 | 13.43 | 111.65 |
| | | PO 10s | 12,008 | 61.67 | 48.39 | 92.21 |
| 100 | 13.04 | GNMA 10.5s | 36,110 | 98.33 | 93.92 | 108.21 |
| | | IO 11s | 9,003 | 41.18 | 23.53 | 80.84 |
| | | PO 10s | 15,243 | 60.07 | 49.64 | 83.49 |
| 200 | 10.89 | GNMA 10.5s | 41,911 | 93.80 | 90.24 | 100.20 |
| | | IO 11s | 11,327 | 40.50 | 27.32 | 64.19 |
| | | PO 10s | 16,764 | 56.46 | 47.55 | 72.47 |
| 300 | 6.50 | GNMA 10.5s | 45,413 | 89.27 | 86.69 | 92.66 |
| | | IO 11s | 12,660 | 39.81 | 30.55 | 51.96 |
| | | PO 10s | 17,892 | 52.73 | 46.18 | 61.33 |
| 400 | −4.48 | GNMA 10.5s | 47,873 | 85.03 | 84.16 | 86.07 |
| | | IO 11s | 13,467 | 38.64 | 35.56 | 42.35 |
| | | PO 10s | 18,884 | 49.38 | 47.18 | 52.02 |

Source: Shearson Lehman Hutton Mortgage Securities.

repurchase agreements; interest rate swap agreements impose additional overcollateralization requirements. The haircut or margin determines the market-imposed upper limit on the financial leverage of the transaction, i.e., the minimum size of the net cash investment. In fact, the high degree of leverage obtainable through collateralized borrowing in the reverse repo market is one of the most attractive features of

**EXHIBIT 15**
**IMPACT OF CHANGES IN THE REINVESTMENT RATE ASSUMPTION**

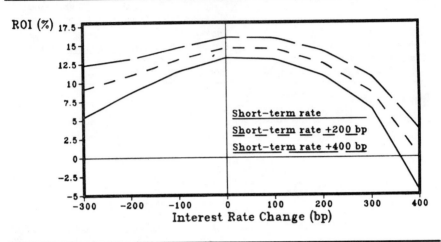

Source: Shearson Lehman Hutton Mortgage Securities.

SATs. Although investors in other capital market transactions have long been sensitive to margin requirements and future margin calls, little conventional mortgage arbitrage analysis focuses on sensitivity to and risks associated with fluctuating margin requirements.

Margin calls that result from a devaluation of the market value of assets force the investor either to sell assets or to increase the quantity of collateral. Depending on opportunity costs, margin calls can have an adverse effect on transaction returns. Conversely, as asset values increase, less overcollateralization is necessary and capital is freed for other purposes.

The magnitude of the margin call impact depends on the deterioration/appreciation of the market value of collateral and the opportunity cost of capital relative to available borrowing costs. If the reinvestment opportunity is the same as the borrowing cost (as in the base case simulation for LFI), margin calls do not significantly affect the simulated performance measures. The importance of margin calls increases as the available reinvestment opportunities improve. Rising interest rates generally damage returns and falling rates enhance returns.

*Horizon Risk*

Like most investments, a SAT's performance is affected by the length of the period over which it is held. For example, holding a 10-year Treasury zero coupon bond until it matures carries virtually no risk on a before-tax basis. The investor receives the anticipated internal rate of return regardless of market conditions (except in the

**EXHIBIT 16**
**IMPACT OF HORIZON PERIOD UNDER THREE INTEREST RATE SCENARIOS**

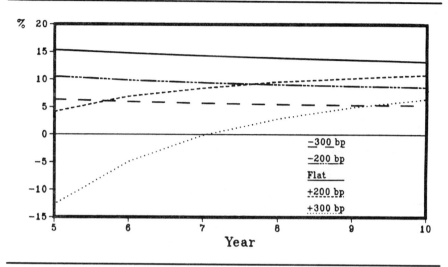

Source: Shearson Lehman Hutton Mortgage Securities.

case of default). However, as the horizon is lengthened or shortened, total return varies. SATs are heavily influenced by the length of the horizon: increasing the holding period reduces the risks associated with terminal asset values and enlarges the importance of reinvestment and yield basis relationship assumptions. Exhibit 16 illustrates the impact of various horizon periods on simulation ROIs. Reducing the holding period generally improves ROIs as rates fall and decreases returns as rates rise. This reflects the relative importance of the SAT liquidation value for total return. Lengthening the horizon reduces the importance of terminal asset valuation and increases the importance of reinvestment return. Asset sales in the declining rate scenarios do not improve returns as much as in the rising rate scenarios, because the amount of assets outstanding is reduced as a result of rapid prepayment rates.

### Cyclical Interest Rates

This SAT simulation analysis has so far assumed that interest rates rise and fall to a specified level or remain unchanged. SAT investors also need to assess the impact of cyclical changes in interest rates—for example, interest rate scenarios that rise and then fall, or conversely, fall and then rise. This type of analysis is particularly useful for SATs that contain securities with option attributes. For mortgage securities, particularly derivative securities, cyclical interest rate analysis provides important insight into the performance characteristics of the SAT. Such an analysis is depicted for LFI in Exhibit 17.

**EXHIBIT 17**
**IMPACT OF CYCLICAL INTEREST RATES**

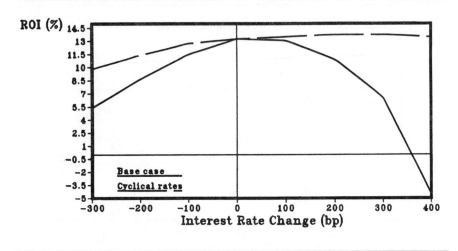

Source: Shearson Lehman Hutton Mortgage Securities.

In Exhibit 17, cyclical interest rates are simulated by assuming that interest rates initially rise or fall, depending on the scenario, at a rate of 100 basis points per year, the same assumption as in the base case analysis. Once the interest rate scenario has fully phased in, however, interest rates are assumed to reverse direction and return to the initial level. In the rising rate scenario, for example, interest rates rise 300 basis points over the first three years and then fall 300 basis points to the initial level. As might be expected, cyclical interest rates enhance the simulation measures from the base case, noncyclical interest rate scenarios. In general, this transaction performs best in a stable interest rate environment. Constraining the interest rate scenarios to return to initial levels should therefore improve returns in relation to the noncyclical scenario analysis. In relative terms, improvement is greatest in the rising rate scenarios because of more favorable pricing on larger balances. The larger balances occur because more of the assets are remaining in the rise-and-fall scenarios than in the fall-and-rise scenarios.

### Rebalancing

Rebalancing reflects the need to modify some of the components of the SAT position to adjust the hedge to changing market conditions. As such, rebalancing addresses three concerns. It may be an effort to counteract the development of duration mismatches in an originally well hedged position. (A significant market move can lead to a divergence in asset and liability durations.) Rebalancing may also redress errors in initial matching, or it may address the need for adjustment due to a change in management's perceptions about interest rate direction and prepayments. In the last case, the SAT structure is positioned to benefit from the anticipated move rather than to immunize returns.

The ability of rebalancing to enhance returns depends upon whether management is proactive or reactive. If reactive—management examines the SAT position after the economic risk has become a reality—rebalancing is less driven by market opportunities than it is by the tax advantages of capital versus ordinary gains/losses since the damage has already been done. If the decision is proactive—management has successfully anticipated market moves—rebalancing is guided by the underlying economic value of the transaction. The realized gains/losses are then achieved through liquidations or greater net interest income. SAT investors must recognize that simulation is a static approach, necessarily requiring frequent reexamination as market conditions change.

Assets and/or liabilities can be liquidated or purchased to alter the performance of the SAT. Often analysis of total return starts with marking the SAT position to current market prices and examining the market net worth of the transaction (book performance is also analyzed). Such an approach typically evaluates net worth under the efficient market assumptions that assets can be traded freely, and that the firm can purchase its debt in the open market at prevailing fair market value. While these assumptions may be unrealistic, they provide a starting point for analysis. Section V of this article examines alternative performance profiles for SAT investors. These strategies can, in many cases, complement existing A/L positions to reflect management's current policies.

## V. ACHIEVABLE PERFORMANCE PROFILES

One of the major advantages of SATs over other investment strategies is their flexibility for structuring transaction performance profiles to match investor needs. This structuring depends on the use of static measures such as duration and convexity models, and iterative analysis through simulating transactions, until the desired performance profile is achieved with an acceptable risk/reward trade-off. Most often, the hedging strategy maintains a stable return profile over a wide range of interest rates. However, a stable return is not always an attainable or in some cases a desirable objective, especially when assets with embedded options like mortgage securities are hedged with instruments that lack counteractive option attributes themselves. Given the wide variety of assets and liabilities, any number of performance profiles can be achieved. Transactions can be structured to capture gains on volatility or stability in interest rates, to produce returns relatively unaffected by interest rates, or to take on a bullish or bearish outlook by creating call- or put-like and long or short positions.

Exhibit 18 shows a sampling of the reward profiles that can be achieved through SATs. In regular SATs like the LFI example, returns are greatest when rates remain unchanged and poorest when volatility increases. This return profile can be attractive for financial institutions wishing to boost yields in the current environment when rates are believed to be somewhat stable over the life of the transaction. In essence, the institution can create a short straddle position (see Exhibit 18a). The maturity-matched transaction for LFI is an example of this type of transaction. Less frequently, transactions are structured to capture returns on the volatility of the interest rate environment. The investor sets up an A/L return structure resembling a long straddle position in options (see Exhibit 18b). Returns are lowest when rates remain unchanged and improve as volatility increases. This is a useful strategy for thrifts confident that change will occur, but unsure of its direction.

Long straddle positions generally require use of derivative mortgage-backed securities as well as interest rate caps and floors to structure returns. Premium-backed IOs, which rally dramatically in rising rates but offer fairly low—often negative—flat interest rate yields, can be used to offset current coupon or discount POs to achieve these profiles. As rates fall, the premium-backed IOs decrease in value only marginally, since prepayments fail to increase from already high levels. The premium-backed POs, on the other hand, rally dramatically when prepayments accelerate and these securities, when purchased at a discount, return principal at par. As rates rise, the POs deteriorate, but the gains on premium-backed IOs offset these losses.

Another common approach is to structure SATs to offer relatively stable or flat returns across a wide range of interest rate scenarios. This is a standard hedging approach used by institutions to rebalance individual transactions. This reward structure can be achieved by employing a variety of standard, derivative, and adjustable rate assets and liabilities to flatten the returns across the desired interest rate spectrum. Achieving stable returns often comes at the cost of lower returns, particularly in stable interest rate scenarios (see Exhibit 18c).

Another familiar structuring technique is to pattern returns to perform well in a bull market and to falter only moderately in a bear market, a call-like structure (see Exhibit 18d). As rates fall, the arbitrage becomes more and more profitable; conversely, as rates rise, losses are capped. Interest rate floors, discount pass-throughs, and CMO bonds can be used to structure this type of transaction.

A put-like position on interest rates may also be tailored (see Exhibit 18e). As rates rise, so do returns. As rates fall, returns decline and level off. Interest rate caps and premium-backed IOs approximate a put profile.

Various instruments can be used to capture bullish and bearish outlooks (see Exhibit 18f). Of the assets discussed earlier, interest only strips, premium coupon securities, CMO residuals, and interest rate caps may be used for bearish outlooks. Discount coupon securities, principal only strips, and interest rate floors accommodate bullish outlooks. On the liability side—particularly for fixed-rate payers in swaps—swaptions, callable swaps, term reverse repurchases, and other term fixed-rate types of financing enhance high interest rate environment returns. Also, interest rate floors may be sold. (See Appendix A for a description of these investment vehicles.) Using short-term funding such as CDs, short-term reverses, and Federal

**EXHIBIT 18**
**ACHIEVABLE PERFORMANCE PROFILES**

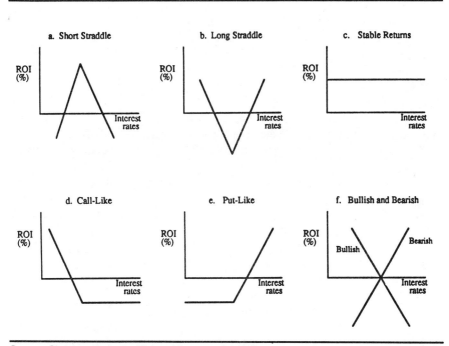

Source: Shearson Lehman Hutton Mortgage Securities.

Home Loan Bank Board advances improves falling interest rate returns. Swaps likewise may be shorted (investors pay floating and receive fixed rates) to reduce asset/liability exposure in a falling interest rate environment.

## VI. CONCLUSION

To meet targeted growth and income levels, financial institutions often enter into structured arbitrage transactions (SATs). However, institutions must fully examine the risk/reward structure of these investments in the context of alternative opportunities and in relation to their existing balance sheets. Simulation analysis examines the risks inherent in the SAT asset/liability position. For assessing SATs, institutions should use measures that reflect their objectives and are good and consistent indicators of performance. The ROI, the IRR, and the net effective margin are the best indicators of relative value. Specific combinations of A/L positions can be created from the instruments available in the capital markets to fit an institution's preferred profile of interest rate performance and credit exposure.

## APPENDIX A.   DERIVATIVE MBS AND INTEREST RATE OPTIONS AS ASSET AND LIABILITY TOOLS

The following is a sampling of the various assets and liabilities that can be employed in SATs. These tools, when used together, can create SAT investments that complement an institution's existing balance sheet.

### ASSETS FOR SATs

**Derivative Mortgage Securities** The performance characteristics of derivative mortgage securities can be utilized to fit the SAT profile to the investor's objectives. In fact, combinations of these securities often produce a better performance profile than less exotic securities.

Derivative securities have a variety of effects on SAT return profiles, including

- modifying the duration of the asset portfolio, thereby decreasing the need for more costly hedging techniques;
- enhancing expected returns;
- improving the stability of returns over different interest rate environments and/ or altering the performance profile to reflect the investor's needs;
- altering the prepayment sensitivity of the asset mix; and
- modifying the convexity attributes of the portfolio.

Useful derivative securities for SATs include stripped securities of both interest only (IO) and principal only (PO) types, CMO residuals, and inverse floating rate tranches from CMOs.

Coupon only type securities (IO stripped securities and servicing fees, both excess and normal) offer a negative interest rate play depending on collateral characteristics. Because their value increases as interest rates rise and falls as rates decline, these securities have a negative mortgage duration. Thus, their value often increases when more traditional fixed-income securities decrease in value. Furthermore, IO type securities with sufficiently low projected prepayment rates also offer very high returns. Given these characteristics, coupon only securities often provide an inexpensive alternative to using swaps in a SAT; they offer rising interest rate protection by hedging the asset side of the transaction.

Principal only type securities (PO stripped securities and deep discount REMIC/ CMO bonds) offer a positive interest rate play for hedging assets in structured arbitrage. As rates fall, principal only strips increase in value. The performance of these derivative mortgage securities depends, like that of IOs, on the characteristics of the underlying collateral. The performance profile is most importantly influenced by the relationship between the mortgage coupon and current market interest rates, i.e., whether the underlying pass-through collateral is priced at near current (par value), discount, or premium coupon. Using principal only strips protects transactions as interest rates fall, in much the same way as using very short-term liabilities; in combination with other hedging vehicles, they can prove useful in stabilizing transactions.

Residuals from REMIC/CMOs with fixed coupons are, like IOs, essentially coupon only type securities. Unless the CMO is considerably overcollateralized, the residual cash flow is the coupon differential between the collateral and the CMO tranches. Consequently, as interest rates increase and prepayments slow, the residual enjoys greater dollar income. This is largely because the spread income (the difference between the collateral income and CMO bond expense) is earned on a larger balance. Conversely, a drop in rates triggers a dramatic decrease in returns.

For REMIC/CMO residuals with floating rate classes, however, the return variability is moderated. The bearishness of the residual is dampened because higher rates must be paid on the floating rate tranches when interest levels rise, despite the larger outstanding balance. The return on the residual is maximized when LIBOR falls and mortgage rates rise—a steepening of the yield curve.

Moderation of residual returns is largely a function of the weight of the floater tranche in the overall structure and the type of bond payment—sequential or simultaneous. Simultaneous payment structures impart a stabilizing effect for the life of the CMO. Sequential returns are somewhat more volatile as tranches mature and return characteristics change.

Floating rate CMO residuals offer high projected yield with returns that rally in a moderately bullish environment. On the other hand, hedging sizeable asset positions may require equity holdings in several different CMO trusts, and are more difficult to leverage.[9]

CMO reverse floater bonds (reverse floaters) offer an extremely bullish play and improve SAT returns in falling interest rate environments. Reverse floater returns are inversely related to short-term interest rates. For example, for a given rise in the index, the coupon declines by some prearranged multiple. Reverse floaters offer a highly leveraged bullish play.

**Other Types of Assets** Other assets are employed in SATs, including project and commercial loans, asset-backed securities, and 15- and 30-year pass-throughs—both agency and private. With some of these assets, particularly commercial loans, credit issues have to be considered in addition to interest rate risk management.

Corporate bonds included in SATs, particularly when the acquisition is timed to take advantage of inter-sector yield aberrations, impart falling interest rate return

---

[9]SATs share many parallels with CMOs. A noteworthy exception, however, is that CMOs distribute the entire burden of prepayment/reinvestment risk to the bondholders. From the standpoint of residual interests in the CMO, prepayment risk manifests itself as loss of spread income. Equity interests in SATs, on the other hand, bear the entire brunt of the prepayment option.

protection, similar to deep discount MBS. The critical variable here is the credit risk of the bond, which can seriously undermine the fundamental objective of a high and reliable cash flow stream. However, corporate bonds that are call protected are typically subject to less reinvestment risk.[10]

**Interest Rate Caps and Floors** Interest rate caps and floors provide a rich array of call and put option opportunities in SATs. Buying an interest rate cap requires that a fee (premium) be paid initially in exchange for the right to receive payments if rates rise above a specified level (the strike). Payments received equal the difference between the prevailing rate level and the strike based upon the principal value. Cap value rises with interest rates. The risk in a falling rate environment is limited to the up-front premium. Thus, caps can be useful in hedging SATs against bearish interest rate scenarios. The purchase of interest rate floors, on the other hand, provides returns which rally as interest rates fall, with losses stopped out at the cost of a premium in rising rate environments. The premium is paid in exchange for the right to receive payments if rates fall below the specified strike. Floors have the same bullish impact on returns as some PO strips. Aside from their speculative potential, caps and floors are extremely useful in stabilizing transactions that might otherwise offer skewed returns. For accounting purposes, the premium or cost of purchasing caps and floors can be amortized over the life of the agreement.

## *LIABILITIES FOR SATs*

Short-term floating and fixed-rate financing provides varying degrees of protection against interest rate fluctuations in SATs. Various forms of financing are available for integrated hedging.

**Short-Term Floating Rate Financing** Among various short-term vehicles for financing the overall transaction are reverse repurchase agreements, dollar roll agreements, Federal Home Loan Bank Board (FHLBB) advances, certificates of deposit (CD) funding, money market preferred stock (MMP), and term repurchases.

A reverse repurchase agreement is a short-term collateralized financing, though the contractual arrangement calls for a sale and subsequent repurchase of the pledged securities. Interest rates are quoted on a simple interest basis. Reverses generally provide inexpensive floating rate funds, with no associated transactions costs. Most SATs begin by initially reversing in the securities. Over time the reverse is usually

---

[10]The 1986 Tax Reform Act reduced the test for thrifts from 82% in qualifying real estate assets to 60%. Additionally, it decreased the value of the preferential tax rate available to thrifts meeting the qualifying asset test. The act increases the relative attractiveness for SATs of nonqualifying assets such as corporate bonds.

rolled over, depending on the targeted leverage and the market value of the collateral. However, the full amount of the collateral cannot be funded by the loan; a certain amount of overcollateralization, or haircut, is required on the funding. The haircut for agency-backed mortgage pass-throughs is usually about six price points of the face value of the securities pledged.

Dollar roll agreements are transactions in which an institution sells a pass-through security to a dealer, and agrees to repurchase a similar security in the future for a predetermined price. A dollar roll amounts to a short-term financing because the thrift has use of the sale proceeds for the term of the agreement, similar to a reverse repurchase. Dollar roll agreements offer low rates useful in SATs because the dealer does not have to return exactly identical securities at the end of the term; similar securities may be substituted in their place.

Federal Home Loan Bank Board advances are an extremely price-competitive source of financing for a wide variety of collateral. Pass-through MBS, as well as adjusted multifamily, commercial, and whole loans are all eligible as collateral for the financing. Although the Federal Home Loan Bank Board discourages reliance on advances and enforces substantial prepayment penalties, advances may provide an effective financing over their maturity. Overcollateralization, however, is substantial—generally between 140% and 200%—and often dramatically diminishes returns on the SAT. In addition, up-front fees are required for advance funding.

Certificates of deposit offer an uncollateralized financing alternative for SATs. Dealers generally require high fees initially, as it is difficult to lock in CD rates quickly. CD borrowing may be set up for long-term financing, but it is hard to arrange CDs in large denominations for longer maturities. The interest rate charged on the borrowing is set by conditions in the CD market, and varies somewhat depending on the size of the issue and the credit quality of the borrower.

Money market preferred (MMP) stock is sold at par every 49 days at a rate similar to commercial paper. Because this stock pays dividends rather than interest, it offers a dividend tax advantage to purchasers. Rates are generally about 70% to 90% of the AA commercial paper rate, including the tax effects of the MMP. Companies that issue MMPs often have large net operating losses and take advantage of tax effects by using equity instead of debt against their write-offs. As a result, the credit quality of MMP issuers makes swaps somewhat less frequent in conjunction with SATs. This type of financing has recently become less attractive due to new tax legislation.

**Long-Term Financing** Long-term financing alternatives used to fix rates in structured arbitrage include swaps, swaptions, callable swaps, caps and floors, and longer maturities on some of the above forms of financing.

An interest rate swap is an agreement to pay fixed rates in exchange for floating rates. Market quotations on the fixed side are expressed as spreads to Treasuries, and on the floating side at LIBOR. The net result of borrowing short and covering short financing with floating rate interest swap receipts is to fix costs on liabilities over the maturity of the swap agreement.

A swaption is a forward swap agreement whereby the purchaser pays an initial fee for the option to enter into a swap at a later date at a specified rate. Investors that do not wish to enter into a swap agreement at the outset of a SAT can hedge against rising interest rates for the cost of the swaption premium. A swaption requires a greater initial investment, but provides for the option of locking in favorable financing costs at a specific date.

The callable swap agreement allows the fixed-rate borrower to terminate the swap at no penalty between the call date and maturity. The call premium as an up-front fee may be amortized over the life of the swap. The callable swap, like the standard swap, allows the purchaser to hedge against rising interest rates, yet it averts the high costs of an unexpected downward rate movement.

Selling interest rate caps and floors provides a financing vehicle that improves returns in relatively stable interest rate scenarios. Selling a floor improves returns for flat and rising rate environments, but if rates fall the transaction returns suffer. Selling a cap enhances flat and falling rate scenarios, with declining returns if interest rates rise.

Selling swaps short provides an interesting twist on the use of fixed-rate financing because the investor pays floating rates and receives fixed-rate financing. These swaps dramatically boost stable interest rate scenario performance and improve declining rate returns in SATs. In rising rate environments, however, they affect the transaction in much the same way as discount PO assets: as rates rise returns are reduced.

Though many assets and liabilities have been described in this appendix, many others go unmentioned. The combination of A/L positions available is virtually limitless.

## APPENDIX B.    ACCOUNTING FUNDAMENTALS FOR MBS

Statement 91 of the Financial Accounting Standards Board (SFAS 91, "Accounting for Nonrefundable Fees and Costs Associated with Originating or Acquiring Loans and Initial Direct Costs of Leases") contains the generally accepted accounting principle relating to income recognition on nonpar securities and amortization of issuing costs including explicit call premiums. Although SFAS 91 is fairly broad in scope, the generic accrual convention is the level yield method. The underlying economic rigor stems from the ability of this method to recognize the income implications when security prices deviate from par. For discount securities, the income recognition method is identical to that of zero coupon bonds where the return of investment is tied to principal maturity.

In its application to mortgage securities, SFAS 91 also emphasizes prepayments and the earlier than anticipated return of principal. For premium securities, particularly coupon only type securities, the Emerging Issues Task Force (EITF) at its May 21, 1987 meeting concluded, regarding issue number 86-38, that Statement 91 applies to interest only type securities also. Earlier in a consensus opinion reached at its December 4, 1986 meeting, however, the EITF had adopted a conservative variant of SFAS 91, which is more in agreement with SFAS 5, "Accounting for Contingencies." Also, the EITF recommended that SFAS 91 be applied with anticipations of prepayments. Although SFAS 91 allows for two different approaches in application of the level yield method—no prepayments anticipated, or prepayments anticipated—the latter provides a more accurate recognition of income, particularly when prices deviate significantly from par. The EITF, however, did not modify its prior consensus on excess and normal servicing fee type assets.

# Forward Prices and Dollar Rolls

STEVEN R. SCHULMAN, PH.D.
PRINCIPAL
FINANCIAL STRATEGIES
SECURITY PACIFIC MERCHANT BANK

## I. INTRODUCTION

Mortgage-backed pass-through securities issued by GNMA, FHLMC, and FNMA are actively traded in the secondary market on a forward delivery basis. A *dollar roll* is mortgage market parlance for a short-term financing technique which involves the simultaneous sale and repurchase of pass-through securities in the forward market. Once an understanding of the proper valuation and market determinants of forward price relationships is acquired, dollar rolls will be readily grasped and one can take full advantage of this financing technique.

Agency pass-throughs traded for forward delivery are termed TBA's by market participants. TBA is an acronym for "To Be Announced." This nomenclature derives from the fact that the seller of a TBA has some latitude in selecting securities to meet delivery obligations and is not required to notify the buyer until just prior to delivery regarding the specific securities that will be delivered. The Public Securities Association has set standards for "good delivery." TBA settlements must conform to these standards unless both buyer and seller agree to other terms at the time of the trade. PSA standards govern the settlement date, number of pools, and principal balance. As of this writing, the key standards established by PSA for settlement and clearing of TBA's are:

- Securities must have identical coupons and be issued by the same agency under the same program.

- For coupons greater than or equal to 12%, a maximum of four pools per $1,000,000 principal amount must be delivered.
- For coupons less than 12%, a maximum of three pools per $1,000,000 principal amount must be delivered.
- Sellers may over-deliver or under-deliver by 2.499999%.
- Settlement dates: Tuesday preceding third Wednesday of month for FHLMC and FNMA 30-year securities with coupons greater than 10%, third Wednesday of month for GNMA I and GNMA II 30-year securities with coupons greater than 10%, as well as all Midgets, Gnomes, Dwarfs, and all GNMA mobile homes, Monday following third Wednesday for all 30-year GNMA, FNMA, and FHLMC securities with coupons less than or equal to 10%, and all GNMA GPM's.

For example, a seller of one million GNMA 9% TBA's for January is obligated to deliver on the Monday following the third Wednesday in January no less than $975,000.01 and no more than $1,024,999.99 of principal balance of GNMA 9% from no more than three different pools. Should the TBA seller hold a large inventory of deliverable securities, the seller is free to deliver, and should deliver, the least desirable securities as long as they conform to delivery requirements. For example, the seller should deliver the slowest paying discount securities and the fastest paying premium securities in inventory.

## II. FORWARD PRICING

The essence of valuing a TBA is very similar to valuation methods for any forward or futures contract. However, there are some additional complications introduced by the uncertainty of mortgage cash flows and the contractual obligations of "good delivery." An investor who owns a GNMA 9% mortgage and sells a GNMA 9% TBA three months forward has created a synthetic short-term instrument. The return on this three-month investment should be the same as other three-month investments of similar credit quality. The investor receives three months of principal and interest cashflows from the GNMA 9%. By selling the security three months forward, the investor has locked in a sale price and thus eliminated all price risk from holding the security. The return earned over the holding period is known as the "implied cost of carry." Instead of holding the security for three months, the investor could sell the security and invest the proceeds at the three-month rate. Forward prices will tend to adjust so that investors are indifferent between: (1) continued holding of a security and selling it for forward delivery, or (2) selling the security outright and investing the proceeds in a money market instrument. This indifference level represents the fair value of a forward contract. An arbitrage opportunity exists if a forward price is too rich or too cheap relative to the cost of funds. If the forward price is too high, an investor can borrow short-term funds, invest in GNMA 9's and sell the forward earning a return greater than the cost of carry. Conversely, if the forward price is too low, an investor could sell the security outright and invest the proceeds at the short-term rate, and then buy the security forward.

The pricing relationship between actual GNMA's and GNMA forwards is readily extended to the relationship between forwards for different delivery dates. For example, by selling a March GNMA 9% TBA and buying a June GNMA 9% TBA, a transaction is entered which permits a GNMA 9 holder to borrow funds for three months. At March delivery, the borrower makes delivery of GNMA 9's at the agreed upon price. Three months of principal and interest cashflows are foregone in exchange for use of the cash proceeds. In June the securities are repurchased at the agreed upon June price. This transaction is a *dollar roll*. The difference between this transaction and a conventional transaction in the repo market is that the identical securities are unlikely to be returned. Any securities conforming to "good delivery" may be returned. Thus, different pools of GNMA 9's, with different prepayment histories, may be received in June than those delivered in March. When the near forward is bought and the more distant forward is sold, this is termed "buying the roll." This roll might be quoted as "down 20" meaning that the more distant TBA would be sold twenty 32nds below where the near TBA is purchased. This spread is referred to as the *drop*. A price for the March TBA is agreed upon by both parties, and two tickets are written: A Buy ticket at the agreed upon March price and a June Sell ticket at a price twenty 32nds below the March invoice.

Before we discuss some of the complications, let's work through a numerical example of a dollar roll (see Exhibit 1). Assume that a November GNMA 9 TBA is priced at 94 and that the November-December roll is quoted "down 6." The reinvestment rate is 7.3%. Also assume a conditional prepayment rate (CPR) of 4% and a remaining term of 27 years and 9 months. Regular settlement for a November 1987 TBA is the 17th and for a December TBA is the 15th of the month.

**EXHIBIT 1**
**ROLL ANALYSIS GNMA 9%**

*Sell security in November and reinvest proceeds at 7.3% for one month:*

| | |
|---|---|
| Sale of $1,000,000 in principal at 94 | 940,000.00 |
| 16 days accrued interest | 4,000.00 |
| Total proceeds | 944,000.00 |
| Interest on proceeds *(28 days at 7.3%)* | 5,359.82 |
| Future value on 12/15 | 949,359.82 |

*Hold Security in November and sell December TBA:*

| | |
|---|---|
| Mortgage Interest Payments | 7,500.00 |
| Scheduled Principal Payments | 617.69 |
| Unscheduled Principal Payments *(4% CPR)* | 3,393.95 |
| 995,988.36 remaining balance at 93-26 | 934,361.58 |
| 14 days accrued interest | 3,485.96 |
| Future value on 12/15 | 949,359.18 |

As can be seen from Exhibit 1, an investor selling GNMA's in November and investing the proceeds at the available short-term rate will realize a return within 64 cents of the alternative of holding the security for an additional month and selling at the December TBA price. Thus if the drop between November and December TBA prices is six 32nds, an investor will be indifferent between continued holding of the GNMA 9 and selling it. Other things being equal, this indifference level represents the fair price for a TBA. Using the assumptions in our example, a December TBA price that is greater or less than 93-26 will result in an arbitrage opportunity as the alternatives of continued holding versus selling and investing short term will produce different returns.

### Dollar Roll Breakeven Calculations

The *breakeven forward price* given reinvestment rate is calculated as follows:

$$
F_{t+k} = \frac{B_t(F_t + A_t)\left(1 + \frac{rd}{360}\right) - (B_{t+k} + A_{t+k}) - \left(\sum_{n=1}^{k} C_n\left(1 + \frac{rd_n}{360}\right)\right)}{B_{t+k}}
$$

where

$F_t$ = forward price divided by 100 for delivery at time $t$.

$B_t$ = principal balance at time $t$.

$C_n$ = cashflow, including scheduled and unscheduled principal (at the expected prepayment rate), as well as all interest, at time $n$.

$A_t$ = accrued interest at time $t$.

$d$ = days in holding period; $d_n$ is equal to days between receipt of cashflow $n$ and end of holding period.

$r$ = cost of funds.

The *implied cost of carry* given forward prices is calculated as follows:

$$
r = \frac{B_{t+k}(F_{t+k} + A_{t+k}) + \left(\sum_{n=1}^{k} C_n\right) - B_t(F_t + A_t)}{B_t(F_t + A_t)\frac{d}{360} - \left(\sum_{n=1}^{k} C_n\right)\frac{d_n}{360}}
$$

A quick approximation of the forward price given the cost of funds which can be computed on any scientific or financial hand calculator with natural log functions is as follows:

$$F_{t+k} = F_t e^{d(s-y)/365}$$

where $e$ is the base of natural logarithms, $s$ is the continuous short-term rate, and $y$ is the continuous yield of the mortgage using the assumed CPR. Other terms are as previously defined. This approximation assumes continuous compounding and ignores the exact timing of cashflows but nonetheless furnishes a surprisingly good estimate of forward prices. To use this approximation it is important to use CPR-adjusted continuous interest rates. The effective cost of funds can be solved for given forward prices by rearranging terms in the above equation:

$$s = y + \left(\frac{365}{d}\right) * \log_e\left(\frac{F_{t+k}}{F_t}\right)$$

Using this formula for our previous numerical example furnishes a price of 93.80, which differs by less than 1/64th from the exact price (93-26) obtained from the arbitrage breakeven analysis.

## III. SUPPLY AND DEMAND

In an arbitrage-free world, market forces should maintain price differentials between months that properly reflect the cost of funds. However, several factors cause deviations from the breakeven value for a TBA. Supply and demand is by far the most significant cause of departures from breakeven values. The breakeven arbitrage valuation method presented above, in fact, establishes a lower limit on the size of the price differentials between months.

Dealers of mortgage-backed securities, may, for a variety of reasons, establish large short positions, particularly in the nearest delivery months. This often occurs when another dealer is accumulating a large position in a particular coupon as collateral for a CMO. If a dealer does not possess a large enough inventory of the security to meet delivery obligations, the dealer finds himself in a "short squeeze" situation. To obtain the requisite amount of securities to cover the short position, the dealer may bid up the roll beyond its economic value. When this occurs, and it is not an uncommon event, holders of the security that is in demand by dealers are in the enviable position to obtain substantially below market short-term funds. Holders obtain this cheap financing by entering a dollar roll agreement with a dealer. The holder sells securities for front month delivery and simultaneously agrees to buy a longer dated TBA.

How much of a price differential the dealer is willing to sustain, i.e., his pain threshold, is ultimately limited by the *cost of fail*. When a dealer, or any other market participant, does not make "good delivery" on a short TBA position, they are technically in a "fail to deliver" situation. If a dealer fails to deliver for one week, one week's additional interest is owed the buyer. For $1,000,000 of GNMA 9's, the cost of failing for 7 days is $1750 or $250 per day. The cost of failing on a particular coupon for one month (in 32nds) is:

$$\text{Cost of Fail} = (\text{coupon} /12) *32$$

Thus while the arbitrage breakeven analysis establishes the lower limit on drop values, the upper limit on the size of a one-month drop will be the cost of fail. If the drop were larger than the cost of fail calculated in the above formula, it would be cheaper for the short seller to actually fail than to obtain securities through an exceedingly expensive roll transaction.

## IV. DELIVERY OPTION

A seller of a TBA, under PSA "good delivery" guidelines, has the option to over-deliver or under-deliver on the principal balance by 2.499999%. Thus on a $1,000,000 trade, the seller is entitled to call back (under-deliver) 2.5% or put (over-deliver) to the buyer an additional 2.5%. In other words, when selling a TBA, an investor is also buying a call on $25,000 and buying a put on $25,000 principal amount. In options parlance, the short seller is long a straddle on 2.5% of the traded amount. Other things being equal, the drop between months obtained by the arbitrage breakeven argument should be augmented by the dollar value of the straddle purchased.

A TBA buyer is implicitly short the option straddle and should expect to pay less than the breakeven fair value as compensation for the additional risk incurred. As volatility increases, the imbedded options increase in value due to the enhanced probability of exercise. Thus as volatility increases, forward prices decline, drop values increase, and the implied cost of carry declines. This is illustrated in Exhibit 2.

## V. OTHER FACTORS

Other factors that affect the implied cost of funds are prepayments, shape of the yield curve, price levels, and reinvestment rates. An increase in prepayments during the holding period increases returns on discount securities, and thus decreases the implied cost of carry. Consequently, to obtain the same internal rate of return on a mortgage roll, an increase in prepayments will result in a larger drop for discounts. The converse holds true for premiums. An increase in prepayments reduces holding period returns thus increasing the implied cost of carry. To obtain a similar implied

**EXHIBIT 2**
**ONE-MONTH DROP AND DELIVERY OPTION VALUES**

|  | GNMA Coupon | | | | |
|---|---|---|---|---|---|
|  | 7.5 | 9 | 10.5 | 12 | 13.5 |
| Price | 86-04 | 94-00 | 102-12 | 107.26 | 110.20 |
| Volatility | 11 | 10 | 8 | 4 | 2.5 |
| Age *(months)* | 86 | 27 | 22 | 38 | 57 |
| CPR | .5 | 4 | 10 | 17 | 33 |
| Drop *(32nds)* | 4 | 6 | 7 | 6 | 1.5 |
| Cost of Fail *(32nds)* | 20 | 24 | 28 | 32 | 36 |
| Cost of Funds | 7.16 | 7.30 | 7.18 | 7.32 | 7.30 |
| Option Value *(32nds)* | 1.7 | 1.7 | 1.5 | .7 | .5 |
| Option-Adjusted Cost of Funds | 6.38 | 6.60 | 6.59 | 6.66 | 7.13 |

cost of carry from rolling premiums undergoing an increase in prepayments, drop values must decline.

As the yield curve steepens, the positive carry earned by holding mortgages that are funded short term increases. As a consequence, the implied cost of carry declines and drop values will increase to compensate. Conversely, as the yield curve flattens, the price differential between months will decrease. If the yield curve inverts, and short term borrowing and lending rates exceed mortgage yields, the drop will become negative and longer dated forwards will trade at a premium to shorter forwards. In a positively sloping yield curve environment, longer dated TBA's will always be priced cheaper than near dated TBAs. This is due to the positive carry earned by holding mortgage-backed securities.

Although not immediately obvious, the absolute price level of a dollar roll also has an effect on the implied cost of carry if prepayments are held constant. If the size of the drop is held constant, an increase in the price level will reduce the cost of funds. This can be seen from the implied cost of carry equation. Since the size of the drop is held constant, but the denominator is increased, the ratio, and therefore *r* must decrease. For example, a roll transaction with a drop of six 32nds will have a lower cost of funds if the price level of the front month is 97 than if the front month is 96. The reason for this is that the value of the stream of cashflows coming from prepayments is a function of the difference between par and the current price of the security. Thus, the lower the price of the security, the greater the value of prepayments and the higher the opportunity cost of not owning the front month. This holds true for rolls on premiums as well. The cost of prepayments to premium holders is less the lower the dollar price of the security. Hence, for a given level of prepayments, whether for premiums or discounts, the lower the price level of a roll, the higher the opportunity cost of not owning the front month, and the higher the implied cost of funds.

Most of the factors discussed in this article which affect the implied cost of funds and the size of the drop between months are summarized in Exhibit 3. In Exhibit 3, all variables except the effect listed on the left are assumed to be held constant.

**EXHIBIT 3**
**COST OF FUNDS AND DROP SENSITIVITY**

|  | Implied Cost of Funds | Drop |
|---|---|---|
| Increase Drop | decrease | |
| Increase COF | | decrease |
| Yield Curve Steepens | decrease | increase |
| Increase Price Levels | decrease | decrease |
| Increase CPR-Premiums | decrease | decrease |
| Increase CPR-Discounts | increase | increase |
| Increase Volatility | decrease | increase |

## VI. SWAPPING DOLLAR ROLLS

Although a dollar roll is itself an arbitrage, it is possible to swap dollar rolls and arbitrage rolls against each other. Swapping rolls between coupons and or agencies may be very attractive at times. Differences in supply and demand may cause some rolls to be cheap and other rolls to be relatively rich. Hence, it may be possible, for example, to borrow cheap funds by selling a FNMA 11 roll and earn a much higher return by buying a GNMA 9.5 roll.

## VII. CONCLUSION

Mortgage forward agreements (TBA's) have been shown to be priced on a cost of carry basis similar to forwards on other financial instruments. Valuation is complicated primarily by prepayments and several delivery options held by the seller of a forward. A dollar roll transaction is a financing technique involving the simultaneous sale and purchase of mortgage TBA's for different delivery months. Due to dealer demand for particular coupons, opportunities to obtain exceptionally low cost financing often are made available in the dollar roll market.

# Asset Backed Securities

ANDREW S. CARRON
DIRECTOR
FIRST BOSTON CORPORATION

WAYNE OLSON
VICE PRESIDENT
FIRST BOSTON CORPORATION

NELSON F. SOARES
VICE PRESIDENT
FIRST BOSTON CORPORATION

## I. INTRODUCTION

Asset backed securities are pass-through securities backed by loans, leases, or installment contracts on personal property (not real estate) such as computers and automobiles. This new generation of securities was introduced by First Boston in 1985 with the sale of lease-backed notes by Sperry Lease Finance Corporation. Investors are attracted to asset backed securities for the following reasons:

- Credit quality—Asset backed securities have high credit ratings, based on recourse provisions covering many times the historical loss rates on the underlying assets.
- Yield—Asset backed securities offer investors yields that exceed those on bonds of comparable maturity and quality.

- Liquidity—Rapid market growth has encouraged the development of a liquid secondary market.
- Relatively predictable cash flows—Asset backed securities carry some prepayment uncertainty, but unlike mortgage securities, most of the principal repayment comes in the form of predictable scheduled amortizations.
- Prepayment consistency—The portion of the principal returned in the form of prepayments is generally stable and is not as affected by changes in market interest rates as are prepayments on mortgage securities.
- Maturity—Asset backed securities have final maturities ranging from 3 to 5 years at the time of issue, with the average time to receipt of principal (average life) ranging from 1 to 3 years.

## II. STRUCTURE

Asset backed securities bear a close structural relationship to mortgage pass-throughs, as the following description of the GMAC 1985-A Grantor Trust issue will demonstrate. The GMAC issue, a pass-through security backed by automobile loans, is fairly representative of the asset backed securities that emerged in 1985.

The GMAC 1985-A Grantor Trust issue is an asset backed security that offers investors an undivided interest in a trust formed by General Motors Acceptance Corporation. To establish the trust, GMAC pooled newly originated installment sale contracts on new automobiles and light trucks. The installment sale agreements in the pool have scheduled maturities of three, four, and five years. The interest rates on the underlying loan contracts exceed the pass-through rate of interest on the security. All contracts call for full amortization of principal over the term to maturity through virtually equal monthly installments.

Investors receive monthly interest on the outstanding balance. The securities have a payment delay identical to that of GNMA I mortgage pass-throughs: interest and principal for each month is remitted to investors on the fifteenth day of the following month. Investors receive a full month's interest on any prepayments. GMAC, as servicer, advances principal and interest for delinquent receivables. Under a limited guaranty agreement, GMAC agrees to repurchase defaulted receivables up to a maximum recourse level of 5% of the remaining pool balance.

Because the GMAC 1985-A Grantor Trust issue is structured as a single class grantor trust, each investor receives a pro rata portion of principal and interest every month. The amount of principal contained in each receipt will depend on the amortization and prepayment rate of the underlying collateral. Faster prepayments will shorten the average life of the issue. (Because principal is returned in small amounts over the life of the bond, investors look at the average life of the initial principal rather than the final maturity as with a bullet-maturity bond.)

To date, there have been two forms of Credit Card ABS: a sale using certificates of ownership of the credit card receivables and a borrowing using notes collateralized by receivables. The two structures have many common features.

The Credit Card ABS issuer continues to service the receivables for which it receives a servicing fee. Generally, no notification is given to cardholders that their accounts are included in the transaction. The receivables of a specified set of accounts are included in the transaction. Generally, more receivables are included than those actually allocated to the Credit Card ABS investors. The additional receivables supply a buffer for seasonality and attrition, so that the total amount of receivables is always at least as great as the investors' interest in the receivables.

For a specified period (the revolving period), Credit Card ABS do not amortize principal. Instead, principal from the receivables is retained by the issuer to reinvest in additional receivables. The length of the revolving period largely determines the average life of the issue.

Interest on the Credit Card ABS is paid monthly on the 15th day of the following month to give the servicer time to process reports on the receivables. Principal repayments on the Credit Card ABS are distributed monthly with the interest payment during the amortization period, which follows the end of the revolving period. The amount of principal distribution is determined as cardholder payments are received on the receivables. Because monthly payment rates are relatively stable, principal is repaid in approximately equal installments.

Credit Card ABS depend, in part, on the rapid pay-out of investor principal to protect the investor against loss in the event of a deterioration in the receivables portfolio. Prescribed pay-out events result in the Credit Card ABS amortizing prematurely. Pay-out triggers include such events as delinquencies or losses above prescribed levels, insolvency of the issuer or a significant decline in portfolio yield. A guaranty, which may be from a third party or from the seller (except in the case of non-recourse asset sales by banks), is provided to protect against credit loss. Fraud losses are generally borne by the seller as a cost of servicing.

Since credit cards constitute "accounts" or "general intangibles" under the Uniform Commercial Code, there is no need for a trustee to take physical possession of any account documents to perfect a security interest in the receivables. The administrative burden is therefore less than with many other asset backed transactions.

## III. ASSET BACKED OBLIGATIONS

Asset backed obligations are debt instruments secured by loans, leases, or installment contracts; they have multiple classes, or tranches, that receive principal repayments in sequence. The asset backed obligation is similar to a collateralized mortgage obligation (CMO) in the same way that an asset backed security is similar to a mortgage backed security. Asset backed obligations offer investors most of the advantages of asset backed securities, plus greater cash flow predictability.

The first asset backed obligation was offered in October 1986 by Asset Backed Securities Corporation, a subsidiary of First Boston. The Series 1 offering totaled $4 billion—the largest non-government debt issue in history. Automobile loans originated by GMAC provided the collateral for the transaction, which was further supported by a limited guaranty from GMAC, a letter of credit from Credit Suisse, and the equity of the Asset Backed Securities Corporation.

Like asset backed securities, the principal and interest payments on the underlying loans or contracts provide the cash flow for bond holders. Like CMOs, principal payments on all the collateral are applied exclusively to the first tranche until it is retired, then to the second tranche, and so forth until the last tranche is paid down. The second and later tranches receive interest only until they, in turn, become the currently paying tranche. In the case of the Series 1 issue, the three tranches had average lives of 1.1, 2.2, and 3.0 years.

The Asset Backed Securities Corporation Series 1 issue was designed so that prepayments are reinvested rather than paid out as received. Therefore, principal is redeemed on a fixed, predetermined schedule and there is no prepayment uncertainty. Asset backed obligations can also be structured to pass through prepayments, giving them some degree of cash flow uncertainty.

## IV. SELLERS

Asset Backed Securities collateralized by automobile loans have been sold by many of the finance companies affiliated with automobile manufacturers: General Motors Acceptance Corporation, Ford Motor Credit Company, Chrysler Financial Corporation through the special-purpose entity, Chrysler Auto Receivables Company, and Nissan Motor Acceptance Corporation. Other automobile lenders have also sold these securities in the public market: Valley National Financial Corporation, Marine Midland Bank, Home Federal Savings and Loan Association, Western Financial Savings Bank, and Empire of America. Securities backed by computer leases have been sold publicly by Sperry Lease Finance Corporation. Securities backed by credit card loans, agricultural equipment, and boat loans have also been issued.

## V. RISK CONSIDERATIONS

The collateral for the securities is pledged to a trustee for the benefit of the certificate holder; the trustee is generally a commercial bank with a high credit rating. Security for the bonds is provided primarily by the collateral, usually with limited recourse to the seller. In the case of default on individual loans servings as collateral, the seller agrees to repurchase them at par up to a maximum amount net of the guarantor's recoveries on the loans, typically ranging from 5% to 10% of the original balance.

Based on data provided by the U.S. Federal Reserve Board, the risk on securities backed by automobile loans appears to be relatively small. Delinquency rates have been fairly stable historically, averaging between 1.5% and 2.5% during the past 20 years. The actual amount of the loss from these delinquencies has been substantially lower due to the ability to recover losses through automobile repossessions. Thus the guarantees provided for these securities appear more than sufficient to cover any defaults.

Most asset backed securities have some type of credit enhancement to assure the performance of the issuer/servicer. This can be in the form of a letter of credit, insurance bond, limited guaranty, overcollateralization, or reserve fund. All publicly issued asset backed securities are rated by the major agencies. The GMAC 1985-A certificates are rated Aa1 by Moody's and AA + by Standard & Poor's.

## VI. PREPAYMENTS

Loans and contracts underlying asset backed securities may be paid off in advance of scheduled maturity, and in fact most such loans are prepaid. In many cases, the option to do so rests entirely with the obligor. When a loan prepayment occurs, the principal is passed through on a pro rata basis to the certificate holders, retiring that portion of their principal that is attributable to the loan that has prepaid. Unexpectedly high prepayment will make the average life of a security shorter than expected, while prepayments lower than anticipated will have the opposite effect. Thus, it is necessary to understand and predict the rate of prepayments in order to evaluate asset backed securities. The following discussion pertains to issues backed by automobile loans, because they represent the largest part of the market. Aside from the particular features of automobile loans, the general principles apply to all asset backed securities.

### *Causes*

Most prepayments on automobile loan issues result from retirement in full of a contract. Fom the investor's point of view, the most significant causes of prepayments issues are as follows:

1. Sale or trade-in of the vehicle will ordinarily necessitate repayment in full.
2. Repossession of the vehicle by the lender or servicer will normally be followed within a few weeks by sale of the vehicle and repayment of the contract. To the extent that an investor is covered by recourse, insurance, or other guarantees of repayment, a repossession results in a full prepayment that is indistinguishable from other types of prepayment.
3. Loss or destruction of the vehicle by collision, theft, or confiscation normally requires repayment of the contract. All automobile receivables backing publicly issued securities require the obligor to carry insurance covering the most common casualties and require the servicer to "force place" such insurance on the vehicle should the obligor allow his policy to lapse.
4. Voluntary prepayment occurs when the obligor decides to retire the obligation with cash.
5. Refinancing occurs when a borrower takes out a new loan to pay off the existing obligation. Refinancing is a much less important source of prepayment in the market for consumer installment sale contracts than in the mortgage market, as discussed below.

6. Death of the obligor may cause the repayment of the loan from insurance proceeds if the obligor has carried credit life insurance.
7. Provisions in public transactions permit or require the servicer to repurchase contracts from the pool under the certain conditions not associated with borrower prepayment. There are typically many such provisions, falling into the categories of breach of warranty, renegotiation of contracts, and administrative convenience.

Although the average life of individual receivables can vary widely from one month to several years, the average life of a credit card receivables portfolio is very stable and depends on both the type and payment terms of the credit card. Credit Card ABS yields are relatively insensitive to changes in the monthly payment rate on the securitized credit card receivables. Forecasts of monthly payment rates are less significant a factor in determining yields of ABS backed by credit card receivables than those backed by mortgages or automobile loans. Credit Card ABS cash flows depend on the statistical properties of the receivables more than ABS backed by automobile loans because the payment terms on credit cards are often more flexible. To understand the nature of Credit Card ABS cash flows, it is important to understand the receivables, the issuer, and the structure.

### Refinancing

Because of the relatively short maturity and small balance of the typical automobile receivable, refinancing of a high rate obligation by a lower rate one is less common in the automobile market than in the mortgage market. Refinancing of a mortgage normally occurs when interest rates fall significantly after a fixed-rate loan contract has been signed. The incentive to refinance an automobile installment sale contract, however, is not strong because the monthly payment savings are very small. Also, loan rates are higher on used cars than on new cars, which also discourages refinancing of new car loans.

Lower financing activity works to the advantage of the asset backed security holder, since a large drop in rates does not produce the massive prepayments that most mortgage securities would experience. This is significant because prepayments harm the investor most in low interest rate environments, as discussed in the next section.

### Importance to Investors

Prepayments on asset backed securities are advantageous to the investor when it is possible to reinvest in securities of similar quality and maturity at a higher rate than was earned on the original investment. They are disadvantageous if market rates at the time of the prepayment are lower than the rate on the original securities. This is equivalent to saying that an investor profits when a discount instrument is called at par and loses when a premium instrument is called at par. Since prepayment rates on Asset Backed Securities are insensitive to changes in the level of interest rates, investors may expect advantageous prepayments to occur as frequently as disadvantageous ones.

*Analysis*

First Boston conducted an analysis of prepayment rates on automobile loans held in the GMAC portfolio over a three-year period. The primary finding of the study is that prepayment rates were remarkably insensitive to interest rates over the period from March 1982 through January 1985. During this period, there were wide fluctuations in interest rate levels as well as in many measures of macroeconomic activity, such as GNP growth and car sales. The consistency of prepayments through the ups and downs of the financial markets minimizes the concern about the prepayment risk of automobile pass-throughs. Prepayments on asset backed securities are more stable and more predictable than prepayments on mortgage backed securities.

Two patterns emerged from the results. First, prepayments are generally higher for high rate contracts than for low rate contracts. Second, prepayment rates are not consistently dependent upon market interest rate levels. The average prepayment rate in the moderate rate environment was higher than that in the low rate environment. Also, the difference in prepayment rates on automobile reeivables between the 14% and 9½% environments was far less dramatic than has been observed in the mortgage markets. The data suggest that refinancings are not very common for automobile receivables.

Contracts on used vehicles tend to prepay faster than those on new vehicles, and 36-month contracts tend to prepay faster than 48-month contracts. While absolute levels of prepayments differ among these categories, however, the prepayment rates within each category are consistent over a wide rantge of interest rate environments. As a result of this analysis, First Boston has devised a prepayment model specifically for automobile receivables, known as the absolute or ABS model. The name for the model refers to both the absolute measure used and the asset backed securities it was designed to analyze. The measurement of prepayments is discussed further in the appendix.

## VII. MEASURING EFFECTIVE MATURITY

Buyers of asset backed securities are generally interested in two statistics that summarize the nature of their investments. The first, the yield or rate of return of the investment, will be addressed below. The other is the life of the investment, or the time span over which the rate of return is realized.

In the simplest sense, the life of a pass-through security may be measured as the time until final maturity. Most of the principal amount in such a security, however, is retired well before final maturity due to scheduled amortization and prepayments. Investors have found it desirable to quantify the effective lifetime of a pool in a way that accounts for its principal paydowns. There are two traditional approaches to this problem, known as average life and duration.

The *average life* of a security is the average number of years that each dollar of principal will be outstanding. Stated differently, it is the number of years that each dollar of principal in a pass-through pool can be expected to survive. Average life is computed as the weighted average time to receipt of all of the principal payments, using as weights the dollar amount of the principal received at the respective points in time. The average life of a term bond is therefore equal to its maturity. Securities with periodic principal payments have average lives shorter than their maturities.

The *duration* of a security is also stated in years. Duration is computed as the weighted average time to receipt of the present value of all projected cash flows (principal and interest), using as weights the present value of the cash received at the respective points in time. Thus, duration is similar to average life, except that instead of measuring the time it takes to recover principal, duration measures the time it takes to recover price. The duration of a zero coupon bond is therefore equal to its maturity. Securities with periodic interest and/or principal payments have durations shorter than their maturities.

*Modified duration* is used as an index of price sensitivity. When duration is divided by a simple factor (equal to one plus yield per period), the result is known as modified duration. The greater the modified duration of an investment, the more volatile is its price with respect to any given change in yield. One desirable property of modified duration is its direct relation to volatility—if one security has twice the modified duration of another, it also will have twice the volatility.

Measured in terms of either average life or duration, effective maturity falls as prepayment rates increase. But average life and duration of automobile receivables do not vary significantly with changes in prepayment rates. The reason for this prepayment insensitivity as compared to that of mortgage pass-throughs or CMOs is that new 36- to 60-month receivables have much faster scheduled principal amortizations than do new 30-year mortgages, and therefore the prepayments are a smaller percentage of the total principal payment received. For example, a typical new 30-year mortgage might be expected to return only 10% of its principal in the form of scheduled amortization before prepayment, whereas for a new 60-month automobile loan the figure would be roughly 60%. This gives every automobile pass-through the equivalent of a guaranteed minimum sinking fund. In sum, lower duration variability means that even if prepayments varied as much on automobile receivables as on residential mortgages (which they do not), the investor's total return would not be as greatly affected as with mortgage securities.

## VIII. MARKET VALUE RESPONSE TO CHANGES IN INTEREST RATES

Unlike mortgage backed pass-through securities, which perform very differently from traditional bonds, asset backed securities closely resemble a noncallable bond in terms of price changes relative to interest rate changes. There is a slight difference in performance between asset backed securities and term bonds. This justifies a slight yield premium for asset backed securities over term bonds of comparable quality, although this difference is not nearly as great as that between many mortgage-backed securities and high quality term bonds.

The market price response of a debenture is convex; that is, the distribution of returns is biased in the investor's favor. For a given decline in yield, the investor's profit is generally greater than the loss that would be created by an equal increase in yield. An asset backed security has this desirable investment characteristic, although to a lesser degree than a debenture of comparable quality and average life. The automobile pass-through should have a price performance very close to that of straight debt.

## IX. YIELD MEASUREMENT

The generally accepted yield measurement for asset backed securities, as for mortgage securities, is projected cash flow yield. The yield will depend not only on the coupon and the price but also on the prepayment assumption. Therefore, yield tables for asset backed securities generally display several yields for each price, corresponding to different prepayment assumptions the investor might use.

Asset backed securities do not generally yield their coupon (pass-through) rates when priced at par. This is the result of two factors, which act in opposite directions:

(a) Yields are stated on a corporate bond equivalent (CBE) basis. This involves an upward adjustment to reflect the advantage to the investor of monthly receipt and reinvestment of cash flows, compared with the semiannual payment frequency of corporate and government bonds, or the annual payments of Eurobonds. A monthly yield of 8% is equal to a semiannual yield of 8.13% and an annual yield of 8.30%.

(b) There is generally a 14-day delay in the remittance of payments to investors beyond the date on which interest is accrued. This is the same payment delay as found on GNMA pass-through securities. The delay serves to reduce the investor's yield relative to an otherwise identical security with no payment delay. When the security is priced at parity (discussed below), the yield reduction typically ranges from 16 to 24 basis points. The yield reduction is greater when the security is priced at a discount and smaller when the security is priced at a premium.

There is a price at which the yield does not vary with prepayment rates and is in fact equal to the coupon restated to its corporate bond equivalent. This price is known as the parity price. It behaves like par on a callable corporate bond: below parity, yield increases with prepayment; above parity, yield declines with prepayment.

## X. CONCLUSIONS

Asset backed securities have been issued at yields of up to 100 basis points greater than Treasury securities with a comparable average life. Investors should be attracted to these instruments because of their yield advantage, high credit quality, short and predictable maturities, and growing liquidity.

### APPENDIX: CASH FLOWS ON ASSET BACKED SECURITIES

Although prepayment of a given loan occurs only once in its life, prepayments in a pool of many such receivables will tend to occur during each month of the pool's life. With each contract representing only a small fraction of the total pool balance, its prepayment in a given month reduces the remaining principal only slightly. The rate at which individual contract prepayments draw down the balance of a pool is called the prepayment rate or prepayment experience of the pool.

As previously noted, contract balances are reduced not only by prepayment but also by scheduled monthly principal amortization. Accordingly, the fraction of a pool's original principal balance that remains at any given point in time (termed the "pool factor") may be expressed as the product of two other numbers: (1) the fraction of the original contracts remaining (not prepaid), or the "survival factor," and (2) the fraction of the representative contract that remains unamortized, or the "contract balance."

The aggregate prepayment rate over any given time interval from origination is defined as one minus the survival factor. Since the survival factor times the contract balance equals the pool factor, as stated above, the aggregate prepayment rate is one minus the ratio of the pool factor to the contract balance.

To state this algebraically, let

PF    = Pool Factor
SF    = Survival Factor
CB    = Contract Balance
PR    = Prepayment Rate

All numbers are expressed as decimal fractions. For example, 15% is expressed as 0.15.

Since
    $PF = SF \times CB$
it follows that
    $SF = PF/CB,$
and since
    $PR = 1 - SF$
it follows that
    $PR = 1 - PF/CB.$

To illustrate these relationships, assume that a pool is originally composed of 10,000 contracts, each with an original balance of $10,000, giving an initial pool balance of $100,000,000. Each contract is fully amortizing over an original term of 36 months at an annual percentage rate of 7%. Further assume that 130 contracts (1.3% of the original number) prepay each month. The cash flows for this pool are displayed in Exhibit 1 and shown in graphical form in Exhibit 2.

For simplicity, this example describes the cash flows on the pool of loans used to support an asset backed security, not the security itself. The cash flows on the asset backed security would be similar, except for the following:

1. A delay (generally 14 days) in the receipt of cash flow; and
2. The retention of a fee by the servicer. Thus, loans with a 7% interest rate might typically be packaged into a security with a 6.3% interest rate; the difference of 0.7% is retained to compensate the servicer for the costs and risks of collecting the monthly payments from the borrowers.

In month 1, cash flow is copmosed of the following components:

a. Interest $= 1/12$ of 7% on the starting balance of $100,000,000 $= $583,333 (Column B).
b. Scheduled Principal $=$ Balance of loans (Column A $= $100,000,000) times the monthly interest rate (7%/12); divided by the quantity:

$$[1 + \text{monthly interest rate } (7\%/12)]^{\text{Remaining Term (36 months)}} - 1$$

This is the standard annuity formula. The result is as follows:

$$\frac{\$100,000,000 \times 7\%/12}{(1 + 7\%/12)^{36} - 1} = \$2,504,376 \text{ (Column C)}$$

c. Unscheduled Principal (Prepayments) $=$ Number of loans prepaid (1.3% ABS $\times$ 10,000 loans in original pool $=$ 130 loans) times average balance per loan prepaid (Column H $= $9749.56) $= $1,267,443 (Column D).

Total cash flow is therefore $4,355,152 (the sum of Columns B, C, D). The principal balance is reduced by $3,771,819 (the sum of Columns C and D) to $96,228,181. For month 2, the process is repeated:

a. Interest $=$ 1/12 of 7% on the starting balance of $96,228,181 $= $561,331.
b. Scheduled Principal $=$ Balance of loans (9,870 loans $\times$ $9,749.56 per loan $=$ $96,228,157) times the monthly interest rate (7%/12) divided by $[1 + (7\%/12)]^{35} - 1 = $2,486,238.

**EXHIBIT 1**
**CASH FLOW OF A HYPOTHETICAL ASSET BACKED SECURITY—$100,000,000—36 MONTHS—7%**

| Month | Starting Balance (A) | Gross Interest (B) | Scheduled Principal (C) | Unscheduled Principal (D) | Total Principal (E) | Ending Balance (F) | Pool Factor (G) | Average Balance (H) | Contract Balance (I) | Number of Contracts (J) | Survival Factor (K) | ABS Rate (L) | SMM Rate (M) |
|---|---|---|---|---|---|---|---|---|---|---|---|---|---|
| 0 | | | | | | | | $10,000.00 | 1.00000 | 10,000 | 1.00000 | | |
| 1 | $100,000,000 | $583,333 | $2,504,376 | $1,267,443 | $3,771,819 | $96,228,181 | 0.96228 | 9,749.56 | 0.97496 | 9,870 | 0.98700 | 1.300% | 1.300% |
| 2 | 96,228,181 | 561,331 | 2,486,238 | 1,234,696 | 3,720,934 | 92,507,247 | 0.92507 | 9,497.66 | 0.94977 | 9,740 | 0.97400 | 1.300 | 1.317 |
| 3 | 92,507,247 | 539,626 | 2,467,804 | 1,201,758 | 3,669,562 | 88,837,685 | 0.88838 | 9,244.30 | 0.92443 | 9,610 | 0.96100 | 1.300 | 1.335 |
| 4 | 88,837,685 | 518,220 | 2,449,069 | 1,168,629 | 3,617,698 | 85,219,987 | 0.85220 | 8,989.45 | 0.89895 | 9,480 | 0.94800 | 1.300 | 1.353 |
| 5 | 85,219,987 | 497,117 | 2,430,032 | 1,135,305 | 3,565,337 | 81,654,650 | 0.81655 | 8,733.12 | 0.87331 | 9,350 | 0.93500 | 1.300 | 1.371 |
| 6 | 81,654,650 | 476,319 | 2,410,690 | 1,101,788 | 3,512,478 | 78,142,172 | 0.78142 | 8,475.29 | 0.84753 | 9,220 | 0.92200 | 1.300 | 1.390 |
| 7 | 78,142,172 | 455,829 | 2,391,039 | 1,068,075 | 3,459,114 | 74,683,058 | 0.74683 | 8,215.96 | 0.82160 | 9,090 | 0.90900 | 1.300 | 1.410 |
| 8 | 74,683,058 | 435,651 | 2,371,077 | 1,034,165 | 3,405,242 | 71,277,816 | 0.71278 | 7,955.11 | 0.79551 | 8,960 | 0.89600 | 1.300 | 1.430 |
| 9 | 71,277,816 | 415,787 | 2,350,801 | 1,000,057 | 3,350,858 | 67,926,958 | 0.67927 | 7,692.75 | 0.76927 | 8,830 | 0.88300 | 1.300 | 1.451 |
| 10 | 67,926,958 | 396,241 | 2,330,207 | 965,751 | 3,295,958 | 64,631,000 | 0.64631 | 7,428.85 | 0.74289 | 8,700 | 0.87000 | 1.300 | 1.472 |
| 11 | 64,631,000 | 377,014 | 2,309,293 | 931,244 | 3,240,537 | 61,390,464 | 0.61390 | 7,163.42 | 0.71634 | 8,570 | 0.85700 | 1.300 | 1.494 |
| 12 | 61,390,464 | 358,111 | 2,288,056 | 896,536 | 3,184,592 | 58,205,872 | 0.58206 | 6,896.43 | 0.68964 | 8,440 | 0.84400 | 1.300 | 1.517 |
| 13 | 58,205,872 | 339,534 | 2,266,493 | 861,626 | 3,128,119 | 55,077,753 | 0.55078 | 6,627.89 | 0.66279 | 8,310 | 0.83100 | 1.300 | 1.540 |
| 14 | 55,077,753 | 321,287 | 2,244,600 | 826,511 | 3,071,111 | 52,006,642 | 0.52007 | 6,357.78 | 0.63578 | 8,180 | 0.81800 | 1.300 | 1.564 |
| 15 | 52,006,642 | 303,372 | 2,222,374 | 791,193 | 3,013,567 | 48,993,075 | 0.48993 | 6,086.10 | 0.60861 | 8,050 | 0.80500 | 1.300 | 1.589 |
| 16 | 48,993,075 | 285,793 | 2,199,813 | 755,668 | 2,955,481 | 46,037,595 | 0.46038 | 5,812.83 | 0.58128 | 7,920 | 0.79200 | 1.300 | 1.615 |
| 17 | 46,037,595 | 268,553 | 2,176,913 | 719,935 | 2,896,848 | 43,140,746 | 0.43141 | 5,537.97 | 0.55380 | 7,790 | 0.77900 | 1.300 | 1.641 |
| 18 | 43,140,746 | 251,654 | 2,153,671 | 683,995 | 2,837,666 | 40,303,080 | 0.40303 | 5,261.50 | 0.52615 | 7,660 | 0.76600 | 1.300 | 1.669 |
| 19 | 40,303,080 | 235,101 | 2,130,084 | 647,845 | 2,777,929 | 37,525,152 | 0.37525 | 4,983.42 | 0.49834 | 7,530 | 0.75300 | 1.300 | 1.697 |
| 20 | 37,525,152 | 218,897 | 2,106,149 | 611,483 | 2,717,632 | 34,807,519 | 0.34808 | 4,703.72 | 0.47037 | 7,400 | 0.74000 | 1.300 | 1.726 |

| | | | | | | | | | | | | | |
|---|---|---|---|---|---|---|---|---|---|---|---|---|---|
| 21 | 34,807,519 | 203,044 | 2,081,861 | 574,910 | 2,656,771 | 32,150,748 | 0.32151 | 4,422.30 | 0.44224 | 7,270 | 0.72700 | 1.300 | 1.757 |
| 22 | 32,150,748 | 187,546 | 2,057,219 | 538,124 | 2,595,343 | 29,555,406 | 0.29555 | 4,139.41 | 0.41394 | 7,140 | 0.71400 | 1.300 | 1.788 |
| 23 | 29,555,406 | 172,407 | 2,032,218 | 501,122 | 2,533,340 | 27,022,065 | 0.27022 | 3,854.79 | 0.38548 | 7,010 | 0.70100 | 1.300 | 1.821 |
| 24 | 27,022,065 | 157,629 | 2,006,856 | 463,905 | 2,470,761 | 24,551,304 | 0.24551 | 3,568.50 | 0.35685 | 6,880 | 0.68800 | 1.300 | 1.854 |
| 25 | 24,551,304 | 143,216 | 1,981,128 | 426,471 | 2,407,599 | 22,143,705 | 0.22144 | 3,280.55 | 0.32805 | 6,750 | 0.67500 | 1.300 | 1.890 |
| 26 | 22,143,705 | 129,172 | 1,955,032 | 388,819 | 2,343,851 | 19,799,854 | 0.19800 | 2,990.91 | 0.29909 | 6,620 | 0.66200 | 1.300 | 1.926 |
| 27 | 19,799,854 | 115,499 | 1,928,565 | 350,947 | 2,279,512 | 17,520,342 | 0.17520 | 2,699.59 | 0.26996 | 6,490 | 0.64900 | 1.300 | 1.964 |
| 28 | 17,520,342 | 102,202 | 1,901,722 | 312,854 | 2,214,576 | 15,305,766 | 0.15306 | 2,406.57 | 0.24066 | 6,360 | 0.63600 | 1.300 | 2.003 |
| 29 | 15,305,766 | 89,284 | 1,874,500 | 274,538 | 2,149,038 | 13,156,728 | 0.13157 | 2,111.83 | 0.21118 | 6,230 | 0.62300 | 1.300 | 2.044 |
| 30 | 13,156,728 | 76,746 | 1,846,896 | 236,000 | 2,082,896 | 11,073,832 | 0.11074 | 1,815.38 | 0.18154 | 6,100 | 0.61000 | 1.300 | 2.087 |
| 31 | 11,073,832 | 64,597 | 1,818,906 | 197,236 | 2,016,142 | 9,057,690 | 0.09058 | 1,517.20 | 0.15172 | 5,970 | 0.59700 | 1.300 | 2.131 |
| 32 | 9,057,690 | 52,837 | 1,790,526 | 158,246 | 1,948,772 | 7,108,918 | 0.07109 | 1,217.28 | 0.12173 | 5,840 | 0.58400 | 1.300 | 2.178 |
| 33 | 7,108,918 | 41,469 | 1,761,754 | 119,029 | 1,880,783 | 5,228,134 | 0.05228 | 915.61 | 0.09156 | 5,710 | 0.57100 | 1.300 | 2.226 |
| 34 | 5,228,134 | 30,497 | 1,732,585 | 79,583 | 1,812,168 | 3,415,966 | 0.03416 | 612.18 | 0.06122 | 5,580 | 0.55800 | 1.300 | 2.277 |
| 35 | 3,415,966 | 19,926 | 1,703,016 | 39,907 | 1,742,923 | 1,673,043 | 0.01673 | 306.98 | 0.03070 | 5,450 | 0.54500 | 1.300 | 2.330 |
| 36 | 1,673,043 | 9,759 | 1,673,042 | 0 | 1,673,042 | 0 | .00000 | .00 | .00000 | 5,320 | 0.53200 | 1.300 | 2.385 |

**EXHIBIT 2**
**CASH FLOW ON A 7% ASSET BACKED SECURITY ASSUMING A 1.3% ABS PREPAYMENT RATE, 0% SERVICING FEE, AND $100,000,000 ORIGINAL PRINCIPAL BALANCE**

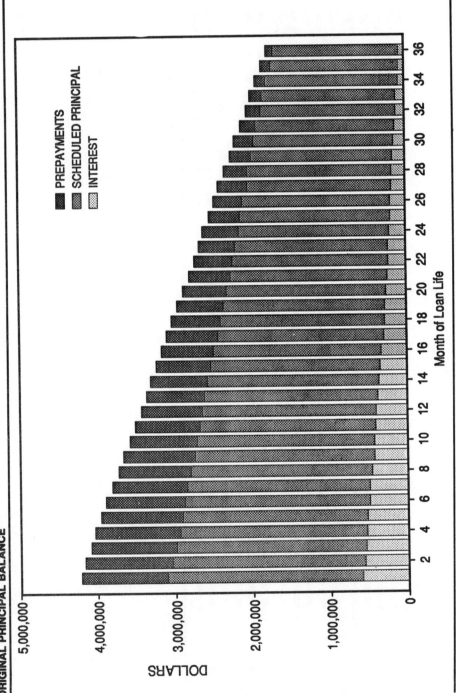

c. Unscheduled Principal (Prepayments) = Number of loans prepaid (1.3% ABS × 10,000 loans in original pool = 130 loans) times average balance per loan prepaid ($9,497.66) = $1,234,696.

This process continues for the entire 36 month contract life of the loans.

## ABS Experience

It is convenient to state prepayment rates over a standard interval, such as monthly. In the previous example, 2,340 contracts have prepaid in 18 months. Therefore, on average 130 contracts have prepaid each month. As there were 10,000 contracts to begin with, this represents 1.3% of the original number of contracts which have prepaid on average each month. The interim ABS rate for any given month within the interval is simply the difference between the beginning and ending survival factors for the month.

This measure of prepayment rates is termed the absolute model of prepayments, because it measures prepayments in each month as an absolute number of contracts, expressed as a fraction of the original number. The model was designed by First Boston specifically to measure prepayments on pools of consumer installment sale contracts on automobiles. The model reflects historical experience on such assets better than do the prepayment models commonly used in the mortgage market. This observation has been confirmed in studies by First Boston of liquidation rates in several portfolios of automobile receivables.

## SMM Experience

A prepayment measure commonly used in the analysis of mortgages is the SMM or Single Monthly Mortality model, which was developed specifically to measure prepayments on pools of home mortgages. This measure is a mortality rate, in which each month's prepayments are expressed as a fraction of the loans remaining at the end of the previous month. In this sense, it is a relative (or conditional) rather than an absolute rate—relative to the number of survivors remaining each month rather than to the fixed reference point of the original number of loans.

The SMM model regards the survival factor as the product of a series of monthly survival factors. For any given month within the interval, the interim SMM rate is the difference between the beginning and ending survival factors for the month (the interim ABS rate), divided by the beginning survival factor.

The cumulative and interim SMM rates will always be higher than the corresponding ABS rates, for a given interval of a given pool's life (except for the first month, during which they are equal), because the SMM rate is applied to a declining number of loans while the ABS rate is always applied to the original number.

The SMM model was developed because estimates of mortgage pool prepayment rates derived in SMM terms tended to be more accurate than those using previously available models. The ABS model is used for automobile receivables at First Boston because SMM rates tend to rise over time within the life of most pools of automobile receivables. The ABS rate tends to be more consistent over a pool's life, and is therefore a better indicator of future behavior than the SMM rate.

# PART V

# Futures and Interest Rate Agreements

# Treasury Bond and Note Futures: Pricing and Portfolio Management Applications

TIMOTHY J. LORD, PH.D.
VICE PRESIDENT
FINANCIAL FUTURES AND OPTIONS GROUP
MERRILL LYNCH CAPITAL MARKETS

## I. INTRODUCTION

In recent years, the global capital markets have become increasingly volatile. This has resulted in greater uncertainty and risk associated with the management of fixed income portfolios and the issuance of debt. Responding to this, money managers have increasingly relied on the derivative product markets to preserve portfolio values and achieve acceptable yields, and liability managers to hedge unanticipated increases in the cost of debt.

This article describes the Treasury bond and futures markets and their use in hedge and yield enhancement strategies. Emphasis is placed on pricing and relative value relationships, and their impact on the performance of cash-futures trades.

Section II develops a methodology for pricing futures contracts based on "cost of carry" relationships and arbitrage trading. Two key measures of relative value between cash and futures prices—the "implied repo rate" and the "basis"—are discussed. Section III explores the impact on futures prices resulting from changes in market conditions. These include changes in the "cheapest-to-deliver" bond,

545

changes in yield spread, futures embedded options, and the delivery-month supply of the cheapest-to-deliver bond. Each of these is analyzed for its potential effect on futures prices, hedging, and trading. Section IV addresses issues that confront portfolio managers who may need to hedge fixed income securities, or seek enhanced portfolio yields. Measures of portfolio risk such as duration, convexity, and basis point value are defined, and their use in constructing hedge ratios and targeting portfolio performance are explored. Finally, the concepts introduced throughout this article are summarized by two applications: an example of a short futures hedge of a Treasury bond, and a synthetic security created by combining a money market instrument and a long futures position. Appendix A summarizes the contract specifications and delivery procedures, and Appendix B contains a glossary of futures terminology.

## II. FUTURES PRICING AND RELATIVE VALUE

Prices of Treasury bond and note futures contracts are linked to prices in the Treasury cash market by arbitrage relationships.[1] This section explores these relationships, including key measures of relative value between cash and futures prices. Those who are unfamiliar with the contract specifications may refer to Appendix A.

### The Invoice Price and Conversion Factor

The bond futures contract specifies delivery of an 8% coupon bond. Bonds with other coupons can also be delivered, but only at a premium or discount (depending on the coupon and maturity) to an 8% bond.[2] The price per $100,000 face value at which an eligible bond can be delivered is called the invoice price. It is calculated as:

$$\begin{array}{c}\text{Invoice price} \\ \text{per contract}\end{array} = \left[ \begin{array}{ccc} \text{Futures} & \times & \text{Conversion} \\ \text{Price} & & \text{Factor} \end{array} \right] \times \$1{,}000 + \begin{array}{c}\text{Accrued} \\ \text{Interest}\end{array}$$

The conversion factor is a quality adjustment mechanism that takes into account a bond's coupon and maturity, relative to the 8% bond specified by the contract. The conversion factor system for invoicing bonds effectively broadens the supply of bonds that are deliverable against the futures market. Just as a commodity producer can deliver (at a premium or discount) grain of various grades against the commodity futures contracts traded in Chicago, a government securities dealer can deliver bonds with various coupons and maturities against the bond contract. The premium or discount depends on the bond's conversion factor.

---

[1] While the concepts contained in this article pertain to both Treasury bond and ten-year note futures, most of the discussion is cast in terms of the bond contract.

[2] A total of 30 T-bonds and 17 T-notes are deliverable against the June '88 bond and ten-year note futures contracts, respectively.

Calculating the conversion factor is a two-step process. First, the remaining time to maturity (time to call if callable) of the bond is calculated from the first day of the delivery month and then rounded down to the nearest quarter. Second, given this maturity (call), the conversion factor is calculated as the price (rounded to four decimal places, with par equal to 1.0) at which the bond yields 8%. Calculated in this manner, the conversion factor is greater than 1.0 for bonds with coupons greater than 8%, equals 1.0 for 8% coupon bonds, and is less than 1.0 for bonds with coupons less than 8%.

What is the conversion factor of the non-callable 7¼% bond due May 15, 2016, deliverable against the June '88 futures contract? Rounded down to the nearest quarter as of June 1st, the time remaining to the maturity of this bond is 28 years and zero quarters. Given this maturity, the price (per dollar) of a 7¼% bond to yield 8% is 0.9167. This is the conversion factor for the 7¼% bond relative to the June '88 contract. Given a futures settlement price of 87¹⁶/₃₂, the invoice price for this bond is equal to $80,211.25 (87¹⁶/₃₂ × 0.9167 × $1000), plus accrued interest at delivery.

### Arbitrage and Futures Pricing

The primary component of the invoice price is the futures price. It is determined both by supply and demand in the futures market and by arbitrage that links futures prices to prices of cash market securities. This arbitrage is important, because it provides a framework for assessing relative value between the two markets. This section examines a simple arbitrage trade and shows how the futures price is linked to the cash market.

Suppose a trader buys a bond that is deliverable against the futures contract, and finances the position with borrowed funds. Simultaneously, he sells a futures contract with the intention of delivering the bond against the contract. What would the trader expect to earn on this arbitrage transaction consisting of a long bond, a financing position and a short futures contract. The answer is zero, if the cash and futures markets are "fairly priced." Futures are said to be fairly priced when there is no potential to make arbitrage profits by establishing simultaneous positions in the cash and futures markets. The zero profit arbitrage relationship between cash and futures prices is:

$$\text{Profit} = (FP \times CF) + C - F - CP = 0$$

where: 
$FP$ = Futures price
$CF$ = Conversion factor for the bond purchased
$C$ = Coupon income[3]
$F$ = Financing cost of the bond
$CP$ = Cash price of the bond

---

[3]Coupon income includes coupons received (if any), reinvestment of coupons, and net accrued interest (accrued received at futures delivery minus accrued paid at settlement).

If the cash or futures market is not fairly priced, a trader could earn a positive profit by taking a short position in the overvalued market and a long position in the undervalued market. This would tend to drive prices down in the overvalued market and up in the undervalued market, reestablishing the equilibrium relationship between cash and futures prices. Thus, the potential for arbitrage is central in determining the relative value relationship between cash and futures prices.

Two useful relationships can be defined, by rearranging terms:

$$CP - (FP \times CF) = C - F \tag{1}$$

The difference between the bond's cash price and the futures price times the conversion factor is related to the difference between the coupon income and cost of financing the bond. The left-hand side of this equation is commonly referred to as the "gross basis" and the right-hand side as the "carry." These are key measures of relative value.

$$FP = \frac{CP - (C - F)}{CF} \tag{2}$$

The futures price can be expressed in terms of the cash price.[4] It generally reflects the coupon yield of the underlying bond relative to its term financing rate in the cash market. This is commonly referred to as a "cost of carry relationship." This terminology derives from the commodity markets, in which physical commodities such as grain can be "carried" over time, prior to their delivery against a futures position. Typically, the carrying charge for physical commodities includes costs of storage, transportation, insurance, and interest. For Treasury securities, the carrying charge is the cost of financing a cash market position. The repurchase (repo) market provides the primary source of financing Treasury securities; consequently, futures prices are closely linked to term repo rates.

These factors also determine the forward price of a bond. The forward price is the expected value of a bond. It generally reflects current and future supply and demand, as well as the cost of carrying a bond over time. If a bond's total coupon income exceeds the cost of financing it, the forward price is at a discount to its spot price. The forward price is at a premium if the cost of financing is higher than the coupon income. On the simplest level, the theoretical futures price equals the forward price of a bond divided by its conversion factor.

---

[4]The bond's cash price can also be expressed in terms of the futures price: CP = (FP × CF) + (C - F). Some traders believe that futures prices are a more accurate representation of value than cash prices, because the futures market is often more liquid than the cash market. This equation can be useful to assess cash values in terms of the futures market.

## Futures Pricing Example

In Exhibit 1, the theoretical futures price is calculated for a 9% 29-year bond (conversion factor = 1.1121), for two yield curves, one positive and the other negative. There is no reinvestment of coupons.

**EXHIBIT 1**
**THEORETICAL FUTURES PRICE**

|                | Positive Yield Curve | Negative Yield Curve |
|----------------|----------------------|----------------------|
| Cash Price     | 100                  | 100                  |
| Coupon         | 9.0%                 | 9.0%                 |
| Coupon Income  | $2,250               | $2,250               |
| Repo Rate      | 6.0%                 | 12.0%                |
| Finance Cost   | $1,500               | $3,000               |
| Carry          | $750 ($23/32$nds)    | −$750 (−$24/32$nds)  |
| Forward Price  | 99-08                | 100-24               |
| Futures Price  | 89-08 (99-08/1.1121) | 90-19 (100-24/1.1121) |

Consider the case of a positive yield curve. The coupon income on a $100,000 face value 9% bond for three months amounts to $2,250. Given a 6% repo rate, the cost of financing that bond over the same period is $1,500. Therefore, the coupon income exceeds the cost of financing, resulting in a positive carry equal to $750 (2,250 − 1,500) or $24/32$nds of a point. The "fair" futures price is obtained by subtracting the carry from the bond's cash price, and dividing the result by the conversion factor. In terms of the equation derived earlier, the futures price is:

$$FP = \frac{100 - 24/32}{1.1121} = 89^8/32.$$

The futures price reflects fair value in the following sense: If the bond is purchased at par, the futures is sold at $89^8/32$, and the position is financed for three months at 6.0% then there is zero expected profit on the trade if the bond is delivered against the contract. The positive carry is equal to the capital loss between the current cash price and the futures invoice price.

We have developed a simple pricing framework based on arbitrage for determining the fair value of a futures contract in terms of the cash market. It is predicated on the notion that arbitrage traders will sell in the overvalued market and buy in the undervalued market if prices get out of line. The section that follows analyzes two strategies that are commonly employed to take advantage of price misalignments.

### Cash and Carry Trades

If futures prices are overvalued relative to the cash market, traders can establish the cash and carry trade. This trade consists of a long position in cash bonds, a financing position and short futures contracts. (It is equivalent to the arbitrage transaction posed earlier.) The cash and carry trade is a long basis trade; that is, long in the cash market and short in the futures market. As traders purchase bonds and sell futures contracts, the futures price tends to decline relative to the bond's cash price. The ability of traders to execute these transactions, whenever futures prices appear overvalued, tends to establish a ceiling on the futures price relative to the price of the cash bond.

Moreover, the cash and carry trade is related to synthetic short-term investments created by shorting futures against long bond positions. If the return to such a trade is high enough, it may become an attractive alternative to other short-term investments. This trade involves an investment of funds (in the cash bond), whereas the cash and carry trade is a leveraged arbitrage transaction.

Conversely, if futures prices are undervalued relative to the cash market, arbitrage traders can transact the reverse of the cash and carry trade. This short basis trade involves shorting bonds in the cash market, investing the cash generated from the short position in the repo market and buying futures contracts. As traders take advantage of this arbitrage, their purchase of futures contracts tends to raise the futures price relative to the bond's cash price. This tends to create a floor under the futures price relative to prices in the cash market.

The reverse cash and carry trade is related to synthetic bond trades consisting of a long futures position coupled with a short-term investment. If futures are undervalued, the return on the synthetic bond can be higher than returns in the cash bond market. Section IV examines such yield enhancement strategies in more detail.

To assess whether futures are rich or cheap to the cash market and to gauge the expected profitability of the trades discussed above, traders often rely on various measures of relative value. One such measure is the implied repo rate.

### The Implied Repo Rate

The gross rate of return on the cash and carry trade, assuming the cash bond is delivered against the short futures position, is called the implied repo rate. It can be calculated at the outset, because both the purchase price (cash market) and the sale price (futures market) are known. The formula for the implied repo rate is:

$$\text{Implied Repo Rate} = \frac{\text{Cash In} - \text{Cash Out}}{\text{Cash Out}} \times \frac{360}{n}$$

where:   Cash In   =   The sum of the invoice price, coupons received (including reinvestment) and accrued interest received at delivery.

Cash Out   =   The current cash price plus accrued interest paid at settlement.

The implied repo rate is annualized according to the number of days (n) between the settlement date of the cash market purchase and the future delivery date. The delivery date is usually assumed to be the final business day of the delivery month if the yield curve is upward sloping, or the first day of the delivery month if it is downward sloping.[5] The implied repo rate is quoted on a simple interest, 360-day year basis to make it comparable to other money market rates.

Relative value can be determined by comparing the implied repo rate to the term repo rate.[6] An implied repo rate that is "too high" relative to the term rate suggests that the futures price is overvalued relative to the cash market. In this case, the cash and carry trade may be profitable. Conversely, an implied repo rate that appears "too low" suggests that the futures price is undervalued, signaling that the reverse cash and carry trade may be profitable.

In practice, the implied repo rate is typically 100 to 300 basis points below the term repo rate. This is illustrated in Exhibit 2 which shows the term and implied repo rates for the cheapest-to-deliver bond versus the March '88 futures contract during the year prior to expiration.[7] During that period, the implied repo rate averaged about 200 basis points less than the term repo rate until the stock market break in mid-October 1987, after which the spread temporarily increased.

An implied repo rate that is less than the term repo rate does not necessarily suggest that futures prices are undervalued. It may reflect the fact that traders with short futures positions can decide when to deliver during delivery month as well as which eligible bond to deliver, whereas traders who are long futures have little control over what bond they will get and when they will receive it. The latter are compensated for this uncertainty by a lower price on the contract, which in turn leads to a lower implied repo rate. These issues are described in more detail when futures embedded options are covered in Section III. The implied repo rate is a yield-based measure of relative value. Some traders prefer to assess relative value in terms

---

[5]This assumption is made because, once the sale price is established (via the short futures position), there is an incentive to hold the cash position longer if it earns positive carry (upward sloping yield curve), and to deliver earlier if it has negative carry.

[6]The precise criteria for relative value depends on market conditions, including the evaluation of embedded delivery options (to be discussed in Section III), and may change as market conditions change.

[7]The cheapest-to-deliver bond is defined as the bond that is most likely to be delivered against the futures contract. The futures prices tends to track the price of this bond. This is discussed in more detail in a later section.

**EXHIBIT 2**
**TERM VS. IMPLIED REPO RATES**

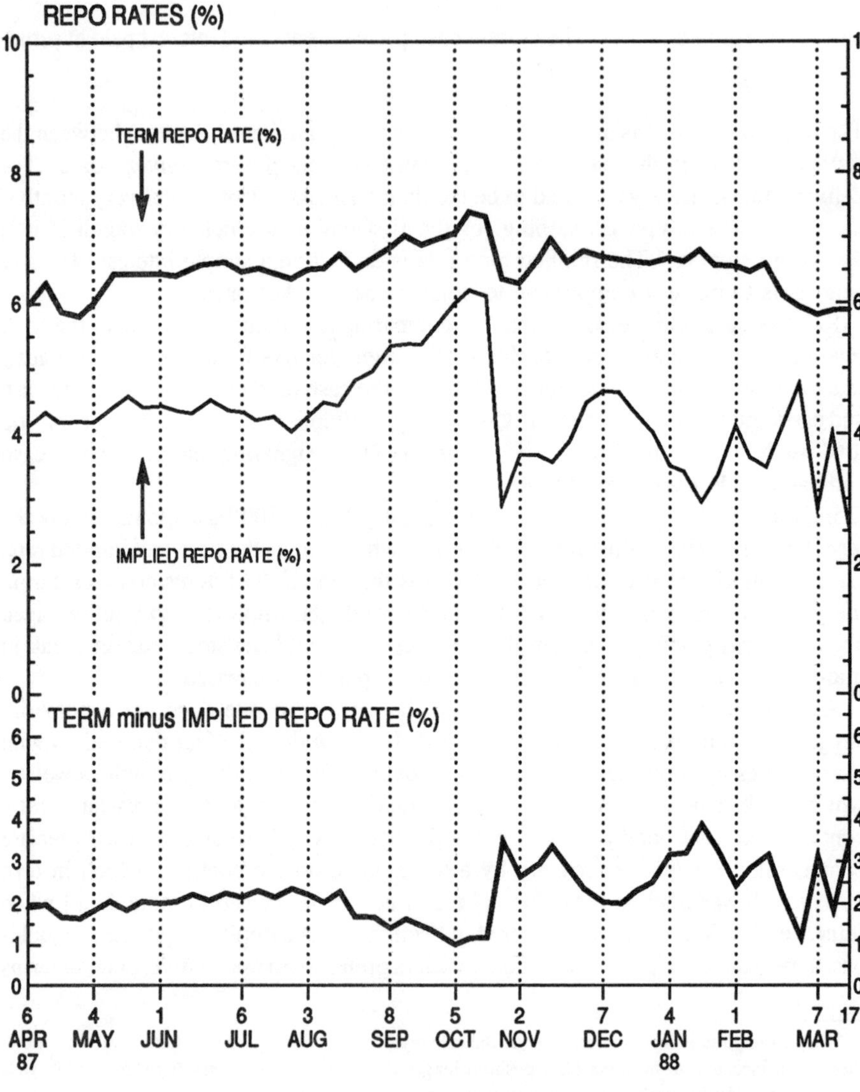

REPO RATES (%)

MARCH 1988 T-BOND FUTURES VS. CHEAPEST-TO-DELIVER T-BOND

of price, because both the cash and futures markets are quoted in this way. The basis is a price-based measure of relative value.

### Basis and Carry

The gross basis is equal to a bond's cash price minus the product of the futures price times the bond's conversion factor. This product is often referred to as the "parity price." It is equivalent to the bond's forward price implied by the futures market. Carry is equal to a bond's coupon income minus the cost of financing the bond. Net basis is equal to the gross basis minus carry. Gross basis and carry, which were derived earlier from the zero profit arbitrage equation, are repeated here:

$$\text{Gross Basis} = CP - (FP \times CF) \quad \text{Carry} = (C - F)$$

Over time, the gross basis of the cheapest-to-deliver bond tends to converge towards zero, because the parity price tends to converge to the bond's cash price at delivery. If the yield curve is positively sloped, the parity price is at a discount to the bond's cash price, reflecting positive carry. For the basis to converge to zero, the parity price must rise relative to the cash price. The reverse holds if the yield curve is negatively sloped.

These relationships are illustrated in Exhibit 3. Notice that the convergence may be more or less than expected if the futures price is over or undervalued. The incremental convergence due to price misalignments (represented by the difference between the solid and dashed lines) is the true cost or gain of a hedge. Suppose the yield curve is positively sloped (top panel). If the futures are undervalued (right diagram), the convergence is larger than expected, representing an incremental cost to a short futures position but a gain to a long futures position. The reverse holds if figures are overvalued. Most yield enhancement strategies are designed to take advantage of incremental convergence, by selling futures when they are overvalued or buying them when they are undervalued. One such strategy is analyzed in more detail in Section IV.

The gross basis of the 7¼% bond due May 2016 versus the March '88 bond futures contract is illustrated in Exhibit 4. The top panel shows the cash and parity price of the bond; the bottom panel the gross basis between them. During the year prior to the contract's expiration, the gross basis declined from about $175/32$nds towards zero, except for a brief period in mid-October 1987 when prices of fixed income securities surged. The gross basis increased because futures prices rose more slowly then cash prices, partly as a result of price limits that temporarily went into effect in the futures market.

Traders often have relative value in mind when they speak of the basis. For example, the expression "the basis is 16 over carry" means that the gross basis is $16/32$nds higher than carry for the underlying bond. What is the implication for

**EXHIBIT 3**
**CONVERGENCE**

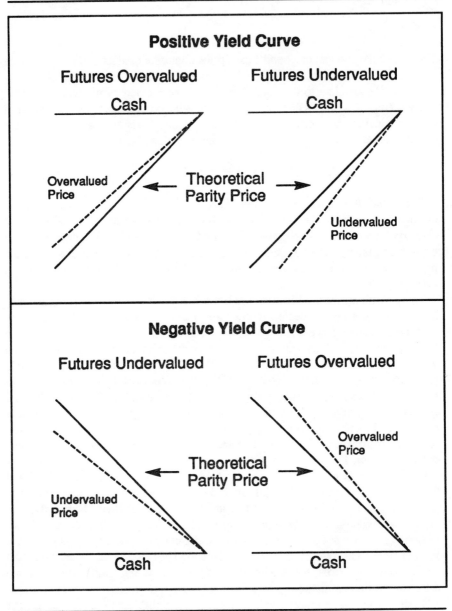

relative value? Does a gross basis that is higher than carry imply that the futures contract is undervalued? Not necessarily, for the same reason (discussed earlier) that a low implied repo rate does not always suggest undervaluation. The short's option to choose which bond to deliver and when to deliver it tends to lower the futures price, resulting in a gross basis that is typically higher than carry. This is illustrated in Exhibit 5 which shows the basis and carry for the 7¼% bond due May 2016 versus the March '88 futures contract, during the year prior to expiration. The net basis shows the amount by which the gross basis exceeds the carry.[8] In addition to evaluating the expected profitability of cash and carry trades, the two measures of relative value—implied repo rate and basis—can also be used to determine which of the bonds eligible for delivery is most likely to be delivered.

### Cheapest-to-Deliver Bond

Although a number of bonds are eligible for delivery against a given futures contract, some issues are more likely to be delivered than others. Traders with short futures positions can decide which bond to deliver against the futures contract. Generally, they choose the bond that maximizes profit (or minimizes loss) upon delivery; that is, the bond with the lowest cash market value relative to its futures invoice price. This bond, often referred to as the cheapest-to-deliver bond, usually exhibits the highest implied repo rate and the lowest net basis. The futures price tends to track the price of this bond.

There are two factors that tend to favor one (or a select group) of the bonds for delivery against the futures contract. The first results from biases in the futures conversion factor. The bias, which depends on the level of the market, tends to favor as the cheapest-to-deliver bond low coupon, long-term bonds when market yields are above 8% and high coupon, short-term bonds when yields are below 8%.[9]

This is illustrated in Exhibit 6, which shows the adjusted delivery price (cash price divided by conversion factor) for two bonds across a range of yields centered around 8%.[10] In general, the adjusted delivery price of the cheapest-to-deliver bond tends to equal the futures price at delivery, because the gross basis on this bond tends to

---

[8]A bond's net basis can be related to its implied repo and financing rates as follows: net basis = (financing rate − implied repo rate) × (n/360) × (market value + accrued interest), where $n$ is the number of days from settlement to delivery.

[9]The bias results from the discounting method used to calculate the conversion factors. Using 8% as the discount rate when market yields are above that level tends to inflate the conversion factors for bonds with distant cash flows (long-term, low coupon bonds) relative to those for bonds with nearby cash flows (short-term, high coupon bonds), favoring the former as cheapest to deliver. The reverse occurs when yields are below 8%.

[10]The exhibit reflects the assumption that the yields on the bonds are identical.

**EXHIBIT 4**
**CASH PRICE, FUTURES PARITY PRICE, AND GROSS BASIS**

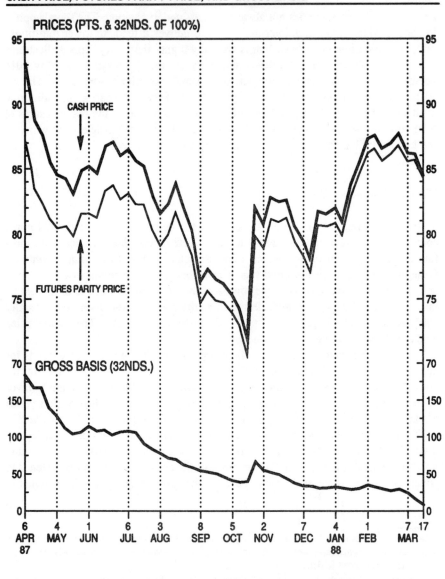

PRICES (PTS. & 32NDS. OF 100%)

CASH PRICE

FUTURES PARITY PRICE

GROSS BASIS (32NDS.)

MARCH 1988 T-BOND FUTURES VS. 7 1/4% OF 5/15/2016

**EXHIBIT 5**
**GROSS BASIS, CARRY, AND NET BASIS**

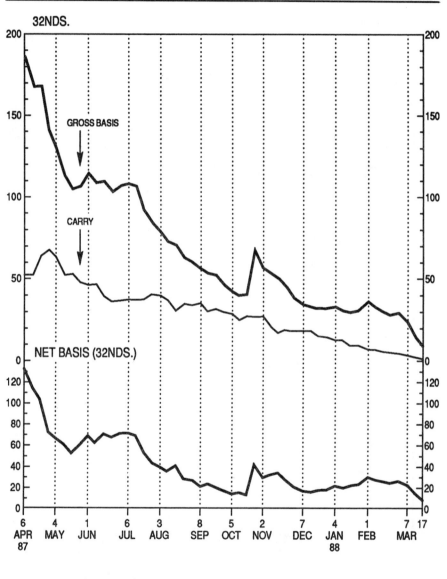

MARCH 1988 T-BOND FUTURES VS. 7 1/4% OF 5/15/2016

**EXHIBIT 6**
**CHEAPEST-TO-DELIVER BOND**

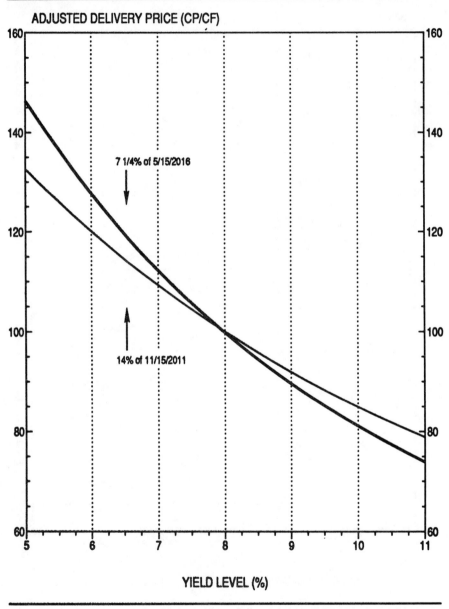

ADJUSTED DELIVERY PRICE (CP/CF)

7 1/4% of 5/15/2016

14% of 11/15/2011

YIELD LEVEL (%)

converge to zero.[11] The adjusted delivery price for most other bonds tends to be higher, because the basis on these does not converge to zero. The bond with the lowest adjusted delivery price is cheapest to deliver. Of the two bonds represented in the exhibits, the low coupon, long-term bond (7¼%, due 2016) is cheapest to deliver at yields above 8%, whereas the high coupon, shorter term bond (14%, due 2011, callable in 2006) is cheapest to deliver at yields below 8%. Changes in the level of the cash market can result in switches in the cheapest-to-deliver bond. This can have a significant impact on the performance of futures hedges and arbitrage transactions, and generally benefits traders who have short futures positions. This is explored in more detail in Section IV.

The second factor is yield spreads in the cash market. In general, high yielding bonds such as premium bonds or callable bonds can be more desirable to deliver than low yielding bonds, because they can be acquired at a lower cost in the cash market relative to their invoice price. An example of the effect of yield spreads on what is cheapest to deliver is shown in Exhibit 7.

**EXHIBIT 7**
**EFFECT OF YIELD SPREADS ON CHEAPTEST-TO-DELIVER BOND**
**(EVALUATION DATE: 01/28/88; MARCH '88 FUTURES PRICE: 93-09)**

|                | *12%*   | *7¼%*  | *7¼%*  |
| -------------- | ------- | ------ | ------ |
| Yield          | 8.66    | 8.66   | 8.50   |
| Cash Price     | 131,750 | 85,125 | 86,656 |
| Invoice Price  | 130,370 | 85,511 | 85,511 |
| Coupon Income  | 1,845   | 1,095  | 1,095  |
| Profit & Loss  | 465     | 1,481  | −50    |

At equal yields (8.66%), the 7¼% bond is cheapest to deliver, because it has a larger profit if delivered against the March '88 contract. The delivery profit ($1,481) is calculated as the invoice price plus coupon income minus the cash price ($85,511 + $1,095 − $85,125). If the yield on the 7¼% bond declines to 8.50% (column 3), the 12% bond becomes cheapest to deliver, because it has the larger delivery profit.

The relative importance of the conversion factor bias versus yield spreads in determining which bond is cheapest to deliver depends on the level of the market. At some yield levels, for example around 8%, yield spreads predominate. At others, the conversion factors are more important. At all levels, the two factors can either offset or enhance one another.

---

[11]In a previous section, it was noted that a bond's parity price tends to converge to its cash price at delivery as the gross basis declines to zero; that is, $(FP \times CF) = CP$. It is equivalent to assert that the adjusted delivery price (of the cheapest-to-deliver bond) equals the futures price; $FP = (CP/CF)$.

## A Generalization of Relative Value to Calendar Spreads

The pricing and relative value concepts discussed thus far are summarized in Exhibit 8. The two key measures—the implied repo rate and the basis—can be used to assess relative value between cash and futures prices.

**EXHIBIT 8**
**MEASURES OF RELATIVE VALUE**

| Futures Price vs Cash Price | Implied Repo Rate vs Repo Rate | Gross Basis vs Carry | Futures Arbitrage Trade |
|---|---|---|---|
| Overvalued | Too High | Too Low | Cash & Carry (Buy Basis) |
| Undervalued | Too Low | Too High | Rel. Cash & Carry (Sell Basis) |

These measures can also be used to assess relative value within the futures markets. For example, suppose the implied repo rate on the nearby contract is "too low" relative to that on a deferred month contract, indicating that the former is undervalued relative to the latter.[12] A trader could take advantage of this by going long the calendar spread; that is, by purchasing the nearby contract and selling the deferred contract.

Futures calendar spreads tend to reflect implied repo rates expected to prevail in the future. By purchasing the calendar spread, a trader can lock in today a future implied repo rate. This occurs because the calendar spread eventually can become a cash and carry trade if the trader accepts delivery on the nearby contract, finances the position, and continues to maintain the short position in the deferred contract. This is illustrated in Exhibit 9 which shows repo rates implied by the Jun-Sep '88 and Sep-Dec '88 calendar spreads.

A trader who is long the Sep-Dec '88 calendar spread on April 19th can lock in a future implied repo rate of 6.17%, by accepting delivery on the Sep '88 contract, while maintaining a short position in the Dec '88 contract. This assumes that the 7¼% bond delivered on the Sep '88 contract is held for three months and then delivered against the short position in the Dec '88 contract. The implied repo rate is calculated as before, where "cash in" is equal to the sum of the total invoice amount on the Dec '88 contract ($80,537.01), plus coupon income including reinvestment at 6.50% ($3,926) on the 7¼% bond during the period from September 30th to December 30th, the assumed delivery dates. "Cash out" is equal to the total invoice amount on the Sep '88 contract ($83,165.62).

---

[12]This assumes that the cheapest-to-deliver bond is identical for both contracts, which is usually the case in practice. If this is not true, the implied repo rate does not necessarily reflect relative value between contract months.

**EXHIBIT 9**
**T-BOND FUTURES CALENDAR SPREADS AND IMPLIED REPO RATES (EVALUATION DATE: APRIL 19, 1988)**

| Futures Contract Month | Futures Price | Cheapest to Deliver Bond | Cash Price | Conv. Factor | Total Invoice Amount | Total Coupon Income | Repo Rate Implied by Calendar Spread |
|---|---|---|---|---|---|---|---|
| June '88 | 88.22 | 7¼ | 82.03 | 0.9167 | 82,206 | 0 | 4.61% (Jun-Sep) |
| Sep '88 | 87.23 | 7¼ | 82.03 | 0.9177 | 83,165 | 3,926 | 6.17% (Sep-Dec) |
| Dec '88 | 86.26 | 7¼ | 82.03 | 0.9177 | 80,537 | | |

In general, repo rates implied by calendar spreads should tend to reflect similar expectations implied in other markets. For example, a case can be made that the repo rate implied by the Sep-Dec '88 bond futures spread is related to the rate on the Sep '88 T-bill futures contract. Both are estimates of three-month rates beginning in September. Of course, comparisons such as this should be evaluated with caution, because factors unique to each market can affect prices differently. In addition, expiration dates may differ across contracts, making the comparison more complicated. Nonetheless, some traders establish calendar spreads against positions in other markets to take advantage of perceived discrepancies across markets.

## III. FACTORS THAT CAN AFFECT CASH AND FUTURES PRICES

Having developed the fundamental pricing and relative value relationships between cash and futures markets, this section explores various factors that can affect those relationships and, consequently, the outcome of futures hedges and arbitrage trades. In particular, we analyze the impact of changes in the cheapest-to-deliver bond, changes in yield spreads, delivery month options, and the delivery-period supply of the cheapest-to-deliver bond.

### Changes in the Cheapest-to-Deliver Bond

Traders with short futures positions can decide which eligible bond to deliver. Most traders assume that the short will deliver the cheapest-to-deliver bond, because it results in the greatest profit (or smallest loss).

Changes in the level of the cash market can cause a switch in what is cheapest to deliver. High coupon, short duration bonds tend to become increasingly cheaper to deliver as yields fall; whereas low coupon, long duration bonds tend to become cheaper to deliver as yields rise (Exhibit 6). This results from the conversion factor bias discussed earlier. Changes in supply and demand, which alter yield spreads, can also cause a switch in what is cheapest to deliver. Because the choice of which bond to deliver is at the option of the short, a change in this bond generally benefits traders who are short futures and works to the disadvantage of those who are long.[13]

A switch in the cheapest-to-deliver bond tends to depress the futures price relative to what it would otherwise be. That is, if the switch occurs in a bear market, the futures price can fall by more than expected, because the contract tends to track longer duration bonds, which fall faster in down markets. Conversely, if the switch occurs in a bull market, the futures price can rise by less than expected, because the contract tends to track shorter duration bonds which appreciate more slowly. The end result is that the futures price tends to exhibit less "positive convexity" than most

---

[13]The exception to this rule occurs when shortages of the cheapest-to-deliver bond occur during the delivery month. A shortage of this bond tends to force traders who are short futures to offset their shorts at higher futures prices, or to deliver more expensive bonds to the benefit of traders who are long futures.

bonds in the cash market.[14] This can benefit portfolio managers who sell futures to hedge cash portfolios, because futures prices can fall faster than cash prices in a bear market, resulting in a hedge gain that exceeds a cash market loss. In a bull market, the loss on a short futures position can be smaller than the cash gain, because futures prices can rise more slowly than cash prices.

Of course, just as a switch benefits a portfolio manager who is short contracts, it reduces the return on trades that consist of long futures positions. As we shall see in Section IV, a switch in the cheapest-to-deliver bond can offset some of the yield advantage of a synthetic bond created by combining Treasury bills with a long position in undervalued futures contracts.

### Changes in Yield Spreads

Shifts in relative supply and demand for bonds in the cash market often result in yield spread changes. This can affect the outcome of futures hedges or arbitrage trades, because the corresponding change in relative prices between cash and futures can lead to unequal gains and losses on the two positions.[15] An increase in the yield spread (defined as the yield of the cheapest-to-deliver bond minus that of the cash position) generally enhances the return on a short future hedge, because the futures price falls relative to the price of the cash position. In contrast, a decrease in the yield spread can reduce the effectiveness of a short hedge. These effects, which are summarized in Exhibit 10, are reversed for long futures positions.

**EXHIBIT 10**
**IMPACT OF YIELD SPREADS ON FUTURES HEDGES**

|  | Yield Spread Increases | Yield Spread Decreases |
|---|---|---|
| Short Futures Hedge | POSITIVE | NEGATIVE |
| (Long basis trade) | (basis increases) | (basis decreases) |
| Long Futures Hedge | NEGATIVE | POSITIVE |
| (Short basis trade) | (basis increases) | (basis decreases) |

Exhibit 11 illustrates the yield spread between the 13¼% bond due May 2014 (callable in 2009) and the 7¼% bond due May 2016. High coupon bonds such as the 13¼% bond were cheapest to deliver during most of 1986 and the first quarter of 1987. The exhibit shows that the yield spread declined by about 60 basis points between June 1986 and March 1987. During the bull market of 1985 and 1986,

---

[14]Convexity is discussed in Section IV.

[15]Yield spread changes only affect futures hedges or basis trades in which the cash position consists of bonds that are not cheapest to deliver.

**EXHIBIT 11**
**YIELD SPREAD**

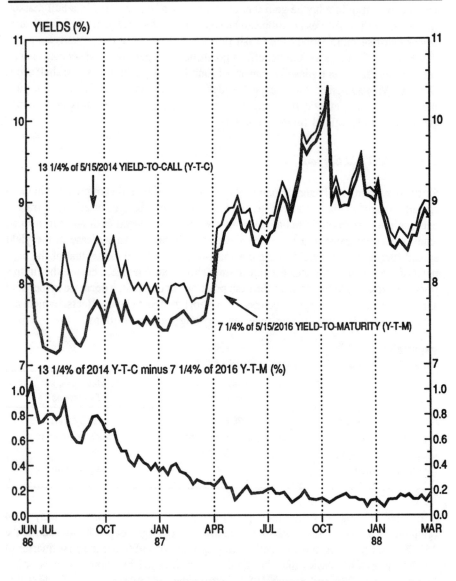

YIELDS (%)

13 1/4% of 5/15/2014 YIELD-TO-CALL (Y-T-C)

7 1/4% of 5/15/2016 YIELD-TO-MATURITY (Y-T-M)

13 1/4% of 2014 Y-T-C minus 7 1/4% of 2016 Y-T-M (%)

JUN JUL      OCT      JAN      APR      JUL      OCT      JAN      MAR
86                    87                                  88

13 1/4% OF 5/15/2014 VS. 7 1/4% OF 5/15/2016

foreign investors had aggressively purchased low coupon, on-the-run bonds, pushing yield spreads up; but, in the second half of 1986 and in 1987, the spreads narrowed as other investors took advantage of higher yields by purchasing high coupon off-the-run bonds. The resulting decline in the yield spread hurt traders who were short futures against long positions in low coupon bonds, but benefited those with long futures positions. This is examined in more detail in Section IV.

### Futures Embedded Options

It was suggested earlier that a switch in the cheapest-to-deliver bond tends to benefit traders who are short futures, to the disadvantage of those who are long. The ability to switch bonds can be thought of as a put option held by the short, both during and prior to the delivery month. In addition, there are two options held by the short that arise only during the delivery month. These options arise from the design of the futures contracts, and are generally of less overall significance than changes in the cheapest-to-deliver bond. Nonetheless, a thorough understanding of them is important.

Traders who sell futures in effect have dual positions: they are short contracts and long put options. They pay for those options implicitly by their willingness to receive a futures price that is generally lower than the equilibrium price implied by the arbitrage analysis discussed in Section II. The lower price compensates those who buy futures for their uncertainty regarding which bond will be delivered and on which day during the month delivery will occur. From either point of view, the delivery options tend to depress the futures price. As was noted earlier, this tends to lower the implied repo rate relative to the financing rate and increase the gross basis relative to carry.

Changes in the value of the embedded options can affect the futures price and hence the performance of arbitrage trades and hedges. For example, an increase in market volatility can increase the value of the embedded options and thereby depress the futures price relative to the underlying cash market. This section describes the two delivery month options mentioned above. They are known as the "wildcard" and "end-of-month" options.

### The Wildcard Option

The wildcard option arises, because, for delivery purposes, the short must deliver $100,000 face value of securities for each futures contract (see Appendix A for a summary of delivery procedures). If the futures hedge ratio is not equal to one, the par value of the bonds held is unequal to the size of the short futures position.[16] Depending on the value of the hedge ratio, the difference between the par value of

---

[16]Hedge ratios are often calculated based on measures of price sensitivity such as duration or basis point value. These measures and other issues related to the hedge ratios are discussed in Section IV.

the cash position and that of the futures must be eliminated, either by buying or selling the residual bonds in the cash market or by liquidating the residual futures contracts by an offsetting transaction. For example, if 12 contracts are sold to hedge a core position of $1 million face value of bonds, delivery against the futures would require that $200,000 of additional bonds would have to be purchased to erase the deficit against the short position. The amount by which the hedge ratio (per $100,000 face value of cash bonds) is greater or less than one is called the "tail" of the hedge. In the example above the tail is two contracts.

It is the tail of the hedge that is the basis for the wildcard delivery option. The option arises because clearing members of the Chicago Board of Trade have until 8:00 P.M. Chicago time to notify the Chicago Board of Trade Clearing Corporation of intent to deliver.[17] While the invoice amount is based on the 2:00 P.M. (Chicago time) futures settlement price, the cash market is open for an additional two or more hours. The advantage to the short of the wildcard option is being able to reference the 2:00 P.M. futures invoice price until 8:00 P.M., even if cash market prices change in the meantime.

If the hedge ratio is greater than one, the tail consists of a deficit of bonds relative to the futures position. If prices in the cash market decline by a sufficient amount after the futures close, the cash equivalent of the futures tail can be purchased at the lower late afternoon price and delivered at the previously set invoice price. In effect, the short has a put option to deliver the bonds at the invoice price. What about the case where the hedge ratio is less than one and the tail consists of an excess of bonds? In this case, the short has a call option. It can be exercised if prices in the cash market rise after 2:00 P.M. by selling the excess bonds at the higher late afternoon price instead of at the futures invoice price. These options and the conditions necessary for exercise are summarized in Exhibit 12.

**EXHIBIT 12**
**WILDCARD DELIVERY OPTIONS**

| Futures Close | Cash Close | Last Notice |
|---|---|---|
| Chicago: 2:00 PM | About 4:00 PM | 8:00 PM |

| HEDGE RATIO (H) | BOND TAIL | OPTION TYPE | WHEN EXERCISED |
|---|---|---|---|
| H>1 | Deficit | Put | Cash Prices Fall |
| H<1 | Excess | Call | Cash Prices Rise |

The wildcard option exists on each trading day starting with the first intention day (two business days prior to the first business day of the delivery month) and extending to the day preceding the last trading day of the futures contract. On the last trading day, the futures position is usually "squared up" for delivery purposes in order to match the cash position on a dollar for dollar basis (one contract for each

---

[17]A clearing member may require its accounts to indicate their intent to deliver prior to 8:00 P.M.

$100,000 face value on bonds). There is no futures trading and no mark-to-market during the last seven business days of the delivery month.[18]

Exercise of the wildcard option depends on two factors: the bond's gross basis and its tail. In general, the delivery profit on the tail must be larger than the dollar value of the gross basis for the option to be profitably exercised. This is illustrated in Exhibit 13, which shows the price changes necessary for profitable exercise of the wildcard option of several deliverable bonds. The first three columns list the coupon, maturity, and 2:00 P.M. cash price on the bonds deliverable against the March '88 futures contract on March 15, 1988. The hedge ratio, invoice price, and gross basis are shown in the next three columns. The futures tail, price change necessary for profitable delivery, and strike price are also shown.

For the 10⅜% bond, the March 15th gross basis is equal to about ⁷/₃₂nds, indicating a $21,875 (7 × $31.25 × 100) delivery loss (per $100,000) on the core position. Assuming the hedge ratio is equal to 1.2326, the tail on this bond is equal to 0.2326 (1.2326 − 1) contracts. For each futures contract outstanding, there is a deficit of $23,260 of cash bonds. For delivery of this bond to be profitable, its late afternoon cash price must fall by ³⁰/₃₂nds (6.99/0.2326) to 114.12. At any price below this, the delivery profit of the tail exceeds the loss from delivering the core position at the invoice price.

### The End-of-Month Option

Treasury bond and note futures cease to trade at noon Chicago time on the eighth business day prior to the end of the delivery month. A trader who is short futures at that time must deliver $100,000 par value of an eligible bond against each outstanding contract, sometime between the last day of trading and the final delivery day. Because there is no daily mark-to-market of futures contracts after the last trading day, most arbitrage positions are "squared up" prior to that time; that is, one futures contract for each $100,000 par value of bonds held, regardless of the coupon or maturity.

The end-of-month option arises following the last trading day, because subsequent changes in relative prices in the cash market can make it profitable to swap the bond originally intended for delivery for another and to deliver it instead.[19] In a bear market, it can sometimes be profitable to swap into a higher coupon (higher factor) bond, and in a bull market into a lower coupon (lower factor) bond. Exhibit 14 illustrates how the option can be exercised.

---

[18]Mark-to-market is the daily settlement process whereby futures gains are credited to the margin account and futures losses are debited.

[19]Shifts in relative supply and demand are the primary cause of changes in relative prices. Changes in the overall level of the market can also lead to realignments between prices to the extent that the initial values and durations among bonds are unequal.

# EXHIBIT 13
## FUTURES WILDCARD OPTION PRICE CHANGES REQUIRED FOR PROFITABLE DELIVERY

Evaluation Date: March 15, 1988
Last Trade Date: March 22, 1988

March '88 Futures Contract
2:00 PM Futures Price: 93.12

| Deliverable Bonds Coupon | Maturity/Call Date | 2:00 PM Price | BPV Hedge Ratio | Futures Invoice Price | Gross Basis (32nds) | Bond Futures "Tail" | Price Change (32nds) | Late PM Strike (32nds) |
|---|---|---|---|---|---|---|---|---|
| 10.375 | Nov-07 | 115.10 | 1.2326 | 115.03 | 6.99 | 0.2326 | −30 | 114.12 |
| 12 | Nov-08 | 130.28 | 1.3920 | 130.23 | 5.10 | 0.3920 | −13 | 130.15 |
| 13.25 | May-09 | 143.19 | 1.5221 | 142.27 | 23.66 | 0.5221 | −45 | 142.06 |
| 7.25 | May-16 | 86.02 | 1.1052 | 85.19 | 14.90 | 0.1052 | −142 | 81.20 |
| 7.5 | Nov-16 | 88.26 | 1.1400 | 88.05 | 20.73 | 0.1400 | −148 | 84.06 |

**EXHIBIT 14**
**END OF MONTH DELIVERY OPTION**

| | BOND 1 | BOND 2 | BOND 3 | Profit due to Swap |
|---|---|---|---|---|
| Futures Price | 100 | 100 | 100 | |
| Factor | 0.5 | 1.0 | 1.5 | |
| Invoice Price | 50 | 100 | 150 | |
| | | prices remain unchanged | | |
| Cash Price | 51 | 100 | 151 | |
| Delivery P/L | −1 | 0 | −1 | 0 |
| | | subsequent price decline | | |
| Cash Price | 47 | 95 | 142 | |
| Delivery P/L | 3 | 5 | 8 | +3 |
| | | subsequent price increase | | |
| Cash Price | 53 | 105 | 157 | |
| Delivery P/L | −3 | −5 | −7 | +2 |

The exhibit shows the delivery profit and loss for three bonds, assuming that prices remain unchanged, decline, or increase. The futures price is equal to 100, and the invoice price for each bond is fixed. Bond 1 has a conversion factor of 0.5, an invoice price of 50, and an initial cash price of 51, resulting in a delivery loss of minus one. Bond 2 has a factor of one, and its invoice price is equal to its cash price. Bond 3 has a factor of 1.5, an invoice price of 150 and a cash price of 151, resulting in a delivery loss of minus one. Thus, Bond 2 is cheapest to deliver, because it has a delivery loss of zero, versus minus one for the other two bonds.

Assume that just before the close of futures trading, a trader buys $100,000 face value of Bond 2 and sells one futures contract. Six days later (last intention day), the trader can decide whether to deliver Bond 2 (at a zero loss) or to swap out of Bond 2 in order to deliver one of the other bonds. If prices remain unchanged, it will not make sense to swap, so Bond 2 will be delivered, and the "profit due to swap" is zero.

Now assume that relative shifts in supply and demand result in unequal price declines for each of the bonds subsequent to the close of futures trading. Bond 3 declines to 142, Bond 2 to 95 and Bond 1 to 47. Recalculation of the Delivery P&L at the new prices reveals that Bond 3 is now cheapest to deliver. It has a delivery profit of 8, compared to 5 for Bond 2 and 3 for Bond 1. At these prices, a trader who is short futures against a long position in Bond 2 can profit by swapping Bond 2 for Bond 3 and delivering it instead. Bond 2 is sold for 95 (a loss of 5), Bond 3 is purchased for 142 and delivered at the futures invoice price of 150 (a gain of 8). The "profit due to swap" is 3 $(8-5)$.

Suppose that instead of falling, all prices rise by unequal amounts. Bond 1 exhibits the smallest dollar increase, followed by Bonds 2 and 3. At the higher price levels, Bond 1 is cheapest to deliver. It has the lowest loss upon delivery, $-3$, compared to $-5$ for Bond 2, and $-7$ for Bond 3. This time, it is profitable to swap from Bond 2 to Bond 1. Bond 2 is sold for 105 (a gain of 5), and Bond 1 is purchased for 53 and delivered at the futures invoice price of 50 (a loss of $-3$). The "profit due to swap" is 2 $(5-3)$.

Notwithstanding the slope of the yield curve, optimal delivery usually occurs on the final delivery day. This results from the fact that it can be profitable to swap bonds more than once, depending on market conditions. In the example above, Bond 3 is substituted for Bond 2 following a price decline. This results in a "locked up" profit of 3. If market prices rise following the swap, profits can be further enhanced by swapping back to Bond 2, or, if prices rise enough, to Bond 1. A volatile market raises the possibility that profits due to delivery swaps can be multiplied by swapping more than once. This provides an incentive to delay delivery to the end of the month. At the same time, the slope of the yield curve can also affect the timing of delivery. If it is positively sloped, there is an incentive related to positive carry to make delivery at the end of the month. If it is negatively sloped, there is an incentive due to negative carry to deliver earlier. This can offset some of the value of the option.

One measure that can be used to determine if it is profitable to swap the cheapest-to-deliver bond for another bond is the difference between their invoice prices. The swap to a higher factor bond is usually profitable only if the difference between the cash prices (when the swap occurs) is less than that between the invoice prices. In Exhibit 14 the difference between the invoice prices of Bonds 3 and 2 is 50 (150 − 100). Thus, a swap to Bond 3 is profitable only if the difference at the new price level is less than 50. Indeed, the exhibit shows that it is 47 (142 − 95), hence the swap is profitable. For lower factor bonds, a swap is usually profitable only if the cash price difference is larger than that of the invoice prices. In Exhibit 14, it is 52 (105 − 53), resulting in a profit on the swap.

Exhibit 15 illustrates how prices in the cash market must change to make a swap from the cheapest-to-deliver bond to other deliverable bonds profitable. The cheapest-to-deliver bond (shown as "CTD" in the top row) is the 10⅜% due November 2012 (callable 2007), priced at 113.14 on March 22, 1988 (the close of futures trading). Its conversion factor is 1.2326 and the invoice price is 113, plus accrued interest. This is based on the March '88 futures contract, priced at 91$^{22}$/$_{32}$. Similar information for several other deliverable bonds is listed below the cheapest-to-deliver bond. The invoice price differential between each bond and the cheapest-to-deliver bond is shown in the column third from the right. The minimum price change required for a profitable delivery swap and the associated strike price are shown in the last two columns.[20] For example, the invoice price differential of the 7¼% bond relative to the 10⅜% bond is −28$^{31}$/$_{32}$. The price of the 7¼% bond must fall by $^{25}$/$_{32}$nds to a level of 83$^{19}$/$_{32}$ before it is profitable to swap from the cheapest-to-deliver bond.

## The Supply of Deliverable Bonds

The original intent in giving traders with short futures positions the option to deliver more than one bond issue against a futures contract was to increase the supply of deliverable bonds. It was thought that this would prevent shortages of deliverable supply and avoid adverse effects on futures prices during the delivery period.

Nonetheless, futures prices can be affected if the open interest is high relative to the supply of the cheapest-to-deliver bond.[21] A lack of supply of this bond tends to force traders who are short futures to either cover their positions by offsetting transactions at higher prices, roll into deferred month contracts, or to deliver bonds that are not cheapest to deliver. This tends to work to the disadvantage of the short

---

[20]The exhibit reflects the assumption that relative prices change according to the relative basis point values among bonds. Basis point value, discussed in more detail in Section IV, is the change in the value of a bond given a one basis point change in yield.

[21]Open interest is the total of futures contracts (one side only; that is, long or short) that have been entered into but not yet liquidated by offsetting transactions or fulfilled by delivery.

**EXHIBIT 15**
**END-OF-MONTH OPTION PRICE CHANGE REQUIRED FOR PROFITABLE DELIVERY SWAP**

| | | | *Evaluation Date: March 22, 1988* | | | | *Last Delivery: March 31, 1988* | | |
| | | Deliverable Bonds | | *Futures Settlement Price: 91.22* | | | | | |
| CTD: | Coupon 10.375 | MAT/Call Nov-07 | Price 113.14 | Conv. Factor 1.2326 | Futures Invoice Price 113.00 | Invoice Price Difference N.A. | Price Change* N.A. | Strike Price N.A. |
|------|--------|---------|--------|--------|--------|--------|--------|--------|
| 1) | 7.25 | May-16 | 84.12 | 0.9167 | 84.02 | −28.31 | −0.25 | 83.19 |
| 2) | 12 | Aug-08 | 128.26 | 1.3976 | 128.05 | 15.04 | −2.07 | 126.19 |
| 3) | 13.25 | May-09 | 141.00 | 1.5299 | 140.09 | 27.08 | −1.20 | 139.12 |
| 4) | 7.5 | Nov-16 | 87.01 | 0.9442 | 86.18 | −26.14 | 0.13 | 87.14 |
| 5) | 12.5 | Aug-09 | 134.12 | 1.4560 | 133.16 | 20.15 | −2.27 | 131.17 |

*Points and 32nds. Assumes relative prices change according to relative basis point values.

and to the benefit of the long. Most traders who intend to deliver against their short positions try to acquire the cheapest-to-deliver bond by the beginning or middle of the delivery month. Those who wait until the end can experience difficulty in acquiring the bond if the available supply has been reduced. This can occur if the bond has been stripped, "locked up" in portfolios, or goes "on special" (that is, it has a low repo rate in the market).

Delivery data indicates that, on occasion, bonds that are more expensive than the cheapest-to-deliver bond are tendered, because of shortages of the latter. This is illustrated in Exhibit 16 which shows deliveries against the March '87 bond contract. A total of 14,428 deliveries occurred, but less than a third of those was accounted for by the 14% bond due November 2011, even though many traders considered it to be cheapest to deliver. Shortages of that bond forced some traders to deliver more expensive bonds, such as the 12% bond due 2013.

### Summary of Pricing and Relative Value

The discussion thus far has concentrated on futures pricing and relative value relationships. More often than not, these are dominant factors in the formulation of futures strategies. As a result, it is important to understand how cost-of-carry and arbitrage relationships determine relative value between cash and futures prices, and how to assess whether one market is rich or cheap in relation to the other. We developed two measures of relative value, the implied repo rate and the net basis, that are often used to gauge the expected profitability of futures strategies. They can also be used to determine which bond is cheapest to deliver.

Of course, the performance of futures trades can be affected by changes in market conditions, particularly if such changes cause a switch in the cheapest-to-deliver bond or shifts in yield spreads. Delivery-month options embedded in the futures contract and shortages of the cheapest-to-deliver bond can also influence the outcome of futures trades. Traders should be aware of the impact these factors can have on futures hedges and arbitrage transactions.

In Section IV, we turn to applications of futures contracts to portfolio management. These include selling futures to hedge a portfolio of bonds, and buying futures to create a synthetic bond that can sometimes yield more than similar bonds in the cash market. Each of these applications is analyzed in the context of the pricing and relative value relationships discussed earlier and in terms of the factors that can affect trade performance.

## IV. APPLICATIONS TO PORTFOLIO MANAGEMENT

T-bond and note futures are widely used by portfolio managers to alter portfolio duration and convexity in anticipation of changes in the level of the market, to

**EXHIBIT 16**
**DELIVERIES AGAINST THE MARCH '87 BOND FUTURES CONTRACT**

| Coupon and Maturity | March | | | | | | | Total |
|---|---|---|---|---|---|---|---|---|
| | 2-24 | 25 | 26 | 27 | 30 | 31 | | |
| 14% 2011 | 0 | 0 | 1 | 581 | 670 | 3,484 | | 4,736 |
| 13⅞% 2011 | 0 | 0 | 0 | 120 | 208 | 1,227 | | 1,555 |
| 13¼% 2014 | 0 | 0 | 0 | 0 | 293 | 1,212 | | 1,505 |
| 12¾% 2010 | 0 | 1 | 1 | 1,400 | 1,039 | 2,894 | | 5,335 |
| 12½% 2014 | 0 | 0 | 0 | 0 | 0 | 2 | | 2 |
| 12% 2013 | 0 | 0 | 0 | 0 | 0 | 1,293 | | 1,293 |
| 11¾% 2014 | 0 | 0 | 0 | 0 | 0 | 2 | | 2 |
| Total | 0 | 1 | 2 | 2,101 | 2,210 | 10,114 | | 14,428 |

*Source:* Commodity Futures Trading Commission.

reduce risk through hedging, and to enhance yields via the creation of synthetic securities. The sections that follow review several measures of portfolio price risk, including basis point value and modified duration. These are often used to construct hedge ratios and evaluate the sensitivity of hedged portfolios. Using these measures, we examine three applications of futures to portfolio management: 1) targeting portfolio duration, 2) selling futures to hedge a bond, and 3) buying futures to create a synthetic security.

### Duration, Convexity, and Basis Point Value

Duration, convexity, and basis point value are often used to measure the price risk of bond portfolios. The duration of a bond measures the sensitivity of a bond's price to changes in yield. Macaulay duration is a unit-free value that measures the percentage change in price given a percentage change in yield. Modified duration, which is closely related, measures the percentage change in price given a level change in yield.[22]

Duration is often expressed in years. The duration of a zero coupon bond is equal to its maturity. This is a useful benchmark, because duration is often used to compare coupon bonds to their zero coupon equivalents. For example, a coupon bond with a duration of 10 years has a similar price sensitivity to yield changes as a 10-year zero coupon bond.

While it is common to express duration in terms of years, it is more intuitive to think of it as a measure of price risk or volatility. In this regard, modified duration is particularly useful, because it measures the percentage affect on price for a change in yields. Aside from scale factors that adjust for units of price versus yield, modified duration is calculated as the change in price with respect to a change in yield, divided by price plus accrued interest:

$$D = (dP/dY)/(P + AI)$$

where:

$D$ = Modified duration
$dP/dY$ = Change in price ($P$) with respect to a change in yield ($Y$)
$(P + AI)$ = Price plus accrued interest ($AI$)

A modified duration of 10 means that a one basis point decline in yield results in a 10 basis point increase in the bond's price; that is, the bond's price increases by 0.1% of its market (not face) value plus accrued interest. Modified duration is illustrated in Exhibit 17 which shows the relationship between yield and percentage price changes for a hypothetical 30-year zero coupon bond. The slope of the line is the measure of the modified duration. For example, if yields drop by one percentage point, the

---

[22]Macaulay duration $= (dP/dY)(1 + Y/2)/(P + AI)$ and modified duration $=(dP/dY)/(P + AI)$, where $(P + AI)$ = price plus accrued interest, $Y$ = annual yield and $dP/dY$ denotes the change in price with respect to a change in yield.

**EXHIBIT 17**
**MODIFIED DURATION**

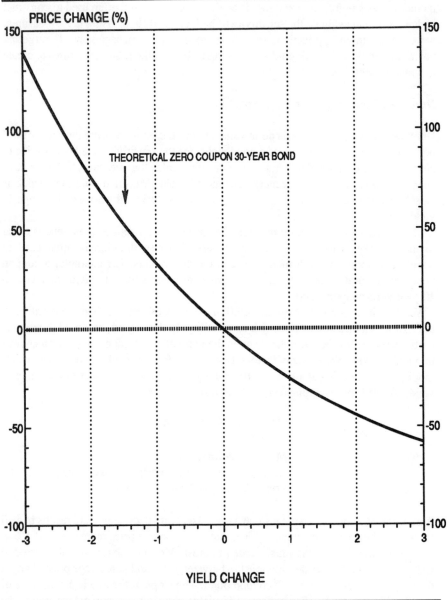

PRICE CHANGE (%)

THEORETICAL ZERO COUPON 30-YEAR BOND

YIELD CHANGE

market value of the bond increases by about 30% suggesting a modified duration of 30.

The duration of a bond or portfolio of bonds is affected by several factors, including the bond's coupon, maturity, and yield. Given equal maturities and yields, high coupon bonds have shorter durations than low coupon bonds, because relatively more of their cash flows come earlier in the life of the bond. An increase in maturity generally increases duration. For zero coupon bonds, duration increases one-for-one with maturity. For most other bonds, duration increases at a decreasing rate as maturity increases.

The level of yields can have an inverse effect on duration for non-callable bonds. This is illustrated in Exhibit 17 which shows that duration increases as yields decline and falls as yields increase. The variability of duration as yields change reflects the nonlinear relationship between a bond's price and its yield. This variability is often referred to as convexity.

Convexity is a measure of the relationship between a bond's duration and yield. Positive convexity means that the duration is inversely related to the level of yields. Conversely, negative convexity means that duration is positively related to the level of yields. The price/yield relationship in Exhibit 17 exhibits positive convexity. Duration increases as yields fall, and decreases as yields rise. This can be a desirable property for a bond portfolio, because it suggests that bond prices rise at an increasing rate as yields fall, and decline at a decreasing rate as yields rise. In contrast, negative convexity implies that prices rise at a decreasing rate as yields fall, and fall at an increasing rate as yields rise. There is usually a trade-off between yield and convexity. Bonds that have positive convexity tend to yield less than bonds that have negative convexity. Examples of bonds that can exhibit negative convexity include mortgage backed securities and callable corporate bonds.

Basis point value measures the dollar change in the value of a bond for a one basis point change in yield. It is the change in price with respect to yield, adjusted for scale factors:

$$BPV = dP/dY$$

where:       $BPV$ = Basis point value
             $dP/dY$ = Change in price ($P$) with respect to a change in yield ($Y$)

A basis point value of $800 per million means that if a bond's yield drops by one basis point, its value rises by $800 per million face value. As a measure of risk, basis point value is closely related to modified duration. The former measures the dollar price risk and the latter measures the percentage price risk for a change in yield. Modified duration is equal to basis point value (per $1 million face) divided by price (as a percentage of par) plus accrued interest; $D = BPV/(P + AI)$. For example, if a bond is priced at par (with zero accrued interest), its modified duration equals its basis point value per $1 million divided by 100. As measures of price risk, modified duration and basis point value are often used to calculate hedge ratios.

### The Hedge Ratio

Hedge strategies are usually constructed so that dollar gains or losses on the hedge position offset as closely as possible those on the cash market position being hedged. To achieve this goal it is important to determine the proper hedge ratio; that is, the number of contracts to buy or sell. Hedge ratios reflect market conditions at the time they are calculated, and may need to be adjusted as those conditions change. One formula for determining a hedge ratio for a bond portfolio is:

$$H = \frac{BPV_p}{BPV_F} \times \text{Beta}$$

Where:        $H$ = Number of futures contracts to buy or sell
              $BPV_p$ = Total basis point value of the portfolio
              $BPV_F$ = Basis point value per futures contract
              Beta = Yield regression coefficient (discussed below)

The ratio of the basis point values accounts for differences in the price sensitivities to yield changes of the cash and futures positions. The numerator reflects the basis point value of the cash position, at current market prices. The basis point value of the futures is usually equal to that of the cheapest-to-deliver bond (per $100,000) divided by its conversion factor.

Depending on when the hedge protection is desired, the calculation of $BPV_F$ may vary. To provide immediate protection, the hedge ratio can be constructed with a $BPV_F$ that equals the current BPV of the cheapest-to-deliver bond divided by its conversion factor and multiplied by the quantity $(1 + rn/360)$, where $r$ is the implied repo rate and $n$ is the number of days to the delivery of the futures contract. To provide protection as of a horizon date equal to the futures delivery date, the $BPV_F$ can be set to the horizon $BPV$ of the cheapest-to-deliver bond divided by its conversion factor. In practice, many hedgers use the current BPV of the cheapest-to-deliver bond divided by its conversion factor. The accuracy of this approach appears to be adequate given the imprecise nature of hedge performance in the face of changes in cash-futures relationships over time. A hedge ratio constructed in this manner tends to equate dollar changes in the value of the bond with those of the futures position for equal shifts in yields.[23]

However, yields do not necessarily shift in tandem. To account for this in the hedge ratio, Beta can be included to reflect the yield relationship between the cash bonds being hedged and the cheapest-to-deliver bond. Determined by historical yield regressions, it measures the average change in the yield of the hedged bond

---

[23]Modified duration can also be used to calculate hedge ratios, replacing the $BPV$ in the hedge ratio formula. However, it should be multiplied by the market value plus accrued interest of the bond to convert the ratio from percentage changes to a ratio of dollar changes.

(the dependent variable) for a change in the yield of the cheapest-to-deliver bond (the independent variable). If yields on the cash position and the cheapest-to-deliver bond move in tandem, Beta is close to 1.0 and has little effect on the hedge ratio.[24] If the yield on the cash position moves more (Beta>1.0) or less (Beta <1.0) than that of the cheapest-to-deliver bond, the inclusion of Beta will alter the hedge ratio. In practice, hedgers often ignore Beta, unless the correlation between yields is known to be significantly different than one-to-one.

Exhibit 18 shows a regression scatter plot of yield changes between GNMA 10% mortgage-backed securities and 7¼% Treasury bonds due May 2016. The regression statistics and exhibit reflect daily yield changes during the last six months of 1987. The slope of the regression line (often referred to as the Beta coeffcient) is 0.69, indicating that, on average, yields on the GNMA security changed by 69 basis points for every percentage point change of the 7¼% bond.[25] This is reflected in the "regression fit" line that has a lower slope than the 45 degree line representing one-to-one changes. Care should be exercised when interpreting yield change regressions and incorporating Beta into hedge ratios, because there is no assurance that historical experience will be repeated in the future.

### Targeting the Performance of a Bond Portfolio

Duration and convexity can be used as gauges by which to target the performance of a bond portfolio. For example, if the market is expected to rally, portfolio managers may wish to increase the duration and convexity of their portfolios to enhance their performance in a bull market. Conversely, if interest rates are expected to rise, it may be prudent to shorten the duration of the portfolio as a bear market hedge. These considerations give rise to the notion of targeting the duration of a portfolio.

Duration targeting can be accomplished in the cash market by restructuring the portfolio, in the futures market by buying or selling futures contracts, or in both markets by combining cash and futures positions. For example, in the cash market, duration can be increased by replacing short-term securities with longer term, lower coupon bonds. It can be reduced by swapping low coupon, long-term bonds for higher coupon, shorter term bonds, or by increasing the percentage of cash held in the portfolio.

There are disadvantages to targeting duration by restructuring the portfolio. First, it can be costly due to the illiquidity of securities held in the portfolio. Second, some managers face institutional constraints to restructuring, because of potential tax liabilities or accounting problems associated with the realization of capital gains and losses. Third, the portfolio may be constructed so as to meet the cash flow requirements of long term liabilities.

---

[24] If the cash bond being hedged is the cheapest-to-deliver bond, Beta equals one and the term has no effect on the hedge position.

[25] As measured by the $R^2$ shown in the exhibit, yield changes on the 7¼% bond account for about 77% of the variance of yield changes on the GNMA security.

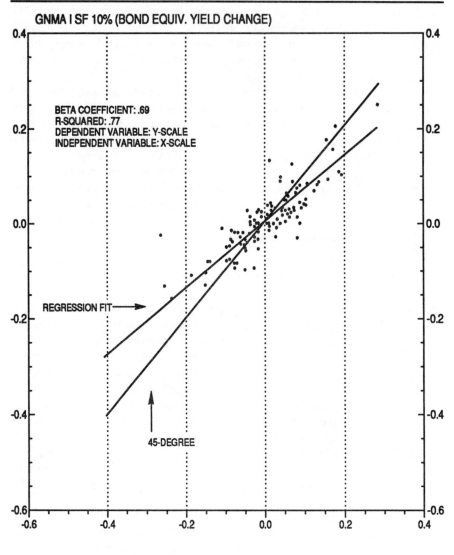

GNMA I SF 10% (BOND EQUIV. YIELD CHANGE)

BETA COEFFICIENT: .69
R-SQUARED: .77
DEPENDENT VARIABLE: Y-SCALE
INDEPENDENT VARIABLE: X-SCALE

REGRESSION FIT

45-DEGREE

7 1/4% OF 5/15/2016 (YIELD-TO-MATURITY CHANGE)

Treasury bond and note futures can at times provide a more effective means to target portfolio duration than by restructuring in the cash market. Strictly speaking, a futures contract has no duration, because the purchase or sale of a contract involves no investment. Nonetheless, a long futures position increases basis point value, thereby increasing portfolio duration. A short futures position reduces basis point value, shortening duration.

The number of futures contracts required to achieve a desired portfolio modified duration can be expressed as:

$$N = 100 \; \frac{(D_H - D_P) \times (MV + A)_p}{BPV_F}$$

where:

$N$ = Number of futures contracts needed to achieve the desired portfolio modified duration

$D_H$ = Target modified duration of the hedged portfolio

$D_p$ = Modified duration of the unhedged portfolio

$(MV+A)_p$ = Market value and accrued interest of the portfolio in millions of dollars

$BPV_F$ = Basis point value of the futures in dollars

The duration of a portfolio can be targeted by adjusting the number of futures contracts held in the portfolio. For example, consider a $100 million portfolio consisting of four $25 million bonds as shown in Exhibit 19. The information reflects market conditions on Mach 15, 1988.

The top panel lists the price, face value, total market value (including accrued interest), basis point value, and modified duration for each bond, the aggregate portfolio, and the March '88 futures contract. (Basis point values are per $1 million for each bond, per $100 million face for the aggregate portfolio, and per contract for the futures.) The portfolio has a market value plus accrued interest of $116.211 million, a total basis point of $108,356, and a modified duration of 9.324. The basis point value of the June '88 bond futures is $85.64 per contract (assuming the cheapest to deliver is the 10⅜% bond).

The bottom panel shows the number of futures contracts needed to achieve the modified duration targets listed in the left column. For example, the number of futures contracts needed to reduce the modified duration from 9.324 to 5 is:

$$\text{Sell } 587 = 100 \; \frac{(5-9.324) \times 116.211}{85.64}$$

A short position of 587 June '88 bond futures contracts reduces the portfolio modified duration to 5; a short position of 1,265 contracts reduces it to zero.

Notice that the hedge ratio defined earlier ($H = BPV_p/BPV_F$) is a special case of

**EXHIBIT 19**
**TARGETING PORTFOLIO MODIFIED DURATION**

| Bond Portfolio | Price | Face Value ($MM) | Total Value ($MM) | Basis Point Value | Modified Duration |
|---|---|---|---|---|---|
| 7¼% (5/15/16) | 86.02 | 25 | 22.119 | 934 | 10.559 |
| 8⅞% (8/15/17) | 103.26 | 25 | 26.130 | 1,108 | 10.600 |
| 10⅝% (8/15/12) | 115.10 | 25 | 29.690 | 1,042 | 8.773 |
| 14% (11/15/11) | 148.14 | 25 | 38.272 | 1,250 | 8.166 |
| Total Portfolio | N.A. | 100 | 116.211 | 108,356 | 9.324 |
| June '88 Futures | 92.10 | 0.1 | N.A. | 85.64 | N.A. |

| Target Duration | Futures Contracts | |
|---|---|---|
| 20 | Buy | 1,449 |
| 15 | Buy | 770 |
| 10 | Buy | 92 |
| 5 | Sell | 587 |
| 0 | Sell | 1,265 |

the duration target formula, where the target duration $(D_H)$ is equal to zero. In this case, the numerator, $(0 - D_p) \times (MV + A)_p$, is equal to $BPV_p$. Most futures hedges are constructed in this manner to fully protect the portfolio from changes in yields. The next example examines such a hedge and the impact of yield spread changes on hedge performance.

### Selling Futures to Hedge a Bond

In this example, the cash portfolio consists of the 7¼% bond due May 2016. The price of this bond and the cheapest-to-deliver bond (10⅜% bond due November 2012, callable in 2007) underlying the June '88 futures contract are shown in the top panel of Exhibit 20, which reflects market conditions on March 15, 1988. The futures price is 92¹⁰/₃₂. The bottom panel shows how the hedged portfolio is affected (in terms of the gross basis and the total return on the net position) one month later by changes in the level of the market and by changes in the yield spread between the 10⅜% and the 7¼%.

The hedge ratio for each million dollars of the hedged bond is approximately 11 contracts. This is calculated by dividing the basis point value of the 7¼% bond ($934 per million face) by the basis point value of the futures contract ($84.73). The latter is equal to the basis point value of the cheapest-to-deliver bond ($104.20 per $100,000) divided by its conversion factor (1.2310).[26]

The body of the exhibit illustrates how the hedge is affected on the horizon date by changes in the level of the market holding the yield spread constant (rows), or by changes in the yield spread holding the level of the market constant (columns).

Changes in the level of the market do not have a significant impact on the effectiveness of the hedge.[27] The highlighted row shows the horizon price of the 7¼% bond, its basis against the June '88 futures, and the annualized total return of the hedged position, over a range of futures prices assuming the yield spread remains constant at 16 basis points. While the price of the hedged bond varies by over six points along the row, the total return is relatively stable, indicating that the short futures position is an effective hedge of the 7¼% bond.[28] The return on the hedge is about three percent, roughly five percentage points less than the yield on the 7¼% bond. The hedged position yields less, because the short futures position, in effect, turns the 7¼% bond into a synthetic money market instrument that yields an amount that reflects the implied repo rate of the futures contract.

Changes in the yield spread (left column) between the 10⅜% bond and the 7¼% bond can have a significant impact on the outcome of the hedge. This is illustrated in

---

[26]When hedging the cheapest-to-deliver bond, the hedge ratio is equal to its conversion factor, because the basis point values cancel: $H = BPV/(BPV/CF) = CF$.

[27]This example assumes that there is no change in the cheapest-to-deliver bond.

[28]Total return is defined as the rate of return on the net position, including changes in the bond price, coupons received (if any), accrued interest, and changes in the value of the futures position. The total return is expressed on a 360-day basis, because the hedged position is equivalent to a money market security.

# EXHIBIT 20
## SHORT FUTURES HEDGE OF 7¼% T-BOND DUE MAY 2016

Evaluation Date: March 15, 1988
Horizon Date: April 15, 1988

BPV Hedge Ratio (Per $MM): 11.03
June '88 Futures Price: 92.10

| C-T-D: Hedged: | Coupon | Call or Maturity | Price (32nds) | Yield | (BPV) ($MM) | Factor | Basis (32nds) |
|---|---|---|---|---|---|---|---|
| | 10.375 | Nov-07 | 115.10 | 8.73 | $1,042 | 1.2310 | 53.63 |
| | 7.25 | May-16 | 86.02 | 8.57 | $ 934 | 0.9167 | 46.07 |

### Horizon Futures Price

7.25% Bond
Implied Cash Price, Basis, and Annualized Hedge Returns

| Yield Spread | 89.10 | 90.10 | 91.10 | 92.10 | 93.10 | 94.10 | 95.10 |
|---|---|---|---|---|---|---|---|
| 0.31 | 82.23 | 84.27 | 85.31 | 87.03 | 88.07 | 89.11 | 90.15 |
| | 59 | 66 | 72 | 79 | 85 | 92 | 99 |
| | 21.41 | 21.49 | 21.65 | 21.89 | 22.20 | 22.60 | 23.06 |
| 0.26 | 83.09 | 84.12 | 85.16 | 86.19 | 87.23 | 88.27 | 89.31 |
| | 45 | 51 | 57 | 63 | 70 | 76 | 83 |
| | 15.39 | 15.34 | 15.36 | 15.46 | 15.64 | 15.89 | 16.22 |
| 0.21 | 82.27 | 83.30 | 85.01 | 86.04 | 87.08 | 88.11 | 89.15 |
| | 31 | 37 | 43 | 48 | 55 | 61 | 67 |
| | 9.43 | 9.24 | 9.13 | 9.10 | 9.14 | 9.25 | 9.44 |
| 0.16 | 82.13 | 83.16 | 84.19 | 85.21 | 86.25 | 87.28 | 88.31 |
| | 17 | 23 | 28 | 34 | 39 | 45 | 51 |
| | 3.52 | 3.20 | 2.96 | 2.79 | 2.69 | 2.67 | 2.72 |
| 0.11 | 81.31 | 83.02 | 84.04 | 85.07 | 86.09 | 87.12 | 88.16 |
| | 3 | 8 | 14 | 19 | 24 | 30 | 36 |
| | -2.34 | -2.79 | -3.16 | -3.46 | -3.69 | -3.85 | -3.94 |
| 0.06 | 81.18 | 82.20 | 83.22 | 84.24 | 85.27 | 86.29 | 88.00 |
| | -10 | -6 | -1 | 4 | 9 | 15 | 20 |
| | -8.15 | -8.72 | -9.22 | -9.66 | -10.02 | -10.31 | -10.53 |
| 0.01 | 81.04 | 82.06 | 83.08 | 84.10 | 85.12 | 86.14 | 87.17 |
| | -24 | -20 | -15 | -10 | -6 | -1 | 5 |
| | -13.90 | -14.60 | -15.23 | -15.80 | -16.29 | -16.72 | -17.07 |

the highlighted column of Exhibit 20. The hedge is initiated when the yield on the 10⅜% bond is 16 basis points higher than that on the 7¼% bond. An increase in this spread to 31 basis points increases the basis to $^{79}/_{32}$nds from $^{34}/_{32}$nds, enhancing the annualized total return on the hedged position to 29.89%. A decline in the yield spread results in a lower basis and a less effective hedge. As was noted earlier, changes in yield spreads can cause a switch in the cheapest-to-deliver bond and this too can affect the outcome of a hedge. Many traders analyze yield spreads carefully prior to hedging, because of their importance in determining the performance of a hedge.

Yield spreads are also important for cross-hedges. A cross-hedge occurs when the cash market security being hedged is (significantly) different than the futures contract, either in terms of maturity or market sector. For example, a short position in T-bond futures against a portfolio of corporate bonds is a cross-hedge, because the futures tracks a Treasury security whereas corporate bonds are privately issued. This type of hedge is sensitive to changes in yield spreads between market sectors. Cross-hedges that consist of short bond futures positions tend to benefit if Treasury yields rise relative to those on the bonds being hedged, but are less effective if they decline. The reverse tends to hold for cross-hedges that consist of long futures contracts.

### Buying Futures to Create a Synthetic Bond

Portfolio managers can benefit from undervalued futures by selling bonds from their portfolio, and replacing them with synthetic securities created by purchasing Treasury bills (or some other short-term security) and bond futures. Overvaluation of the delivery options embedded in the contract and the natural tendency for government securities dealers to be short futures to hedge their inventories are two factors that sometimes contribute to undervaluation of the contract.

In a previous section on basis and carry relationships, it was noted that yield enhancement strategies are often designed to take advantage of incremental convergence, by selling futures when they are overvalued or purchasing them when they are undervalued. This is analyzed more closely in the following example that compares the one-year rate of return on equal-dollar investments ($100 million) in two alternatives. They are: a) an 8⅞% bond due August 2017, and b) a synthetic investment consisting of a long position in a one-year T-bill maturing March 16, 1989, coupled with a long position of 1244 March '89 bond futures. Under most conditions, the synthetic investment yields more than the 8⅞% bond, because the additional convergence of the undervalued March '89 futures contract makes it advantageous to be long futures.

The comparison between the two alternatives is summarized in Exhibit 21, which shows the impact on their annualized returns due to changes in yield levels, yield spreads, and a switch in the cheapest-to-deliver bond. The exhibit reflects prices as of March 15, 1988. At that time the 10⅜% bond due November 2012 (callable in 2007) was cheapest to deliver.

**EXHIBIT 21**
**SYNTHETIC BOND CREATED WITH FUTURES (ANNUALIZED RETURNS)**

| (1) Yield Change | (2) 8⅞ Coupon | (3) Synthetic CTD Const 10⅜% | (4) Synthetic CTD Switch to 7¼% | (5) Synthetic Yield Sprd −.15 B.P. | (6) Synthetic Yield Sprd +.15 B.P. |
|---|---|---|---|---|---|
| −3.00 | 50.12 | 47.61 | 47.61 | 49.86 | 45.41 |
| −2.00 | 33.54 | 33.80 | 33.80 | 35.75 | 31.90 |
| −1.00 | 19.87 | 21.82 | 21.82 | 23.51 | 20.16 |
| 0.00 | 8.51 | 11.38 | 11.38 | 12.85 | 9.93 |
| 1.00 | −0.99 | 2.26 | 0.80 | 3.55 | 0.99 |
| 2.00 | −9.01 | −5.94 | −8.39 | −4.72 | −7.11 |
| 3.00 | −15.83 | −13.35 | −16.20 | −12.30 | −14.37 |

The first column shows potential changes in yields (in percentage points) on March 15, 1989, one year after the position is initiated. The second and third columns depict the corresponding annualized returns for the 8⅞% bond and the synthetic investment, respectively. If yields remain unchanged on the horizon date, the one-year return on the synthetic bond is 11.38%, nearly three percentage points higher than the yield on the 8⅞% bond (8.51%). The synthetic investment yields more due to the incremental convergence of the undervalued futures contract.

If yields remain stable throughout the one-year period, a significant switch in the cheapest-to-deliver bond is unlikely. On the other hand, if yields rise significantly (corresponding to a yield change of roughly plus 1.0 or more), the long duration 7¼% bond due May 2016 is likely to become cheapest to deliver.

The effect of the switch is shown in column four. In a bull market, returns for the synthetic are greater than the 8⅞% bond (comparing columns 2 and 4) until yields drop by about 200 basis points or more, at which point the longer duration of the 8⅞% bond causes it to have the better return. However, this assumes that the hedge ratio remains unchanged; if one adjusts for being under-hedged by purchasing additional contracts (or out-of-the-money futures call options), returns on the synthetic would increase commensurately. In a bear market, the cheapest-to-deliver bond switches to the 7¼% bond due May 2016. Despite its long duration, the synthetic security continues to perform better than the 8⅞% bond until yields rise by 300 basis points.

Column 5 shows the effect on the synthetic position due to a 15 basis point decrease in the yield spread between the 10⅜ and 8⅞% bonds, assuming the cheapest-to-deliver bond remains the 10⅜% bond across all yield scenarios. A decrease in the spread enhances the return to the synthetic position regardless of changes in the level of rates, because it causes the futures price to rise relative to that of the 8⅞% bond. Conversely, if the spread increases by 15 basis points (column 6), the synthetic's returns are reduced.

Historical data on the performance of synthetic long bonds relative to comparable cash market bonds is shown in Exhibit 22. It compares the predicted and actual

**EXHIBIT 22**
**SYNTHETIC LONG BOND TRADE—HISTORICAL RESULTS**

| (1) Start Date | (2) End Date | (3) Start Long Bond | (4) Start C-T-D Bond | (5) End CTD C-T-D Bond | (6) Actual Change in L.B. Yld | (A) Actual L.B. Return | (B) Pred. Synth. Return | (C) Actual Synth. Return | (B)−(A) | (C)−(A) |
|---|---|---|---|---|---|---|---|---|---|---|
| 03/19/86 | 03/18/87 | 9.25-16 | 12.375-04 | 12.75-10 | −0.37 | 12.08 | 13.87 | 15.59 | 1.79 | 3.51 |
| 04/23/86 | 04/22/87 | 9.25-16 | 14-11 | 12.5-14 | 1.09 | −3.46 | −1.25 | 0.88 | 2.20 | 4.34 |
| 05/21/86 | 05/20/87 | 9.25-16 | 14-11 | 12.5-14 | 1.55 | −8.10 | −6.16 | 0.21 | 1.95 | 8.31 |
| 06/18/86 | 06/17/87 | 7.25-16 | 13.875-11 | 13.25-14 | 1.07 | −3.85 | −1.92 | 5.49 | 1.93 | 9.34 |
| 07/16/86 | 07/15/87 | 7.25-16 | 14-11 | 13.25-14 | 1.49 | −8.17 | −6.86 | −0.70 | 1.31 | 7.47 |
| 08/20/86 | 08/19/87 | 7.25-16 | 14-11 | 7.5-16 | 1.86 | −11.23 | −10.08 | −6.11 | 1.15 | 5.12 |
| 09/17/86 | 09/16/87 | 7.25-16 | 14-11 | 7.25-16 | 2.11 | −12.03 | −10.37 | −6.19 | 1.66 | 5.84 |
| 10/15/86 | 10/14/87 | 7.50-16 | 13.875-11 | 7.25-16 | 2.45 | −14.12 | −12.95 | −10.34 | 1.17 | 3.78 |
| 11/19/86 | 11/18/87 | 7.50-16 | 13.25-14 | 7.25-16 | 1.57 | −8.41 | −5.63 | −2.89 | 2.78 | 5.52 |
| 12/17/86 | 12/16/87 | 7.50-16 | 14-11 | 7.25-16 | 1.78 | −10.27 | −7.63 | −4.69 | 2.64 | 5.58 |
| 01/21/87 | 01/20/88 | 7.50-16 | 14-11 | 7.25-16 | 1.47 | −7.61 | −5.09 | −2.91 | 2.52 | 4.70 |
| 02/18/87 | 02/17/88 | 7.50-16 | 13.25-14 | 10.375-12 | 0.92 | −2.00 | 1.64 | 3.20 | 3.64 | 5.20 |

returns of the outstanding long bond versus synthetic alternative. Columns 1 to 6 contain data that describe the long bonds, cheapest-to-deliver bonds, and actual changes in yields that occurred during the periods relevant to each trade. The remaining columns compare the projected and actual returns on the cash and synthetic positions.

For the trade beginning on 06/18/86 (fourth row), the return on the actual long bond (7¼% bond due 2016) was negative 3.85%, corresponding to an increase in its yield equal to 1.07%. The projected return for the synthetic position (given the same yield change) was negative 1.92%, almost two percentage points higher than the return on the long bond. Due to actual yield spread changes that benefited the synthetic position relative to the long bond, the actual return was 5.49%, more than nine percentage points higher. During the holding period of this trade, the yield on the 13¼% bond due 2014 (the ending cheapest-to-deliver bond) declined by about 60 basis points relative to the yield on the 7¼% bond. This is illustrated in Exhibit 11.

As with most cash-futures trades, the performance of the synthetic long bond trade is sensitive to yield spread changes in the cash market. Assuming that yield spreads are stable, the expected yield advantage of the synthetic bond relative to the long bond currently appears to be in the range of about one to three percentage points.

## V. CONCLUSION

Treasury bond and note futures are widely used to control risk and enhance yields. To use futures effectively, it is important to understand how futures prices are linked to those in the cash market. This article has attempted to shed light on the relationship between cash and futures prices, the factors that can affect those prices and the performance of selected cash-futures strategies.

Treasury bond and note futures can be used flexibly to achieve the goals of asset and liability managers. For many portfolio managers, futures are the primary means to protect the value of cash bonds, and can sometimes be used to enhance yields. For liability managers, a short futures position can be just the right tool to lock in borrowing costs before rates go higher. Regardless of the objective, an assessment of relative value between cash and futures prices based on the concepts presented in this article is strongly recommended prior to executing trades.

## APPENDIX A: CONTRACT SPECIFICATIONS AND DELIVERY PROCEDURES

### Contract Specifications

The contract specifications for the Treasury bond and note futures are shown in Exhibit A-1. Some of these šuch as price limits or trading hours may vary. At the time of this writing, daily trading limits on the bond and note contracts are 3 and 2 points, respectively, and trading hours are 8:00 a.m. to 2:00 p.m. Chicago time Monday through Friday, and 5:00 p.m. to 8:30 p.m. Sunday through Thursday during the evening session.

**EXHIBIT A-1**
**CONTRACT SPECIFICATIONS**

|  | *Treasury Bonds* | *Ten-Year T-Notes* |
|---|---|---|
| Trading Unit | U.S. Treasury Bonds with $100,000 face value. | U.S. Treasury Notes with $100,000 face value. |
| Deliverable Grade | U.S. Treasury bonds which have an actual maturity at least 15 years if not callable; and, if callable, are not so for at least 15 years. | U.S. Treasury notes with an original maturity of not less than 6½ years and not more than 10 years. |
| Delivery Months | As determined by the Exchange (currently March, June, September, and December). | |
| Delivery Method | By Federal Reserve book-entry transfer system. Invoice is adjusted for coupon rates and maturity or call dates. Accrued interest is prorated. | |
| Settlement | Based on conversion factor whereby the price at which a bond or note with this time to maturity (time to call if callable) with the same coupon rate as this issue will yield 8%. The time to maturity (time to call if callable) of a given issue is calculated in three month increments from the first day of delivery month (that is, 15 years and 5 months = 15 years and 1 quarter. | |
| Minimum Price Fluctuation | 1/32 of a point ($31.25 per contract.) | |
| Trading Limits* | Trading limits are set by the Board of Directors of the Chicago Board of Trade, and can change depending on market conditions. January 1, 1987 limits: | |
|  | 96/32 above and below the previous day's settlement price. | 64/32 above and below the previous day's settlement price. |

*Trading limits do not apply to trading in the current month on or after the first notice day thereof.

## *Delivery Procedures*

Delivery is a three day process to allow those involved—the Long, the Short, The Clearing Corporation, and the banks—to make the necessary notifications and arrangements in an orderly manner.[29] Making and taking delivery is accomplished by completing a series of steps in an established sequence by a stated time.

The first step in the procedure (prior to the actual three day delivery sequence) occurs when the Long notifies the Clearing Corporation of all open positions two days prior to the first business day of the delivery month.

On Position Day (day 1 in the delivery sequence) the Clearing Corporation receives notice of intention to deliver from the seller (Short Clearing Member). The Short has the option of when to initiate the delivery process during delivery month.

On Intention Day (day 2) the Clearing Corporation matches the Short Clearing Member with the oldest outstanding Long Clearing Member position, and invoicing occurs.

On Delivery Day (day 3) title to bonds or notes is transferred from the seller (Short Clearing Member) to the buyer (Long Clearing Member), by book-entry procedure.

These procedures are summarized in Exhibit A-2.

## APPENDIX B: GLOSSARY OF TERMS

**Arbitrage.**  Simultaneous purchase of cash securities or futures in one market against the sale of cash securities or futures in the same or a different market; to profit from a discrepancy in prices.

**Basis.**  Gross basis is the difference between a bond's cash price and its (futures) parity price. Net basis is equal to gross basis minus carry.

**Bear Market.**  A market in which prices are declining.

**Beta (or Beta Coefficient).**  A statistical measure of the relationship between the prices or yields of two securities.

**Bull Market.**  A market in which prices are rising.

**Call Option.**  An option which gives the option buyer the right to purchase (go "long") the underlying futures contract at the strike price on or before the expiration date.

**Carry.**  The difference between the coupon income (including reinvestment of coupons and net accrued interest) of a bond and the cost of financing that bond.

---

[29]The delivery process is shortened to two days on the next to last business day of the delivery month.

**EXHIBIT A-2**
**DELIVERY PROCEDURES**

| | Clearing Corporation | Short | Long | Bank |
|---|---|---|---|---|
| First Position Day | | | Two (2) days prior to first business day of delivery month. Long advises the Clearing Corp. of all open long positions by using a *Long Position Report Card* which is updated during the delivery month as changes occur. | |
| Day 1 Position Day | | **By 8:00 pm\*** Short advises Clearing Corp. of his intention to make delivery by submitting a *Delivery Notice* and a *Delivery Tender Card*. | | |
| Day 2 Intention Day | **By 8:30 am\*** Clearing Corp. matches short to oldest Long & notifies both parties by sending a *Delivery Assignment Notice* to Long and a *Notice to Seller* to Short. | **By 2:00 pm\*** Short invoices Long by sending him a *Delivery Invoice*. | **By 4:00 pm** Long provides Short with banking information necessary for transfer of Bonds or Notes against payment. | |
| Day 3 Delivery Day | | **By 10:00 am\*\*** Short deposits Bonds or Notes to be transferred by his bank to Long via the Fed system. | **By 1:00 pm\*\*** Long deposits federal funds to be transferred by his bank to Short via the Fed system. | The two banks representing Short and Long, simultaneously transfer Bonds or Notes to Long and payment to Short via the Fed System. |

\*For deliveries occurring on the last business day of the delivery month, Position Day and Intention Day may occur on the same day. In such cases, the deadline for *Delivery Notices* is extended to 2:00 p.m. on Intention Day. Upon receiving the *Delivery Notices* the Clearing Corporation shall promptly match the Long with the Short, and provide notices to Long and Short Clearing Members. The deadline for submitting invoices by the Short is extended to 3:00 p.m. on Intention Day.
\*\*If it is a banking holiday, the transfer must be completed by 9:30 a.m. the next banking business day.

**Cash Market.**  A market in which commodities, fixed income and equity securities are traded for current delivery.

**Clearing Corporation (or Clearing House).**  The futures exchange entity, whose function it is to clear (match) all purchases and sales and to assure the financial integrity of all futures and options transactions. Once a trade has been cleared, the Clearing Corporation becomes the buyer to every seller and the seller to every buyer.

**Clearing Member.**  A member of the Clearing Corporation. Clearing members include brokerage firms, trading companies and some individuals. All trades of a non-clearing member must be registered and eventually settled through a clearing member.

**Closing Price (or Range).**  The price (or price range) recorded in the trading place in the final moments of a day's trade that are officially designated as the "close." (See Settlement Price.)

**Closing Transaction.**  A purchase or sale that offsets an existing position. That is, selling a futures contract that was previously purchased or buying back a futures contract that was previously sold. (See Opening Transaction.)

**Conversion Factor.**  A factor relevant to Treasury bond and note futures that attempts to translate a bond eligible for delivery into the standard grade specified by the contract (that is, an 8% bond).

**Convergence.**  The movement of the futures invoice price towards the price of the underlying cash instrument as the delivery date approaches. Until the settlement date draws near, there is a natural difference between the cash and futures invoice price (the basis) due to the cost of carry.

**Cost of Carry.**  The cost of holding a commodity over time. Includes financing cost, storage and security. In the case of interest-bearing securities, "positive carry" exists when a security's coupon income exceeds its short-term financing cost, and "negative carry" exists when the financing cost exceeds the coupon income.

**Cross Hedge.**  Hedging a commodity with a futures contract in which the underlying commodity differs from the commodity being hedged. Example: hedging mortgages with Treasury bond futures.

**Daily Settlement.**  Futures participants are charged for their losses or credited for their gains at the end of each trading day. (See mark-to-market.)

**Delivery.**  The tender and receipt of the actual security in settlement of a futures contract.

**Delivery Month.**  The specified month within which a futures contract matures and can be settled by delivery.

**Delivery Notice.**  The written notice given by the seller of his intention to make delivery against an open short futures position on a particular date. This notice, delivered through the clearing house, is separate and distinct from the warehouse receipt, book entry or other instrument that will be used to transfer title.

**Delivery Price.**  The price fixed by the clearing house at which deliveries on futures are invoiced and the price at which the futures contract is settled when deliveries are made. (See Settlement Price.)

**First Notice Day.**  The first day on which notices of intention to deliver actual commodites against futures market positions can be received. First notice day can vary with each commodity and exchange.

**Forward Contract.**  A contractual agreement between two parties to exchange a commodity at a set price on a future date. Differs from a futures contract because most forward commitments are not exchange traded or standardized, and carry the risk related to the credit worthiness of the other side of the transaction. Forward contracts are generally not marked-to-market as are futures.

**Futures.**  A standardized contract, traded on an organized exchange, to buy or sell a fixed quantity of a defined commodity at a set price in the future. A clearinghouse takes the other side of the transaction, removing much of the credit risk. Positions can easily be closed by taking the other side in the open outcry auction of the exchange.

**Futures Commission Merchant (FCM).**  Individuals, associations, partnerships, corporations and trusts that solicit or accept orders for the purchase or sale of any commodity for future delivery on, or subject to the rules of, any contract market and that accept payment from or extend credit to those whose orders are accepted. FCMs must be registered with the Commodity Futures Trading Commission.

**Futures Contract.**  A contract traded on a futures exchange for the delivery of a specified commodity or financial instrument at a future time. The contract specifies the item to be delivered and the terms and conditions of delivery.

**Futures Price.**  The price of a particular futures contract determined by open competition between buyers and sellers on the trading floor of the exchange.

**Hedge.**  The buying or selling of offsetting positions in order to provide protection against an adverse change in price. A hedge may involve having positions in the cash market, the futures market and/or options.

**Initial Margin.**  Customer's funds or securities put up as collateral for a guarantee of contract fulfillment at the time a futures market position is established.

**Invoice Price.**  The futures price times the conversion factor times $1,000, plus accrued interest. The invoice price is related to the parity price which is equal to the futures price times the conversion factor.

**Last Notice Day.**  The final day on which notices of intent to deliver on futures contracts may be issued. Occurs on the second to last business day of the month for T-bond and note futures.

**Last Trading Day.** Day on which trading ceases for the maturing (current) delivery-month futures contract. Occurs on the eighth to last business day of the delivery month for T-bond and note futures. On this day, trading ceases at noon (Chicago time) and the settlement price remains fixed for the remainder of the delivery month.

**Long.** The position which is established by the purchase of a futures contract. The holder of such a position is sometimes referred to as "the long."

**Long Hedge.** A hedge in which the futures contract is bought (a long position).

**Long Basis.** A trading position consisting of a long position in cash market securities that are hedged with a short position in the futures market.

**Margin.** The sum of money which must be deposited and maintained in order to provide protection to both parties of a trade. The Exchange establishes minimum margin amounts. FCMs often require margin deposits that exceed Exchange minimums. In turn, FCMs post and maintain margins, with the Clearing Corporation.

**Margin Calls.** Additional funds which may be required of the long or short if there is an adverse price change or if margin requirements are increased.

**Mark-to-market.** The daily settlement process whereby futures gains are credited to the margin account and futures losses are debited. The calculation of futures gains and losses is based on the futures settlement price. (See daily settlement.)

**Notice Day.** Any day on which notices of intent to deliver on futures contracts may be issued.

**Notice of Delivery.** A notice given through the clearinghouse expressing intention to deliver the commodity. Chicago Board of Trade notices are called "intentions to deliver."

**Open Interest.** The sum of futures contracts (long or short, but not both) in one delivery month or one market that has been entered into and not yet liquidated by an offsetting transaction or fulfilled by delivery.

**Opening Transaction.** A purchase or sale which establishes a new position. (See Closing Transaction.)

**Parity Price (Futures Parity Price).** Equal to the futures price times the conversion factor for a particular bond or note.

**Position.** An interest in the market, either long or short, in the form of one or more open contracts.

**Price Limit.** Maximum price advance or decline from the previous day's settlement price permitted for a commodity in one trading session.

**Put Option.** An option which gives the option buyer the right to sell (go "short") the underlying futures contract at the strike price on or before the expiration date.

**Settlement Price.** The daily price at which the clearing house clears all trades and settles all accounts between clearing members for each contract month. Settlement prices are used to determine both margin calls and invoice prices for deliveries.

**Short.** The position created by the sale of a futures contract or option (either a call or a put) if there is no offsetting position. The holder of such a position is sometimes referred to as "the short."

**Short Hedge.** A hedge that involves the selling (shorting) of a futures contract. A short position guards against a price decrease in the underlying commodity; a short position in interest rate futures protects the hedger from rising rates.

**Short Basis.** A trading position consisting of a short position in cash market securities hedged with a long position in the futures market.

**Spread.** A position consisting of both long and short futures of the same or different class. Examples include calendar spreads (consisting of a long position in one contract month and a short position in another) and the "NOB" (Notes over Bonds) spread (consisting of a position in the note futures against an opposing position in the bond futures).

**Strike Price.** The price at which the holder of the call (put) may exercise his right to purchase (sell) the underlying futures contract.

**Variation Margin.** Payment required upon margin call.

# Implied Duration and Hedge Ratios for a Treasury Bond Futures Contract

ROGER G. CLARKE, PH.D.
MANAGING DIRECTOR AND
CHIEF INVESTMENT OFFICER
TSA CAPITAL MANAGEMENT

## I. INTRODUCTION

One technique commonly used to calculate the appropriate hedge ratio between a bond position to be hedged and a Treasury bond futures contract is to take the ratio of their respective price changes for a given change in interest rates.[1] This ratio gives the proportion of futures contracts to use in hedging the bond position. Since the change in the price of the bond for small changes in interest rates is proportional to the bond's modified duration, it is sometimes useful to express the hedge ratio in terms of the bond's duration.

---

[1] See Robert W. Kopprasch, "Understanding Duration and Volatility," Chapter 5 in Frank J. Fabozzi and Irving M. Pollack (eds), *The Handbook of Fixed Income Securities* (Homewood, IL: Dow Jones-Irwin, 1987).

Equation (1) expresses the well-known relationship between the price change in a bond paying interest semi-annually and a small change in its yield to maturity.[2]

$$\frac{dP}{d(1+y/2)} = \frac{-PD}{(1+y/2)}$$

$$= -PD^*$$

(1)

where   $P$   = the current price
      $y$   = the yield to maturity of the bond
      $D$   = Macaulay duration
      $D^*$ = Modified duration

$$= \frac{D}{(1+y/2)}$$

The futures contract on a Treasury bond does not have a duration in the traditional sense according to Macaulay's definition using the expected cash flows. However, the price of the future is linked to the price of the cheapest-to-deliver Treasury bond through the cash and carry arbitrage relationship. With this pricing relationship we can calculate an implied duration for the future. The future's implied duration can then be used to construct an appropriate hedge ratio for a particular bond B to be hedged using the futures contract. The hedge ratio is given as the negative of the ratio of the respective price changes between the bond being hedged and the futures contract. Using equation (1) we can write the hedge ratio in terms of their respective durations as:

$$h = \frac{-dB}{dF}$$

$$= \frac{-BD_B^*}{FD_F^*} \frac{d(1+y/2)}{d(1+i/2)}$$

(2)

$$= \frac{-BD_B^* \delta_B}{FD_F^*}$$

---

[2]The original notion of duration can be found in Frederick Macaulay, *Some Theoretical Problems Suggested by the Movements of Interest Rates, Bond Yields and Stock Prices in the United States Since 1856*, National Bureau of Economic Research, 1938. The extension of duration to its modified form can be found in John R. Hicks, *Value and Capital*, Clarendon Press (Oxford), 1939.

where $B$    = the price of the bond to be hedged (including accrued interest)
       $D_B^*$    = the modified duration of bond B
       $y$    = the annual yield to maturity of bond B
       $F$    = the current futures price
       $D_F^*$    = the implied modified duration of the future
       $i$    = the annual yield to maturity on the cheapest-to-deliver Treasury bond of the futures contract
       $\delta_B$    = the sensitivity of a change in y to a change in $i = dy/di$

## II. THE IMPLIED DURATION OF A FUTURES CONTRACT

The cash and carry arbitrage relationship keeps the price of the Treasury bond future closely tied to the price of the cheapest-to-deliver Treasury bond.[3] If the future is priced greater than its fair value, there is an incentive to sell the overvalued future and borrow to buy the underlying Treasury bond for future delivery against the futures contract. Such an arbitrage would give a higher than fair market rate of return. To prevent this the future must be priced fairly. The arbitrage possibilities help keep the futures price linked to the price movement of the cheapest-to-deliver Treasury bond.[4] Equation (3) indicates that the price of the future is grossed up by the amount of interest which must be paid to finance the purchase of the Treasury bond but is reduced by the amount of interest earned on the bond itself. The conversion factor $f$ is needed to convert the cheapest-to-deliver bond into an equivalent 8% coupon. The fair market value of the future is given as:

$$F = \frac{P(1 + rt/360) - C(a + t)/360}{f} \tag{3}$$

where $C$    = annual coupon payment on the cheapest-to-deliver bond
       $t$    = actual number of days to futures expiration
       $a$    = number of days of accrued interest in the current purchase price
       $f$    = bond conversion factor on the cheapest-to-deliver bond
       $i$    = annual yield to maturity on the cheapest-to-deliver bond
       $r$    = annual implied repo rate based on the cheapest-to-deliver bond
       $P$    = price of the cheapest-to-deliver bond including accrued interest

---

[3]A discussion of the cash and carry relationship can be found in the article by Timothy Lord in this book ("Treasury Bond and Note Futures: Pricing and Portfolio Management Applications").

[4]The arbitrage relationship is somewhat less precise than implied here because as interest rates change the cheapest-to-deliver bond can also change. The relationship is also influenced by some embedded options the short seller has because of the choice of delivery time. The future often appears to be priced cheap as a result of these embedded options. For a discussion of this phenomenon see Frank Jones and Beth Krumholz "The Cheapness of the Treasury Bond and Note Futures Contract" (Kidder Peabody and Co., Inc.), March 1985.

As the yield to maturity on the cheapest-to-deliver bond changes, the price of the bond will change and cause a change in the future price. If we define the implied duration of the futures contract as

$$D_F^* = \frac{-1}{F} \frac{dF}{d(1+i/2)} \, , \tag{4}$$

the appendix shows that the implied duration of the futures contract can be written in terms of the bond's duration as

$$D_F^* = \frac{P}{fF} [D^*(1+rt/360) - \delta_r t/180]$$

$$= \frac{fF + C(a+t)/360}{fF(1+rt/360)} [D^*(1+rt/360) - \delta_r t/180] \tag{5}$$

where $\delta_r = dr/di$

The top equation expresses the modified duration in terms of the current price of the cheapest-to-deliver bond and the futures price while the second equation expresses the relationship just in terms of the current futures price.

Both equations indicate that the implied modified duration of the futures is a function of the duration, conversion factor and coupon rate on the cheapest-to-deliver bond, the implied repo rate, and the relative rate change between the yield to maturity and the implied repo rate. The second form of the equation results from using the relationship between the fair value of the future and the price of the cheapest-to-deliver bond in equation (3).

Several special cases result from the general form of equation (5). If the implied repo rate does not change with a change in yield to maturity, $\delta_r = 0$, equation (5) reduces to

$$D_F^* = \frac{PD^*(1+rt/360)}{fF}$$

$$= \frac{D^*(fF + C(a+t)/360)}{fF} \tag{6}$$

Since $C \geq 0$, the implied duration of the future will usually be greater than or equal to that of the underlying cheapest-to-deliver bond.

Alternatively, if there is a level shift in interest rates such that the change in the annualized implied repo rate is equal to the change in the yield to maturity, $\delta_r = 1$, we have

$$D_F^* = \frac{P}{fF} \; [D^*(1+rt/360) - t/180]$$

$$= \frac{fF + C(a+t)/360}{fF} \; [D^*(1+rt/360) - t/180]$$

(7)

Consequently, the implied duration for the future is reduced when the implied repo rate changes. This occurs because an increase in the implied repo rate increases the futures price due to increased borrowing costs independent of a change in the price of the underlying bond as yield to maturity changes. If both rates change in the same direction, the change in the implied repo rate will produce effects in the opposite direction from that of a change in yield to maturity and therefore decreases the sensitivity of the future to the change in yield to maturity.

### III. AN EXAMPLE

To illustrate the application of the modified duration formula consider the implied duration of a future selling at 71 9/32 with 53 days to expiration. The cheapest-to-deliver bond is the 7-7/8 of 2007. Its price is 70 31/32 and has a conversion factor of .9881. The accrued interest on the bond is $3.71875 from 170 days of accrued interest.

Using equation (3) to solve for the implied repo rate gives

$$1 + rt/360 = 1.00835$$

or alternatively,

$$r = 5.672\%.$$

If we assume that the implied repo rate remains constant, the implied duration of the future would be

$$D_F^* = 1.069 \; D^*$$

Consequently, the implied duration of the future is nearly 7% greater than that of the bond itself. The duration of the bond is approximately 8.13 which gives an implied duration for the future of

$$D_F^* = (1.069)\ 8.13 = 8.69$$

If we assume a level shift in the interest rates, the implied duration using equation (8) would be

$$D_F^* = (1.069)\ D^* - .31 = 8.38$$

Equation (1) gives the hedge ratio to match the price change in an arbitrary bond B with a futures contract tied to the cheapest-to-deliver bond P. This equation is perfectly general and can be used in constructing a hedge for an arbitrary bond position. The hedge ratio will depend on both the duration of the bond to be hedged and that of the cheapest-to-deliver Treasury bond as well as their relative interest rate volatilities.

For example, a hedge can be constructed for the 12-1/2% Treasury bond of 2014. The duration of the bond is approximately 8.19 while that of the future we calculated as 8.69. If we assume that the repo rate remains constant and the respective yield changes between the bond to be hedged and the cheapest-to-deliver bond are equal ($\delta_B = 1.0$), the appropriate hedge ratio would be:

$$h = \frac{-BD_B^*\delta_B}{FD_F^*}$$

$$= \frac{-108.0(8.19)(1.0)}{71.28(8.69)}$$

$$= -1.43$$

Consequently, a short position in 143 futures contracts would be required to hedge the exposure in 100 bonds of $100,000 face value each.

If the bond to be hedged is the same as the cheapest-to-deliver Treasury bond for the future, however, equation (2) reduces to

$$h = \frac{-PD^*}{FD_F^*} \tag{8}$$

$$= \frac{-fD^*}{D^*(1 + rt/360) - \delta_r t/180}$$

With the additional simplification that the implied repo rate doesn't change ($\delta_r = 0$), the hedge ratio in equation (8) reduces to

$$h = \frac{-f}{1 + rt/360} \qquad (9)$$

Using data from the examples we constructed previously gives the hedge ratio for the future against its underlying cheapest-to-deliver security in equation (9) as

$$h = \frac{-.9881}{1.00835}$$

$$= -.973$$

Consequently, to hedge the price movement in the equivalent value of 100 bonds (the 7⅞ of 2007), each with $100,000 of face value, a short position in 97 futures would be required.

If it were assumed that the implied repo rate would change equally along with the change in yield to maturity, equation (8) would give the hedge ratio as

$$h = \frac{-.9881(8.13)}{8.13(1.00835) - .294}$$

$$= -1.02$$

To create the hedge under this assumption would require 102 futures to hedge the equivalent value of 100 bonds, each with face value of $100,000. More futures are required because the future has a somewhat smaller duration and therefore, more are required to hedge the same change in value for the underlying bond.

## APPENDIX: DERIVATION OF THE MODIFIED DURATION FOR A FUTURES CONTRACT

As the yield to maturity on the cheapest-to-deliver bond changes, the price of the bond will change and cause a change in the futures price. Taking the derivative of the futures price in equation (3) with respect to change in the bond's yield to maturity gives:

$$\frac{dF}{d(1+i/2)} = \frac{1}{f}\left[ \frac{dP}{d(1+i/2)}(1+rt/360)+P\frac{d(1+rt/360)}{d(1+i/2)} \right]$$

$$= \frac{1}{f}\left[ \frac{dP}{d(1+i/2)}(1+rt/360)+P\delta_r t/180 \right]$$

where $\delta_r = dr/di$                      (A1)

Substituting equation (1) into equation (A1) for the duration of the cheapest-to-deliver bond gives

$$\frac{dF}{d(1+i/2)} = \frac{-P}{f}\left[ D*(1+rt/360)-\delta_r t/180 \right] \qquad (A2)$$

If we define the implied modified duration of the future as

$$D_F^* = \frac{-1}{F}\frac{dF}{d(1+i/2)} \qquad \text{A3)}$$

we can write the modified duration of the future in terms of the duration of the bond as

$$D_F^* = \frac{P}{fF}\left[ D*(1+rt/360)-\delta_r t/180 \right]$$

$$= \frac{fF+C(a+t)/360}{fF(1+rt/360)}\left[ D*(1+rt/360)-\delta_r t/180 \right]$$

                                                             (A4)

In the second equation the relationship between the futures price and the price of the cheapest-to-deliver bond is used to substitute for the bond price P.

# The Bond Buyer Municipal Index Coefficient and Its Implications for Trading

Jane Sachar Brauer, Ph.D.
Vice President
Derivative Products Group
First Boston Corporation

## I. INTRODUCTION

The Bond Buyer 40 Bond Index (BBI) is the index off of which the municipal futures contract trades. It consists of 40 actively traded long municipal bonds, which are combined using yield conversion factors applied to each bond and a coefficient applied to the overall basket.

Considerable confusion surrounds the calculation of the BBI, especially with regard to the role of the coefficient. This article explains how the Index is constructed, how the coefficient enters into the price of the Index and how changes in market yields cause the price to decrease as bonds move in and out of the Index. Along the way, we will consider some tactical implications for trading positions.

This work was done while the author was at Goldman Sachs.

To understand the role of the coefficient, keep in mind Equation (1), which is the formula for the Index price:

$$BBI = \frac{1}{40} \sum \frac{\$ \text{ price of bonds}}{\text{conversion factor}} \times \text{coefficient} \qquad (1)$$

We will consider each of the main elements of the formula in turn and then review the implications for trading strategies.

## II. THE CONVERSION FACTOR

The price of each bond in the Index is altered through the use of a conversion factor to make all of the bonds somewhat comparable. This is to prevent bonds trading at higher prices from having excessive weight, relative to bonds trading at lower prices, in the calculation of the price of the Index. The factor is based on the price that would be required for each bond to yield 8% to the par call. For example, the factor for an 8% bond is 1.000. A 7% bond with a 14-year par call has a dollar price (in decimal) of $91.67 at an 8% yield, and therefore a conversion factor of 0.9167. The conversion factor is used to create a converted price, which equals the price divided by the factor. The actual price of the bond is divided by the conversion factor to create an 8%-equivalent "conversion price."

## III. THE COEFFICIENT

Unlike the conversion factor, which is calculated separately for each bond, the coefficient is used only once in the calculation of the overall Index. However, it is changed twice a month when new bonds replace existing bonds in the Index.

The coefficient is used to ensure that the substitution of new bonds into the Index—with different prices from the bonds that are dropped—does not change the value of the Index at the time of substitution. Although, on the surface, it may seem as though the price/yield relationship may be maintained by the inclusion of both conversion factors and the coefficient, the coefficient actually has the effect of decreasing the Index price.

## IV. EXAMPLE

Let us demonstrate this effect with a simple example. For simplicity, assume that we start with an Index price of $100, the market is at 8%, the Index consists of one 8% bond, and the coefficient is 1.00. All prices are quoted in decimal.

Let us look at what happens to the price of the Index when the market goes from 8% to 7% and then back to 8%.

*Assumptions to start:*

Index price = $100
Market level = 8% (as above)
N = 1
Index consists of one 8% bond with a 10-year 102 call and 14-year par call
Conversion factor = 1.00
Coeffecient = 1.00

Now we assume the market level changes from 8% to 7%. At this level, the 8% bond is priced to the premium call. The price of the Index is found by Equation (2).

$$\frac{\text{bond price}}{\text{conversion factor}} \times \text{coefficient} = \frac{\$108.11}{1.0} \times 1.0 = \$108.11 \qquad (2)$$

Let us assume that the market level stays at 7% until it is time to update the Index. At this time, the 8% bond is replaced in the Index by a 7% par bond. The conversion factor of a 7% bond with a 10-year 102 call and 14-year par call is 0.9167 (see Section II above). The converted price of the bond is $100/.9167 = $109.09

It would be a misrepresentation of value in the municipal market to say that the Index went from $108.11 to $109.09. The Index should stay at $108.11 until a change occurs in the price of one or more of the included bonds.

Therefore, to smooth the Index, a new coefficient has to be calculated to ensure this continuity at the time of substitution. Any change in the Index price will then reflect a movement in the market rather than the addition of a new bond.

The new coefficient is derived from the calculation that maintains the pre-substitution price of the updated Index as shown in Equation (3).

$$\$108.11 = \frac{\text{new bond price}}{\text{conversion factor}} \times \text{new coefficient}$$

$$= \frac{\$100}{.9167} \times \text{new coefficient} \qquad (3)$$

Solving for the new coefficient in Equation (4), we get:

$$\frac{\$108.11 \times .9167}{\$100} = .9910 \qquad (4)$$

Alternatively, the new coefficient can be expressed by Equation (5):

$$\frac{\text{old index with coefficient}}{\text{new index without coefficient}} = \frac{\$108.11}{\$109.09} = .9910 \qquad (5)$$

Now we assume that the market moves back to 8% and the Index is being updated. The 7% bond is now trading to maturity and is priced at $88.69. The converted price of the bond is $88.69/.9167 = $96.75 and the price of the Index is $96.75 × 0.9910 = $95.88 (below the original price of $100 at the start of this example).

The discount 7% bond is now replaced by an 8% par bond. The converted price of the 8% bond is $100/1.0 = $100.00 and the coefficient is $95.88/$100 = 0.9588. Therefore, the price of the Index is maintained at $100/1.0 × .9588 = $95.88

Suppose the market for par bonds is 7%. The coefficient will be greater than 1.00 if the premium bond priced to the call (the old bond) is higher in price (i.e., lower in yield) than 6.8%. For example, if the 8% bond is priced at $111.75 (6.60%), the coefficient will be $111.175/$109.09 = 1.0191. If the bond priced to the call is higher in yield than 6.8%, the coefficient will be less than 1.00.

In summary, as the market moves up and down between 8% and 7%, the Index rises to 108.11% and falls to 88.69% of its previous level. The net effect is a relative change of 1.0811 × .8869 = .9588. Two market swings have decreased the Index to 95.88% of its original price. As Exhibit 1 shows, after six more similar movements (to 7% and back to 8%), the price decreases to 84.52% of the original price. This "shrinking coefficient" effect is one reason why it is not possible to convert the price of the Index to a meaningful yield.

**EXHIBIT 1**
**PRICE CHANGES AS MARKET MOVES BETWEEN 8% and 7%**

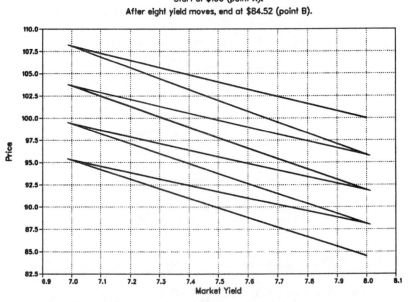

Start at $100 (point A).
After eight yield moves, end at $84.52 (point B).

Goldman Sachs & Co.—Financial Strategies Group

## V. HISTORICAL MOB LEVELS

The shrinking coefficient is also a reason why the MOB spread (Municipal Over Bond, or the spread between municipal futures and Treasury futures) of $-140$ thirty-seconds has a different interpretation from the MOB of $-140$ a year earlier. The price of the Index underlying the municipal future cannot be related to one particular yield level.

As an example, let us observe in Exhibit 2 several days when the MOB was between 138 and $-142$. Notice how different the yield ratios were between the general municipal market, respresented by electric revenue bonds, and Treasuries. Compared to the cheapest-to-deliver Treasury for most of the period, the yield spread ranged from $-.104$ to .782 and the ratio from 1.012 to .914.

Thus, for the same MOB spread, the yield spread was considerably higher and the ratio considerably lower in the latter period. This result holds up regardless of the level of the MOB. Also shown in Exhibit 2 are ways in which the MOB was between $-5$ and 5. But notice how different these yield ratios have been ranging between .927 and .880 for the ratio of electric revenue bonds to the cheapest-to-deliver Treasury.

**EXHIBIT 2**
**COMPARISON OF MUNICIPAL AND TREASURY YIELDS WHEN THE MOB WAS WIDE OR CLOSE TO ZERO**

| Date | (1) Elec Rev Bonds | (2) UST 14's 2011 | (3) UST 30 Yr | Spread (2)-(1) | Spread (3)-(1) | Ratio (1)/(2) | Ratio (1)/(3) |
|---|---|---|---|---|---|---|---|
| | | | when 140 < MOB < −138 | | | | |
| 06/16/86 | 8.700 | 8.596 | 7.435 | −0.104 | −1.265 | 1.012 | 1.170 |
| 07/07/86 | 8.000 | 8.236 | 7.152 | 0.236 | −0.848 | 0.971 | 1.119 |
| 04/14/87 | 8.625 | 9.022 | 8.403 | 0.397 | −0.222 | 0.956 | 1.026 |
| 05/22/87 | 8.950 | 9.401 | 8.918 | 0.451 | −0.032 | 0.952 | 1.004 |
| 10/23/87 | 9.000 | 9.581 | 9.105 | 0.581 | 0.105 | 0.939 | 0.988 |
| 03/16/88 | 8.290 | 9.072 | 8.592 | 0.782 | 0.302 | 0.914 | 0.965 |
| | | | when −5<MOB<5 | | | | |
| 03/31/86 | 7.450 | 8.037 | 7.481 | 0.587 | 0.031 | 0.927 | 0.996 |
| 09/04/86 | 7.625 | 8.408 | 7.408 | 0.783 | −0.217 | 0.907 | 1.029 |
| 10/07/86 | 7.750 | 8.505 | 7.538 | 0.755 | −0.212 | 0.911 | 1.028 |
| 12/03/86 | 7.400 | 8.180 | 7.316 | 0.780 | −0.084 | 0.905 | 1.012 |
| 01/19/87 | 7.150 | 8.141 | 7.330 | 0.991 | 0.180 | 0.878 | 0.975 |
| 03/13/87 | 7.150 | 8.136 | 7.493 | 0.986 | 0.343 | 0.879 | 0.954 |
| 04/02/87 | 7.550 | 8.521 | 7.903 | 0.971 | 0.353 | 0.886 | 0.955 |
| 08/26/87 | 8.310 | 9.447 | 8.986 | 1.137 | 0.676 | 0.880 | 0.925 |

## VI. IMPLICATIONS

### Adding Alternative Minimum Tax (AMT) Bonds

If an 8% AAA general obligation bond (GO) at 8.00% (converted price of $100) is replaced by an 8% AMT bond at 9.10% (converted price of $88.75/1.000 = $88.75), the coefficient would be $1/.8875 = 1.1268$ of its previous value. When shifting from GOs to revenue bonds, lowering the credit, or introducing AMT bonds, the effect is to raise the coefficient. As the composition of the Index shifts back and forth from GO to revenue bonds, while the credit mix varies, the coefficient will shift up and down. However, the introduction of AMT bonds into the Index, a new development, has permanently raised the coefficient relative to the period before AMT bonds existed.

### Some Things to Notice

When the market traded up and down in our example, the coefficient decreased. This is because the conversion factor converts in a manner similar to that of a 14-year bond. But in this example, the bond traded up less (like a 10-year callable bond) and traded down more (like a 30-year bond). So in each case, we removed a bond with a converted price that was lower than the converted price of the bond we added. This method tends to lower the coefficient, whether bonds trade up or down. However, this effect causes the coefficient to fall more rapidly when bonds trade down than when they trade up. The market has generally risen since the Index began in December 1983, but the coefficient has slipped to only .94. In a falling market it may slip somewhat faster.

### When to Put on a MOB Trade

Buying the MOB means buying municipal futures and selling Treasury futures. Selling the MOB means buying Treasury futures and selling municipal futures. The decision to put on a MOB trade should be made on the basis of relative yields and market outlook, not on the absolute level of the difference between the municipal and Treasury futures prices. This difference is due to the coefficient, to the absolute yield level, and to the difference in the dollar durations of bonds in the Index and bonds deliverable on the Treasury futures.

### The Effect of the Coefficient on Hedging a Municipal Portfolio or Adjusting the MOB

The coefficient affects the price sensitivity, or dollar duration, of the Index, as do the particular bonds included in the Index (premium or discount). Therefore, when the Index changes twice a month, hedge ratios always need to be recalculated. The coefficient is merely another feature that must be considered when calculating these hedge ratios. For example, if the coefficient decreases, making the dollar duration of the municipal future lower, you may need to increase your municipal futures position.

To calculate the correct weighting for the MOB, you must also take into account the relative movements of municipals versus Treasuries. For example, if municipal yields move less than Treasury yields, the price sensitivity of the municipal future may be less than the price sensitivity of the Treasury future, even if the dollar durations of the two instruments are identical. If the municipal future is less price sensitive than the Treasury future, then the MOB (traded one municipal for one Treasury future) will deteriorate in a market rally and improve in a market retreat. Suppose that you want to buy the MOB in anticipation of municipals outperforming Treasuries, without a view on general market direction. You should use the dollar duration and relative yield volatilities in determining the correct proportion of municipals to Treasuries.

## VII. CONCLUSION

We have shown that the coefficient affects the Index by shrinking it. This directly affects the value of the Index relative to historical levels, as well as price sensitivity of the futures contract. Those who understand this effect will have a competitive advantage when hedging or trading with the municipal futures contract.

# Interest Rate Caps and Floors: Tools for Asset/Liability Management

Victor J. Haghani
Vice President
Salomon Brothers Inc

Robert M. Stavis
Vice President
Salomon Brothers Inc

## I. CAP AND FLOOR MECHANICS

Asset and liability managers' awareness of their increased vulnerability to adverse interest rate moves has spurred tremendous growth in the market for protected interest rate agreements (caps and floors) over the past several years.[1] In recent years

The authors would like to thank those in the Bond Portfolio Analysis Hedge Group and the Hedge Management Unit who contributed ideas for this article. In particular, Rick Stuckey and Nancy Noyes provided useful suggestions and material. Kannan Ayyar played a major role in developing the numerical examples. In addition, we would like to thank Laura Davey and Michelle Murphy for their editorial assistance.

Mr. Stavis is currently a Managing Director of the DAVCO Group, a New York-based money management firm.

[1] The generic term protected interest rate agreement in this context includes all hedging contracts designed to limit risk in an asymmetric manner. These include caps (ceilings), floors and collars. In this article, we will not discuss guaranteed-rate programs, which effectively convert a floating rate to a fixed rate, eliminating both the risk of a change in the rate in one direction and any benefit from a movement in the opposing direction.

as the fixed-income markets have become nearly as volatile as the equity markets, the cost of making an incorrect interest rate judgment has risen dramatically. Consequently, both asset and liability managers have sought new strategies to limit risk. Two vehicles that have proven quite successful in managing interest rate risk are caps and floors.

A protected interest rate agreement can be defined as a contract that, for a fee, grants the right to benefit fully from a rate move in one direction, while being exposed to only limited risk if the rate goes the opposite way. The asymmetric nature of the contract leads to two types of agreements. The most popular is the interest rate cap, which is used to set a maximum level, or cap, on a short-term rate index. The purchaser of the cap will be compensated if the index goes above a certain level, known as the strike level. The other type of agreement is the interest rate floor, which sets a minimum rate on some index.[2] An asset manager may purchase a floor to guarantee some minimum return on a floating-rate asset. For a predetermined fee, the guarantor of the floor would pay the purchaser whenever the index is below a certain level on a given set of dates.

## Market Description

The market for caps and floors can be viewed as an outgrowth of the over-the-counter market in fixed-income options. Caps and floors are private agreements entered into by two distinct parties. As in all over-the-counter transactions, participants are required to manage the credit risk of their counterparties.

Because most cap and floor agreements are private, it is difficult to estimate the size of the existing market. However, the volume of cap transactions that resulted from the issuance of capped floating-rate notes does give some indication of the market size. Market participants believe that these transactions comprise only a small part of the entire market, yet in the last nine months of 1985, floating-rate debt issuers created more than $4.5 billion of caps. The issuer sells a capped floating-rate security, which represents a liability up to but not above the cap level. The issuer then sells an interest rate cap, using the proceeds to lower the effective rate on the debt. The combination of selling a capped floating-rate note and an interest rate cap leaves the issuer with a package of floating-rate debt. This gives the investor a capped floating-rate asset and also creates a large volume of interest rate caps with specific terms, not tailored to the specific needs of individual investors.

Several factors are behind the sharp growth in the cap and floor market. First, in addition to facing more interest rate risk, asset and liability managers are being judged on shorter and shorter performance horizons. Hedging has become more important in the everyday management of assets and liabilities; long- or short-term rates are no longer the only choices. Asset and liability managers must examine a

---

[2]These two agreements are analogous to purchasing a strip of put options or a strip of call options on short-term rates, respectively.

whole menu of hedged and unhedged alternatives.[3] Asymmetric hedging with caps and floors may be particularly attractive, because for a known fee, it allows a manager to "always be right" in choosing between long and short rates. There has also been an increased understanding of the options and option-like risks embedded in a variety of other asset and liability products, particularly in the fields of mortgage and insurance products. Now that they are more aware of these risks, people have sought new methods of protection.

With the increased involvement in hedging programs, the volume of futures and options trading has surged. Because it is easy to hedge in the futures markets, with its low transaction costs and negligible credit risk, futures have become a popular hedge vehicle for symmetric protection from interest rate exposure. Managers desiring optional protection also benefit from the increased liquidity in futures, since futures market liquidity is important to the options market. Speculators taking on options positions, in turn, use the futures market to hedge their exposure.

The development of the interest rate swap market has led issuers and investors to search the full interest rate spectrum for relative value. And, since the duration of the desired security can be altered, this can be done regardless of the rate outlook. Because it establishes a direct relationship between variable rates and fixed rates, the swap market is often the benchmark against which other strategies, particularly those involving caps and floors, are judged.

Finally issuers' and investors' increased reliance on short-term, variable-rate securities has also spurred growth in this market. In a positive yield curve environment, issuers are naturally attracted to shorter-term financing. In 1980, debt issuances with maturities of less than three years (including floating-rate notes, commerical paper and extendable notes) made up only 19% of all financing in the United States; by 1985, the same maturities comprised almost 40% of corporate debt. As is always the case with variable-rate financing in a positive yield curve environment, the benefits of lower rates today must be weighed against the risk of higher rates in the future. Interest rate caps allow issuers to effectively finance at rates near short-term levels while setting bounds on their interest rate exposure.

### Basics of the Contract

Before the premium required to enter into an interest rate protection agreement can be determined, the purchaser must select the characteristics of the contract. The following five terms need to be specified.

1. *Underlying Index.* Caps and floors can be created on many short-term indexes in a variety of maturity ranges; for instance, caps can be purchased on one-, three- or six-month LIBOR. Caps and floors can be set on the following

---

[3]See Robert Kopprasch, Cal Johnson and Armand Tatevossian, "Strategies for the Asset Manager: Hedging and the Creation of Synthetic Assets," in Frank J. Fabozzi and T. Dessa Garlicki (eds.), *Advances in Bond Analysis and Portfolio Strategies* (Chicago, IL: Probus Publishing, 1987).

indexes; LIBOR, commercial paper, average daily prime rate, Treasury bills, certificates of deposit (CDs), and DATES.

2. *Term of the Agreement.* Caps and floors generally are structured with terms of between three months and 12 years.

3. *Frequency of the Agreement.* The frequency pertains to two aspects of the agreement. First, it defines the spacing of the "determination dates" on which the level of rates will be compared with the strike level of the cap or floor to determine what, if any, payment will be made. Virtually any frequency can be used, although monthly, quarterly and semiannual are most common. Second, frequency refers to the payment dates. The payments to the cap or floor holder generally occur on the next business day after the determination date, although payment in arrears is also possible. Because these agreements are private, other structures can be established; for example, there could be a cap that protects a series of weekly liabilities with a rate set weekly off three-month LIBOR. This cap could entail quarterly payments, which would be easier to process than weekly payments. Caps or floors on rate averages can also be created to match a frequently reset instrument. A liability that is based on a daily reset could be protected with a cap on the average of the index over each month.

4. *Strike Level.* This level determines the point where the agreement will begin to provide protection. Usually, one fixed level applies to the entire program, although the level can change over time in a predetermined way.

5. *Amount Underlying the Agreement.* Like the strike level, the amount underlying the contract can be constant or it can change over time. A declining schedule is often used when protecting an asset or liability that has an amortization feature. For instance, a borrower with a series of loans whose outstanding balance changes over time can purchase a cap with a variable schedule to match the terms of the loans.

A fee for the cap or floor program is determined based on the terms of the cap or floor chosen by the purchaser. It is generally paid in a single payment, at the onset of the program, but it can also be paid with a set of periodic payments.

Should the holder of a cap or floor want to terminate early, the contract may be sold back to the grantor, thus allowing the holder to recover some of the initial cost of the contract. Alternatively, the contract can be offset by taking an opposite position in a cap or floor with identical terms. Where the payment structure is periodic, the present value of unpaid premium must be incorporated into the buyback arrangement.

The process of determining the appropriate terms for a cap or floor generally involves an analysis of the risk associated with the position to be hedged. This will provide the basis for selecting the terms of the cap or floor. For example, a real estate developer might be considering a project that would involve a three-year floating-rate loan based on three-month LIBOR. The loan would have a quarterly draw schedule with interest due quarterly. The developer could protect himself from higher future interest rates by purchasing a cap agreement with a term of three years, quarterly resets and based on three-month LIBOR. The amount underlying the agreement would be an increasing balance based on the quarterly draw schedule. Lastly, the developer would have to determine a strike level.

There is always a trade-off between strike level and premium paid for cap and floor agreements. Unlike the other components of the aforementioned cap (which were chosen to match a specific liability), the strike level is chosen to provide an appropriate risk/return trade-off. The choice of strike level is a decision similar to the selection of the amount deductible under an insurance policy. As there is a trade-off between the amount of deductible and the premium paid for insurance, there is also a trade-off between strike level and the premium paid for a cap. A cap with a high strike rate costs less, but it does not provide protection as early as a cap struck at a lower level. The choice of strike rate ultimately will be based on the purchaser's market outlook and tolerance for risk.

### Calculation of the Payment Flows

The calculation of the payment to be made to the holder of a cap or floor from the grantor is made on each determination date of the agreement. For a cap, if the rate being protected is above the strike rate, a payment will be made to the cap holder. If the rate is at or below the strike rate, no payment is made. The amount of payment exchanged when an interest rate cap pays off is equal to the amount of interest that would be paid on the underlying amount at the prevailing market rate, less the amount of interest that would be paid on the underlying amount at the strike rate. In the case of a rate floor, a payment is made only when the short-term index is below the strike rate. In order to determine the amount of the payment, if any, it is necessary to know the exact source of reference for the rate in question (such as Reuters LIBOR fixing or the Federal Reserve Statistical Release H15, for example), as well as the appropriate quotation (discount, bond-equivalent) and daycount conventions.

Caps and floors are structured to protect the holder from adverse changes in a specific index. It is important to make the distinction between the index being protected and the issuer's cost of funds (or realized return for an asset). Protection does not extend to an issuer's quality spread. For instance, an issuer who hedges a series of one-month commercial paper borrowings with a cap is not protected from a change in the market's demand for credit quality spread. This risk is symmetric; that is, it can have either a favorable or unfavorable impact on the issuer's realized cost of funds.

### An Example of a Typical Interest Rate Cap

Since interest rate caps are the most common type of protected rate agreement, we will use a cap to demonstrate the mechanics of the contract. A typical cap agreement could have the following terms:

| Underlying Index: | Three-Month LIBOR |
|---|---|
| | (Reuters Monitor Money Rates Service) |
| Term of Cap: | Three Years |
| Rate Determination: | Quarterly |
| Cap Level: | 8.00% |
| Payment Frequency: | Quarterly, In Arrears |
| | (CD, Actual/360) |
| Underlying Amount: | $100 Million |
| Up-Front Fee: | $1.850 Million, or 1.85% of Par |

In this agreement, the guarantor would pay the holder of the cap during any quarter when three-month LIBOR was over the 8% cap level on the determination date. As an example, if LIBOR were quoted at 9% on the determination date, the payment would be calculated in the following way:

$$\left[\frac{\text{Reference Rate}}{360} \times \text{Days in Period} \times \text{Principal Amount Protected}\right] -$$

$$\left[\frac{\text{Cap Level}}{360} \times \text{Days in Period} \times \text{Principal Amount Protected}\right] =$$

$$\left[\frac{9.00\%}{360} \times 92 \times \$100,000,000\right] -$$

$$\left[\frac{8.00\%}{360} \times 92 \times \$100,000,000\right] = \$255,556$$

In this case, the guarantor would pay the holder of the interest rate cap $255,556. If LIBOR were at or below the strike rate of 8%, no payment would be made.

### Payoff and Profit Pattern of Caps and Floors

Before analyzing the impact of a cap or floor over the entire life of the agreement, it is useful to examine one payment period in isolation. Exhibit 1 shows the annualized payment the holder of the cap would receive based on the level of the short-term index on the determination date. For rates above 8%, the holder of the cap receives the quarterly equivalent of the difference between the current rate and the 8% strike rate. For rates under 8%, no payment is made. To determine the profit pattern of the cap, it is necessary to account for the premium paid at the start of the program.

**EXHIBIT 1**
**PAYOFF PATTERN OF CAP AT END OF ONE PAYMENT PERIOD**

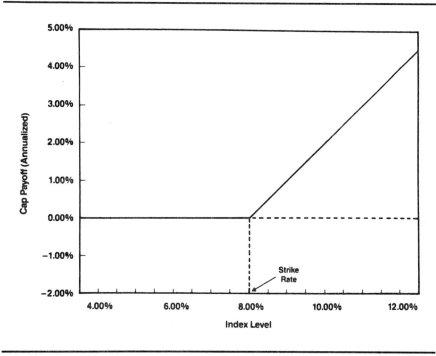

The impact of the premium over the life of a cap or floor can be determined by amortizing it over the program's life.[4] In the previous example, the fee of 1.85% of par is amortized over 12 quarterly periods at a fixed rate of 8%. This calculation gives a CD-equivalent periodic fee of 0.17%, or 0.69% annualized. By apportioning the equivalent periodic premium to each period, it is possible to draw the profit pattern (annualized) for a single payment period as shown in Exhibit 2. The premium is recovered where the profit is equal to zero, which requires the index to be above the cap level at the end of the period.

The payoff pattern of an interest rate floor with a strike rate of 8% for one period is shown in Exhibit 3. For rates below the floor level, the holder of the floor is paid the difference between the floor rate and the index level. For rates above the floor, no payment is made. The profit pattern for one period of the floor, which is derived by subtracting the amortized premium from the payoff pattern shown in Exhibit 3, is illustrated in Exhibit 4. In the case of the floor, the break-even level (where the

---

[4]In principle, each of the individual capped periods has a different premium associated with it, but for ease of analysis, we will determine one single periodic fee. This periodic fee is simply the annuity whose present value is equal to the up-front premium paid for the caps.

**EXHIBIT 2**
**PROFIT PATTERN OF CAP AT END OF ONE PAYMENT PERIOD**

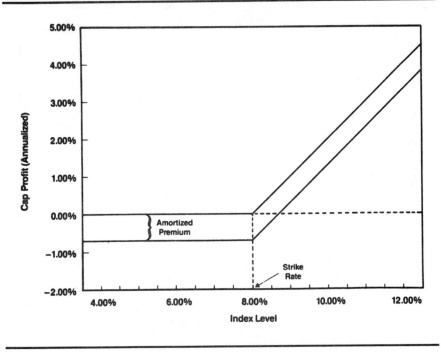

premium is recovered and the profit is zero) requires the index to be below the floor level on the determination date by the annualized periodic cost of the floor.[5]

This analysis examines the cap and floor in isolation. In practice, caps are usually used to put a ceiling on short-term liability exposure, and floors are often purchased to hedge the return to floating-rate assets. Most of the following analysis will be based on the combination of caps and short-term liabilities, which will be referred to as *capped liabilities,* and the combination of floating-rate assets and floors, which will be referred to as *protected assets.*

The effective interest expense of a combination of a variable-rate liability and an interest rate cap are shown in Exhibit 5. The effective cost of a capped liability for any level of the short-term index has three components. The first is the actual interest expense, which is represented by the diagonal line in Exhibit 5 (this includes the issuer's quality spread, which is assumed to be zero in these examples). The second component is the payment, if any, received from the cap, which has the

[5]The payoff pattern of the cap is analogous to the intrinsic value pattern at expiration of a put option, while the floor is equivalent to the intrinsic value pattern of a call option at expiration.

**EXHIBIT 3**
**PAYOFF PATTERN OF FLOOR AT END OF ONE PAYMENT PERIOD**

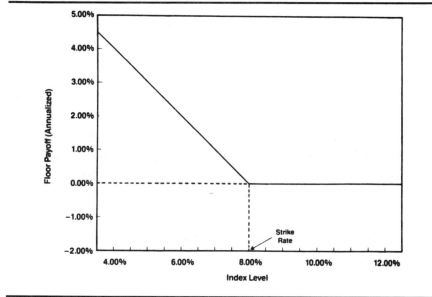

**EXHIBIT 4**
**PROFIT PATTERN OF FLOOR AT END OF ONE PAYMENT PERIOD**

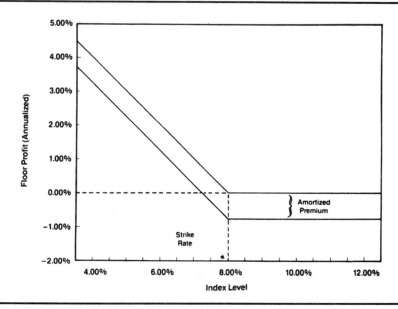

pattern shown in Exhibit 1. The third component is the amortized cost of the cap. The combination of these components results in an asymmetric pattern of effective interest expense, which is measured on the left-hand vertical axis of Exhibit 5. For index levels above the strike rate of 8%, say 10%, the issuer would be paid the quarterly equivalent of the difference between the index and the strike rate—in this case, 2%. Thus, the effective cost to the issuer is 10%, less the payment of 2%, plus the amortized cost of the cap of 0.69%, which equals 8.69%. This represents the worst-case cost of funds for the issuer. For levels below 8%, the effective cost to the issuer is simply the index level plus the amortized cost of the cap.

The alternative to hedging a variable-rate liability with interest rate caps is to fix the cost of funding by buying an interest rate swap or simply to issue fixed-rate debt. Therefore, it is relevant to compare the cost of the capped liability with the cost of fixed-rate funding available at the onset of the program. The horizontal line in Exhibit 5 represents the benchmark fixed rate. The right-hand axis of Exhibit 5 shows the savings or loss versus fixed funding that the issuer experiences in each period. To the extent that the effective capped rate is less than the fixed rate, the issuer has positive savings. The issuer suffers losses versus fixed-rate funding when the effective interest expense is greater than the fixed rate.

Viewed from this perspective, the caps provide the issuer with protection against higher rates. Although the result may seem somewhat counter-intuitive, the issuer benefits most when the caps do not pay off.

**EXHIBIT 5**
**EFFECTIVE INTEREST EXPENSE OF VARIABLE-RATE LIABILITY PLUS 8% CAP AND SAVINGS VERSUS FIXED-RATE FUNDING**

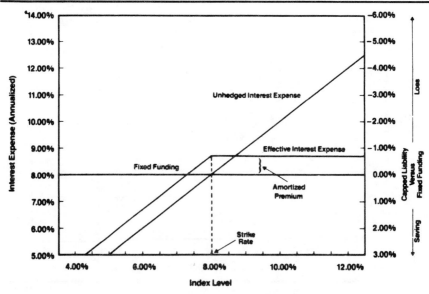

Exhibit 6 shows the effective coupon income from the combination of a floating-rate asset, such as a Eurodollar floating-rate note (FRN), plus an interest rate floor, net of the cost of the floor. The effective interest income of a protected asset has three components similar to those of effective interest expense of a capped liability. The first is the unhedged coupon level, which is simply equal to the index level plus any spread to the index provided by the FRN, which is assumed to be zero in this example. The second component is the payoff, if any, from the floor. The sum of the unhedged coupon and the floor payoff, if any, must be decreased by the cost of the floor agreement, which results in the asymmetric pattern shown in Exhibit 6. The profit or loss versus the benchmark fixed rate can be read off the right-hand vertical axis of the chart. It is the vertical distance between the horizontal line and the kinked pattern of effective interest income. The protected asset provides the highest returns under a scenario of high interest rates, in which the floor does not pay off.

### *Analyzing a Cap or Floor Over Its Full Term—The Use of Scenario Analysis*

Although it is important to understand the return characteristics of caps and floors for a single payment period, it is even more important to understand the risk/return patterns of caps and floors over their entire lives. Therefore, we must begin to consider them as a strip of protection agreements, with one covering each payment

**EXHIBIT 6**
**EFFECTIVE INTEREST INCOME OF FLOATING-RATE ASSET PLUS 8% FLOOR AND PROFIT VERSUS FIXED-RATE INVESTMENT**

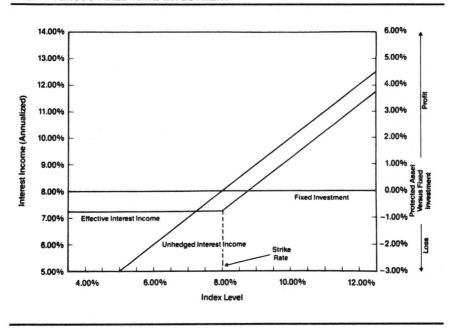

period. It thus becomes necessary to create scenarios of short-term interest rate movements over the term of the contract, rather than just at the end of one payment period, as we did previously. Since there is an infinite number of hypothetical rate scenarios, it is impossible to analyze all of the cases, so representative examples must be chosen. The choices should demonstrate maximum downside risk and give some measure of upside potential. A break-even scenario is necessary to be able to roughly separate favorable from unfavorable scenarios.

For ease of reference, and since there is not a significantly better simple alternative, all scenarios used in the following analysis will have the following structure: The short-term index begins at its current level, and, by the beginning of the first protected payment period, rises or falls to a constant level (plateau level), where it remains for the life of the program. Thus, a scenario can be referenced either by the change in the short-term index required to take the index to the plateau level or by the plateau level itself. Although the plateau scenario analysis provides useful insights, other approaches involving interest rate probability distributions may be more appropriate as a means of quantifying the expected risk/return trade-off implied by investor or borrower expectations.

After devising appropriate short-term rate scenarios, it is possible to determine the performance of a capped liability or a protected asset for each scenario. This scenario performance can then be compared with some fixed-rate benchmark that was available at the onset of the program.[6] Situations in which the scenario outcome is worse than the fixed rate (lower for unprotected assets, higher for capped liabilities) will be termed "unfavorable," and situations where the scenario outcome is better than the fixed rate will be referred to as "favorable." The previously described cap will be used to illustrate this point:

## Terms of Cap

| | |
|---|---|
| Underlying index: | Three-Month LIBOR |
| Term of Cap: | Three Years |
| Rate Determination: | Quarterly |
| Cap Level: | 8.00% |
| Payment Frequency: | Quarterly, In Arrears |
| Underlying Amount: | $100 Million |
| Up-Front Fee: | $18,500/$1 Million or 1.85% of Par |
| Cost Amortized Over Term of Cap: | $1,749 per Quarter Per Million |
| | 69 CD Basis Points Per Year |
| Market Data: | |
| Starting LIBOR Level | 6.50% (CD, Actual/360) |
| Three-Year Fixed | |
| Funding Level | 8.00% (Semiannual, 30/360) |

---

[6]This can be the cost of fixed debt, term investment yields or the interest rate swap rate.

**Worst-Case Scenario** Since the buyer of a cap or floor has limited risk, a worst-case scenario can be specified that will represent the maximum loss the buyer can suffer. The set of worst-case scenarios covers all cases where the short-term index is at or above the cap level of 8.00% on every determination date. For simplicity, in the following worst-case scenario, the short-term index will rise immediately to 100 basis points above the cap level and remain there throughout the term of the cap. The flows based on a $100 capped liability associated with this worst-case scenario, given that the cap premium will be accounted for by amortizing the cost over the life of the program, are shown in Exhibit 7. The worst-case cost of funds is the internal rate of return of the net flows.[7] In this example, the worst-case cost of funds is 8.75% (semiannual bond equivalent).

**EXHIBIT 7**
**WORST-CASE SCENARIO**

| Quarter | LIBOR Rate | Liability Cash Flow | Cap Payoff | Capped Cash Flow | Cap Cost Amortized @ 8.00% SA | Net Cash Flow |
|---------|-----------|--------------------|-----------|-----------------|-------------------------------|---------------|
| 0 | | − 100.00 | | | | 100.00 |
| 1 | 6.50% | 1.65 | 0.00 | 1.65 | 0.17 | 1.82 |
| 2 | 9.00 | 2.28 | − 0.25 | 2.03 | 0.17 | 2.20 |
| 3 | 9.00 | 2.28 | − 0.25 | 2.03 | 0.17 | 2.20 |
| 4 | 9.00 | 2.28 | − 0.25 | 2.03 | 0.17 | 2.20 |
| 5 | 9.00 | 2.28 | − 0.25 | 2.03 | 0.17 | 2.20 |
| 6 | 9.00 | 2.28 | − 0.25 | 2.03 | 0.17 | 2.20 |
| 7 | 9.00 | 2.28 | − 0.25 | 2.03 | 0.17 | 2.20 |
| 8 | 9.00 | 2.28 | − 0.25 | 2.03 | 0.17 | 2.20 |
| 9 | 9.00 | 2.28 | − 0.25 | 2.03 | 0.17 | 2.20 |
| 10 | 9.00 | 2.28 | − 0.25 | 2.03 | 0.17 | 2.20 |
| 11 | 9.00 | 2.28 | − 0.25 | 2.03 | 0.17 | 2.20 |
| 12 | 9.00 | 102.28 | − 0.25 | 102.03 | 0.17 | 102.20 |

| | |
|---|---|
| Internal Rate of Return (Semiannual Bond Equivalent) | 8.75% |
| Internal Rate of Return (CD Quarterly) | 8.54% |

Instead of going through the process of the internal rate of return calculation, the worst-case cost of funds can be estimated as the cap level plus the amortized cost of the cap. Using the numbers from Exhibit 7 for illustration, this approximation would be the strike rate of 8.00% plus the amortized cost of the cap of 69 basis points, or

---

[7]In fact, it can be argued that the cap cost should be amoritzed at the same worst-case cost of funds rate that is being determined, allowing only for an iterative solution.

8.69%, which is 15 basis points higher than the actual internal rate of return of 8.54%.[8]

A worst-case scenario can also be calculated for a protected asset. The floor return on a protected asset occurs when the index is at or below the strike rate on the floor agreement on every determination rate. As with the caps, an exact worst-case return can be calculated by setting out all the cash flows and determining their internal rate of return.

**Break-Even Scenario** A break-even scenario for a protected asset or capped liability is defined as a rate scenario for which the cap or floor buyer would be indifferent between the protected short-term rate and locking in the fixed rate over the life of the program. Using the scenario structures defined previously, we arrive at the most conservative of all possible break-even scenarios. In practice, rates may follow paths that on average are more adverse than the break-even scenario, and the protected rate program will still compare favorably with a fixed rate. Thus, the plateau scenario is a conservative dividing line between favorable and adverse scenarios, because it does not recognize the added value of a strip of independently excersizable agreements, as opposed to protection on the average index level over the period.

The break-even scenario for the aforementioned cap is shown in Exhibit 8. A liability issuer would be indifferent between capped-rate debt and fixed-rate debt in this case, where LIBOR increases 70 basis points to 7.20%. Here, the break-even scenario is found by laying out the exact cash flows and adjusting LIBOR rates until the break-even condition is met. However, there is a short-hand estimate the break-even index level, akin to that used for the worst-case level. For a capped liability, the available fixed rate is converted into the quotation convention of the capped index, and the amortized cost of the cap is subtracted from that rate.[9] We will use the data from Exhibit 9 to illustrate. The fixed rate of 8.00% converts to 7.81% quarterly CD equivalent. Subtracting the 69 basis points of the cap cost gives a rate of 7.12%, which is only eight basis points from the true breakeven of 7.20%.

---

[8]When the starting short-term index is not equal to the cap level, a further adjustment must be made. The calculation must take account of the fact that the first payment (which is usually not protected) is made at the current index level, not the strike level. The amount by which to alter the first approximation is the difference between the strike level and the current level of the index, amortized at the strike rate over the life of the cap. In this example, since the current index level is below the strike level, this amount should be subtracted (added if the strike is below the index) to lower the worst-case cost of funds. In our example, the difference between the strike rate and the initial index level is 1.5%. This difference for one quarter, amortized over the three-year period, is 14 basis points per year. Subtracting from the 8.69% gives an approximate worst-case cost of 8.55% on a quarterly CD basis. In semiannual bond-equivalent terms, this is 8.76%, which represents a one-basis-point deviation from the true net cost of funds shown in Exhibit 7.

[9]Again, this rate must be adjusted to reflect the fact that the first-period interest expense is equal to the current level of the index and is not capped. The adjustment is analagous to the one made in the worst-case scenario.

**EXHIBIT 8**
**BREAK-EVEN SCENARIO**

| Quarter | LIBOR Rate | Liability Cash Flow | Cap Payoff | Capped Cash Flow | Cap Cost Amortized @ 8.00% SA | Net Cash Flow |
|---|---|---|---|---|---|---|
| 0 | | −100.00 | | | | 100.00 |
| 1 | 6.50% | 1.65 | 0.00 | 1.65 | 0.17 | 1.82 |
| 2 | 7.20 | 1.82 | 0.00 | 1.82 | 0.17 | 2.20 |
| 3 | 7.20 | 1.82 | 0.00 | 1.82 | 0.17 | 2.20 |
| 4 | 7.20 | 1.82 | 0.00 | 1.82 | 0.17 | 2.20 |
| 5 | 7.20 | 1.82 | 0.00 | 1.82 | 0.17 | 2.20 |
| 6 | 7.20 | 1.82 | 0.00 | 1.82 | 0.17 | 2.20 |
| 7 | 7.20 | 1.82 | 0.00 | 1.82 | 0.17 | 2.20 |
| 8 | 7.20 | 1.82 | 0.00 | 1.82 | 0.17 | 2.20 |
| 9 | 7.20 | 1.82 | 0.00 | 1.82 | 0.17 | 2.20 |
| 10 | 7.20 | 1.82 | 0.00 | 1.82 | 0.17 | 2.20 |
| 11 | 7.20 | 1.82 | 0.00 | 1.82 | 0.17 | 2.20 |
| 12 | 7.20 | 101.82 | 0.00 | 101.82 | 0.17 | 102.20 |

| | |
|---|---|
| Internal Rate of Return (Semiannual Bond Equivalent) | 8.00% |
| Internal Rate of Return (CD Quarterly) | 7.81% |

**EXHIBIT 9**
**COST OF CAPPED LIABILITIES UNDER TWO CAP LEVELS**

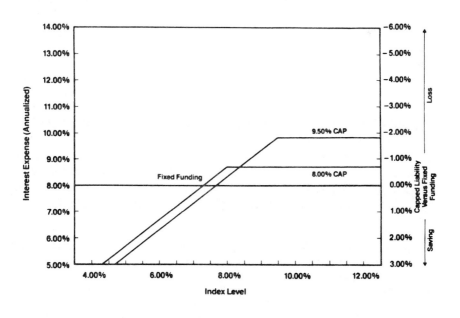

The break-even scenario brings to light a phenomenon that often occurs in a positively sloped yield curve. The break-even scenario for the caps is above the current index level. This means that rates can rise and the capped short-term rate can still be cheaper than fixed funding. This is because the fixed rate is higher than the short-term index level (a positively sloped yield curve), and this difference provides a "buffer" for a slight rise in short-term rates. So, although it is common to associate short-term funding with an expectation of stable or falling rates, a somewhat bearish outlook on short-term rates can be reconciled with a short-term funding plan when the yield curve is sufficiently positively sloped. More precisely, for a capped liability, the spread between the fixed rate and the short-term index must be greater than the cost of the cap, otherwise a fall in rates from the current level will be required to offset the cap premium. When the yield curve is flat or inverted (short-term rates higher than long-term rates), the break-even scenario for a capped floating-rate liability versus the fixed rate will always require a fall in the short-term index.

Although this analysis is couched in terms of a capped liability, it is also important to calculate a break-even scenario for variable-rate assets combined with interest rate floors. The break-even scenario for a protected asset is the scenario under which the return to the asset plus floor combination is equal to the benchmark fixed rate. In a positively sloped yield curve environment, the break-even point will always require the short-term index to rise to a level sufficiently above the benchmark fixed rate to offset the cost of the floor. Only in an inverted yield curve environment would the break-even scenario encompass an average level of rates below the current index.[10]

### Comparing Risk/Return of Different Cap and Floor Strikes

Different strike levels provide different balances between upside potential and limited downside risk. The worst-case and break-even scenarios provide enough information to compare the risk/return trade-offs of caps and floors of different strikes.

The cost of funds for one payment period of a variable-rate liability capped at either 8% or 9.5% is shown in Exhibit 9. The horizontal axis measures the level at which the index plateaus at the end of the first period. For all rate changes that leave the index above the strike rate, the cost of funds is constant and equal to the worst-case cost of funds. Rate changes that leave the short-term index below the strike rate represent lower costs of funds than the worst case. The lower the rate, the lower the

---

[10]In some cases, there will be no break-even point, because the cap or floor and floating rate always dominate the fixed rate. Protected rate agreements may be very attractively priced, or short-term securities may be very attractive relative to available fixed rates. For short-term liabilities plus caps, the worst-case cost of funds is below the fixed-rate issuance level; for the floating-rate asset plus floor combination, this means the worst-case return is greater than the fixed rate available. Such a situation is a rare market opportunity, the manifestation of an inefficiency that market forces usually eradicate with time.

cost of funds. The right-hand vertical axis shows savings or loss of the capped liability versus fixed funding. The point at which the line crosses the fixed funding level represents the break-even scenario. Where the short-term index is below the break-even rate, the cost of funds will be lower than the fixed cost of funds represented by the horizontal line.

By comparing the patterns of the capped liabilities, it is clear that the 8% cap limits the downside risk more than the 9.5% cap. The worst-case cost of funds under the 8% cap is lower than it is under the 9.5% cap; therefore, the 8% cap costs more than the 9.5% cap. Thus, the premium of the 9.5% cap will be recovered under smaller favorable rate moves than those required to recover the cost of the 8% cap. The break-even level for the 9.5% cap is therefore higher than the break-even for the 8% cap—that is, it is closer to 8% than the break-even point for the 8% cap.

The performance of a floating-rate asset and an interest rate floor can be analyzed in a similar way. The risk/return profile of the short-term asset plus floor combination for strike levels of 8% and 6.5% is shown in Exhibit 10. The worst case occurs when rates are equal to or lower than the floor rate for the duration of the floor. When the index is above the floor level, the return to the protected asset increases proportionately with increases in the index level. As with the capped liabilities, the floor that provides less protection—namely, the 6.5% floor—has greater downside risk, and because it costs less, will perform better on the upside.

**EXHIBIT 10**
**RETURN TO PROTECTED ASSET UNDER TWO FLOOR LEVELS**

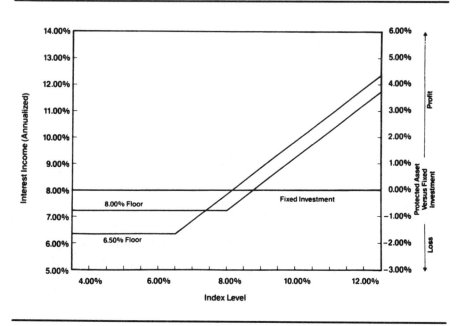

**EXHIBIT 11**
**RATE SCENARIOS IN HISTORICAL PERSPECTIVE**

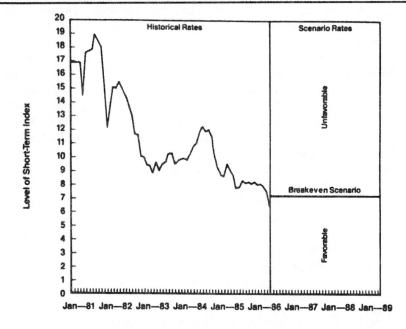

Given the risk/return patterns in Exhibits 9 and 10, the potential cap or floor buyer can choose the appropriate financing or portfolio structure, reflecting market view and tolerance of risk. In this respect, it is useful to combine the scenarios that we have described with a historical perspective in Exhibit 11. This allows the user to assess rate scenarios and market views in the context of the relevant market parameters.

## II. APPLICATIONS OF CAPS AND FLOORS

Interest rate protection agreements have many applications other than capping short-term liabilities and putting a floor on floating-rate assets. Since caps and floors are available in long maturities (they are regularly structured for periods of 12 years, and can be as long as 20 years, whereas exchange-traded options on fixed-income securities typically are not available with any liquidity over a one-year horizon), they are well suited for hedging long-term options embedded in existing securities, or simply for expressing a longer-range view of rate levels and the volatility of rates.

## Capped Liabilities and Protected Assets

Fixed-income asset and liability managers have traditionally faced two classes of instruments: fixed rate or variable rate. Interest rate caps and floors offer a new alternative that combines the most desirable features of both: a protected variable rate. In addition to providing an asymmetric risk/return profile, strategies involving caps and floors allow market participants to capture relative value along the yield curve. The swap markets have shown that perceptions of value in different maturity sectors relative to a common benchmark may vary considerably. Swapping techniques allow issuers and investors to capitalize on these market opportunities. In this light, protected interest agreements offer an asymmetric way to tap the same opportunities.

Some investors/issuers are also limited in terms of maturity. Highly leveraged issuers such as real estate developers, for instance, may not have favorable access to the long-term credit markets. In the past, they have been limited to variable-rate vehicles. Often, these issuers do not even have access to interest rate swaps as a means of fixing their variable-rate liabilities. Caps provide an alternative—and sometimes the only—means to limit their interest rate exposure. Likewise, corporations often can issue commercial paper or Euro-CDs at tighter spreads to Treasury rates, and can use interest rate protection agreements to cap the risk of rising rates. Issuers in this case would be open to the risk of widening quality spreads and would only be protecting the level of the index capped.

Another way of using caps to capture relative value has emerged in the tax-exempt market: Caps and floors on tax-exempt short-term rates have recently become available. This allows municipal issuers to capture relative value in the short-term sector, while retaining rate protection against higher future rates. In this area, caps are available in maturities as long as 20 years, making them excellent candidates to combine with long-term, adjustable-rate municipal financings. On the asset side, managers who can invest only in short-term and floating-rate securities can now put a lower bound on rates far into the future, still without investing in long-term securities. Many commercial and money center banks with large floating-rate note portfolios have used floors to guarantee a minimum return on their assets.

Caps and floors are also used in managing the asset/liability mismatch that many financial institutions face. For instance, a thrift funding a fixed-rate commercial real estate loan portfolio with short-term deposits can manage the gap risk by extending the duration of the short-term liabilities with interest rate caps.

Protected assets and capped liabilities have been the most common use of caps and floors to date. Therefore, the analysis has concentrated on the use of caps and floors in conjunction with variable-rate vehicles to create capped liabilities and protected assets. However, when fixed-rate securities provide better relative value than variable-rate securities, capped liabilities and protected assets as previously described can be created in another way.

Synthetic capped liabilities can be created by combining a fixed-rate financing and a floor to provide the same risk/return profile as a capped liability. This combination of fixed financing plus a floor can have identical cash flows to a capped liability when the cap and floor are struck at the same level. It is also possible to create a synthetic protected asset by purchasing a fixed-rate asset and a cap.

### Hedging Long-Term Embedded Options

Just as caps and floors can be used to create asymmetric patterns of return, they can also be used to negate, or hedge, an asymmetric return pattern of a security that includes some form of optional structure. The most straightforward use of caps and/ or floors as a hedge is to offset caps and/or floors associated with existing securities. For example, issuers of capped floating-rate notes often sell a cap against the liability, resulting in a straight variable-rate liability. If the cap sold has the same terms as the cap embedded in the capped floating-rate notes, this is a perfect hedge. In addition, if the buyer of the cap values it more than the seller, it is possible for the seller to finance below normal levels.

In contrast to the direct hedging application, caps and floors can also be used to cross-hedge securities with other optional characteristics similar to, but not exactly the same as, caps and floors. For instance, fixed-rate residential mortgage-backed securities include an option for the borrower to prepay the principal outstanding. This feature affects the price response of the mortgage to yield changes. When the mortgage is trading around par, the price appreciation under a decline in rates is limited, since lower rates will encourage prepayments. Increases in rates, on the other hand, decrease prepayments and thereby make the security more volatile on the downside. Strategies involving short-term financing of a mortgage portfolio hedged with interest rate swaps (paying fixed and receiving the floating index) have often provided significant yield pickups.[11] However, this is not a perfect hedge. For instance, under large decreases in rates, the loss on the interest rate swap outweighs the limited gain on the mortgage. To alleviate this mishedge, some of the interest rate swaps can be replaced with interest rate caps. Under yield increases, the caps provide the same protection as swaps; under declines in rates, however, the caps are not as onerous as the interest rate swap.

### Interest Rate Collars

Since their development, protected interest rate agreements have progessed beyond simple caps and floors. Often an issuer (or investor) reduces the net cost of buying a cap (or floor) agreement by selling a floor (or cap) to create an interest rate collar. A

---

[11]See Michael Waldman, "Constructive Uses of Fixed-Rate Mortgages: Arbitrage Opportunities for Financial Institutions," in Frank J. Fabozzi (ed.), *Mortgage-Backed Securities: Strategies, Applications and Research* (Chicago, IL: Probus Publishing 1987).

**EXHIBIT 12**
**COLLARED FLOATING-RATE NOTE**

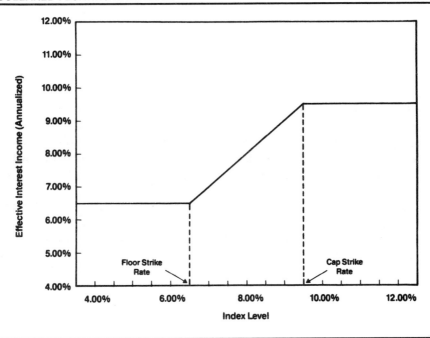

range forward is a special type of collar in which the strike rates are chosen so as to make the fees on the two transactions offset each other. The collar and range forward agreements leave some interest rate risk in between the two strike levels, but they eliminate risk from very large rate moves.

The effective coupon for one payment period from the combination of a floating-rate note plus an interest rate collar, contingent on the level of the index on the determination date, is shown in Exhibit 12. The investor constructs the interest rate collar by buying a floor struck at 6.5% and selling a cap struck at 9.5%. In this example, the proceeds from the sale of the cap exactly match the cost of the purchase of the floor. The result is a floating-rate security that pays a minimum of 6.5% if the index is at or below 6.5% and a maximum of 9.5% if the index is at or above 9.5% on the determination date. If the index is between 6.5% and 9.5%, the effective coupon is simply the index rate.

The interest rate collar causes the duration of the synthetic collared floating-rate note to be greater than the duration of the floating-rate note in isolation. If rates increase, all else constant, the synthetic will be worth less due to the greater likelihood of below-market interest payments as the effective coupon reaches a ceiling imposed by the cap component of the collar. If rates decline, the synthetic will be more valuable because of the increased potential for above-market interest payments, because of the floor set by the collar.

## III. DETERMINANTS OF VALUE

The ultimate determinant of the attractiveness of a cap or floor is its cost. To decide on the terms of a contract (or whether one should be used at all), it is necessary to understand the determinants of value. Cost depends on a combination of the prevailing market conditions and the terms of the contract itself. Furthermore, as market conditions change, it is often desirable to offset a cap before its expiration. Insofar as a cap or floor is used as a hedging instrument, it is important to understand the relative impact of changing market factors on its value, as well as how aging will affect its price.

Although the pricing of caps and floors draws heavily on options pricing theory, it is possible to describe the determinants of value in a more intuitive way. In the following section, we address two issues: First, the relationship of caps, floors and interest rate swaps, explaining why the interest rate swap market provides the appropriate fixed rate to be used for analysis. Second, we describe how changes in the terms of a cap or floor—namely, strike level, length of protection and frequency—as well as the expected volatility of the index and market fixed-rate levels affect value.

### Relationship of Caps, Floors and Interest Rate Swaps

As we illustrated in Section I, there are similarities between the profit and payoff patterns for caps and floors; in particular, Exhibits 2 and 6 have the same pattern. In the standard options framework, puts and calls are related to each other through the price of the underlying security. In the case of caps and floors, the common denominator is the interest rate swap.[12]

We will illustrate with a simple example. Assume a flat yield curve with both the short-term index and the five-year interest rate swap level at 8%. It is possible to show that a five-year cap is equivalent to a position of a five-year floor plus a long position in a par interest rate swap with a fixed semiannual coupon of 8% (that is, paying 8% fixed and receiving the floating index every six months), when both the cap and the floor are struck at the swap rate and if the fixed rate is paid on the same basis as the floating. It can be demonstrated that these positions will generate the same cash flows under any market scenario.

For rates above the cap level, say 10%, the holder of the cap will be paid the

---

[12]See Robert Kopprasch, John Macfarlane, Daniel Ross and Janet Showers, "The Interest Rate Swap Market: Yield Mathematics, Terminology and Conventions," Chapter 58 in Frank J. Fabozzi (ed.), *The Handbook of Fixed Income Securities* (Homewood, IL: Dow Jones-Irwin, 1987).

difference between the index and 8%, which is 2%. The floor and the swap combination generates the same cash flow. Since rates are above 8%, the floor by itself generates no income, while the swap entitles the holder to the difference between the 8% fixed outflow and the 10% floating index, also a net payment of 2%. For rates below the cap level, say 6%, the cap holder receives no payment. The holder of the floor plus the swap also experiences no net cash flow. The floor generates a positive cash flow equal to the difference between 8% and the index level, 2%, which is just enough to cover the shortfall on the interest rate swap between the fixed payment outflow of 8% and the floating payment received, 6%. At exactly 8%, none of the securities generates cash flows.

Since these two positions are equivalent, the cost of the two portfolios should be the same. Thus, the cost of the cap will be the same as the cost of the interest rate swap plus the cost of the floor. Since an at-the-market swap is a par swap, no swap fee would pass between the two parties, and the cost of the floor would equal the cost of the cap.

For ease of reference, we will define the situation where the relevant interest rate swap fixed rate is equal to the cap and floor strike rates expressed using the same quotation convention as representing an "at-the-money" cap or floor.[13] A cap will be termed in the money and a floor out of the money when the strike rate is below the relevant swap rate. Where the strike rate is above the swap rate, the cap will be termed out of the money and the floor in the money.

There is a more general relationship between caps, floors and swaps. The cost of a cap at a given strike rate is equal to the cost of the floor at the same strike rate, plus the cost (positive or negative difference from par) of an appropriate interest rate swap. The swap must be structured with the fixed coupons of magnitude and frequency equal to the strike rate and the floating coupons identical to the index and frequency underlying the cap.[14]

Given the central role of interest rate swaps in the relative pricing of caps and floors and their widespread use for converting floating indexes to fixed-rate equivalents, generally the swap rate, when available, is the best choice for a benchmark fixed rate. It facilitates the separation of the analysis of the relative value of the interest rate protection agreements from the assessment of the relative value of the underlying security to be hedged with the contract. Sometimes, however, the relevant interest rate swap rates are not available, such as in the tax-exempt sector, or may not be appropriate—where the particular index or maturity is illiquid, for

---

[13]The first payment period of a variable-rate security is usually not protected by a cap or floor, since the interest rate at the beginning of the period is known. This means that if the starting short index level does not equal the fixed rate, there will not be parity in price between the floor and cap struck at the swap rate. The positive (negative) spread between the strike rate and initial level of the floating index will increase (decrease) the cost of the cap relative to the floor.

[14]Again, this value must be adjusted to account for the difference, if any, between the starting level of the index and the strike level of the described contract.

example. In these cases, a fixed rate may be obtained from an estimation of the level that would be available on an equivalent fixed-rate security reflecting the index under question.

## Impact of Changes in Valuation Parameters

**Strike Rate** The strike rate is the threshold that short-term rates must cross before the contract starts to pay off. For caps, the higher the cap level, the higher rates must go before the cap provides a benefit, and hence, the less valuable the cap is to the buyer. For caps identical in all respects except strike level, the one with the higher strike rate will have the lower value.

For floor agreements, the strike rate has a similar effect, but in the opposite direction. The higher the strike level, the greater the value of the floor agreement. If a floor with a higher strike level did not command a higher cost, it would be possible to purchase the floor at the higher rate and sell the floor at the lower rate, generating fee income without assuming any risk. This transaction would be repeated until the price of the floor with the higher strike rate is above the price of the floor struck at the lower level.

**Market Rates** The level and structure of market interest rates have an important impact on the price of caps and floors. Whereas the strike rate does not change over the life of the agreement, market interest rates will continually change, making them the parameter most likely to significantly alter the value from day to day. Although the link between the yield curve and the value of caps and floors is complicated, and beyond the scope of this article to rigorously describe, it is possible to make some basic observations on this relationship.

By using a benchmark fixed rate that reflects the conversion of the short-term index into a fixed rate, it is possible to show how changes in its level, with all else constant, will affect the value of caps and floors.[15] A flat yield curve will be used as a starting point. The primary effect of higher available fixed rates is to increase the value of a cap and decease the value of a floor.

To understand the general impact of changes in market rates, it is necessary to recognize the source of value of a protected interest rate agreement. At a minimum, the value of a cap expressed in basis points per annum can be estimated as the greater of zero and the fixed rate minus the cap level (this is analogous to the measure of intrinsic value in the standard options context). Before the expiration of the cap, where the fixed rate is close to the cap level, the value of the cap will be significantly greater than this mininum value to reflect the value of the desirable asymmetric

---

[15]In fact, the forward levels of the index underlie the valuation of caps and floors. For this analysis, however, we will take the forward rate structure as given and assume that a change in the fixed rate will cause an equivalent change in each forward rate.

payoff pattern of the cap (this value is termed "time premium" in the standard options context). However, for fixed rates well above or below the cap level, the additional—or "time"—value of the cap will be close to zero. Well below the cap level, the chance of the cap paying off becomes remote, and the value of the cap is near zero. Well above the cap level, the risk if rates go down is the same as the potential if rates go up by a similar amount. Since the buyer of the cap does not enjoy the protection of an asymmetric risk pattern, there is little incremental value in the cap over the minimum value given reasonable rate moves in either direction.

The same analysis can be applied to the valuation of floor agreements. The minimum value of the floor expressed on an annualized basis is equal to the floor level less the fixed rate for interest rate levels below the strike rate, and zero when the fixed rate is above the floor rate. The floor value will be above the minimum value except for rate levels far from the strike rate, where the value of the floor will be close to its minimum value for the reasons described for the cap. These observations are shown in Exhibit 13, where the value of an 8% cap and an 8% floor can be read off the vertical axis. It should be noted that over most rate levels, the value of caps or floors changes by an amount less than the change in the underlying rate (this is akin to the hedge ratio, or delta, of an option). For every basis point increase in market rate levels, the annualized value of the cap will usually increase by less than one basis point. For low rate levels, the ratio of increase in annualized cap value to increase in market interest rates will be lower than the value of that ratio for higher market rate levels. The value of a floor behaves in a similar way. The annualized value of a floor will generally increase by less than one basis point for every one-basis-point decrease in market interest rates, and, the deeper the floor is in the money, the higher that increase will be. Combined with the time to maturity of the cap or floor, this measure can be used to arrive at a measure of the sensitivity of up-front value to parallel shifts in interest rates. Such a measure is useful in hedging applications where the objective is to equate the sensitivity to changes in rates of a hedge vehicle with the price sensitivity of the target security.[16]

There is also a secondary effect of a change in market interest rates. The level of market rates affects value through its use in discounting future cap or floor payoffs. The absolute impact of changes in these discounting factors is greater the longer the term and the greater the up-front value of the contract. With floors, the primary and secondary impact of a change in interest rates work in the same direction: Higher rates lower the up-front cost of the floor on both counts. Caps, on the other hand, experience opposing forces from changes in rates. For a rise in rates, the primary effect is to raise the cost of the cap, while the secondary discounting effect is to lower its cost. In aggregate, over reasonable rate levels, the primary effect is dominant: Higher market rates cause higher cap values.

---

[16]This measure can be used to determine the implied modified duration of a capped liability or a protected asset. See Robert Kopprasch, "Understanding Duration and Volatility," Chapter 5 in *The Handbook of Fixed Income Securities*.

**EXHIBIT 13**
**VALUE OF CAPS AND FLOORS VERSUS FIXED-RATE LEVEL**

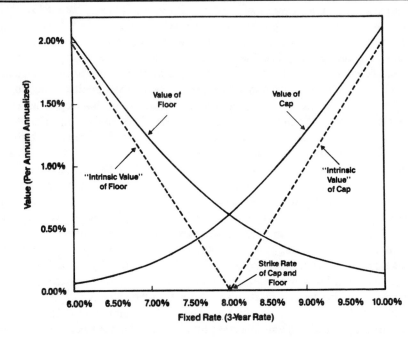

We have done this analysis assuming parallel yield curve shifts. In practice, however, the shape of the yield curve is continuously changing. Although a detailed analysis of the impact of this changing structure on the value of protected interest rate agreements is beyond the scope of this article, two points should be noted in connection with this issue. The first is that, as long as the benchmark fixed rate stays constant, changes in the shape of the yield curve will have a similar impact on caps and floors, because of the link between caps and floors through the interest rate swap market. The second is that increased positive and increased negative steepness in the yield curve, given a constant benchmark fixed rate, both tend to increase the price of caps and floors.

**Volatility of Short-Term Rates** The cost of a cap or floor reflects the market's expectation of future variability of the index underlying the protection agreement. Since caps and floors represent a return pattern of limited downside risk and virtually unlimited upside potential, higher variability of interest rates always translates into higher value. On the upside, higher payoffs become more likely. This outweighs the impact of the increased probability of larger unfavorable moves, since the downside risk is limited to payoffs of zero.

The expected volatility of rates is the only determinant of the value of caps and floors that is not measurable outside the context of the protected interest rate agreement market. This is no coincidence, since the market for caps and floors is the only forum for the expression of expectations of the volatility of short-term rates over long horizons. Of course, these expectations are not formed in a vacuum, as market participants use various forecasting methods to develop their views. Popular approaches include the measurement of the historical volatility of relevant market interest rates, as well as the monitoring of volatility expectations expressed in other markets, including the exchange-traded options markets.

**Length of Term of Protection Agreement** In addition to the role it plays in determining the relevant market parameters to use in the valuation process, the time to maturity of caps and floors affects their value in three ways.

The first effect is that more payment periods will be protected. This will always increase the up-front cost of both caps and floors.

The second is that it determines the horizon over which rates can move. Exhibit 14 demonstrates the relationship of time and volatility by describing an envelope within which there is a 95% probability that the short-term rate will lie at any given time horizon, assuming a flat yield curve at 8%, and volatility of the short-term index of 20% annually. The probability that the short-term index will be above the

**EXHIBIT 14**
**95% CONFIDENCE BAND OF FUTURE SHORT-TERM RATE LEVELS**

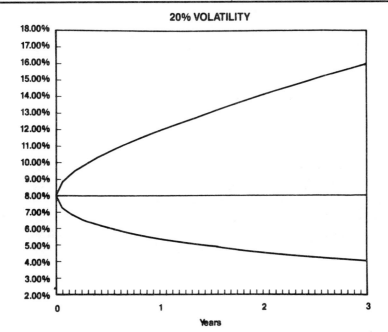

cap level increases with time. Thus, it should be evident that the longer the term of the contract, the greater the absolute amount of protection afforded the buyer—and hence, the greater the cost of the cap or floor.

The third effect of the term of the agreement concerns the discounting of the potential benefits of the agreement. Expected payoffs in the more distant future are worth less than equivalent nominal benefits to be received earlier.

These three effects do not all work in the same direction. Nevertheless, the first two will always dominate the third, so that increasing the term of a cap or floor will always increase its value. This is relevant not only to the initial choice of terms of a cap or floor, but also when analyzing the offset of a protection agreement before expiration.

**Frequency** The payment frequency of a cap or floor affects the extent to which the buyer of a cap or floor can benefit from volatility in rate levels. The more frequent the payment periods, the greater the possibility of interim index levels that will generate cash inflows, as each payment period represents an independently exercisable option. Hence, a cap or floor with a greater number of independent payment periods tends to have a higher expected value than the same agreement with a lower frequency. This is not to say that the higher frequency contract always outperforms the contract of identical terms with a lower payment frequency, since under many scenarios the lower payment frequency agreement may actually outperform the one with the higher frequency. In practice, it is usually appropriate to match the frequency of the agreement with the frequency of the security that is being hedged. A cap or floor with higher frequency also may be more valuable, because the first period is often not protected by a cap or floor, since the starting rate is known at the start of the program. Since an agreement with a higher frequency has shorter periods, the nonprotected period will be shorter. For example, while a one-year quarterly cap covers only three quarters one year, a one-year monthly cap covers 11 months, and should, therefore, be more valuable.

## IV.  SUMMARY

Interest rate cap and floor agreements are important and flexible tools for asset and liability management. Over the past several years, the breadth and depth of the protected interest rate agreement market have expanded dramatically to meet the hedging needs of issuers and investors. This market will likely continue along its current path of integration into the fixed-income capital market and will be used increasingly as a means of capturing relative value.

# Index